# Understanding Islamic Finance

# Understanding Islamic finance

"Muhammad Ayub has provided the most comprehensive treatment to date of the contracts, products and systems used in Islamic finance. He explores how the concepts are rooted in the Islamic economic system in a way that will appeal to academics while at the same time giving a coherent account of the products that finance practioners should find helpful."

—Professor Rodney Wilson, Director of Postgraduate Studies, Durham University

"The author has rendered a great service to the field of Islamic finance through this painstaking encyclopedic effort that could have only been undertaken by a dedicated scholar-teacher-trainer like Dr Ayub. This detailed compilation of the views of the four majority jurisprudential schools of thought in Islam on matters relating to financial transactions, presented and explained in clear language and applied to contemporary developments in Islamic banking and finance, is highly useful to students and practitioners of Islamic finance. The book is of particular significance for financial engineers who wish to design financial instruments compatible with the requirements of Islamic jurisprudence"

—Dr Abbas Mirakhor, Executive Director, IMF Washington DC

"Understanding Islamic Finance is the fruit of many years of hard work by the author based on his understanding of Islamic law and the principles of Islamic economics. Islamic economic system being a rule-base system can be understood very well when viewed as a set of contracts. Therefore, this book provides the vital bridge between the legal foundation and the theory of economic and financial systems in Islam. This bridge helps the reader better understand Islamic finance."

—Dr Zamir Iqbal, World Bank, Washington DC

*About the author*

**MUHAMMAD AYUB** is Director of Training, Development and Shari'ah Aspects at IIBI, London. Formerly, he was with the State Bank of Pakistan (central bank) where he headed the Islamic Economics Division and Shari'ah Compliance Division as Senior Joint Director in the Research and Islamic Banking Departments. He also served as Head of Islamic Banking at NIBAF, the training wing of SBP. Besides contributing a large amount of material on the subject, he has been serving as a Master Trainer on theory and practice of Islamic finance.

For the last two decades, he has been involved in R&D for the Islamic Banking Industry, Product Development, IB Prudential regulations, Risk Management, Shari'ah related controls and audit of Islamic banking institutions.

For other titles in the Wiley Finance Series
please see www.wiley.com/finance

# Understanding Islamic Finance

**Muhammad Ayub**

John Wiley & Sons, Ltd

*Other Wiley Editorial Offices*

John Wiley & Sons Inc., 111 River Street, Hoboken, NJ 07030, USA

Jossey-Bass, 989 Market Street, San Francisco, CA 94103-1741, USA

Wiley-VCH Verlag GmbH, Boschstr. 12, D-69469 Weinheim, Germany

John Wiley & Sons Australia Ltd, 42 McDougall Street, Milton, Queensland 4064, Australia

John Wiley & Sons (Asia) Pte Ltd, 2 Clementi Loop #02-01, Jin Xing Distripark, Singapore 129809

John Wiley & Sons Canada Ltd, 6045 Freemont Blvd, Mississauga, ONT, L5R 4J3, Canada

Wiley also publishes its books in a variety of electronic formats. Some content that appears in print may not be
available in electronic books.

Anniversary Logo Design: Richard J. Pacifico

*Library of Congress Cataloging in Publication Data*

Ayub, Muhammad, 1951–
    Understanding Islamic finance / Muhammad Ayub.
        p.   cm. — (Wiley finance series)
    Includes bibliographical references and index.
    ISBN 978-0-470-03069-1 (cloth : alk. paper)
    1. Finance—Islamic countries.   2. Finance—Religious aspects—Islam.   3. Economics—Religious
aspects—Islam.   I. Title.
    HG3368.A6A98 2007
    332.0917′67—dc22                                                    2007035537

*British Library Cataloguing in Publication Data*

A catalogue record for this book is available from the British Library

ISBN 978-0-470-03069-1 (HB)

Typeset in 10/12pt Times by Integra Software Services Pvt. Ltd, Pondicherry, India

*In the Name of Allah,*
*the Most Merciful, the Most Beneficent*
*For my youngest daughter, Wardah*

# Contents

**PART II    CONTRACTUAL BASES IN ISLAMIC FINANCE    99**

# List of Boxes and Figures

## Boxes

# Figures

# Foreword

The last decade has seen an unprecedented growth not only in the practice of Islamic banking and finance but also in the literature on Islamic finance. This book, however, is not merely another addition to the available literature. It has a marked distinction. It not only places theory and practice in one place along with Sharīʿah (Islamic law) underpinnings, but also provides an objective assessment of conformation of the practice to the theory. A good coverage of recent innovation in Islamic financial products is also a distinguishing feature of this book.

Islamic finance is a subject that has now been recognized as a distinct academic discipline to be included in the curricula of economics, business, finance and management faculties of institutions of higher learning. There are several universities and institutions, both in Muslim and other countries, that are teaching courses on Islamic banking and finance. These teaching programmes, however, have been seriously constrained by the non-availability of a standard textbook to be followed. I can say with confidence that this book carries the status of a textbook to be prescribed in the senior levels of undergraduate programmes as well as in graduate programmes in the relevant faculties.

Islamic finance is still a new subject. There is great interest in conducting research on different aspects of its theory and practice in the contemporary set-up. Students of economics and finance keenly look for topics of research in this field. The analytical approach adopted in this book is conducive to bringing to light potential areas of research. Thus, research students in the area of Islamic finance should find this book a must read.

The author of the book has a long experience of research in the State Bank of Pakistan (the central bank of the country), which has played, during the last decade, a significant role in promoting Islamic finance in the country. By virtue of his position in the research department of the State Bank of Pakistan, he has a very valuable insight into the operations of Islamic banks as well as their feasibility to survive in competition with the conventional banks in the country. His approach in presenting the material in this book is very pragmatic.

The book, thus, is a useful guide to all those who would like to establish an Islamic bank or would like to work in Islamic financial institutions.

I congratulate the author as well as the publisher in bringing out this useful book.

**M. Fahim Khan**
Division Chief
Islamic Research and Training Institute
Islamic Development Bank
Jeddah, Saudi Arabia

# Preface

Islamic scholars have been critically examining the modus operandi of modern commercial banks ever since their establishment in the Muslim world in the last decade of the nineteenth century. As time passed, the consensus emerged among the scholars that the system was against the principles of Sharīah, mainly because of paying/charging returns on loans and debts. Keeping in mind that direct or indirect intermediation between resource surplus and resource deficit units was necessary to fulfil the growing needs of human societies and for the development of business and industry, Islamic scholars and economists started offering conceptual models of banking and finance as a substitute for the interest-based financial system by the middle of the twentieth century.

Institutions offering Islamic financial services started emerging in the 1960s in isolation, but the movement of Islamic banking and finance gained real momentum with the establishment of Dubai Islamic Bank and the Jeddah-based Islamic Development Bank in 1975. In the evolutionary process, the initial theoretical model of two-tier Mudarabah developed into a versatile model enabling the Islamic financial institutions (IFIs) to conduct trading and leasing business to earn profit and pass on a part of the same to the savers/investors. To complete the cycle of Islamic finance, institutions offering Takaful services started emerging in 1979 as a substitute for the modern insurance system.

While the increasing involvement of the Sharīah scholars, creative work by research institutions like the IRTI (IDB) and the issuance of Sharīah Standards by the AAOIFI (Bahrain) provided a critically needed base to the emerging financial discipline, participation of the world's top banking institutions like HSBC, BNP Paribas and Citigroup in the 1990s provided a driving force to transform it from a niche discipline to a global industry. The establishment of the Islamic Financial Services Board (IFSB) in 2002, as a standard-setting institution, also paved the way for making Islamic finance a globally acceptable proposition. It provided impetus for the promotion and standardization of financial operations of Islamic financial institutions (IFIs), involving consultations among the relevant regulating authorities and the international financial institutions. The emergence of Sukuk as investment and liquidity management instruments in the last six years not only tended to complete the investment cycle in the emerging financial structure, but also provided a powerful driving force for its development, with huge potential ahead.

The above progress reveals that the Islamic finance industry has crossed the significant milestone of having increasingly wider acceptance at a global level. The amazing development so far, the present state of affairs and the challenges ahead give rise to some crucial considerations for the experts, policymakers and practitioners in Islamic finance. First, the rapid growth of the industry over the last decade has enhanced the demand for committed, devoted and professionally trained personnel for Islamic banking operations. Second, the industry, as it has emerged, is facing a credibility challenge on the grounds of lack of awareness among the public and also due to the general perception that Islamic banks' present framework, with a reliance on debt-creating modes like Murabaha, might not be helpful in realizing the objectives that its pioneers had visualized for transforming the interest-based financial system to a system compatible with the tenets of the Sharīah.

Bankers, the business community, industrialists, Sharīah scholars and the general public need to know what Islamic finance is, what its features are and how it works. In particular, students of business and finance, the product developers for the emerging industry and the personnel involved in operations need to have proper knowledge of the principles of Islamic finance, the essential requirements of different Islamic modes of financing and how they can be applied to various operations and services of banks and financial institutions. Accordingly, the availability of any comprehensive book, covering both theory and practical aspects of Islamic finance, is regarded a prerequisite for promoting Islamic banking and finance.

In the above scenario, I was asked by John Wiley & Sons to produce a write-up that could serve as a textbook for students, bankers and all others who want to understand the philosophy, modes, instruments and operations of Islamic banking and financial institutions. I accepted the challenge and worked on the outline, covering Islamic economics as the basis of Islamic finance, principles of Islamic finance, the main features of Islamic commercial law, modes, products and procedures to be adopted by Islamic financial institutions and the role Islamic finance can play in the development of the financial system and economies. The book contains discussion on the basic modes, followed by the procedures that IFIs are using or may adopt to fund a variety of clients, ensuring Sharīah compliance. Practical and operational aspects covering deposit and fund management by Islamic banks involving financing of various sectors of the economy, risk management, accounting treatment and the working of Islamic financial markets and instruments have been discussed in suitable detail.

The external reviewer of Wiley, while giving his expert opinion on the original manuscript, suggested adding a chapter on appraisal of common criticism of Islamic banking and finance. Although such discussions were there in scattered places in the book, covering all criticism and misconceptions about the principles and operations of Islamic banks in one chapter in the final manuscript will hopefully help readers to remove confusion, besides adding value to the book.

In preparing the book, I have benefited from the traditional books of Islamic jurisprudence, the literature available so far on Islamic banking and finance, resolutions of the Islamic Fiqh Council of the OIC – the highest body representing Sharīah scholars of all major Islamic countries, the Sharīah Standards developed by the AAOIFI and rulings of the Sharīah boards of some Islamic banks. As such, it reflects the consensus/mainstream viewpoint relating to principles of the Islamic financial system, modes of financing and their essential Sharīah requirements that are recognized on a wider scale and are the bases for Islamic banking practices in the Middle East and other parts of the world. In places, the minority view in respect of some products has also been included to give a measure of dissent.

Among those who accept the prohibition of interest, there are two approaches: according to the mainstream approach, IFIs can use both categories of Islamic modes, while some believe that Islamic banking, in letter and spirit, means only Shirkah-based transactions. The latter perception is that Islamic finance, which was originally conceived as a two-tier Mudarabah, has shifted to debt-creating modes that are almost similar to the interest-based products of the banks, and as such, Islamic banks' business also yields fixed returns as in the case of the interest-based system. According to the mainstream approach, however, the issue of mode selection is one of a preference for some over others and not one of prohibition of debt-creating/fixed-return modes, and hence IFIs can use both categories of modes subject to observance of the Sharīah rules relating to trade and lease transactions and keeping in mind the risk profile of the savers/investors and the nature of business, profitability and cash flow of the entrepreneurs seeking facilities from the Islamic banks.

The message this author intends to convey is that IFIs need to carefully observe the principles of Islamic finance with Sharīah inspiration while using any of the permitted modes. It is, however, a fact that an important factor determining the integrity of their operations, besides Sharīah compliance and the professional competence of their incumbents, is the possible impact of Islamic banks' operations on the clients and the society or economy. A common question faced by the practitioners is whether the Islamic banking in vogue will be able to remove distortions created by the interest-based system, even in the long run. It requires, on the one hand, that the role of partnership modes and equity-based capital in Islamic banks' operations needs to be enhanced and, on the other hand, the stakeholders need to be educated and apprised that all Islamic modes can play a positive role in development and capital formation, if used by banks observing the Sharīah rules. Further, banking is only one part, though the most strategic one, of the overall system of finance and economics. Fiscal, credit and monetary policies of the states have a crucial impact on the financial business in any economy. This would require the creation of real-asset-based money only and promoting retail and corporate financial services on the basis of fair play and risk-sharing. Therefore, for sustainable and all-pervasive development of economies and the welfare of human beings as a whole, the real-asset-based system of finance with care for socio-economic ethics needs to be introduced gradually on a wider scale.

I hope that the work in hand will prove to be a useful source material for understanding the principles, modes and operations of Islamic finance for all those who want to have such knowledge, especially those who intend to apply it for providing Sharīah-compliant solutions to investors and fund users.

I pray to the Almighty to accord His acceptance to this effort, made solely to spread knowledge about and promote observance of the injunctions of the Sharīah in economic and financial dealings, and make this book a means of disseminating the concept of Islamic banking and finance, forgiving me for any inadvertent errors and omissions.

Muhammad Ayub
Director
Training, Development and Shariah Aspects
Institute of Islamic Banking and Insurance (IIBI)
London

# Acknowledgements

Credit for this work primarily goes to my friend Riaz Ahmad, who introduced me to John Wiley & Sons, and to Caitlin Cornish, Senior Commissioning Editor for the Finance list at Wiley, who asked me to produce a textbook on Islamic finance. Other people at Wiley, who persistently persuaded me to carry on the work, include Emily Pears and Vivienne Wickham and the rest of the editorial staff of this wide-range publishing house. I am deeply obliged to all of them and also to the external reviewer who examined the first version of the manuscript and suggested the addition of a chapter "An Appraisal of Common Criticism of Islamic Banking and Finance", which added value to the book.

I have extensively benefited from the scholarly works of a number of institutions and individuals in the preparation of the book. The institutions include: the Islamic Fiqh Council of the OIC, Jeddah (their resolutions); the Accounting and Auditing Organization for Islamic Financial Institutions (AAOIFI), Bahrain (Sharī'ah and accounting standards); the Council of Islamic Ideology, Pakistan (report on elimination of interest from the economy, June 1980); the Federal Shariat Court, Pakistan (judgement on Riba, November, 1991); the Shariat Appellate Bench of the Supreme Court of Pakistan (judgement on Riba, December, 1999, along with scholarly discussions on all related issues).

A large number of publications of the Jeddah-based Islamic Development Bank's Islamic Research and Training Institute (IRTI) provided me with an extensive opportunity to study various conceptual and practical aspects of Islamic banking and finance. The institute deserves my deep appreciation and gratitude. I must gratefully appreciate the invaluable services of Dr Ahmad Mohamed Ali, President of the IDB, in rendering the IRTI a reference point for anyone desirous of understanding conceptual and operational contours of the emerging Islamic finance industry. The scholars associated with IRTI from whose works I especially benefited include: Dr M. Umer Chapra, Dr Mabid Ali Al-Jarhi, Dr Monzer Kahf, Dr M. Fahim Khan, Dr Munawar Iqbal, Dr Tariqullah Khan, Dr Ausaf Ahmad and Dr Habib Ahmed.

Scholarly works of a large number of other personalities also helped me a lot in the preparation of this book. I pay my profound gratitude to all of them. The following names come instantly to my mind: Dr Muhammad Nejatullah Siddiqi, Shaikh Siddiq M. Al-Amen Al-Dhareer, Justice Muhammad Taqi Usmani, Dr Wahbah Zuhayli, Dr Mahmoud Amin El-Gamal, Dr S.M. Hasanuz Zaman, Dr Abbas Mirakhor, Dr Mohammed Obaidullah, Dr Mohsin S. Khan, Dr Nadeem ul Haque, Dr Zamir Iqbal, Dr Ziauddin Ahmad and Dr M. Tahir Mansoori.

A large number of specialists and practitioners helped me to gain clarification on conceptual issues and practical aspects of Islamic banking and finance. I wish to record my thanks and gratitude to all of them. The following deserve special mention: Mr Hassan Kaleem, Sharīah Advisor, Al Baraka Bank, Pakistan; Mr Muhammad Najeeb Khan, Sharīah Advisor, Habib Metropolitan Bank, Pakistan; Mr Anwar Ahmad Meenai, Head Islamic Banking Division, National Bank of Pakistan; Mr Mohammad Sajid, CEO, JS Finance, Jahangir Siddiqi & Co., Karachi; Mr Ashar Nazim and team, The Capital Partners, Karachi; Mr Omer Mustafa Ansari, Ford Rhodes Sidat Hyder & Co., Karachi; Mr Muhammad Faisal Shaikh, Head Product Development, Bank Islami Pakistan; Mr Ahmad Ali, Head Product Development, Meezan Bank, Pakistan.

My very special thanks are due to Dr S.M. Hasanuz Zaman, former Chief, Islamic Economics Division of the State Bank of Pakistan and Ch. Rashid Ahmad Javed, former Director of the State Bank of Pakistan, who gave a thorough reading to a number of chapters of the book and suggested needed amendments/improvements.

While I am greatly obliged to all of the above-mentioned institutions and scholars, I am solely responsible for any inadvertent mistakes.

I would also like to record my thanks to Mr Riaz Riazuddin, Economic Advisor, State Bank of Pakistan, who encouraged me to take up the Wiley project I was initially hesitant to accept because of my official responsibilities at the State Bank and the volume of work required to accomplish the job. I would be rather ungrateful if I did not take this opportunity to pay thanks to the State Bank of Pakistan and its training arm (the National Institute of Banking and Finance, or NIBAF), where together I spent 27 years and got the opportunity to pursue my research work in Islamic economics, banking and finance.

Mr Bashir Ahmad Zia, Chief Librarian, and other staff of the library of the State Bank of Pakistan also deserve my gratitude for providing me the opportunity to consult books and journals from time to time. Their facilitation helped me a lot in the completion of the project. Indeed, I am deeply obliged to all of them.

Last, but not least, my thanks are also due to Muhammad Yousuf, my long-associated colleague at the State Bank and NIBAF, for composing and re-composing the manuscript and helping me to produce this work in an orderly manner.

Muhammad Ayub

# Part I
## Fundamentals

# 1

# Introduction

## 1.1 ECONOMIC SCENARIO IN THE NEOCLASSICAL FRAMEWORK

Since the failure of the centralized economic system of the East in the 1980s, the efforts of economists, experts, policymakers and governments around the world have been focused on strengthening market forces to achieve optimal economic growth and sustainable development at national and global levels. However, despite some trivial development, market forces have failed to achieve balanced and equitable growth, not only at individual countries' level but also regionally among both developed and developing countries.

While the capitalist system, canonized at Bretton Woods in 1944, allowed a free hand to the capitalist countries and within them the firms and individuals to maximize their profits with minimal consideration of the human aspects, norms and ethics, the post-Bretton Woods system, based on excessive creation of monies, particularly the US Dollar, resulted in "oceans" of poverty around the world.[1]

Communism was the opposite of capitalism as far as the capitalization of resources was concerned, while ownership was hypothetical and control was centralized. Due to this extremist unbalanced behaviour, it had to go after completing its short cycle of less than a century.

Capitalism does not monopolize all resources directly but through several diversified media with different levels and distribution controls, like a master–slave set-up. Due to strong political and institutional support at international level, effectively giving veto to big powers over the activities of the IMF and the World Bank, neocapitalism has taken a longer time cycle, but as all limits have been crossed, it could at any time lead to collapse, inflicting heavy losses on the global economy.

"Greed" – the unbridled pursuit of wealth – has become the most popular slogan of individuals and particularly of the corporate world, leaving the masses to misfortune. Money created out of nothing has strengthened the exploitation mechanism and widened the gap between the haves and the have-nots. The resultant economic scenario has led to the following concerns for mankind:

---

[1] The gold standard remained in practice in some shape up to 1944, when the Bretton Woods agreement was signed by the then 35 sovereigns, linking all currencies with the US Dollar in a fixed ratio and declaring them redeemable at one ounce of fine gold for 35 dollars. But in 1971 even the gold–currency link was abolished. Gold, instead of being a unit of account for determining the prices of all other currencies, became a normal commodity whose worth was expressed in terms of units of account or paper currency. All currencies depreciated, followed by the Dollar's depreciation. But the Dollar, being a reserve currency, was used as a blatant tool for exploitation of the whole world with the support of the main international financial institutions. See Perkins, 2004, pp. 212–213.

- human behaviour guided only by self-interest – no concern for behavioural aspects;
- no discipline in the creation of high-powered money, leading to unjust and exploitative payment systems and illegitimate control over the resources of weaker individuals and nations;
- contradictory policies – leaving the crucial functions of providing health, education and the basic needs of the masses to a market characterized by forces like "self interest", liberalization and deregulation, under the banner of alleviating poverty and increasing literacy levels, etc. is clearly contradictory;
- no or dubious concern for human dignity and rights;
- no care for the weak and the oppressed classes;
- no concern for justice, fair play and equity;
- the influential and the elite exploiting the weak – leading to a phenomenal concentration of wealth together with large-scale hunger and poverty;
- unhindered unethical practices like deceitful advertisements to allure consumers, leading to hefty salary packages for the marketing "experts" and leaving the real contributors to national and global production and the consumers at the mercy of market forces.

The following remarks of Keynes about harmony between private and social interests aptly sum up the actual situation in the world and lend support to the above view:

> "The world is not so governed from above that private and social interests always coincide. It is not so managed here below that in practice they coincide. It is not a correct deduction from the principles of economics that enlightened self-interest always operates in the public interest. Nor is it true that self-interest generally is enlightened; more often individuals acting separately to promote their own ends are too ignorant or too weak to attain even these." [2]

## 1.2   CONVENTIONAL DEBT: A RECIPE FOR EXPLOITATION

The grim situation briefly portrayed above is not limited to the poor or the least developed countries in Africa, Asia and other areas of the planet. Inequity has become the hallmark and the most serious problem facing mankind in all societies. Masses of people in almost all emerging/developing, Islamic and non-Islamic, and even developed and industrialized economies are facing the same fate. The interest-based financial system is a major hurdle in achieving distributive justice. It is creating unrepayable debt – making a class of people richer and leaving others poorer and oppressed.

Excessive debt and its servicing are the striking features of the interest-based mechanism: yesterday's debt can be repaid by taking out more debt today. It is not only stifling economic growth but also crippling the efforts made by the World Bank, IMF and other donors to reduce poverty in poor countries. It also distorts the payments systems, on account of which the concern for just and fair incomes and earnings is being accorded the least consideration. No one cares who is going to pay the debt: which future generations and from where? This kind of behaviour – avoiding the payment of currently owed debt – is not acceptable under any divine religion. In Islamic Sharī´ah, debt liability is subject to strict accountability on the Day of Judgement.

The economic problems of underdeveloped countries (UDCs) have emanated largely from their excessive debt accumulation. The cost incurred in the form of interest has to be paid by

---

[2] Keynes, 1926. Also see Chapra, 1992, pp. 53–54.

successive governments through increasing rates, taxes and charges on consumption goods and utilities. For servicing the debts, governments raise taxes without providing any socio-economic amenities or quid pro quo. Their foreign exchange earnings, including export proceeds and remittances of expatriates, are also consumed by debt servicing.

This has led to an ever-increasing share of risk-free capital, vis-à-vis risk-based capital and business, resulting in business failures, unemployment and, ultimately, gross inequalities of income and wealth. It has exerted disastrous effects by reinforcing the tendency towards wealth accumulation in fewer hands together with large-scale hunger and poverty. The unproductive and wasteful spending both by individuals and governments, which the interest-based mechanism and easily available credit have the tendency to promote, has led to a decline in savings, real investments and employment opportunities. The system, combined with inflation, becomes a recipe for economic instability and chaos. This affects the poor and the middle class, who together comprise the major part of the population, and thereby the level of national savings, leading the economies into a vicious circle of poverty and gross injustice.

So-called debt relief packages have failed to resolve the real issue of poverty alleviation. In the recent past, debt relief has been provided to 27 countries, most of which are from Sub-Saharan Africa. According to a World Bank report, the debt stock of these countries has been reduced by two-thirds.[3] Due to such efforts, the external debt burden of developing countries as a group has decreased to some extent (from 45 % of GNI in 1999 to about 40 % in 2003) but that has not been universal and there are many countries that have not been provided any relief. In addition, the aggregate declines in external indebtedness of developing countries have been offset by rises in domestic debts, exposing them to enhanced risks with regard to the scale of the overall debt burden arising from higher interest rates on domestic borrowing in almost all developing countries. Further, trade barriers imposed by developed countries on the products of poor and developing countries have not been lifted, which smacks of an exploitative approach on the part of the rich nations.

Leaving aside the poor and developing countries, even the developed countries have become accustomed to the bane of debt. On account of the continued and repeated current account deficits of the United States, it has been transformed from a significant international investor in the 1970s to the world's largest debtor country. As of today, only US nationals are apparently immune from the devastation of debt and that is by dint of the US Dollar being the major reserve currency, despite the fact that it has become a zero-saving nation with unparalleled individual, institutional and national debt. In 2004, while the US deficit was $668 billion, or 5.7 % of GDP, its net external liabilities were estimated at over $2.7 trillion (23 % of US GDP, or 7.5 % of world GDP). In 2005 it jumped to $805 billion and is likely to hit 12 % of GDP by the end of the decade.[4] American national debt has passed $9 trillion. The late eminent columnist Art Buchwald termed it "The $9-trillion heist".[5]

The real story of modern empire, writes John Perkins, is that it "exploits desperate people and is executing history's most brutal, selfish and ultimately self-destructive resource-grab."

---

[3] World Bank, 2005, p. 25.

[4] *The Economist*, 18th March, 2006.

[5] *Daily Dawn*, Karachi, 20th April, 2006. In a survey of the world economy, *The Economist* (London) asks, "Why did American investments abroad perform so much better than foreign investments in America? The main reason is the Dollar. It is the world's reserve currency, and America – unlike many other debtors – can issue bonds in its own currency. Virtually all America's foreign liabilities are denominated in dollars, whereas around 70 % of its foreign assets are in foreign currencies." (24–30th September, 2005).

The empire that spends trillions of dollars created out of thin air on wars and for bribing the corrupt has not been able to spend the mere 40 billion dollars that, as per United Nations estimates, would be sufficient to provide clean water, adequate diets, sanitation services and basic education to every person on the planet.[6] "Part of America's current prosperity is based not on genuine gains in income, nor on high productivity growth, but on the borrowing from the future", states *The Economist* under the caption of "Danger time for America" in its issue of 14th February, 2006.

The system has generated inequality at alarming levels, even in developed countries like the US and Britain. As a national objective, therefore, GDP growth no longer makes such obvious sense.[7] In the US, inequality has increased since 1973, as demonstrated by the Gini coefficient – a measure of inequality of income distribution in an economy. It increased from 0.394 in 1970 to 0.408 in 1990 and to 0.462 in 2000. The current value of the Gini coefficient in the US resembles its value in developing countries. The same is the case in Britain. Emerging economies like China are also facing the same problem of inequity and a widening gap between the haves and the have-nots, despite the highly impressive performance of macroeconomic indicators.

Financing of the huge deficit with the fragile global politics could seriously destabilize the international markets and economies. Up until now the system has worked because the US has the right to print dollars. As long as the world accepts the Dollar as the standard currency, excessive debt does not pose a serious problem. However, if another currency comes along or any of the US creditors like Japan or China decide to call in their debts, the situation may become out of control.[8]

Since the collapse of the Bretton Woods system in 1971, the central focus of the IMF policies has been to safeguard the US interests, whatever her policies,[9] which has created so much vulnerability that now its critics are not only the protesters against globalization in various parts of the world, but also senior officials of the IMF in Washington. In the wake of US financial imbalances that placed the global economy at risk, the IMF criticized US economic policies during their spring meetings in 2006, but the US response was to tell the Fund to mind its own business.[10]

## 1.3   GROWTH *PER SE* MAY NOT LEAD TO SOCIO-ECONOMIC JUSTICE

For about half a century, the major objective of economic policy has been to promote growth in the overall pursuit of development and happiness of the population. However, it has been observed that because of rising inequality, growth alone is not a reliable indicator of socio-economic development. Despite growth in many parts of the world, a large number

---

[6] Perkins, 2004 pp. xii, 216.

[7] Ahmad, 2005. Also see *Daily Dawn*, 14th April, 2006; *The Economist*, Special report on inequality in America, 17–23rd June, 2006, pp. 25–27 and on Japan, pp. 31, 32.

[8] Perkins, 2004, pp. 212, 213.

[9] A hazardous policy decided jointly by the US Treasury, IMF and the World Bank in the early 1990s and implemented by the latter two for the benefit of the former, commonly known as the "Washington Consensus", aimed at trade and capital market liberalization. The countries that followed had to suffer. China and India did not follow and devised their own policies; both of them are now the fastest growing economies in the world. Malaysia was also able to control the crisis of the late 1990s as it adopted its own policies without taking advice from the IMF and the World Bank.

[10] See *The Economist*, 22–28th April, 2006, pp. 12, 14, 69, 70.

of people are unemployed, half-fed and ill-treated as a result of unhindered market forces. Steady-state growth models and "trickle-down" theory have demonstrated conclusively that they enhance inequalities of asset distribution by enabling the powerful and better-endowed groups to grow at an even faster rate than which they were growing before, leaving the masses in deeper misery.[11]

John Perkins, in the preface to his book, *Confessions of an Economic Hitman*, while analysing the dangerous world situation, writes: "The idea that all economic growth benefits humankind and that the greater the growth, the more widespread the benefits, ... is of course erroneous ... It benefits only a small portion of the population ... may result in increasingly desperate circumstances for the majority ... When men and women are rewarded for greed, greed becomes a corrupting motivator." He also points to the problems arising from fallacious concepts about economic development.[12]

A number of emerging economies are showing impressive growth rates. But economic growth under neoliberalism is not serving the welfare function; rather it is enhancing poverty because the benefits do not trickle down by themselves, due to distortions created by vested interests in a free market functioning without proper surveillance, disclosure and transparency that, in truth, reinforces skewed income distribution patterns. China, one of the fastest growing economies with a growth rate in double digits, is facing the same problem. The lot of the country's poor, particularly in rural areas, has got worse, as the previous communist system guaranteed certain basic needs including food, health care and primary education. The support systems have collapsed due to the shift to a market-based economic system.[13]

In cases where the wealth and assets are concentrated in big business and industrial segments in urban areas and the countryside is feudalistic, even the impressively high growth rate of the economy and sectors like industry and agriculture will not lead to better income distribution and poverty alleviation. As such, experience has proved that poverty does not reduce even by governments spending on health, education or infrastructure, because the basic tools of exploitation continue to work and such spending is not directed to the fulfilment of the basic needs of the masses. The resultant large-scale poverty is a hurdle to industrial investment and growth, as it lessens the consumers' demand for manufactured goods due to high inequitous income distribution. There must, therefore, be a revolutionary redistribution of assets and income prior to stabilization if the growth is desired to reduce asset distributional inequalities.

The deepening imbalances in external payments in developing and emerging economies and financing needs associated with those imbalances have created serious concerns in global policy circles and the capital markets. This may affect the external finance and commodities in which emerging market economies operate.[14] Any abrupt and disorderly adjustment of the exchange rate of major currencies or rises in interest rates may disturb all major economic indicators in these economies. This would have serious consequences for developing countries.

---

[11] For details on poverty in the world's richest countries see Chapra, 1992, pp. 127–129.

[12] Perkins, 2004 pp. xii, 216, 222.

[13] *The Economist*, 11th March, 2006.

[14] Among the emerging market economies are: China, Hong Kong, India, Pakistan, Malaysia, Indonesia, South Korea, the Philippines, Thailand (in Asia), Egypt, Saudi Arabia, Israel (in the Middle East), Argentina, Brazil, Chile, Mexico, Peru, Venezuela (Latin America), South Africa and Bulgaria, Czech Republic, Estonia, Hungary, Poland, Russian Federation and Slovakia (Eastern Europe).

While it is a fact that there is no short cut method of relieving poor individuals and nations of past debt, policymakers will have to make concrete efforts to change the basis and the procedure of fund mobilization, both from internal and external sources. The solution lies in replacing risk-free with risk-related capital and making efforts to ensure inflow of foreign resources in the form of direct and portfolio investments. Borrowed funds are mainly squandered and it is imperative to replace them with asset and risk-based investments through fully thought-out and long-term proactive policies.

## 1.4  SOCIAL WELFARE ACTIVITIES OF THE STATES

Almost all present governments spend huge amounts of money on social security nets, but that expense does not tend to mitigate the ill effects of the injustice inflicted by the tools of conventional economics and finance and the resultant inequitous distribution of income and resources by unhindered market forces. Imbalances created by the system as a whole cannot be corrected only by a government's selective spending; it rather leads to moral hazard in a number of socio-economic directions. Compared with the problems created by the system, such social welfare activities cannot cater to the needs of the millions of poor or the vulnerable groups in any society.[15] In addition to strengthening, restructuring and expanding the social safety nets to provide support to the deserving segments of society, there must be a big change in the system at a broader level so that weaker groups can get their due share at the stage of production and distribution of wealth and assets among various factors of production.

That is why, despite heavy spending by governments and high levels of technological and industrial development, even the countries with massive resources have been unable to realize their normative goals, due mainly to the fact that there is a conflict between the operative tools of conventional economics and their normative goals. The interest-based system of creation and allocation of funds and market-based monetary policy have been viciously anti-poor and an important cause of unemployment and asset and income distributional injustice at national and global levels. Governments and central banks are becoming more and more passive to the fate of the masses in all economies, facilitating profit maximization by the corporate sector and those who are already rich.

## 1.5  THE MAIN CULPRIT

Obviously, there has been a long list of factors responsible for the failure of the global economic system in amicably solving the economic problems of mankind and ensuring justice, equity and fair play. However, the main two factors are the inefficient modus operandi of economic management with practically no concern over poverty or exploitation of the weak, and the functioning of money, finance and the financial markets that play the most strategic role in creating, distributing and transferring resources and wealth at national and global levels. Governments, in a bid to allow free interaction of market forces, have not been properly fulfilling their overseeing function with the objective of protecting the main

---

[15] Charity, on whatever scale, cannot solve the problem. This is why "Billanthropy" by the biggest charitable foundations (see report by *The Economist*, 1st July, 2006, pp. 69–71) has not been able to make a dent on poverty.

stakeholders and vulnerable segments of society. As a result, vested interests have been creating distortions in the markets to artificially control and determine the supply of goods and transfer of resources to the privileged classes.

As the major tool in the hands of governments is money, one factor that has to be taken care of to realize the overall objective of equitable and sustainable economic growth for welfare of mankind is the area of money and finance. The institution of interest, on the basis of which governments and the public and private sector corporations borrow funds, creates parasites in society and thereby the gap between the rich and the poor keeps on widening. According to the late Yusuf Ali (the eminent translator of the Holy Qur'ān into English): "Whereas legitimate trade or industry increases the prosperity and stability of men and nations, dependence over usury would merely encourage a race of idlers, cruel bloodsuckers and worthless fellows who do not know their own good and therefore are akin to madmen" (translation of verse 2: 275). It is a ground reality that the interest-based system, irrespective of the rate, is creating "idlers" and "cruel bloodsuckers".

The prohibition of interest in all revealed religions that we shall discuss in the following chapters essentially implies that there can be no gain without risk-sharing, which implies that if someone wishes to get a return, he must also be liable for the loss, if any. "No risk, no gain" is actually the basic juristic principle of Sharī´ah and a normative rule of justice. The liability to bear a possible loss can motivate investors to be more careful in making their investments. This can help remove the moral hazard that is associated with risk-free gains on financial investments and, thereby, inject greater discipline into the financial system.

## 1.6   THE NEED OF THE HOUR

There are many opinions about the ultimate cause of the crisis. However, sensible people have long been calling for comprehensive reform of the financial system to help prevent chaos and spread of financial crisis, or at least minimize their frequency and severity. A vast majority of Muslim jurists and scholars believe that the ultimate cause lies in disregarding the prohibition of interest, which is an important teaching of all major religions.

The state of affairs in the global economy and glaring inequalities both at inter and intra national levels necessitate the evolution of a system that could lead to a balanced, sustainable and equitable economic order in the world at large. This requires economists and policymakers to develop an economic system based on the ideals of socio-economic justice and fair play. By fulfilling this mission they would be giving to humanity the message of peace, happiness, welfare and prosperity.

In particular, the economists who have been working on Islamic economics for the last few decades and trying to conceive a model that could lead to balanced and equitable growth that benefits individuals as well as societies must undertake the job with dedication and fervour. While doing this, one thing that they should take seriously is that justice/fair play is the *raison d'etre* of any economic system that is to be sustainable in the long run, and in the Islamic worldview, it cannot be given up for any other consideration whatsoever.

The major element creating injustice is "interest". Replacing this with a risk-related capital and investment mechanism could help solve many socio-economic ills. There are a number of other benefits that can be derived from the prohibition of interest. Among these are the injection of a moral dimension into the financial system along with greater equity and market discipline to make the financial system more equitable, healthier and stable.[16]

## 1.7  ECONOMICS AND RELIGION

Economists have been debating the impact of religion on economic performance for many years. This aspect will be discussed in detail in the next chapter. Here, a brief introduction will suffice.

Whether economics should be mixed with religion is a significant question these days. More specifically, can Islam be helpful in economic development or it is a drag on economic growth? Any detail on this aspect is not within the remit of this book, which has to focus on finance, the most strategic part of any economic system. A large number of scholars have blamed the relative poverty of Muslims today on their religious beliefs. But Marcus Noland, an eminent economist, maintains that this long-standing view is wrong: "There is nothing inherent about these [Islamic] societies that they have to perform poorly," says the economist with the Institute for International Economics in Washington, "If anything, Islam promotes growth . . .".[17]

While discussing the role of religion in economics one must distinguish economics as a science from an economic system. An economic system has to be discussed as a thought based upon any ideology, while economic science should be considered as a science which deals with the creation of wealth. An economic system relates to management of wealth distribution in a society that tends to solve economic problems of various groups by enabling or restricting them from utilizing the means of production and satisfaction. Thus, the system comprises the following three main elements:

1. Ownership of property, commodities and wealth.
2. Disposal of ownership.
3. Distribution of wealth among the people.

Commodities are possessed for their benefits, which represent the suitability of a commodity to satisfy any human need. Goods/assets are possessed as a result of work, inheritance, purchasing/obtaining property for sustenance, governments granting possession of something to the citizens and transfer payments or goods granted as gifts (without giving anything in exchange). From this perspective, the Islamic economic system is different from the other systems only to the extent of ownership and distribution of resources among the factors of production and various groups of society, with a defined role of the State to ensure that injustice is not done to any of the individuals, parties or groups.[18]

Islamic economics, in fact, can promote a balance between the social and economic aspects of human society, the self and social interests and between the individual, family, society and the State. It can effectively address issues like income distribution and poverty

---

[16] For a discussion of the socio-economic benefits of an interest-free system of financial intermediation, see Chapra, 2000a. See also Siddiqi, 1983; Mills and Presley, 1999, pp. 58–72 and 114–120.

[17] http://www.csmonitor.com/cgi-bin/encryptmail.pl?

[18] The term "commodity" includes everything possessed for utilization through buying, leasing or borrowing, whether by consumption, such as an apple, or by usage, such as a car; or through utilizing it like borrowing machinery or leasing a house. Property (Māl) is anything that can be possessed and includes money, such as gold and silver, commodities, such as clothes and foodstuffs, immovable properties, such as houses and factories, and all other things which are possessed. Human effort is a means to obtain the property or its benefit. Therefore, wealth is the property (Māl) and the effort together (Nabhani, 1997, p. 47).

alleviation, which capitalism has not been able to address. At the global level, it may be helpful in eliminating the sources of instability, thus making the world a happier place with harmony among followers of various religions.

In the contemporary world, we have macro-level evidence of distributive justice and development. The trickle-down theory (TDT) adopted in Malaysia during 1957–1970 failed miserably and resulted in the tragedy of 13th May (1969) race riots in the country. Then the Malaysian government adopted a policy which applied the core value of Islam, i.e. justice with fairness, that has contributed significantly to the country's miraculous achievement in the last three decades. Although the government could not fully apply the Sharī'ah principles, it adopted a pragmatic policy (New Economic Policy) that had the twin objectives of eradicating poverty and restructuring society to ensure justice with fairness. This policy of higher growth with distributive justice emerged as a direct response to the failure of the growth alone development policy (TDT) pursued during the 1960s. Success at the macro-level did act as a contributory factor to compensate the failure of some institutions and values at the micro-level.

Based on the principles laid down in the Holy Qur'ān and the Sunnah of the Prophet, Muhammad (pbuh), the Islamic system played a strategic role in the development of human society from the second half of the seventh to the tenth century AD. The early Muslims excelled in all the fields of knowledge of their times, besides understanding and practising the tenets of Islam.

The period from the Pious Caliphate after the demise of the holy Prophet (pbuh) up to the 11th century AD represented the zenith of Muslim glory. Muslims were able to develop and extract wealth from their lands and through their world trade, strengthen their defence, protect their people and guide them in the Islamic way of life.

As the expanding frontiers of the Islamic State gave birth to monetary issues, mercantilism, urbanization and socio-economic problems, they developed the system and theories to resolve the emerging issues. A large number of individual scholars and thinkers of the Middle Ages developed a number of branches of knowledge, including economic principles, that could be considered as the basis of the modern political economy and economic thought. As such, the Medieval Age was considered the golden period of Muslim history.[19]

With intellectual regressiveness, the Muslim civilization began to wither, becoming more and more preoccupied with minor issues. The Industrial Revolution was totally missed. This regressiveness continued until the British and French instigated rebellion against Turkish rule and brought about the downfall of the Ottoman Empire, the last Muslim world power, replacing it with European colonies. It was only after World War II that these colonies became independent.

## 1.8   ISLAMIC PRINCIPLES CAN MAKE THE DIFFERENCE

The above discussion implies that problems have emanated from

1. The unchecked creation of money.
2. A reliance on market forces without any ethical limits.

---

[19] For details on the contribution by Islamic jurists to economics, see Chapra, 2000a, pp. 145–172. The assumption made by Joseph Schumpeter in his book *History of Economic Analysis* (1954) and reference to it by the Nobel Laureate, Douglas North (in his December 1993 Nobel lecture) that the period between the Greeks and the Scholastics was sterile and unproductive and the theory of the "Great Gap" based on this assumption is false and lacks credibility.

3. An emphasis on growth and profit *per se* without regard to the distribution aspect.
4. The negative role of the State and the regulators in allowing the pursuit of greed and unchecked profit.

Islamic principles of economics and finance provide checks for all these factors. They focus on clarity and lack of ambiguity, just and fair treatment for all and care for the rights of others. But these principles are necessarily ethical and, as a ray of hope, some senior policymakers have been witnessed talking about ethics. These principles need to be adopted for the relief of mankind.

Market mechanisms, private property and enterprise, self-interest and competition are integral parts of Islamic economics, just as in the case of a free-market system. After the goods are produced, these are consumed or used in the process of further production through the two main contracts, namely sale/purchase (trading) and leasing, that can be entered into by individuals, partnership firms and corporations. For undertaking these transactions properly, Islamic jurisprudence provides other contracts/subcontracts along with detailed rules.

The fundamental feature of Islamic economics and finance is socio-economic and distributive justice. It also has a comprehensive system of ethics and moral values. It does not allow the destruction of output by, say, dumping into the oceans or burning, to force up or to maintain prices fictitiously at a higher level. Under the effective supervision of the government, markets can function freely under a competitive price mechanism, transparency and disclosures, subject to the condition that they are not distorted by the influential and stronger segments of a society. Within this overall framework, individuals have the right of ownership and freedom of enterprise, and can get return or profit by creating additional value and sharing gains and losses. The State has to undertake an overseeing role so that a closer linkage between real economy and finance can contribute to growth and evenly shared income.

The Islamic economic system prohibits commercial interest, excessive uncertainty, gambling and all other games of chance and emphasizes a social welfare system based on mutual help, character building, behavioural changes, the system of Zakat (the religious obligation of every Muslim who has wealth in excess of his consumption needs at the nonprogressive rate – generally 2.5 % of net wealth or 5 or 10 % in the case of agricultural produce above a minimum limit – Zakat money has to be distributed among the have-nots and the needy as per the tenet of the Holy Qur'ān given in verse 9: 60) and care and dignity for the poor. It accepts the right of capital to enjoy a just return with the condition that it also bears the liability or risk of any loss. Any entitlement to profit or return comes from value addition and bearing the business risk, the nature of which will be different in different business contracts or transactions based on partnership, trading or leasing.

The main principle governing permission to trade/exchange, subject to fulfilment of certain rules, and prohibition of Riba (interest), games of chance or gambling and other illegal contracts is that all gains and receipts in exchange transactions must be accompanied by any consideration stipulated with free will and mutual consent of the parties. Contracts covering various transactions have been classified as commutative and noncommutative (Uqood-e-Mu'awadha and Uqood Ghair Mu'awadha – discussed in Chapter 5). While profit or return is valid in the case of the former, like the contracts of sale and leasing, no return can be taken in respect of the latter, as in the case of gifts, guarantees[20] and loans, as loaning, guaranteeing or gifting are considered by Islamic Sharī´ah as gratuitous and benevolent acts. Loans are granted for timely help of the needy and the debtor cannot be charged any amount over the amount of loan or debt. However, a loan has to be repaid one way or the other until the creditor gives relaxation or the debtor is declared insolvent. Accountability of loans or debts in the Hereafter remains intact, even in the case of insolvency, until the creditor waives the amount of debt.

## 1.9    REGULATING TRADE AND BUSINESS

Islam recognizes the role of markets and freedom of individuals in business and trade. Trade and business practices have contributed a lot to the development of the economies of Europe, the East and Far East. As expressed by Gordon Brown, the then Chancellor of the UK's Exchequer: "It was mainly through peaceful trade that the faith of Islam arrived in different countries".[21] Islamic finance, by offering trade-based models of financial intermediation, can provide an opportunity for closer interaction between Muslim and non-Muslim communities and enhance social cohesion among various societies. It may bring nations and countries closer through trade based on ethical values and some standards of justice and fair play. However Islam also recognizes the possible adverse impact of totally unregulated businesses on the various sections of society, particularly the poor and the disadvantaged.

All of this implies that economists and policymakers should concentrate mainly on two areas to streamline the global economic system and place it on a sound footing. First, the role of government, which has been a highly contested issue between the neoclassical/liberals and the conservatives over the last few decades. In view of the bitter experience of capitalism, with a passive government role resulting in growth for only a few individuals and groups and leaving the majority of human beings in utter poverty, economists should consent as a group that governments must perform an active role, not for conducting various businesses, but for ensuring the proper and smooth functioning of market forces with accountability and transparency, so that vested interests cannot manipulate through their malpractices. Concepts that have emerged in conventional economics and finance in recent years, like ethical finance, green funds and socially responsible investments, tend to imply a closer link between the desirable objectives of any economic system caring for human beings and the world as a whole.

The second area is that of money, banking and finance – financial instruments, institutions and the markets. Islamic finance requires that all financial transactions and the instruments must be represented by genuine assets and business transactions as per their respective rules and norms relating to fair play, transparency and justice. It is true that the gold standard cannot be adopted again, but there must be some foolproof criteria for the creation of money. The principles of Islamic finance – that all financial assets must be based on real assets (not necessarily gold or silver) on the one hand, and that the time factor in business transactions has value only through the pricing of goods and their usufructs on the other – provide the best

---

[20] Guaranteeing a financial obligation for a price involves Riba, which is prohibited. The guarantor is, however, allowed to recover out-of-pocket expenses incurred for providing the guarantee (not including the opportunity cost of the funds for securing the contingent obligation) (council of the Islamic Fiqh Academy, 2000, Resolution No 12(12/2), p. 18.

[21] Brown, 2006, p. 10.

such criteria. This could provide a paradigm shift for financial services by seeking a moral compass for the system based on market forces by linking them with the real economy. The only requirement is that the economists and the people at the helm of affairs start thinking seriously without any preconceived biases and prejudices.

Creating financial assets out of nothing and putting others at undefined risk is tantamount to cheating and fraud, which should no longer be allowed if peace, tranquility and human dignity are the objectives, as the so-called super powers, human rights organizations and other democratic groups often proclaim. There has to be some sound basis for the creation of money, because the absence of such a basis has resulted in injustice and imbalances in the global system and economies. The piling up of fictitious assets without any real economic activity and the unjust transference of risk to others should not be acceptable to minds concerned with human rights and dignity. As such, all financial assets must be based on real assets and business activities.

If the financial system at national and global levels, along with its tools and instruments, was based on a just and equitable foundation, governments could easily formulate and implement policies for the proper functioning of market forces, leading to fair distribution of income and allocation of resources. This would be accomplished indirectly through fiscal, taxation and monetary policies and directly through control over rogue forces to facilitate smooth market functioning. Therefore, economists should proceed to suggesting a proactive facilitative role for regulators and governments. This is particularly required for the functioning of the financial system, as it is like a heart in the human body and the major tool for efficient and balanced flow of resources among various groups in society. It is pleasant to read the then Chancellor of the UK's Exchequer Gordon Brown quoting a Hadith of the holy Prophet (pbuh) relevant to this discussion: "The Ummah, the Muslim global community, is like the human body, when one part feels pain, the other parts must reflect the pain – a truth of relevance in and beyond the Muslim world that emphasizes our duty to strangers, our concern for outsiders, the hand of friendship across continents".[22]

When economists, even many of those sitting in Washington and London, deem the imbalances a huge threat to world development, peace and prosperity, they may call for the application of a system according to which all financial assets have to be based on some real assets and economic activities conducted on the basis of such assets. Applying these principles to the supply and demand of money and management of savings, investments and financial assets could lead to sustainable and equitable growth and development, leading to the happiness of mankind as a whole.

The allocation of funds on the basis of interest needs to be replaced by risk-related placement under the principle of partnership and other contracts based on genuine and valid trading and leasing activities, implying that the fund owners should share both the risk and the return with the users of the funds. All parties to a contract have to undertake respective liabilities for entitlement to profit and the deciding factor is the nature of the transaction. The parties owning risk and reward at various stages in the process of undertaking transactions will charge differently in business activities based on trading, leasing or the Shirkah (partnership) principles. But the risk will have to be borne one way or the other, which can be mitigated but not totally eliminated if profit generated from such a transaction has to be legitimized.

---

[22] Brown, 2006, p. 12.

# 1.10   ISLAMIC FINANCE PASSING SIGNIFICANT MILESTONES

Islamic principles of economics and finance, briefly laid down above, have already proved their ability to attract policymakers and practitioners from all over the world to develop the edifice of an efficient financial system on this basis. From the dawn of the 21st century, Islamic finance has been developing so vigorously that it has evolved from a nascent industry to a global market, where Muslim and non-Muslim are working together and learning from each other for the development of relevant products and services. It has passed the significant milestones of existence, recognition by the global financial authorities and most recently in delivery of sophisticated and lucrative financial services with competitive pricing and sufficient care for Sharī´ah compliance.

All of this was achieved within just 25 years. Until the early 1970s, Islamic banking was an academic dream, of which few people were aware, even educated Muslims; now it has become a widely known practical reality. It made headway in the 1980s as a new system of financial intermediation, in spite of an unfavourable environment and without the help of the auxiliary or shared institutions needed for its successful operation.

Its recognition around the world relates to its workability and viability. It has also attracted the attention of mega international financial institutions, regulators like the Federal Reserve Board, FSA of England, international financial institutions like the IMF and the World Bank and prestigious centres of learning like Harvard and Rice Universities in the United States and the London School of Economics, Loughborough and Durham Universities in Britain, International Islamic Universities in Malaysia and Pakistan and a number of other institutions in Saudi Arabia and Egypt.

Islamic banking and finance is being practised in over 75 countries around the world, with about 550 Islamic financial institutions in the field. A number of international institutions and regional financial centres are playing a crucial role in the standardization of Islamic finance products and thus enhancing its credibility. Almost all multinational conventional finance groups are offering Islamic financial products through specially created subsidiaries or windows. It is a healthy sign of good and ethical business in future that will increase the prosperity and peace of mind of millions of people who were previously either keeping away from the conventional banking system or feeling guilty due to the involvement of interest in their transactions, otherwise prohibited in all revealed religions.

The development of standard-setting bodies and global facilitators like the Accounting and Auditing Organization for Islamic Financial Institutions (AAOIFI), the Islamic Financial Services Board (IFSB), the International Islamic Financial Market (IIFM) and the Liquidity Management Centre (LMC) is providing recognition for Islamic finance and enhancing its credibility to both customers and regulators. Bahrain, Malaysia, Saudi Arabia and Dubai have been serving as its hub for about the last two decades. Now, London and Singapore are also striving to become centres for Islamic finance. Britain's then Chancellor of the Exchequer Gordon Brown told the Islamic Finance and Trade Conference held in London in June 2006 that he wants to make London a global centre for Islamic finance by offering regulatory and tax regime measures to support the creation of Islamic finance products.[23]

Demand for Islamic finance is on the rise, both in Muslim majority and Muslim minority countries. In the UK, for example, the Islamic Bank of Britain (IBB) is working as a

---

[23] Brown, 2006, pp. 11, 15.

full-fledged Islamic bank with seven branches (planned to increase to 12 branches by the end of 2007). The first customer to open an account in the Leicester branch of IBB was a non-Muslim who travelled over 100 miles because of the ethics and transparency offered by an Islamic bank.[24] Besides this, the European Islamic Investment Bank (EIIB), HSBC Amanah, Alburaq (a subsidiary of Arab Banking Corporation), Lloyds TSB, ABC International Bank Bristol & West Building Society, KPMG, Clifford Chance, Norton Rose, Dawnay Day and 1st Ethical are among those offering services also to non-Muslim customers. In Malaysia, about 40 % of Islamic banks' clients are non-Muslims. In the US and North America, a large number of institutions are providing Islamic financial services, mainly to the Muslim community.

Prospects for the future are expected to be better, particularly if the instability that now prevails in the international financial system continues to accentuate and leads to a realization that it cannot be removed by making cosmetic changes in the system but rather by injecting into the system greater market discipline. This discipline is ingrained in Islamic finance principles.

## 1.11   COULD IT WORK TO ACHIEVE THE OBJECTIVES?

The question is: will Islamic economics and finance theories sooner or later reach a point where they provide a better alternative to the world at large? The question is quite a complex one; it has many dimensions to think over and requires courage to fix the targets. Economics is the most strategic part of everyday life – given much emphasis in Islam due to its social implications – but unfortunately it is not being developed and implemented anywhere at State level. Unless the policymakers, regulators and central monetary bodies take solid steps for Research & Development, followed by practical application, any selective and half-hearted application by individual IFIs might not be able to provide a better alternative for governing global finance and economies.

Now the foundations have been laid, if the majority of the world's 1.2 billion Muslim population chose to abide strictly by the tenet of the Sharī'ah, i.e. charging or paying interest is forbidden, many of the Islamic governments, investment institutions and ultimately the bulk of global commerce would transform to the natural instruments of business based on fair play and justice. If the human rights groups and those believing in ethics also joined hands and worked together for the cause they proclaim, many serious issues including hunger, poverty and social conflict could be resolved and the countries and the people could come closer, making the planet a more peaceful place to live.

But the point worth consideration by the experts in Islamic finance is that the system has to be developed to make it not only legally or formally Sharī'ah compliant, but also to change its basis and the mindset of the stakeholders and the market players in such a manner that it could be helpful in realizing the objective proclaimed by the pioneers of Islamic finance theory. The message this author wants to convey is that Islamic financial institutions which look at the products offered by the conventional system and mould them to see how they can formally or legally fit in the Islamic perspective without regard to their impact on various segments in society can only undermine the integrity of the Islamic theory

---

[24] Piranie, 2006, p. 24 (paper presented at the IFTC, 2006).

of finance. Compliance to principles should be Sharī´ah inspired and must, therefore, be the foremost consideration before the product developers, implementers and regulators.

Good ethics, which play an important role in the functioning of Islamic finance theory, are missing in present human society, including Islamic countries. In this area, governments, academicians and other opinion makers will have to do a lot of work to persuade the policymakers and educate the masses not to compromise on the rules of fair dealing and justice, both at national and international levels. It may take a long time, but we have to move in the right direction if the objective is to be realized sooner or later.

Keeping in mind the low ethical standards in almost all present societies, it will be a challenging task, but if conducted with dedication and effective coordination on a large scale, it is not impossible. Islamic countries have to set the precedent by applying the system in line with its principles vehemently and vigorously so that others have no choice but to follow it. In addition to raising risk-based capital at national levels, inflow of borrowed capital needs to be replaced with direct and portfolio investment. Governments will have to do a lot in this regard, especially by playing a facilitation role while ensuring that vested interests do not exploit the masses in general and the weak and the poor in particular. There has never been a "perfect" society in all respects, and there will not be in future. Always there have been elements creating distortions. It is the State that has to save the masses and society from such rogue elements or vested interests.

## 1.12  ABOUT THIS BOOK

This book relates to one part of the agenda prescribed above and that is deliberating upon the principles and the practices of Islamic finance. A financial system provides operating tools and instruments to an economic system, on the basis of which it tends to achieve its objectives. Likewise, Islamic finance is only one, but the most effective, part of the overall Islamic economic system and not the all-conclusive part. Its importance as the most effective part, however, has to be recognized because the flow of money, and thus transfer of resources, to various segments in a society is controlled by the banking and financial system, which, at its current stage of development, works like the blood circulating in the human body.

As regards the interpretation of the tenets of the Sharī´ah, the book represents the main-stream view of Islamic finance for the reason of its recognition at a wider scale and also because it is the basis for Islamic banking practices in the Middle East and other parts of the world. The Sharī´ah principles, accounting, risk management and other performance standards as being developed by the standard-setting institutions like the AAOIFI and the IFSB, are also based on the mainstream view. This should not be taken as a big problem for readers or the system, as practices based on the minority view in respect of a few concepts are in the process of transformation to make them compatible with the mainstream view and philosophy.

The challenges facing Islamic finance include educating and creating awareness among the stakeholders on a large scale and convincing people that the theory of Islamic finance is workable on a sustainable basis. A number of myths occupy peoples' minds about the Islamic financial system. Removing those myths and promoting Research & Development is crucial in promoting the system. Policymakers, bankers, the business community, industrialists, Sharī´ah scholars, students of business schools and the people at large need to know what

Islamic finance is, what its features and philosophy are and how it works. In particular, the product developers, those responsible for implementation and also the financial experts need to be familiar with the essential requirements of different Islamic modes of business, enabling them to provide financial services relating to retail, corporate and government sectors ensuring Sharī´ah compliance and the best operating procedures. This book is an effort in this regard to make available a textbook-type resource to students, bankers, the business community and the general public. Hopefully it will be useful in providing a sound understanding about the principles of Islamic finance and how they work to form a viable system.

The nature, scope, objectives and main features of the Islamic economic system are discussed briefly, just to lay a foundation for discussion while studying and understanding the Islamic financial system. The main body of the book is devoted to explaining the philosophy and concepts of Islamic finance, how it has to be applied at the micro-level and what its prospects and challenges are. The book comprises three parts, each part spanning a number of chapters.

Part I discusses the need for, basis and overall structure of Islamic economics, presenting a framework under which the Islamic financial system is supposed to work. It explains the philosophy and the main features of Islamic finance that form the basis of operations for Islamic financial institutions (IFIs). The major prohibitions that IFIs are required to observe are also discussed in this part. As the prohibition of Riba is the least controversial issue, more emphasis in discussion has been given to the connotation of the term Riba and how it encompasses various forms of present-day business and finance.

Part II provides an overview of the Islamic law of contracts and elaborates upon basic requirements of various transactions to be undertaken by IFIs, enabling readers to understand what the nature of various contracts is. While conventional banks' main function is loaning, Islamic banks' activities pertain to trading, leasing and other real sector business through a number of business structures. Rules of trading and loans and debts are, therefore, crucial for Islamic banking practitioners. Spanning three chapters, this part explains the components of major contracts like those of sale, loans and debts and some related subcontracts like Hawalah (assignment of debt) Kafalah (guarantee/surety) and Rahn (pledge).

Part III, the most strategic part, gives an overview of financial products in conventional and Islamic perspectives and discusses the main Islamic modes of business and investment and how they have to be used by IFIs as modes of financing. Explanations of the concepts of credit and forward sales (Murabaha–Mu'ajjal, Salam and Istisna'a), leasing of assets and services (Ijarah), partnership-based modes like Musharakah, Mudarabah and Diminishing Musharakah are followed by the procedures that IFIs could adopt for respective modes to facilitate a variety of clients, ensuring Sharī´ah compliance.

Chapter 13 discusses some accessory contracts that could be used by IFIs (along with other main contracts) like Wakalah (agency), Tawarruq (acquiring cash through trade activities), Ju'alah (stipend or reward for doing any defined job) and Istijrar (repeat sale/purchase or supply contract).

Chapter 14 contains some guiding principles on the application of the system on both the deposit and the asset sides, the issues involved in product development, deposit management and financing of specific areas.

Chapter 15 discusses the most vital and recently emerging topics in Islamic finance – Sukuk and securitization, elaborating upon the concepts and discussing the procedures. It explains how the concept of Sukuk can be used to realize the huge potential of Islamic finance.

Chapter 16 is devoted to the concept, practice and potential of Takaful – the Islamic alternative to insurance – the development of which is necessary to complete the cycle of Islamic banking and finance.

Islamic banking theory, as well as practice, is subject to a large number of objections and criticism, not only by those who have doubts about the prohibition of modern commercial interest, but also by those who visualize an ideal and absolutely "pure" system having socio-economic benefits within a given timeframe. Chapter 17 is devoted to the appraisal of such criticism.

Chapter 18 – The Way Forward – concludes the book by discussing the prospects, issues and challenges facing the Islamic finance movement and how and to what extent it can play its role for the socio-economic development of societies.

# 2

# Distinguishing Features of the Islamic Economic System

## 2.1 INTRODUCTION

The global economic scenario as described in Chapter 1 necessitates the evolution of a system that could lead to a balanced, sustainable and equitable economic order in the world at large for the benefit of individuals and societies. Islamic economic principles can become a basis for promoting a balance between the social and economic aspects of human society, the self and social interests, and between the individual, family, society and the State. At the global level, it could be helpful in eliminating sources of instability, thus making the world a happier place with harmony among followers of various religions.

Although the aspects directly related to the subject of this book pertain to banking and finance, it is worthwhile to discuss the overall framework of Islamic economics within which the Islamic financial system is supposed to work. Accordingly, this chapter will discuss the fundamentals of the Islamic economic worldview having a direct or indirect impact upon the business of Islamic financial institutions and the markets.

## 2.2 ISLAMIC SHARĪ´AH AND ITS OBJECTIVES

Before we discuss economics and economic aspects of human beings in the light of Islamic Sharī´ah (Sharī´ah in brief) we should explain what Islamic Sharī´ah is and what its objectives (Maqāsid) are. This is because all business and financial contracts in the framework of Islamic finance have to conform to the Sharī´ah rules with the objective of helping to achieve Maqāsid al Sharī´ah. Sharī´ah refers to a code of law or divine injunctions that regulate the conduct of human beings in their individual and collective lives. In addition to some general rules there are some specific branches of these injunctions which are: Aqāid, or matters of belief and worship; Akhlāq, or matters for disciplining one's self; Ahkam, or socio-economic and legal systems; Frāidh, or obligations; and Nawāhi, or prohibitions. Islamic economics directly or indirectly deals with all these disciplines.

### 2.2.1 Sources of Sharī´ah Tenets

The primary source of the divine law is the revelation – the Holy Qur'ān and Sunnah of the holy Prophet (pbuh) (Muslims believe in terms of Qur'ānic injunctions that an established Sunnah of the prophet is based on the revelation).[1] Accepting the revelation as the source of tenets and information requires complete submission to Sharī´ah rules. According to Islamic

---

[1] See, for example, verses 3 and 4 of Surah 53 of the Holy Qur'ān.

belief, the Qur'ān is the last revealed book from the Almighty, free from any tampering until the Hereafter (Qur'ān; 15: 9); obedience to the injunctions contained in it is considered necessary by all Muslims, at least conceptually. The Sunnah, which consists of the sayings of and the actions done and/or approved by the holy Prophet (pbuh), is an equally important source of information in Islamic law. The importance of sticking to the Sunnah is obvious from the following verse of the Holy Qur'ān: Allah says, "Indeed you have in the Messenger of Allah an excellent example for the one who hopes in Allah and looks to the Last Day" (33: 21). The Exalted also says: "So if you obey him (i.e. Muhammad, pbuh), only then you will be guided" (24: 54). Almost all Muslims believe that obedience to the orders of the holy Prophet is necessary for being a Muslim.

The other sources of Sharī'ah tenets are Ijma'a (consensus) and Qiyās (analogy), which are based on Ijtihad. Ijtihad, the mental effort of scholars having juristic expertise to find solutions to emerging problems and issues, and Qiyās, or finding solutions through analogy in the light of the text of the Qur'ān and Sunnah, are the secondary sources for derivation of rules and regulation for any upcoming events or issues. Ijma'a of the Companions of the holy Prophet is considered by the overwhelming majority of Muslims an important source for the derivation of laws subsequently. The general welfare/interest (Maslaha-e-Mursalah) of human beings and 'Urf (prevalent practice) are also important tools in the hands of Islamic jurists that are kept in mind for deciding the Sharī'ah position of various contracts and activities without compromising on the basic tenets contained in the Qur'ān and Sunnah. The jurists, Sharī'ah scholars, Sharī'ah boards of Islamic banks and other institutions dealing with Sharī'ah matters are required to suggest solutions and issue edicts regarding various activities on the basis of the above sources of Sharī'ah.

Sharī'ah rules can be divided into Dos (orders to undertake any act) and Don'ts (prohibition from some acts), which can further be divided into the rituals (matters of worship) that are considered as rights of Allah (SWT) and the matters for disciplining human life that constitute the rights of human beings. While the former acts (rituals or matters relating to belief and worship in the form of Frāidh or obligations) have to be accomplished strictly according to the Sharī'ah tenets, the latter matters that pertain to socio-economic rights and obligations are governed by the rule of "General Permissibility" (Ibāhatul Asliyah), which means that all acts and things which have not been expressly prohibited by the original sources of Sharī'ah are permissible. It is pertinent to observe, however, that while Allah (SWT) may like to forgive any of the lapses by Muslims in respect of His rights (first category), lapses in respect of the rights of human beings would have to be forgiven only by the aggrieved person(s). Further, it is a cardinal principle of Islam that everyone is accountable for his acts and the accountability is individual, both in rituals and in socio-economic contracts.

### 2.2.2  Objectives (Maqāsid) of Sharī'ah

The study of objectives is significant, as they reflect the spirit of the Sharī'ah and help jurists in determining the prohibition or permissibility of any matters on the basis of Ijtihad and Qiyās. Catering to the well-being of the people in the worldly life as well as in the Hereafter or relieving them of hardship is the basic objective of Sharī'ah. Islam takes a positive view of life considering man as the viceroy of God. Virtue does not mean abandoning the beauties of life, but enjoying those while remaining within the framework of the values through which Islam seeks to maximize human welfare. It requires living a morally responsible life, earning only by fair means and considering wealth as a stewardship for which account is to be rendered to Allah Almighty.

According to conventional economics, livelihood is the fundamental problem of man and economic development is the ultimate goal of human life. According to Islamic economics, livelihood is necessary and indispensable but is not the true and the only purpose of human life; the life hereafter is the real factor to be taken care of. This way, Islam also caters for the welfare of man in the Hereafter. Wealth in all its possible forms is created by Allah, it belongs to Allah; He has delegated the right of property to man for use and He has the right to demand that man subordinates his use of wealth to the commandments of Allah. "He it is who made you vicegerents in the earth" (6: 165) and "does the man think that he will be just left to himself" (75: 36). Wealth has to be used in such a way that it ensures success in this world and the world hereafter.

The overall objective of Sharī´ah behind these injunctions is the happiness and well-being of human beings in this world and the world hereafter. The concept of happiness from the Islamic perspective is different from the concept of pleasure – the major objective of positive economics. Accordingly, everything which guarantees well-being and fulfils the supreme interests of mankind is included in the objectives of Sharī´ah. These objectives have been identified by jurists like Ghazāli, Shātbi and subsequently by Tahir ibne Ashoor by an inductive survey of the Holy Qur'ān and Sunnah. The objectives can be divided into primary and secondary objectives.

*Primary Objectives*

The primary objectives that Sharī´ah tends to realize are the protection and preservation of:

1. Religion.
2. Life.
3. Progeny – family unit.
4. Property.
5. Intellect.
6. Honour.

The protection of religion means achieving the purpose of worship of Allah (SWT). In Islam there is a comprehensive system of beliefs and Sharī´ah makes it the responsibility of the State to implement Sharī´ah requirements in respect of beliefs.

The protection and preservation of human life refers to the sanctity of life as emphasized in the Qur'ān and Sunnah. There is the law of Qisās to punish those who cause any harm to human life. This objective also refers to the provision of basic necessities to all human beings.

The protection of progeny or the family unit relates to marriage and the family institution, whose purposes are: procreation, protection against lack of chastity and the proper upbringing of children, enabling them to become good human beings and Muslims and to bring peace and tranquility to society. Means to realize this objective are the promotion of the marriage contract, tenets relating to family life and the prohibition of adultery.

The protection of wealth and property refers to the sanctity of the wealth of all members of society, with an emphasis on valid (Halal) earning and discouragement of a concentration of wealth leading to a vast gap between the poor and the rich and the inability of the former to meet their basic needs of food, health and fundamental education. For this purpose, Islam provides a comprehensive law governing Mu'āmalāt or transactions among members of a society.

The promotion of human intellect refers to acquiring knowledge, thus enabling people to differentiate between good and bad and to play their part in enhancing the welfare of human society as a whole.

The protection of human honour and dignity refers to the prohibition of false accusations, the right to privacy and the sanctity of private life.[2]

*Secondary Objectives*

The above primary objectives of Sharī´ah lead to a number of secondary objectives, which are:

1. The establishment of justice and equity in society.
2. The promotion of social security, mutual help and solidarity, particularly to help the poor and the needy in meeting their basic needs.
3. The maintenance of peace and security.
4. The promotion of cooperation in matters of goodness and prohibition of evil deeds and actions.
5. The promotion of supreme universal moral values and all actions necessary for the preservation and authority of nature.

Relating the objectives of Sharī´ah with human welfare, Muhammad Umer Chapra, an economist at the Jeddah-based Islamic Development Bank (IDB), contends:

"However, if well-being were to be defined in a way that rises above the materialist and hedonist sense and incorporates humanitarian and spiritual goals, then economics may not be able to avoid a discussion of what these goals are and how they may be realized. These goals may include not only economic well being, but also human brotherhood and socio-economic justice, mental peace and happiness, and family as well as social harmony. One of the tests for the realization of these goals may be the extent to which social equality, need fulfilment of all, full employment, equitable distribution of income and wealth, and economic stability have been attained without a heavy debt-servicing burden, high rates of inflation, undue depletion of nonrenewable resources, or damage to the ecosystem in a way that endangers life on Earth. Another test may be the realization of family and social solidarity, which would become reflected in the mutual care of members of society for each other, particularly the children, the aged, the sick, and the vulnerable, and absence, or at least minimization, of broken families, juvenile delinquency, crime, and social unrest."

He adds:

"The spiritual and humanitarian goals stated above are of equal, if not of greater importance . . . The material and the spiritual aspects of well-being are not, therefore, independent of each other. They are closely interrelated. Greater family harmony may help raise better individuals to operate in the market, and better social harmony may create a more conducive environment for effective government and accelerated development. If this is true, then the emphasis on serving self-interest and maximizing wealth and consumption may have to be toned down to some extent to serve social interest and optimize human well-being. Some uses of resources that serve self-interest and fit well into the hedonist framework may have to be reduced to fulfil the needs of all individuals in society and thereby promote family and social harmony."[3]

---

[2] For further details, see Chapra, 2000a, pp. 115–125 and Mansoori, 2005, pp. 11, 12.
[3] Chapra, 2000a, pp. 4–8. (Also published in *The Journal of Socio-economics*, **29**, pp. 21–37).

Hence, from the study of the Qur'ān and Sunnah, some basic socio-economic rights of human beings have been identified. These rights are:

1. The right to safety.
2. The right to be informed.
3. The right to choose.
4. The right to be heard.
5. The right to satisfaction of basic needs.
6. The right to redress.
7. The right to education.
8. The right to a healthy environment.

Islam requires rulers and various regulators in the system to protect the masses from harm and hardship caused by unscrupulous factors in society through strong and effective laws, and they should be respected in the sense of fulfilment of all socio-economic rights. The State must also curb institutional and other malpractices.

## 2.3   WHY STUDY ISLAMIC ECONOMICS?

A cursory look at the above objectives will reveal that economic aspects or matters relating to the sustenance of human beings command a central place in the realm of Sharī'ah. Man is largely concerned in his life with two main aspects, namely material resources/means of sustenance and religious beliefs. Studying economics is important for the dual purpose of having better sustenance and religious imperatives. Islam does not like the concept of the "pious person" as distinct from the "worldly person". It enjoins a system of devotions/worship as well as guides on the economy, political affairs and international relations. Regarding this integrated approach, the Holy Qur'ān says:

> It is not righteousness that ye turn your faces towards East or West; but it is righteousness to believe in Allah and the Last Day, and the Angels, and the Book and the Messengers; to spend of your substance, out of love for Him, for your kin, for orphans, for the needy, for the wayfarer, for those who ask, and for the ransom of slaves; to be steadfast in prayer, and practise regular charity, to fulfil the contracts which we have made; and to be firm and patient, in pain (or suffering) and adversity, and throughout all periods of panic. Such are the people of truth, God fearing. (2: 177)

Professor Dr Anis Ahmad explains beautifully the implications of the above verse of the Holy Qur'ān by saying:

> "While the verse begins with a reference to spending substantially for one's kin, it immediately refers to orphans, the needy, travellers and others who may fall in to the category of strangers.... An objective analysis of the Qur'ānic teachings informs us about the social and human dimensions of the Qur'ānic message. A book which does not want any human being to be enslaved politically, economically, culturally and educationally, is relevant for all human beings. Muslims and others should directly undertake an unbiased, critical and objective analysis of the Qur'ān so as to understand its message to humanity. The ethic-centric approach of the Qur'ān makes its teachings valuable and relevant for all who are concerned with the future of humanity. It offers the most reliable way of building a sustainable and peaceful world order."[4]

---

[4] Ahmad, Anis, 1997.

Thus, Islam emphasizes fair and equitable distribution of resources and meeting the needs of economically feeble people as part of devotion, worship and faith. It induces its followers to relate their piety (Taqwa) with social realities. It persuades a person to share the blessings and bounties of Allah with others as a matter of obligation by declaring that Taqwa encompasses not only the love of Allah, but also the love of fellow human beings, who should be treated as part of an extended human family. This refers in a way to the need to study the economic aspects of mankind.

M.A. Mannan has indicated seven reasons or socio-economic imperatives for the study of Islamic economics, which are broadly covered by the above two factors. These imperatives are ideological, economic, social, ethical, political, historical and international. To him:

> "The significance of the study of Islamic economics lies in its balanced focus on the production of goods and services as well as other determinants of the 'quality of life' for which value judgement may be needed within the Islamic value framework. Accordingly, Islamic economics being an integrated body of knowledge does overlap with other disciplines such as religion, sociology, political science in a much more significant way than secular economics. The fact is that Islamic economics cannot remain neutral between different ends. It is concerned with what is and what ought to be, in the light of the Sharī´ah. Therefore, it involves the study of social, political, ethical and moral issues affecting the economic problems directly or indirectly."[5]

The Islamic world as a whole is underdeveloped and backward when compared to the Western developed countries. Some Muslim economists have been emphasizing for many years the study and development of Islamic economics to help the underdeveloped countries come out of the vicious circle of poverty, ignorance and illiteracy. But the backwardness and underdevelopment of the Muslim world is not the only imperative for the study of Islamic economics. The global socio-economic situation in the world, which indicates the failure of all secularist systems, also calls for finding any better alternative for solving the problems of massive underdevelopment and injustice in the world, where the rich and the affluent, both in the developed and the developing world, have increasingly become accustomed to "hyper-consumption", leaving billions of human beings starved, illiterate and lacking any socio-cultural position. This luxurious and conspicuous/lavish consumption has led to a general trend of spending to enhance social status as well as to get pleasure.[6]

As a direct result of this trend, "Trickle-down" and all other economic theories that referred to automatic care of the poor when the growth rate or national income rises have failed. The Western concept of the welfare state has now been replaced by "the least government is the best government". The market is now the engine of economic growth and State intervention in removing income disparities between households and various groups in society is more of a myth than a reality. This system is producing poverty.

Even the normative part in modern capitalist economies is the outcome of the Enlightenment movement, the worldview of which was basically secularist. It considered all the revealed truths of religion as "simply figments of the imagination, nonexistent, indeed at the bottom priestly inventions designed to keep men ignorant of the ways of Reason and Nature". This weakened the hold of religion and the collective sanction it provides to moral values, and thus deprived society of morally-oriented filtering, motivating and restructuring mechanisms.[7]

---

[5] Mannan, 1984.
[6] *The Economist*, London, 24th December–6th January, 2006, pp. 66, 67.
[7] Chapra, 1996, p. 14.

As the main theme of the Islamic economic system revolves around care for the poor and socio-economic justice, studying Islamic economics should be a strategic activity for economists and policymakers. The Islamic economic system can be studied properly only in the context of the Islamic way of life as a whole. The Holy Qur'ān gives broad principles of values regarding the economic aspects of man's life, like an owner's attitude towards his property, society's attitude towards the needy, the cooperative basis of the economic relationship and the bias against a concentration of wealth. The individual must be mindful of other ends while planning for economic ends. He has to subject each and every activity to thorough scrutiny, avoiding all those forms which are injurious to social interest.

### 2.3.1   The Role of Islamic Economists

The early Islamic jurists mainly advised individuals and rulers on behaviour in economic matters and economic policies. In the later period, they also analysed such economic thoughts as trading, prices, money, profit-sharing, taxes, development, etc. They gave special importance to ethics and moral purposes and focused on justice, need fulfilment, efficiency, freedom, growth and development. Those who did work of outstanding nature included Imams of juristic schools of thought like Abu Hanifa, Malik, Shafii, Ahmad ibn-e-Hanbal, Zaid bin Ali, and others like Muhammad bin Hasan al Sheibani, Abu Yusuf, Yahya bin Adam, Abu Ubaid, Qudama bin Jafar, Ali ibn Muhammad Al Mawardi, Nizamul Mulk Tusi, Nasiruddin Tusi, Abu Hamid Muhammad Ghazali, Ibn Taymiyah, Ibn Qayyim, Ibn Khaldun, al Maqrizi and Shah Waliullah. The contributions from a few of the jurists are briefly given hereunder:

- Ibn Khaldun's[8] empirical social inquiry gave him the unique perception of causal interdependence of political and economic power as well as pressures which are generated by vested interests in an organized society.
- With regard to the activity of public and private sectors in an economy, it may be relevant to point out that Ibn Khaldun, in his Muqaddamah (literally an "Introduction to History", which has been described by the renowned historian Professor Arnold Toynbee as "the greatest work of its kind that has been created by any man in any time or place") strongly supported free private enterprise and advocated that "capitalists amongst the inhabitants of cities need rank and protection". He was against government meddling with the market mechanism by inequitable taxation or by direct participation in production and distribution. He believed that a State monopoly in commerce and agriculture ruins the economy.
- Ibn Khaldun anticipated Adam Smith in his theory of labour value; Malthus for the theory of population and Keynes for a normative role for the State. He also presented a coherent theory of economic growth. As such, he can be treated as the founder of economic science. His ideas on the market system, production, exchange and consumption of wealth, macroeconomics, taxation, role of the government, money, labour, etc. provide a valuable study of economic thought and the system.
- Ibn Khaldun states: "The finances of a ruler can be increased and his financial resources improved only through the revenue from the taxes. The revenue from taxes can be

---

[8] Abu Zayd, Waliyuddeen 'Abdur Rahmaan Ibne Muhammad, popularly known as Ibn Khaldun – the greatest Muslim social scholar of the Middle Ages (AD 1332–1406). For his contribution to economics, see Boulakia, 1971. Also see a note on him at http://www.islamicissues.info/essays_others.html.

improved only through the equitable treatment of people with property and regard for them... other means taken by the ruler, such as engaging in commerce and agriculture, soon turn out to be harmful to the subjects, to be ruinous to revenue and to decrease cultural activities". Also, like Adam Smith, Ibn Khaldun noticed that productivity depends on the extent of the market, division of labour and specialization.

- With his profound historical, political and economic insight, Ibn Khaldun warned that the growth of absolute power in the State is the cause of decline of economic prosperity. For, according to him, absolute power has to be preserved by expanding bureaucracy, the army and the police, which have to be supported by increased taxation, confiscation and, worst still, by direct interference of the State in economic activity by engaging in commerce and industry.

- Ibn Taymiyah[9] discussed the concepts of Thaman-e-mithl (normal/market price or wage), economic freedom, pricing in the market, the role of the ombudsman and the functions of the government in the development of a smooth and just socio-economic order.

- The thirteenth century Memorandum of Nasiruddin Tusi laid down guidance for the Mongol kings on the financial administration of the then Iran.

- Shah Waliullah discussed basic principles on production and exchange of wealth.[10]

With regard to the contribution of the Islamic world to trade and economics in the Middle Ages, Maurice Lombard, in his book *The Golden Age of Islam* (originally published in 1971 in French and translated into English in 1975) writes:

"The Muslim East provided the driving force behind economic and cultural life; the West was a Void – an area in which all commercial and intellectual activity had ceased after the decline and fall of Rome and the subsequent barbarian invasions.... Great ports provided the Muslim World with ships, dockyards, and seafaring populations. There were three enormous complexes: first, shipping in the Persian Gulf and the Red Sea, which Arab and Persian sailors opened up towards the Indian Ocean and which was complemented by the river-boats of the Euphrates and Tigris; next, the ports of Syria and Egypt, foremost of which was Alexandria, backed by the river-boats of the Nile; finally, the ports on the Sicilian Strait and the Strait of Gibraltar, supported by the river-boats on the Guadalquivir. Caravan towns also possessed transport systems which dominated the Mesopotamian routes (running westwards towards Syria and eastwards towards Iran and central Asia), the Arabian routes, and the Berber trading routes crossing the Sahara. (p. 8)

The centre of the Muslim World was situated in the Isthmus region, bounded by the Persian Gulf, the Red Sea, the Mediterranean, the Black Sea, and the Caspian Sea. It was, therefore, set at the intersection of two major economic units: the Indian Ocean area and the Mediterranean area. These two territories, united in Hellenistic times but later split into two rival worlds, the Roman–Byzantine and the Parthico–Sassanian, were now reunited by the Muslim conquest, so as to form a new, vast territory which was economically one. This unity rested on large-scale trading relations along caravan and maritime routes, on one main currency, the Muslim Dinar, and one international commercial language, Arabic.... Finally, the unity mentioned above was helped by the reintroduction into world trade of the great consumer markets of the western Mediterranean... " (p. 9)

With regard to the growth of money in the Islamic economy in the 10th century, he says:

"Finally, monetary economy was important, and was expressed in an abundant minting of dinars made possible by the influx of new gold and the development of credit, which doubled the circulation

---

[9] For the contribution of Ibn Taymiyah, see Ahmad, 1961.

[10] For details on the contribution by Islamic jurists to economics, see Chapra, 2000a, pp. 145–172; Siddiqi, 2002.

of currency. In the ninth century, . . . the growth of wealth and commercial transactions was so great that actual cash could be seen changing hands in the smallest townships where, hitherto, simple barter had been the only method in use. And so the enlarged area of money circulation was matched by a greater power wielded by town over country."

Referring to the fall of the Muslim world he says:

"(it) received a mortal blow in the form of the crises, the disturbances, the invasions of the second half of the eleventh century. They impeded the powerful flow of trade, thereby provoking the decline of the cities. Henceforward the Muslim World was not a united whole, but divided. There was a Turkish Islam, a Persian Islam, a Syrian Islam, an Egyptian Islam, and a Maghreb Islam. Gone was the single Muslim civilization and in its place was a resurgence of regional particularisms, embodied in a number of different Muslim civilizations. (pp. 10, 11)

However, even during its economic decline, the Muslim World long continued to influence the world in the realms of science, medicine and philosophy. It played a conspicuous part in medicine especially, not only during the Renaissance but right up to the nineteenth century." (For detail, see pp. 236–239).

After the start of the Renaissance movement in the late 19th century, Islamic economics started re-emerging as an intelligent academic pursuit. Scholars like Syed Qutab, Syed Abul A'ala Mawdudi, Hifzurrehman Sweharvi, Muhammad Yusufuddin, Syed Baqar Sadre, and Dr Hameedullah can be considered pioneers and scholars of the first generation in the Modern World who initiated the process of defining modern economic thought in the light of the principles of Islam. Formal work on Islamic economics in the modern world that has led to a vigorous revival of Islamic economic thought has been done by a large number of economists, notable among which are Anwar Iqbal Qureshi, Ahmad al Najjar, Nejatullah Siddiqi, Sheikh Mahmud Ahmad, Mahmud Abud Saud, Muhammad Umar Zubair, Monzar Kahaf, S.M. Hasanuz Zaman, Anas Zarqa, M.A. Mannan, Mohamed Ali Elgari, M. Umer Chapra, Abbas Mirakhor, Mohsin S. Khan, Fahim Khan, Munawar Iqbal, Khurshid Ahmad and many others.

Contemporary Islamic economists (of the second and the third generation) have discussed almost all areas of modern economics including market forces, production, distribution, consumption and allocation of resources, efficiency, scarcity, choice and opportunity cost, the role of money, individual–society–State relationships, individual self-interest, the welfare economy, mutual help (social welfare function), ethics and, last but not least, government budgeting and finance and the economic responsibility of the State.

Considerable work has been done by well-known economists including Mohsin Khan, Abbas Mirakhor, Zuber Iqbal, Nejatullah Siddiqi, Anas Zarqa, Monzar Kahaf and other Islamic economists of the second and third generations, as mentioned above, on various segments of economic management. These works largely pertain to interest-free banking and interest-free investment and production. Also, a good deal of work has been done on fiscal policy, Zakat, auditing and accounting, banking regulations and supervision.

But all of these are segments and have not been put together into a comprehensive model. These segments (with variations) are being practised/implemented in several countries. However, even in the contents and implementation of these segments, there is a lack of uniformity. This is yet another problem which needs to be addressed both at scholarly and operational levels.

The work is being done in different areas. But, Islamic economics in the form of a complete model and a welfare function may take a longer time. It is obvious that where value judgements are involved, quantification, and hence uniformity, is not possible, with clear implications for both the formulation and implementation of policies. Before this is done, Islamic economics can be introduced in parts only. This choice rests with individual countries.

## 2.4   ISLAMIC ECONOMICS: WHAT SHOULD IT BE?

To understand the possible structure of Islamic economics, enabling a society to realize the objectives identified above, we may first of all discuss the concepts of economics proper and normative economics. Economics proper, which is also called positive economics, is concerned exclusively with the scientific explanation of behaviour under conditions of scarcity. It is a science, value neutral and is concerned with empirical and not normative aspects. Even where it deals with values and purposes, it deals with them objectively as facts, which, along with other relevant data, determine what is or may be, but not what should be. It describes, but does not prescribe. The definition of "Economics" by Lionel Robbins is an example of positive economics.[11]

The second kind of economics is normative or welfare economics, which is sometimes called "political economy". In the case of normative economics, policy recommendations must involve some value judgements. The Islamic approach is that economic development and creation of abundant wealth are means to satisfy human needs and support society. These are not sought for boasting or spending in offence, arrogance or oppression. Linking this world with the Hereafter, Islam enjoins Muslims to seek the Hereafter through what they earn and not to forget their share of the worldly life. The Holy Qur'ān says:

> "And seek the abode of the Hereafter in that which Allah has given you, and do not neglect your portion of worldly life, and be kind as Allah has been kind to you, and seek not disorder/corruption in the earth". (28: 77)

Therefore, Islamic rules of economics make it binding for human beings not only to abide by the Sharī´ah tenets relating to dos and don'ts but also to keep in mind the impact of their activities on others and society as a whole. To realize the goal, the State should try to control the wants of the people through a filtering process, motivate the people to abstain from activities injurious to others and restructure the socio-economic system for the transfer of resources from one use/sector to others to ultimately realize the dual objective.[12]

It is the welfare content which makes normative economics different from positive economics. Broadly, welfare economics comprises the aims, goals and aspirations of society and these are reduced into the utilitarian principle of greatest satisfaction of the maximum number of people in society. Islamic economics tries mostly to remove injustice and inequality for promoting progress. To realize the objective, it accepts the basic concomitants of the system of market economy, like the innate right of ownership, freedom of enterprise and the competitive environment in business and industry. However, the vision of Islam in this regard is different from the role models of present market systems which have become outdated with the march of events. The Sharī´ah indicates the directions of transformation towards a social order of justice, well-being, security and knowledge, but it does not impose these laws. It tends to provide equal chances to all for earning a livelihood leading to equitable, not equal, distribution of income and wealth, just like blood in the human body that

---

[11] Robbins, 1962.
[12] Chapra, 2000a, pp. 357–369.

is not distributed among various organs of the body equally because of the different nature of the jobs rendered by each organ.

It is also because of the noncoercive nature of Sharī´ah that the market is relied upon as a natural phenomenon of ethical human transformation. The holy Prophet (pbuh) categorically discouraged intervention for price fixation as long as price fluctuations occurred due to market forces alone. But when undue monopolistic and unjust pricing, production and distributional practices were existent, Al-Hisbah (the institution of the ombudsman) was empowered as a social regulatory body to check these imbalances for purposes of re-establishing a better semblance of market-driven exchanges in the light of the just order that Sharī´ah aims at in society at large.

### 2.4.1   Islamic Economics Defined

Islamic economics has been defined differently by different economists/scholars, keeping in mind specific aspects of human life. To Ibn Khaldun, economics meant the desire for food and other requirements and efforts to obtain them; and a science which deals with management of households and cities in accordance with dictates of reason as well as ethics, so that the masses may be directed towards a behaviour that leads to the preservation and performance of their species.

Mohsin S. Khan, a senior economist at the IMF, says:

"Broadly speaking, the term 'Islamic Economics' defines a complete system that prescribes a specific pattern of social and economic behaviour for all individuals. It deals with a wide-ranging set of issues, such as property rights, incentive system, allocation of resources, types of economic freedom, system of economic decision-making and proper role of the government. The over-riding objective of the system is social justice and specific patterns of income and wealth distribution and consequently economic policies are to be designed to achieve these ends."

S.M. Hasanuz Zaman, an IDB Laureate in Islamic economics, has critically examined definitions by a number of scholars and given his own definition:

"Islamic Economics is the knowledge of application of injunctions and rules of the Sharī´ah that stop injustice in the acquisition and disposition of material resources in order to provide satisfaction to individuals and enable them to perform their obligations to Allah and society."[13]

This implies that Islamic economics is a social science which studies the economic problems of people in the light of the values of Islam. One way of looking at Islamic economics would be the use of resources for the welfare of the people within the framework of Sharī´ah. Once a framework of the Sharī´ah has been adopted, it will determine various aspects of economic management like the contents of production, trade, finance, distribution and many other things.

Islamic economics deals with issues like how to create, distribute, own and enhance property and wealth, how to spend and dispose of it for the benefit of individuals as well as societies. The means of production of goods are almost the same for all nations, as economic science is universal for all nations. As such, an Islamic economy would also be producing/providing all goods and services required for the "welfare" of mankind. But the economic system that determines how to distribute the wealth and how to possess, spend or dispose of it, is different for different nations depending upon their ideology, and here lies

---

[13] Hasanuz Zaman, 2000.

ιne difference between the Islamic economic system and the capitalistic or the socialistic systems.

The integrated model of the Islamic social framework is based, among other things, on the following criteria, which provide a positive motivation for economic activities, steered by the concept of a fair balance between material and spiritual needs and between the individual's and social needs:

1. Equilibrium between work and worship.
2. Human equality.
3. Mutual responsibilities in society.
4. Distributive justice.
5. Balanced and beneficent use of the "bounties of God".
6. Limited sovereignty of individuals in terms of "self interest" for the benefit of fellow beings and society.
7. The principle of co-existence.
8. The freedom of conscience.

## 2.5   PARAPHERNALIA OF ISLAMIC ECONOMICS

The objective of the Islamic economic system, like any other economic system, is the realization of efficiency and equity in allocation and distribution of resources, for which it recognizes the role of market forces and the freedom of individuals. But it also recognizes the possible adverse impact of the totally unregulated market on various sections of society, particularly the poor and the disadvantaged. The pure materialistic "positive" approach has never been capable of serving social interests and realizing such goals. The "invisible hand" of market forces, as contended by Adam Smith, has failed to fulfil the social obligations required for the ultimate socio-economic outcome of human actions. Hence, Islamic economics provides ample room for State intervention to achieve an optimal mix of functioning of market players guided by individual self-interest and serving the social interest by the State's facilitation and overseeing activities.

The urge for maximization of wealth by individuals without taking care of its impact on the well-being of others or society as a whole cannot generate long-term sustainable growth and well-being of individuals or societies. Therefore, both positive and normative objectives are to be realized through market functioning supported by State facilitation and intervention aimed at realization of socio-economic goals like need-fulfilment, an optimum and stable growth rate, equitable distribution of income and wealth with class and ecological coherence.

As indicated above, an economic system has to be discussed as a thought based upon any ideology, while economic science should be considered a science which deals with the creation of wealth. An economic system relates to the management of wealth distribution in a society and enables or restricts its members from utilizing the means of production and satisfaction. Production of goods and services and their distribution among various groups in society, sources of funds for the State and their spending were the main areas of Islamic economics and the system up to the Middle Ages. Commercial activities of that period depicted a number of techniques of production, distribution, trade, payment and mobility of money and credit.

Thus, the system comprises the following three main elements:

1. Ownership of commodities and wealth.[14]
2. Transfer of the ownership.
3. Distribution of wealth among the people.

The variables and thoughts used in economic analysis include the determinants of the level of income and employment, money and banking, fiscal and monetary policies, national income accounting, economic growth, demand and supply of money and stability. Details may also include expenditure, the savings–investment relationship, the savings–income relationship, consumption and investment functions, the potential level of output, employment, labour force and profit as aggregate variables. All these determinants will correspond to principal Islamic values and tenets.

The abolition of interest (Riba), promotion of trading and other real business activities, establishment of profit-sharing as a tool, the application of Zakat and avoidance of wasteful consumption (Isrābf) along with an effective overseeing role of the State constitute the key macroeconomic features of an ideal Islamic economy. Study of these variables would indicate the state of any Islamic economy, its stability, weaknesses and strengths and various relationships among producers and users of resources.

### 2.5.1   Ownership of Resources and Property Rights

Islamic economics, based on the paradigm of socio-economic justice, takes its roots from the belief that all resources in the world belong to its Creator, One God; human beings are holding these resources in trust. Behaving as vicegerent of the Creator, they are free to earn and spend the wealth according to His orders given to mankind through His Messengers. Man has to enjoy and use wealth under Allah's command. Islam has given the individual the freedom to earn a livelihood. Likewise, Islam has given every individual the right to enjoy whatever wealth he has earned by legal means and whatever wealth he has received through the Islamic law of inheritance.

Ownership by man is thus Divine permission for utilizing the goods and assets. The Holy Qur'ān says: "And give them from the Māl of Allah, which He gave to you." (24: 33). It also says: "And spend from what He put you in charge of" (57: 7). As such, Islam has set the limits and the means through which individuals, groups, the public and the State can possess property in such a way that acquisition in varying degree is within reach of all the people, despite disparities in their abilities. These limits are in terms of the quality or the means of acquiring and not in terms of quantity of wealth, as this resists human beings' strife to work diligently. Limits in terms of quality are necessary, otherwise human greed could corrupt the economy and cause chaotic relationships in society. It also conforms to human nature so as to satisfy their basic needs and enable people to benefit from comforts.

The following are the means of possessing goods: work, inheritance, purchasing/obtaining property for sustenance, properties granted as gifts and the State granting possession of something to the citizens. To facilitate the acquisition of property and wealth, Islam has indicated legal means of ownership and its transfer through a variety of contracts. General

---

[14] The term commodity includes everything possessed for utilization through buying, leasing or borrowing, whether by consumption, such as an apple, or by usage, such as a car, or through utilizing it, like borrowing machinery or leasing a house. Property (Māl) is anything that can be possessed and includes money, such as gold and silver, commodities, such as clothes and foodstuffs, immovable properties, such as houses and factories, and all other things which are possessed. Human effort is a means to obtain the property or its benefit. Therefore, wealth is the property (Māl) and the effort together. (Nabhani, 1997, p. 47).

rules for these contracts have also been defined in detail with the possibility of resolving any contemporary issues through Ijtihad, subject to observance of allowed limits. These rules allow man to utilize the resources by consuming them, benefiting from them or exchanging them via a number of contracts like sale, loan, lease or gift. Rules pertaining to investment of wealth/property have also been laid down.

Along with property rights, income and profit entitlement are established in Islamic economics. This must occur through the effort, work or taking responsibility (Dhamān) and distribution by means like partnership, trade, joint ventures, loans, various vehicles of transfer incomes like grants and Zakat and the control of waste. Hence, the Islamic economy has a linkage between the market functions of productive involvement and growth and the institutional functions of policy and control.

### 2.5.2  Islamic Welfare Approach

The concept of welfare in Islam is neither exclusively materialistic nor absolutely spiritual. It has rather dovetailed the spiritual and material aspects of life so that they may serve as a source of mutual strength and as the foundation of true human welfare and happiness.

Study of the teachings of the Holy Qur'ān and Sunnah leads us to some basic principles of the economic system of Islam, which encourage human beings' development, enforce justice, stop exploitation and tend to set up a contented and satisfied society that can be termed a real welfare society. In addition to achieving optimum produce in both public and private sectors, allocation and distribution of resources and produce must take a course that fulfils the basic human needs of all, irrespective of the colour, race and/or creed of the people. The fulfilment of basic needs makes society tranquil, comfortable, healthy and efficient, and able to contribute properly towards the realization and perpetuation of human welfare. On account of the crucial importance of need fulfilment, it needs to be discussed in detail.

As indicated above, the economic system of Islam tends to ensure the satisfaction of all the basic needs (food, clothing and housing) of every individual, without any distinction, and to provide resources to enjoy from living in a particular society. So individuals and society are both important to make a contented and happy economy and society. All individuals are linked with one another by certain relationships in social and economic dealings. Therefore, the standard of living in an Islamic society has to be raised by securing the basic rights for every individual in terms of need fulfilment side by side with enabling them to secure comforts and prosperity.

In order to meet the basic needs of each and every member of a society, Islam urges all to earn and seek the provisions for use by mankind. Islamic economy achieves this objective by obliging each capable person to work, enabling him to fulfil his and his dependents' basic needs. A number of verses of the Holy Qur'ān and traditions of the holy Prophet (pbuh) reveal that Islam obliges individuals to earn and use the wealth so as to develop the economy for the betterment of society. It is the State's responsibility to take measures and adopt policies to enable those who are willing to work and anxious to work to find employment.

The principle backed by self-interest alone as a secular core value is in direct conflict with the core Islamic value of "moderation", which would mean necessities of life together with some comforts aimed at minimizing the hardships of life. Hence, items of luxury and conspicuous consumption are not encouraged in the Islamic worldview of development.

If some individuals are unable to earn and fulfil their needs, Sharī´ah obliges their fellow beings – depending upon the nature of the relationship like neighbours, relatives, etc. – to support them in fulfilling their basic needs. If there is nobody to support such people, Islam obliges the State to be responsible for the support of all citizens, particularly mentally or physically disabled people and the destitute. The holy Prophet has said: "The Imam (ruler) is incharge (Rā´iee) and he is responsible for his citizens."

As regards basic needs, there is total agreement among Islamic economists that it is the most important objective of the Islamic distributive policy. However, there may be some difference of opinion as to which needs should be guaranteed and how these should be fulfilled. Nevertheless, maximization of Falah (welfare in this world and the Hereafter) has firm relevance with the Islamic concept of development, which can be achieved through obedience to Allah (SWT) in worship (Ibādāt) as well as Mu'āmalāt, including all kinds of economic activities related to production, consumption, exchange and distribution. As long as seeking the pleasure of Allah is set as the final goal, the latter will be in perfect conformity with the former.

This describes the contents of the Islamic welfare function, incorporating a collection of value judgements covering all noble things in life. However, by going beyond material welfare and for a reward in the world hereafter, these elements of the welfare function are virtually impossible to quantify. That is what constitutes the greatest challenge for Islamic economists. As pointed out by Umer Chapra:

> "There is, however, no theoretical macroeconomic model that would show how the Islamic values and institutions, and different sectors of the economy, society and polity would interact to help realize the vision. . . . The field where very little progress has been made is microeconomics. It has not been possible to establish the relationship among the macroeconomic goals and the behaviour of different economic agents and the kind of socio-economic and political reform that the realization of goals may require."[15]

### 2.5.3  The Factors of Production

The Qur'ānic injunctions on distribution of wealth help a lot in introducing a broader basis of the distribution of income and wealth and require that in the process of distribution, none of the factors of production is deprived of its share nor does it exploit any other. Land, labour and capital jointly create value. As a result, the land-owner, the labourer and the owner of capital should jointly share the produce. The distinctive feature of the Islamic system is that capital has to bear the loss, if any. In addition to this, Islam compulsorily retains a portion of the produced wealth as Zakat for those who are prevented from contributing their share in production due to any social, physical or economic handicap.

Capitalism has four factors of production:

1. Capital – the produced means of production – its compensation is "interest".
2. Land that includes all natural resources – things which are being used as means of production without having previously undergone any process of human activity – its compensation is the rent.
3. Labour – any effort or physical exertion on the part of human beings – its compensation is wages.

---

[15] Chapra, 2000b, pp. 21–37.

4. The entrepreneur or organization – which brings together the other three factors, makes use of them and bears the risk of profit and loss in production – its compensation is "profit".

The factors of production in Islamic economics are:

1. Capital – includes those means of production which cannot be used in the process of production until and unless they are either wholly consumed or completely altered in form during the production process; it cannot fetch any rent. "Profit" is compensation of capital in the Islamic framework, but it comes with responsibility or liability. So the profit on any capital is the residual revenue of a business conducted with that capital after making payment to all other parties; if the residual is negative, the capital owner has to suffer a loss that is the shortfall in the principal employed in the business.
2. Land – all such means of production which are used in the process of production in such a way that their corpus and original form remains unaltered. Their compensation is rental; these can be lent or leased. For example, an owner of a factory would claim rent of land and that of the installed machinery and plant; similarly, owners of houses, vehicles, machines, etc. are entitled to rent.
3. Labour – that is, human exertion, whether physical or mental and also includes organization and planning. Its compensation is wages.

Profit, according to Islamic theory, is the result of the productivity of capital that an entrepreneur has invested or a reward for his workmanship or for shouldering responsibility. It is not a reward for capital or for enterprise *per se*. An entrepreneur who, for example, brings together factors like land, labour, machinery and uses his own financial resources (money capital), has to pay wages and rental for the use of land or machinery as per agreed terms; he will make a profit on his capital or reward for his entrepreneurship only if there is some residual after payment of the rental, wages and other expenses on raw materials, etc.

If the money capital is taken as a loan, the entrepreneur is bound to repay the same amount of loan without any addition or shortfall, irrespective of the fact that he earned a profit or incurred any loss in the business. In a case where the whole or a part of the money capital is taken from anyone else who wants a profit on it, and the business suffers a loss, the money capital would pro rata reduce and the provider of the capital would be obliged to accept the shortfall or erosion of the whole amount. Therefore, a capital provider or an entrepreneur is not entitled to profit simply by virtue of being a capital owner or an entrepreneur. All participants in a joint business have similar rights and liabilities according to the nature of the activity or the terms of the agreement.

The above discussion is suggestive of five factors of production, namely: land, capital, labour, management and responsibility/liability. While land as a factor of production includes all nonconsumable assets that can be rented, the concept of capital requires some detail. This is so because of a different treatment of capital in the conventional economic theory which narrows down the concept by restricting capital to borrowed money; hence its claim on interest, which is discarded by Islam. Money itself is not recognized as capital and as such it cannot earn a profit in itself. It cannot claim the rent as it is consumed and its form changes when it is used. As the provider of funds is liable to loss, if any, he is an entrepreneur as well. He will get a profit/loss for his capital and wages/remuneration for his entrepreneurship/labour. If he does not manage the business himself and provides capital to any other individual/group of individuals for any business, he will have a share in the profit while the manager of the business will get "wages" in the form of a share in the profit. But if the business suffers a loss, the capital owner will bear the loss while the manager's labour will be wasted.

The responsibility to get a job done is also a factor; it may be taken by a single person or a group of people joining together as business partners. A number of financers may join together to contract a partnership and pursue any business of their choice, themselves or through hired managers. They may also get the job done by signing subpartnerships with other contractors or companies. They would all share the profits of such business. They may also assign the job to big business organizations and firms to complete different jobs on an offered bid price. The reward for taking the responsibility to coordinate the services and supplies and get the work done according to the terms of the contract is also profit.

### 2.5.4  Restrained Individual Freedom

The "laissez faire" that is the basis of conventional economics has a built-in possibility of distortions in the smooth functioning of the market economy, mainly on account of the unbridled "profit motive" leading to a focus on enrichment without any care for the impact on others or society. Even though the Great Depression and the resultant Keynesian revolution tended to undermine this faith in the efficacy of market forces, the recent disenchantment with a large government role in the economy has restored it and there is a call for liberalism or return, as early as possible, to the classical model with "minimum" government intervention.[16]

State intervention with a secular approach cannot produce long-term solid results for society either. This is because the "profit motive" in the absence of any ethical norms, finds loopholes for misdeeds, injustice and corruption. Even socially undesirable professions like gambling and sex-related industries become part and parcel of public policy, leading to socio-economic problems as most capitalists invest their money in lucrative unhealthy practices and not in socially desirable sectors like education, health, housing and commodity producing sectors including agriculture and industry.

Islamic economics is not devoid of money matters, because those form the greater part of any economy. However, it maintains a balance between production and consumption and cares about distribution. It draws a line of demarcation between good and evil or lawful and unlawful. The overall message that we derive from the literature on the philosophy and the nature of the Islamic economic system is that it is a means to achieve development in terms of complete human personality from all dimensions – material, world and ethical, of individuals and of society as a whole. It pays due attention to causes, effects and consequences of actions.

There are certain curbs and some checks imposed by Sharī'ah on consumers' behaviour. Individuals are not at large to exercise their own will in terms of choice. Some basic rules have been laid down to govern intensity of wealth-gaining and income-consuming activities of society. It does not stand neutral as regards ends and means. It is religion-based, valuation-oriented, morality-judged and spiritually-bound. It is positive and normative science, as it links materialistic and moralistic requirements of changing nature. Thus, the scope of Islamic economics is the administration of scarce resources in human society in the light of the ethical concept of welfare in Islam.

---

[16] Chapra, 1992, p. 17.

All types of work except those leading to indecency or socio-economic loss to other individuals and society are permissible. A basic principle of the Islamic legal system is that an activity or a commodity that is not prohibited through the Sharī´ah texts is permissible. Thus, man has to observe the prohibitions only. Islamic economics would mean undertaking all activities individually or collectively that are not prohibited and that could add to the welfare and happiness of human beings.

The most important prohibitions in the field of economics are the prohibition of interest, hazard and gambling due to their extremely harmful impacts on society. Such limitations are necessary for the fulfilment of the overall objectives of the Sharī´ah for making society happy and satisfied, both materially and spiritually.

### 2.5.5   Liberalism versus State Intervention

The individual self-interest of conventional economics leads to maximization of wealth and want satisfaction, independent of its impact on the rest of society. The concept of "positiveness" has been expressed in terms of unrestrained individual freedom, making economics "entirely neutral between ends". Further, it is believed that market forces will themselves create "order" and "harmony", and lead to "efficiency" and "equity". The government should hence abstain from intervening.

The concept of Pareto efficiency in conventional economics is based on the assumption that the market will automatically take care of "equity" and that the market equilibrium will be a Pareto optimum, leading to realization of normative goals at least in the long run. It leads to the common belief of modern economics that any intervention in the framework of Pareto optimality would lead to less efficient results. This framework is, however, based on some assumptions like harmony between individual preferences and social interest, equal distribution of income and wealth, a true reflection of the urgency of wants by prices and perfect competition. Since no real world market is likely to satisfy these assumptions, there is a considerable distortion in the expression of priorities in the markets. Hence, the Pareto efficiency or Pareto optimality concept that generates conflict in society does not fit properly in the philosophy of Islamic economics. It reflects a built-in bias against the realization of normative goals if reliance is placed primarily on prices for allocation and distribution of resources.[17]

Society is for the individuals who are responsible for their actions and accountable to the one creator for their conduct. The individual has a right to participate in economic activities for his sustenance and the tasks relating to social well-being, subject to the limitations and injunctions of the Qur'ān and the Sunnah. The crucial involvement of individuals for the collective benefit of society has been aptly described by the holy Prophet (pbuh) in a parable, as reported by Imam Bukhari in his "Sahih" and as given below:

"Those who accept and abide by the limits ordained by Allah and those who transgress may be likened to two groups sharing a boat; one group occupying the upper deck and the other the hold. Whenever those in the hold required water they had to go up to draw it. So they thought among themselves; why not have a hole in the bottom and thus save inconvenience to those in the top? Now if those on the top do not dissuade and prevent them, all are lost. If they do, all are saved."

---

[17] Chapra, 2000a, pp. 67, 68.

This shows that society cannot remain as a silent spectator to any harmful act of individuals and individual freedom does not imply unrestricted power to endanger the health of society as a whole. Social authority in the form of the State is recognized by Islam for the prevention of exploitation and moral degeneration as well as for the promotion of the material and spiritual interests of men and women. The Holy Qur'ān says: "O ye who believe! Obey Allah, obey the Messenger and those of you who are in authority." Thus, a purposeful relationship based on goodwill and cooperation is found in the individual–State relationship. The rulers cease to deserve obedience should they transgress the Sharī´ah. The holy Prophet has said: "Obedience, (to rulers) is not valid where a disobedience to Allah is involved".

As such, Islamic economics requires balanced growth in any society encompassing both material and spiritual satisfaction of the individual as well as society. Material wealth, industrial inventions, technological development, etc. are important factors in Islamic economics, but the spiritual and social aspects like the patterns of relationships amongst human beings and between man and God and the emerging perceptions about affairs of life are equally important factors, leading to optimal realization of the objectives of the Islamic Sharī´ah. The State can introduce necessary laws to ensure social justice and to put an end to economic exploitation and oppression and the Holy Qur'ān gives the Islamic State the necessary legal authority to do so (see Qur'ān; 22: 41).

The Islamic economic system gives an important overseeing role to the State and regulators in order to create harmony between individuals and social benefits. Freedom available to individuals for undertaking economic activities does not mean that anyone can engage in trade and business that is harmful to society. Belief in one God and accountability in the life Hereafter is the central point of all human activities, which can mainly be divided into the rights of the Creator and the rights of fellow beings. All human beings are accountable to Him in the Hereafter with regard to both types of rights and will be rewarded or punished according to the individuals' deeds without any injustice.[18]

In an Islamic economy, the State is bound to take measures not to allow forces with vested interests to distort the functioning of market forces.[19] A large number of references from the Holy Qur'ān and the Sunnah reveal that Islam has accepted the law of demand and supply as a principle but has subjected it to some limitations to avoid any moral and social ills and problems. The ultimate objective of an Islamic economy is to establish social justice. The other objectives, such as best use of resources, freedom of work and business, meeting the requirements of the deprived and establishing human dignity, etc. are only there to assist in achieving the ultimate objective. Therefore, it is not lawful to allow the operation of such economic activities that might disturb the balance and real and genuine economic and social justice.

The literature on Islamic economics emphasizes four types of action by government in economic life. These are:

1. Ensuring compliance with the Islamic code of conduct by individuals through education and, whenever necessary, through compulsion.
2. The maintenance of healthy conditions in the market to ensure its proper functioning.

---

[18] See Holy Qur'ān, 2: 281.
[19] See Chapra, 2000a, pp. 69–72.

3. Modification of the allocation of resources and distribution of income affected by the market mechanism by guiding and regulating it as well as direct intervention and participation, if needed, in the process.

4. Taking positive steps in the field of production and capital formation to accelerate growth.

The Islamic State can impose some limitations with a view to avoiding distortions and keeping in mind the well-being of society as a whole. All members of a society, regardless of differences in gender and religion, are allowed to undertake any of the permissible (Halal) businesses, but this is subject to the condition that it should not harm others. Once the Pious Caliph, Umar Farooq (Allah be pleased with him) asked a person who was selling a commodity at a much lower price than the market price to increase the price/rate or to leave the market.

Ibnul Qayyim has explained the functions of an Islamic State in the following words:

"Allah has sent down Prophets and revealed Books to establish justice which is the fundamental and basic objective of the whole creation. Everything revealed by Allah proves that the ultimate goal of revelation is the establishment of a just and balanced way of life. In whatever way the law may be made it must aim at establishing justice and fair play. The most important thing is the purpose and objective of law and not how it has been derived or enacted. But Allah, by giving us a number of laws, has set examples and reasonable basis for framing and enacting laws. The lawful government policies and directives are, therefore, considered a part of Sharī'ah and not a violation of it. To define them as government policies is only a matter of terminology, but these are, in fact, a part of Sharī'ah; the only condition is that such government policies and directives must be based on justice and fair play." (Ilāmul Muwaqqi'in)

It is, therefore, established that the responsibility of the government is to maintain a balance of economic activities and services. If the balance is distorted by economic agents with vested interests, the State has to restore the balance. Qur'ān's disapproval of the concentration of wealth (59: 7) and emphasis on justice (14: 90) is beyond any doubt. On account of this, one of the important duties of an Islamic government will be to recover wealth usurped through illegal means and return it to its genuine owners or to deposit it with the State exchequer. For checking all irregularities, Islamic economics introduces the institution of "Hisbah" that must be run by people of high integrity.

Umer Chapra has listed the following functions of the State in the field of economics and finance:[20]

1. Eradication of poverty, maintaining law and order, ensuring full employment and achieving an optimum rate of growth.
2. Economic planning.
3. Ensuring social and economic justice.
4. Stability in the value of money. This is vitally important not only for the continued long-term growth of an economy but also for social justice and economic welfare. The Holy Qur'ān says: "And give full measure and weight with justice" (6: 152). "So give full measure and weight without defrauding men in their belongings and do not corrupt the world after its reform" (7: 85; see also, 11: 84–85, 17: 35 and 26: 181). Money being a measure of value, any continuous and significant erosion in its real value may be interpreted in the light of the Qur'ān to be tantamount to corrupting the world because of

---

[20] Chapra, 1979, pp. 12–20.

the adverse effect this erosion has on social justice and general welfare, which are among the central goals of the Islamic system. In the mutually interdependent global economy of today, it may not be fully possible for the small and open economy of an individual Muslim country to achieve the desired stability. However, what it does imply is that an Islamic state should itself be clear about its role with respect to price stability and should be determined to contribute whatever it can to the attainment of that goal.[21]

5. Harmonizing international relations and national defence. The Islamic State should encourage and support any constructive move towards peace, and should honour all treaties and agreements to which it is a partner. Nevertheless, it should do its utmost to strengthen its defence so as to prevent or frustrate any aggression against its faith, territory, freedom and resources.[22]

As a corollary, governments and the central banks/monetary authorities would be required to ensure that banking and non-banking financial institutions function smoothly and the interests of all stakeholders, particularly small savers and the masses in general, were protected and the cartels and monopolies did not exploit them. Regulators would also ensure that the institutions did not get involved in antisocial activities injurious to individuals, society and human beings at large.

Leaving the most strategic sector of money and finance to market forces without any effective overseeing role is bound ultimately to generate disastrous effects for the long-term health of economies. Governments/regulators must devise and adopt fiscal and monetary policies in their respective ambits in such a way that an expected rate of return emerging from real sector business in the economies becomes the benchmark and an effective signal for the efficient allocation of funds to various sectors.

## 2.6  SUMMARY

Banking and finance are parts of economics or the economic system, as the rules governing activities of banks and financial institutions stem from the overall economic framework in which these institutions operate. It is, therefore, worthwhile to discuss the structure of Islamic economics under which the Islamic financial system is supposed to work. In this chapter we have discussed the fundamentals of the Islamic economic worldview having direct or indirect impact upon the business of Islamic financial institutions and markets.

All economic and financial contracts in the framework of Islamic finance have to conform to the Sharī´ah rules, with the objective of helping to achieve the well-being of people in the worldly life as well as in the Hereafter. Hence, studying economics is important for the dual purpose of having better sustenance and the religious imperatives. The sources of rules dealing with economic aspects of human beings are the Holy Qur'ān and Sunnah of His last Messenger, Muhammad (pbuh). In addition to the Qur'ān and Sunnah, Ijma'a, Qiyās and Ijtihad provide a hierarchical framework of sources of rules governing Islamic economics and finance.

---

[21] Chapra considers that borrowing from the central bank should be the last resort, as it generates inflation unless accompanied by a corresponding increase in the supply of goods and services. However, according to the principle that a smaller sacrifice may be imposed to avoid a larger sacrifice and that the smaller of two evils may be tolerated, borrowing from the central bank may also be defended under certain special circumstances, even if there is no corresponding rise in output. Also see Chapra, 1985.

[22] See Holy Qur'ān; (8: 60) and (2: 190).

Islam has provided basic principles for the economic activities of human beings. In the Middle Ages, Muslim scholars provided the driving force behind the then economic activities and cultural life. Contemporary Islamic economists have discussed almost all areas of modern economics; but all these are segments that need to be put together into a comprehensive model.

Profit, according to Islamic theory, is the result of the productivity of capital that an entrepreneur has invested or a reward for his workmanship or for shouldering responsibility. As capital provider he has to bear the loss, if any, and as entrepreneur he has to pay the wages, rentals and other expenses and gets the residual, if any. All participants in a joint business have similar rights and liabilities according to the nature of the activity or the terms of the agreement.

Islamic rules of economics make it binding for human beings not only to abide by the Sharī´ah tenets relating to dos and don'ts but also to keep in mind the impact of their activities on others and society as a whole. To realize the goal, the State should facilitate business in such a way that various stakeholders and parties involved do not exploit each other. To ensure that the basic needs of all are fulfilled, it should try to maintain socio-economic justice and to control the wants of the people through a filtering process, motivate the people to abstain from activities injurious to others and restructure the system for transfer of resources from one use/sector to others to ultimately realize the dual objective of balanced growth with need fulfilment.

Islam adopts a balanced approach between an individual's freedom and the well-being of society. It likes the market mechanism to balance the demand and supply of goods for the dispensation of economic justice, the ultimate benefit of society and for the efficient allocation of resources. All efforts made for self-interest which are not in harmony with social interests are antisocial activities and, therefore, not allowed. In other words, for the smooth functioning of the global economic system and welfare of mankind, there is a need to reform the institutional set-up to the effect that private and social interests coincide. This is feasible only if the socio-economic system of all societies is organized such that fair dealing is ensured with all factors of production and that all channels of unjust earnings are effectively closed.

For the smooth and proper functioning of the banking and finance sectors, governments and regulators should be obliged to perform an effective overseeing role to ensure that market forces and different stakeholders do not exploit one another. For justice, fairness and the longer term health of the system, they have to ensure that monetary growth is "adequate" and not "excessive" or "deficient".

# 3

# The Main Prohibitions and Business Ethics in Islamic Economics and Finance

## 3.1  INTRODUCTION

In the previous chapter we discussed the main features of Islamic economics and the Islamic economic system, with the objective of distinguishing them from conventional economics. Now we proceed to discuss the fundamentals of Islamic business and finance, including the basic prohibitions, encouragements, norms and ethics governing economic and business activities in the framework of the Sharī´ah.

Islam has constrained the freedom to engage in business and financial transactions on the basis of a number of prohibitions, ethics and norms. Besides some major prohibitions, Islamic law has prescribed a number of other norms and boundaries in order to avoid inequitable gains and injustice. As Sharī´ah compliance is the *raison d'etre* of the Islamic financial system, concern for the Sharī´ah tenets should dominate all other concerns of Islamic financial institutions. It is only through the compliance of Islamic banking operations with the norms and the principles of the Sharī´ah that the system can develop on a sustainable basis and can ensure fairness for investors, the business community and institutions.

This chapter is organized to include discussion of the major prohibitions and norms that determine the overall limitations, working beyond which would create Sharī´ah compliance problems for Islamic financial institutions and observance of which is necessary for the integrity and credibility of the Islamic finance movement. The prohibitions that we shall discuss here include that of Riba, commonly known as "interest" in conventional commercial terminology, Maisir and Qimār (gambling) and Gharar or excessive uncertainty about the subject matter and/or the price in exchanges and the norms and ethics of business and finance in the Islamic framework. These norms and ethics require that all economic agents in a society must avoid injustice and unfair dealing with others and that harm should not be inflicted upon anyone. Invalid contracts on account of any contractual deficiencies are not the subject of this chapter but will be discussed in Chapter 5. Similarly, principles and features of Islamic banking and the financial system will be discussed separately in the next chapter.

## 3.2  THE BASIC PROHIBITIONS

As a rule, Islamic law does not recognize transactions that have a proven illegitimate factor and/or object. For that purpose, Sharī´ah has identified some elements which are to be avoided in commerce or business transactions. In this regard, the prohibition of Riba, Gharar and gambling is the most strategic factor that defines invalid and voidable contracts and demarcates the overall limits which should not be crossed. We will elaborate upon these one by one.

### 3.2.1  Prohibition of Riba

It is important to observe at the very beginning that there is no difference of opinion among Muslims about the prohibition of Riba and all Muslim sects consider indulgence in Riba-based transactions a severe sin. This is because the primary sources of Sharī´ah, i.e. the Holy Qur'ān and Sunnah, strongly condemn Riba. However, there have been differences regarding the meaning of Riba or what constitutes Riba, which must be avoided for the conformity of economic activities to the tenets of the Sharī´ah.

There are a number of myths and much confusion, even among devoted and pious Muslims. While some liberal Muslims consider that commercial interest is not Riba prohibited by Islam, many pious and devoted Muslims have the belief that any prefixed return in all types of transactions is Riba and therefore prohibited. Many in the business community consider that in Islamic banking, costless money should be available. A number of economists and policymakers believe that the profit margin on credit sales by Islamic banks resembles Riba.

These myths have to be removed, particularly among the three main stakeholders, i.e. Sharī´ah scholars, academicians and bankers. If they properly understand and accordingly educate the masses, only then will people in general have firm confidence about the concepts and the working of the new system. Therefore, besides the prohibition of Riba, we will discuss the connotation of Riba to explain what types of transactions Islamic banks have to avoid.

*Prohibition of Riba in the Qur'ān and Sunnah*

A number of verses of the Holy Qur'ān expressly prohibit Riba. Although some indications of displeasure against Riba were given in the Makkah period, the express prohibition was imposed by Islam sometime before the battle of 'Uhad in the year 3 AH.[1] Final and repeated prohibition came in the year 10 AH, about two weeks before the passing away of the holy Prophet (pbuh). From the Holy Qur'ān, verses on Riba in order of revelation are given below:

- **Surah al-Rum, verse 39**
  "That which you give as Riba to increase the people's wealth increases not with God; but that which you give in charity, seeking the goodwill of God, multiplies manifold." (30: 39)
- **Surah al-Nisa', verse 161**
  "And for their taking Riba although it was forbidden for them, and their wrongful appropriation of other people's property. We have prepared for those among them who reject faith a grievous punishment." (4: 161)
- **Surah Al-e-Imran, verse 130**
  "O believers, take not doubled and redoubled Riba, and fear Allah so that you may prosper. Fear the fire which has been prepared for those who reject faith, and obey Allah and the Prophet so that you may get mercy." (3: 130)
  (This verse contains a clear prohibition for Muslims and it can firmly be said that it is the first verse of the Holy Qur'ān through which the practice of Riba was forbidden for Muslims in express terms. This was sometime around the battle of 'Uhad).[2]

---

[1]  Ibn Hajar, 1981, **8**, p. 205.
[2]  Shariat Appellate Bench, 2000, Justice Taqi Usmani's part, paras 11–24.

- **Surah al-Baqarah, verses 275–281**

  — "Those who take Riba shall be raised like those who have been driven to madness by the touch of the Devil; this is because they say: 'Trade is just like interest' while God has permitted trade and forbidden interest. Hence those who have received the admonition from their Lord and desist, may keep their previous gains, their case being entrusted to God; but those who revert, shall be the inhabitants of the fire and abide therein forever." (275)

  — "Allah deprives Riba of all blessing but blesses charity; He loves not the ungrateful sinner." (276)

  — "O, believers, fear Allah, and give up what is still due to you from Riba if you are true believers." (278)

  — "If you do not do so, then take notice of war from Allah and His Messenger. But, if you repent, you can have your principal. Neither should you commit injustice nor should you be subjected to it." (279)

  — "And if the debtor is in misery, let him have respite until it is easier, but if you forego it as charity, it is better for you if you realize." (280)

  — "And be fearful of the Day when you shall be returned to the Allah, then everybody shall be paid in full what he has earned and they shall not be wronged." (281)

The above verses indicate the clear prohibition of Riba. Verses of Surah al-Baqarah, given in bullet point 4 above, not only describe the prohibition of Riba, but also give a comprehensive principle for determining whether a transaction involves Riba or not. About the background of the revelation of verses 278 and 279 of this set of Qur'ānic tenets, Shaikh Taqi Usmani says:

> "After the conquest of Makkah, the holy Prophet (pbuh) had declared as void all the amounts of Riba that were due at that time. The declaration embodied that nobody could claim any interest on any loan advanced by him. Then the holy Prophet (pbuh) proceeded to Taaif, which could not be conquered, but later on the inhabitants of Taaif, who belonged mostly to the tribe of Thaqif, came to him and after embracing Islam surrendered to the holy Prophet (pbuh) and entered into a treaty with him. One of the proposed clauses of the treaty was that Banu Thaqif would not forego the amounts of interest due on their debtors but their creditors would forego the amounts of interest. The holy Prophet (pbuh) instead of signing that treaty simply ordered to write a sentence on the proposed draft that Banu Thaqif will have the same rights as other Muslims have. Banu Thaqif, having the impression that their proposed treaty was accepted by the holy Prophet (pbuh), claimed the amount of interest from Banu Amr Ibn-al-Mughirah, but they declined to pay interest on the ground that Riba was prohibited after embracing Islam. The matter was placed before Attaab ibn Aseed (God be pleased with him), the Governor of Makkah. Banu Thaqif argued that according to the treaty they were not bound to forego the amounts of interest. Attaab ibn Aseed placed the matter before the holy Prophet (pbuh) on which the following verses of Surah al-Baqarah were revealed:
>
>> 'O those who believe, fear Allah and give up what still remains of the Riba if you are believers. But if you do not do so, then listen to the declaration of war from Allah and His Messenger. And if you repent, yours is your principal. Neither you wrong, nor be wronged.' (278–279)
>
> At that point of time, Banu Thaqif surrendered and said that they had no power to wage war against Allah and his Messenger".[3]

---

[3] Shariat Appellate Bench, 2000, Justice Taqi Usmani's part of Judgement, paras 23, 24, pp. 528, 529; quoting from Ibn Jarir, Jami-al-Bayan, 3: 107; Al-Wahidi, Alwasit, 1: 397 and Al-Wahidi, Asbab-al-Nuzool, Riyadh, 1984, p. 87.

A large number of traditions of the holy Prophet (pbuh) pertain to various aspects of Riba, like its prohibition, the severity of its sin and its forms. For the sake of brevity, we will give here only some of them to derive important implications and rules relating to transactions in the present age. In line with the verses of the Holy Qur'ān, the following Ahādith (traditions) of the holy Prophet (pbuh) reiterate the prohibition of Riba:

1. From Jabir (Gbpwh): "The Prophet (pbuh) cursed the receiver and the payer of interest, the one who records it and the witnesses to the transaction and said: 'They are all alike [in guilt]'."[4]
2. From Anas ibn Malik (Gbpwh): "The Prophet said: 'When one of you grants a loan and the borrower offers him a dish, he should not accept it; and if the borrower offers a ride on an animal, he should not ride, unless the two of them have been previously accustomed to exchanging such favours mutually'."[5]
3. Zaid B. Aslam reported that interest in pagan times was of this nature: "When a person owed money to another man for a certain period and the period expired, the creditor would ask: 'you pay me the amount or pay the extra'. If he paid the amount, it was well and good, otherwise the creditor increased the loan amount and extended the period for payment again."[6]
4. The holy Prophet (Pbuh) announced the prohibition of Riba in express terms at the occasion of his last Hajj, which was the most attended gathering of his Companions. The Prophet said: "Every form of Riba is cancelled; capital indeed is yours which you shall have; wrong not and you shall not be wronged. Allah has given His Commandment totally prohibiting Riba. I start with the amount of Riba which people owe to my uncle Abbas and declare it all cancelled". He then, on behalf of his uncle, cancelled the total amount of Riba due on his loan capital from his debtors.[7]
5. The holy Prophet (Pbuh) said, "Gold for gold, silver for silver, wheat for wheat, barley for barley, dates for dates and salt for salt – like for like, equal for equal, and hand to hand; if the commodities differ, then you may sell as you wish, provided that the exchange is hand to hand."[8]
6. Bilal (Gbpwh) once visited the Messenger of Allah (pbuh) with some high quality dates, the Prophet (pbuh) inquired about their source. Bilal explained that he traded two volumes of lower quality dates for one volume of that of the higher quality. The Prophet (pbuh) said: "This is precisely the forbidden Riba! Do not do this. Instead, sell the first type of dates, and use the proceeds to buy the others."[9]
7. A man deputed by the holy Prophet (pbuh) for the collection of Zakat/Ushr from Khyber brought for him dates of very fine quality. Upon the Prophet's asking him whether all the dates of Khyber were such, the man replied that this was not the case and added that he exchanged a Sa'a (a measure) of this kind for two or three (of the other kind). The holy Prophet replied: "Do not do so. Sell (the lower quality dates) for dirhams and then use

[4] Muslim, Kitab al-Musaqat, Bab la'ni akili al-riba wa mu'kilihi; also in Tirmidhi and Musnad Ahmad.
[5] Baihaqi, 1344 H, Kitab al-Buyu', Bab kulli qardin jarra manfa'atan fa huwa riban.
[6] Malik, 1985 chapter on Riba fiddayn (No. 418), Tradition No. 1362, p. 427.
[7] Al-Khazin, 1955, 1, p. 301.
[8] Muslim, 1981, Kitab al Musaqat, chapter on Riba.
[9] Ibid.

the dirhams to buy better quality dates. (When dates are exchanged against should be equal in weight."[10]

## Riba in Loans/Debts

From the above references from the Qur'ān and Sunnah we can derive a number of results regarding the severity of the sin of Riba, its forms and its connotation. First, indulging in Riba-based transactions is tantamount to being at war with Allah (SWT) and His Messenger, which no one should even think of. Not only the lenders but also borrowers and other parties involved commit sin by paying interest or by giving a helping hand in interest-based business. If a destitute is constrained to borrow on interest in case of compulsion to fulfil his basic food needs, there is the possibility of granting limited permission to borrow on interest. But a person who takes advantage of interest-based loans for luxurious consumption or for the development of his businesses is culpable as per the above tenets.

What the Qur'ānic verses have discussed is the Riba on loans and debts. As is discussed in detail in Chapter 5, a loan (Qard) is any commodity or amount of money taken from any other person with liability to return or pay back the same or similar commodity or amount of money when demanded back by the creditor. A debt (Dayn) is a liability to pay which results from any credit transaction like a purchase/sale on credit or due rentals in Ijarah (leasing). The amount of debt has to be paid back at a stipulated time and the creditor (in case of debt) has no right to demand payment of the debt before the mutually agreed time. The principle that the Holy Qur'ān has given in verses 2: 278 and 279 is that in both loans and debts, the creditor has the right to the Ra'asul-māl (principal amount) only; in the former case, exactly the amount given as the loan and in the latter case, the liability or the amount of debt generated from the credit transaction. Any amount, big or small, over and above the principal of loan or debt would be Riba. As conventional banks' financing falls into the category of loans on which they charge a premium, it falls under the purview of Riba as prohibited by the Holy Qur'ān. As such, there should be no doubt that commercial interest as in vogue is Riba in the light of the principle given by the Holy Qur'ān.

The word "Riba", meaning prohibited gain, has been explained in the Holy Qur'ān by juxtaposing it against (profit from) sale. It explains that all income and earnings, salaries and wages, remuneration and profits, usury and interest, rent and hire, etc. can be categorized either as:

- profit from trade and business along with its liability – which is permitted; or
- return on cash or a converted form of cash without bearing liability in terms of the result of deployed cash or capital – which is prohibited.

Riba, according to the criterion, would include all gains from loans and debts and anything over and above the principal of loans and debts and covers all forms of "interest" on commercial or personal loans. As such, conventional interest is Riba. It is interest or Riba on loans and debts which we discuss in detail below.

---

[10] Ibid.

*How to Distinguish*

The question arises, how does one distinguish between various types of transactions to judge their permissibility or prohibition? The answer lies in differentiating the contracts on the basis of their nature; all real sector business transactions involve:

1. Sale/purchase that may be either cash or credit.
2. Loaning.
3. Leasing.

When executed, these transactions have different implications in respect of transfer of ownership, risk and liability.

In Bai', or sale, ownership of the commodity being sold is transferred to the buyer just at the time the sale is executed and this transfer is definite and permanent. It makes no difference whether the payment of the price is on the spot or deferred. This ownership transfer is against on-the-spot or credit payment that may also involve a profit margin for the seller. In the case of Salam, a special kind of forward sale, although goods have to be delivered at a future stipulated time, both parties are obliged to give/take ownership at a specified time on agreed terms, irrespective of whether the price rises or falls at the time of delivery. If the transaction is that of a gift (Hibah), ownership of assets will transfer there and then on a permanent basis free of any payment.

A loan, which is always free of any charge in Islamic finance, leads to the temporary transfer of ownership of goods/assets free of any payment, meaning that the debtor is liable to return or pay back the same asset to the creditor. Riba (in loans or debts) also means the temporary transfer of ownership of goods/assets, but that transfer involves payment of interest, which is prohibited.

Ijarah is a totally different transaction in that ownership of the leased asset does not transfer and only the usufruct of the asset is made available to the lessee against the payment of rent. As ownership remains with the lessor, he is entitled to rental and is also liable for expenses relating to ownership and loss of the asset, if any. It is important to observe, however, that anything which cannot be used without consuming its corpus, or which changes its shape altogether in the process of its use, cannot be leased out, this includes yarn, money, edibles, fuel, etc. Yarn, when used, takes the form of cloth; it can be bought and sold but not leased. That is why, in Islamic finance, taking rent on leasing of assets like houses, vehicles, etc. is permissible while charging rent on money is prohibited.

Hence, we have to determine whether a transaction is that of a sale or a loan; and if it is a credit sale, at what time the sale transaction is executed and generates a debt, after which the seller will not be in a position to charge any addition over the price. Verse 2: 275 of the Holy Qur'ān has very important implications in respect of payment of debts/liabilities arising from credit transactions. It reports the usurers saying: "The sale is very similar to Riba." Their objection was that one can increase the price of a commodity in the original transaction of sale because of its being based on a deferred payment, which is treated as a valid sale. But if they add to the due amount after the maturity date and the debtor is not able to pay, it is termed Riba, while the increase in both cases is similar.[11] The Holy

---

[11] This is specifically mentioned by famous exegetist Ibn-abi-Hātim in his Tafsir, 1997, p. 545. Sayyuti and Ibne Jarir Tabari have also reported a similar situation of Riba involvement in which a person sold any commodity on credit; when the payment was due and the purchaser could not repay that, the price was enhanced and the time for payment extended (Sayyuti, 2003 and Tabari, n.d., p. 8).

Qur'ān's reply to the above approach is that "God has permitted trading and prohibited Riba," meaning that so long as price is not stipulated, parties can bargain; once the sale is executed and liability in the form of a payable price determined, this becomes a debt which has to be paid without any increase or further income to the seller.

The principle that anything over and above the amount of loans and debts amounts to Riba is also proved by the above tradition numbers 2 and 3. While the second tradition prohibits one from taking even a small benefit from the debtor, the latter indicates that debt liability cannot increase in the case of a payment default by the debtor. Tradition number 3 reflects both the cases of simple loans and debts arising from credit transactions. One can bargain on price keeping in mind the credit period given for payment of the price, but when the credit price is settled and liability generated, the principle is the same for loans or debts – there should be no increase over the receivable amount.

On the basis of the clear text of the Qur'ān and Sunnah as given above, the word "interest" is now commonly understood as Riba, although Riba is a much wider term than "interest". While "interest", which is a monetary charge levied for the use of money for the sake of money, is always Riba, the latter (Riba) is not restricted to only interest. Riba also applies to nonmonetary exchanges and includes sale/exchange transactions, which has important implications even today, particularly in respect of foreign exchange transactions. This we shall explain in the following sections.

*Some Misconceptions*

Owing to the fact that interest is a focal point in modern economic life, and especially that it is embedded in the operations of existing financial institutions, a number of scholars have been interpreting it in a manner which is radically different from the understanding of the majority of Muslim scholars throughout the history of Islam and that is also sharply in conflict with the categorical statements of the holy Prophet (pbuh). Islam accepts no distinction, in so far as prohibition is concerned, between "reasonable" and "exorbitant" rates of interest and thus what came to be regarded as the difference between usury and interest, or between returns or bonuses on loans for consumption and those for production purposes and so on.[12] Below, we briefly give some misgivings and their possible replies.

According to some scholars only a specific form of Riba, i.e. Riba al-jahiliyyah that was prevalent at the time the Holy Qur'ān was revealed, falls under the Qur'ānic prohibition. Riba al-jahiliyyah, according to them, was when the lender asked the borrower at the maturity date if he would settle the debt or swap it for another larger debt of longer maturity period.[13] The difference between the maturity value of the old and new debt amounted to Riba. These scholars say that if some charge is added to the loan at the very beginning, it will not be Riba. This is, however, not correct, as a number of forms of Riba were prevalent in the pre-Islamic period, including addition over loans and debts, and all of them were prohibited by Islam.

It may be noted that even if we accept that only the stated form of Riba was present, the conventional system of time-based compounding of debt still clearly falls into that category. Interest on loans/deposits as applied by conventional banks is rather worse than that form of

---

[12] Translation of the Holy Qur'ān by Ali, 1989, p. 115.

[13] Ahmad, 1995. For a rejoinder to this paper, see *Journal of Islamic Banking and Finance*, Karachi, January–March, 1996, pp. 7–34.

Riba which was charged only when the borrower was not able to return the loan at maturity, as present-day interest is charged both at the beginning when the transaction is executed and in the case of overdue payments.

Sometimes it is misunderstood that only a high rate of interest is prohibited and any normal charge on loans or debts does not come under the purview of prohibition. On the basis of verse 3: 130 (given earlier) it is argued that a loan involves Riba only if it carries the condition of doubling and redoubling, and the word "Riba" refers only to usurious loans on which an excessive rate of interest is charged by the creditors, which entails exploitation. It is added that modern banking interest cannot be termed "Riba" as the rate of interest is not excessive or exploitative.

However, the argument is not tenable as per the tenets of the Holy Qur'ān. The Qur'ān makes it very clear that in a loan transaction, and for that matter a trade transaction culminating in a debt contract, any addition chargeable to the principal amount is Riba. The Qur'ān says: "If you repent, then you have your principal only". Believers have been ordered to give up whatever amount of Riba is outstanding. Otherwise they will be considered at war with Allah and his Prophet (pbuh). Further, "rate" is a relative term and any rate will, over time, double and redouble the principal; hence, any addition over the amount of debt *per se* is prohibited, irrespective of the rate.[14]

Exegetist Ibne Jarir Tabari, while explaining verse (2: 279) says that creditors are entitled to only the original amount of debt without any addition or profit.[15] *Daaera-e-Maarif al Islami* (*the Encyclopaedia of Islam in Urdu*) has given a convincing argument to clarify this confusion: "Allah says in Surah Al-Māidah 'and sell not Signs of Allah for a low price' (5: 44). Would this mean that selling the Signs of Allah for a high price is permissible? Definitely not! Similarly, the verse 3: 130 will not permit one to charge any rate or anything over and above the principal of a receivable."[16]

It is also argued by a few that Umar the Great (Gbpwh) stated that the Prophet (pbuh) passed away before giving any specific direction with regard to differences of opinion about the meaning of Riba. The Shariat Appellate Bench (SAB) of the Supreme Court of Pakistan has discussed this issue in detail in its judgement and concluded that Umar the Great (Gbpwh) had not even the slightest doubt about the prohibition of Riba Al-Nasiah that is involved in all types of modern commercial laws.[17]

In addition, it is argued that there was no commercial interest in Arabia at the time of revelation of the Holy Qur'ān; only a particular form (may be on consumption loans) was prohibited. This also is not correct. The SAB has elaborated upon this aspect in detail, as evidenced by some of their findings that we reproduce below:

"It is not to say that commercial or productive loans were not in vogue when Riba was prohibited. More than enough material has now come on the record to prove that commercial and productive loans were not foreign to the Arabs, and that loans were advanced for productive purposes both before and after the advent of Islam.

All kinds of commercial, industrial and agricultural loans advanced on the basis of interest were prevalent in the Byzantine Empire ruling in Syria, to the extent that Justinian, the Byzantine

---

[14] For details see Shariat Appellate Bench, 2000, pp. 557–564; Zaman, 1966, pp. 8–12.
[15] Tabari, n.d., pp. 26, 27.
[16] University of the Punjab, 1973, **10**, p. 172.
[17] Shariat Appellate Bench, 2000, pp. 539–543.

Emperor (527–565 AD) had to promulgate a law determining the rates of interest which could be charged from different types of borrowers.

The Arabs, especially of Makkah, had constant business relations with Syria, one of the most civilized provinces of the Byzantine Empire. The Arab trade caravans used to export goods to and import other goods from Syria.

The above material is more than enough to prove that the concept of commercial loans was not alien to the holy Prophet (pbuh) or his companions when Riba was prohibited. Therefore, it is not correct to say that the prohibition of Riba was restricted to consumption loans only and it did not refer to commercial loans.

The SAB concluded:

"It is thus clear that the permissibility of interest can neither be based on the financial position of the debtor nor on the purpose for which money is borrowed, and therefore, the distinction between consumption loans and productive loans in this respect is contrary to the well-established principles".[18]

Some people favour an interest-based system on the basis of the "Principle of Necessity". However, adverse impacts of interest on the world economy in general and the economies of developing countries in particular imply that it is the biggest threat to the developing economies, a belief also held by many renowned economists.[19]

Interest is sometimes legalized on account of inflation and decreases in the purchasing power of lent money. This is also not a valid argument. When any currency depreciates, it makes no difference whether it is in the pocket of someone who has lent some money or it is with the borrower/debtor – depreciation equally affects money in the pocket of a person and money with the person to whom he has given the credit. If a person lends for the reason that the money in his pocket will lose its value while lending, i.e. it would be beneficial for him on account of indexation, this would also involve interest on the basis of the rule that all loans that seek benefit involve Riba. Therefore, indexation of financial obligations also leads to Riba.[20]

Finally, the supporters of interest argue that today's debtors are not poor people; charging interest from them is not unjust. However, this argument strengthens the case against interest because the relatively richer class takes funds at cheaper rates vis-à-vis their profits. They give a small part of the profit in the form of interest to the banks, which is treated as an expense and ultimately charged to the consumers. Thus, the rich become richer leaving the poor poorer. If some of them incur loss, they are bound to suffer that loss. To avoid this they often resort to unethical practices, causing harm to society as a whole. Interest leads to exploitation by any of the parties, i.e. debtor or creditor, and hence it is prohibited irrespective of who is the exploiter in any particular transaction. The conventional financial system has become a means for exploiting savers or depositors and the general public.

## Riba in Sale/Exchange Transactions

The last three traditions given above relate to the prohibition of Riba in sale or exchange contracts. In particular, the fifth tradition forms the basis of elaborate juristic rules on Riba

---

[18] Shariat Appellate Bench, 2000, pp. 546–557.
[19] Shariat Appellate Bench, 2000, pp. 194–195.
[20] For details on this aspect, see the work by the following authors: Federal Shariat Court, 1992, paras 154–234; Hasanuz Zaman, 1993.

prohibition in sale contracts and other exchange transactions. This type of Riba is termed "Riba Al-Fadl".

Exchange rules are different for different contracts and types of assets. We have briefly discussed contracts in the preceding section. Assets could be consumables, durables, monetary units or media of exchange like gold, silver or other currencies, shares representing pools of assets, etc. Goods other than monetary units are traded on market-based pricing. Gold, silver or any monetary units (Athman) are governed by specific rules that have been discussed by jurists under the caption of Bai' al Sarf (sale of Athman). Usufructs and services are covered by the rules of Ijarah or Ujrah (leasing/hiring of services). Loans and debts are governed by the rules relating to their repayment and assignment.

The well-known Hadith on the exchange of six commodities and the other traditions about the exchange of low quality dates for a lesser amount of better quality dates deal with Riba in exchange transactions and have far-reaching implications in respect of business activities in the Islamic framework. Later jurists have extended the scope of this kind of Riba to other commodities on the basis of analogical reasoning (Qiyās) and the 'Illah (effective cause) of prohibition.

According to the rules of exchange of monetary units (Bai' al Sarf), if any article is sold for an article of the same kind, the exchange must be on the spot (without delay) and the articles must be equal in weight. In this context, jurists have held lengthy discussions, keeping in mind the two types of 'Illah that play an effective role in the exchange: the unit of value (Thamaniyyah) and the edibility. The commentator of Sahih Muslim, Imam Nawavi has summarized these rules in the following way:

- When the underlying 'Illah of the two goods being exchanged is different, shortfall/excess and delay both are permissible, e.g. the exchange of gold for wheat or dollars for a car.
- When the commodities of exchange are similar, excess and delay both are prohibited, e.g. gold for gold or wheat for wheat, dollars for dollars, etc.[21]
- When the commodities of exchange are heterogeneous but the 'Illah is the same, as in the case of exchanging gold for silver or US Dollars for Japanese Yen (medium of exchange) or wheat for rice (the 'Illah being edibility), then excess/deficiency is allowed, but delay in exchange is not allowed.

In the present scenario, the major 'Illah, or cause, on the basis of which one may extend the rules of Riba to other commodities by analogy is their being used in lieu of money. There is consensus among scholars that the rules of Riba apply to anything that serves the function of money. This may be gold, silver, any paper currency or IOUs.

## Connotation of the Term Riba

On the basis of the above detailed discussion, we are now in a position to explain what the term Riba connotes in the perspective of present-day business and finance. The literal meaning of Riba is excess and in the terminology of the Sharī'ah, it means an addition, however slight, over and above the principal of a loan or debt. Nasiah means delay or delaying the delivery of a commodity in a contract. The term Riba Al-Nasiah, therefore,

---

[21] The nature of the transaction must be kept in mind; this prohibition is for business or sale transactions. Nonremunerative contracts (Uqood Ghair Mu'awadha) like Qard and Dayn are exempt from this rule.

means the benefit or excess that arises from the delay of counter value in an exchange based on loans or sales. More precisely, it is the potential benefit to be derived during the period of delay stipulated for either of the exchanged/counter currency values. Riba Al-Nasiah relates to loan transactions and is also termed Riba Al-Qur'ān. Riba Al-Fadl that relates to exchange/sale transactions is the quality premium in the exchange of low quality for better quality goods of the same genus, e.g. in the exchange of dates for dates, wheat for wheat, etc.

Hence, Riba includes both usury and interest as used in modern commercial terminology. The word "interest" by and large has now been accepted and is understood as Riba. Conventional banks' loan transactions carrying interest involve both Riba Al-Nasiah and Riba Al-Fadl – an extra amount of money is paid at the time when payment becomes due as per the loan contract.

Keeping in mind all types of transaction, a broader definition of Riba would be the following:

> "Riba means and includes any increase over and above the principal amount payable in a contract obligation, not covered by a corresponding increase in labour, commodity, risk or expertise."

This definition requires that all accruals should correspond to liability and risk and excludes from Riba the profit charged in trading and Shirkah, commission or service charged in Ujrah and Wakalah and the rentals charged in Ijarah.

The definition of Riba by Justice Wajihuddin Ahmad, a member of the Shariat Appellate Bench of the Supreme Court of Pakistan, which he indicated in his separate part of judgement, is worth mentioning:

> "Riba in Islam encompasses every return and all excess arising purely in consideration of time allowed for the use of money or of any other thing of value lent as also every such increase on goods exchanged violative of any or all of the mandates of saw'am-bi-sawaa' (meaning equal for equal), Mithlam-bi-mithlin (like for like) and Yadam-bi-yadin (hand to hand or on the spot), where the exchange, subject to the ahādith, is of like commodities for at least that in Yadam-bi-yadin, if such exchange be in dissimilar articles."[22]

### Prohibition of Riba in Other Revealed Religions

It is pertinent to observe that Islam is not alone in prohibiting Riba. The institution of interest is repugnant to the teachings of all revealed religions and from the purely religious point of view, there have never been two views about its prohibition. Similarly, none of the revealed religions has accepted "interest" as the cost of using capital as commonly understood in conventional economics. A detailed discussion of the tenets of various religions on Riba is not the purpose of this chapter. We shall refer to this aspect only briefly.

Debate has been ongoing for a long time with regard to bank interest or commercial interest and whether it is Riba or not. The majority of ancient philosophers and Greek and Roman thinkers forbade interest in their day. The Old and the New Testaments similarly prohibited it.[23] The logic as to why religions, including Islam, have prohibited interest is that it exerts disastrous effects on human societies by reinforcing the tendency of wealth accumulation in fewer hands. It leads to an ever-increasing share of risk-free capital vis-à-vis risk-related capital, resulting in business failures, unemployment and ultimately to gross

---

[22] Shariat Appellate Bench, 2000, p. 425.
[23] For details, see Shariat Appellate Bench, 2000, Taqi Usmani's part, paras 37, 38.

inequalities of income and wealth that are bound to end up in social strife and economic chaos. Islam is opposed to exploitation in every form and stands for fair and equitable dealings among all human beings.[24]

Riba, the term used for any rate of return on the principal of loans/debts, has been erroneously divided into two parts, i.e. the permitted cost of capital use and the prohibited high rates. In English terminology, the Latin word "usury" was used as the equivalent of Riba. It means the use of anything and in the case of loans it means the use of borrowed capital; hence, usury means the price paid for the use of money. In medieval times, the word "interest" was identified as something different from usury. The *Encyclopedia Britannica* has dealt in detail with the split of Riba into two parts. Division was made by the King (and the Church) of England in 1545 into a legal maximum that was termed interest and another over and above the legal maximum. The confusion was confounded by the inception of paper money/fiduciary money/token money.

The movement for the acceptability of "interest" on theoretical grounds was launched effectively by Calvin and Molinaeus in the middle of the sixteenth century. With the development of trade and commerce, opportunities for investment of money increased and economists and experts started justifying interest, at least on loans for commercial and productive purposes. The movement gathered momentum with the advent of the Industrial Revolution in the eighteenth century and ultimately overshadowed all arguments and rationale from those who tried to defend the Divine prohibition of interest and save mankind from its disastrous effects. *EH Net Encyclopedia* has concluded the following in this regard:

"Most nations continue to regulate usury, which is now, in the West, defined as contracting to charge interest on a loan without risk to the lender at an interest rate greater than that set by the law. However, moral arguments are still being made about whether or not contracting for any interest is permissible. Because both the Bible and the Qur'ān can be read as forbidding usury, there will always be moral, as well as social and economic reasons for arguing about the permissibility of lending at interest.[25] "

The views of J.L. Hanson, expressed in his *Dictionary of Commerce and Economics*, are worth quoting here:

"Usury: A term now restricted to the charging of a very high rate of interest on a loan, but formerly used in connection with interest whether the rate charged was high or low. The medieval church, following the law of Moses and the writings of Aristotle and other Greek philosophers, condemned the payment of interest on a loan as usury and unjust. The usury laws passed in the sixteenth century prohibited a rate of interest in England in excess of 5 per cent." (pp. 470–471)

## The Rationale for the Prohibition of Interest

Different quarters have expressed different opinions with regard to the rationale or purpose of prohibiting interest by the Sharī'ah. As a whole, socio-economic and distributive justice, intergenerational equity, economic instability and ecological destruction are considered the basis of the prohibition of interest. Keeping in mind all relevant texts and the principles of Islamic law, the only reason that appears convincing is that of distributive justice, because the prohibition of Riba is intended to prevent the accumulation of wealth in a few hands;

---

[24] For the antisocial impact of the institution of interest see Somerville, 1931; Cannan *et al.*, 1932; Dennis and Somerville, 1932.
[25] http://eh.net/encyclopedia/article/jones.usury.

that is, it is not to be allowed to "circulate among the rich" (Holy Qur'ān, 59: 7). Then the major purpose of Riba prohibition is to block the means that lead to the accumulation of wealth in the hands of a few, whether they are banks or individuals.

To many people, the matter of Riba prohibition is simply a matter of ritual obedience. Sharī'ah text prohibits Riba, therefore it should be taken as prohibited; it is not necessary to know the rationale. Some say that prohibition of Riba prevents a life of luxury, prohibits hoarding and leads to broad-based development. Still others believe that it prevents injustice and, therefore, injustice is the only cause of prohibition. On this basis they differentiate between interest and usury and claim that modern commercial interest is not oppressive as it was in the past. They hold this viewpoint for vagueness of the term (Zulm), as it provides flexibility in expressing opinions freely. However, it is not right to stress only this reason.

The rationale for prohibition of charging interest from someone who is constrained to borrow to meet his essential consumption requirements is obvious. But interest on loans taken for productive purposes is also prohibited because it is not an equitable form of transaction.[26] When money is invested in a productive undertaking, the amount of profit that may accrue is not known beforehand and there is also the possibility of a loss. Therefore, the charging of a fixed and predetermined rate of interest on loans for productive purposes cannot be morally justified. Justice demands that the provider of money capital should share the risk with the entrepreneur if he wishes to earn a profit. Thus, there is a basic difference between Islam and capitalism in regard to the treatment of money capital as a factor of production. Whereas in the capitalistic system, money capital is treated on a par with labour and land, each being entitled to a return irrespective of profit or loss, this is not so in Islam, which treats money capital on a par with enterprise.[27]

The institution of interest creates parasites in society and thereby the gap between the rich and the poor keeps on widening. According to Allama Yusuf Ali (the eminent translator of the Holy Qur'ān into English): "Whereas legitimate trade or industry increases the prosperity and stability of men and nations, dependence over usury would merely encourage a race of idlers, cruel bloodsuckers and worthless fellows who do not know their own good and therefore are akin to madmen". The distinction between "usury" and "interest" in this context is meaningless. Any rate, i.e. anything above zero, would lead to exploitation in the long run, as can be witnessed in the case of developing countries where all economic problems happen to be the direct result of an interest-based system – low levels of savings, heavy budgetary deficits, inflation along with recession, high debt servicing and unemployment. What is considered a reasonable rate today may be regarded as "usurious" tomorrow. And what may be "usurious" today, may be treated as just "interest" tomorrow because of the inflation rate prevailing in an economy. The distinction between interest and usury is made just to deceive mankind and to allow the same old robbery in a more presentable form.

The general view of conventional economists has been that interest plays an important role in promoting savings, investment and economic development. However, this is not the case in a real sense and the reality on the ground indicates the reverse. The level of savings in an economy is determined by a large number of factors – the rate of return on savings being just one determinant. The income level in any economy, the pattern of income distribution, the rate of inflation, stability in the economy and fiscal measures of the government are much more important than the role of interest in savings and investment. Similarly, the

---

[26] See Council of Islamic Ideology (CII), 1980, pp. 7, 8.
[27] Ahmad, 1993.

conventional view that borrowing enhances productivity and capacity to repay is not true. Many economists have been pointing out for a long time the harmful impact of the institution of interest on national and global economies.[28]

The interest-based financial system is creating unrepayable debt – making a class of people richer and leaving others poorer and oppressed. Today, all developing countries are caught up in a sophisticated debt trap owing to the most striking feature of the interest-based mechanism: yesterday's debt can be repaid by taking out more debt today. The unproductive and wasteful spending both by individuals and governments, which the interest-based and easily available credit system has the tendency to promote, has led to a decline in savings, real investment and employment opportunities in almost all countries around the world. The system, combined with inflation, becomes a recipe for total economic instability. This affects the poor and the middle class, which comprise the major part of the population, and thereby the level of national savings.

It has been proved by empirical evidence that credit, compared with equity, does not play any critical role in modern investment and business spending. Contrary to the popular misconception, a major part of funds which finance business needs in the US, for example, are raised as equity (and not loans) on the open market, i.e. common stocks. Kester (1986) lists debt-to-equity ratios for major categories of business in the US and Japan, and shows that most of these ratios are substantially below unity, so that equity financing is much more prevalent than debt financing. This amount of debt would be reduced even further were it not for the artificial tax advantage of debt-based financing in these countries (since interest payments can be written off). Mohsin S. Khan (1986) has shown that interest-based credit increases the risk of banking crises. If collateral is sufficient, modern banks will finance projects even with poor feasibility. This results in business failures.

It is a proven fact and also a ground reality that, at the global level, debt has been used by capitalist countries and the multilateral institutions as a tool of control. The Ottoman Empire was subjected to European influence through the institution of interest-based debt.[29] The role of the IMF and the World Bank is also to subjugate the indebted countries to the will of the rich countries. *The Economist*, against the backdrop of America's war against terrorism after September 11, 2001, puts the caption: "The IMF and the World Bank: Bribing Allies" and contends that the two institutions that are driven by political considerations have become a part of America's arsenal.

James Robertson has succinctly explained how the interest-based system works to favour the rich and what role the present money system plays in the following words:

"The pervasive role of interest in the economic system results in the systematic transfer of money from those who have less to those who have more. Again, this transfer of resources from poor to rich has been made shockingly clear by the Third World debt crisis; but is applied universally. It is partly because those who have more money to lend get more in interest than those who have less; those who have less often have to borrow more; and partly because the cost of interest repayments now forms a substantial element in the cost of all goods and services...When we look at the money system that way and when we begin to think about how it should be redesigned to carry out its functions fairly and efficiently as part of an enabling and conserving economy, the arguments for an interest-free inflation-free money system for the twenty-first century seem to be very strong."[30]

---

[28] For details see Siddiqi, 1981, pp. 47–51, Ahmed, 1967, pp. 171–196.

[29] Zaman and Zaman, 2001, p. 71 (quoting from Blaisdell, 1929).

[30] Robertson, 1990, pp. 130, 131. For further details, see Shariat Appellate Bench, 2000, Taqi Usmani's part of judgement, paras 132–179.

An interest-based system generates unemployment because capital and wealth flow in the direction of high and risk-free return without regard to the efficiency of the fund-borrowing sectors. Thus, it has a built-in tendency to increase risk-free capital vis-à-vis risk-based capital. Why would a person invest his own resources to establish a factory, wherein he will have to deal with unionized labour and many other problems, when he can earn a high return by investing money in any risk-free financial paper issued by the government to meet its revenue expenditures? This results in recession, unemployment, bankruptcies and stagflation.

Wayne A.M. Visser and Alastair McIntosh of the Centre for Human Ecology have described the extensive history of the critique of usury and come to the conclusion that the present global economic system is more usurious/interest-based than ever before. In their opinion, the reasons cited in the critique of usury seem more pressing and relevant now than ever:

> "In particular, it is the belief of the authors that individuals or organisations in the West with money to invest, especially those which like to consider themselves as being ethical, might have rather more to learn from Islam than is generally acknowledged. But first, society needs to be re-conscientised to the relevance of the age-old usury debate in modern times."[31]

### Riba and other Factor Payments

The guaranteed reward on capital in the form of interest marks a fundamental difference between the manner in which the Islamic and conventional economic systems view and use money. Capital as a factor of production in Islamic finance constitutes those things which can be used in the production process only if they are wholly consumed, such as gold or silver in the past and/or money in the present age. In other words, they cannot be lent or leased. Therefore, one cannot derive any benefit from money unless one gives it up in exchange for commodities or services using the structure of any of the valid contracts of sale or lease.

Capital in the above perspective is entitled to profit provided it also takes liability of the risk of loss. Fixed assets like buildings and machinery have claims on rent. Labour includes all sorts of human effort, rendered both physically and mentally, and is entitled to wages/salaries. The entrepreneur gets his reward for his physical as well as his mental exertion and not in exchange for the liability of the risk of loss of capital. Islam views the risk of loss as being attributable to capital that is money itself.

Hence, there is no place for "interest". That is to say, a person who wants to invest his money in any business must take the risk of loss, only then is he entitled to profit. The one who provides land gets rent or revenue, and the provider of labour gets a salary or wages. Should any joint business fail, the provider of capital would lose his money, the provider of land would lose rent and the provider of labour would lose salary. If a man owns his business, he gets or loses all three rewards. Details about this aspect have been given in Chapter 2.

### 3.2.2  Prohibition of Gharar

The second major prohibition is that of Gharar, which refers to the uncertainty or hazard caused by lack of clarity regarding the subject matter or the price in a contract or exchange. A sale or any other business contract which entails an element of Gharar is prohibited.

---

[31] Visser and McIntosh, 1998, pp. 175–189. Also: http://www.alastairmcintosh.com/articles/1998_usury.htm#_ednref3.

"Gharar" means hazard, chance, stake or risk (Khatar). Khatar/Gharar is found if the liability of any of the parties to a contract is uncertain or contingent; delivery of one of the exchange items is not in the control of any party or the payment from one side is uncertain. In the legal terminology of jurists, "Gharar" is the sale of a thing which is not present at hand or the sale of a thing whose "Aqibah" (consequence) is not known or a sale involving hazard in which one does not know whether it will come to be or not, e.g. the sale of a fish in water, or a bird in the air. Material available about Gharar in the literature on Islamic economics and finance is far less than that on Riba. However, the jurists have tried to discuss different aspects to determine whether or not any transaction would be non-Sharī´ah compliant due to the involvement of Gharar.

Uncertainty cannot be avoided altogether in any business. Risk-taking is rather a condition for the entitlement to profit in business. The problem, however, was that the extent of uncertainty making any transaction Haram had not been clearly defined. Lately, scholars have differentiated between Gharar-e-Kathir and Gharar Qalil (too much and nominal uncertainty) and declared that only those transactions that involve too much or excessive uncertainty in respect of the subject matter and the price in a contract should be prohibited. Therefore, although it has been more difficult to define than "Riba", a consensus has emerged in the recent past regarding its extent rendering any transaction valid or void. Accordingly, Gharar is considered to be of less significance than Riba. While the slightest involvement of Riba makes a transaction non-Sharī´ah-compliant, some degree of Gharar in the sense of uncertainty is acceptable in the Islamic structure of business and finance.

However, many areas still need Ijtihad, particularly in terms of Takaful operations, the secondary market for Sharī´ah-compliant securities and the possible involvement of various derivatives in Islamic finance.

Imam Malik defines Gharar as the sale of an object which is not present and thus whose quality of being good or bad is not known to the buyer: as in the sale of a runaway slave or an animal which has been lost by its owner, or the sale of an offspring still in the womb of its mother,[32] or buying of olives with olive oil, or sesame with sesame oil or butter with butter oil. These are all illegal sales according to Imam Malik because of the involvement of the element of chance.

As indicated above, Gharar includes ambiguity/uncertainty about the end result of a contract and the nature and/or quality and specifications of the subject matter of the contract or the rights and obligations of the parties, possession and/or delivery of the item of exchange. In other words, it relates to uncertainty in the basic elements of any agreement: subject matter, consideration and liabilities. The sale of a thing over which the seller has no control, like an escaped animal or any bird flying in the air, or a contract in which the price has not been finalized or the future performance date is not known involves Gharar, making the transaction illegal. In some other cases, however, jurists differ slightly about the coverage of Gharar.[33]

A number of Companions of the holy Prophet (pbuh) have reported the prohibition of Bai' al Gharar from the holy Prophet. While a number of books of Hadith and Islamic jurisprudence mention this special form of prohibited Bai', the term Gharar is generally used as a cardinal principle of Islamic law on Bai'. For example, Imam Bukhari in his Sahih,

---

[32] Malik, 1985, p. 422. See also Tirmidhi, 1988, No. 1252. It is important to observe that while an offspring of a cow in its womb cannot be sold, the price of the cow is indirectly increased due to its conception and that is valid according to the jurists.
[33] Al-Dhareer, 1997, pp. 9–11; Hassan, 1993, pp. 47, 48.

has not reported the Hadith on Bai' al Gharar but captioned a chapter "Al Gharar Sale and Habal-al-Hablah" (i.e. sale of what is in the womb of the animal). Under this heading, he reports the Hadith forbidding the Habal-al-Hablah and trading by "Mulamasah" (sale by touching) and "Munabadhah" (e.g. bartering items without inspection). Al 'Ayny, in his Sharah on Bukhari, has explained why the reference to Gharar is contained only in the heading of a chapter, which does not include a Hadith on Gharar as such. He says that the Hadith forbids the Habal-al-Hablah sale, which is a form of Gharar. Thus, Imam Bukhari refers to the multiple forms of Gharar, of which he has singled out "Habal-al-Hablah", a device by which a particular item refers to all items of similar description.[34] From this, the jurists derive the general legal principle that a contract must not be doubtful and uncertain as far as the rights and obligations of the parties are concerned, otherwise it would be tantamount to deceiving any of the parties. The object of the contract must be precisely determined, price and terms must be clear and known (Ma'lum). This is generally true of all objects which can be measured, counted or weighed and which are subject to the prohibition of Riba.

According to Sharī'ah scholars, to become prohibited, a hazard or uncertainty would be major and remunerative, e.g. when involved in sale contracts it should affect the principal aspects of the contract, and it may not be the need of any valid contract like that of Salam and Istisna'a. Gharar can be avoided if some standards of certainty are met, such as in the case of Salam, where a number of conditions are required to be fulfilled. The vendor must be able to deliver the commodity to the purchaser. Therefore, Salam cannot be conducted in respect of those goods that are normally not available in the market at the stipulated time of delivery. It is prohibited to sell any undeliverable goods. The commodity must be clearly known and its quantity must be determined to the contracting parties.

As indicated above, Gharar relates more to "uncertainty" than to risk as used in commercial terminology. This uncertainty relates to the existence of the subject matter, rights of or benefits to the parties and the consequences of the contract. Some jurists apply it to cases of doubtfulness, e.g. whether or not something will take place. This excludes "unknown" objects.[35] On the other hand, the Zahiri school of thought applies it only to the unknown to the exclusion of the "doubtful". Thus, according to Ibn Hazm, Gharar in sales occurs when the purchaser does not know what he has bought and the seller does not know what he has sold.[36] However, the majority of jurists include both the unknown and the doubtful to render a transaction Gharar-based and thus prohibited. In particular, the Malikites widen the scope of Gharar on the basis of which eminent contemporary scholar Shaikh Al-Dhareer has classified the principles covering Gharar under the following headings:[37]

I.   Gharar in the terms and essence of the contract includes:

(a) Two sales in one.
(b) Downpayment ('Arbūn) sale.
(c) "pebble", "touch" and "toss" sales.[38]

---

[34] Al-Ayny, n.d.
[35] Al-Dhareer, 1997, p. 10; cf Ibn Abideen, n.d., iv/147.
[36] Ibn Hazn, 1988, **8**, pp. 343, 389, 439.
[37] Al-Dhareer, 1997, pp. 10, 11.
[38] Referring to selling the lot of cloth upon which the stone thrown will fall ( Bai' al Hasat) or clothes with unspecified quality of cloth, size and design.

(d) Suspended (Mu'allaq) sale.

(e) Future sale.

II  Gharar in the object of the contract includes:

(a) Ignorance about the genus.

(b) Ignorance about the species.

(c) Ignorance about attributes.

(d) Ignorance about the quantity of the object.

(e) Ignorance about the specific identity of the object.

(f) Ignorance about the time of payment in deferred sales.

(g) Explicit or probable inability to deliver the object.

(h) Contracting on a nonexistent object.

(i) Not seeing the object.

In order to avoid uncertainty, Islamic law denies the power to sell in the following three situations:

1. Things which, as the object of a legal transaction, do not exist.
2. Things which exist but which are not in possession of the seller or the availability of which may not be expected.
3. Things which are exchanged on the basis of uncertain delivery and payment.

Such transactions are prohibited to avoid fraudulent activities, disputes and injustice in trade, as a sale involving Gharar may cause a vendor to consume or erode the property of others unlawfully. Abdullah ibn Abbas (Gbpwh) extended the prohibition of Bai' al Gharar to Bai' al-Ghāib (the sale of absent or concealed goods). The latter contract is considered as falling within the notion of Gharar, since the object of sale is uncertain and the purchaser has the right of option (Khiyār) to revoke the contract upon sight.

Examples of Gharar are: ignorance about the species being sold, about the quantity of the object and the price, lack of specification of the item being sold, e.g. saying: "I sell you one of the houses of this project" without specifying that house, sale of debt (assignment without recourse to the seller) is prohibited as realization of the debt in the future is not certain, ignorance of the time of payment in deferred sales, contracting on a nonexistent object and/or the inability to deliver the object, indicating more than one price or option in a contract unless one is specifically chosen. As this uncertainty may lead to undue benefit to one party at the cost of the other, Gharar sometimes also implies deceit.

Gharar also means deception through ignorance by one or more parties to a contract. The following are some more examples of Gharar:

1. Selling goods that the seller is unable to deliver, as this involves counterparty or settlement risk. This is why, for goods to be covered under the subject of Salam (which is permitted), it is necessary that the relevant commodity might be available in the market at least at the time when delivery has been stipulated.
2. Making a contract conditional on an unknown event, such as "... when it rains".
3. Two sales in one transaction in such a way that two different prices are given for one article, one for cash and one for credit, without specifying at which price one buys the item with the understanding that the sale is binding on the buyer at either price; or selling

two different articles at one price, one for immediate remittance and the other for a deferred one while the sales are conditional upon one another.

4. Making the contracts too complex to clearly define the benefits/liabilities of the parties. That is why the holy Prophet (pbuh) has prohibited combining two sales in one. Shaikh Siddiq Al-Darir opines in this regard: "... the two sales are concluded jointly as when the seller says: 'I sell you my house at such a price if you sell me your car at such a price'. Such a sale is forbidden because of Gharar in the contract: the person who sells the item at a hundred in cash and at a hundred and ten a year hence does not know which of the two sales will take place and he who sells his house provided the other would sell him his car does not know whether this contract will be accomplished or not, since the fulfilment of the first sale is conditional upon the fulfilment of the second. Gharar exists in both cases: in the first case, the sale price is not specified; in the second, the sale may or may not take place."

5. Selling goods on the basis of false description.

6. All contracts where value-relevant information is not clearly available to the parties. A number of invalid sales are included in this category. It may include:

— Selling known or unknown goods against an unknown price, such as the sale of milk in the udder of a cow; selling the contents of a sealed box; or someone may say: "I sell you whatever is in my pocket".

— Selling goods without proper description, such as selling the lot of cloth upon which the stone thrown will fall (Bai' al Hasat) or clothes with unspecified quality of cloth, size and design.

— Selling goods without specifying the price, such as selling at the "market price".

— Selling goods without allowing the buyer to properly examine the goods.[39]

Jahl (ignorance or nonclarity about the parties or their rights and obligations, the goods or the price) is also a part of Gharar. The absence of Jahl requires that the commodity must be defined and its specifications clearly indicated. The purchaser should know about the existence and condition of the goods and the vendor should be able to deliver them on the agreed terms and at the agreed time. In other words, one should not undertake anything or any act blindly without sufficient knowledge, or risk oneself in adventure without knowing the outcome or the consequences.

The general principles for avoiding Gharar in sales transactions that can be concluded from the above discussion are: the contracts must be free from excessive uncertainty about the subject matter and its counter value in exchanges; the commodity must be defined, determined and deliverable and clearly known to the contracting parties; quality and quantity must be stipulated; a contract must not be doubtful or uncertain so far as the rights and obligations of the contracting parties are concerned; there should be no Jahl or uncertainty about availability, existence and deliverability of goods and the parties should know the actual state of the goods.

### 3.2.3  Prohibition of Maisir/Qimār (Games of Chance)

The words Maisir and Qimār are used in the Arabic language identically. Maisir refers to easily available wealth or acquisition of wealth by chance, whether or not it deprives the

---

[39] For all these traditions, see Muslim, 1981 book of sales.

other's right. Qimār means the game of chance – one gains at the cost of other(s); a person puts his money or a part of his wealth at stake wherein the amount of money at risk might bring huge sums of money or might be lost or damaged. While the word used in the Holy Qur'ān for prohibition of gambling and wagering is "Maisir" (verses 2: 219 and 5: 90, 91), the Hadith literature discusses this act generally in the name of "Qimār".

According to the jurists, the difference between Maisir and Qimār is that the latter is an important kind of the former. "Maisir", derived from "Yusr", means wishing something valuable with ease and without paying an equivalent compensation ('Iwad) for it or without working for it, or without undertaking any liability against it, by way of a game of chance. "Qimār" also means receipt of money, benefit or usufruct at the cost of others, having entitlement to that money or benefit by resorting to chance. Both words are applicable to games of chance. References from the Holy Qur'ān in this regard are:

- "O you who believe! intoxicants and gambling, sacrificing to stones, and divination by arrows, are abominable actions of Satan; so abstain from them, that you may prosper." (5: 90)
- "Satan intends to excite enmity and hatred among you with intoxicants and gambling, and hinder you from the remembrance of Allah, and from prayer; will ye not then abstain?" (5: 91)
- "They ask thee concerning wine and gambling. Say: 'In them is great sin and some benefits for people; but the sin is greater than the benefits'." (4: 219)

Gambling is a form of Gharar because the gambler is ignorant of the result of the gamble. A person puts his money at stake wherein the amount being risked might bring huge sums of money or might be lost or damaged. Present-day lotteries are also a kind of gambling.

According to Pakistan's Federal Shariat Court (FSC), a lottery in which coupons or tabs are given and inducement or incentives are provided by an uncertain and unknown event depending on chance, or disproportionate prizes are distributed by the drawing of lots and where a participating person intends to avail themselves of a chance at prizes is repugnant to the tenets of the Sharī'ah. The FSC adds that a scheme wherein the investors' money is safe and intact, but the prizes to be given are related to interest generated from capital accumulated through it, is also repugnant to the tenets of the Sharī'ah due to the involvement of Qimār.

Maisir and Qimār are involved in a number of conventional financial transactions and bank schemes/products which Islamic banks have to avoid. Conventional insurance is not Sharī'ah-compliant due to the involvement of both Riba and Maisir. Governments and public/private sector corporations mobilize resources on the basis of lottery and draws, which come under the banner of gambling and are, therefore, prohibited. Present futures and options contracts that are settled through price differences only are covered under gambling.

In Webster's dictionary, a lottery has been defined as "a distribution of prizes by lots or chance". In practice, a number of forms of lottery are prevalent, some of which might be valid, but the majority are invalid from the Sharī'ah point of view. It is necessary to have a test to decide which are permitted and which are not. An analysis of the Qur'ānic verses and the holy Prophet's traditions would show that in valid lotteries, no one should have any personal right or vested interest in the matter and no one should be deprived of what he had already had or contributed to the process. Further, if the exigency of a situation dictates that some out of them have to forego any right or fulfil any liability, the solution in the absence of any other valid or agreed formula is not to decide arbitrarily but through drawing of lots, as in the case of the holy Prophet Younus (pbuh).[40]

Again, wherever a donor, grantor or a man in authority has to select some people who have equal footing in order to confer some right, privilege or concession on them, the matter could be decided by drawing of lots. Such a form of lottery in such cases is permissible. Sometimes, entrepreneurs offer products whereby, when sold for a price, any additional product is given to the purchaser as an incentive, without any scheme of drawing of prizes or lots. This is also permissible as the purchaser knows what he is purchasing and the vendor knows what he is offering for sale and what its price is. The price being known and the property being sold are available for inspection and there is no element of chance. Such a sale, though induced and publicized with a reward to attract customers, is not hit by any provision or tenets of the Sharī´ah.

However, wherever it is a question of causing loss to some in the drawing of lots with the result that others benefit at the cost of those who lose, it will be the prohibited type. A lottery in which the incentive provided to the investors is disproportionate prizes distributed by drawing of lots, or where a participating person intends to avail themselves of a chance at prizes, is repugnant to the injunctions of Islam.[41]

In some other schemes, tickets, coupons or tabs are given on the purchase of the product, leading further to the drawing of lots. In such cases the inducement is by an uncertain and unknown event, depending on chance, and such a promotion of sale is clearly hit by the injunction of Islam, generally prohibiting gambling, wagering and swearing. Exaggerated publicity and misstatements tend to deceive the clients by giving the impression that everyone will become a millionaire, while the probability of the "bumper prize" is one or two in hundreds of thousands and for even the lowest prizes is one in many thousands of wagers.

Another aspect worth discussion is that such schemes involve Riba, Gharar and Jahl in addition to Qimār or gambling. The proceeds of such schemes take the form of debt and the prize paid is a part of the predetermined additional payment made by the banks (borrower) to the lender. While the winners of prizes take the interest money through lottery, the non-winners wait for their chance. According to the Sharī´ah principles, if the intention of a purchaser of an exhibition ticket is basically to win the prize, the buyer of the ticket will be a sinner. Therefore, not only the money pooled for prizes is illegal, but the method of its distribution through the lottery system also resembles gambling.

Most of the lotteries operated by governments, financial institutions and NGOs are repugnant to the tenets of the Sharī´ah because the incentives provided to the investors are not the profits accruing on the investment but disproportionate prizes distributed by drawing of lots. Besides, the attraction is not to give a helping hand to charitable and philanthropic purposes but to avail oneself of a chance at prizes, thereby disobeying the commandment of the Holy Qur'ān on the subject.

More relevant to a discussion on financial institutions are lotteries or prize-carrying schemes/bonds that banks launch from time to time. Can Islamic banks launch any such bonds or schemes? We discuss this aspect below.

In prize bond schemes, although investors' money may remain safe, the prizes are related to the interest generated from the capital so accumulated. Precalculated interest is distributed among the bondholders. There is also the aspect of the chance for a few to get a prize without

---

[40] See details of this incident in any Tafsir of the Holy Qur'ān in verse 10: 97.
[41] For details, see Ayub, 1999, pp. 34–42; cf. Pakistan, PLD, 1992, SC pp. 157–159.

undertaking any liability or doing work for it, at the cost of other bondholders. Therefore, conventional prize-carrying schemes are repugnant to the tenets of the Sharī´ah due to the involvement of both Riba and Maisir.

Banks running such schemes normally do not give any return to the participants of the scheme. Some others give a very meagre return to general participants of the scheme and give the difference between the meagre rate given to the majority of the participants and huge prizes to a few out of hundreds of thousands of participants. This causes loss to the majority to give undue advantage to some of the participants of the schemes. Moreover, the attraction in these schemes is to avail oneself of a chance at a prize and become a millionaire overnight. It is not only un-Islamic but also against the common norms of morality and sound economic principles. Such schemes divert the flow of scarce resources from real sector economic activities to games of chance and speculation.

## 3.3    BUSINESS ETHICS AND NORMS

In addition to the major prohibitions, including Riba, Gharar and gambling, the Islamic Sharī´ah has enunciated a set of principles that provide a basic framework for the conduct of economic activities in general, and financial and commercial transactions in particular. The Holy Qur'ān and the Sunnah refer to a number of norms and principles which govern the rights and obligations of parties to the contracts. Principles enunciating justice, mutual help, free consent and honesty on the part of the parties to a contract, avoiding fraud, misrepresentation and misstatement of facts and negation of injustice or exploitation provide grounds for valid contracts.[42]

These norms are related to the accountability of human beings before Allah (SWT) and therefore have different implications from those of the norms of mainstream business ethics. Islam teaches belief in the Hereafter, which requires that man should not usurp anyone's rights. It is a principle of Sharī´ah that while Allah (SWT) may pardon the faults committed against His rights (neglect of worship, for example), he does not pardon the harm done by a man to fellow beings or even to other creatures. So, giving people their due right is the cardinal principle of the Islamic system of ethics. Some encouragements like benevolence, purification of income, proper transparency and disclosures, documentation of transactions leading to precision about the rights and liabilities of the parties and comprehensive ethics requiring care for others are also part of the Islamic framework of business norms. Below, we briefly give some important norms.

### 3.3.1    Justice and Fair Dealing

The foremost principle governing all economic activities is justice, which means fair dealing with all and keeping a balance. Justice keeps the sky and the earth in their right places and is the cementing force between various segments in a society. The Holy Qur'ān says: "...And let not the enmity and hatred of others make you avoid justice. Be just; that is nearest to piety..." (5: 8). Stressing this point, the Qur'ān further says: "You who believe stand steadfast before Allah as witness for (truth and) fair play" (4: 135). This makes the point clear that whoever believes in God has to be just with everyone – even with enemies.

---

[42] For details, see Hasanuz Zaman, 2003.

In another place, the Qur'ān says: "And eat up not one another's property unjustly (in any illegal way, e.g. stealing, robbing, deceiving, etc.) nor give bribery to the rulers that you may knowingly eat up a part of the property of others sinfully" (2: 188).

Islam thus requires that the rights and obligations of any person are neither greater nor lesser in any way than the rights and obligations of other people. Business rules are equally applicable to all. No one can take the property of others wrongfully. In his celebrated speech at the time of the last pilgrimage, the holy Prophet (pbuh) declared the inviolability of the rights of human beings in all the three categories of person, property and honour.

In the early Islamic era and subsequently up to the Middle Ages, a lot of emphasis was given to the character building of the masses to ensure justice, fair play with one another and the resultant harmony in society. Many remarkable events of justice and equity are recorded in Islamic history. It was through this deep sense of true justice and equality that Islam played a remarkable role in the development of human society. A number of norms and good practices stem from the overall principles of fair play and justice. These are briefly discussed below.

### Honesty and Gentleness

Honesty, truthfulness and care for others are the basic lessons taught to Muslims by the Sharī'ah, with relatively more emphasis in respect of business transactions. The holy Prophet (pbuh) has said: "The truthful and honest merchant shall be with the Prophets, the truthful and the martyrs on the day of Resurrection." He also said: "It is not lawful for a Muslim to sell to his brother something defective without pointing out the defect". Cheating others and telling lies is considered a great sin. Allah's Apostle used to invoke Allah in the prayer saying: "O Allah, I seek refuge with you from all sins, and from being in debt." Someone said: "O Allah's Apostle! You very often seek refuge with Allah from being in debt". He replied: "If a person is in debt, he tells lies when he speaks, and breaks his promise when he promises."[43] This does not mean that taking a loan is prohibited; the holy Prophet (pbuh) borrowed for himself and also for the Islamic State, as is discussed in Chapter 7. The emphasis is on honesty and speaking the truth and avoiding the sinful act of telling lies; so loans should be taken out only in the case of severe personal or genuine business need.

Ibn Umar (Gbpwh) narrates: "A man came to the Prophet (pbuh) and said: 'I am often betrayed in bargaining.' The Prophet advised him: 'When you buy something, say (to the seller): "No deception".' The man used to say so afterwards". In the case of deception one is entitled to rescind the contract. Similarly, Ghaban, which means misappropriation or defrauding others in respect of specifications of the goods and their prices, is prohibited with the purpose of ensuring that the seller gives the commodity as per its known and apparent characteristics and charges the fair price. The Holy Qur'ān says: "Fill the measure when you measure, and weigh with a perfectly right balance." (17: 35; also verses 86: 1–6).

Another feature of a good businessman is that he avoids harshness and is gentle with other parties and stakeholders. As reported by Imam Bukhari, Allah's Apostle said: "May Allah have mercy on a person who is gentle when he sells, when he buys and when he demands his rights." The person who is liable to pay or undertake any liability is duty bound not to react even if the person who has some right to receive becomes aggressive in demanding

---

[43] Reported by Tirmizi, Darmi, Ibn Majah and others.

his right. Creditors have also been encouraged to be gentle and even give more time if the debtor is really in trouble.

The holy Prophet once said: "Whoever takes the money of the people with the intention of repaying it, Allah would (arrange to) repay it on his behalf, and whoever takes it in order to spoil it, then Allah would spoil him." A man demanded his debts (in the form of a camel) from the holy Prophet in such a rude manner that his Companions intended to harm him, but the Prophet said: "Leave him, no doubt, for he (the creditor) has the right to demand it (harshly). Buy a camel and give it to him." They said: "The camel that is available is older/better than the camel he demands." The Prophet said: "Buy it and give it to him, for the best among you are those who repay their debts handsomely."

It is important to observe, however, that the nature of treatment in the institutional set-up of business is different from any individual-to-individual business relationship. If someone waives the debt payable by any destitute or a person with a genuine problem, he is doing a noble job, as per the instructions of the Holy Qur'ān. But institutions like banks, which manage public money as a trust, cannot and should not give a free hand to those who wilfully default in fulfilling their obligations. That is why all Islamic banks have been allowed by their Sharī'ah boards to impose fines on defaulters with the objective of disciplining their clients and as a deterrent against wilful default. Abu Huraira narrates: "Allah's Apostle said, 'Procrastination (delay) in repaying debts by a wealthy person is injustice'." The amount of fine or penalty is used for charitable purposes and is not credited to the P & L Account of the banks. This aspect is discussed in more detail in Chapter 7.

### Prohibition of Najash

Bidding up the price without an intention to take delivery of the commodity is termed "Najash" and is not permissible. The Prophet (pbuh) has said: "A Nājish (one who serves as an agent to bid up the price in an auction) is a cursed taker of Riba."[44] As reported by Hakim in his Sahih, the Prophet said: "If anyone interferes in the market to create a rise in prices, God has right to cast him face down in Hell." This practice is not only unethical, but also harmful for society, as it creates distortions in the market.

### Prohibition of Khalabah (Misleading Marketing)

Khalabah means misleading, like pursuing unaware and simple clients by overprojecting the quality of a commodity. It is prohibited due to being unethical: one presents his product in such a way that factually it is not so. Accordingly, manipulation and excessive marketing not based on facts about the wares are prohibited. As reported by Imam Muslim in his Sahih, the holy Prophet said: "Refrain from swearing much while selling or doing business, for it may increase business (in the beginning) but brings destruction (ultimately)." Misleading advertising is covered under this prohibition.

### Disclosure, Transparency and Facilitating Inspection

The Sharī'ah attaches great importance to the role of information in the market. One must give ample opportunity to the client to see and check the commodity that he is going to buy.

---

[44] Ibn Hajar, 1981 (Bab al Najash).

Inaccurate or deceptive information is forbidden and considered a sin. The holy Prophet said: "Deceiving a Mustarsal (an unknowing entrant into the market) is Riba".[45] The concealment of any information vital for the contract is tantamount to a violation of the Islamic norms of business and the informationally disadvantaged party in a contract has the right to rescind the contract.

A number of traditions of the holy Prophet (pbuh) stress the need for proper information and disclosure and prohibit such practices that may hinder information about the value and quality of the commodities to the buyers and the sellers. Keeping silent and not letting the buyer know of any defect that is in the knowledge of the seller is considered dishonesty. The holy Prophet (pbuh) once passed by a man who was selling grain. He asked him: "How are you selling it?" The man then informed him. The Prophet (pbuh) then put his hand in the heap of grain and found it wet inside. Then he said: "He who deceives other people is not one of us."

At the time of the holy Prophet (pbuh), when market information was not available to the people of far-flung tribes who used to bring their produce for sale to the towns, the holy Prophet said: "Do not go in advance to meet Rukbān (grain dealers coming to the town to sell goods) to buy their goods, nor should one of you sell over the head of another nor increase the price to excite another to buy Najash" (Sahih Bukhari). This tenet of the holy Prophet means that the grain dealers should come to the town's market and sell their wares at a price determined by the forces of demand and supply. All parties in the market must have enough information about the quality, value of the product, purchasing power of the clients and demand for the product. The wares being sold should be capable of inspection to enable both parties to reasonably know the benefits in case the contract is finalized. For the purpose of transparency, therefore, transactions should be executed within the market or the place where people are aware of the demand and supply situation and are in a position to trade taking into account all relevant information.

Holding any value-related information or structuring a contract in such a way that parties to the contract are not aware of the specifications of the subject matter or its counter value amounts to Gharar and Jahl, which are prohibited as discussed earlier. Hence, the Islamic ethical system requires that all information relevant to valuation of the assets should be equally accessible to all investors in the market. It is consistent with the parties' right to have necessary information and freedom from misrepresentation.

### 3.3.2  Fulfilling the Covenants and Paying Liabilities

Out of twelve commandments given to Muslims by the Holy Qur'ān in Surah Bani Israel, a few relate to fulfilling covenants and not usurping the wealth of the weak in society. "And keep the covenant. Lo! Of the covenant it will be asked" (17: 34).

Business and financial contracts result in rights and liabilities of the parties and the liable party must fulfil the liability as per the agreement or the contract. Sharī´ah emphasizes fulfilment not only of contracts but also promises or unilateral agreements. One of the symbols of hypocrites indicated by the Sharī´ah is that they do not fulfil their promises. We shall discuss this aspect in detail in Chapter 5. It is pertinent to indicate briefly that contemporary scholars unanimously consider promises binding. In Islamic finance, the concept of promise is invoked in Murabaha to Purchase Orderer, leasing, Diminishing Musharakah, etc. In all

---

[45] Suyuti, al-Jami' al-Saghir, under the word ghabn; Kanz al-'Ummal, Kitab al-Buyu', **2**, p. 205.

these arrangements, if the promisor does not fulfil the promise, the promisee has the right to recover the actual loss incurred by him due to the breach of promise.

### 3.3.3   Mutual Cooperation and Removal of Hardship

Mutual help, solidarity and joint indemnification of losses and harm are other important norms of the Islamic economic framework compared to the conventional economic structure, where cut-throat competition causes a number of unethical practices like fraud and forgery. Islam cherishes that a person helps others in times of need and prohibits any such action that may cause any loss or harm to others. The Holy Qur'ān says: "Assist one another in the doing of good and righteousness. Assist not one another in sin and transgression, and keep your duty to Allah" (5: 2). The holy Prophet has encouraged mutual assistance by saying: "The Believers, in their affection, mercy and sympathy towards each other are like one human body – if one of its organs suffers and complains, the entire body responds with insomnia and fever" (Sahih Muslim).

Accordingly, a number of practices or schemes of mutual help like 'Āqilah, Dhamān Khatr al-Tariq, etc. that were prevalent in the pre-Islam period were validated by Islam. 'Āqilah (kin or persons of relationship) was a custom in some tribes at the time of the holy Prophet (pbuh) that worked on the principle of shared responsibility and mutual help. In case of natural calamity, everybody used to contribute something until the disaster was relieved. Similarly, this principle was used in respect of a blood money payment, which was made by the whole tribe. In this way, the burden and the losses were distributed. Under Dhamān Khatr al-Tariq, losses suffered by traders during journeys due to hazards on trade routes were indemnified from jointly created funds. Islam accepted this principle of reciprocal compensation and joint responsibility. This principle is the foundation of the institution of "Takaful" – an alternative to conventional insurance in Islamic finance.

### 3.3.4   Free Marketing and Fair Pricing

Islam provides a basic freedom to enter into any type of Halal business or transaction. However, this does not imply unbridled freedom to contract. Exchange is permitted only when undertaken in permissible commodities and according to the rules and principles laid down by the Sharī´ah in respect of various types of transactions like Bai', Ijarah and services. Jurists have discussed these rules in detail and we shall also elaborate upon them in the relevant places in this book.

Islam envisages a free market where fair prices are determined by the forces of demand and supply. Prices will be considered fair only if they are the outcome of genuinely free functioning of market forces. There should be no interference in the free play of the forces of demand and supply, so as to avoid injustice on behalf of suppliers of goods and consumers. The holy Prophet has prohibited Ghaban-e-Fahish, which means selling something at a higher price and giving the impression to the client that he is being charged according to the market rate.

The price of any commodity is determined by keeping in mind the input and production costs, storage, transportation and other costs, if any, and the profit margin of the trader. If a person starts selling his goods in the market at less than the cost price out of his piety and philanthropy, he will be creating problems for others, as a result of which the supply of that commodity may suffer in the future and ultimately people may suffer. That is why the second Caliph of Islam, Umar (Gbpwh), asked a trader who was selling at less than the market price to raise the rate to the market level or leave the market. Islam cherishes philanthropy, but requires that it must not create problems for genuine businesses.

However, if parties with vested interests hinder the proper functioning of market forces or indulge in hoarding for creating artificial scarcity, the State or the regulators are duty bound to take proper steps to ensure that the forces of demand and supply work genuinely and there is no artificial manipulation. Therefore, to safeguard the interests of all stakeholders, the Islamic state should not allow the creation of distortions.[46] However, permission to interfere is subject to the condition that it is intended to remove market anomalies caused by impairing the conditions of free competition.

Islamic banks will have to follow the rules prescribed by the Sharī´ah for trading and other business. With regard to principles concerning operations in the market, the Jeddah-based Council of the Islamic Fiqh Academy of the OIC in its fifth session (10–15th December, 1988) held that:

1. The basic principle in the Qur'ān and the Sunnah of the holy Prophet (pbuh) is that a person should be free to buy and sell and dispose of his possessions and money, within the framework of the Islamic Sharī´ah in accordance with the divine Command: ("O you who believe! Consume not each other's property in vanities, unless there is trade based on mutual acceptance").
2. There is no restriction on the percentage of profit which a trader may make in his transactions. It is generally left to the merchants themselves, the business environment and the nature of the merchant and of the goods. Care should be given, however, to ethics recommended by Sharī´ah, such as moderation, contentment and leniency.
3. Sharī´ah texts have spelt out the necessity to keep the transactions away from illicit acts like fraud, cheating, deceit, forgery, concealment of actual features and benefits which are detrimental to the well-being of society and individuals.
4. Government should not be involved in fixing prices except only when obvious pitfalls are noticed within the market and prices due to artificial factors. In this case, the government should intervene by applying adequate means to get rid of these factors, the causes of defects, excessive price increases and fraud.

### 3.3.5 Freedom from Dharar (Detriment)

This refers to saving others from any harm due to a contract between two parties. The concept of rights and liabilities is there in Islam like other systems. Of course, the rights are much more strongly enforced in the Islamic framework, with a provision of right/option for the informationally disadvantaged party to reverse its position. The State and regulators are duty bound to ensure fair play and justice for all and that the forces with vested interests do not create hardship for the masses.

If the regulators come to the conclusion that the majority of investors are naïve and irrational, they can take a paternal approach to protect them from the unhealthy practices of any of the market players. They also need to provide the general public necessary information about the nature of business activities. Even if relevant information is available to them, they may lack the ability to properly analyse that information, and may take irrational investment decisions. Investors may also over-react to any disinformation and behave in an irrational

---

[46] See Maududi, 1991, **2**, pp. 15, 16 (under interpretation of verse 17: 34, 35).

way. In such cases, the State needs to take proper steps to guide the general investors so as to protect them from losses that could be possible due to unhealthy practices in the market.

If a contract between two parties executed with their mutual consent is detrimental to the interests of a third party, the latter may enjoy certain rights and options. A case in point is the pre-emptive right (Shuf'ah) of a partner in joint ownership. This pre-emptive right may be extended by analogy to a situation where existing minority shareholders in joint stock companies could be adversely affected by any decision of the controlling shareholders, such as selling additional stocks to the public, effecting a change in management, mergers and acquisitions, etc.[47]

## 3.4  SUMMARY AND CONCLUSION

We have discussed the fundamental Islamic prohibitions, their implications for various transactions, some encouragements regarding economic behaviour and Islamic commercial ethics that have important bearing on financial transactions in the framework of Sharī´ah. Riba, Gharar and games of chance are the main prohibitions which have to be avoided for the conformity of transactions with the tenets of the Sharī´ah. In addition to these prohibitions, Islam has prescribed a moral/behavioural standard that is almost common in all civilized societies of the world.

Effort has been made to ascertain what constitutes Riba. Any increase over the principal amount of a loan/debt against nothing but time is Riba. As a logical corollary to the prohibition of Riba, the Sharī´ah has prohibited all benefits accruing to a person without any labour, risk or expertise. Any person who wishes to earn profit on his monetary investment must bear the loss or damages accruing to the business where his money capital has been used.

Lending in Islam is a virtuous activity since the lender has to give away the lent goods/money to the borrower for the period of the loan without seeking any compensation. If the value of that loan decreases due to inflation, it is as if the lender has done a larger virtue. The Holy Qur'ān encourages giving extra time to borrowers who are in difficulty or faced with financial constraint. Therefore, the Fiqh Academy of the OIC has categorically ruled out as strictly forbidden the commonly suggested solution of the indexation of a lent amount of money to the cost of living, interest rates, GNP growth rates, the price of gold or some other commodities. However, one can lend in terms of gold or any other currency which is considered not vulnerable to inflation. In this case too, debt liability cannot increase due to inflation.

Gharar means excessive uncertainty in any business or contract about the subject of a contract or its price, or mere speculative risk. It leads to the undue loss of one party and the unjustified enrichment of the other. It includes ambiguity/uncertainty about the ultimate result of a contract and the nature and/or quality and specifications of the subject matter of the contract or the rights and obligations of the parties. A sale or any other business contract which entails an element of Gharar is prohibited. According to Sharī´ah scholars, to become prohibited, a hazard or uncertainty would be major, remunerative, it should affect the principal aspects of the contract, and it may not be the need of any valid contract like that of Salam and Istisna'a.

---

[47] Obaidullah, n.d., p. 13.

Gharar can be avoided if some standards of certainty are met. In the case of a valid Salam, a number of conditions are required to be fulfilled. The vendor must be able to deliver the commodity to the purchaser. It is prohibited to sell any undeliverable goods. The commodity must be clearly known and its quantity must be determined to the contracting parties. Jahl (ignorance) is a part of Gharar and means lack of clear understanding of the specifications about the very nature of the contract or the subject matter.

The holy Prophet (pbuh) has prohibited some types of sale due to the Gharar element. Most of these forms are rarely of concern in the present-day economic system. However, many contemporary financial transactions like forwards, futures, options and other derivative securities involve major Gharar to an extent which renders them invalid. Similarly, the contracts where both the price and the commodity are to be delivered at a future date remain inconclusive, and therefore invalid, due to the element of Gharar.

Gambling is a form of Gharar because the gambler is ignorant of the result of the gamble. Governments and public/private sector corporations mobilize funds on the basis of lotteries and draws, which come under the banner of gambling and are, therefore, prohibited. Draw-based prize schemes launched by financial institutions are also repugnant to the tenets of the Sharī´ah due to the involvement of both Riba and Maisir.

Transactions should conform to certain ethical standards, e.g. trustworthiness in business transactions and generosity in bargaining. Acts like false swearing, lying and hiding facts in any bargains must also be avoided. Fair dealing encompassing honesty, straightforwardness, free consent and negation of misstatement, misrepresentation and exaggerated description of products are important pillars of business ethics as per Islamic Sharī´ah. Sharī´ah does not approve of publicity which leads to concealing facts about the business, exaggeration about the product or the financial position of any entity.

# 4

# The Philosophy and Features of
# Islamic Finance

## 4.1  INTRODUCTION

Islamic banking and finance has been conceived as banking and finance in consonance with
the ethos and value system of Islam. Hence, it is governed, in addition to the conventional
good governance and risk management rules, by the principles laid down by the Islamic
Sharī´ah. In the 1980s, the term "interest-free banking" was used to describe an alternative
system to the conventional interest-based system. But the term "interest-free banking" is
a narrow concept, denoting a number of banking instruments or operations which avoid
interest. Islamic banking, a more general term, is expected not only to avoid interest-based
transactions, but also to avoid Gharar, also prohibited in the Islamic Sharī´ah, and other
unethical practices and to participate in achieving the goals and objectives of an Islamic
economy.

The above nature of business demarcates the philosophy and features of the emerging
discipline in the world of finance. In this chapter we shall be discussing the basic features of
Islamic finance directly affecting the products, instruments, institutions and markets in the
framework of business and finance. This includes avoiding interest, involvement in genuine
trade and other business, Kharaj bi-al-Daman and other requirements for profit entitlement
in various kinds of businesses, money earning money versus risk-based business and their
impact on banks, depositors and the fund users.

## 4.2  THE PHILOSOPHY OF ISLAMIC FINANCE

Islamic economics, of which Islamic finance is an important part, is broadly based on
some prohibitions and encouragements. The prohibition of Riba and permission to trade, as
enshrined in verse 2: 275 of the Holy Qur'ān [Allah has allowed (profit from) trade and
prohibited Riba], drive the financial activities in an Islamic economy towards asset-backed
businesses and transactions. This implies that all financial transactions must be representative
of real transactions or the sale of goods, services or benefits. In addition, Islam has also
prescribed a moral/behavioural standard that is almost common in all civilized societies of
the world.

The structure of Islamic finance revolves around the prohibition of any return derived
on a loan/debt (Riba) and the legality of profit. Riba – commonly known as interest – is
an increase taken as a premium from the debtor. It represents the return on transactions
involving exchange of money for money, or an addition, on account of delay in payment, to
the agreed price on sale debts/debts. The Sharī´ah has prohibited it as it generates imbalances
in the economy. As all transactions involving interest payments are strictly prohibited, debt

contracts cannot be sold at a premium or discount, and exchange transactions of money or goods representing money like gold and silver must be equal for equal and hand to hand. While the term "equal for equal" is obvious, meaning that any increase on one side would be Riba, the exchange of money as business must also be hand to hand, because otherwise, a person can take benefit by the use of money/currency which he has received while he has not given its counter value from which the other party could take benefit.

In the context of Islamic finance, a loan will be considered only a monetary or financial transaction where only funds exchange hands with a guarantee for repayment in full without any return for the creditor. It will not be considered an investment. Investment in the Islamic context is not merely a financial or monetary transaction in which the transfer of funds is the only activity. Investment will be considered only if it becomes a part of real activity or is itself a real activity. Thus, purchasing a bond issued by a government or corporation or making a deposit in a conventional bank in the form of a loan will not be considered investment, because they are merely financial transactions and no real activity is involved. However, if the funds are used to purchase real goods or services and then sell them on at a profit, this use of funds will be treated as investment. But using the funds borrowed on interest for buying or building a physical asset is not a permissible activity. Similarly, buying and selling a financial document will not be an investment because no real activity by the holder is involved in this exchange. As such, while earning on loans is prohibited by virtue of it being interest, any return on investment is permissible and allowed.

In loan transactions, the exchange must be of equal amounts. If the borrowed commodity is fungible, as currency notes are, exactly its like is to be repaid; and in the case of nonfungible goods, the loan contract will be made in terms of money.[1] In the case of two similar goods, the condition of excess payment of either is prohibited, even when it is a transaction of sale, not a loan. The excess has been termed Riba. Thus, if one ton of wheat or 1000 dollars are borrowed, one ton of wheat or 1000 dollars will be repaid; any excess shall be usurious. Currency notes represent Thaman (price) and trading in Thaman has been declared by the holy Prophet (pbuh) as usurious except when exchanged hand to hand and also equal for equal (in case of similar currencies).

In addition to the negation of interest, Islamic finance does not approve involvement in excessive risk-taking or any games of chance that also lead to exploitation and loss to both or any of the parties to the contracts and to human society as a whole. One should sufficiently know what one is giving and what one is getting in exchange in a contract. This implies that certainty about the subject matter and its exchange value, transparency, disclosure and free consent of the parties for entering into the contract are the important factors in Islamic business and finance. A number of principles and rules stem from the above given philosophy of Islamic finance and these are discussed below.

### 4.2.1 Avoiding Interest

Keeping in mind the two verses of the Holy Qur'ān (II: 275, 279), jurists and Sharī'ah scholars have developed a criterion that serves as a fundamental building block of the Islamic theory of finance and economics. The most important feature of that theory is avoiding interest or any *ex ante* return derived on a loan/debt (Riba). The lender, according

---

[1] According to the Hanafites, only fungible goods may be lent or borrowed. Other schools of Islamic Fiqh, however, allow lending of every kind of property; and in case similar is not available, its price will be paid to the lender (Al Jaziri, 1973, **2**, p. 679).

to Sharī´ah tenets, has to give away the lent goods/money to the borrower for the period of the loan without seeking any worldly compensation. Therefore, Islamic banks will not take or give any loan or enter into contracts seeking any increase over the principal of loans or debts created as a result of any credit transaction. Buying/selling goods, both on cash payment and credit, for the purpose of earning profit is permissible. Pricing the goods, keeping in mind the time given for payment of the price in credit transactions, is also acceptable with the condition that it should not involve any addition or enhancement to the principal amount of the debt created as a result of the sale transaction. This aspect has been discussed in detail in Section 4.6 while discussing the concept of time value of money.

This implies that once any debt is created, the seller cannot demand more than the credit price stipulated in the sale or other contracts. Those who were involved in usurious transactions at the time the Holy Qur'ān was revealed protested and argued that lending on interest was like an act of trade and that they should be allowed to add more and more so long as the debtor did not pay. They were admonished through the revelation in the Holy Qur'ān that while "trade" was permitted, "Riba" was forbidden. Any increase over the receivable of the sale was Riba and in loans or debts they were entitled to their principal sums only. Therefore, lending on interest is alien to Islamic banks and financial institutions. In case of any debts created by way of trade or Ijarah transactions, they are not allowed to charge anything over and above the principal of the debt. They are not allowed to charge costs of funds or rent on money in short-, medium- or long-term loans, overdrafts, guarantees, financing against bills, receivables or other instruments or sell their debt instruments.

### 4.2.2  Avoiding Gharar

Avoiding Gharar is another main principle of Islamic finance. Gharar, as discussed in detail in the previous chapter, refers to entering into a contract in absolute risk or uncertainty about the ultimate result of the contract and the nature and/or quality and specifications of the subject matter or the rights and obligations of the parties. Gharar is also involved if there is a lack of adequate value-relevant information (Jahl) or there is inadequacy and inaccuracy of any vital information which leads to uncertainty and exploitation of any of the parties. Deceit, fraud or deliberate withholding of value-relevant information is tantamount to Gharar. Islamic banks should not engage in any bargain in which the result is hidden, as they would not be certain whether the delivery could or would be made, which is necessary for the completion of any genuine business transaction.

The current practices of financial institutions and insurance companies in the futures and options markets are un-Islamic because of the elements of Gharar, interest, gambling, etc. The transactions of contemporary stock markets, if cleansed of these elements, would be Islamic.

The prohibition of Gharar requires Islamic banks not to engage in speculative trade in shares, short-selling, discounting of bills and securities or trading in unidentified items. Similarly, Islamic investment banks' involvement in IPOs of joint stock companies would require care to avoid Gharar, as information asymmetry between the investors and promoters in the early stages of companies' establishment may involve Gharar. Trading in derivatives also involves Gharar and, therefore, is a grey area for Islamic banks.

### 4.2.3   Avoiding Gambling and Games of Chance

Another kind of activity which IFIs have to avoid is gambling/games of chance, which again have been discussed in detail in the previous chapter. All instruments like prize bonds or lotteries in which coupons or tabs are given and inducement or incentives are provided by an uncertain and unknown event depending on chance, or disproportionate prizes are distributed by drawing of lots or where the participating persons intend to avail themselves of chance at prizes are repugnant to the injunctions of Islam. Similarly, a scheme wherein the investors' money is safe and intact, but the prizes to be given are related to interest generated from capital accumulated through it, does not conform to the injunctions of Islam due to involvement of both Riba and Qimār.

Gambling is involved in a number of financial transactions and conventional banks' schemes/products, which Islamic banks have to avoid. Conventional insurance is not Sharī'ah-compliant due to the involvement of both Riba and Maisir. Governments and public/private sector corporations mobilize resources on the basis of lotteries and draws, which come under the banner of gambling and are, therefore, prohibited. Present futures and options contracts that are settled through price differences only are covered under gambling. More relevant to the discussion in this regard are lotteries or prize-carrying schemes/bonds that conventional institutions launch from time to time. This is because only a small number of the participants of such schemes get a prize at the cost of other bondholders, without undertaking any liability or doing work for it.

### 4.2.4   Alternative Financing Principles

In the absence of interest as a basis of financing, Islamic banks have a number of techniques and tools to do their business. Briefly, they will invoke the participation and sharing principle applicable in Musharakah, Mudarabah and their variants, the deferred trading principle applicable in respect of credit and forward sales (Mu'ajjal and Salam), a combination of techniques like Shirkah and Ijarah, Murabaha and Salam/Istisna'a, etc. and return-free loans in specific situations and in consultation with various stakeholders.

Below we give the major forms of Islamic finance so that readers can easily understand the discussion with respect to the philosophy of Islamic banking:[2]

1. Mudarabah is a partnership arrangement in which one party provides capital to the partnership while the other party provides entrepreneurial skills. Any loss is borne by the financier; any profit is shared by the partners according to a pre-agreed ratio.
2. Musharakah, another PLS arrangement, may take the form of a permanent equity investment, a partnership in a specific project having a fixed duration or a diminishing partnership (the bank's share is reimbursed over time by the company acquiring funds), especially for housing and other fixed asset financing that could be leased.
3. Murabaha–Mu'ajjal involves acquiring goods upon a customer's demand or otherwise and their credit sale at a profit margin. It results in debt covering the cost plus a profit margin. This debt has to be paid back irrespective of profit or loss to the person or institution that purchased on credit and suffered loss or the wares destroyed in his ownership. To this effect, we come across a very important reference relating to the period of the second Pious Caliph of Islam Umar (Gbpwh). As reported by Ibn-e-Jarir Tabari (d. 310 AH),

---

[2] All these techniques are discussed in Part III.

"Hind bint-e Utbah came to Umar and asked for a loan of 4000 (dinars) from the public exchequer so that she could trade with it and became liable to pay back the same. After getting the amount, she went to the area of banu kalb and engaged in trading; but she suffered loss. Umar (Gbpwh) said the loan could not be waived as it was from the public exchequer."[3]

4. Salam involves providing funds against the forward purchase of precisely defined goods with prepayments.
5. Ijarah involves leasing an asset and receiving rentals; so long as the asset is on lease, the lessor owns the asset and the risk and reward of its ownership.
6. Istisna'a involves engaging a person that could also be a financing agent to manufacture or construct and supply an item at some future date for an explicit sum on periodic payment. The agent contracts with a manufacturer to produce the commodity and the customers make payments to cover the production price and the profit margin.

We can distribute the above modes into a number of categories, as given in Table 4.1, which also shows the salient features of the various modes in terms of liquidity, rate of return (known or unknown) and the nature of collateral or guarantee. The rate of return for the banks is known in credit sales like Murabaha, Musawamah and in Ijarah. However, the risk profile of trade and Ijarah is different and in the case of the latter, the bank will have to bear the asset risk and the ownership related expenses. The net return in Ijarah would, therefore, be quasi fixed.

**Table 4.1** Features of various Islamic financing tools

| Type of contract | Liquidity | Guarantee | Rate of return |
| --- | --- | --- | --- |
| Debt-creating modes | | | |
| Qard al Hasan | — | Collateral | Nil |
| Credit sales | Non-liquid | Collateral | Known |
| Salam | Non-liquid | Collateral | Unknown/known |
| Istisna'a | Non-liquid | Collateral | Unknown/known |
| Semi-debt modes | | | |
| Ijarah | Liquid | Collateral | Known |
| Sharing modes | | | |
| Musharakah | Liquid | Penalty for misconduct | Unknown |
| Restricted Mudarabah | Liquid | Penalty for misconduct | Unknown |
| General Mudarabah | Liquid | Penalty for misconduct | Unknown |

The return is basically unknown in Salam and Istisna'a, as the bank cannot ascertain in advance the price at which it will sell the asset when delivered under these contracts. But it could be known to the bank to some extent, with the possibility of any change in income, if it enters into a parallel contract or a promise with any party for disposal of the asset at any stipulated price. If the promisor is unable to purchase the asset for any reason, the bank's income will certainly be affected. In the case of sharing modes, the return rate is not known in advance.

---

[3] Federal Shariat Court (FSC) Judgement, PLJ, 1992, FSC, 153 (cf Tabari, Ibne Jarir, Tarikh al Umam, **5**, pp. 29, 30). Also in University of the Punjab, 1973, **10**, p. 775.

*Security/Collateral*

In all debt-creating modes, banks may ask the client to furnish security in the form of a mortgage, a lien or a charge on any of his existing assets. In a forward purchase, banks can ask the client to furnish security to ensure that he shall deliver the commodity on the agreed date. In PLS modes, the bank can also ask for security against the nonperformance of the contract. But the bank is not entitled to enforce the collateral in the case of loss in the business if loss has occurred without any misconduct or negligence on the part of the client partner.

*Liquidity*

The feature of liquidity means the possibility or ease with which the bank can sell the related assets to get cash when needed. As Murabaha receivables cannot be sold like debt instruments are sold in conventional finance, they are considered non-liquid assets. The same is true of Salam and Istisna'a. Assets or instruments representing assets in Ijarah or sharing modes are liquid because the same can be sold in the secondary market.

### 4.2.5    Valid Gains on Investment

All gains on investment or principal of a business are not prohibited.[4] On the basis of the overall principles indicated by the Sharī´ah, scholars have identified methods of gainful deployment of surplus resources with the objective of enhancing their value. Profit has been recognized as a "reward" of capital and Islam permits gainful deployment of surplus resources. The *ex post* profit, allowed by the Sharī´ah, symbolizes entrepreneurship and the creation of additional wealth. However, along with the entitlement to profit, the liability of risk of loss rests with the capital itself; no other factor can be made to bear the burden of the loss on capital.

Financial transactions, in order to be permissible and for the purpose of earning profit, should be associated with tangible real assets. In the Islamic framework, money itself is not recognized as capital, and as such it cannot earn a profit in itself. The provider of funds is an entrepreneur as well. He will get a profit/loss for his capital and a wage/remuneration for his entrepreneurship/labour.[5] If he does not manage the business himself and provides capital to any other individual/group of individuals for any business, he will have a share in the profit while the manager of the business will get "wages" in the form of a share in the profit. But if the business suffers a loss, the capital owner will bear the loss while the manager's labour will go wasted. Thus, earning of profit, depending upon the outcome of the business, is permissible. Keeping in mind this principle, it can be said that one can earn profit on his investment or financing but that has to be related to certain assets exposed to direct or indirect business risk.

---

[4] Islam not only encourages investment for the purpose of gain but also considers the productive investment obligatory. The holy Prophet is reported to have said: "He who sells a house [without need], but does not invest the proceeds in something similar, God will not bless the proceeds". Caliph Umar used to say: "He who has wealth, let him develop it and he who has land let him cultivate it". See Chapra, 1993, p. 98.

[5] Labour means both human bodily and mental exertion. Thus, entrepreneurship is not an independent factor of production.

*All Pre-fixed Returns are not Riba*

It is also not necessary for the sake of Sharīʿah compliance that income from any investment/transaction should be variable. In a number of structures it could be fixed and even then Sharīʿah compliant.

To ascertain the Sharīʿah position of any types of transaction, we will have to look at their nature. If it is a loan or a credit transaction culminating in a debt, such loans/debts cannot fetch any increase whatsoever. In the sale of goods or their usufructs, however, one can make a profit as per the rules of the Sharīʿah relating to the respective transactions. In trade, a person can sell any commodity, not including money, for one price on a cash-and-carry basis and for a higher price on a deferred payment basis. Cash or credit prices in the market should be determined by market forces. However, this is subject to certain conditions, the fulfilment of which is necessary to differentiate between interest and legitimate profit. The following points may be kept in mind to differentiate various transactions in terms of deciding their permissibility or otherwise:

- Baiʿ (sale/purchase of goods) means the definite transfer of ownership of goods to the buyer against the payment of a price that can be on the spot, delayed (in a credit sale) or in advance (in Salam). The risk and reward relating to the sold goods will belong to the buyer, who will be required to pay the price irrespective of the manner in which he has used them or the profit/loss to him in business. As such, Islamic banks will have no recourse to the sold goods for the purpose of Murabaha rollover. The banks price the goods and the debt is created; now the goods belong to their clients, they have no right to re-price them.
- Hibah (gift) means the permanent transfer of ownership of assets free of any payment. After having given a gift, one cannot take it back except with the consent of the person to whom the gift was given.
- Riba (Al-Nasiah) means giving something or money temporarily to others' ownership against payment; this involves interest and is therefore prohibited. If this temporary transfer of ownership of goods/assets is free of any payment, it is called Qard al Hasan/Tabarruʿ and Islam encourages this activity.
- Ijarah refers to the transfer of the usufruct of assets against payment of rent. Rental is allowed subject to the condition that the lessor bears the risk and expenses relating to ownership of the leased asset. There should be no confusion in this regard about interest vis-à-vis the concept of rent in Ijarah (leasing). It might be argued, for example, that as per approved Sharīʿah principles, predetermined rent including a time value of money is allowed; therefore, a predetermined time value of money in loans/debts should also be permitted by analogy. This argument does not have any substantive basis. The rent in leasing is calculated on the basis of the capacity of the asset to give usufruct, which is, in principle, uncertain. Hence, it remains uncertain how much time value of money is actually realized until the asset has completed its economic life. The lessor, as owner of the leased assets, is also the owner of the risk and reward associated with that asset. Further, anything which cannot be used without consuming its corpus during its use cannot be leased out, like money, yarn, edibles, fuel, etc., because when an asset no longer exists, how can the lessor bear the ownership-related risk? All such things/assets, the corpus of which is not consumed with their use, can be leased out against fixed rentals. As such, one can lease out his asset to others for use against fixed/stipulated rental(s). While aeroplanes, ships, houses, motor vehicles, etc. can be leased out against

fixed rentals, money/goods representing monetary units, edible items, petrol, etc. cannot be leased out; such items can be sold/bought or loaned and in the latter case exactly their like has to be given back or repaid.

The above discussion implies that Islamic banks can charge a fixed profit if they engage in trading and leasing. In loaning, however, or in the case of any debt or receivable emerging from credit transactions, they cannot charge any amount over and above the amount of the loan or the debt once created.

*Variable Rates on Investments*

Partnership-based modes (Musharakah, Mudarabah and their variants, collectively called Shirkah) give variable returns to the investors. Shirkah is the major mode used by Islamic banks for mobilizing deposits and funds from savers/investors, who get a variable return based on the result of the business conducted by the banks with their funds. Use of these modes on the assets side would yield a variable return for the banks. However, products can be structured in such a way that investors get a quasi-fixed return. This is possible when Shirkah-based investment is attached to fixed earning modes like trade and Ijarah. Examples are Diminishing Musharakah on the basis of Shirkatulmilk and securitization through Shirkah.

The business risk involved in Shirkah-based modes is more than the risk in trade or Ijarah-based modes discussed above. The partners of a business conducted on the basis of Shirkah are at liberty to determine, with mutual consent, the ratio of profit allocation for each of them. The loss to be suffered by each partner must be exactly in the proportion of his investment. As the risk is high, normally the profit is also high in such modes. A number of empirical studies have proved that Shirkah-based or equity financing is widely used in various parts of the world and has many advantages over debt-based financing.[6] However, Islamic banks and financial institutions have not yet fully explored the potential of Shirkah-based investments.

*Benchmarks/Reference Rates*

Financial institutions, while working in a competitive and regulated environment, require reference rates or scales for executing and pricing the contracts. Benchmarks make administration and regulation by the banks' management and the central banks easy, effective and transparent. Different benchmarks are required for different kinds of financial contracts. Juristic rules underlying the theory of Islamic finance accept the presence of such benchmarks. In Fiqh literature, we come across discussions on Ujratul-mithl (matching wage), Ribh-al-mithl (matching rate of profit), Qirād mithl (matching rate in Qirād/Mudarabah) and Musaqat mithl (matching rate in crop sharing). Sharī'ah scholars allow banks to get service charges on loans provided by them on the basis of Ujratul-mithl.[7] The word "mithl" is used to denote a remuneration or compensation which has to be given in case the underlying contract(s) become voidable (Fāsid) due to nonfulfilment of any condition required for valid contracts of Bai', Ijarah or Shirkah. This indicates a rate of wage, hire or return generally

[6] See Zaman and Zaman, 2001.
[7] Usmani, 1999, p. 147.

payable in the situation when a party to the contract has done some job or undertaken a responsibility but is not entitled to any remuneration due to any problem in contractual terms; he is then paid any customary compensation. This implies a generally prevalent rate in the market at any point in time. Such rates of return, prevalent in the market under varying situations of business, are taken for granted as a guiding indicator.[8]

For conventional finance there is only one benchmark or reference rate (the interest rate). Islamic finance requires two benchmarks: one for debt/semi-debt contracts and the other for non-debt (equity) contracts. Therefore, two reference scales are needed: the price (mark up/rent) reference scale and the sharing ratio reference scale, through the central bank Mudarabah ratio or inter-bank Mudarabah ratio.

The benchmarks should be decided by market forces provided there are no distortions of a gross nature. Islamic banks working in parallel with conventional banks normally use the same benchmark as the conventional banks are using. According to the Sharīʿah scholars, using any interest-based benchmark for the pricing of goods and their usufruct in trade and Ijarah-based activities of Islamic banks does not make their operations un-Islamic so long as other rules of trade and Ijarah are applied.[9]

### 4.2.6   Entitlement to Profit – With Risk and Responsibility

The assumption of business risk is a precondition for entitlement to any profit over the principal. The important Sharīʿah maxim: "Al Kharaj bi-al-Daman" or "Al Ghunm bil Ghurm" is the criterion of legality of any return on capital, meaning that one has to bear loss, if any, if he wants to get any profit over his investment. Profit has to be earned by sharing risk and reward of ownership through the pricing of goods, services or usufruct of goods.

Investment in the Islamic context is not merely a financial or monetary transaction in which transfer of funds is the only activity. Investment, both by banks' depositors and the financial institutions, will be considered only if it is a part of real activity or is itself a real activity. This is because money has the potential for growth when it joins hands with entrepreneurship. In itself, it is not recognized as capital and, therefore, it cannot earn a return.

In all economic activities there could be some commercial risk and one has to bear that risk for the validity of the profit or earnings. In other words, the return on invested funds that plays a productive role in any business is a factor in the willingness and ability to cause "value addition" and bear the risk of a potential loss in the business. Reward should depend on the productive behaviour of the business where funds are used, implying that interest, lotteries, gambling, etc. are prohibited, because return in respect of them either does not accept the business risk or is based on pure luck, chance or hazard.

In debt-creating modes, Islamic banks will face credit/party risks, ownership transfer risks, market risks, commodity risks, price or rate of return risks, legal and documentational risks and other mode-specific risks. Remaining within the Sharīʿah principles, Islamic banks are allowed to take risk mitigation/management measures. Hence, risk can be mitigated but not totally eliminated. Transfer of commercial risk to anyone else without transferring the related reward is not permissible.

---

[8] For details, see Hasanuz Zaman, paper read at IRTI, IDB upon getting the IDB Prize on Islamic Economics.

[9] Usmani, 2000a, pp. 118–120.

The principle is that ownership cannot be separated from the risk of related loss. This has important implications for various transactions. In loans, there is no entitlement to any profit because the creditor gets back the full amount, irrespective of the nature of use by the debtor or the fact the debtor incurred loss in his business which he undertook with the borrowed money. In trade, so long as the asset remains with the seller, he has to bear the risk of its destruction; as soon as he sells it, the risk is transferred to the buyer and in the case of a credit sale, the buyer has to pay the price at the settled time even if the asset is destroyed for any reason. He can mitigate the risk by way of Takaful but it will have no link with his liability to pay the price. In Ijarah, the lessor is entitled to rent only when he keeps the asset in usable form by incurring ownership-related expenses and undertakes the risks associated with the asset.

The business risk involved in Shirkah-based modes is far more than that involved in trading modes like Murabaha, Salam and Ijarah, because in Shirkah, all business loss has to be borne by the capital while the manager or the entrepreneur loses his labour in the case of loss in a joint business. For depositors in Islamic banks, risk stems from the failure of business and uncertainty regarding the level of profit to be shared. This risk does not discourage depositors; rather it justifies the profit and as such we see that Islamic banks' deposits are increasing continuously. For banks, financing on the basis of Shirkah involves risk because clients could disguise the profits and they may lose even the principal, because loss in Islamic finance means loss of capital and not any decrease in the expected profit.

Although investment depositors participate in PLS, there arises the question of whether they should bear only the market risks or also the risks related to fraud, carelessness, mismanagement and loan concentration. There is, however, a consensus that the depositors should not be burdened on account of negligence and follies on behalf of the management. Experts consider it desirable to protect them against these risks to raise their confidence in the financial system and to make the banks' management as well as the supervisory authorities more careful in their risk management and regulation of the banks respectively.

### 4.2.7 Islamic Banks Dealing in Goods not in Money

Conventional banks deal in money: they get money from the public as loans and pay them interest; they give advances to needy people or firms in the form of money and charge them interest. In domestic or foreign trade financing activities or even in the case of finance lease, goods are also involved, but they have no concern with the goods or assets themselves; their main concern is with financing the purchase of goods and for that purpose they also deal in documents to facilitate the trading of goods. As such, there is a famous quote in conventional banking: "Banks deal in documents not in goods". They undertake no responsibility or risk in respect of the subject of the contracts and their counter payments or price.

In contrast, Islamic banks deal in goods and documents and not in money. They use money only as a medium of exchange for purchasing the goods for the purpose of leasing or selling onward, thereby earning income or profit. In this process they also use documents for executing sale and lease contracts, keeping in mind the Sharī´ah principles and facilitating the operations.

The above discussion reveals that Islamic banks intermediate between savers/investors and fund users by involving certain goods and assets or papers representing ownership of real assets. In Salam or Murabaha, for example, the banks deal in certain commodities, not money. They purchase the goods directly or through their agent (under a Wakalah arrangement), at their own discretion for maintaining inventory, or upon an order by their client. The banks take on ownership and the related risks and then sell them at cost plus a profit margin, just like traders. After the execution of a sale, the risk transfers to the clients who will be bound to pay the price at the settled time. In Istisna'a, the manufacturers manufacture the asset and deliver it to the bank along with all related assets and market risks.

In Salam, they receive goods against which they have made prepayments; after that, the asset risk and the price risk is theirs and not the Salam seller's. Contemporary scholars have suggested a parallel contract of Salam whereby a bank may sell a commodity purchased through Salam for the same date of delivery or even the quantity. Scholars are of the view that as long as the original and the parallel Salam contracts are not linked together or made conditional on each other in any way, there is no restriction on the terms of the parallel Salam contract, which is a new and independent contract that should be honoured regardless of whether the first Salam contract is honoured or not.

Involvement in forward trading of goods on the basis of Salam and Istisna'a not only has great potential for developing the agricultural and rural micro-finance market, but also for making the future of the majority of people living in rural areas secure. However, forward foreign exchange operations with delayed payment of any of the currency of exchange and most types of financial futures are not available in the Sharī'ah-compliant system, because these instruments are hedging strategies of the interest-based system. The spot foreign exchange market can function without any problem.

In Ijarah, Islamic banks have to deal in physical assets; they purchase the assets for lease to the clients. So long as the asset remains on lease, its ownership and related risks/expenses remain with the bank; if the asset is damaged without any fault on the part of the lessee and it is not able to deliver the normally intended benefit, the bank's right to receive rental will cease. For transfer of the asset's ownership to the lessee, there must be a separate sale or gift agreement with all related conditions.

In Musharakah- and Mudarabah-based investments, Islamic banks' earnings depend on the result of economic activity undertaken by the client, and they will share the profit as per agreed ratios and bear the loss as per their share in the capital of Shirkah business.

In addition to the above business activities, Islamic banks may provide services against service charges or management fees. However, they cannot receive any fee on lending operations as cost of funds, as that would amount to Riba. Similarly, any penalty in case of default by the clients in paying their debts will not be credited to their Profit & Loss Sharing Statements.

Islamic banks also earn non-fund-based income. Besides the charges for transfer of funds or making payments on behalf of clients, they may engage in fund management against fixed fees under the contract of Wakalatul Istismar as a part of their non-fund-based activities. Under this arrangement, all profit/loss will be that of the client(s) and the banks will be entitled to a fixed management fee against their service for managing the clients' investment.

### 4.2.8 Transparency and Documentation

Islamic banks and financial institutions are required to adopt transparency, disclosure and documentation to a greater extent than the conventional banks. Lack of transparency in respect of Murabaha transactions, where Islamic banks are required to provide all details of the cost/price and the payment mode, may render the transaction non-Sharī'ah compliant.

The Holy Qur'ān enjoins us to write down and take witnesses in all transactions that involve credit one way or the other. Similarly, the holy Prophet (pbuh) himself encouraged disclosure of all features of goods being traded and the competitive environment in which people get sufficient information about goods and their prices in the market. The Islamic banks' disclosure standards are stringent because their role is not limited to a passive financier concerned only with interest payments and loan recovery. Islamic financing modes are used to finance specific physical assets like machinery, inventory and equipment. Hence, clients of Islamic finance must have business which should be socially beneficial, creating real wealth and adding value to the economy rather than making profit out of antisocial or merely paper transactions.

An Islamic bank is a partner in trade and has to concern itself with the nature of business and profitability position of its clients. To avoid loss and reputational risk, the Islamic banks have to be extra vigilant about their clientele. As such, I believe Islamic banks are less likely to engage in illegal activities such as money laundering and financing of terrorism than conventional banks.

### 4.2.9  Additional Risks Faced by Islamic Banks

Even though Islamic banks can genuinely take collateral for extending finance, they cannot rely on it heavily because of the risks associated with various transactions. They are, therefore, under obligation to carry out a more careful evaluation of the risks involved. The additional risks that Islamic financial institutions have to face are asset, market and Sharī´ah non-compliance risks, greater rate of return risks, greater fiduciary risks, greater legal risk and greater withdrawal risk.

Asset risk is involved in all modes, particularly in Murabaha (before onward sale to the client), Salam (after taking delivery from the Salam seller) and Ijarah, as all ownership-related risks belong to the bank so long as the goods are in its ownership. In Shirkah-based modes, risk is borne as per the share in the ownership. Certain developments in the economy or the government's trade policy may affect the demand and prices of goods, leading to asset, price and rate of return risks. Receivables created under Murabaha cannot be enhanced even if the general market rate (benchmark) rises. In the case of non-Sharī´ah compliance, not only would the related income go to the Charity Account, but it may also lead to creditability risk for an Islamic bank, which in turn may lead to withdrawal risk and the "contagion effect" for the Islamic finance industry. Banks' involvement in physical assets may also lead to greater legal risks than the conventional banks have to face.

The results of a survey of 17 Islamic financial institutions conducted by Khan and Habib (2001) confirms that Islamic financial institutions face some risks arising from profit-sharing investment deposits that are different from those faced by conventional financial institutions. The bankers consider these unique risks more serious than the conventional risks faced by financial institutions. The Islamic banks feel that returns given on investment deposits should be similar to those given by other institutions. They strongly believe that the depositors will hold the bank responsible for a lower rate of return and this may cause withdrawal of funds by them. The survey also shows that Islamic bankers judge profit-sharing modes of financing and product-deferred sales (Salam and Istisna'a) to be more risky than Murabaha and Ijarah.

The survey further reveals that while Islamic banks have established a relatively good risk management environment, the measuring, mitigating and monitoring processes and internal controls need to be further upgraded. The growth of the Islamic financial industry will, to a large extent, depend on how bankers, regulators and Sharī´ah scholars understand the inherent risks arising in these institutions and take appropriate policies to cater for these needs. The problems facing Islamic banks, as identified by the survey, include lack of money market instruments and a legal and regulatory framework that is not supportive to them and could be a source of systemic risk.

Mitigation of the risks would require special expertise and sound knowledge of Sharī´ah rules, lest it may lead to non-Sharī´ah compliance. Sharī´ah has identified the responsibilities/liabilities of the parties in respect of every contract and one cannot avoid that responsibility/liability. Thus, Islamic banks can manage risk to a certain limit beyond which they will have to take up the risk/loss. In Ijarah, the risk of asset loss (if not due to any negligence of the lessee) will be that of the bank, it cannot ask the lessee to bear the risk in addition to paying the rent.[10] The bank will have to bear the cost of managing the risk, although it can build such costs into rentals with the free and mutual consent of the lessee and subject to related juristic rules. In Mudarabah, the bank, as a Mudarib, cannot get any remuneration if the Mudarabah business incurs loss.

For goods purchased under Salam, the bank can transfer the price and asset risk to any other party through Parallel Salam. But the responsibility of the original and the parallel contracts will remain independent of each other. The bank can also mitigate the asset and market risk by entering into a promise to purchase by any prospective buyer.

Risk of default by clients can be mitigated by putting a penalty clause in the contract to serve as a deterrent; the amount of penalty would go to the Charity Account. This is the case in all modes except Istisna‘a, where the bank can insert a clause for a decrease in the price of the asset in case of a delay in delivery. This clause is termed "Shart-e-Jazāi" in Islamic jurisprudence. The logic behind this provision in the case of Istisna‘a is that manufacturing/construction of any asset depends, to a large extent, on personal effort, commitment and hard work by the manufacturer, who may start work on contracts with other people, while in the cases of Murabaha and Salam, one party has to pay the deferred liability that has been defined and stipulated in the contract.

## 4.3   DEBT VERSUS EQUITY

After discussing the basic ingredients of Islamic finance, we take up some related aspects that will be helpful in fully understanding the philosophy of Islamic finance theory.

It transpires from the above discourse that debt has to remain a part of Islamic finance. Islamic financial institutions, while providing a financial facility through trading activities, create debt that is genuinely shown in their balance sheets. So the issue is not one of "debt versus equity" but one of putting greater reliance on equity and subjecting the debt to the principle of Sharī´ah that debt, once created, should not increase on the basis of conventional opportunity cost theory.

In many areas of business, Shirkah-based modes either cannot be used or are not advisable, keeping in mind the risk profile of the investors. For example, a widow may require an Islamic banker to invest her money in less risky but Sharī´ah-compliant business because she is not in a position to bear the risk of loss that could arise in Shirkah-based business.

---

[10] This is based on an important juristic rule: Al Ujrah wal Dhamān Lā Tajtami‘ān ( Wage/rent and liability/responsibility do not add up together).

The bank, as a trustee, would be bound to invest funds of such risk-averse investors in trade and Ijarah-based activities. This gives rise to debt.

In line with the writings of the pioneers of the present movement of Islamic finance, many authors, both economists and financial experts, have been saying that Shirkah or equity-based modes are the only modes which can serve as an alternative to interest in the Islamic framework. But this is not the case. Debt has existed forever, and will remain an important part of individuals' and nations' economics. The holy Prophet (pbuh) himself incurred debt, both for personal and also the State's requirements, as will be discussed in Chapter 7. The only point to be taken care of is that a debt should not carry "interest". Therefore, debt creating modes like Murabaha, Salam and Ijarah will remain as operating tools in the hands of Islamic financial institutions. The issue is not the permissibility of debt-creating modes, but a preference for equity-based modes over debt-creating modes.

Therefore, the aim is to create a healthy balance between debt-based and equity-based financing for the prosperity of the economy and society. An economy with a heavy reliance on debt could be highly risky. It is commonly said, for example, that in the US, personal and public debt has reached a point where it is a cause for concern with respect to the stability of the economy, a state which would have been reached already if not assisted by the twin factors of the US being the only super power in the world and the US Dollar being the reserve currency. The policies of the international financial institutions like the IMF, the World Bank and the WTO are also helping the US economy to survive, in spite of incurring heavy debts at the cost of the global economy.

## 4.4  ISLAMIC BANKING: BUSINESS VERSUS BENEVOLENCE

Islamic banks do business just like their counterparts on the conventional side, with the difference of keeping in mind Sharī´ah compliance aspects. There has been a myth in some circles that Islamic banks need to work as social security centres, providing only return-free loans or charity to the needy and for benevolence. This myth has to be removed because business and benevolence are two separate things. Individuals have the right to spend for benevolence out of their income, for which they will be rewarded in the Hereafter as per Sharī´ah tenets. But the banks that hold depositors' money as a trust are not allowed to dole out the trust funds at their discretion.

Normally, the "middle class" in all societies keeps funds in banks that are used by business groups, who are generally affluent and relatively richer than the masses in a society. Islamic banks are doing business with the available funds and passing on a part of the income to the fund owners – depositors or investors. Any bank may like to provide return-free loans out of its own (equity) funds or accumulated "Charity Fund" with the approval of the Sharī´ah advisor, or engage in other social security activities, but this should not negatively affect its fiduciary responsibilities towards the depositors. To fulfil these responsibilities, banks will undertake trading and Ijarah business, provide agency-based services against fees and adopt all risk mitigation techniques remaining within the limits imposed by the Sharī´ah.

Islamic banks sell goods purchased by them at a profit, lease assets against rentals and share the profit (or bear the loss) accruing from Shirkah-based investments. They help society to develop by facilitating asset-based investment and the supply of risk-based capital. Subject to the policies of their boards and in consultation with stakeholders, they can also take part in social and welfare activities, but this will not reflect their normal course of business.

## 4.5   EXCHANGE RULES

Islamic banks' activities, as discussed above, involve the exchange of goods for money, which may take a number of forms like simultaneous exchange on the spot, spot delivery and deferred payment and spot payment with deferred delivery. For such exchange contracts, the Sharī'ah has advised exchange rules that are quite different from the rules applied in conventional finance, which are very flexible due to the absence of any Sharī'ah-related limitations. The most strategic difference between Islamic and conventional rules is that in the latter case, both items of exchange in a transaction can be delayed/deferred and the goods purchased and even the "options" sold onward without taking ownership of the underlying assets or possession of the related risk.

In Islamic finance, only one of the items of an exchange contract can be delayed and goods not owned or possessed cannot be sold. Exchange rules are different for different contracts and types of wealth. Goods other than gold, silver and monetary units, durable assets and shares representing pools of assets can be exchanged with money at market-based pricing with at least one item of the exchange delivered on the spot. Gold, silver or any monetary units (Athman) are subject to the rules of Bai' al Sarf, i.e. equal for equal and hand to hand in the case of homogeneous currency, and hand to hand in the case of different units of currency being exchanged. Usufruct and services (leasing/services) can be exchanged with rentals/wages to be paid in advance, on the spot or deferred. Loans/debts have to be paid without premium and discount and cannot be sold, except by recourse to the original debtor and at face value.

The famous Hadith of the holy Prophet (pbuh) regarding the exchange of six commodities, i.e. gold, silver, wheat, barley, dates and salt, has laid the foundation of these rules. These commodities belong to two categories: two, gold and silver, can serve as monetary units while the remaining four are edible goods. On this basis, jurists have identified two causes ('Illah) of prohibition and held detailed discussions on the rules in respect of application to other goods, reaching consensus on a number of aspects.

The OIC Fiqh Council in its eleventh session (14–19th November, 1998) resolved: "It is not permissible in Sharī'ah to sell currencies by deferred sale, and it is not permissible, still, to fix a date for exchanging them. This is evidenced in the Qur'ān, Sunnah and Ijmā'." The Council observed that contemporary money transactions are major factors behind the financial crises and instability in the world and recommended: "It is incumbent upon Muslim governments to exercise control over money markets and to regulate their activities relating to transactions in currencies and other money-related transactions, in accordance with the principles of Islamic Sharī'ah, because these principles are the safety valve against economic disaster".

Explaining the rules of exchange, the OIC Fiqh Council in its ninth session (1–6th April, 1995) resolved the following regarding crediting a sum of money to the bank account of a customer, in the following cases:

1. Where a sum of money has been credited to the account of the customer, either directly or through a bank transfer.
2. Where a customer contracts a sale of "Sarf" by purchasing a currency for another currency standing in his own account.
3. Where the bank, by order of the customer, debits a sum of money from his account and credits it to another account, in another currency, either in the same bank or in another bank, no matter whether it is credited in favour of the same customer or in favour of any

other person. But it is necessary for the banks to keep in mind the Islamic rules governing the contract of "Sarf".

If such crediting takes some time to enable the beneficiary to draw the amount so credited, this delay can be allowed, provided that it does not exceed the usual period normally allowed in such a transaction. However, the beneficiary of such crediting cannot deal in the currency during the allowed period until the crediting takes its full effect by enabling the beneficiary to draw the amount.

Explaining the relevance of this Hadith, Imam Nawavi, an eminent commentator of Sahih Muslim,[11] says that (in the case of all commutative contracts) when the effective cause ('Illah) of prohibition of exchange of two commodities is different, a shortfall/excess or delay in payment are both permissible, as, for example, in the sale of gold or dollars for wheat (the former being a medium of exchange and the latter an edible item); when the commodities are similar, an excess/deficiency or delay in payment are both prohibited, e.g. gold for gold or wheat for wheat; when the commodities are heterogeneous but the 'Illah is the same, as in the case of the sale of gold for silver or Rupees for Dollars (the common 'Illah being their use as media of exchange) or of wheat for rice (the common 'Illah being edibility), then an excess/deficiency is allowed while a delay in payment is not allowed. As such, futures trading in commodities like gold and silver that serve as Thaman is forbidden.

After analysis of the Fiqh literature on the exchange of similars, we come across the following significant points:

- Exchange should be without any "excess". It follows that the debt contract must be settled with reference to the "original legal standard". Money is used as a medium of exchange.[12]
- Since the value of money can rise as well as fall during inflation and deflation respectively, the settlement of a debt contract should be made in terms of the original date of agreement, which can be taken as a base year.[13]

We need to keep in mind the difference between the natures of sale and loan contracts. An exchange in the form of loans, which intrinsically means a delay in repayment, must be of equal amounts. This is because loaning is a virtuous act in which exactly the same/similar amount has to be returned. If the borrowed commodity is fungible, as currency notes are, exactly its similar is to be repaid; in the case of nonfungible goods, the loan contract needs to be made in terms of money and in the case of two similar goods, the condition of excess payment of either is prohibited, even when it is a transaction of exchange/sale, not a loan.

While barter transactions are very rare in the modern age and banks are not likely to engage in such activities, foreign exchange dealings are included in the normal activities of banks and financial institutions. It is imperative, therefore, that when a sale transaction is taking place among currencies, the exchange has to take place instantly and not on a deferred basis. There are numerous traditions of the holy Prophet (pbuh) to this effect.

As regards currency futures, some scholars forbid them while others distinguish between the following two cases: the first is where one currency is delivered on the spot and the other

---

[11] Discussion on 'Illah can be seen in *Sahih Muslim* with annotation by Nawavi, 1981, **11**, pp. 9–13. For the juristic views of various scholars, see Al Muhallah, **7**, pp. 403–426.

[12] A famous Hadith about the dates of Khaiber may be referred to in this regard. In order to avoid Riba, dates of low quality were sold in the market and then with the money received, dates of good quality bought (Muslim, 1981, **11**, pp. 20, 21).

[13] The holy Prophet advised a Companion accordingly (regarding stipulating price in dinars (gold) but paying in dirhams (silver); Ibnul Qayyim, 1955, **4**, p. 327).

is delayed; this is forbidden. The second, that is permitted, involves the future exchange of both currencies at the previously agreed rate. Therefore, forward cover in currencies can be taken in the form of a promise only for fulfilling the real exchange needs of the traders and not for making speculative gains. The client would enter into a promise with the bank to sell or purchase a certain amount of currency against the foreign currency at the agreed rate, but the actual exchange of both currencies would be simultaneous.

Some scholars from the Indo-Pak subcontinent have suggested the use of Salam in Fulus (coins of inferior metals).[14] However, the forward sale or purchase of currencies in the form of Salam is not a valid contract. As described earlier, paper money can be used only as a price; it cannot serve as a commodity to be sold in Salam. The counter values to be exchanged in Salam include the price on the one hand and the commodity on the other. The commodity is to be deferred in Salam and if the price is also deferred, the Salam contract will mean the exchange of debt against debt, which is prohibited. If the price in Salam is in US $, for example, and the commodity to be sold is Rupees, it will be a currency transaction, which cannot be made through Salam because such an exchange of currencies requires simultaneous payment on both sides, while in Salam, delivery of the commodity is deferred.

## 4.6   TIME VALUE OF MONEY IN ISLAMIC FINANCE

There is almost a consensus among Sharī´ah scholars that the credit price of a commodity can genuinely be more than its cash price, provided one price is settled before separation of the parties.[15] According to many jurists, the difference between the two prices is approved by the Nass (clear text of the Sharī´ah). The Islamic Fiqh Academy of the OIC and Sharī´ah boards of all Islamic banks approve the legality of this difference. This is tantamount to the acceptance of time value of money in the pricing of goods. What is prohibited is any addition to the price once agreed because of any delay in its payment. This is because the commodity, once sold (on credit), generates debt and belongs to the purchaser on a permanent basis and the seller has no right to re-price a commodity that he has sold and which does not belong to him.

As this is an aspect of far-reaching implication for Islamic finance, we may discuss it in detail. Jurists allow the difference between cash and credit prices of a commodity, considering it a genuine market practice. Both time and place have their impact on the price. A commodity sold for 100 dollars in a posh area might be available for 50 dollars in a middle class residential area. Similarly, an object with a price of 100 dollars in the morning might be available for 50 in the evening. This is all acceptable in Sharī´ah if caused by genuine market forces. Similarly, it is quite natural that the credit price of a commodity is more than its cash price at a point in time, while in forward contracts like Salam, the future delivery price is less than the spot price.

The concept of time value of money in the context of Sharī´ah is also established from the fact that Sharī´ah prohibits mutual exchanges of gold, silver or monetary values except when it is done simultaneously. This is because a person can take benefit from use of a

---

[14] For detail see Usmani, 1994, pp. 38–42.
[15] Shariat Appellate Bench, 2000, pp. 476–477. Also see Thani, Ridza and Megat, 2003, p. 35.

currency which he has received while he has not given its counter value from which the other party could take benefit.

The contract of Salam also provides ample illustration of the concept of time value of money through pricing of goods. Salam is a forward contract which enables a commodity to be bought for immediate payment of the price and future delivery. The basic element of this contract is that the price paid in advance for future delivery of the goods is genuinely less than the cash-n-carry price at the time the Salam contract is executed.

It further transpires from the Sharī´ah tenets that time valuation is possible only in business and trade of goods and not in the exchange of monetary values and loans or debts. Islamic economics has the genuine provision of converting money into assets on the basis of which one can measure its utility, but loaning is considered a virtuous act from which one cannot take any benefit. While it concedes the concept of time value of money to the extent of pricing in credit sales, it does not uphold generating rent to the capital as interest does in credits and advances, leading to a rentier class in a society. Valuation of the credit period for pricing the goods or their usufruct is different from the conventional concepts of "opportunity cost" or the "time value". As such, "mark-up" in trade is permissible provided the Sharī´ah rules relating to trade are adhered to, but interest is prohibited due to being an increase over any loan or debt. Therefore, no time value can be added to the principal of a loan or a debt after it is created or the liability of the purchaser stipulated. Time is invaluable; once wasted, it cannot be refurbished. So it should not be compared with money, which, if stolen or snatched, can be restored. In business, however, one keeps in mind the time factor as a natural phenomenon to strike a fair balance between the forces of demand and supply. We will discuss this aspect in Chapter 6.

On the basis of the above rationale, an overwhelming majority of Islamic economists believe that economic agents in an Islamic economy will have a positive time preference and there will be indicators available in the economy to approximate the rates of their time preferences, generally determined by the forces of demand and supply. There is no justification to assume a zero rate of time preference in an Islamic economy, as made in a number of studies on investment behaviour in the Islamic perspective.

## 4.7  MONEY, MONETARY POLICY AND ISLAMIC FINANCE

Money is the most strategic factor in the functioning of any financial system. The status, value, role and functions of money in Islamic finance are different from those in conventional finance. In the conventional system, money is considered a commodity that can be sold/bought and rented against profit or rent that one party has to pay, irrespective of the use or role of the lent money in the hands of the borrower. As this is not the case in Islamic finance, the philosophy, principles and operation of Islamic finance differ to a large extent from the principles and operation of conventional finance.

Experts in Islamic economics concede the advantages of money as a medium of exchange. The holy Prophet (pbuh) himself favoured the use of money in place of exchanging goods with goods. The prohibition of Riba Al-Fadl in Islam is a step towards the transition to a money economy and is also a measure directed at making barter transactions rational and free from the elements of injustice and exploitation.

### 4.7.1   Status of Paper Money

As the banking and financial system revolves around money, this author decided to discuss the matter of money as a part of the chapter on the features of Islamic finance. The present form of money has evolved over time from various types of goods used as money and metallic money to paper and electronic money. Money in the present form, or the currency notes in vogue, are a kind of Thaman (a unit of account to serve as the price of anything), just like gold and silver used to be in the past. In this form it is wanted only for exchange and payments and not for itself, as it has no intrinsic value. Accordingly, the present fiat or fiduciary money represents monetary value for all purposes of making payments; the currencies of all countries are unlimited legal tender and creditors are obliged to accept them for recovery of debt.

Linking money to productive purposes brings into action labour and other resources bestowed by Allah (SWT) to initiate a process from which goods and services are produced and benefits passed on to society.

Therefore, paper money is subject to all the tenets of Sharī´ah relating to Riba, debts, Zakat, etc. One cannot sell a 10 dollar bill for 11 dollars because the bill represents pure money and has no intrinsic value. Notes of any particular currency can be exchanged equal for equal. Currency notes of different countries are considered monetary units of different species and therefore can be exchanged without the condition of equality but subject to the conditions of Bai' al Sarf (currency exchange), briefly discussed in foregoing paragraphs, i.e. hand to hand.

The Shariat Appellate Bench of Pakistan's Supreme Court says in this regard: "Today's paper money has practically become almost like natural money equal in terms of its facility of exchange and credibility to the old silver and gold coins. It will, therefore, be subject to the injunctions laid down in the Qur'ān and the Sunnah, which regulated the exchange or transactions of gold and silver".[16] The Islamic Fiqh Council of the OIC in its third session (11–16th October, 1986) also resolved that paper money was real money, possessing all the characteristics of value, and subject to Sharī´ah rules governing gold and silver vis-à-vis Riba, Zakat, Salam and all other transactions.

### 4.7.2   Trading in Currencies

Paper currencies cannot be sold or bought like goods having intrinsic value. The Sharī´ah has treated money differently from commodities, especially on two scores: first, money (of the same denomination) is not held to be the subject matter of trade, like other commodities. Its use has been restricted to its basic purpose, i.e. to act as a medium of exchange and a measure of value. Second, if for exceptional reasons, money has to be exchanged for money or it is borrowed, the payment on both sides must be equal, so that it is not used for the purpose it is not meant for, i.e. trade in money itself. In the context of trading in goods, as distinct from exchange of various currencies, Shaikh M. Taqi Usmani in SAB Judgement says: "The commodities can be of different qualities. Therefore, transactions of sale and purchase are effected on an identified particular commodity. Money has no quality except that it is a measure of value or a medium of exchange. All units of money of the same denomination are one hundred per cent equal to each other. If A has purchased a commodity

---

[16] Shariat Appellate Bench, 2000, pp. 269–273.

from B for Rs.1000/= he can pay any Note(s) of Rupee amounting to Rs.1000...". This real nature of money, which should have been appreciated as a fundamental principle of the financial system, remained neglected for centuries, but it is now increasingly recognized by modern economists. Professor John Gray (of Oxford University), in his recent work *False Dawn*, has remarked:

> "Most significantly perhaps, transactions on foreign exchange markets have now reached the astonishing sum of around $1.2 trillion a day, over fifty times the level of world trade. Around 95 percent of these transactions are speculative in nature, many using complex new derivatives, financial instruments based on futures and options.... This virtual financial economy has a terrible potential for disrupting the underlying real economy, as seen in the collapse in 1995 of Barings, Britain's oldest bank."

The evil results of such an unnatural trade were pointed out by Imam Al-Ghazali 900 years ago in the following words:

> "Riba (interest) is prohibited because it prevents people from undertaking real economic activities. This is because when a person having money is allowed to earn more money on the basis of interest, either in spot or in deferred transactions, it becomes easy for him to earn without bothering himself to take pains in real economic activities. This leads to hampering the real interests of humanity, because the interests of humanity cannot be safeguarded without real trade skills, industry and construction."[17]

### 4.7.3   Creation of Money from the Islamic Perspective

The monetary and credit policies in any economy have a great impact on the functioning of its financial system through their impact on the quantity and value of money. As against bullion money, paper or fiduciary money can be created simply by ledger entries or the issuing of paper securities and without regard to a corresponding increase in goods and services in an economy. This leads to distortions and exploitation of a segment in society by others. In the Islamic financial system, where exploitation of one by another is strictly prohibited, the supply or growth of money/credit should match the supply of goods and services. There might be some minor mismatches, but persistent mismatches are not consistent with the principle of Islamic finance, as they generate distortions in the payments system and injustice to any of the parties to the contracts.

Of all the features of Islamic financial instruments, one stands out distinctly – that these instruments must be real asset-based. This means that Islamic banks are not able to create money out of nothing or without the backing of real assets, as is the case in the conventional system today. They can only securitize their asset-based operations for the purpose of generating liquid funds, transferring thereby their ownership to the security holders along with their risk and reward. The financing of government budget deficits by Islamic banks and financial institutions will not be possible until the governments have sufficient real assets to raise funds in a Sharī'ah-compliant manner or for the conversion of debt stock into Sharī'ah-compliant securities.

To ensure this, it is important for the regulators to monitor the three sources of monetary expansion namely, financing of government budgetary deficits by borrowing from the central bank – the major source of expansion, the secondary credit creation by commercial

---

[17] Shariat Appellate Bench, 2000, Taqi Usmani's part of Judgement, paras 135–152.

banks and the exogenous factors. The central bank would gear its monetary policy to the generation of growth in the money supply, which is neither "inadequate" nor "excessive" but just sufficient to exploit fully the capacity of the economy to supply goods and services for broad-based welfare.

Commercial banks' deposits constitute a significant part of the overall money supply. These deposits may be "primary deposits", which provide the banking system with the base money (cash-in-vault + deposits with the central bank) or "derivative deposits", which, in a proportional reserve system, represent money created by commercial banks in the process of credit extension and constitute a source of monetary expansion. Since derivative deposits also lead to an increase in money supply, the expansion in derivative deposits needs also to be regulated if the desired monetary growth is to be achieved. This could be accomplished by regulating the availability of base money to the commercial banks and restricting the banks from making the "cash reserves" ineffective through their reserve-sweep programmes.[18]

Corrective measures would be needed to set aside the impact of exogenous factors as far as possible. These measures would include the use of monetary tools, e.g. mopping up liquidity in case the money supply increases due to capital inflows and investing the funds in commodity-producing avenues so that the increase in money supply is matched by an increase in the supply of goods and services with a proper gestation period and in the long run.

The whole discussion on the creation of money and credit in the available literature on Islamic finance is centred on the assumption that the Islamic finance model is based on a two-tier Mudarabah or Shirkah system for the mobilization and use of funds. Although the Islamic banking system in vogue is not based on this model and Islamic banks are using fixed-income modes, yet it is worthwhile to briefly discuss the stance of Islamic economists on this important area with far-reaching implications.

The institution of credit and bank money has been an important key issue discussed by Islamic economists. Early writers on Islamic economics saw something morally wrong in credit money. Some doubted its need and ascribed its proliferation to the vested interests of the banks that gain a lot out of thin air or of no air at all, create an artificial purchasing power and take advantage of the demand for it. This demand is also illicitly created by those who have managed to liquidate their assets and prefer to enjoy a guaranteed income against their withheld money. They advocate a 100% reserve system. Such economists say that if any extra money is needed for financing fresh transactions, it should be issued by the central bank.

Those who favour credit creation have argued that in the Islamic system of banking, credit will be created only to the extent that genuine possibilities of creating additional wealth through productive enterprise exist. Demand for profit-sharing accommodation will be limited by the extent of the available resources and the banks' ability to create credit will be called into action only to the extent of this demand, subject to the constraint imposed by profit expectations that satisfy the banks and their depositors. They say that credit should not be ascribed in any way as being the child of interest, as banks' ability to create credit is independent of the terms and conditions on which it is created.

All Islamic economists, however, realize that interest is the villain and if a measured amount of credit and money is generated in the market without the involvement of interest,

---

[18] For the latest tactics of conventional banks in creating fictitious money and their impact, see Hatch, 2005.

it may not be harmful for the financial and payment systems. Abolition of interest will, to a large extent, curtail the harmful features of the creation of credit by banks. They argue that the crucial question with regard to causation of trade cycles is related to the role of interest in such a credit system and not credit creation as such. Under an interest-based system, the entrepreneur has to aim at a rate of profit which may be three times as high as the rate of interest or even higher. This high pitching of profits forces him to either raise the price of the product or lower the wages of labour. Whatever proportion is assigned to either of the alternatives, effective demand is slashed. The remedy suggested by these economists recommends reshaping the credit structure so that loans cease to command any interest and profits get reduced to the level where they pay only for the labour of the enterprise.

Under a Shirkah-based, interest-free system, it should not be difficult to conclude that possibilities for overexpansion will be sufficiently limited, especially as the liability to losses will attach to the banking system – the creator of credit. The relationship of an Islamic bank with its clients is that of a partner, investor or trader, and not of a creditor or debtor, as in a conventional bank. Islam lays stress on equitable sharing of profit and loss between capital and enterprise that should be by mutual consent. Working along these lines, the Islamic commercial banks will be creating credit as their counterparts do in the present system. Creation of credit by the banks depends on the public habit of keeping their income and savings in the form of bank deposits and making the most of their payments through cheques. This enables the bank to meet public demand for cash by keeping a fractional reserve against their deposits. The overall volume of credit fluctuates as banks' cash reserves change due to changes in the public demand for cash or the central bank's policies.[19]

### 4.7.4   Currency Rate Fluctuation and Settlement of Debts

IFIs create debts/receivables by way of trade and leasing-based modes. What impact inflation has on their receivables is an area of important discussion. Before deliberating upon the Sharī´ah position of linking the debts with any money or a commodity, it is pertinent to observe that, even in conventional finance, indexation is not normally used to make up the loss occurring due to inflation. Conventional institutions rather make a provision for a floating rate in the agreements, keeping in mind the future inflationary pressures. As such, any new rate is applied on the remaining period, while it does not affect the liability already accrued.

Islamic banks are not allowed as a rule to link any debt or receivable for the purpose of indexation. In certain modes/products, however, they are allowed to stipulate a floating or variable rate. But this does not affect any debt liability already created. For example, in Ijarah, Islamic banks can charge rental at a higher rate, if already provided for in the agreement, for any remaining period of the lease; but the rentals for a particular period once accrued cannot be indexed.

The issue of indexation will be deliberated upon in detail in Chapter 7. Here, we shall give only a brief overview of the Sharī´ah position on indexation. The clear injunctions of the Holy Qur'ān and Sunnah reveal that if the financial contribution takes the form of a loan or a debt, it is to be paid back exactly in the same kind and quantity, irrespective of any change in the value of the concerned currency or price of the commodity lent or borrowed,

---

[19] For further details on various aspects of money see Chapra, 1985, pp. 195–208; Al Jarhi, 1983; Choudhury, 1997, pp. 71–103, 286–291.

at the time of return of the loan. This principle is applicable not only for loans and debts but also for credit, barter, deferred exchange of currency, delayed payment of remuneration after devaluation or revaluation, indemnity and a change in the unit of currency at the time of redemption of the loan.

However, if the currency of the debt becomes extinct or is not available for any reason, its counter value will be paid to repay the debt and the rate will be that of the due date. For example, a credit sale executed on 1st July generates a debt of ten Saudi Riyals (SR) payable on 31st December. On the due date, i.e. 31st December, the purchaser is liable to pay SR 10 irrespective of the Riyal's value in terms of any other currency. If the debtor is obliged to pay in Rupees for any reason, the exchange rate will be that which is prevailing on 31st December because he was liable to pay Saudi Riyals on that date.

A change in the value of money, particularly a depreciation of currencies normally termed inflation, is a general feature of most of present-day economies. The main cause of this depreciation is the unlimited creation of money and credit, creating liabilities for debtors in general and hitting future generations in particular.

Governments and central banks have used a variety of measures to combat inflation, including indexation of wages and financial obligations used largely in Latin American countries in the 1980s. But these measures could not control prices and inflation rose in a number of countries to over 2000 % per annum. Ultimately, they had to revise the strategy and adopt policies other than indexation for combating inflation.

In Islamic finance it is also sometimes argued that indexation should be adopted to counter inflationary pressures or that repayments may be made after taking into account the impact of inflation on the purchasing power of money. Experience has shown, however, that indexation is neither a substitute for interest nor has it been able to control the vagaries of inflation. The Nass (clear text) of the Holy Qur'ān (2: 279) allows only the principal of a loan and debt and declares any addition over it as Riba. In the presence of the Nass, the idea of linking loans/debts to the purchasing power of money cannot be justified on the basis of Ijtihad, because Ijtihad is carried out only where the guidance of the Qur'ān and Sunnah does not exist. This approach is further discussed below.[20]

In the past, the value of bullion money was represented by its content. The value of debased money or paper money is represented by official commitments rather than its physical content. During an inflationary period, the intrinsic characteristics of money, i.e. its role as a medium of exchange and as a unit of account, remain intact. Only the relative characteristics change, i.e. the future value of money in terms of its exchange value; but this has been changing since the introduction of money, even in respect of full-bodied coins. The value of silver dirhams depreciated in terms of gold dinars in the time of the early Caliphate.[21] But we do not find any reference in the whole literature on Islamic economics and finance to the concept of indexation in that era.

Shaikh Taqi Usmani, as Judge of the Shariat Appellate Bench, has also refuted the argument that interest is paid to compensate the loss that a lender suffers due to inflation.[22] He nullified the suggestion that indexation of loans can be a suitable substitute for interest-based loans. In this respect he says:

---

[20] For details, see Usmani, 1999, pp. 110–114.

[21] See, Maududi, 1982/1991, **1**, pp. 382, 383 (4: 92).

[22] Shariat Appellate Bench, 2000, pp. 593–596.

"But without going into the question whether indexation of loans is or is not in conformity with Sharī´ah, this suggestion is not practical so far as the banking transactions are concerned. The reason is obvious. The concept of indexation of loans is to give the real value of the principal to the financier based on the rate of inflation, and therefore, there is no difference between depositors and borrowers in this respect. It means that the bank will receive from its borrowers the same rate as it will have to pay to its depositors, both being based on the same measure, i.e. the rate of inflation. Thus, nothing will be left for the banks themselves, and no bank can be run without a profit".

The learned Justice has admitted the problems created by inflation and has also referred to various suggestions given by different quarters for solving the problem.[23]

With regard to the impact of change in the purchasing power of any currency on a debt, the OIC Fiqh Council in its fifth session (10–15th December, 1988) resolved the following:

"It is significant that a fixed debt is repaid in its own currency and not by its counter value, because debts are settled in the same currency. Thus, it is not permitted to attach fixed debts, whatever their source, to currency fluctuation".

## 4.8   SUMMARY

We have discussed the central ingredients of Islamic finance and some relevant aspects that could be helpful in achieving Sharī´ah compliance for Islamic banks' transactions. The term "Islamic finance" or "Islamic banking" simply refers to a state of affairs wherein the financial institutions and the clients have to fulfil the relevant principles of Islamic jurisprudence. Some conditions have been put in place to ensure that contracts do not contain the elements of Riba, Gharar and Qimār – the main prohibitions as discussed in Islamic law.

Some of the major characteristics of Islamic banking can be described as follows: Islamic Sharī´ah does not prohibit all gains on capital. It is only the increase stipulated or sought over the principal of a loan or debt that is prohibited. Islamic principles simply require that the performance of capital should also be considered while rewarding the capital. The prohibition of a risk-free return and permission to trade, as enshrined in verse 2: 275 of the Holy Qur'ān, makes the financial activities in an Islamic set-up real asset-backed with the ability to cause "value addition".

Profit has been recognized as "reward" for (use of) capital and Islam permits gainful deployment of surplus resources for enhancement of their value. However, along with the entitlement to profit, the liability of risk of loss on capital rests with the capital itself; no other factor/party can be made to bear the burden of the risk of loss. Therefore, financial transactions, in order to be permissible, should be associated with goods, services or benefits. While at a micro level this feature of Islamic finance leads to the generation of real economic activity and stable growth, at a macro level it can be helpful in creating better discipline in the conduct of fiscal and monetary policies.

The Islamic banking system is based on risk-sharing, owning and handling of physical goods, involvement in the process of trading and leasing and construction contracts using various Islamic modes of business and finance. As such, Islamic banks deal with asset management for the purpose of income generation. They have to prudently handle the unique risks involved in the management of assets by adherence to the best practices of corporate

---

[23] Shariat Appellate Bench, 2000, p. 593.

governance. Once the banks have a stable stream of Halal income, depositors will also receive stable and Halal income.

Islamic banks reflect the movement towards eliminating the role of interest in human society, in keeping with the teachings of Islam and other major religions. They mobilize resources through Sharī´ah-compatible ways. The most important of these are demand and investment deposits as well as shareholders' equity. Demand deposits normally do not participate in profit or loss to the banks and their repayment is guaranteed. In contrast with this, investment deposits are mobilized on the basis of profit/loss sharing. This should motivate the depositors to monitor the affairs of their banks more carefully and to punish them by withdrawing their deposits if the banks' performance is not up to their expectations. Islamic banks are, therefore, under a constraint to manage their risks more effectively.

If the banks, with the money mobilized on the Shirkah principle, conduct business keeping in mind the Sharī´ah principles of trade and lease, their business will be Islamic and the return earned and distributed among the savers/investors will be Halal. They have to avoid Riba – earning returns from a loan contract or selling debt contracts at a discount or premium – Gharar – absolute risk about the subject matter of the contracts or the price – gambling and chance-based games and general prohibitions and unethical practices.

The rules pertaining to currency exchange contracts (hand to hand and in equal quantity in case of homogeneous currency) have also been discussed. Violation of these rules will result in Riba Al-Fadl (where the quantity of hand-to-hand exchanged money is different) or Riba Al-Nasiah (where money is exchanged for money with deferment).

This chapter has also explained that money has the potential for growth when it joins hands with entrepreneurship. Therefore, money has time value, but this can be manifested in sale/leasing contracts only. Accordingly, a person can sell any commodity for one price on a cash-and-carry basis and for a higher price on a deferred payment basis. However, this is subject to certain conditions, the fulfilment of which is necessary to differentiate interest from legitimate profit. What is prohibited is any addition to the price once mutually agreed because of any delay in its payment. This is because the commodity once sold, even on credit, belongs to the purchaser on a permanent basis and the seller has no right to re-price a commodity that he has sold and which no longer belongs to him. It further transpires that time valuation is possible only in business and trade of goods and not in exchange of monetary values and loans or debts. Loaning is considered in Sharī´ah a virtuous act from which one cannot take any benefit. The discussion in the chapter leads to an important conclusion that valuation of the credit period based on the value of the goods or their usufruct is different from the conventional concepts of "opportunity cost" or "time value".

Islamic economics has the genuine provision of converting money into assets, on the basis of which one can measure its utility. While it concedes the concept of time value of money to the extent of pricing in credit sales, it does not uphold generating rent to the capital as interest does in credits and advances, leading to a rentier class in society. Hence, economic agents in an Islamic economy will have positive time preference and there will be indicators available in the economy to approximate the rates of their time preferences, generally determined by the forces of demand and supply. There is no justification to assume a zero rate of time preference in real sector business in an Islamic economy.

Besides trading, Islam allows leasing of assets and getting rentals against the usufruct taken by the lessee. All such things/assets, the corpuses of which are not consumed with their use, can be leased out against fixed rentals. The ownership in leased assets remains with the lessor, who assumes the risks and gets the rewards of his ownership.

Other salient features of Islamic finance are:

- Differentiating between trading (definite transfer of ownership of goods against payment of price), loaning (temporary transfer of ownership of goods/assets free of any payment) and leasing (transfer of usufruct of goods against payment of rent).
- All gains on principal are not prohibited and the deciding factor is the nature of the transaction.
- Lending is a virtuous act – not a business.
- Islamic banking is a business; lending will not be its regular business. Rather, banks will be facilitating production and trade just like any business ventures, charging profit from the business community and giving ex post returns to savers/investors, getting management fees/shares for their services.
- Entitlement to profit is linked with the liability of risk of loss that comes with the capital itself. Profit is earned by sharing the risk and reward of ownership through the pricing of goods, services or benefits.

The discussion in this chapter has aimed at removing the myths about Islamic banking. Major findings in this regard are:

- A fixed return in the pricing of goods and their usufruct, subject to fulfilment of the relevant Sharī´ah essentials, is permissible.
- Islamic banking is also a business to be conducted by the funds mobilized primarily from the middle class of the economy. This does not mean the availability of cost-free money. Islamic banks earn through trade, lease and services and the income is distributed among the suppliers of funds on the basis of defined principles.
- It is absolutely normal that in trade, the cash and credit prices of a commodity are different, provided one price is settled before finalization of the contract and there is no change in the liability thus created.
- While trade profit is permissible, any excess payment sought on loans or debts is prohibited due to being Riba. The profit margin that banks charge in their trade operations is permissible if the trading principles given by Islam are taken care of.
- It is true that the preferable modes for financing operations by banks are Shirkah-based modes (Musharakah and Mudarabah). But trading and lease-based modes are also permissible. Banks can use all of these modes, keeping in mind the risk profile of the savers/investors and cash flow and profitability of the fund users.

# Part II
## Contractual Bases in Islamic Finance

# 5
# Islamic Law of Contracts and Business Transactions

## 5.1 INTRODUCTION

Islam considers the property of people as sacred and inviolable as their life and honour. To ensure this, it forbids the unlawful devouring of others' property by way of theft, embezzlement, usurpation, bribery, cheating and all other unlawful means of acquiring wealth. These proscriptions are in addition to the main prohibitions like Riba, Gharar and Qimār, which are considered major causes for usurpation of others' property. In addition, different transactions have different features that need to conform to the tenets of the Sharī´ah. Contracts that do not conform to these tenets or that involve any of the above prohibited elements are regarded as invalid. As Islamic banks and financial institutions are dealing in goods by entering into contracts like sale, leasing, partnership, suretyship, agency, assignment of debt, mortgages, etc., it is worthwhile discussing in detail the overall framework of the Islamic law of contracts to ascertain the permissibility/validity or nonvalidity of their operations.

This chapter deals with the general principles of contracts, the elements of contracts, conditions of subject matter, qualification of contracting parties, classification of contracts with regard to validity, the nature of remuneration or compensation in contracts or consideration of the contracts and the causes and effects of invalidity.

## 5.2 MĀL (WEALTH), USUFRUCT AND OWNERSHIP

Contracts deal with goods/wealth (Māl), usufruct of goods and transfer of ownership of the goods/usufruct from one to another party. It is pertinent, therefore, to briefly describe all of these concepts.

Wealth is anything that is useable and has legal and material value for the people. It means that anything considered Māl from a juristic point of view should be of value, possessable and it should have a legitimate use. It also includes abstract and intangible rights (like trademarks and intellectual property).[1] In addition to other goods, fiduciary money is also a kind of Māl. It serves as a medium of exchange or the standard by which the value of other goods is measured but in itself it is not a subject matter of sale.

Māl or property in Islamic commercial law is divided into movable and immovable, fungible and nonfungible and finally determinate ('Ain) and indeterminate (Dayn) categories. 'Ain is a specific or determinate type of Māl while Dayn is a nonspecific or indeterminate property. In contracts, when a person is to get a certain/specific property from other, this

---

[1] Mustafa Zarqa, cf. Mansoori, 2005, p. 190.

is determinate or 'Ain. When a nonspecific unit of any kind of property is to be taken, it is regarded as Dayn. Hence, gold, silver, currency, grain, oil and the like are kinds of indeterminate or Dayn property; while giving counter delivery in exchange contracts one can give any units of these items. Legally, Dayn is the responsibility or obligation of a person to another person that has to be fulfilled by paying any units of the relevant property equivalent to the obligation.[2]

With respect to the exchange of goods, Islamic law distinguishes between Mabi' (the subject of sale) and Thaman (price). Currency notes and debt certificates are not a valid subject of sale (in exchange of homogeneous currencies). They represent Thaman, serve as a medium of exchange, but cannot adopt the role of a commodity, as their exact utility cannot be assessed before they are actually spent. These are issued by the State or its authority and people accept them with full confidence, as they accepted gold/silver in the past. Nobody accepts the notes taking them as exchangeable for gold or silver. Further, the notes are unlimited legal tender while gold (in the past) was limited currency. They are like "Fulus" that had value more than their intrinsic value.[3] A commodity, on the other hand, is the principal object of sale from which the benefit is ultimately to be derived in lieu of a price as settled between the contracting parties.

Accordingly, ownership can be any of the following categories of assets and can be acquired through contracts, succession or addition to the existing owned assets of someone:

1. Ownership of assets (Milk ul'Ain).
2. Ownership of debt (Milk ud Dayn).
3. Ownership of usufruct (Milk ul Manf'at).

If a person gets ownership of 'Ain (the asset itself), he gets ownership of its Manf'at also, but not the other way round, meaning that getting usufruct of something does not mean ownership of the asset itself, as in the case of Ijarah where usufruct is transferred to the lessee and the ownership remains with the lessor. If an Ijarah contract involves transfer of ownership as an automatic impact of lease, the contract is void.

Milk ul'Ain is definite and not related to time, meaning that when someone gets ownership of an asset through purchase, the asset is subject to his discretion; his ownership cannot be ended or done away with, but can be transferred with his free will and according to any valid contract as per the respective juristic rules. For example, a buyer of a commodity on credit becomes the owner of that commodity and the seller, after execution of the sale, has no jurisdiction to take it back from the purchaser; he can only ask for payment of the debt or the credit price. As such, the concept of transfer of ownership of an asset, as distinguished from the transfer of its usufruct, is of immense importance for Islamic banks, as it determines the liability, right, risk and reward for them in their asset-based operations.

Milk ul Manf'at is related to time, meaning that usufruct of any asset against rental can be taken or given for a specified time. Thus, a valid Ijarah (lease) contract always needs stipulation about the lease period.

An important categorization of goods is that of fungible (Zwatul Amthāl or Mithli) and nonfungible (Zwatul Qiyam or Qimi) goods. An article is said to be Mithli if all of its units are similar, like wheat or rice of particular varieties or vehicles of a given trademark. People choose any of their units while the purchasing price of all units in the market is

---

[2] For details, see Rahim, 1958, pp. 261, 325.
[3] Usmani, 1994, pp. 26–28.

the same. A commodity belongs to a dissimilar category if its like is not available in the market and each of its units has a different value due to differences in quality or otherwise, like paintings, gems and buildings. This categorization is important for Islamic financial institutions because, for example, Salam can be conducted for Mithli goods, while Istisna'a is used for Qimi goods.

For transfer of the ownership of goods or their usufruct through trade, lease or gift, jurists have laid down certain rules, keeping in mind the text of the Qur'ān and Sunnah and remaining within the general framework of the Sharī´ah for guidance of the people. While ownership is transferred in a sale to the buyer, it remains with the lessor in Ijarah. While "sale and buy-back" (Bai' al 'Inah) is prohibited according to the majority of jurists, "sale and lease-back" is allowed by almost all. These aspects are explained in detail in relevant chapters.

### 5.2.1 Defining Various Related Terms

Various Arabic terms are used to denote transactions and contracts and convey the meaning of undertaking a contractual obligation. These terms are: Mithāq, 'Ahd or W'adah and 'Aqd.

#### Mithāq

Mithāq means a covenant and refers to an earnest and firm determination on the part of the concerned parties to fulfil the contractual obligations; it has more sanctity than ordinary contracts. The word Mithāq has been used in the Holy Qur'ān in a number of places.[4]

Examples of Mithāq are the treaties in the early Islamic era between Muslims and other nations and the contract of marriage. The Holy Qur'ān refers to the covenant between God and human beings (13: 20), treaty between nations or groups (8: 72 and 4: 90) and the contract of marriage (4: 21). As such, this term has more relevance with religious and social covenants than with economic or financial contracts.

#### 'Ahd or W'adah

'Ahd refers to a unilateral promise or an undertaking, although sometimes it also covers a bilateral obligation. The Holy Qur'ān has used this word in both senses.[5] The Qur'ān says: "And fulfil every 'Ahd, for every 'Ahd will be inquired into (on the Day of Judgement)" or "(But righteous) are those who fulfil the contracts, which they have made". 'Ahd is also termed W'adah in the Fiqh literature.

#### 'Aqd (Contract)

'Aqd, which lexically means conjunction or to tie, is synonymous with the word "contract" of modern law. Murshid al-Hayran has defined it as the conjunction of an offer emanating from one of the two contracting parties with the acceptance by the other in a manner that it affects the subject matter of the contract. According to Majallah al-Ahkam al-Adliyyah, an 'Aqd takes place when two parties undertake obligations in respect of any matter. It is

---

[4] See verses 4: 21; 4: 90; 8: 72; 13: 20.
[5] See verses 2: 40; 2: 177; and 17: 40.

effected by the combination of an offer (Ijab) and acceptance (Qabul). Al 'Inayah has defined 'Aqd as a legal relationship created by the conjunction of two declarations, from which flow legal consequences with regard to the subject matter. Among modern jurists, Abd al-Razzaq al-Sanhuri defines 'Aqd as the concurrence of two wills to create an obligation or to shift it or to relinquish it.[6]

An analysis of the above definitions would reveal that a contract involves: the existence of two parties; the issuance of an outward act depicting internal willingness; an offer (Ijab) and acceptance (Qabul). Further, there must be a legal union between the two declarations regarding the subject matter or the contractual obligations.[7]

'Aqd, therefore, implies obligation arising out of a mutual agreement. The term 'Aqd has an underlying idea of conjunction, as it joins the intention as well as the declaration of two parties. The Holy Qur'ān has used the word in this sense: "O believers! fulfil your contracts ('Uqud)."[8]

'Aqd is used in two senses: in the general sense, it is applied to every act which is undertaken in earnestness and with firm determination, regardless of whether it emerges from a unilateral intention such as Waqf, remission of debt, divorce, undertaking an oath, or from a mutual agreement, such as a sale, lease, agency or mortgage. In this sense, 'Aqd is applicable to an obligation irrespective of the fact that the source of this obligation is a unilateral declaration or agreement of the two declarations. In the specific sense, it is a combination of an offer and acceptance, which gives rise to certain legal consequences.[9]

Of the above three terms, Islamic law relating to business generally deals with 'Ahd/W'adah (promise) and 'Aqd (contract). Islamic financial institutions presently enter into promises in respect of a number of transactions, some of which are:

- Murabaha to Purchase Orderer, wherein the client places an order with the bank to purchase for him a well defined asset and promises to buy the same at cost plus the bank's profit margin.
- Ijarah Muntahia-bi-Tamleek, in which the bank or the client promises with the other party to sell or purchase the asset at the end of the lease period or transfer the ownership to the client through the contract of Hibah (gift). Similarly, the concept of W'adah is used while issuing Sukuk on the basis of Ijarah.
- Sale and lease-back is allowed subject to the fulfilment of certain conditions and in this transaction, promise is a crucial ingredient.
- Diminishing Musharakah, in which case the client promises to redeem the bank's investment by periodically purchasing the bank's share in the joint asset or the bank promises to sell its part of ownership in the asset.
- Disposal of goods purchased through Salam, in which case an Islamic bank, after executing a Salam contract for forward purchase of a well-defined product, gets a promise from any trader that the latter will buy it on stipulated terms and conditions. Islamic banks also take promises from their clients to sell the banks' Salam assets when received as their agents at any given price.

---

[6] Mansoori, 2005, pp. 19–23.
[7] Mansoori, 2005, pp. 20, 21.
[8] (1: 5). Also see 2: 235; 5: 88.
[9] For details see Mansoori, 2005, pp. 19–23.

• Similarly, for disposal of assets manufactured/constructed under Istisna'a, banks take promises to buy from other parties.

'Aqd (contract) is the most crucial tool for Islamic banks for both deposits and asset sides. They enter into Amānah, Qard (loan), Shirkah, or Wakalah contracts with savers or depositors and Bai', Ijarah, Ujrah, Shirkah, Wakalah, Kafalah, Ju'alah and Hawalah contracts with those who avail themselves of the financing facility from them. It is, therefore, pertinent to discuss in detail the concepts of W'adah (promise) and 'Aqd (contract).

## 5.3   GENERAL FRAMEWORK OF CONTRACTS

Islamic law is related to the methodology of the Sharī'ah in dealing with Ibādāt (devotional acts) and Mu'āmalāt (transactions). Ibādāt are held to be universal truths that are unaffected by time and space. The Mu'āmalāt are matters pertaining to individuals interacting among themselves. They may change with changes in time and space. Imam Ibn Taymiyah explains the difference between Ibādāt and Mu'āmalāt in the following words:

> "The acts and deeds of individuals are of two types: Ibādāt, whereby their religiousness is improved, and Adāt or Mu'āmalāt (transactions), which they need in their worldly matters. An inductive survey of the sources of the Sharī'ah establishes that devotional acts are sanctioned by express injunctions of the Sharī'ah. Thus, what is not commanded cannot be made obligatory. As regards transactions, the principle governing them would be permissibility and absence of prohibition. So nothing can be prohibited unless it is proscribed by Allah (SWT) and His Prophet (pbuh) in the overall framework."[10]

This provides a reasonable degree of liberty to the jurists in finding solutions to emerging problems and issues in entering into contracts and transactions and business dealings with one another.

Mu'āmalāt, in turn, pertains to two types of activities, i.e. social and economic and/or financial. This chapter deals with the second category of activities, relating one way or another to transactions and human activities in respect of production, exchange and distribution of economic resources.

Income is generated either through production of goods or providing services by way of sale of goods, their usufruct or expertise. Businesses are conducted in various structures like that of sole proprietorship, partnership (Shirkah), agency (Wakalah) or labour (Ujrah) or forms like sale and lease. All such activities are subject to the observance of certain rules, making the transactions valid and legally enforceable. These rules together constitute the Islamic law of contracts.

A basic rule of Islamic law is that the factor to be considered in Mu'āmalāt or social and economic contracts is the apparent wording, any format or writing of the contract. Only that will have legal consequences; any party who has entered into a contract cannot say that it was not his intent (Niyyah). The law will enforce what he has agreed with the other party. In devotional acts (Ibādāt), on the other hand, it is the intent, meaning or Niyyah of the person doing any devotional act that matters and not mere words.

The validity of the contract requires that its motivating and underlying cause should be according to the requirements of the Sharī'ah. All contracts which promote immorality or

---

[10] Ibn Taymiyah, Fatawa al Kubra, cf, Mansoori, 2005, pp. 3, 4.

are against public policy, are harmful to a person or property of a third party or which are forbidden by law are deemed to be void. A sale or hiring of a weapon to a criminal who will use it to kill innocent people is invalid, when the seller or the lessor is aware of his intention.

## 5.4   ELEMENTS OF A CONTRACT

A contract comprises the following elements: the existence of two parties who must be capable of entering into contracts, i.e. they must be mature and sane; an offer (Ijab) and acceptance (Qabul); a legal (Sharie) basis of union between the two declarations and the contractual obligations; and free from all prohibited factors. Muslim jurists in general hold that, intrinsically, the essential elements of a contract are threefold and if these elements are not found properly, the contract is invalid:

- the form, i.e. offer and acceptance (Sighah);
- the contracting parties ('Aqidain);
- the subject matter (Ma'qud 'alayh).

According to Sanhuri, who has included some other factors, there are seven components in a contract:[11]

- the concurrence of offer and acceptance;
- the unity of the Majlis (session/meeting) of a contract;
- plurality of the contracting parties;
- sanity or the power of distinction of the contracting parties;
- subject matter susceptible to delivery;
- the object (Mahall) defined;
- the beneficial nature of the object, in that trade in it is permitted as per Sharī'ah rules.

### 5.4.1   Offer and Acceptance: Form of the Contract

The form (offer and acceptance) is the procedure or the means by which a contract is made. Juristic rules require that the offer should be in clear language and unconditional. There should be conformity of the offer and acceptance on the subject matter and the consideration and issuance of the offer and its acceptance should be in the same session. We briefly discuss these rules in the following paragraphs.

An offer (Ijab) is the necessary condition of a valid contract. It has been defined as a declaration or a firm proposal made first with a view to creating an obligation, while the subsequent declaration is termed acceptance (Qabul). Ijab signifies the willingness of a party to do something positive. Islamic law is silent on whether the willingness of a party to abstain from a thing also constitutes Ijab or not. The Council of Islamic Ideology in Pakistan is of the view that only the commission of an act forms Ijab. Abstinence from an act cannot be regarded as Ijab. Pakistan's Federal Shariat Court is of the opinion that a contract may be to do anything or to abstain from doing it. This definition conforms to the meaning of

---

[11] Mansoori, 2005, p. 25.

Ijab as given in the Contract Act of 1872 in English law, which says: "When one person signifies to another his willingness to do or to abstain from doing anything with a view to obtaining the assent of that other person to such an act or abstinence, he is said to make a Proposal".[12]

Offer and acceptance can be conveyed in a number of ways, namely: by words, by gesture or indication or by conduct. There is no difference of opinion among jurists with regards to the conclusion of contracts through words. They have not fixed particular words for the formation of a particular contract. Whatever conveys the meaning with clarity is considered sufficient for the formation of a contract. It is all the same whether the words are explicit or implicit.

An offer is considered cancelled in the following cases:

- withdrawal of the offer by the maker;
- death of a party or loss of its capacity to enter into the contract;
- termination of the Majlis, i.e. contractual session, without concluding the contract;
- destruction of the subject matter;
- lapse of the time fixed for acceptance.

It is a requirement of Islamic law that acceptance should conform to the offer in all its details and that it should be accepted in the same meeting if the offer is made to be effective from that session. The requirement of unity of session for "offer and acceptance" has been interpreted in different ways. This requirement is based on a saying of the holy Prophet (pbuh): "The contracting parties have the right of option (to finalize or not) until they separate."[13] Despite some minor differences of opinion, jurists are of the view that a contract must be completed by offer and acceptance in the same meeting until one party acquires for itself the right to think over, to ratify or to revoke the contract later.[14] The option of stipulation (Khiyar al- Shart) is a mechanism provided by Islamic law to overcome the problem caused by the restriction of unity of the session. This option makes a contract nonbinding for the party which has acquired that right for a specified period.[15]

The Federal Shariat Court of Pakistan, in this regard, has observed:

"A narrow interpretation of Majlis would mean that the offer of the promisor should be accepted without any delay and without giving the promisee any opportunity to think or consult someone in order to make up his mind. This may be practicable in small transactions but will fail in bigger transactions, which may require considerable inquiry. Thus, if an offer is made for sale of a factory, it will require inquiry into the title, power to sell, value of machinery, value of building, its liabilities, if any, profitability, etc. If the Majlis is interpreted to mean a single session, no one will consider purchasing a property . . . ."

The Hadith (as given above) simply means that if the two parties agree to enter into a contract in one meeting, each of them shall have a right to retract from it until they separate. It also means that an offer must be taken seriously. To some modern scholars, the word "meeting" is only a legal fiction, in that whatever time is taken by the promisee to communicate his acceptance may be called a continuance of the same meeting.[16]

---

[12] Mansoori, 2005, p. 26.

[13] Bukhari, Sahih, Kitab al Buyu.

[14] Mansoori, 2005, p. 30.

[15] The concept of Khiyar (the option to rescind a sale contract) is discussed in detail in Chapter 6.

[16] For further detail see Mansoori, 2005, pp. 30, 31.

As such, if a seller makes an offer to a potential buyer: "I sell you this commodity for so much", but the buyer does not answer him before they separate, the sale is not concluded and the offer no longer exists. However, if the buyer gets a specified time from the seller, they can conclude the sale within that time on the basis of that offer.

It may be observed that the requirement of unity of session does not apply to the contracts of agency, gift and appointment of an executor for the property of any minor.

### 5.4.2   Elements of the Subject Matter

The subject matter of a contract may include the object of the contracts, a commodity or the performance of an act. The contractual obligation of one party according to Islamic law is the consideration for the contractual obligation of the other party. Detailed conditions in respect of subject matter in various types of contracts are different, but on the whole, the subject matter should be existing/existable, valuable, usable, capable of ownership/title, capable of delivery/possession, specified and quantified and the seller must have its title and risk. If a nonexistent thing is sold, even with mutual consent, the sale is void according to the Sharī´ah.

Accordingly, short-selling has been prohibited by almost all scholars. Similarly, the subject of a contract should not be a thing which is not normally used except for a nonpermissible purpose. The subject matter of an exchange contract must have value of some kind. The "usufruct" of an asset is considered property and thus can be the subject matter of an exchange transaction. A commodity which has not yet come into existence or is not deliverable, and the seller does not know as to when it could be delivered (like an animal which is missing or a stolen car), cannot be sold in order to avoid Gharar.

On the same basis, a contract for sale of a debt or a receivable is not valid because the seller of the debt (creditor) does not know whether and when the debtor will pay the debt. But, if it is subjected to the rules of Hawalah (assignment of debt) with recourse to the original debtor, it is valid. In Salam (the sale of goods with prepayment and deferred delivery), the sale of a nonexistent commodity is allowed because all details about the commodity and delivery are pre-agreed and Gharar is removed.

Conditions regarding the subject matter are discussed below in some detail:

- The basic attributes of the merchandise should consist of pure materials, which should be objects of intrinsic/legal value having some use. The commodity, service or performance must not include things prohibited by the Sharī´ah like wine, pork and intoxicants. It must be ritually and legally clean and permissible. It is further required that the purpose of the contract and the underlying cause should also not be contrary to the objectives of the Sharī´ah. Therefore, a contract to operate a brothel or a gambling house is not valid because in the former case the contract is contrary to the preservation of the family unit, progeny and offspring, which is an objective of the Sharī´ah, and in the latter case, the objective is opposed to the preservation of property and amounts to devouring others' properties wrongfully. Further, since immortality is prohibited in Islam, any contract or transaction that entails these evils or promotes them is also forbidden.
- Legality of the subject matter requires that the commodities should be owned by someone. It also requires that it should be free from legal charge. Thus, an asset mortgaged with a creditor cannot be sold until redemption of the asset upon payment of the debt.
- The subject matter should fulfil the objective of the contract. Thus, perishable goods like vegetables cannot be the subject of a pledge. Similarly, public roads and parks cannot be

the subject of a sale contract because these are meant for the benefit of the public and not for individuals.

- The subject matter should not be harmful to the contracting parties or the public in general. As such, producing and trading in intoxicants like heroin, etc. is not a valid subject for contracts.

## Precise Determination of Subject Matter

The subject matter should be precisely determined with regard to its essence, quality and value. Determination can be made either by pointing or by detailed specification. In some cases, jurists allow a sale even if the goods have not been examined. In such a case the buyer is granted the option of sight after the contract. Thus, there can be two ways to determine the subject matter:

1. The subject matter is known and specified when the parties to the contract see and examine it at the time of the contract. If the subject matter is present in the session, the majority view is that its examination is necessary.
2. Sale by description. If the asset or property to be sold is known, like a house of the seller who has only one house, a description highlighting its specifications is deemed to be sufficient. However, if the seller has a number of apartments almost similar to each other, then identification of the specific unit is necessary for the contract to be valid. If an owner of a shopping mall says to a person: "I sell one of the shops to you" and the person accepts it, the contract is voidable unless the shop intended to be sold is specifically identified or pointed out to the buyer.

The consideration of a contract or the price must be agreed and fixed at the time of executing the exchange transactions. If the price is uncertain, the contract is void. For example, if the seller says to the buyer: "Take this (asset) and I will charge you its price in the market, or I shall tell you the price later", or he says: "If you pay within a month the price will be $100, and if within two months you will be charged $105", and the buyer agrees without stipulating any one final price, the transaction is not valid.

The measuring unit of the price should also be known, e.g. any legal tender or currency, etc. Special care is needed in barter sales because in cases of uncertain price, sales would not be valid. The ownership of the goods being sold remains with the seller until delivery is made. In this respect, there should be a formal event that signifies the point at which a contract is concluded, for example a handshake or a signature. At this point, ownership, along with its risk and reward, is transferred to the buyer, who is liable to pay the price either immediately or at a later specified date if the contract involves credit.

## Possession and Certainty of Delivery of the Subject Matter

The capacity to deliver the subject matter of the contract at the time of the conclusion of the contract is an essential condition of a valid contract. If such a capacity is lacking, the contract is void. The holy Prophet (pbuh) is reported to have said: "He who buys foodstuff should not sell it until he has taken possession of it". It is reported that the Companion Hakim ibn Hizam had bought some commodities in the times of Umar ibn al-Khattab (Gbpwth), and intended to sell them to others. Umar ordered him not to sell the commodities before taking their possession. Zayd ibn Thabit, Abdullah ibn Umar and Abdullah ibn 'Abbas

(Gbpwth) held the same view as that of 'Umar. Their interpretation implies that the vendor must be the real owner of the goods and, as such, the owner of their risk and reward. As regards the liability in case of damage, successors like Ta'aus and Qatadadh opined that if the goods were damaged before being paid for (in a cash sale), they belonged to the vendor. But if they were damaged after the purchaser had promised to take them, they belonged to the latter and the former had to replace them. Further, according to Muhammad ibn Sirin, if any party in the contract makes a precondition for the replacement of damaged goods, the liability for such replacement is on the one who made it.[17]

Therefore, the subject matter of the sale must be in the possession (Qabza) of the seller at the time the sale is executed. In the case of Salam, certain conditions have been put in place to rule out the possibility of nondelivery of the goods in a normal business scenario. For example, only those commodities that are normally available in the market at the time when delivery has to be made can become the subject of Salam, so that the Salam seller can get them from the market for delivery to the Salam buyer if he himself is unable to produce them as per the agreed specifications. In Istisna'a, it becomes the responsibility of the manufacturer/seller to supply the specified asset at the agreed time.

Possession of the subject matter by the seller means that it must be in the physical or constructive possession of the seller when he sells it to another person. Constructive (Hukmi) possession means a situation where the possessor has not taken the physical delivery of the commodity, yet the commodity has come into his risk and control and all the rights and liabilities of the commodity are passed on to him, including the risk of its destruction. In the case of immovable assets, any legal notice of transfer or mutation is sufficient.

## 5.5   BROAD RULES FOR THE VALIDITY OF MU'ĀMALĀT

### 5.5.1   Free Mutual Consent

All transactions, in order to be valid and enforceable, must be based on free mutual consent of the parties. The consent that is required for the formation of a valid contract is free consent. Consent obtained through oppression, fraud and misperception renders a contract invalid as per Islamic law. It also requires that consenting parties have certain and definite knowledge of the subject matter of the contract and the rights and the obligations arising from it. Accordingly, inspection of the subject matter and proper documentation of the transaction, particularly if it involves credit, have been encouraged and emphasized.

Practices like Najash (false bidding to prices), Ghaban-e-Fahish (charging exorbitant prices while giving the impression that the normal market price has been charged), Talaqqi-al-Rukban (a city dweller taking advantage of the ignorance of a Bedouin by purchasing his goods at a far lower price before the latter comes to the market) and concealing any material defect in the goods or any value-related information in trust sales like Murabaha have been strictly prohibited so that the parties can decide with free will and confidence.

### 5.5.2   Prohibition of Gharar

All valid contracts must be free from excessive uncertainty (Gharar) about the subject matter or the consideration (price) given in exchange. This is particularly a requirement of all

---

[17] Al-Sanani, 1972, **8**, p. 28, cf. Hassan, 1993, p. 34.

compensatory or commutative contracts. In noncompensatory contracts, like gifts, some uncertainty is affordable. Gharar conveys the meaning of uncertainty about the ultimate outcome of the contract, which may lead to dispute and litigation. Examples of transactions based on Gharar are the sale of fish in water, fruits of trees at the beginning of the season when their quality cannot be established or the future sale of not fully defined or specified products of a factory which is still under construction.[18]

In order to avoid uncertainty, valid sales require that the commodity being traded must exist at the time of sale; the seller should have acquired the ownership of that commodity and it must be in the physical or constructive possession of the seller. Salam or Salaf and Istisna'a are the only two exceptions to this principle in Sharī'ah and exemption has been granted by creating such conditions for their validity that Gharar is removed and there is little chance of dispute or exploitation of any of the parties. These conditions relate to the precise determination of quality, quantity, price and the time and place of delivery of the Salam goods.

Another relevant example of avoiding uncertainty is that of the sale of debt, which, *per se*, is not allowed even at the face value, because the subject matter or the amount of debt is not there and if the debtor defaults in payment, the debt purchaser will lose. Therefore, discounting of bills is not allowed as per Sharī'ah rules. However, subjecting it to the rules of Hawalah (assignment of debt) will validate the transaction, because under the rules of Hawalah, the purchaser of debt (if it is on the face value) will have recourse to the original debtor and Gharar is removed.

Other examples of Gharar-based invalid transactions are short-selling of shares, the sale of conventional derivatives and the insurance business. Futures sales of shares, in which delivery of the shares is not given and taken and only a difference in price is adjusted, trading in shares of provisionally listed companies or speculation in shares and Forex business, in which only the difference is netted and delivery does not take place, are other examples of Gharar-based transactions.

However, speculation *per se*, which means sale/purchase keeping in mind possible change in prices in the future, is not prohibited. It is only such sales that may involve the sale of nonexistent and not owned goods/shares and Maisir/Qimār that are prohibited.[19]

### 5.5.3   Avoiding Riba

As discussed in detail in previous chapters, Riba is an increase that has no corresponding consideration in an exchange of an asset for another asset. The increase without corresponding consideration could be either in exchange or loan transactions. As Islamic banks and financial institutions are involved in real sector trading activities as well as the creation of debt as a result of credit transactions, they must give special consideration to avoiding Riba lest their income might go to the Charity Account due to non-Sharī'ah compliance. In the conventional sense, the cost of funds amounts to Riba and they have to make profit by way of pricing the goods or usufruct of assets and not by lending.

---

[18] Already discussed in detail in Chapter 3.
[19] Usmani, 1999, pp. 74, 75, 89–91.

### 5.5.4   Avoiding Qimār and Maisir (Games of Chance)

Qimār includes every form of gain or money, the acquisition of which depends purely on luck and chance. Maisir means getting something too easily or getting a profit without working for it. All contracts involving Qimār and Maisir are prohibited. Present-day lotteries and prize schemes based purely on luck come under this prohibition. Dicing and wagering are rightly held to be within the definition of gambling and Maisir. Therefore, Islamic banks cannot launch any such schemes or products.[20]

### 5.5.5   Prohibition of Two Mutually Contingent Contracts

Two mutually contingent and inconsistent contracts have been prohibited by the holy Prophet (pbuh). This refers to

1. The sale of two articles in such a way that one who intends to purchase an article is obliged to purchase the other also at any given price.
2. The sale of a single article for two prices when one of the prices is not finally stipulated at the time of the execution of the sale.
3. Contingent sale.
4. Combining sale and lending in one contract.

In order to avoid this prohibition, jurists consider it preferable that a contract of sale must relate to only one transaction, and different contracts should not be mixed in such a way that the reward and liability of contracting parties involved in a transaction are not fully defined. Therefore, rather than signing a single contract to cover more than one transaction, parties should enter into separate transactions under separate contracts.

Islamic banks may come across a number of transactions in which there could be inter-dependent agreements or stipulations that have to be avoided. The combination of some contracts is permissible subject to certain conditions:

- Bai' (sale) and Ijarah (leasing) are two contracts of totally different impacts; while ownership and risk are transferred to the buyer in Bai', neither ownership nor risk transfer from the lessor to the lessee. It is necessary, therefore, that lease and sale are kept as separate agreements. In Islamic banks' Ijarah Muntahia-bi-Tamleek (lease culminating in transfer of ownership to the lessee), the relationship between the parties throughout the lease period remains that of the lessor and lessee and the bank remains liable for the risks and expenses relating to ownership. Transferring ownership risk to the lessee during the lease period would render the transaction void. However, one of the parties can undertake a unilateral promise to sell, buy or gift the asset at the termination of the lease period. This will not be binding on the other party.
- Shirkah and Ijarah can be combined, meaning that a partner can give his part of ownership in an asset on lease to any co-partners. Jurists are unanimous about the permissibility of leasing one's undivided share in a property to any other partner.[21] However, sale of ownership units to the client in Diminishing Musharakah will have to be kept totally separate, requiring "offer and acceptance" for each unit.

---

[20] Already discussed in detail in Chapter 3. Also see Saleh, 1986.
[21] Usmani, 2000a, p. 86.

- Musharakah and Mudarabah can also be combined. For example, banks manage depositors' funds on the basis of Mudarabah; they can also deploy their funds in the business with the condition that the ratio of profit for a sleeping partner cannot be more than the ratio that their capital has in the total capital.
- Contracts of agency (Wakalah) and suretyship (Kafalah) can also be combined with sale or lease contracts, with the condition that the rights and liabilities arising from various contracts are taken as per their respective rules. As per present practice of Islamic banks, Wakalah is an important component of Murabaha, Salam and Istisna'a agreements.
- Islamic banks can structure products by combining different modes subject to the fulfilment of their respective conditions. For example, they can combine Salam or Istisna'a with Murabaha for preshipment export financing. Diminishing Musharakah is also a combination of Shirkah and Ijarah, added by an undertaking by one party to periodically sell/purchase the ownership to/from another partner.

Similarly, the exchange of two liabilities is prohibited. Transactions between two parties involve an exchange of any of the following types: corporeal property for corporeal property, corporeal property for a corresponding liability or a liability for another liability. Each one of these can be immediate for both parties or delayed for both or immediate for one party and delayed for the other. In this way, Ibn Rushd has identified nine kinds of sales.[22] Out of the above categories of exchange, an exchange involving delay from both sides is not permitted as it amounts to the exchange of a debt for a debt, which is prohibited. That is why full prepayment is necessary for valid contracts of Salam. Some further details on "two deals in one transaction" are given in Chapter 6.

### 5.5.6   Conformity of Contracts with the Maqasid of Sharī'ah

The injunctions of the Sharī'ah are directed towards the realization of various objectives for the welfare of mankind. The objectives of the Sharī'ah have been emphasized in a large number of the texts of the Qur'ān and Sunnah. Any contract or transaction that militates against any of these objectives is invalid in Sharī'ah. It is quite obvious that the rights of fellow beings have to be honoured in respect of all transactions. The rights of Allah (SWT) in Sharī'ah also refer to everything that involves the benefit of the community at large. In this sense, they correspond with public rights in modern law. Therefore, any contract should not be against the benefits of the public at large.[23]

### 5.5.7   Profits with Liability

This principle states that a person is entitled to profit only when he bears the risk of loss in business. It operates in a number of contracts such as the contract of sale, hire or partnership. Any excess over and above the principal sum paid to the creditor by the debtor is prohibited because the creditor does not bear any business risk with regard to the amount lent. In sale and lease agreements, parties have to bear risk as per the requirements of the respective contracts.

---

[22] Ibn Rushd, 1950, 2, p. 125.
[23] Mansoori, 2005, pp. 11, 12.

### 5.5.8  Permissibility as a General Rule

Everything that is not prohibited is permissible. The principle of permissibility establishes the fact that all agreements and conditions contained in them are permissible as long as they do not contradict any explicit text of the Qur'ān or Sunnah.

Individuals are not always in a position to conduct exchange transactions on a spot payment basis. Many times, one of the two counter values to an exchange transaction is not exchanged simultaneously, as happens in credit (Mu'ajjal) or forward (Salam) transactions. The validity of these transactions requires certain rules. Such contracts are discussed in detail in various other chapters.

## 5.6  W'ADAH (PROMISE) AND RELATED MATTERS

In W'adah or 'Ahd, one party binds itself to do some action for the other. 'Ahd generally does not create legal obligation but in certain cases it becomes legally binding and enforceable. This is where the promisee has incurred some expenses or taken some liability as a result of the promise. Contingent promises are also considered binding.

Keeping in mind the intricacies of present-day business, particularly when conducted by Islamic banks, contemporary scholars have reached the consensus that W'adah is enforceable by law until and unless the promisor is not in a position to fulfil it on account of any *force majeure*. If nonfulfilment is due to any wilful act of the promisor, he has to make good the loss to the promisee.[24] For example, A promises to sell next month a house to B (a bank) for $100 000, but subsequently he sells the house to C before the month elapses. A would be liable to make up any actual loss incurred by the bank, since it might have made arrangements to lease the house or to sell it or to use it for accommodation for its staff and thus incurred costs.

Let's say A asks bank B to purchase for him a motor car and promises to buy it from B at $20 000. After B purchases it for the total cost of $18 000, A backs out; B sells it in the market for $17 000. Now the net loss of $1000 will have to be borne by A, which the bank can recover from his security or token money (Hamish Jiddiyah).

The rationale behind this consensus decision is that, in many cases, binding promises become a genuine requirement, the fulfilment of which does not amount to violation of any basic Sharī'ah tenet. For example, importers need to hedge their foreign exchange needs, but since forward contracts of gold, silver or any monetary units are not allowed as per Islamic principles relating to Bai' al Sarf, they can do this through unilateral promise by any of the parties. Thus, they can take foreign currency forward cover for genuine business activities allowed by the Sharī'ah scholars on the basis of promise and simultaneous exchange of the currencies at the agreed time.

Some scholars have criticized Islamic banks for treating the "promise to purchase" by the client as binding. But as it does not involve violation of any major Sharī'ah principle, many edicts have declared it binding, keeping in mind the practical problems in finalization of contracts. Quoting the arguments of both sides, Dylan Ray concludes:

> "Having examined these Fatwas, it seems clear that from the point of view of the medieval Fiqh sources, the only correct view is that the promise to purchase ought not to be binding.

---

[24] For details see Vogel and Hayes, 1998, pp. 125–128.

However, modern Muslim jurists do not at all consider themselves bound by their predecessors, and most Islamic banks consider the promise to purchase as binding. Further, they require collateral against the possibility of the promise being dishonoured. This reasoned departure from medieval Fiqh demonstrates that important developments are occurring in the way Islamic judgements are constructed. These developments are creating a degree of conflict among Islamic legal scholars, and objections have been raised against the Murabaha transaction as it is currently practised."

In the opinion of this author, it does not involve any conflict. It seems that Ray has not thoroughly read the position and importance of promise in Islamic Sharī'ah. Many traditional jurists, particularly the Malikis, Hanbalis and some Hanafi and Shafi'e, and almost all contemporary jurists have accepted the legal effectiveness of promise if understanding between the promisor and the promisee takes place in commercial dealings with mutual consent. According to them, fulfilling a promise is mandatory and a promisor is under moral as well as legal obligation to fulfil his promise. In this regard, Shaikh Taqi Usmani says:

"This view is ascribed to Samurah b. Jundub, the well-known companion of the holy Prophet 'Umar B. Abdul Aziz, Hasan al-Basri, Sa'id b. al-Ashwa', Ishaq b. Rahwaih and Imam Bukhari. The same is the view of some Maliki jurists, and it is preferred by Ibn-al-Arabi and Ibn-al-Shat, and endorsed by al-Ghazzali, the famous Shafi'e jurist, who says the promise is binding if it is made in absolute terms. The same is the view of Ibn Shubruma".[25] The third view is presented by some Maliki jurists. They say that in normal conditions, promise is not binding, but if the promisor has caused the promise to incur some expenses or undertake some labour or liability on the basis of promise, it is mandatory on him to fulfil his promise for which he may be compelled by the courts.[26]

Further, this does not contradict any Nass (text) of the Qur'ān or Sunnah and therefore can be accepted on the principle of Ibāhatul Asliyah.

The Islamic Fiqh Academy of the OIC has made the promise in commercial dealings binding with the following conditions:

1. The promise should be unilateral or one-sided.
2. The promisor must have caused the promisee to incur some liabilities or expenses.
3. If the promise is to purchase something, the actual sale must take place at the appointed time by the exchange of offer and acceptance. Mere promise itself should not be taken as the actual sale.
4. If the promisor backs out of his promise, the court may force him either to purchase the commodity or pay actual damages to the seller. The actual damages will include the actual monetary loss suffered by him, but will not include the opportunity cost.[27]

According to the majority of scholars, Muwa'adah or Mu'ahidah (bilateral promise) is not allowed in situations where 'Aqd is not allowed (e.g. forward currency contracts), and thus not enforceable by law. However, some scholars of the subcontinent consider bilateral promise as enforceable by law except for the bilateral promises in transactions like short-selling of currencies or shares of joint stock companies. Notwithstanding the binding nature of promise, the difference between a contract ('Aqd) and a bilateral promise is that the ownership in bilateral promise is not transferred at the time of signing the promise, while in

---

[25] Al Muhallah, 8: 28; Bukhari, al-Sahih, al Shahadat; Ghazali, 3: 133, cf. Usmani, 2000a, p. 122.

[26] For detail see Usmani, 2000a, pp. 120–126.

[27] OIC Fiqh Academy, 5th Conference, Resolution Nos. 2 and 3.

'Aqd, not only the ownership transfers but also the rules of inheritance apply as soon as it is executed.

The binding nature of promise has important implications for Islamic banks' operations in respect of Murabaha to Purchase Orderer, Ijarah-wal-Iqtina', Diminishing Musharakah, which is used by many Islamic banks in the world for housing finance, and for the disposal of goods purchased by banks under Salam/Istisna'a.

### 5.6.1   Token Money (Hamish Jiddiyah) and 'Arbūn

In the case of binding promises, Islamic banks take token money from the promisee clients, which is the amount taken from them to convey seriousness in purchasing the relevant commodity/asset. In Arabic, this is called Hamish Jiddiyah – the margin reflecting the firm intention of the promisee. Banks hold token money as a trust and adjust it in price at the time of the execution of the sale. This means that Hamish Jiddiyah is taken before the execution of an agreement, as against 'Arbūn, which is taken from the buyer as part of the price after execution of the sale agreement. In cases where the bank undertakes some activities and incurs expenses in purchasing the asset for onward sale to the promisee, and the latter fails to honour the "promise to purchase", the bank can recover the actual loss from the promisee; the excess/remaining amount of Hamish Jiddiyah will have to be given back to the client. The actual loss does not cover the loss in respect of "cost of funds".[28] 'Arbūn is the earnest money given at the time of execution of the sale as part of the price.

Such amounts are also taken in tenders, in which the bidders show their intention to purchase an asset at a certain price and instantly give a part of it to the seller who has called the bid. If the bid is accepted, the amount becomes part of the price. So the amount is treated as a trust until the time of bidding and the nonsuccessful bidders have the right to get it back. Bidders can cover actual damage sustained in the bidding process.[29]

The seller, after execution of the sale against a part payment, has the right to retain the whole amount of 'Arbūn if the other party has failed to perform within the period stipulated in the agreement. The AAOIFI, however, considers it preferable to refund the amount over and above the loss actually sustained by the seller.[30]

In recent years, 'Arbūn has become a subject of intensive research in respect of finding any alternative to the conventional options. It therefore warrants some detail. Imam Malik has defined 'Arbūn in the following words: "It is when a person buys a slave or rents an animal and says to the seller or the owner of the animal, 'I will give you one dinar or one dirham or more or less and if I ratify the sale or the rent contract, the amount I gave will be part of the total price. And if I cancel the deal, then what I gave will be for you without any exchange'."[31] He considers this deal invalid.

Two traditions are reported with regard to 'Arbūn in various books of Hadith, one prohibiting and the other allowing 'Arbūn sale. But both of these are considered weak and unauthenticated. Among the main schools of Islamic Fiqh, only the Hanbali school considers Bai' al 'Arbūn a legal contract. They rely mainly on the report from Naf'i Ibnal Harith,

[28] AAOIFI, 2004–5a, No. 5, p. 66.
[29] AAOIFI, 2004–5a, pp. 65, 66, 76.
[30] AAOIFI, 2004–5a, pp. 65, 66, 76.
[31] Al-Baji, 1332AH, **4**, p. 158.

an officer at Makkah deputed by Caliph Umar (Gbpwh), which states that he bought from Safwan Ibn Umayyah a prison house for Caliph Umar (Gbpwh) for four thousand dirhams on condition that if the Caliph approved of it, the deal would be final, otherwise Safwan would be given four hundred dirhams.[32]

The majority of contemporary jurists are of the view that if a buyer in actual sale transactions stipulates by his free will and without any duress that he will either finalize the deal within so many days or the sale will be considered cancelled and the seller will get the amount given in advance, it could be considered legal. But open options, even in valid sales, wherein the parties have no intention to buy and want profit simply by transferring risk to the other party, are against the basic philosophy of Islamic finance. That is why conventional options have not been accepted as genuine instruments in Islamic finance. We shall discuss this in detail in Chapter 8. Here, we can briefly say that the concept of 'Arbūn is acceptable to the extent of part payment after finalization of the deal. Its legality as a separate sale, i.e. Bai' al 'Arbūn, and its implications for the legality of conventional options are not acceptable, in general, to scholars.

## 5.7   TYPES OF CONTRACTS

Contracts can be classified with respect to a number of perspectives. With respect to validity or otherwise as per Sharī'ah rules, jurists in general divide contracts into two types, namely: valid (Sahih) and invalid (Batil) contracts. A valid contract is one that satisfies all of its conditions, while an invalid contract is one in which one or more conditions for legality are violated.[33]

Hanafis, however, divide contracts into three categories of valid (Sahih), voidable/defective (Fāsid) and void (Batil). Thus, they divide the void contracts into defective/irregular (Fāsid) and invalid categories.[34] If one studies the details of these categories in books by the Hanafi jurists, one may face some confusion regarding this categorization unless deep understanding is developed by thorough and extensive study. That is why Zuhayli, while discussing voidable contracts according to Hanafis, says:

> "I have distinguished between examples of invalid and defective sales to avoid confusion, in contrast to what most books of Hanafi jurisprudence discuss under the heading of defective sales. The majority of such books use the term 'defective sales' to mean the more general category of 'defective and invalid sales', i.e. all sales that are legally prohibited. It is also common for the authors of such books to use the term 'defective' (Fāsid), when they really mean 'invalid' (Batil). The reader is then forced to infer their meaning from the surrounding text or by telling statements such as their saying: 'thus the contract does not become valid' in the case of invalid sales, and 'thus the contract returns to being valid' in the case of defective ones."

In the following pages, we will be discussing the three categories as described by Hanafis because these provide more options for practitioners to apply the Islamic law of contracts in modern-day operations.

---

[32] Ibnul Qayyim, 1955, **3**.
[33] Zuhayli, 2003, **1**, p. 74.
[34] For details see Zuhayli, 2003, pp. 71, 72.

### 5.7.1   Valid Contracts

The validity of any contract depends on the legality or illegality of the subject matter, the existence and precise determination of the subject matter, delivery or the ability to deliver the subject matter without involvement of excessive uncertainty and precise determination of the price or consideration in a contract.

A valid contract is one which is in accordance with Islamic law, both as regards its 'Asl (fundamental components, nature or essence) and Wasf (accessory circumstances or external attributes). A contract is deemed valid when all elements of the contract (form or offer and acceptance, the subject matter and the contracting parties) are found to be in order; the conditions of each element have been met and it is free from external prohibited activities like Riba, Gharar, etc. The form of the contract requires conformity between offer and acceptance, their issuance in the same session and the existence of Ijab until the issuance of Qabul. It also requires that parties to the contract must be sane and mature in age and that the subject matter must be permissible, in existence, deliverable and known. (Petty purchases of edibles by children that do not create any rights or liabilities for any of the parties are exempt; however, the seller has to ensure that the children do not get involved in harmful things. Similarly, day-to-day transactions in which offer and acceptance is implied are exempt.)

A valid contract assigns all its effects which the Sharī´ah has determined for it. It becomes effective (Nafiz) upon execution if not suspended (Mawquf), in which case it is enforced upon the removal of the cause of suspension. Some jurists, including Hanafis, Malikis and some Hanbalis, are of the view that the effectiveness of a valid contract can be delayed until the happening of a future event. To them, a valid contract can be either Nafiz (immediately effective) or Mawquf (suspended or tied to any future event). According to Shawafi'e and some of the Hanbalis, however, a valid contract must be effective immediately upon its execution. A Nafiz contract is one in which the elements are found to be in order, the conditions are met, the external attributes are legal and it is not suspended or dependent upon ratification.

*Contracts Effective Instantly or from a Future Date*

Jurists allow the contracts of Ijarah and Istisna'a (manufacturing upon order) to become effective from a future date because a person does not own usufructs immediately as he does in the case of a sale contract, but he owns them gradually, so time is considered in such contracts. Kafalah (suretyship) and Hawalah (assignment of debt) are also considered to be contracts effective from a future date. A Kafil is not required to pay debt immediately when the contract is concluded. So it is valid if the surety were to say to the creditor: "If your debtor has not paid off his debt to you by the beginning of next month, I will make the payment". Similarly, agency, divorce and Waqf are valid from a future date. A contract of bequest, by its nature, also admits delay, as it cannot be enforced in the life of the legator. The contract of Ijarah can be either immediately enforceable or made effective from any future date.

The contract of sale is immediately enforceable in the opinion of all jurists, thus it is not permissible to say: "I sell you this house at the beginning of next year". The jurists see in this postponement and delay an element of Gharar. It is like a contract which is contingent upon an uncertain event, where the parties do not know whether it will occur or not. In this regard, Siddiq al Dharir observes: "Indeed the only Gharar in a future contract lies in the possible lapse of interest of either party, which may affect his consent when the time set therein comes. If someone buys something by 'Aqd Mudhaf (effective from future) and his circumstances change or the market changes bringing its price down at the time set for fulfilment of contract, he will undoubtedly be averse to its fulfilment and will regret entering into it. Indeed the object may itself change and the two parties may dispute over it". It is pertinent to note that Ibn al-Qayyim and Ibn Taymiyah do not subscribe to the majority viewpoint. They maintain that 'Aqd Mudhaf is permissible, without distinction between a sale contract and a leasing contract.[35]

To avoid any juristic issue, contemporary scholars suggest arranging a unilateral promise for regular contracts in the future.

### Mawquf (Suspended) Contracts

The following may be causes for suspending the effects of a valid contract:

1. Defective capacity of any of the parties, e.g. a transaction by a minor which has the likelihood of both benefit and harm is valid subject to ratification, which may be accorded by the guardian after the transaction and before the minor attains puberty, or by the minor himself after puberty if the guardian did not object before his attaining puberty. The status of such a contract is that if ratification is granted, it acts retrospectively from the date of the contract, but if ratification is refused, the contract becomes void.
2. Lack of proper authority, i.e. the person acting as agent does not have proper authority over the principal – the contract by a Fuduli (a person who is neither guardian nor agent, or if he is an agent, he transgresses the limits prescribed by the principal). It is also subject to ratification as in case 1 above.
3. The right of any third party. If the owner sells a property mortgaged by someone, it will be subject to ratification by the mortgagee. If a house owned by A is mortgaged with a bank, A cannot sell it, and if he enters into a contract to sell it, it will be a Mawquf contract. The bank would demand that his debt be paid first. It is important to observe that before ratification, the buyer has the right to revoke the contract but the mortgagor/seller has no right to revoke the contract of sale made by him.

### Binding (Lāzim) and nonbinding Contracts

Contracts which are Sahih and Nafiz can be divided into Lāzim (binding) and Ghair Lāzim (nonbinding) contracts. A Lāzim contract is one in which none of the parties has the unilateral right to revoke (without the consent of the other) unless an option (Khiyar-al-Shart) has been granted to a party by virtue of which the right to revoke can be exercised. A contract is Ghair Lāzim if any of the parties has a right to revoke it without the consent of the other. There are two reasons why a contract might be nonbinding or revocable:

1. The nature of the contract. Some contracts are nonbinding by nature; both parties are allowed to revoke independently. Examples of such contracts are Wakalah (agency), Kafalah (suretyship), Shirkah (partnership), Wadi'ah (deposits or Amānah), and 'Āriyah (commodity given for use without any compensation or rent). These contracts are terminable by any of the parties. But if the parties mutually agree that none of them will

---

[35] For further details, see Mansoori, 2005, pp. 181–185.

terminate up to a specified period, the contract will no longer be revocable unilaterally. Accordingly, in Islamic banks' investment deposits based on the Shirkah principle, the banks can restrict the depositors to withdrawal before the settled date by putting a clause to this effect in the agreement, i.e. the account opening form. Shareholders of joint stock companies also cannot terminate their shareholding. They can simply transfer their part through the sale of shares in the market.

2. An option (Khiyar-al-Shart) stipulated in the contract prevents it from becoming Lāzim until the time of Khiyar is over. The party possessing the Khiyar of recession can revoke the contract within the period of the option without the consent of the other party.[36]

### 5.7.2 Voidable (Fāsid) Contracts

A contract that is legal in its 'Asl, i.e. it has all the elements of a contract, but is not legal in its Wasf, i.e. with respect to external or nonessential attributes of the contract, will not necessarily be void, rather it will be voidable or Fāsid, and can be regularized or validated by removing the cause of irregularity.

If a contract is structured in a way that is prohibited, it can, under certain circumstances, be rectified by removal of the objectionable clause, or it may result in the entire contract being annulled. If conditions of less importance, like minute specifications of subject matter, are not fulfilled, the contract will be capable of ratification, but will be void due to defect until the defect is removed or compliance with the Sharī'ah conditions is achieved. If the defect is rectified, the contract becomes valid.

*Causes of Irregularity in Voidable (Fāsid) Contracts*

Causes of invalidity are of two types:

1. Intrinsic causes which relate to the basic elements of the contract, such as unlawfulness or nonexistence of the subject matter, or the absence of contractual capacity in any of the parties.
2. Extrinsic causes that relate to Wasf, i.e. external attributes such as Riba or Gharar contained in the contract.

It is pertinent to note that Riba and Gharar are causes of irregularity of a contract in Hanafi law, while in other schools they are causes of invalidity of a contract. However, even in Hanafi law, a Riba- or Gharar-based contract is not enforceable and only removal of the term involving Riba or Gharar would validate it. For some detail, the following may be the major factors rendering contracts irregular or voidable:

- Defective consent. The majority of jurists hold that a contract made under coercion is a void or Batil contract. However, Hanafi jurists consider it a voidable or Fāsid contract which can be regularized by ratification. In other words, it is a suspended contract which is subject to ratification. Ratification of an irregular contract is possible before possession as well as after it.

---

[36] Mansoori, 2005, p. 82.

- Lack of any value-relevant information (Gharar or Jahl). If the contract lacks any such information for any of the parties that may lead to dispute, the contract is Fāsid. The lack of information affecting the validity of contracts can be of the following types:

  — Relating to the subject matter, e.g. indeterminate object in a sale contract or unidentified/not sufficiently defined asset in an Ijarah contract. In Ijarah Mosufah bil Zimmah,[37] which is permissible, the asset might not be exactly identified but should be sufficiently described as to leave no ambiguity regarding the use or usufruct to be taken.
  — Lack of information about consideration, e.g. one definite price is not settled or the price is kept subject to change at the discretion of any or both of the parties.
  — Lack of information about the time of performance in sale, lease and other binding contracts. A partnership contract is not invalidated due to indeterminacy of the period, because a partnership is a nonbinding contract in its origin.
  — Lack of information about the guarantee, surety or the pledge. It is necessary that in the case of a credit, the security, guarantee or the pledge must be identified and made known to the creditor.

- Defect due to any invalid condition not being collateral to the contract or not admitted by the commercial usage or which gives benefit to one of the parties at the cost of another. Invalid and defective conditions may make a transaction voidable.[38] The following types of conditions may be deemed to be invalid or not permissible:

  — When it is against the purpose of the contract, such as stipulating that the buyer will not sell the asset he is purchasing or he will not rent it out, or stipulating in a marriage contract that the husband will not establish a matrimonial relationship with his wife.
  — When it is expressly prohibited by the Sharī´ah, like selling an article on the condition that the purchaser will sell something else to the buyer or lend him some money or make him a gift. Such conditions are prohibited because Islamic law expressly prohibits the combination of (i) two mutually inconsistent contracts and (ii) a loan and a sale. A genuine credit sale of any commodity is one transaction and, therefore, perfectly permissible in Islamic law.
  — When it is against the commercial usage, such as a condition by the purchaser of corn that the seller will grind it, or a condition by a buyer of a piece of cloth that the seller will sew it.
  — When it is advantageous to one party at the cost of the other party. For example, where the seller reserves for himself an advantage from the sale, such as the condition that he shall reside in the house sold for a period of two months after the sale, or he will lend him some money.[39]

It is pertinent to note here that these irregular conditions affect only compensatory contracts, such as contracts of sale, hiring, etc., and do not affect gratuitous contracts, such as

---

[37] In Ijarah Mosufah bil Zimmah, the lessor undertakes to provide a well-defined service or benefit without identifying any particular units of asset rendering the related service. For example, an Islamic bank may require a transporter to pick up and drop its officers from their houses to the office on air-conditioned vans of a defined nature. In this case, any particular van is not hired, neither will the destruction of any van terminate the lease contract; the lessor has to arrange the vans as per the agreement.

[38] There are three types of conditions according to Hanafis: valid, defective and invalid; see Zuhayli, 2003, 1, pp. 123–131.

[39] Mansoori, 2005, pp. 157–163.

loan, gift, donation, Waqf, or contracts of suretyship, such as Kafalah, mortgage, Hawalah (assignment of debt) or the contract of marriage. Irregular conditions in the latter contracts do not invalidate them. Only the invalid condition is abrogated. The other part of the contract remains valid and effective.

Joint ventures in early Islamic society traditionally took the form of Shirkah and Mudarabah in trade and industry and Muzara‘a and Musaqat in agriculture. A valid Shirkah entitled the parties to a share in the profits of business. If the contract of Shirkah or Mudarabah failed to comply with legal requirements, it was treated as void (Batil) or voidable (Fāsid) depending upon the nature of violation. It was here that the jurists distinguished between the functions of different factors and assigned to them different portions of income according to the role that they had played in the process of production or in providing the service.

In such voidable contracts, the parties that help in production or assist the rendering of service are allowed a matching wage, except the capital provider, who claims the residual. As payment of wages and other charges supersedes the calculation of profit, the owner of capital may be a loser if the earnings do not exceed this liability. In order to protect the owner from this situation, jurists have introduced the concept of matching the rate of profit (Ribh-al-mithl), matching rates in Mudarabah, etc. in addition to the concept of matching wages.

## Some Forms of Voidable Contracts

Hanafi jurists have identified some forms of Fāsid or voidable contracts. These are:

- Bai‘ al-Majhūl (lacking any material information). This refers to a sale in which the object of sale or its price or the time of payment remains unknown and unspecified.
- Contingent contract. This is a contract that is contingent upon an uncertain event. For example, A says to B: "I sell to you my house if X sells to me his house".
- Sales contract effective from a future date. A sale becomes effective as soon as it is executed. If a contract says that the sale will come into effect from a future date, it will be voidable and will be of no effect.
- Bai‘ al-Ghāib. This is a sale of an item which is not visible at the meeting of the parties; the seller has title over the subject matter but it is not available for inspection of the parties because it is elsewhere. This has to be regularized by seeing. However, if the parties are satisfied with the description of the item of sale and there is no chance of Gharar, the contract is valid.
- Sale contract with unlawful consideration. This refers to a sale whose consideration or price is something prohibited by Islamic law, such as wine or pork.
- Two sales in one. This is where a single contract relates to two sales, such as selling one commodity for two prices, one being cash and the other a credit price, thus making the contract binding against one of the two prices without specifying either.[40]

## Legal Status of the Fāsid (Voidable) Contract

A voidable contract must be revoked without the consent of either party. Therefore, no rights or obligations arise. However, if the cause of defect or irregularity is removed, the contract

---

[40] For detail see Zuhayli, 2003, **1**, pp. 102–123.

becomes valid. The legal position of such a contract depends upon whether the goods have been delivered or not. For example, if the subject of sale, not previously identified, is mutually identified, the sale contract is valid. If a lender has put the condition of interest in a loan contract, the condition of charging interest is invalid and if this condition is removed, the loan contract becomes valid and the debtor has to pay only the principal sum of the loan. Here, the rule may be kept in mind that noncommutative contracts (like the contract of loan) do not become void with a void condition. Only the condition has to be removed.

If the buyer in a voidable sale (due to unidentified subject matter, for example) takes possession of an item or an object with the consent of the seller, ownership will pass on to him and he will be liable to pay the value agreed with mutual consent or the market value and not necessarily the price fixed in the earlier agreement. In this regard, Majallah points out: "In Bai' Fāsid, where the buyer has received the object with permission of the seller, he becomes the owner."[41] However, the parties can still revoke it if the buyer has not disposed of it. In such a case, if the seller wishes to get the commodity back, he must first pay the purchase money to the buyer. Until such recompense, the goods are held by the purchaser as a pledge. But if the buyer has disposed of the property by onward sale or donation or added or subtracted from it, or changed it in such a way that it can no longer be regarded as the same object, then there is no right for either party to annul the contract. Thus, where the buyer has sold the property, this second sale is valid and legally enforceable; it cannot be obstructed in Islamic law by the fact that the first sale was irregular.[42]

As such, a valid contract can be differentiated from a voidable contract in the following manner:

- Ownership in a valid contract is transferred from the seller to the purchaser by mere offer and acceptance, whereas in a voidable contract it is transferred to him by possession taken with the consent of the seller.
- In a voidable sale, the value of the commodity, i.e. its market price, is admissible, whereas in a valid contract, an agreed price is paid. In a voidable lease contract, the lessor is entitled to equitable and proper rent (according to the market rate) and not to the rent specified in the original lease agreement. Similarly, in a voidable partnership, each partner gets the profit in proportion to his capital and not according to the agreement.

### 5.7.3   Void (Batil) Contracts

Contracts that do not fulfil the conditions relating to offer and acceptance, subject matter, consideration and possession or delivery, or involve some illegal external attributes are considered void (Batil). In other words, if major conditions relating to the form of the contract (acceptance does not conform to the offer, or the offer does not exist at the time of acceptance, etc.), parties to the contract (sane and mature), possession and deliverability of the subject matter are not fulfilled, the contract is Batil.[43]

The sale of a thing having an element of absolute uncertainty or speculation is not valid, for example, the sale of milk in the udder of a cow is not a valid sale. Similarly, a sale with unknown consideration and until an unknown period, the sale of a dirham for two

---

[41] Al-Atasi, 1403 AH, Majallah, Article 371.
[42] Mansoori, 2005, pp. 87–89. Also see for detail Zuhayli, 2003, 1, pp. 139–144.
[43] Mansoori, 2005, pp. 90–94.

dirhams, bidding over the bid (after the two parties have reached an agreement on the price)[44] and contracts actuated by fraud or deceit are examples of invalid contracts. In contrast, permissible forms of Bai' include Salam (or Salaf), selling through bidding, Bai' al Khiyar (option to rescind), Musawamah (bargain on price), Murabaha (bargain on profit margin), etc.

A Batil contract does not give rise to any effect, i.e. the buyer will not have the title to the subject matter; the seller will not have the title to price or the consideration; ownership will not transfer and the transaction will be null and void. If delivery of the goods has already been made, the same would have to be returned to the other party regardless of whether such illegality was known to the parties. If the buyer sells the goods to a third party after taking delivery, the original seller cannot be prevented from claiming the goods. The reason is that ownership cannot be transferred through a contract that is Batil. This Hukm is clearly different from that of a Fāsid contract, which has been discussed above.

## 5.8 COMMUTATIVE AND NONCOMMUTATIVE CONTRACTS

With respect to the consideration or counter value in exchange, contracts are of two types. The first are Uqood-e-Mu'awadha, or compensatory/commutative contracts, as a result of which one party can get remuneration or compensation – like sale, purchase, lease and Wakalah contracts. The other kind is that of Uqood Ghair Mu'awadha or noncommutative contracts, wherein one cannot get any return or compensation – like contracts of loan (Qard), gift (Tabarru/Hibah), guarantee (Kafalah) and assignment of debt (Hawalah). Any consideration in the contracts of loans, guarantee, against guarantee *per se* and assignment of debt would be illegal.

### 5.8.1  Uqood-e-Mu'awadha (Commutative Contracts)

Among commutative contracts (sale, hire and manufacturing), sale contracts can be further classified as follows:

Classification according to object:

- Bai' Muqayadhah (barter sale);
- Bai' al Hāl (simultaneous exchange of goods for money, spot sale);
- Bai' al Sarf (exchange of money or monetary units);
- Bai' Salam (sale with immediate payment and deferred delivery);
- Bai' Mu'ajjal (deferred payment sale, commonly known as a credit sale);
- Bai' Mutlaq (normal sale of goods for money, also called absolute sale).

Classification according to price:

- Bai' Tawliyah (resale at cost price);
- Bai' Murabaha (resale at cost price plus profit – bargaining on profit margin);

---

[44] Imam Malik says regarding prohibition of bidding against each other and outbidding. "There is no harm, however, in more than one person bidding against each other over goods put up for sale." He said: "Were people to leave off haggling when the first person started haggling, an unreal price might be taken and the disapproved would enter into the sale of the goods. This is still the way of doing things among us."

- Bai' Wadhi'ah (resale with loss); (The above three forms of sale are termed Buyu'al Amanat or trust sales)
- Bai' Musawamah (sale without any reference to the original cost price-bargaining on price).

Ijarah or the contract of hiring is divided into:

- Ijarat al Ashkhas (rendering services);
- Ijarat al Ashya (letting things).

Istisna'a (contract of manufacturing).
Wakalah can be both commutative and noncommutative contracts.

## 5.8.2    Uqood Ghair Mu'awadha (Tabarru') or Gratuitous Contracts

The main feature of these contracts is the donation of property. The donor transfers ownership of any property to a party without consideration. The following contracts fall under this category:

- Hibah (gift);
- Wasiyyah (bequest);
- Waqf (endowment);
- Kafalah (guarantee);
- 'Āriyah (loan of usable item free of any charge);[45]
- Loan (Qard);
- Hawalah (assignment of debt).

Among these contracts, Kafalah, Qard and Hawalah are directly relevant to Islamic banking operations, but they cannot charge any profit against these contracts *per se*. However, they can charge fees for other services provided on the basis of Wakalah or Ju'alah. For example, while issuing L/Cs, guarantees, etc., banks can charge for their services depending upon expenses incurred for issuing guarantees. These charges can be amount-based (possibly slabs) but not time-based.

## 5.8.3    Legal Status of Commutative and Noncommutative Contracts

Compensatory/commutative contracts like sale, purchase, lease and other remunerative agreements become void by inserting any void condition. Noncompensatory/voluntary agreements do not become void because of a void condition. The void condition itself becomes ineffective. For example, a person enters into an interest-based loan; the condition of charging interest on the loan would be void but the loan contract will remain effective, the debtor will have to repay the loan/debt as it becomes due. Similarly, Gharar (uncertainty) does not invalidate noncompensatory contracts; for example, jurists indicate that donation of a stray or unidentified animal or fruit before its benefits are evident or a usurped commodity is permissible, but their sale is not valid.

---

[45] For example, the holy Prophet (pbuh) took iron chest plates on the basis of 'Āriyah at the time of Ghazwa-e-Hunain; Mubarakpuri, 1996, p. 563 (Abu Daud, 1952, Kitab al Buyu').

## 5.9  CONDITIONAL OR CONTINGENT CONTRACTS

As a general rule, conditional contracts are not valid. This, however, requires some detail and some conditions could be acceptable. We find discussion in the Fiqh literature on three types of stipulations/conditions:

1. T'aliq – conditions which suspend a contract to any future event.
2. Idafa – an extension that delays the beginning of any contract until a future time.
3. Iqtiran (concomitance) that varies the terms of the contract.[46]

In all these cases the contract may or may not be void even if the condition is void. Various jurists differ with regard to the result of stipulation. Both Hanafis and Hanbalis allow some delay in beginning contracts like lease of agency (where property is transferred only over time) until any future event, but not for sale.[47]

As regards concomitant conditions, all schools consider whether the condition agrees to or is in conflict with the purpose of the contract. For example, a stipulation that the buyer pays the price or the seller transfers full title is a valid stipulation. They also approve the condition that the buyer will pay in certain coins/currency or provide a pledge as security. However, they do not approve a condition that the buyer will never resell the object. The conditions that pose problems are those by which any of the parties gets an additional benefit. Here, jurists differ but Ibn Taymiyah has taken a practical approach by rejecting only those conditions which are in contradiction with the Qur'ān and Sunnah or the Ijma'a, or which contradict the very object of the contract.

As regards the overall view of different schools of thought, Hanbali jurists emphasize the supremacy of the discretion of contracting parties and allow every condition and stipulation as long as it does not contradict any text from the Qur'ān or the Sunnah. The Hanafi, Shāfi'ī and Maliki jurists divide conditions into valid, irregular and void.

Valid conditions are those that confirm the effects attributed to juridical acts by the Sharī'ah and which are admitted explicitly by it, such as the option of stipulation (Khiyar al-Shart) reserved for a party to revoke or ratify a contract within specified days. Such a condition is valid because the Sharī'ah has sanctioned the option of stipulation and the option of inspection (Khiyar al-Ru'yah). The stipulation to sell on the condition that the seller will not hand over the goods to the buyer unless he pays the price is also a valid condition, because it stresses and confirms the effects of the contract and realizes its objective.[48]

A condition in aid of a contract is valid, like a sale with a condition that the vendor in the cash sale will have possession of the property when the price is paid, or a sale on condition that the buyer should pledge something to the vendor as security for the price.[49] Similarly, any condition which is customary to embody in a contract will be upheld.[50] If a Fāsid (invalid) condition is put into a contract that is otherwise valid, the condition will be void while the contract will be valid and enforceable, i.e. without regard to that condition.[51]

---

[46] Sanhuri 3: 134–172; cf Vogel and Hayes, 1998, p. 100.

[47] Al-Atasi, 1403 AH, Majallah Articles 408–440; Ibn Qudama, 1367 AH, **6**, pp. 6–7.

[48] Mansoori, 2005, pp. 157–163.

[49] Al-Atasi, 1403 AH, Majallah Articles 186, 187.

[50] Tirmidhi, 1988, No. 1276. (Jaber bought a camel from the holy Prophet and a condition of a ride to the home was put into the contract). Also, Al-Atasi, 1403 AH, Majallah, Article 188.

[51] Nisai, n.d., **7**, p. 300.

A condition which is not of advantage to either party is regarded as superfluous and cannot be enforced. A condition which is repugnant to a contract or transfer of ownership but is of advantage to one of the parties will make the transaction debauched if made an inseparable part of it.[52]

A void condition is any condition which directly infringes any rule of the Sharī´ah, or inflicts harm on one of the two contracting parties or derogates from completion of the contract. We can therefore conclude our discussion on the subject of conditions in contracts by stating that a condition or stipulation which is not against the main purpose of the contract is a valid condition. Similarly, a condition which has become a normal practice in the market is not void provided it is not against any explicit injunctions of the Holy Qur'ān or Sunnah. For example, a condition that the seller will provide five years' guarantee and one year's free service is not void, neither is the availability of a warranty against defective goods a problem. Similarly, conditions may be imposed in a sale regarding the service or repair of any manufactured item sold to a buyer. The parties can give each other an option to cancel a transaction during a given period after the conclusion of that transaction.

## 5.10  SUMMARY

All commercial transactions must be governed by the respective rules and norms of Islamic ethics, as enunciated by the Sharī´ah. The Islamic system disapproves of any exploitation or injustice on the part of any of the parties involved. To achieve this objective, the Sharī´ah has advised some prohibitions and recommended some ethics. Detailed study of the rules and norms reveals that Islamic finance is, in essence, an ethical system and ethics need to be an inseparable part of the system.

What is not prohibited is permissible. Therefore, all contracts are valid unless they violate the text of the Holy Qur'ān or Sunnah of the holy Prophet (pbuh), or are in conflict with the objectives of the Sharī´ah.

A property is either a specific existent object ('Ayn), e.g. a house, or an object defined generically or abstractly by an obligation (Dayn). One can subdivide sale according to the types of Mabi' being exchanged. The mode of Murabaha can be used in trading of 'Ayn and merchandise and not in credit documents or Dayn.

The prohibition of sale of a debt for a debt affects when obligations (to perform or to pay) are delayed, and when such obligations may be bought, sold or otherwise transferred. In a transaction, any of the two counter values can be postponed, i.e. payment of the price, or delivery of the commodity. While the former is a credit sale or Bai' Mu'ajjal, the latter refers to a future sale wherein the goods sold are to be supplied later against prepaid price (Salam).

Any contracts must be made as explicit as possible in order to avoid Gharar and injustice to any of the parties. A clause in the contract allowing a change in liability beyond the control of the liable party would be unjust, e.g. the client in Murabaha agrees that the bank can change his liability whenever the latter likes, or the client agrees to automatic compensation for the bank in case of his failure to meet the liability.

Commercial contracts have to be concluded at a price that is agreed mutually without uncertainty or hazard (Gharar) with regard to the subject matter and the counter value or

---

[52] Vogel and Hayes, 1998, p. 101; Al-Atasi, 1403 AH, Majallah, Article 189.

consideration and the seller's ability to deliver. A valid contract must comprise the following intrinsic elements:

- The form, i.e. offer and acceptance, which can be conveyed by spoken words, in writing or through indication and conduct. The acceptance should conform to the offer in all its details.
- The contracting parties, who must have the capacity for execution.
- The subject matter, which must be lawful, in actual existence at the time of the contract and should be capable of being delivered and precisely determined either by description or by inspection/examination.

If the contract is one of sale, it must be noncontingent and effective immediately, because the sale of goods attributable to the future is void in the opinion of the majority of scholars.

The arrangement of "two contracts into one contract" is not permissible in Sharī´ah; therefore, we cannot have the agreement of hire and purchase in one contract, we can only undertake/promise to purchase the leased asset.

Promise in commercial transactions can be binding or nonbinding. It can be legally enforceable, particularly if the promisee incurs some expenses or liability as required by the promise. Therefore, if the promisor backs out from fulfilling the promise, the other party can claim for the actual loss that could arise due to nonfulfilment of the promise.

The validity of the contract requires that its motivating and underlying cause should be according to the requirements of the Sharī´ah. All contracts that promote immorality or are against public welfare, are harmful to a person or property of a third party or which are forbidden by law are deemed to be void.

Generally, Islam prohibits all transactions that depend just on chance and speculation, those in which the rights of the contracting parties are not clearly defined and those that enable some to amass wealth at the expense of others and which could result in litigation. Such transactions involve appropriation of other's wealth without right or justice. Practices like Riba, Gharar, fraud, dishonesty, false assertions and breach of contracts and promises also lead to injustice. In every instance of prohibited business conduct one can discern an element of injustice, either to one of the contracting parties or to the general public. In some such cases, the injustice may not be apparent, yet it is always there. In order to nip evil in the bud, Islam seeks to block all those channels that eventually lead to injustice.[53]

---

[53] For further details on Islamic law see: Hassan, 1993; Qadri, 1963, pp. 97–113.

# 6

# Trading in Islamic Commercial Law

## 6.1 INTRODUCTION

The growth in wealth is an acknowledged pursuit approved by the Sharīʿah and both society and individuals are encouraged to increase their wealth. This growth or development takes place through the production of goods and exchange of values among parties in the market. Further, Islamic law does not limit profits or fix prices; it promotes the free flow of goods in an open environment for achieving such goals. All that Islamic law requires human beings to do for establishing a just economic system is to avoid Riba and Gharar along with fulfilling some other rules and principles of business to ensure that "the (wealth) may not make a circuit between the wealthy among you".[1] While Riba is strongly prohibited in Islamic law, trading is not only permitted, but also encouraged. Study of the Holy Qur'ān and the Sunnah of the holy Prophet (pbuh) reveals that Islam is favourably inclined to promote commercial and trading activities.[2]

Islamic banks have to operate on the basis of profit and not Riba, and the profit can be earned mainly through activities in three areas: trading, leasing and PLS contracts. Accordingly, we have to distinguish profit from Riba and then find out the rules prescribed by the Sharīʿah for earning legitimate profit. In this chapter we shall discuss various aspects and general rules for Baiʿ/trading that may be applied for trade-based modes like Baiʿ Murabaha, Muʿajjal, Salam, Istisnaʿa, etc. Since banks' funds invested through these modes take the form of a debt, these can be regarded as debt-creating modes of financing and the finance-user stands obliged to pay back the entire amount (or its equivalent, in cases of Baiʿ Salam), like a debt.

While both trading and Riba-based activities generate returns and increases in the capital, the increase generated by the former is welcome, whereas that generated by Riba is forbidden. The Arabs engaged in trading and were used to a number of false/wrong practices. The Sharīʿah condemned those practices and imposed various restrictions to make the trade activities legal, just and decent. It is, therefore, an issue of paramount importance that any increase/addition/growth to be termed "Riba" should be clearly distinguished from the increase in one's wealth as a result of trading, and the rules of trading and tradable goods be identified to make trade transactions distinct from Riba-based transactions.

---

[1] Holy Qur'ān, 59: 7.
[2] Holy Qur'ān, verses 4: 29, 10: 67, 14: 33, 16: 12, 17: 12, 28: 73, 45: 12, 61: 73–77, 62: 10, 78: 11, etc.

## 6.2   BAI' – EXCHANGE OF VALUES

Literally, Bai' means exchange of one thing with another; one thing being the subject matter (Mabi') and the other being price (Thaman). The Majallah, a code of Islamic commercial law based on the Hanafi Fiqh, defines a sale as "the exchange of property for property", and in the language of the law, it signifies an exchange of property for property with mutual consent of the parties, which is completed by declaration and acceptance.[3] Legally, Bai' refers to giving ownership of a commodity to another person in compensation of the other commodity. The seller gives ownership of the commodity to the buyer on a permanent basis in exchange for the price.

The word Bai' in its widest meaning stands for any bilateral contract. In that sense, a simple word for Bai' would be "exchange". This may involve all types of business and any exchange. But all exchanges that lead to Riba are unanimously prohibited. This is why, contracts for interest-based loans are excluded from the definition of valid Bai' according to the jurists.[4] Similarly, exchanges based on Gharar or absolute uncertainties are void. The literature of Hadith and Fiqh contains mention of many types of Bai' that have been prohibited by the holy Prophet (pbuh). The common factor of all such prohibited types is that they contained the elements of Riba, deception and/or Gharar. A sale, to become valid, must be free from all false and prohibited practices. The main features of a valid sale are shown later in Figure 6.2.

There is confusion among some people that conventional banking business is also a form of Bai' and therefore permissible in Sharī'ah. During the hearing of the Review Petition in the Riba case in Pakistan by the Supreme Court of Pakistan, the Counsel of the petitioners argued: "The word Bai' used in verse 2: 275 (of the Holy Qur'ān) includes sale, business, trade, investment, bargaining, etc; therefore, the present-day banking business is covered by the term Bai'."[5] No doubt the referred verse of the Holy Qur'ān highlights the wider meaning of Bai' – in broad terms it means business of a particular kind, means of making a living/earnings, a job or occupation. But it also provides a general principle governing permissibility: all exchanges are permitted except those involving Riba. We explain this in the following paragraphs.

Different exchanges involve different rules in respect of the liabilities and benefits for the parties to exchange, ownership rights, etc. Exchange in the form of trading involves the reciprocal exchange of property rights along with usufruct. In Ijarah, which is termed the sale of usufruct, the lessor gives usufruct against rental but retains ownership along with the liabilities relating to ownership. In loans, there is a temporary but complete transfer of ownership (along with usufruct) to the borrower, who can use the loaned item like his other possessions, but he has to give it back. Shirkah involves sharing of ownership and benefit/loss among the partners.[6]

In trade, as soon as a sale agreement takes place, ownership of the subject matter is transferred to the buyer, irrespective of whether he has made a cash payment or has to pay in the future according to an agreed schedule. In the latter case, the buyer is liable to pay the

---

[3] Al-Atasi, 1403 AH, Majallah, Article 105.

[4] For details see Al Jaziri, 1973, **2**, pp. 290–300.

[5] Ayub, 2002, pp. 230–232.

[6] Ibn Hazm (1988), while differentiating Bai' and Ijarah, says that Bai' makes the purchaser owner (of al 'Ain); Ijarah does not make him the owner. Ijarah of those things that are consumed with use is not valid, **7**, p. 4, No. 1287.

agreed price and not the commodity. In a loan, the item/commodity of loan is transferred to the borrower and he gets ownership of the item with full discretion about its use. But he has to repay a similar item/commodity or the money.

While Riba-based loaning involves the definite right of return, Bai' yields risk-based return. In other words, "risk and reward" is an essential ingredient of trade, which is inherent in all trading activities. A transaction becomes usurious if it involves an exchange of two counter values such that ownership in the item exchanged is passed on to the other party who has to repay it with any excess; e.g. if A gives $1000 to B for his use and B uses it for consumption or in his business and then returns $1000 to A, it will be a loan transaction; it will become usurious if A is required to pay any extra amount, $1050 for example.

Accordingly, rules are specific to every exchange (these have been explained in Chapter 4). A trade transaction requires the transfer of complete and instant ownership that is irreversible once finalized. It means that the seller excludes the commodity from his ownership and gives it to the buyer on a permanent basis, while in loans, ownership is transferred for a specified period and exactly its similar has to be paid back.[7]

When the genera of the goods to be exchanged in trading are different, delivery of one of the exchanged items can be delayed, as in a credit sale or as in advance payment for purchase of wheat through Salam. If gold or any currency is exchanged for wheat or any other commodity, there is no Riba; if wheat is exchanged for barley, Riba is found if delivery of one is delayed, because they are species of the same genus.[8]

Loan transactions, on the other hand, have to be executed on an equal basis for the purpose of repayment. All banking transactions are covered under this rule and their unequal exchange is tantamount to Riba. Therefore, as conventional banks deal in money, their transactions cannot be termed as Bai' in the strict sense.

In this respect, renowned Hanafi jurist Sarakhsi says: "Trade is of two kinds: permitted (Halal), which is called Bai' in the law; and prohibited (Haram), which is called Riba. Both are types of trade. Allah Almighty informs us, through the denial of the disbelievers, about the rational difference between exchange (Bai') and Riba, and says: 'That is because they said Bai' is like Riba'. Almighty, then, distinguishes between prohibition and permission by saying: 'And Allah has permitted sale and prohibited Riba'."[9] Therefore, contemporary Muslim scholars also do not include loaning in the meaning of the term Bai', particularly because present-day money is fiat money and not bullion money that had intrinsic value and that was traded in the past in addition to serving as a medium of exchange.

## 6.3    LEGALITY OF TRADING

Trade is one of the commendable professions among innumerable lawful sources of earnings and Islam has put a tremendous emphasis on it for the acquisition of wealth. The Holy Qur'ān has permitted this in the words: "Allah hath allowed trading and prohibited Riba."[10] This aspect is further confounded by the fact that the Prophet (pbuh) himself, the Companions and the eminent Imams and jurists conducted trading. The Holy Qur'ān says: "O you who

---

[7] Al Jaziri, 1973, **2**, pp. 290, 291, 300–302.
[8] Muslim, 1981, with annotation by Nawavi.
[9] Al-Sarakhsi, n.d., **12**, p. 108.
[10] Holy Qur'ān, 2: 275.

believe! Do not devour your property among yourselves falsely except that it be trading by your mutual consent".[11]

The holy Prophet (pbuh) also gave it much importance by saying: "That one of you takes his rope and then comes with a load of wood upon his back and sells, it is better than to beg of men whether they give or reject him".[12] While encouraging truthfulness in trade, he observed that the truthful merchant (will be rewarded by being ranked) on the Day of Resurrection together with the Prophets, the truthful ones, the martyrs and the pious people.[13] The holy Prophet also said: "The best earnings are those of the businessman who does not tell a lie when he speaks; does not misappropriate the trust; does not break the word if he promises; does not cavil while making purchases; does not boast while selling his goods; does not prolong the period of repayment of loan; and does not cause difficulty to his debtors!" Further: "The best type of earning is Bai' based on truth and earnings of one by his own hands".

### 6.3.1 Trade (Profit) versus Interest: Permissibility versus Prohibition

Inference can be made from the Holy Qur'ān (verses 2: 275, 276) that Riba on loans and debts must not be equated with trade or profit from sale. It is significant to note that the mention of the permissibility of trading in the verse precedes the prohibition of Riba, which fact signifies that the alternative to Riba is trading. Islamic banks' trading activities are sometimes criticized on two grounds: one, banks are intermediaries and as such they should not get involved in trading and other real sector activities; two, their charging a price more than the cash price in the market is equivalent to interest-based financing.[14] Both objections are invalid because the business of banking and finance has never been static to any particular structure and subject to proper risk management; an Islamic bank can adopt any modus operandi of business keeping in mind the Sharī'ah compliance aspects. Even conventional banks take part in real business activities, the best example of which is Merchant Banking in Germany. Therefore, Islamic banks' trading activities, fulfilling all conditions prescribed in Islamic commercial law, should not be equated with interest. Below we will discuss the second aspect in detail.

An important difference between a trade's profit and Riba is that the former is a result of real investment activity in which the business risk is allocated more evenly among all the parties involved, whereas in Riba-based business, reward is guaranteed to a party leaving the other party in risk. As such, Riba-based transactions do not fulfil the important Sharī'ah principle of "Al-Kharaj bi-al-Daman", which signifies that one can claim profit only if he is ready to take liability – bear the business risk, if any. The rationale of this principle is that earning profit is legitimized by engaging in an economic activity and thereby contributing to the development of resources and society.

The profit margin earned by a trader is justified firstly because he provides a definite service in the form of seeking out, locating and purchasing goods for his client, for which he is allowed to charge a certain amount of profit, and secondly, he takes business risk in

---

[11] Holy Qur'ān, IV: 29.

[12] Bukhari (Al Asqalani), **5**, p. 46, No. 2373.

[13] Abu Hanifah, n.d., **II**, p. 351. The Prophet is also reported to have said: "Allah will let the man enter the paradise who is an easy purchaser (in bargaining), an easy vendor (in selling), an easy debtor (in repaying the debts) and an easy creditor (in lending and demanding back the loans)." Ibn Hajar, 1998, **4**, p. 388.

[14] See Kazmi, 2004.

obtaining the goods, like damage in storage or in transit and market and price risks. All these activities and risks justify his earning a profit, even if the margin of profit in the case of a credit sale of a commodity is more than the margin involved in the cash market price of that commodity. The Sharīʿah permits a trader to sell for cash or on credit subject to the condition that the price, once agreed between the parties at the time of bargain, is not changed, even if the payment is not made by the due date.

On the other hand, earning money from money on the basis of interest creates a rentier class, giving a smaller and smaller share of the national produce to those doing real work for the creation of wealth in the economy. Islamic financial institutions, while undertaking trade services, have to fulfil the conditions required for valid sales.

The permissibility of a higher credit price than the cash price will be discussed in a subsequent section of this chapter.

## 6.4   TYPES OF BAIʿ

With respect to legality, there are a number of types of Baiʿ that can be valid (Sahih), void (Batil), voidable (Fāsid) and suspended (Mawquf). We have discussed these in detail in the previous chapter. The Hanafi jurists, in particular, have categorized sale into Baiʿ Nafiz or Sahih, Baiʿ Batil and Baiʿ Fāsid, on the basis of certain rules.[15] While Batil means a contract in which ownership title is not transferred and, therefore, is not Sharīʿah-compliant and not enforceable, Fāsid refers to a contract that involves any violation of Sharīʿah rules that is not of a severe nature, and if parties to the contract are agreed and some modifications are made, it is considered enforceable. If the transfer of title is subject to any specific conditions, it is a Mawquf, or suspended, sale.[16]

The most important type of valid Baiʿ is exchanging any commodity with money on the spot or at credit (Baiʿ al Mutlaq). The exchange of various kinds of money or goods representing money, e.g. gold, silver, Dollars, Rupees, etc., is called Baiʿ al Sarf. The exchange of goods with goods is called barter (Baiʿ al Muqāyaza).[17] Other forms are: Muʾajjal, where the price of the property is deferred to a future but definite time; and Salam, when a sale contract is made by immediate payment against the future delivery of the commodity. All types of Baiʿ have their own rules to become acceptable modes of business in Sharīʿah. Various forms of Baiʿ with respect to the counter values, which have already been defined in Chapter 5, are shown in Figure 6.1.

## 6.5   REQUIREMENTS OF A VALID SALE CONTRACT

Islamic banks have to undertake trade that is governed by some rules, as per the Islamic Sharīʿah. The rules broadly pertain to proper offer and acceptance by the respective parties, free consent of the seller and buyer, legality of the wares and anything used as a medium of exchange, the importance of record-keeping in business, security, discharging one's due in full, fulfilment of promise, etc (Figure 6.2). A sale must be prompt and absolute because a sale attributed to a

---

[15]  Al Jaziri, 1973, **2**, p. 300; Usmani, 2000b, pp. 71–80.
[16]  Al Jaziri, 1973, **2**, p. 292.
[17]  Al Jaziri, 1973, **2**, pp. 290–300.

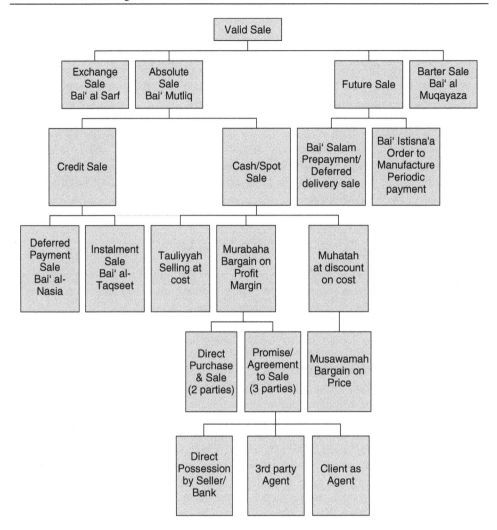

**Figure 6.1** Forms of Bai' with respect to counter values

future date or a sale contingent on a future event is void/voidable and the parties will have to execute it afresh when the future date comes or the contingency actually occurs.

The approved forms of Bai' reflect the main principles of mutual consent of the parties and justice, with an emphasis on good manners, leniency and honesty. Mutual consent can exist only when there is volition, truthfulness as against coercion, fraud and lying. Justice includes imperatives like fulfilment of promise and contracts, correct weights and measures, clear and definite stipulation of price, nature and amount of work, wages and payments, honesty and sincerity.[18] Good manners prescribed by the Sharī'ah in conducting any business include politeness, forgiveness, due compensation and removal of hardship faced by others.[19]

---

[18] For various conditions see Al Jaziri, 1973, pp. 318, 324, 325, 327, 330, 336.

[19] Al-Zoor (wrong/false statements) has been included by the holy Prophet among the Kaba'ir (Tirmidhi, 1988, p. 2, No. 965); Al Jaziri, 1973, **2**, p. 305.

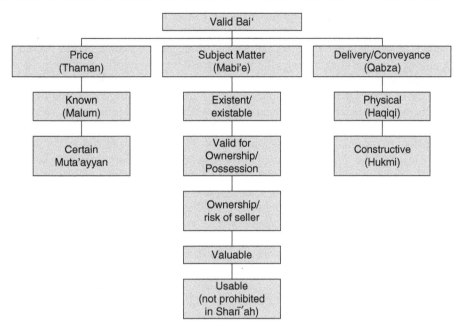

**Figure 6.2**    Elements of valid Bai'

The seller and the buyer must have an understanding and sufficient discretion; the commodity sold and its price should be known to both parties, it should have value in law and must be in existence and/or it must be susceptible to delivery of possession, either immediately or at some future time. This last condition is specific to a Salam sale.

### 6.5.1    The Object of the Sale Contract

Jurists have emphasized the clear identification or specification of the subject matter of a sale contract and its definite delivery to the buyer. They require a number of conditions concerning the object, which must be satisfied for a valid sale. As this aspect has already been discussed in detail in the previous chapter, here we shall briefly indicate the main conditions. First, the object must be pure, lawful (Mubāh), clean, wholesome and, of course, marketable and bearing legal value. It must be Māl-e-Mutaqawam (wealth having a commercial value); its underlying cause (Sabab) must be lawful, and it must not be proscribed by Islamic law; it should not be a nuisance to public order or morality. For example, the sale and trading of commodities such as wine or alcoholic products, pork and pork products is prohibited, and contracts involving such commodities are void on the grounds of their illegality.[20] The flesh and bones of animals that have died by other means than ritual slaughter (Halal) cannot be sold. Idols are also forbidden commodities.

Second, the object must be in existence at the time of the contract and the vendor must be the real owner of the commodity to be sold. What is not owned by the seller cannot be sold. For example, if a bank sells to client C a car which is presently owned by factory F, but the

---

[20] Muslim, 1981 with annotation by Nawavi, **11**, pp. 6–8; Tirmidhi, 1988, **2**, p. 27; Al Jaziri, 1973, **2**, p. 293.

bank is hopeful that it will buy it from F and shall deliver it subsequently to C, the sale will be void according to the Sharī´ah. At the most, the bank can make a promise to sell.

A related condition is that of taking possession of the goods before their sale. As reported by Imam Bukhari: "Ibn Umar narrated 'I saw the people buy food stuff randomly (i.e. blindly without measuring it) in the life time of the Prophet and they were punished if they tried to sell it before carrying it into their own houses'." Qastalani in his commentary on Sahih Bukhari reports that before the commodity comes into the possession of the vendee it is not lawful for sale according to Imam Shafi'e, Muhammad and some other jurists.[21] Many jurists, including the Hanafis, have, however, contended that for a lawful sale transaction, it is sufficient that the item of sale must be present and fully known, leaving no room for ignorance or dispute, and that physical possession is not necessary for a valid sale. It is also ascertained in Majallah that delivery of the sale item on the part of the vendor is completed when he sets it aside for the vendee and there is nothing to restrict him from taking physical possession from the vendor whenever he desires.[22]

Accordingly, a purchaser who has not got possession of a commodity cannot sell it onward. For example, if A has purchased a car from B, but B has not yet delivered it to A or to his agent, A cannot sell that car to C and if he sells it before taking its actual or constructive delivery from B, the sale is void.

As discussed earlier, the condition of existence of the sale item at the time of execution of the contract has been mitigated by the authorization of Bai' Salam and Istisna'a contracts, which cover the future supply and future manufacture of goods respectively. Scholars deduce from this permissibility that when the object of a contract is a particular thing, it must be in existence at the time of the contract. Accordingly, if A sells the unborn calf of his cow to B, the contract is void because of Gharar. But where the object is a promise to deliver or to manufacture with given specifications, the object of that promise needs not be in existence at the time of the contract, but must be possible and definite, i.e. it must be capable of being defined in such a way as to avoid Gharar, Jahl or uncertainty about its delivery and dispute about its quality.

Fourth, the object of a sale contract must be capable of certain delivery. Jurists, therefore, have prohibited the sale of a camel which has fled, a bird in the air or a fish in water.[23] As such, a stolen motor vehicle cannot be sold until found and seen by both parties. It is important to indicate that the overriding concern of jurists is to prevent conflict and unjustified profits arising out of uncertain contracts. The condition that, for execution of the contract, the object must be capable of delivery can be understood as an aspect of the right to title, namely that the object must be in the ownership of the person intending to sell and the right to transfer must be legal and its quantity and value must be known. If the object of a contract is a promise to deliver or manufacture a good in the future, the promise must be feasible and the goods to be delivered must be known (defined).

Among examples mentioned by jurists for the inability to deliver is the sale of a debt against another debt, the sale of that which one does not have in one's possession and the sale by a buyer of what he has bought before he takes possession. Similarly, a sale is void if its future existence is uncertain in that it may or may not exist, for example, the sale of what a she-camel may give birth to. However, jurists differ on whether all nonexistent commodities

---

[21] Irshad-al-Sari, Sharah, Sahih Bukhari, **4**, p. 57.

[22] Al-Atasi, 1403 AH, Majallah, Articles 262, 263; Al-Marghinani, *Hidaya*: **3**, pp. 58–59.

[23] Zuhayli, 1985, **4**, pp. 503, 504.

cannot be sold or only those that involve Gharar. Ibn Taymiyah is of the view that there is no evidence to prove that the sale of every nonexistent item is impermissible... there is another cause for the prohibition of the sale of nonexistent objects and that is Gharar. A nonexistent item cannot be sold, not because it is nonexistent but because it involves Gharar. For example, the "sale for years" (also called Mua'awamah), in which fruits of a tree or an orchard are sold for more than one year to come, and the sale of Habl al Hablah is prohibited.[24] Therefore, with regard to the Prophet's saying: "do not sell what you do not possess", scholars contend that what is meant by possession here is the inability to deliver the goods. So, from the seller's part, he must be sure that he can deliver the goods.

Nawavi, in his annotation to Sahih Muslim, has reported that people used to buy from the caravans without weighing, measuring or even estimating precisely.[25] Selling goods onward could be unjust to the buyers, so they were asked to take possession before selling. This is also evident from the words of Imam Bukhari: "Ibn Umar (Gbpwh) narrated 'I saw the people buy food stuff randomly (i.e. blindly without measuring it) in the life time of the holy Prophet (pbuh) and they were punished if they tried to sell it before carrying it into their own houses. Similarly, a heap of grain was purchased, considering it a specific amount, the purchaser was asked first to take delivery of the declared amount and then to sell onward'."[26] The rationale behind this seems to be that the seller should take the risk and reward of his trade activity.[27] So long as the sold commodity remains with the seller – the buyer has neither made payment nor taken its possession, its risk and reward are that of the seller.

Goods subject to Salam and Istisna'a and the conditions required for their permission are the best examples of the permissibility of nonexistent but defined goods. It is commonly understood that Salam goods can also not be sold before taking their possession, and the following Hadith is reported for this: The holy Prophet said: "A person who purchases something on Salam, he should not transfer it to others before its transmutation (taking its possession)".[28] But the sale of Salam goods needs more detail (given in Chapter 10), particularly in view of the fact that the above Hadith is "weak".[29] Salam is an exception and goods purchased through Salam can be sold onward on the basis of (Parallel) Salam. If we were to strictly observe the spirit of this Hadith, Parallel Salam would not be possible. Further, the Salam purchaser undertakes the business risk after the Salam contract is executed; prices may fall or rise, he has to take possession of the goods.

Ibn Hazm explains that whatever a person owns should be taken as if it is in his possession although the commodity might be in Hind.[30] Many other jurists, including the Hanafis, have contended that for a lawful sale transaction, it is sufficient that the item of sale must be present and fully known, leaving no room for ignorance and dispute, and that physical possession is not a necessary condition of a valid sale.[31] It is also ascertained in Majallah that delivery of the sale item on the part of the vendor is completed when he sets it aside for the vendee and there is nothing to prevent the buyer from taking physical possession

---

[24] Tirmidhi, 1988, No. 1335, p. 32, cf. Al-Dhareer, 1997, pp. 31, 32, see also Muslim (x/95, 200), Nisai, n.d., **7**, pp. 293, 294.

[25] Muslim, 1981, with annotation by Nawavi, **10**, pp. 168–169.

[26] Bukhari, Bab al Kail 'alal Baai'i.

[27] Tirmidhi, 1988, No. 1308–1033, p. 25.

[28] Abu Daud 1952, Kitab al Buyoo, *Al Salaf la Yohawal*.

[29] Ibn Hajar, 1998, 3, No. 1203, p. 69.

[30] Ibn Hazm, **7**, 1988, p. 475.

[31] Al-Atasi, 1403 AH, Majallah, Articles 197–200, 262.

from the vendor whenever he desires.[32] Hence, if A has purchased a car from B, who has placed the car in a garage where A has free access and A is allowed to take delivery, real or constructive, from that place whenever he wishes, the car is in the constructive possession of A and if he sells it to C without acquiring physical possession, the sale is valid.

This implies that as the purchaser has taken the liability of the risk, he is considered the owner of the commodity, although the asset/commodity is still in the godown of the seller or even in any other country or area. Hence, if a Karachi-based bank contracts to purchase one hundred thousand bags of fertilizer from a factory in Lahore and the factory sets the bags aside and gives constructive possession to the bank, the bank is considered the rightful owner of the fertilizer and is capable of selling it to any third party. So long as the bags are not sold, the asset, market or price risk will be that of the bank and not of the factory.

However, one can promise to sell something which is not yet owned or possessed. Similarly, one can promise to buy any asset with given specifications. In the case of promise, the actual sale will have to be executed after the commodity comes into the possession of the seller, with proper offer and acceptance, and unless the sale is formally executed, the promise will have no legal consequences. Normally, a promise creates just a moral obligation on the promisor to fulfil his promise, but if the promisee has incurred any liability or expense as a result of the promise and the promisor backs out, the latter should be held responsible for the actual loss to the promisee.

### 6.5.2 Prices and the Profit Margin

As a principle, Islam is not inclined to fix prices or profit margins for traders and leaves them to be settled by the forces of demand and supply. The holy Prophet (pbuh) is reported to have allowed the competitive price mechanism to balance the demand and supply of goods for the dispensation of economic justice, the best ultimate benefit of society and for efficient allocation of resources.[33] The limitations are only to take care of some moral, religious and cultural perceptions and aspirations, which give an important place to the State in ensuring the desired norms.[34]

However, Islam has ordained transparency in respect of features/qualities of the wares and honesty in dealing. In a market where buyers and sellers trade with liberty, the parties can bargain on any price. In Sunan Abu Daud, we come across a very interesting instance. The holy Prophet (pbuh) sent one of his Companions ('Urwah) to purchase for him a goat and gave him one dinar. Urwah went to the market and purchased two goats for one dinar, then sold one of them in the market for one dinar and gave the holy Prophet a goat and also one dinar. The holy Prophet was so happy with his honesty and expertise that he prayed for the promotion of his trade and business.[35]

With regard to pricing, the Islamic Fiqh Council of the OIC, in its fifth session, resolved the following:

---

[32] Al-Atasi, 1403 AH, Majallah, Article 263; Al-Marghinani, *Hidaya*, **3**, pp. 58–59.

[33] Tirmidhi, 1988, No. 1336 (also in Abu Daud, 1952, Kitab al Buyoo).

[34] If suppliers of the goods do not act judiciously and the authorities fail to protect consumer rights, prices can be fixed in consultation with the experts in the relevant field. See Waliullah, 1353 H, **2**, p. 38.

[35] Tirmidhi, 1988, No. 1281, p. 18; Abu Daud, 1952, Kitab al Buyoo, Bab fel Mudarib.

1. The basic principle in the Qur'ān and the Sunnah of the Prophet (pbuh) is that a person should be free to buy and sell and dispose of his possessions and money, within the framework of the Islamic Sharī´ah.
2. There is no restriction on the percentage of profit a trader may make in his transactions. It is generally left to the merchants themselves, the business environment and the nature of the merchant and of the goods. Regard should be given, however, to the ethics recommended by the Sharī´ah, such as moderation, contention, leniency and indulgence.
3. Sharī´ah texts have spelt out the necessity to keep transactions away from illicit acts like fraud, cheating, deceit, forgery, concealment of actual benefits and monopoly, which are detrimental to society and individuals.
4. Governments should not be involved in fixing prices except when obvious pitfalls are noticed within the market and the price, due to artificial factors. In this case, governments should intervene by applying adequate means to get rid of these factors, the causes of defects, excessive price increases and fraud.

The Sharī´ah does not allow excessive profiteering (Ghaban-e-Fahish), which means that a person sells a commodity stating explicitly or giving the impression that he is charging the market price, when actually he is charging an exorbitant price, taking benefit from the ignorance of the purchaser.[36] If the purchaser comes to know afterwards that he has been charged excessively, he has the option to rescind the contract and take back his money. Although jurists in general do not recommend any specific profit rates in trading, we find inferences in books that the maximum profit rate to be charged in trade should be 5 % in respect of wares, 10 % in case of animals and 20 % in real estate.[37]

### 6.5.3  Cash and Credit Prices

In medieval Islamic trade, not only was buying and selling on credit accepted and apparently widespread, but also the credit performed many important functions in trade transitions. We find a lot of detail in Fiqh books on various aspects of trade transactions on credit.

Most jurists believe that the seller can indicate two prices, i.e. one for cash and another for a credit transaction, but one of the two prices must be settled in the same meeting. They, however, qualify this with the condition that the difference should be a normal practice of the market, the aim should be the business of trade and the seller should not resort to the practice of Ghaban-e-Fahish. The following tradition is important in this regard: "The person who makes two bargains in one sale, the lower of the two is lawful for him or he would be charging Riba".[38] Jurists like Semāk, Aozāii and others have interpreted this as a situation where a person declares in the sale contract that in the case of credit, the sale price will be so much, and in the case of cash, so much.[39]

Besides the situation described above, another situation is where the seller declares only one price, the credit price, higher than the price prevalent in the market, and the buyer agrees to buy at that price. Jurists differ regarding the legality of charging this excess on account of the period allowed for the payment of the price. The jurists who disapprove argue that the seller himself may not differentiate between the cash and credit price, but if the purchaser

---

[36] For detail on Ghaban-e-Fahish, see Al Jaziri, 1973, **2**, pp. 570–573.
[37] Al-Atasi, 1403 AH, Majallah, Article 165.
[38] Abu Daud, 1752, **3**, p. 274.
[39] Thanwi, n.d., **14**, p. 273.

feels that he has been charged an excess on account of a delay, the transaction will be usurious. However, other jurists, mostly belonging to Shafi'e and Hanafi schools, deem this form lawful on the grounds that the seller sells the goods on a deferred payment basis and stipulates, at the time of the bargain, the whole price in return for the sale item. This is just like the situation where, for example, a seller declares to the buyer that the price will be $10 if he purchases it today and $11 tomorrow. This is permissible according to all jurists, as the seller has the right to demand the price, keeping in mind the time of the sale contract. The difference in price therein is in lieu of the item of sale and not as a reward for time. They argue that the permissibility of the form under consideration can be derived therefrom. However, when the price is stipulated once, it should not be subject to any change, keeping in mind the period of time given for payment.[40]

Imam Tirmidhi in his Jām'i has also reported that the holy Prophet (pbuh) forbade two sales in one contract. According to Tirmidhi, some jurists have explained this in the sense that a person states: "I sell this cloth for cash for 10 and on credit for 20 (dirhams)" and at separation, one price is not settled. If one of the two prices is settled, it is not prohibited.[41] Tohfatul Ahwazi, Sharah Jām'i al Tirmidhi, explains that if the seller says that he sells the cloth for 10 for cash and 20 on credit, and the buyer accepts either of the two prices; or if a buyer says that he purchases for 20 on credit or the parties separate having settled on any of the prices, the sale will be valid.[42]

Jurist Shukāni explains the above aspect and concludes that if the purchaser in such a situation says: "I accept for 1000 for cash" or "for 2000 on credit", this would be all right.[43] He adds that the 'Illah (effective cause) for prohibition of two sales in one is the nonfixity of the price.[44] He has a separate booklet on the subject wherein he maintains that he reached the conclusion after thorough research.[45]

Shah Waliullah in Muaswwa, Sharah Al Mu'watta, writes that if the parties separate after settlement on one price, the contract is valid and there is no difference of opinion in this regard.[46]

Among scholars of the present age, the late Shaikh Abdullah ibn Bāz, who was the most honoured grand Mufti of Saudi Arabia, permitted instalments sale wherein the credit price could be higher than the cash price.[47]

Jurists allow this difference, considering it a genuine market practice. It is quite natural that in the market, the credit price of a commodity should be more than its cash price at a point in time, while in forward purchase, the future price will be less than the cash price (that is why the Companions asked the holy Prophet (pbuh) about the validity of Salam/Salaf when Riba was prohibited and the holy Prophet allowed it on the condition that the price, quality and delivery of the goods should be stipulated).

In the words of eminent Hanafi jurist Sarakhsi: "Selling on credit is an absolute feature of trade". In discussing the rights of a managing partner in a Musharakah contract, Sarakhsi says: "We hold that selling for credit is part of the practice of merchants, and that it is the

---

[40] Thanwi, n.d., **14**, p. 134; Al Sanani, 1972, pp. 136–137.
[41] Tirmidhi, 1988, No. 1254.
[42] Mubarakpuri, n.d., **2**, p. 236.
[43] Shukāni, n.d., **5**, p. 12.
[44] Ibid.
[45] Shukāni, Shifa al Khilal fe hukm-e-ziadat al thaman al Mujarrad wala'jal.
[46] Waliullah, 1353 H, **2**, pp. 28, 29.
[47] Ibn Bāz, 1995, p. 142.

most conducive means for the achievement of the investor's goal, which is profit. And in most cases, profit can only be achieved by selling for credit and not selling for cash." He further states: "A thing is sold on credit for a larger sum than it would be sold for cash".[48]

The comments of Abraham L. Udovitch on the views expressed by Sarakhsi are worth mentioning: "This statement makes clear as to why there was a greater profit to be derived from credit transactions ... The difference in price between a credit and cash sale also helps explain why the prohibition against usury, to the extent that it was observed, did not exercise any crippling restriction on the conduct of commerce. For, while the difference in the price for which one sells on credit and the price for which one sells for cash does not formally and legally constitute interest, it does fulfil, from the point of view of its economic functions, the same role as interest. It provides a return to the creditor for the risk involved in the transaction and compensates him for the absence of his capital."[49]

Udovitch, however, overstates the case when saying that the difference in the cash and credit prices of a commodity fulfils the same role as interest. Islamic economics has the genuine provision of converting money into assets and then one can measure its utility. While it concedes the concept of time value of money to the extent of pricing in credit sales, it does not generate rent on the capital as interest does in credits and advances, creating a rentier class. Money is a means of exchange. As per the rules of the Sharī'ah, $1000 today will be $1000 tomorrow. However, what matters is the translation of 1000 dollars into an asset, in which case that $1000 asset may be worth more or less in any number of years one may consider. Therefore, value has to be in the context of any asset, in which case it can be higher or lower in the future.

The jurists have also derived argument on the difference between cash and credit prices from the Holy Qur'ān. The Qur'ān has reported nonbelievers saying: "The sale is very similar to Riba." (2: 275) Referring to this verse, Shaikh Taqi Usmani says: "Their objection was that when we increase the price of a commodity in the original transaction of sale because of its being based on deferred payment it is treated as a valid sale; but when we want to increase the due amount after the maturity date and the debtor is not able to pay, it is termed Riba, while the increase in both cases seems to be similar." This objection has been specifically mentioned by the famous commentator of the Holy Qur'ān Ibn-Abi-Hātim: "They used to say that it is all equal whether we increase the price in the beginning of the sale, or we increase it at the time of maturity. Both are equal. It is this objection which has been referred to in the verse ... "[50] The Holy Qur'ān's response to the above thinking of nonbelievers was: "and Allah has permitted trading, and prohibited Riba".

Allamah Sayyuti has quoted from Mujahid that "people used to sell goods on credit; at the time when the payment was due, they used to give extension against enhanced prices. At this, the verse 'Do not eat Riba doubled and redoubled' was revealed."[51] Ibne Jarir Tabari has reported from Qatādah a similar situation of Riba involvement in which a person sold

---

[48] Al Sarakhsi, n.d., **22**, p. 45; cf. Udovitch, 1970, pp. 78, 79.

[49] Udovitch, 1970, p. 80.

[50] Shariat Appellate Bench, 2000, pp. 536–538; Ibn-abi-Hātim reports: ". . . when the payment became due the debtor used to say to the creditor: 'give me more time, I would give you more than your amount', when it was indicated that it amounted to Riba, they used to say that it was all equal whether we increase the price in the beginning of the sale, or we increase it at the time of maturity, both are equal. It is this objection which has been referred to in the verse by saying 'They say that the sale is very similar to Riba'." (Ibn-abi-Hātim, 1997, **2**, Nos. 2891, 2892, p. 545.

[51] Sayyuti, 2003/1423.

any commodity on a credit price payable at any agreed time; when the payment was due and the purchaser could not pay it, the price was enhanced and the time for payment extended.[52]

It can safely be derived from the above discussion that a transaction of credit sale with a price higher than the spot price is acceptable.[53] What is prohibited is that the price, once mutually stipulated, is enhanced due to any delay in its payment. This is because a commodity, once sold, becomes the property of the purchaser on a permanent basis and the seller has no right to re-price a commodity that he has already sold, and also because the price becomes a debt.

The difference in price has become a customary factor due to market competition and the free play of market forces and clients are ready to pay a price for the benefit to be achieved by them of having purchased goods without making cash payments. Therefore, according to many jurists, this aspect is approved by the Nass (clear text of the Sharī´ah) from the Salaf (forebears).[54]

Accordingly, absolute certainty on price is necessary for the validity of a sale. All jurists agree that if one definite price is not stipulated in the case of a credit sale, it will become Riba and therefore unlawful. For example, A says to B: "If you pay within a month, the price is 10 dollars, and if you pay after two months, the price is 12 dollars"; B agrees without absolutely determining one of the two prices. As the price remains uncertain the sale is void, unless any one of the two alternatives is agreed upon by the parties at the time of concluding the transaction.

Another point to be clarified is that a person who has bought an asset on credit can sell it onward after taking its possession, even if he has not made full payment of its price. If a client C purchases a car on Murabaha, with the price payable in five years, from day one, C is the owner of the car and is liable to the bank for the agreed amount according to the agreed schedule. He can sell the car for any reason after one year, for example to Y, who agrees to pay the remaining installments. Although C has not paid all the instalments, this would not be considered a "sale of what he doesn't own".

## 6.6   RIBA INVOLVEMENT IN SALES

Sales contracts could involve Riba Al-Fadl, as discussed in Chapter 3. In this regard, rules for the mutual exchange of homogeneous or heterogeneous commodities have a direct relevance to the rules of trading. The mutual exchange of 'Ayān (commodities of material value in themselves) is subject to rules different from the exchange of Athman (having monetary values or prices). When an article of the kind of Thaman or price is sold or exchanged with an article of the same kind, the law requires that there must be mutual delivery and each of the articles must be equal in weight to the other. The following commonly known Hadith of the holy Prophet forms the basis of discussion on this aspect of exchange: "Gold for gold, silver for silver, wheat for wheat, barley for barley, dates for dates and salt for salt – like for like, equal for equal and hand to hand; if the commodities differ, then you may sell as

---

[52] Tabari, n.d., **6**, p. 8.
[53] Accordingly, the Islamic Fiqh Academy of the OIC and Sharī´ah supervisory boards of all Islamic banks approve the legality of this difference in price.
[54] For details, see *Sahifah Ahl-Hadith* (Urdu), February 24, 1993.

you wish, provided that the exchange is hand to hand".[55] Exchange rules need to be seen in the light of this saying, as discussed in Chapter 4.

The sale and purchase of currencies and foreign exchange dealings are included in the normal activities of banks and financial institutions. It is imperative, therefore, that when a sale transaction is taking place among currencies, the exchange has to take place instantly and not on a deferred basis. In this regard, a normal time required for payment/settlement is allowed by the Sharī´ah scholars provided that it does not become a condition of the exchange. The OIC Islamic Fiqh Academy and the Sharī´ah advisory committee of Al Baraka Bank allow the use of an otherwise Sharī´ah-compliant credit card for the purchase of gold and silver, as an unintentional delay of up to 72 hours does not create a problem in respect of payment.[56]

## 6.7   GHARAR – A CAUSE OF PROHIBITION OF SALES

Gharar is one of the main factors that make a transaction un-Islamic. This subject has been discussed in detail in Chapter 3. Here we shall indicate the overall theme of Gharar and the kinds of sale that have been prohibited on its account.

"Gharar" means hazard, chance, stake or risk. In the legal terminology of jurists, "Gharar" is the sale of a thing which is not present at hand or whose consequence is not known or a sale involving hazard in which one does not know whether it will come to be or not, as in the sale of a fish in water or a bird in the air. From this the jurists derive the general principle that a sale must not be doubtful or uncertain as far as the rights and obligations of the parties are concerned, otherwise it would be tantamount to deceiving the other party. The object of the contract must be precisely determined, and price and terms must be clear and known.

The general principles with regard to avoiding Gharar in sale transactions that have been derived by jurists are: the contracts must be free from absolute uncertainty about the subject matter and its counter value in exchanges. The uncertainty leads to risk but all risks are not Gharar, because business risk is not only a part of life but also a valid requirement for taking a return in exchanges. The requirement is that the commodity must be defined, determined and deliverable and clearly known to the contracting parties; quality and quantity must be stipulated; the contract must not be doubtful or uncertain so far as the rights and obligations of the contracting parties are concerned and the parties should know the actual state of the goods.

This implies that ignorance (Jahl) is also a part of Gharar that has to be avoided. The purchaser should know about the existence and condition of the goods and the vendor should be able to deliver them on the agreed terms and at the agreed time. In other words, one should not undertake anything or any act blindly without sufficient knowledge, or risk oneself in adventure without knowing the outcome or the consequences.

The holy Prophet (pbuh) prohibited all those transactions that involved Gharar (and Jahl). These included, Bai' al-Ma'dum, Bai' al-Mulamasah, Bai' al-Munabadhah, Bai' al Hasat, and similar other contracts involving uncertainty.[57] Imam Malik defines Mulamasah and Munabadhah thus: "Mulamasah is when a man touches or feels a garment, but does not unfold it nor ascertain (its character). Munabadhah is when a man throws to another a

---

[55] Tirmidhi, 1988, No. 1263–1994, also in Bukhari, Muslim, 'Ibn Mājah.
[56] Al Baraka Resolutions, 1995, No. 12/6, p. 193.
[57] Tirmidhi, 1988, Nos. 1252, 1253 (p. 8), 1332 (p. 31), also see Bukhari, Sahih, Kitab al Buyoo.

garment in exchange for a garment that the other throws to him without both of them examining them." Imam Malik, therefore, says that it is not permissible to sell a Persian mantle or shawl which is inside its cover or a Coptic garment in its fold unless they are unfolded and their insides seen, because their sale (in their folded state) is a sale of risk.

Imam Malik did not, however, disallow the well-established practice of selling whole bales of goods on the basis of their description in an accompanying catalogue or list of contents (Barnāmaj), without actually unfolding them, for then it would become impossible to conduct wholesale trade. He, therefore, says: "The sale of bales according to the Barnāmaj is different from the sale of a Persian shawl in its cover or a garment in its fold. The difference between them is (based on) the actual practice and their knowledge with the people, and it continues to be among the allowable sales among the people because the sale of bales according to the Barnāmaj without unfolding is not intended as a risk and has no similarity to Mulamasah".[58]

In the present age, where a large number of goods are made under trademarks or where minute specifications of goods can be stipulated in the contract, there may not be any involvement of Gharar. Many jurists soften this condition in the case of nonedibles.[59] Accordingly, religious boards allow the banks to agree to provide goods other than edibles, after purchasing them from the market.[60]

A common Gharar-based transaction in the present age is that of a book-out contract, in which a person buys an asset and then sells it without taking possession, only getting/paying the difference in the purchase and sale prices. This happens in commodities, stocks and the foreign exchange markets. In particular, a large part of the global foreign exchange markets comprises book-out transactions involving speculation and excessive risk-taking. Exchange does not actually take place and only paper entries give rise to the rights/liabilities of the parties. The Sharī'ah committees and boards have declared such transactions prohibited.[61]

## 6.8    CONDITIONAL SALES AND "TWO BARGAINS IN ONE SALE"

The Sharī'ah does not approve sales that are conditional upon such matters that may or not may happen due to games of chance. In the Fiqh literature, we come across the prohibition of two stipulations in a sale: Shartaan fi Ba'ien, or sale with a stipulation, and Bai'wal Shart, which involves lack of clarity and an unjustifiable benefit to any of the parties. For example, a person says to another: "I will sell you this house if any third person sells me his house".[62] Gharar in this transaction pertains to the time of the meeting, the condition and finalization of the contract. Conditions of gift, marriage, Qard or Shirkah as a part of a sale contract render it a prohibited contract from the Sharī'ah angle.

Hanafi jurists consider such conditional contracts a type of gambling. Ibn Abideen opines that sales that are the instruments of ownership cannot be postponed to the future nor can they be conditional upon realization of an event in the future, as this involves gambling.[63]

---

[58] Malik, 1985, pp. 423, 424.
[59] Tirmidhi, 1988, explanation at No. 1314, p. 26.
[60] Al Baraka, Fatawa, 1997, p. 91.
[61] Al Baraka, Fatawa, 1997, p. 102.
[62] Ibn Qudama has given a number of examples for such sales, 1367 AH, **4**, pp. 234, 235. Also see pp. 225–227.
[63] Ibn Abideen; Mustafa al babi, 1367 H, **IV**, p. 324.

However, Ibn Taymiyah and Ibnul Qayyim allow certain types of suspended sale, not seeing any Gharar in the same. To them, such conditions are permitted to be attached to sales that do not involve Gharar and Riba. Ibn Taymiyah rejects only those stipulations which contradict a clear provision of the Qur'ān, the Sunnah or the scholarly consensus, or which contradict the very object of a contract, nullifying it. Ibn Hazm, in *al-Muhallah*, has maintained seven types of conditions that can be enforced, including Rihn in Bai', delay in payment in a credit sale (with stipulated time of payment), traits or features of the goods to be traded and other conditions mutually agreed upon and not against the rules of Sharī'ah.[64]

The holy Prophet is reported to have said: "unlawful are a sale and a loan (Bai' wal Salaf), or two stipulations in a sale, or a sale of what you do not have."[65] Imam Malik defined Bai' wal Salaf, the contract of selling and lending, as being like one man saying to another: "I shall purchase your goods for such and such if you lend me such and such". If they agree to a transaction in this manner, it is not permitted. If the one who stipulates the loan, abandons his stipulation, the sale is permitted. Shah Waliullah has explained it as co-mingling of a loan with a sale, which involves Jahl/hazard and is therefore not valid.[66] The Prophet (pbuh) is reported to have said: "Prevent them from making . . . a selling and lending (contract) (concurrently) . . . ."[67] Imam Ahmad explained it as if a person gives a loan to someone and then sells to him something at a higher than market price.[68]

Combining contracts which are conditional upon each other confuses the rights and liabilities of the parties and obstructs fair remedies in the event of default, thereby opening a door to Riba and Gharar. In this regard, Ibn Taymiyah is the most liberal, objecting only to the combination of onerous and gratuitous contracts, such as sale and loan (Qard), since by such arrangement parties can easily hide an illegal compensation for the loan. Modern scholars seem to follow this view, since the combination of contracts occurs quite frequently.

One alternative in this regard is to combine contracts informally, without legally conditioning one on the other. Tawarruq, for example, is a transaction whereby a needy person buys something on credit and then immediately, in a separate transaction with another party, sells it for cash. Most scholars have declared this permissible. Such a ruling reflects the fact that behaviour like this cannot be regulated by law but only by moral ruling. Sharī'ah principles require that the exchange value should neither be bunched with gift nor made contingent upon any loan or Shirkah condition. For example, a person, says: "Sell me this; I will give you that much gift in addition to price".[69] This involves Gharar and Jahl and the seller should rather decrease the price so as to determine exactly the counter value paid by the buyer.

## 6.9   BAI' AL'ARBŪN (DOWNPAYMENT SALE)

'Arbūn sale has been defined as a sale of downpayment, with the condition that if the buyer takes the commodity, the downpayment will become part of the selling price, and if he does not purchase the commodity, the advance money will be forfeited.[70] Two traditions of the

---

[64] Ibn Hazm, 1988, **7**, pp. 319–331, No. 1447.

[65] Tirmidhi, 1988.

[66] Waliullah, 1353 H, **2**, p. 28; Nisai with Sharah Al Sayyuti, **7**, p. 295.

[67] Tirmidhi, 1988, No. 1257, p. 9.

[68] Ibn Qudama, 1367 AH, **4**, p. 235.

[69] Al Baraka, 1997 (6: 24), p. 101.

[70] Al-Marghinani, **iv**, p. 232; Al-Baji, 1332 AH, **III**, p. 495.

holy Prophet have been reported in this regard. A Hadith quoted by Imam Malik says that the holy Prophet (pbuh) forbade 'Arbūn sale. According to another Hadith, Zaid ibn Aslam asked the holy Prophet (pbuh) about 'Arbūn as a part of a sale; the Prophet permitted it.

The majority of traditional jurists accept the Hadith prohibiting 'Arbūn sale due to the involvement of Gharar. However, Hanbalis allow it.[71] Later jurists are also divided about its permissibility. Shaikh Al-Dhareer writes in this regard: "Jurists have disagreed on the permissibility of 'Arbūn sale. It was prohibited by the Hanafis, the Malikis, the Shafi'es, the Zaidi Shiites, Abul Khattab of the Hanbali school, and it was reported that Ibn Abbas and Al-Hassan also forbade it. But it was approved by Imam Ahmad who narrated its permissibility on the authority of Umar (Gbpwh) and his son and a group of the followers of the Prophet's Companions (Tabi'een) including Mujahid, Ibn Sirin, Naf'i Bin Abdel Harith and Zaid Ibn Aslam". He has reported Ibn Rushd saying: "The majority of scholars have forbidden it because it involves Gharar, risk-taking and the taking of money without any consideration in return".[72]

Ibn Qudama, a Hanbali jurist, justifies 'Arbūn by comparing it with two similar contracts, one is a transaction by which a buyer asks the seller to rescind a sale and offers the latter a sum of money to do so.[73] He quotes Ibn Hanbal as saying that 'Arbūn is in the same category. The second contract is where a potential buyer pays a potential seller of goods a sum in return for the latter's agreeing not to sell the goods to anyone else. Later, the buyer returns and buys the goods by final sale, deducting the initial payment from the price. The latter sale is valid, since it is free of any condition. Ibn Qudama then hints that in this second transaction, the advance payment would be unearned gain if the final sale were not concluded, and would have to be returned on demand.

We can derive on the basis of the above discussion that in cases of involvement of absolute Gharar or injustice with the buyer (when he committed to purchase, but cannot do so due to any unforeseen happening), downpayment confiscation might not be permissible. However, to the extent of a customary practice wherein parties do business in the market with free consent and any unforeseen events are also taken into account, it would be permissible on the basis of 'Urf. The Islamic Fiqh Council of the OIC and the AAOIFI have also allowed customary downpayment sale with the condition that a time limit is specified.[74]

## 6.10   BAI' AL DAYN (SALE OF DEBT)

A credit document emerging from any transaction of credit sale represents a debt which cannot be sold as per Sharī'ah rules due to the involvement of Gharar and/or Riba. A trader selling a commodity on credit and thus having a bill of exchange, an export bill or a promissory note cannot sell it to an Islamic bank as they could to a conventional bank. As an alternative, the bank can serve as a trader and purchase the commodity from its producer and then sell it to others who need it on credit, keeping a margin for itself.[75] The OIC Fiqh Academy and Sharī'ah scholars in general consider the sale/purchase of such securities or

[71] Zuhayli, 1985, **4**, p. 508.

[72] Al-Monataqa, 4/157; Nehayet al-Mohtaj, 3/459; Al-Moghni, 4/233; al-Bahr Al-Zakhkhar, 3/459; Bedayat al-Mujtahid, 2/162; cf. Al-Dhareer, 1997, pp. 16, 17.

[73] Ibn Qudama, 1367 AH, **4**, p. 233.

[74] Council of the Islamic Fiqh Academy, 2000, pp. 16, 17; AAOIFI 2004–5a, pp. 65, 66, 76.

[75] Al Baraka, 1997, No. 9/12, pp. 152, 153.

documents representing debt at a price other than their nominal value incompatible with the tenets of the Sharī´ah. Even on face value, the sale of debt is allowed only when the purchaser has recourse to the original debtor, as in the case of Hawalah.

"Al Kāli bil Kāli", a maxim in the Fiqh literature forbidding the sale of debt, means the exchange of two things both delayed or exchange of one delayed counter value for another delayed counter value. The practice of Bai' al-Kāli bil Kāli was prevalent among the pre-Islamic Arabs and was also termed Bai' al-Dayn bid-Dayn. What is prohibited by this contract is the purchase by a man of a commodity on credit for a fixed period, and, when the period of payment comes and he finds he is not able to pay the debt, he says: "Sell it to me on credit for a further period, for something additional". The Prophet is reported to have prohibited such a sale. This principle has near universal application and has earned canonical authority in Islamic law as Ijma'a or consensus.

The best example of this practice in the present age is "rollover" in Murabaha, where the banks, in a case of default on the Murabaha receivable, enter into another Murabaha for giving more time to the client and thus charge more on their receivables. All Sharī´ah boards and Sharī´ah scholars prohibit this practice and any return on this account is not considered legitimate income for Islamic banks.

In the early 1980s, banks in Pakistan were allowed to purchase trade bills, considering the same as a Murabaha contract. But the Council of Islamic Ideology and the Sharī´ah Courts in Pakistan disapproved of such transactions. Islamic banks should not trade in such securities and debts for the basic reason that debts/debt instruments are not saleable at a premium or discount.

However, a debt can be assigned or transferred on the basis of "Hawalah", which implies the transfer of debt obligation from the originator to a third party.[76] The difference between the "sale of debt", which is prohibited, and the "assignment of debt", which is permissible, is that in the latter, there is recourse to the assignor or the original debtor if the assignee does not pay the debt for any reason.

The sale of certificates, or Sukuk, is an important area in this regard. As already indicated, an object of sale in the Islamic law of contracts must be a property of value. When a share or certificate is supported by an asset, as evidenced via the securitization process, it is transformed into an object of value and therefore qualifies to become an object of trade, whereby it can be purchased and sold in both the primary and secondary markets subject to the condition that a return on it is based on cash flow from the asset backing the instrument. Investors do have the right to sell such instruments.

Semi-debt instruments like leasing contracts resemble debt in the sense that they obligate the user to a certain specific commitment (rent). Such contracts can be traded under certain conditions since such trading represents the sale of leased assets, which can be conducted on negotiated prices.

## 6.11   AL 'INAH SALE AND THE USE OF RUSES (HIYAL)

Fiqh literature contains mention of a number of legal ruses that people have used to circumvent the prohibition of Riba. Fatāwa Alamgiri, Mahmasāni's Falsafa al Tashri, Shātbi's al

---

[76] Tirmidhi, 1988, No. 1331, pp. 30, 31; Muslim, 1981, **10**, pp. 227, 228.

Mowafaqāt, etc. contain reference to many techniques that people used to make transactions technically permissible.[77]

Joseph Schacht has undertaken extensive work in modern times on the subject of Hiyal. By elucidating types of Hiyal and commenting on works by Shaybani and Khassaf, of the Hanafi Fiqh, and Qazwini, a Shafi'e jurist, Schacht relates a part of Hiyal to casuistry practices that could mislead the people. Study of a vast literature in this regard would reveal that the legality of Hiyal refers to some procedural devices advising people to be careful in making contracts and framing legal statements. The purpose would be to avoid clashes with the law and not to avoid the law. Accordingly, Hiyal, to the extent that they are acceptable, are precautionary devices and a counterpart of Shariat literature.[78]

Mahmasani narrates the following bases for the prohibition of Hiyal:

> "First – the Sharī'ah texts are not aimed at the deeds themselves but rather at the interest which those deeds are intended to serve. Therefore, all acts should be interpreted in the light of their spirit and intent and not by their appearances... Second – attempts at bypassing the law are tantamount to deceit, and deceit is prohibited in Sharī'ah as evidenced by the Qur'ān and the Sunnah... Third – the Prophet, the Companions and the Followers have been quoted in opposition to legal fictions... Ibn Masud and Ibn Abbas, following the example of the Prophet, were reported to have ruled against acceptance of a gift from the debtor before settlement of the debt, because the purpose of a gift under such circumstances was the postponement of payment of the debt and a ruse to legalize interest. Similarly, Muslim jurists, their followers and the doctors of traditions such as Imam Bukhari agreed on the prohibition of legal fictions and on the necessity of avoiding them".[79]

According to Mahmasani, ruses or subterfuges are against the Shari'i spirit and are not permissible. The Shafi'e, Malikis and Hanbalis have declared the use of Hiyal as haram and totally prohibited, while according to Hanafis, only such Hiyal are permissible as are compatible with the spirit of the Sharī'ah. An example of a permissible Shari'i Hilah is that a borrower may sell something to a lender at a price which is less than its actual price, or the borrower may purchase something from the lender at a price higher than its actual price.[80] The purchaser can use the commodity himself or sell it in the market to get cash for other needs. However, this is the practice of real purchase and sale (termed Tawarruq) and different from Bai' al 'Inah that involves buy-back and that has been prohibited by the holy Prophet.

In Fatāwa Alamgiri (Hanafi Fiqh), a Hilah in terms of which a ruser sells a commodity of $1000 payable after a year and then buys the same commodity for $950 on cash payment, has been declared unlawful due to the involvement of the element of Riba. This practice is known as Bai' al 'Inah, defined as a double sale involving "buy-back", by which the borrower and the lender sell and then resell a commodity between them, once for cash and once for a higher price on credit, with the net result of a loan with interest.

Jurists consider 'Inah a stratagem whose function is to attain illegal ends through legal means. Ibn Qudama says: "If a person sells something on credit, it is not permissible to buy that commodity at a price less than the price at which he sold. Similarly, if a person sold something for cash and then purchased on credit at higher than the sale price, it would not

---

[77] Ali, n.d., **10**, p. 355–364.

[78] Schacht, 1964, pp. 81–84, 205–210.

[79] Mahmasani, 1961, pp. 124, 125; for detail see pp. 119–126.

[80] Mahmasani, 1961, p. 122.

be permissible. However, if he purchases at a price less than he sold for cash, it would be permissible".[81]

Although some jurists, particularly Shawafi', allow 'Inah in specific cases,[82] jurists in general have prohibited it. Even the Shafi'es do not give tacit approval for this. Saiful Azhar Rosly and Mahmood M. Sanusi have concluded in a study: "We have argued therefore in the above that the view of Imam Shafi'e has reached a level which is similar to the other Muslim schools, although the methodology which he adopted appears to be different as he considered that when the legal preconditions of the contract are fulfilled, it cannot be cancelled on the account of the intention of the parties. Likewise, this study finds no significant Sharī'ah justification of Bai' al 'Inah."[83]

On this basis, the Sharī'ah committee of Al Baraka has not approved the purchasing of a commodity by a company on credit for $20 and then selling it for cash for $15 to a sister company (holding company) on account of this being Bai' al 'Inah.[84] This means that actually, the commodity has been purchased back by the same seller who undertakes a transaction only to get interest. However, if one of the two companies is not fully owned by the owner of the first company, this would not amount to Bai' al 'Inah, as the commodity has not been sold only to the first seller but also to others. This would be permissible provided there was not any manipulation to circumvent the Riba prohibition.

In fact, in most such cases, no handing over or possession takes place, as had been the case in buy-back-based mark-up operations in the NIB system in Pakistan adopted in the 1980s that were declared non-Sharī'ah-compliant by the Sharī'ah Courts.

Another form of 'Inah is where one person asks another: "Buy for me (from a third party) such and such an object for ten dinars in cash, and I will buy it from you for 12 dinars on credit."[85] This transaction does not necessarily constitute Riba so long as the parties engage in normal trade and ownership is actually transferred. However, Maliki jurists prohibit it on the grounds of blocking the means (to an illicit end) (Sadd al-Zarāi'). Ibn Taymiyah, a Hanbali jurist, in this respect says: "And if the person who requests [that the other buy an object for cash and sell it to him on credit with an increase] aims [by concluding this transaction] at obtaining dirhams (money) against a greater quantity of dirhams at term, and the seller also aims at the same thing, then this is Riba, and there is no doubt as to its prohibition, no matter how it is arrived at. Indeed actions are to be judged by intentions, and each person has his intention".

Ibn Taymiyah goes on to divide 'Inah sales into three groups according to the buyer's intention:

1. He buys the goods (on credit) in order to use them, such as food, drink and the like, in which case this is sale, which God has permitted.
2. He buys the goods in order to trade with them; this is trade, which God has permitted.
3. He buys the goods to get dirhams, which he needs, and it was difficult for him to borrow or sell something on a Salam contract (immediate payment for future delivery), so he

[81] Ibn Qudama, 1367 AH, **4**, pp. 174–177.
[82] See Nawavi in his annotation of *Sahih Muslim*, 1981, **6**, p. 21.
[83] Rosly and Sanusi, 1999.
[84] Al Baraka, 1997, p. 128.
[85] cf. Ray, 1995, p. 56.

buys a good in order to sell it and take its price. This, then, is Tawarruq (a form of 'Inah), which is Makrooh (reprehensible) according to the most eminent of the jurists.[86]

Another variant of sale and repurchase transactions is when a person sells his house and takes the price, but then, for example, the purchaser promises that whenever he gives the price back, the latter will resell the house to him. This is a ruse permitted by Hanafi jurists subject to certain conditions. Such an arrangement, termed Bai' bil Wafa in the Hanafi Fiqh, basically treats the sold asset as collateral until the amount is paid back by the other party to the sale. In this arrangement, a person sells his house and takes the payment; the buyer promises to the seller that whenever the latter gives him back the price of the house, he will resell the house to him. The Hanafi jurists have opined that if the resale of the house to the original seller is made a condition for the initial sale, it is not allowed. However, if the first sale is executed without any condition, but after effecting the sale, the buyer promises to resell the house whenever the seller offers to him the same price, this promise is acceptable and it creates not only a moral obligation, but also an enforceable right of the original seller. Even if the promise has been made before effecting the first sale, after which the sale has been effected without a condition, it is allowed by certain Hanafi jurists.[87]

On the basis of the above, some forms of repurchase promises have been allowed by the Sharī´ah scholars, and Islamic banks provide housing finance through the arrangement of Diminishing Musharakah. Banks purchase a part of the ownership of the client in a plot of land/house and the client promises to repurchase the same after the lapse of a period in which its market value changes, generally one year. The period of one year has been suggested by scholars so that the transaction might not enter into the prohibited category of Bai' al 'Inah or a sale and buy-back arrangement.[88]

## 6.12   OPTIONS IN SALES (KHIYAR)

The Sharī´ah demands that the seller should disclose all the defects in the article being sold. Otherwise the sale is not valid. When a person has made a purchase and was not aware, at the time of sale or previously, of a defect in the article bought, he has an option, whether the defect is small or big, and he may either be content with it at the agreed price or reject it. If a seller has sold an asset as being possessed of some specific quality, and that asset turns out to be without that quality, the buyer has an option to annul the contract. It is to be recognized, however, that the right to exercise an option is not automatic. It has to be specified at the time of entering into the contract. This brings us to another extraordinary peculiarity of Islamic law: the doctrine of option or the right of cancellation (Khiyar).

Even when a sale is duly executed, free from any grounds of illegality, it still may not be absolutely binding on the parties involved if the condition of option is provided in the contract (Khiyar al-Shart).[89] So long as the parties do not leave the place of contract, any of them can cancel the deal (Khiyar al-Majlis). However, if it is stipulated that the contract has been finalized even if the parties do not separate, Khiyar al-Majlis will not be available.[90]

---

[86]   Ibn Taymiyah, fatāwa, 440/29, 431/29; cf. Ray, 1995, pp. 56, 57.

[87]   Usmani, 2000a, p. 88 with reference from Jami'ul-Fusoolain **2**, p. 237 and Radd al-Muhtar, **4**, p. 135.

[88]   Usmani, 2000a, pp. 82–92.

[89]   Al Jaziri, 1973, pp. 339, 340, 357–362; Tirmidhi, 1988, Nos 1268, 1269, pp. 13–15, 16.

[90]   Al Jaziri, 1973, pp. 343–345.

This concept of option is entirely different from the "options" that are simply the rights sold/bought in the conventional derivatives markets. Such transactions do not fulfil the conditions required for a valid sale. We shall discuss options and other derivatives in detail in Chapter 8.

The Sharī'ah literature discusses the concept of option in trade wherefrom we conclude that the informationally disadvantaged party at the time of entering into the contract can have the option to cancel the contract within a specified period. The Prophet (pbuh) himself recommended to one of his Companions to reserve an option for three days in all his purchases. Jurists are unanimous on the validity of this kind of option. However, they differ on options for more than three days.[91] Such option stipulation can be reserved by either of the parties.

Aside from this, the purchaser has an option without any stipulation with regard to things he has purchased without seeing, and also on account of defects in the commodity being sold. The greatest of all defects is the lack of a title or of the right to sell on the part of the seller. The parties can also agree that if payment is not made within three days, the contract will be annulled. This is called an option of payment (Khiyar-e-Naqad). This sale would be valid only if payment was made within the specified number of days.[92]

The following five types of options among various forms discussed in Fiqh books are important:

- Khiyar al-Shart: a stipulation that any of the parties has the option to rescind the sale within so many (specified) days; this is also termed Bai' al Khiyar.
- Khiyar al Ro'yat: an option to be exercised on inspecting the goods – goods, if not according to the contract, can be returned after inspection if such an option has been provided for in the sale agreement.
- Khiyar al 'Aib: an option with regard to defect – goods can be returned if found to be defective; this kind of option is available even if no such condition is stipulated in the contract if the defect was not brought to the notice of the buyer at the time of the contract and the defect caused a visible decrease in the value of the sold commodity.[93] However, if the seller declares at the time of the contract that he will not be held responsible for any defect in the commodity, the contract is valid according to Hanafis.[94]
- Khiyar al Wasf: the option of quality – where goods are sold by specified quality, but that quality is absent, the goods can be returned.
- Khiyar-e-Ghaban: the option relating to price – where goods are sold at a price far higher than the market price, and the client is told or given the impression that he has been charged the market price.

As regards the Khiyar al Ro'yat, jurists differ as to whether the sale of unseen items is binding or not.[95] Ibn Hazm contends that if a person purchases an unseen commodity but the seller has sufficiently described its features and the commodity conforms to those features,

[91] Al Jaziri, 1973, p. 358.
[92] Al Jaziri, 1973, pp. 358, 359.
[93] Al Jaziri, 1973, pp. 381–383.
[94] Al Jaziri, 1973, p. 395.
[95] Ibn Hazm, 1988, 7, pp. 214, 215.

it would be unjust not to purchase the commodity by using Khiyar al Ro'yat.[96] Shaikh Al Dhareer writes in this regard:

> "The Hanafis and the Shafi'is have held in one view that the sale is not binding on the buyer. Upon viewing, he can revoke it or ratify it. It means that he has the option of (rejecting) upon seeing the object even if it is found to be consistent with the manner described; for not seeing the object obstructs the completion of the transaction. Since this sale is known as the sale with the option of seeing, it must include such option. The Malikis and the Shafi'is have held, in one of their views, and so did the Hanbalis, that the sale is binding on the buyer should he find the object corresponding to the way earlier described to him. But if he found it different, he has the option either to ratify the sale or to revoke it. This is a manifestly cogent view".[97]

In Salam and Istisna'a, Khiyar al Ro'yat is not available if the goods are according to the specifications already stipulated.

In the case of Murabaha to Purchase Orderer, the client would have the options of defect and specification/quality. If the assets or the goods required by the client are not according to the stipulated specification or have any material defect, the client will have the right not to purchase the goods as per his promise, and if Murabaha is executed, he will have the right to rescind the sale unless the bank gets a certificate of fitness just at the time of the sale after giving the client sufficient opportunity to examine the asset.

## 6.13  SUMMARY

A valid sale contract must fulfil the following requirements.

1. The parties must enter into the contract voluntarily with full/free consent.
2. Both parties must be fully competent – intellectually sound adults.
3. The subject of the sale must be a property of value acceptable in Sharī´ah – it must be pure, lawful (Mubāh), clean, wholesome and, of course, marketable and having legal and commercial value. From the Sharī´ah perspective, its underlying cause must be lawful and it must not be proscribed by Islamic law nor a nuisance to public order or morality.
4. The seller must be the owner of the object being sold, or he must be authorized to sell by dint of contracts like partnership, agency or guardianship (of a minor).
5. The seller must be in a position to deliver the goods.
6. Both parties must take cognizance of the object of the sale by examining or by adequate description.
7. The price must be precisely determined and known to the parties at finalization of the contract.
8. All permissible goods can be purchased/sold on credit in exchange for cash – the counter values not being homogenous. This means that all goods that are not of the Thaman kind can be sold for currency on credit.
9. The credit price of a commodity can be more than its cash-n-carry price. But the price must be precisely determined when the sale contract is completed. In the case of late payment by the debtor in a credit sale, the seller cannot get any compensation from the buyer.

[96] Ibn Hazm, 1988, **7**, p. 216.
[97] Al-Dhareer, 1997, p. 33 (quoting from Al-Bada'i, 5/392; Al-Muhazzab, I/263; Al-Muntaqa or Al-Muwatta, 4/287).

10. Money cannot be traded as a commodity and financial transactions must be supported by genuine trade or business-related activities.

This chapter has also discussed elements of Gharar and the prohibited sales due to the involvement of Gharar and Riba. The Sharī´ah position of Hiyal (legal ruses) and Bai' al 'Inah have been discussed to describe the possible limits within which products can be developed by Islamic banks. The concept of option (Khiyar) and its relevance to the Islamic banking business has also been discussed in some detail.

# 7
## Loan and Debt in Islamic Commercial Law

### 7.1  INTRODUCTION

Conventional banks receive money from depositors and lend it to borrowers on the basis of interest. In other words, their business relates to loaning based on interest in one way or the other. The superstructure of Islamic banks is based on profit/loss sharing (PLS) or modes that culminate in debts that do not carry interest. They mobilize deposits generally on the basis of profit/loss sharing, with the exception of a small portion comprising current deposits that are generally treated as loans and in some cases Wadi'ah/Amānah (trust). On the assets side, Islamic banks use PLS as well as debt-creating modes based on trading and leasing activities. Practically, a large part of their assets is based on modes that generate debt.

In Sharī´ah, loaning is a virtuous act that does not provide for any compensation for the use of lent money.[1] This implies that the person who takes a loan is obliged to pay only the principal and any demand for an excess would make the loan usurious. It is, therefore, important to discuss the Sharī´ah rules relating to loans and debts and this chapter is dedicated to a discussion in this regard.

Islamic financial institutions (IFIs) create debts as they provide a credit facility in the form of credit sale or lease of assets. Loaning may also be involved in some situations. Areas to be discussed include the objects of loans, the rules of loaning, the repayment of loans and debts, excess payment as gifts, security and surety, responsibilities of the sureties, assignment of debt or Hawalah, punishment to the debtor in case of his (wilful) default, instructions for the creditor and duties of the debtor, the sale of a debt for a debt, prepayment rebate and issues related to insolvency.

### 7.2  THE TERMS DEFINED

The terms used in the Holy Qur'ān, Hadith and Fiqh in this regard are Qard, Salaf and Dayn. While the former two terms relate to the giving or taking of loans, Dayn comes into existence as a result of any other contract or credit transaction. The literal meaning of Qard is "to cut". It is so called because the property is cut off from lender's ownership when it is given to the borrower. Legally, Qard means to give anything having value in the ownership of any other by way of virtue so that the latter can avail himself of the same for his benefit with the condition that the same or similar amount of that thing should be paid back on demand or at the settled time. Jurists are unanimous on this legal definition.[2]

---

[1]  Al Jaziri, 1973, pp. 300, 677–680.
[2]  Ibn Hazm, 1988, **6**, p. 347, No. 1191; Al Jaziri, 1973, pp. 300, 301, 677–680.

The Shariat Appellate Bench (SAB) of the Supreme Court of Pakistan has quoted what Syed Mohammad Tantawi of Al Azhar (Egypt) considers about Qard and Dayn. He says:

"Qard (as a term) is more particular than Dayn, as it is that loan which a person gives to another as help, charity or an advance for a certain time. . . . A Dayn is incurred either by way of rent or sale or purchase or in any other way which leaves it as a debt to another. Duyun (debts) ought to be returned without any profit since they are advanced to help the needy and meet their demands and, therefore, the lender should not impose on the borrower more than what he had lent."[3]

The word "Salaf" literally means a loan which draws forth no profit for the creditor.[4] In a wider sense, it includes loans for specified periods, i.e. short, intermediate and long-term loans. Salaf is another name for Salam, wherein the price of the commodity is paid in advance while the commodity or the counter value is supplied in the future, as specified in the Salam contract that creates a liability for the seller. Qard is, in fact, a particular kind of Salaf. If the amount can be demanded at any time or immediately, it is called Qard or a loan payable on demand.

Therefore, loans under Islamic law can be classified into Salaf and Qard, the former being a loan for a fixed time and the latter payable on demand.[5] Dayn is created as a result of any credit transaction in which one of the counter values is deferred.

Another term used for borrowing goods is 'Āriyah, which means to give any commodity to another for use without taking any return. In this sense, it is also a virtuous act like Qard. The borrowed commodity is treated as a liability of the borrower, who is bound to return it to its owner. In the address of the last pilgrimage, the holy Prophet (pbuh) said: "al 'Āriyah has to be returned, a surety must make good the loss on behalf of the assured and the debts payable must be paid".[6]

The difference between Qard and 'Āriyah is that in the latter, exactly the borrowed commodity has to be returned while in Qard, the similar of the loaned commodity has to be paid by the debtor. In order to prepare for Ghazwa-e-Hunain, some time after the conquest of Makkah, the holy Prophet (pbuh) took as 'Āriyah a number of camels and iron breast-plates from Safwan bin Umayyah. The holy Prophet (pbuh) assured him that 'Āriyah would be paid back in full. While giving back, some of the plates were found to be missing. The holy Prophet asked him how he could compensate him. But Safwan, who had converted to Islam, waived the loss.[7]

The English word "loan" seems to be the counterpart of the word Qard and "debt" that of Dayn. The loans/advances given by the present banking system are covered under any of these two categories. In Murabaha operations by IFIs, goods are sold and Duyun/debts are created, which ought to be returned without any profit over the amount of debt, as all conditions relating to Dayn would be applicable to them.

---

[3] Shariat Appellate Bench, 2000, pp. 217, 218.

[4] Al-Qattan, n.d., p. 357.

[5] Among the jurists, this is the opinion of the Hanafi, Shafi'e and Hanbali schools. To these jurists, Qard is among Duyun Hālah (that can be demanded any time). Particularly, Imam Abu Hanifa is of the view that any Qard can be called back by the lender at any time. The same is the view of Ibn Hazm. According to Malik, when a time is settled for repayment (Qard-e-Muajjallah), the lender cannot demand its earlier payment (Al-Ayni, n.d., Kitab al Ishtiqraz; Ibn Hazm, 1988, 6, pp. 350, 351; Al-Atasi, 1403 AH, 1, p. 439).

[6] Tirmidhi, 1988, p. 20 (Kitab al Buyoo, chapter on al 'Āriyah). For details on 'Āriyah, see Ibn Qudama, 1367 AH, 5, pp. 203–210.

[7] Abu Daud, 1952, Kitab al Buyoo.

The legality of Qard is proved beyond doubt by the Sunnah of the holy Prophet (pbuh) and the consensus of the jurists.[8] At the time of Ghazwa Hunain, the holy Prophet borrowed for the Islamic State forty thousand dirhams from Abdullah Ibn Rabi'ah (Abpwh).[9] Loan advancing by way of Qard, according to the sayings of the holy Prophet, is more pleasing to Allah (SWT) than alms-giving.[10] According to another Hadith, Qard is equivalent to half Sadaqah (charity) (although it is received back in full).[11]

In view of all these definitions and the Sunnah of the holy Prophet, it may be said that Qard is a kind of loan advanced for the benefit of the borrower and the creditor can demand it back any time. Ownership of the loaned goods is transferred to the borrower who can use, buy, sell or donate it as he wishes, like his other belongings.[12] Salaf is used for a loan of fixed tenure, and in that sense it is closer to Dayn and both these types are the liabilities created on account of credit transactions for a fixed tenure.

Loans may consist of any things that are valuable and their similar or substitute becomes payable immediately or on demand in the case of Qard and at the stipulated time in the case of Salaf and Dayn. Further, a Qard should not be conditional upon any other contract like Bai'.[13]

## 7.3    ILLEGALITY OF COMMERCIAL INTEREST

Contemporary Sharī'ah scholars have reached the consensus that modern commercial interest comes under the purview of Riba and no form of loan/debt based on interest is exempt from this prohibition.[14] It is established from the available literature that the Riba prohibited by the Holy Qur'ān included different forms which were practised by the Arabs of Jahiliyyah.[15] Financing on the basis of Riba was a commercial profession of the rich at that time. The common feature of all these transactions was that an increased amount was charged on the principal amount of a debt. At times, this debt was created through a transaction of sale and sometimes it was created through a loan. Similarly, the increased amount was at times charged on a monthly/yearly basis, while the principal was to be paid at a stipulated date, and sometimes it was charged along with the principal. All these forms used to be called Riba.

All loans that embody any benefit over and above the principal as a precondition are void, irrespective of the fact that the condition embodies any gain in quantity or quality. Hanafi jurist Al-Sarakhsi says: "When the accrual of benefit is laid down in the loan contract as a precondition, it would be a loan carrying benefit, prohibited by the holy Prophet".[16] Ibn Qudama in *Al Mughni* opines: "All jurists agree that any loan containing a condition giving effect to an increase in it is illegal . . . it being immaterial whether the increase accrues in

---

[8] Nisai, n.d., **7**, p. 303; Ibn Qudama, 1367 AH, **4**, p. 313 (Baab al Qard).

[9] Nisai, n.d., **7**, p. 314, Kitab al Buyoo, Babal Istiqraz.

[10] Zuhayli, 1985, **4**, pp. 720, 721.

[11] Jassas, 1999, p. 426.

[12] Ibn Hazm, 1988, **6**, p. 350, No. 1196.

[13] Zuhayli, 1985, **4**, p. 720. Any condition that more or less than the loaned amount would be returned would make the loan usurious (Ibn Hazm, 1988, **6**, p. 347, No. 1193).

[14] Shariat Appellate Bench, 2000, pp. 459–463, 522–567; Ayub, 2002, pp. 19–28, 39, 40, 221–260.

[15] See Ibn-abi-Hātim, 1997, No. 2913.

[16] Al-Sarakhsi, n.d., **14**, p. 35.

quantity or in quality".[17] The jurists also agree that if a loan is tied to the condition of increase or any other benefit, it entails Riba, irrespective of whether it is in the form of money or not.[18] Ibn Qudama reports from Ibn al-Munzar: "The jurists are unanimous on the point that any binding on the part of the lender upon the borrower entailing an increase or embodying a gift or a present above the principal is Riba".

It is reported that Ibn Abbas and Ibn Masud (Abpwth) forbade extending a loan entailing benefit because a loan contract is a contract of mutual kindness and closeness. Whenever it contains a clause to effect an increase above the principal, it kills the spirit of lending. There is no distinction in this increase whether it occurs in quantity or in quality, as, for example, if one person lends to another person debased coins in return for un-debased coins, or lends units of currency in return for "better units" in the future, the transactions will become illegal.[19] If it is laid down in the loan contract that the borrower will rent out his house to the lender or he will sell something to him or will extend him a loan on another occasion, it becomes illegal because the holy Prophet (pbuh) has prohibited making a contract of sale involving another contract of loan as a condition, as the lender in this case binds one contract with another contract and this is not permitted.[20]

## 7.4  LOANING AND THE BANKING SYSTEM

Deposits and investments with conventional banks and in government securities are covered under the definition of Qard because not only their principal is guaranteed, but also banks and/or the governments stipulate to pay a return on the deposits/investments that is either fixed or not linked with the outcome of their economic activities. Banks use the amount so mobilized as they wish and are fully liable for their repayment, even in the case of loss to the banks. Current accounts of banks are also categorized as loans because banks are as much liable to the current account holders as to the fixed account holders. On the assets side also, conventional banks' financing mostly takes the form of loans or debts for consumption durables or business activities like working capital finance, trade finance, project finance, BMR, micro and SME finance, government finance, etc. Direct intermediation by the investment banks for facilitating the corporate sector also sometimes takes the form of interest-based transactions.

The majority of writers on Islamic finance hold that banks in the Islamic framework will continue to work as intermediaries.[21] Some Islamic economists have recommended that banks remain as intermediaries, but they should also act as traders or institutions dealing in tangible goods. They may adopt universal banking and holding company models having fully owned subsidiaries/mutual funds for various types of financing operations.[22] Whatever may be their structure, Islamic banks should not be in a position to earn money from money and should be involved in real goods for the purpose of financing. As such, by using trade- and lease-based modes/products, they are creating debt and have to abide by the Sharī´ah rules relating to Dayn.

---

[17] Ibn Qudama, 1367 AH, **IV**, pp. 319, 320.
[18] Jawad 1966, **III**, p. 274.
[19] Ibn Qudama, 1367 AH, **IV**, pp. 319, 320.
[20] Ibn Qudama, 1367 AH, **IV**, p. 320.
[21] Shariat Appellate Bench, 2000, p. 254.
[22] Khan, 1999.

## 7.5   GUIDANCE FROM THE HOLY QUR'ĀN ON LOANS AND DEBTS

The Holy Qur'ān provides guidance on various aspects of loans and debts. It says:

> "O ye who believe! When ye deal with each other, in lending or transactions involving future obligations for a fixed period of time, reduce it to writing. Let a scribe write down faithfully between the parties; let not the scribe refuse to write: as Allah has taught him, so let him write. Let him who incurs the liability dictate, but let him fear his Lord Allah, and not diminish, aught of what he owes. If the person liable is mentally deficient or weak, or unable himself to dictate, let his guardian dictate faithfully and get two witnesses, out of your own men, and if there are not two men, then a man and two women, such as you choose for witnesses, so that if one of them errs, the other can remind her. The witness should not refuse when they are called on (for evidence). Disdain not to reduce to writing (your contracts) for a future period, whether it be small or big: it is juster in the sight of Allah, more suitable as evidence, and more convenient to prevent doubts among yourselves, but if it be transaction which you carry out on the spot among yourselves, there is no blame on you if you reduce it not to writing. But, take witnesses whenever you make a commercial contract; and let neither the scribe nor the witness suffer harm. If you do (such harm), it would be wickedness in you. So fear Allah; for it is Allah that teaches you. And Allah is well acquainted with all things. If you are on a journey and cannot find a scribe, a pledge with possession (may serve the purpose) . . . "[23]

The first part of the above verse deals with transactions involving future payment, while the second part guides on transactions in which payment and delivery are made on the spot. For credit transactions, the Qur'ān recommends witnesses and documentation, while for transactions performed on the spot, no written evidence is required except oral witnesses and even these oral witnesses can be dispensed with if the parties trust each other. Ibn Hazm considers the witnesses necessary in the case of credit transactions.[24] They provide safeguards against disputes that may arise in the absence of documentation and witnesses and allow loan transactions for a fixed or known time period. Transactions involving advance payment such as Salam (whereby a price is paid in advance for a specified commodity to be delivered at an agreed time in the future) and Bai' Mu'ajjal (sale for a price to be paid in the future) are covered under this verse. Hence, the Qur'ān guides one to commercial morality of the highest standard in the most practical manner, as man has been advised to do business as if all transactions are to be carried out as in the presence of God Almighty.

## 7.6   THE SUBSTANCE OF LOANS

The question of which things can be loaned is important for any discussion on the subject. Besides goods serving as Thaman, Qard can be given in all those goods that are Mubāh (permissible), have value and their similar is available, enabling repayment. According to the Hanafi school of thought, a loan should consist of fungibles only (similars of weight and measure).[25] However, as we see in the Sunnah of the holy Prophet, Qard can also be taken of animals, which are not fungibles. The other three schools of thought allow it in terms

---

[23] Holy Qur'ān: 2: 282, 283.
[24] Ibn Hazm, 1988, **7**, pp. 224–226, No. 1415.
[25] Al Jaziri, 1973, pp. 678, 679.

of all such commodities that can be sold except human beings.[26] However, the amount and value of loan should be known without any doubt.[27]

According to the Maliki school, Qard is a loan of something "valuable" granted only as a favour and not by way of 'Āriyah[28] or Hibah (gift) but to recover it in the form in which it was granted. The word "valuable" is specifically used to exclude that which is not valuable from the definition of Qard, and the word "favour" to show that the benefit is for the borrower alone and not for the lender. Under this definition, Qard may consist of anything that is valuable, be it merchandise, animals or similars of weight and that can be the subject of Salam.[29]

## 7.7  REPAYMENT OF THE PRINCIPAL ONLY

Lending/borrowing is, indeed, unavoidable in human life, and, therefore, is permissible in Islam. Had it not been permissible, the holy Prophet would never have set an example of a borrower both for the Islamic State and for private purposes. However, borrowing should not be taken as a means for lavish consumption. In that sense, Islam discourages the act of borrowing.[30] Besides, it has to be borne in mind that a loan must be paid. Debt is not forgiven, even for martyrs. Further, a loan whereby something in excess of the principal is exacted becomes unlawful, as it amounts to Riba. There is no exemption on the basis that a Qard transaction has taken place between a Muslim and a non-Muslim, an employer and an employee or a State and the people.[31] Prohibition of Riba means that money can be lent without any expectation of return over the amount of the principal, and as such, every loan that draws forth or stipulates profit is unlawful.

The holy Prophet (pbuh) has said that after making a loan, the creditor must even refrain from accepting a present from the borrower unless exchange of such presents was in practice between the borrower and the lender before the advancement of the loan.[32] However, some indirect benefits that have become customary that do not involve any cost for the borrower have been considered permissible. For example, jurists see no harm if it is agreed between the parties that the debt will be paid in some other country if it is in the interests of both parties. Ibn Zubair, for instance, used to accept sums of money from the inhabitants of Makkah to be paid in Iraq through drafts drawn upon his brother Mus'ab, who lived in Iraq. To this, Ibn Abbas and Ali (Gbpwth) did not make any objection.[33]

## 7.8  TIME VALUE OF MONEY IN LOANS AND DEBTS

While in trading of goods it is permitted that the credit price of a commodity be different from its cash price, no value can be assigned to the time given for payment of a receivable

---

[26] Muslim with annotation by Nawavi, 1981/1401, **11**, pp. 36–38. For details see also Zuhayli, 1985, **4**, p. 723.

[27] Ibn Hazm, 1988, No. 1203, p. 356; Al Jaziri, 1973, pp. 680–692.

[28] 'Āriyah means gratuitous loan of nonconsumable goods, exactly the same commodity has to be returned after using for the time given.

[29] Al Jaziri, 1973, p. 678; Ibn Hazm, 1988, **6**, pp. 355–357.

[30] The holy Prophet used to pray to Allah Almighty not to be suppressed under debt. (Ibn Hajar, **5**, p. 60). See also Waliullah, 1353 H, p. 56.

[31] Ibn Hazm, 1988, **7**, p. 467, No. 1506.

[32] Ibn Qudama, 1367 AH, **4**, pp. 319–321.

[33] Ibid.

once its amount is mutually stipulated. This is because money is not regarded as a lawful commodity for homogeneous exchange except in equal sums. One hundred dollars have to be exchanged for one hundred dollars only. We have discussed the issue of the time value of money in detail in Chapter 4. It was explained that time valuation is approved by the Sharī'ah in business and trade and not in Qard or Dayn, because the latter are considered virtuous acts from which one cannot take any benefit.

The Sharī'ah does recognize a difference in value due to a time element, and does not prohibit realizing the time value of money in a business. What is prohibited is any claim to the time value of money as a predetermined quantity calculable at a predetermined rate not related to any real sector business. All currency notes (of various denominations) are factually homogeneous in that they all represent purchasing power (as dinars and dirhams did in the time of the holy Prophet) and are legal tender, their genus and 'Illah are also the same. Therefore, a person who is to avoid loaning on Riba cannot resort to the sale or lease of currency notes, as they are not subjects of sale and lease like common goods and assets.

Similarly, government securities and bonds or savings certificates command value as gold or silver commands value and, therefore, are money. While gold or silver may serve as both Thaman and Mabi', bonds or currency notes reflect value only, as the latter have no value in the absence of the government authority and as such cannot serve as Mabi'.

## 7.9   INSTRUCTIONS FOR THE DEBTOR

The foremost duty of the debtor is to repay the loan in fulfilment of the promise or contract made with the creditor.[34] Wilful default or procrastination in payment of due debt has been equated by the holy Prophet to injustice.[35] According to a Hadith, a debtor who is able to pay but does not repay the debt can be arrested and embarrassed.[36] According to another Hadith, the greatest sin after Kabāir, is to leave, after death, unpaid debt where there is no one to pay the same.[37] In the case of Qard, the creditor has the right to ask for repayment even before the date of promise. In desperate circumstances when the debtor is really unable to pay, he should take the creditor into his confidence and regret his inability to pay the debt. The holy Prophet (pbuh) has warned that a believer's soul remains encumbered with the debt until he pays.[38] He also said that the best among people is he who is the best in payment of his liabilities.[39] That is why, the holy Prophet did not offer funeral prayer for a Companion (Gbpwh) until his debt was taken over by someone else.[40] The Sharī'ah even allows punishment of a debtor who does not pay his debt, and if he defaults wilfully, he can be arrested, punished and dealt with harshly.[41]

The huge numbers of nonperforming loans (NPL) of banks at present in almost all countries of the world reveal that borrowers do not make serious efforts to fulfil their responsibility to pay their debts while they continue their lavish lifestyles. According to Islamic teachings,

---

[34] Qur'ān, 17: 34.

[35] Tirmidhi, 1988, No. 1331, pp. 30, 31; Muslim, 1981, **10**, p. 227.

[36] Jassas, 1999, **2**, p. 410.

[37] Jassas, 1999, **2**, p. 425.

[38] Nisai, n.d., **7**, pp. 314, 315; Tirmidhi, 1988, Kitab al Buyoo, Bal al Aflas.

[39] Tirmidhi, 1988, Nos 1061–1063, pp. 30, 31; Muslim, **11**, p. 37; also in Bukhari, kitab al Wakalah.

[40] Bukhari, **4**, pp. 466, 467, No. 2289; **5**, p. 6; Kitab al Hawalah. It was the time when the Islamic State was unable to pay such debts and liabilities.

[41] Bukhari, **5**, p. 62 (Kitab al Istiqraz); Tirmidhi, 1988, No.1339; Nisai, n.d., **7**, pp. 316, 317.

a borrower, while taking loans, must have a firm intention to repay,[42] and if his intention is to blemish or to usurp the loan amount, God (SWT) will spoil him. Islam requires that a debtor should not only pay the debt in time, but also express thanks and pay gratitude to the creditor while repaying the amount.[43] It is also desirable on the part of the authorities to make relevant laws and accounting and auditing standards to minimize the chances of nonpayment of loans or other moral hazard threats in present-day societies.

## 7.10   INSTRUCTIONS FOR THE CREDITOR

The Holy Qur'ān encourages creditors to give more time for payment, or even to waive the loan amount, if the debtor is in dire straits.[44] In a number of traditions, the holy Prophet (pbuh) has encouraged lending by indicating it a highly virtuous act, liked by Allah Almighty.[45] He encouraged creditors to be polite to debtors and to waive a part of the loan. Abu Hadrad, a Companion, was unable to pay a loan that was due to another Companion Ka'ab Ibn Malik (Abpwth). When the latter insisted, the holy Prophet asked him to waive half of the debt, and when he was agreed on this, the debtor was advised to repay the remaining half from wherever he could arrange.[46]

The majority of jurists, particularly the Maliki and Shafi'e jurists, do not allow punishment or arrest of debtors who are really in trouble, and recommend giving more time.[47] Imam Abu Hanifa is of the view that a person who does not pay his debt when it is due, should be put in prison for two to three months; after which, information should be taken about his capability to repay, and if he is really in trouble, he may be acquitted.

In the case of a debt with a settled due date, the creditor cannot ask for earlier repayment so long as the debtor does not transgress the terms and conditions.[48]

However, if the creditor is not inclined to give more time for payment, he cannot be compelled to do so and the debtor would then be required to pay one way or another. A number of instances in the early history of Islam lead us to the point that even a destitute debtor is not entitled to get more time as his right.[49] He will not be remitted of the repayment of debt and whatever he earns over and above his normal food needs, should go towards repayment of the debt.[50]

## 7.11   HUSNAL QADHA (GRACIOUS PAYMENT OF LOAN/DEBT)

Repaying a loan in excess of the principal and without a precondition is commendable and compatible with the Sunnah of the holy Prophet (pbuh). Jabir (Abpwh) says that the Prophet (pbuh) owed to him a debt; "he paid to me and gave me more than the principal".[51] Similarly,

---

[42] Nisai, n.d., **7**, pp. 315, 316; also in Sahih Bukhari, **5**, pp. 54, 55.

[43] While repaying a debt of 40 000 dirhams, the holy Prophet prayed for Abdullah b. Abu Rabiah (Abpwh) and said "thanksgiving and timely payment is the reward for the creditor" (Nisai).

[44] Qur'ān, 2: 282. The holy Prophet has also emphasized it, see Tirmidhi, 1988, No. 1329, p. 30.

[45] Muslim, 1981, **10**, pp. 224, 225 (Kitab al Musaqat), also in Tirmidhi, 1988, Kitab al Buyoo.

[46] Muslim, 1981, **11**, p. 23; Bukhari, **5**, p. 76, No. 2424 (Kitab fil Khosumat); Tirmidhi, 1988, No. 1340, p. 34.

[47] Muslim, 1981, **10**, p. 227.

[48] Ibn Hazm, 1988, **6**, p. 353, No. 1201.

[49] Ibn Hazm, 1988, **6**, pp. 420, 421.

[50] Ibn Hazm, 1988, **6**, pp. 423, 424.

[51] Muslim, 1981, **10**, p. 219; Nisai, n.d., **7**, pp. 283, 284, 318, 319; Ibn Qudama, 1367 AH, **4**, pp. 320, 321.

the holy Prophet ordered to pay a better camel in repayment of a debt as a camel of the age that was borrowed was not available at the time of repayment.

However, gracious repayment of debt is a matter of individual discretion and cannot be adopted as a system, because this would mean that a loan would necessarily yield a profit. All references in the Fiqh literature that we find in favour of gracious payment of debt indicate that addition should not be a precondition, explicit or implicit. But if it is adopted by banks or the government as a system, it would envisage addition, both explicit (in the form of a customary rate) and implicit (an investor would expect that he would get some return that may be in the form of the GNP's nominal rate of growth, for example).

Current account deposits in Islamic banks are considered loans and the bank is bound to return their full amount on call. Banks' income from the business is pooled and allocated to various categories of deposits/liabilities on the basis of weightages, assigned in advance. Current accounts will carry no weightage. As resolved by the Islamic Fiqh Council of the OIC, the liability to return the loan (current deposit) will not be affected by the bank's solvency or otherwise, meaning that the bank will pay the amount of the deposit irrespective of its profit or loss. The predominant Sharīʿah ruling, therefore, is that such accounts are not eligible for a share in profits, as they are not subject to risk and there shall be no return payable on them. The relationship between the depositor and the bank in the case of such deposits is that of a creditor and debtor. Banks may indicate in the account opening form that they will invest the funds deposited under current accounts at their own discretion in any of the Sharīʿah-compliant modes. Further, they will be at liberty to take service charges from the current account holders.

A departure from the general view in this regard is that some Sharīʿah boards have ruled that current accounts may be eligible for gifts but not for profits. The Sharīʿah supervisory board of the Faysal Islamic Bank of Sudan, for example, sees it as permissible to give prizes for deposits that bear no risk and, therefore, cannot get dividends. Such gifts may be given without prior knowledge of the account holders, so long as the prizes are varied and made on a nonregular basis, in order to help mobilize the funds and to achieve a just reward distribution between account holders and shareholders. Most Sharīʿah boards, however, do not favour such arrangements.

Another consideration is that a part of banks' income comprises non-fund income earned from currency transfers or other "customer services". As deposits in the current accounts are an important source of financial strength for banks, they can pass on a part of that income to such depositors as a gift, provided no such prior inducement is given to such depositors and it does not take the form of a system of return or earnings on deposits.

## 7.12  REMITTING A PART OF A LOAN AND PREPAYMENT REBATE

On the subject of remitting a part of the debt against early payment and other concessions to debtors, we come across three traditions of the holy Prophet (pbuh). Two contradictory (in meaning) traditions have been reported by Imam Baihaqi. Briefly these traditions are:

1. When the holy Prophet (pbuh) expelled Bani al Nadhir from Madina, he was told that debts were owed to some of them that had not become due; the Prophet said, "Dhaʿawoo wa Taʿajjloo" (remit a part of the receivable and take that earlier).

2. A Companion, Miqdad bin Aswad said that he gave someone a loan of a hundred dirhams. He needed money when the holy Prophet sent him along with a delegation. He asked the debtor to remit ten and pay ninety dirhams. He accepted and paid ninety dirhams. When the holy Prophet came to know, he said: "You got yourself and the other party involved in Riba".[52]

To reconcile the above two traditions, jurists generally believe that the remitted amount (in the first tradition) related to an amount of Riba that was accrued to Jews of Banu Nadhir. This they derive on the basis of details reported by the eminent jurist Wāqidi about the incident. He writes: ". . . Abu Rafi'i Salam bin al Haqiq had to get 120 dinars from Usaid bin Huzair. He agreed to get the principal of 80 dinars and remitted the excess".[53] This means that the remitted amount in Banu Nadhir's case was that of Riba and not the principal. That is why Imam Malik, while giving the view of Ibn Umar and Zaid bin Thabit (Gbpwth) on this aspect, describes that there is no difference of opinion about the illegality of remitting a part of Dayn payable by anyone and getting the remainder. To Imam Malik, this is just like a person giving more time after a debt becoming due and increasing the amount of debt. It is Riba without any doubt.[54]

The third tradition is reported by Bukhari, Muslim and others according to which the holy Prophet (pbuh) asked his Companion Ka'ab bin Malik to waive half of the debt payable by another Companion Abdullah bin Abi Hadrad while the former was pressing the latter to pay his debt; Ka'ab waived half of the debt. When Abdullah told that he had no resources to pay even half the debt, the Prophet asked him to arrange payment from wherever he could.[55]

Going into details and to resolve the issue, jurists have differentiated between the two categories of loans, i.e. Duyun Hālah (loans that have become due or could be called back at any time) and Duyun Mu'ajjalah (time of payment is settled between creditor and debtor and the debt is not yet due). Remission of a part in the former category (due loans) is allowed by almost all jurists on the rationale that in such loans, delay is not the right of the debtor.[56] It means that if a debt has become due and it has not yet been paid, the creditor can remit a part of the amount for early payment. In this respect, jurists also say that it should not be made a condition. Imam Malik has captioned a chapter, "If a person purchases on credit, it is not permissible to pay less before the due date" and quoted two traditions reported by Zaid b. Thabit and Abdullah b. Umar (Abpwth) not approving discounts on prepayment.

Shah Waliullah, in *Musawwa*, referring to the above two and the tradition of Ka'ab b. Malik and Abu Hadrad (Abpwth), according to which the former waived half of the debt on recommendation of the holy Prophet, has observed that the former two instances relate to debt not yet due while the latter was due debt (Dayn al Hālah). He also explains that time of repayment cannot be stipulated in the case of Qard, while in the case of a credit sale (and Dayn), the payment time can be settled in the contract.[57]

---

[52] Baihaqi, 1344 H, Kitab al Buyoo, **6**, p. 28.

[53] Waqdi, 1966, **1**, p. 374.

[54] Waliullah, 1353 H, Kitabl al Buyu (Riba fil Dayn), **1**, p. 606.

[55] "Ka'ab demanded his debt back from Ibn Abi Hadrad in the Mosque and their voices grew louder until Allah's Apostle heard them while he was in his house. He came out to them raising the curtain of his room and addressed Ka'ab, 'O Ka'ab!' Ka'ab replied, 'Labaik, O Allah's Apostle.' (He said to him), 'Reduce your debt to one half,' gesturing with his hand. Ka'ab said, 'I have done so, O Allah's Apostle!' On that, the Prophet said to Ibn Abi Hadrad, 'Get up and repay the debt, to him.' Muslim, **10**, pp. 219, 220; Bukhari, Kitab al Khasumat.

[56] Jassas, 1999, **2**, pp. 387–392.

[57] Waliullah, 1353 H, **2**, pp. 50, 51.

Some of the later Hanafi jurists distinguish between debts created as a result of Musawamah (bargaining on price) and those payable as a result of Murabaha–Mu'ajjal, wherein a profit margin is added by the seller keeping in mind the credit (payment) period. They say that if the debtor in Murabaha–Mu'ajjal pays earlier than the due date or if the debt becomes due on his death, then the creditor will have to remit the part of debt relating to the remaining period as the profit margin was charged against the time given for payment.[58] They allow this on account of benefit to both parties. The majority of contemporary Sharī'ah scholars, however, do not allow remission for earlier payment in Murabaha operations by banks. The OIC Fiqh Academy, the Sharī'ah committees of Islamic banks in the Middle East and Sharī'ah scholars in general consider that it would be similar to interest-based instalment sales techniques.

The AAOIFI Sharī'ah Standards also prohibit giving rebate to the client on early payment on a contractual basis, as under Murabaha, the price has to be fixed once and for all. However, if there is no commitment from the bank in respect of any discount in the Murabaha price, the AAOIFI standards allow the bank to give a rebate in the case of early payment at its sole discretion.[59] Experts therefore recommend that the matter should be brought to the knowledge of the Sharī'ah advisor, who may decide each case of rebate on merit.

## 7.13  PENALTY ON DEFAULT

The classical jurists were not generally in favour of pecuniary punishment or penalty to a debtor in case of a default in payment. They normally allowed harsh treatment or imprisonment.[60] In the resolutions passed in the early stages of Islamic banking evolution, the religious boards in Islamic banks also did not allow the provision of penalty clauses in Murabaha–Mu'ajjal agreements, giving an automatic right to the bank to impose fines so that Murabaha operations could not become a means of charging interest. According to the juristic rules of the Sharī'ah, the case of a wilful defaulter is similar to that of a usurper (Ghāsib) who is made to return any profit, along with the property, made by him on the usurped property.[61] Therefore, Sharī'ah scholars subsequently allowed imposing a penalty in cases of default by the banks' clients.

A heavy nonperforming portfolio and default on the part of the clients is a serious problem confronting financial institutions all over the world. This problem could be a threat to the success of the Islamic banking system. If clients do not honour their commitment in respect of timely payment of a debt created in an instalment sale, Murabaha or leasing, or do not pay the banks' share of profit in participatory modes, or do not deliver goods at the stipulated time in Salam and Istisna'a, it could cause irreparable loss to the system, the banks and financial institutions and ultimately to the savers and the respective economies.

Some of the classical jurists and almost all contemporary scholars allow punishment (T'azir) of such borrowers in the form of fines. In the opinion of some Maliki jurists, a delaying borrower should be obliged to pay for charitable activities.[62] In view of the

[58] Ibn Abideen, n.d., p. 757; Al-Atasi, 1403 AH, 2, p. 450.
[59] AAOIFI, 2004–5a, No. 8, pp. 122, 132.
[60] Jassas, 1999, 2, p. 411.
[61] Al Baraka, Resolutions (1981–2001), pp. 65, 66.
[62] AAOIFI, 2004–5a, No, 8, p. 132; Al Baraka, Resolutions and Recommendations (1981–2001), No. 12/8, p. 215.

severity of the problem, all Sharī´ah bodies like the Islamic Fiqh Council of the OIC, the AAOIFI, the Shariat Appellate Bench of the Supreme Court of Pakistan, etc. have approved the provision of penalty clauses embedded in contractual agreements that keep a balance between the requirement in view of the severity of the problem and that of the Sharī´ah conditions/principles to keep the fine difference between interest and a Murabaha profit intact. The penalty thus received has to be given to charity.[63]

Banks can claim liquidated damages or compensation for a loss arising from default. However, the amount of compensation should be decided by the court or any independent reconciliation committee, keeping in mind the loss incurred by the bank in profit that it could have earned if it had invested the amount on a similar project during the delay period.[64] The penalty proceeds should be given to charity because penalties on default in repayment cannot become a source of income for the creditor.[65] This implies that liquidated damages to be given to banks in cases of default on the part of the banks' clients should be based on actual loss. If required by any of the parties, the court may reasonably adjust the amount of compensation. The "actual loss" should not be the loss in terms of conventional "opportunity cost". It has to be proved by the bankers themselves to the satisfaction of the court or any arbitrator.

However, some Sharī´ah boards allow Islamic banks to charge from the defaulter the rate realized by them on their Murabaha portfolio during a specific period. They also recommend that the financial condition of the client be taken into account.[66] A Fatwah of the religious supervisory committee of Bank Al Baraka, Sudan says in this regard:

> "It is permissible for the bank and the Murabaha client to agree that the latter would pay compensation for harm he would cause the bank by reason of his delay in payment, on the condition that the harm caused to the bank be material and actual, and that the Murabaha borrower be prosperous (enough to pay) and (deliberately) tardy (in paying the debt). The best means of calculating the amount of this compensation is to base it on the actual profit realized by the bank during the period for which the Murabaha client delayed payment. For example, if the client delayed payment for three months, the bank would take the return on investment it had realized during those three months, and demand compensation from the Murabaha client at this realized rate of return. If the bank did not make any return during the relevant period, it would not demand anything from the client".[67]

In this context we will have to differentiate between Qard and Dayn, as jurists have approved imposing penalties in the latter case only. This means that in the case of a loan (Qard), the creditor should give more time,[68] while if the liability to pay has emerged from any sale or exchange transaction and the client is deferring the payment through dilatory tactics, he can be required to pay a fine, which goes to charity, and even to compensate the bank for a loss through arbitration. According to this approach, the OIC Fiqh Council has differentiated between pure loan contracts and debt contracts involving the performance of certain obligations/acts by the clients, and decided that penalty clauses can be put into the original contracts or in a separate agreement in all financial debt contracts except where the

---

[63] AAOIFI, 2004–5a, No. 8, pp. 122, 132.

[64] Al Baraka, Resolutions (1981–2001), No. 3/2, pp. 65–66.

[65] OIC, Islamic Fiqh Academy, Resolution No. 109 (3/12), pp. 251, 252.

[66] Al Baraka Sudan Fatwah in IIBID, p. 125, also in IAIB, pp. 36–37; cf. Ray, 1995, pp. 50, 182, 183.

[67] In Dalil al fataāwa al Sharī´ah fi- a Māl al Masrafiyya, Cairo: IIBID, 1989, pp 125, 126; cf. Ray, 1995, pp. 182, 183.

[68] It is not permissible to impose a penalty for delay in repayment of Qard al Hasan, Al Baraka, Resolutions (1981–2001), No. 6/11, p. 103.

original commitment is a loan meaning Qardal Hasan, as imposing a penalty provision in a loan contract is usury in the strict sense.[69]

The OIC Fiqh Council also resolved that penalty provision should become null and void when a client proves that his failure to meet an obligation was due to a reason beyond his control, or when he proves that the bank, as a result of his breach of the contract, has incurred no loss.[70]

### 7.13.1 Insolvency of the Debtor

If a debtor does not have enough money to pay his debt(s), he is termed insolvent/bankrupt (Muflis) in Islamic commercial law.[71] In such cases it must be ensured that the debtor is not resorting to fraudulent bankruptcy, in which case he can be pressed and even imprisoned for payment of debt. However, if a person is really in trouble and there is little chance of his ability to pay in the foreseeable future, he can be declared insolvent; all his assets will be sold and the proceeds distributed among the creditors on a pro rata basis. If some of the debts remain unpaid, he must be given time for easement. The State or the regulators of the financial system can play an important role in resolving such issues, as the holy Prophet did in the case of Ibn Abi Hadrad and Jabir bin Abdullah.[72] Jurists differ regarding arresting such an insolvent debtor. According to Imam Malik and Imam Shafi'e, he can be arrested only if there is the possibility that he has some hidden wealth.

If a commodity sold on credit is still with the insolvent buyer in the same condition, the seller has the first right according to a saying of the holy Prophet and according to the majority of the jurists. (Narrated Abu Huraira: "Allah's Apostle said, 'If a man finds his same things with a bankrupt, he has more right to take them back than anyone else'.") Imam Abu Hanifa is in favour of the distribution of its proceeds among all other creditors.[73]

## 7.14   HAWALAH (ASSIGNMENT OF DEBT)

Hawalah literally implies the transfer of something from one person to another or from one situation to another. Legally, Hawalah is an agreement by which a debtor is freed from a debt by another becoming responsible for it, or by shifting the responsibility from one person to another with the effect that a debtor is replaced by another debtor.

Hawalah may be restricted or unrestricted. In restricted Hawalah, the assignee has to pay from the asset or property of the assignor that is in the possession of the assignee. Unrestricted Hawalah is not restricted to payment being made from the assets/property of the assignor/transferor in the hands of the transferee–the assignor (debtor) does not act as creditor to the payer who undertakes to pay from his own funds and has recourse from the assignor provided that the payment was made by the order of the transferor.[74]

Hawalah, or the transfer of debt, is different from the transfer of right in which a creditor is replaced by another creditor. As such, it refers to the endorsement or assignment of debt.

---

[69] Al Baraka, Resolutions (1981–2001), No. 6/11, p. 103, also p. 137.

[70] OIC, Islamic Fiqh Academy, Resolution No. 109 (3/12), p. 252.

[71] Ibn Hajar, 1981, **5**, pp. 62, 63.

[72] Ibn Hajar, 1981, **5**, pp. 310, 311.

[73] Nisai, n.d., **7**, pp. 311–314; Waliullah, 1353 H, pp. 56–58.

[74] Al-Atasi, 1403 AH, Majallah, Articles 673–679.

The Muslim jurists encouraged the Hawalah contract and it was carried to Europe through Spain and Sicily during the crusades of the 12th century of the Common Era.[75]

The contract of Hawalah, together with the contract of al-Suftajah,[76] formed the basis of bill of exchange in Islamic commercial law. The term "Hawalah" also applies to a mandate to pay and denotes the document by which the transfer of debt is completed. In this sense, it also means a promissory note or a bill of exchange. A number of products/services provided by the banking industry today are forms of Hawalah, like cheques, drafts, pay orders, remittances, promissory notes, bills of exchange, ODs, endorsements, etc.

The difference between "sale of debt", which is prohibited, and the "assignment of debt", which is permissible, is that in the latter case, there is recourse to the assignor or the original debtor if the assignee does not pay the debt for any reason. In the sale of debt, the purchaser of the debt instrument has no recourse to the seller of the debt, and therefore, due to the involvement of Gharar and Riba, the sale of debt is prohibited, except in the case where it is subject to the rules of Hawalah.

Hawalah should take effect immediately – it must not be suspended for a period of time or concluded on a temporary basis nor must it be contingent on future unlikely events. However, the assignee will have to pay when the debt becomes due and it is permissible to defer payment of the transferred debt until a mutually specified date.[77]

Hawalah is a noncommutative contract and the assignee cannot take any remuneration for his service. Assignment of debt is, therefore, allowed at the nominal value of the debt/debt instrument with recourse to the original debtor or the assignor if the assignee defaults in payment of the liability.[78] It is a binding contract and not subject to unilateral termination. According to the majority of jurists, the obligation to pay the debt would return to the assignor in the case of bankruptcy or death of the assignee.[79]

No obligation of debt will be left without being paid if the assignee becomes bankrupt, dies, and so on. The Prophet (pbuh) is reported to have said: "Procrastination in paying debts by a wealthy man is injustice. So, if debt is transferred from your debtor to a trustworthy rich debtor, he should agree".[80] The observation made by the Prophet (pbuh) to accept Hawalah by a rich debtor is a recommendation, which is held by the majority of jurists. This Hadith also implies that Hawalah is valid when it is contracted as a result of mutual consent between the assignor and the assignee. Similarly, Wakalah is permissible for the payment of debt, i.e. a person can be appointed as agent to pay the debt.[81]

## 7.15   SECURITY/GUARANTEE (KAFALAH) IN LOANS

As discussed above, a loan must be repaid. The lender can demand some security to which he may have recourse in the event of failure by the borrower to fulfil his obligation. The holy Prophet (pbuh) himself borrowed from a Jew against the security of an iron breastplate

---

[75] See Hassan, 1993, p. 182.

[76] Suftajah was a document through which payment for purchased goods was made in another place through a second party.

[77] For details see Ibn Hajar, 1981, **4**, pp. 464–468.

[78] Al Jaziri, 1973, pp. 259–261, 267–269.

[79] Although jurists of some schools of Fiqh absolve the original debtor or the assignor of the liability to pay, the viewpoint of the majority is more justifiable. See Al Jaziri, 1973, **2**, pp. 259–269; **3**, pp. 290–305.

[80] Muslim, 1981, with Sharah by Nawavi, **10**, pp. 228, 277.

[81] Muslim, 1981, **11**, p. 23.

which was with the Jew at the time of his demise.[82] Islam has laid down broad principles in this regard as well. In the Qur'ān we come across: "If ye are on a journey and cannot find a scribe, Rihn Maqbudah (a pledge) with possession (may serve the purpose)".[83] This is convincing proof of the fact that (i) a pledge is permissible, (ii) it makes no difference whether a person is on a journey or at home, (iii) transactions of this nature can take place even between a Muslim and non-Muslim.

Guarantee is covered under the term "Kafalah" in Islamic commercial law. There are two forms of guarantee: Kafalah, or suretyship, and Rihn, or pledge/surety. The two pre-Islamic contracts used for guarantee or safe return of loans to their owners were approved by the holy Prophet (pbuh) and their elaborated applications were extended by later generations in order to avoid any iniquities to both parties in the contract of loan, especially to the creditor.

Literally, Kafalah means to take on the responsibility for the payment of a debt or for a person's appearance in court. Legally, in Kafalah, a third party becomes surety for the payment of a debt unpaid by the person originally liable. The degree or scope of suretyship should be known and should not come with preconditions. It is a guarantee given to a creditor that the debtor will pay the debt, fine or any other liability.

Rihn, or pledge, is also a security for the recovery of debt if the debtor fails to repay it.

Kafalah and Rihn interrelate in the case of debt, but they have different functions. In the contract of Kafalah, a third party becomes surety for the payment of debt, but in Rihn, the debtor hands over something as a pledge to ensure the payment of debt. Mutual consent/agreement is the basis for the validity of both contracts, as in other business transactions. In addition, Rihn is also regarded as a trusteeship; the creditor has to hold the pledged property as a trust.

A creditor can also ask for personal surety from any third party. This creates an additional liability with regard to the claim. The creditor has the right to demand payment from the debtor and the surety and if the surety is obliged to pay the liability, the debtor is bound to pay the surety.[84] If the debtor does not pay, the surety will have to pay the creditor and for that purpose he is entitled to get Zakat and even charity.[85]

If the guarantor agrees that the debt of the principal debtor would be remitted by him, its effect would be that of Hawalah, or transference of debt. If a delay is granted to the principal debtor for the payment of his debts, the delay is also granted to the surety. But a delay given to the surety is not a delay given to the principal debtor.

A surety agreement becomes enforceable by the offer of surety, provided the claimant is agreeable. It is also lawful to become the surety of a surety. There can be more than one surety at the same time for a single obligation, i.e. joint surety or joint guarantee; each one is liable only for his share of the debt. But if various people become sureties of a debt one after the other, each one of them is liable for the whole debt. If the jointly indebted people become surety for each other, each of them is liable for the whole debt.

A guarantee shall not be effective in the case of goods that are in trust in the hands of the principal debtor. For example, a person cannot furnish as guarantee goods that are pledged to him or assets that he has taken on lease.

---

[82] Muslim, 1981 **11**, pp. 39, 40; Bukhari Sahih, **3**, p. 143 (Kitab al-Rihn); Ibn Qudama, 1367 AH, **4**, p. 326.

[83] Qur'ān, 2: 283.

[84] Al Jaziri, 1973, p. 267.

[85] Qur'ān, 9: 60. The term "Ghārmeen", included in Zakat beneficiaries, broadly means those obliged to pay others' debts as sureties; Muslim, 1981, Kitab al Zakat.

A bank can call for the following types of guarantee to secure its loans:

- letters of guarantee;
- use of cheques (post-dated);
- promissory notes;
- freezing cash deposits;
- third party guarantees;
- Hamish Jiddiyah (earnest money taken from a prospective client to ensure the performance of any assignment or liability by him before execution of the formal contract);
- 'Arbūn (downpayment taken as part of the settled payment taken after execution of the formal contract).

Whatever is valid as the subject of sale can become the subject of a pledge, which is encumbered to the extent of the debt.[86] A share in jointly owned property can also be given as a pledge.[87] The pledger is the owner of the risk and reward of the commodity pledged, as he is the owner, and has given possession only as a guarantee. Accordingly, if the pledge is destroyed/lost without negligence or any fault on the part of the pledgee, the loss is that of the pledger/debtor. The pledgee, being a trustee, cannot be held responsible for the loss of security, and therefore can recover from the pledger what has been lent to him.

### 7.15.1  Risk and Reward in Pledge

As indicated above, a pledger, i.e. a person owing a debt, is the owner of the risk and reward of the commodity pledged. The holy Prophet has said: "Pledge cannot be foreclosed, and it is from the pledger and for him is its Ghunm or accession and upon him is its Ghurm or loss".[88] Accordingly, if the pledge is destroyed/lost without any proven negligence of the pledgee, the loss is that of the pledger/debtor. The pledgee, being a trustee, cannot be held responsible for the loss of security, and therefore can recover from the pledger what has been lent to him. Any excess amount, e.g. over and above the loan amount, belongs to the pledger/debtor. According to a Hadith of the holy Prophet: "Pledge is to cover what it is for"[89] that is, to cover the debt, and therefore security remains bound to the extent of debt.

The words of the holy Prophet that pledge cannot be foreclosed, as given above, do not convey that the pledgee cannot sell it for recovering the debt. These words imply that the pledge should remain redeemable and not be appropriated wrongfully, as was the practice in those days.[90] Imam Abu Hanifa also considers that pledge implies an encumbrance or charge (on property so pledged) to the extent of loan.[91] Accordingly, a provision in the contract that in case of nonpayment of debt, the pledged commodity should be taken over by the pledgee in place of the debt is not valid.[92]

When the duration of a pledge expires, and the debt becomes payable but not paid, the pledgee can apply to the court to have the pledged commodity sold and the debt recovered

---

[86] Ibn Qudama, 1367 AH, **4**, pp. 326, 327; Alusi, Rooh al-Ma'ani, **3**, p. 54; Ibn Rushd, 1950, Kitab al-Rihn.

[87] Ibn Qudama, 1367 AH, **4**, p. 338; Ibn Hazm, 1988, **6**, p. 364, No. 1211.

[88] Bukhari, **5**, pp. 143, 144, Mps/ 2511, 2512; Ibn Qudama, 1367 AH, **5**, p. 326; Jassas, 1999, **2**, pp. 562–565; Shafi'e, 1321 H, **3**, p. 147.

[89] Jassas, 1999, **2**, pp. 562–565; Baihaqi, 1344 H, **6**, p. 40.

[90] Jassas, 1999, **2**, p. 555.

[91] Al Sarakhsi, n.d., **XI**, p. 64.

[92] Ibn Qudama, 1367 AH, **4**, p. 383.

out of the sale proceeds. To avoid any possible trouble and expense, the creditors may have an irrevocable power of attorney to sell the security on behalf of the pledger to recover their dues from the proceeds and remit the extra amount, if any.

### 7.15.2    Benefits from Pledge

A Hadith of the holy Prophet (pbuh) guides us on this aspect of pledge, according to which a pledged animal can be used for riding and its milk consumed in return for what is spent (on it) and its maintenance rests with him who rides it and consumes its milk.[93] This reveals that the pledgee has the right to benefit from the security as it is in his possession and he has to maintain it. No permission of the pledger is required in this regard. However, there is a difference of opinion among jurists as to who should derive benefit from a pledge or security.

Some of the Hanafi jurists hold that it is not at all permissible for the pledgee to benefit from the pledge, even with the permission of the pledger, for it amounts to Riba, but the majority of them maintain that benefit may be derived by the pledgee with the permission of the pledger, provided it is not so stipulated at the time of contract.[94]

According to the Shafi'e school, it is the right of the pledger to derive benefit from the security, as he is the owner of it. The security should remain in the possession of the pledgee except for the periods when it is made use of by the pledger.[95]

According to the Maliki school, the pledger is entitled to benefit from the pledge and its accession. But it is also possible for the pledgee to have such benefit provided that (i) the loan for which security is given is not of the nature of Qard but has resulted from a sale transaction, (ii) the benefit for pledge is stipulated at the time of contract and (iii) that the period of such benefit is specified.[96] Hanbali jurists allow use by the pledgee subject to the permission of the pledger.[97]

Study of the arguments of various schools of Fiqh reveals that the difference of opinion is due to the fact that some jurists attach more weight to the possession by the pledgee, while others lay greater emphasis upon the ownership of the pledge. It is said that permission is necessary to derive benefit, while in certain cases it is not, and again no permission will give the right to benefit when the security is for a loan of the nature of Qard. The benefit is in return for the expenditure on maintenance. Some of the jurists say that the benefit should be in proportion to the expenditure, otherwise it would amount to Riba.[98] This does not lead to any hard and fast rule, because the Prophet, while allowing benefit of the pledged animal, did not mention the minute aspect of equating expenses with the benefit. Putting any condition in the loan contract that the pledgee has the right to benefit from the pledge is not valid.[99] However, to the extent that is possible, any extra income, i.e. over and above the expenses incurred, should go to the pledger.

On this analogy, an Islamic bank as a pledgee may derive benefit from a pledge in return for its maintenance by it. A house, for instance, requires maintenance and the

---

[93] Bukhari, **5**, pp. 143, 144; Ibn Qudama, 1367 AH, **4**, p. 326.

[94] Al Jaziri, 1973, pp. 672–675; Zuhayli, 1985, **4**, pp. 725, 726; Jassas, 1999, pp. 563–567.

[95] Al Jaziri, 1973, pp. 669–671.

[96] Al Jaziri, 1973, pp. 667, 668.

[97] For details of all schools Ibn Qudama, 1367 AH, **4**, pp. 385–391; Al Jaziri, 1973, **2**, pp. 675, 676.

[98] Jassas, 1999, **2**, p. 555.

[99] Ibn Qudama, 1367 AH, **4**, p. 386.

bank can benefit by it on the above principle or charge the pledger a customary rate for its services or even take it on lease and give it to someone for something more. The rental over and above the customary rate of the bank's services should go to the pledger.

Apart from pledge, an Islamic bank has the right of lien, i.e. the right to retain the property belonging to another until a debt due from the latter is paid. This is called a "possessory lien", which seems to be permissible under Islamic law on the analogy of a seller (in cash sales) who has been invested with a right to retain the property sold by him in his possession, until its price is paid to him.[100]

Mortgage, where only the interest in the property is transferred to the mortgagee and not its possession, has not been discussed in traditional books on Islamic law. However, contemporary scholars allow it on the basis of analogy.

## 7.16   BAI' AL DAYN (SALE OF DEBT/DEBT INSTRUMENTS)

Secondary market trading of debt and debt-based securities is possible through Bai' al Dayn, as in the case of a variety of Malaysia-based Sukuk. However, Jamhoor Ulama do not accept this, even though the debt represented by Sukuk is supported by underlying assets. The traditional Muslim jurists are unanimous on the point that Bai' al Dayn with discount or premium is not allowed in Sharī'ah. The overwhelming majority of contemporary Sharī'ah scholars are also of the same view. However, some experts from Malaysia have allowed this kind of sale. They normally refer to the ruling of the Shafi'e school, but they do not consider the fact that the Shafi'ete jurists allowed it only in a case where a debt was sold at its par value.[101]

Rosly and Sanusi (1999) have observed in this regard: "The trading of Islamic bonds at a discount using Bai' al Dayn has been found unacceptable by the Jumhur Ulama' including al-Shafi'e. As such, the position of Malaysian Islamic bonds remains unacceptable among the Middle Eastern jurists, although some Malaysian jurists found this the opposite."[102] The OIC Islamic Fiqh Council, which has the representation of all Islamic countries, including Malaysia, has also approved the prohibition of Bai' al Dayn unanimously without a single dissent.

## 7.17   IMPACT OF INFLATION ON LOANS/DEBTS

The Sharī'ah scholars, Sharī'ah courts, committees and boards of various Islamic banks have not accepted the principle of indexing loans and debts with any currency/basket of currencies or gold.[103] The Federal Shariat Court (FSC) in Pakistan has discussed this issue in detail (paras 153–234 Judgement; 14th November, 1991). In this context, reference has been made to books like Hidaya, Al-Mabsut, Badaa'i al Sanaa'e, Kitabul Fiqh (Al Jaziri), and personalities like Imam Abu Hanifa, Imam Muhammad, Abu Yousuf, Ghazali, the celebrated jurist of the 13th Hijrah century, Ibn Abidin Shami, Pakistan's Council of Islamic Ideology, papers read by prominent Ulama and economists in an international seminar on indexation held in Jeddah and to other eminent scholars of Islamic Sharī'ah.

---

[100] Muslehuddin, 1993, p. 115.

[101] Usmani, 2000a, p. 217.

[102] Rosly and Sanusi, 1999, **1** (2).

[103] Dr S.M. Hasanuz Zaman has produced a monograph *Indexation of Financial Assets: an Islamic Evaluation*, which discusses all relevant aspects of indexation (Hasanuz Zaman, 1993).

After quoting the well-known Hadith of Sahih Muslim regarding Riba on the exchange of six commodities, the FSC says:

"Gold and silver (currency) have been counted among the six commodities about which it has been ordained that the transactions among these commodities must be like for like, equal for equal and hand to hand. If someone borrows Rs.100 from the bank, which have to be paid back after one year, and this amount, after indexation, becomes Rs.120 or so, it would fall into the category of Riba, as enunciated in the aforesaid Hadith and comes within the ambit of Riba Al-Nasiah as well as Riba Al-Fadl".[104]

The FSC also quotes from the renowned Kitabul Fiqh by Al Jaziri:

"Among the points relating to loan or debt is the requirement that the transaction should involve equality. In this way, if a measurable thing is lent, for example wheat, it is necessary to return the same quantity irrespective of increase or decrease in its price. The same rule is applicable to all those things which are lent or borrowed by counting".[105]

In this context, Allama Kasani says that if someone borrows on the condition that he will repay with some benefit over and above the loan, or someone borrows depreciated coins on the condition that he will repay the original coins, the transaction will not be considered legal. The relevant text of Al-Kasani is:

"As far as loan is concerned it is pertinent to mention here that it should not consist of any kind of benefit, if it be so it will not be legal, for example, if someone gave stagnant coins as a loan on the condition that the borrower would pay proper coins or give anything as benefit at the time of the payment of loan. This kind of transaction will not be considered as legal because the holy Prophet (pbuh) prohibited such kinds of loan which bring any kind of benefit. The principle in this respect is that any stipulated benefit in the transaction is Riba, for the reason that this benefit is not in compensation of anything. It is obligatory on every Muslim to prevent himself from actual Riba and the doubt of Riba".[106]

Ibn Qudama has also discussed the question elaborately and stated that the borrower should return the same as he had borrowed, whether there may be an increase in the value or there may be devaluation: "The borrower should pay the same coins or currency, irrespective of any increase or decrease occurred in the currency".[107]

The Shariat Appellate Bench of the Supreme Court of Pakistan has also discussed this issue. The senior most Judge of the Bench, Justice Khalilur Rahman, in this respect says:

"Riba/interest cannot be rationalized on the basis of indexation because all loans and debts are to be settled on an equal basis in terms of the units of loan or object. In the case of paper currency, exchange takes place by counting. If the debt contract amounted to Rs. 1000/- the creditor may claim only Rs. 1000/- by counting – no more, no less. The prohibition of Riba essentially requires that, generally speaking, all like-for-like exchange be executed on an equal basis in terms of the relevant units of exchange. If this does not suit someone, he is free to avoid such an exchange and to pursue an alternative permissible course of action. For example, instead of there being a loan to a needy person to fulfil his consumption or business need, there may be either a Bai' Mu'ajjal or a partnership arrangement between the resource-owner and the needy party. While the need of the

---

[104] Federal Shariat Court, Judgement of 14th November, 1991, para. 182.
[105] Federal Shariat Court, para. 188.
[106] Al-Kasani, 1993, cf. Federal Shariat Court, para. 188.
[107] Ibn Qudama, 1367 AH, **5**, pp. 319, 320, 322, 325.

latter may be fulfilled, concerns of the former may be accommodated through the margin added in the deferred price or automatically adjusted through the realized profits".[108]

While explaining the term "Qard" according to Hanafis, Al Jaziri has given an interesting example: A purchases on credit 4 pounds of meat at qirsh 5 per pound (total amount payable 20 qirsh). If, at the time of payment, the meat's price falls to qirsh 2 per pound, even then A will have to pay 20 and not 8 qirsh.[109] Similarly, Ibn Qudama has observed that all fungibles will have to be returned in the same quantity as borrowed, without consideration for appreciation or depreciation.[110]

Lending in Islam is a generous/gratuitous act and the lender gives away the lent goods/money to the borrower for the period of the loan without any compensation in exchange. If the value of that loan decreases due to inflation, it is as if the lender has done a greater virtue. The Holy Qur'ān encourages giving extra time to borrowers who are in difficulty or faced with financial constraint. Therefore, the Fiqh Council of the OIC has categorically ruled out as strictly forbidden the commonly suggested solution of indexation of a lent amount of money to the cost of living, interest rates, GNP growth rates, the price of gold or some other commodities, etc. However, one can lend in terms of gold or any other currency which is not considered vulnerable to inflation. In that case also, the debt liability cannot increase due to inflation.

An important consideration in this regard is that when a particular currency depreciates, its value decreases across the board; it makes no difference whether a person has lent it or is keeping it with himself in liquid form. If he lends it by indexing with gold, for example, in order to avoid a decrease in its value, it would imply that he has drawn benefit from the loan as the debtor would make good the deficiency in his amount of money while money kept in his own coffer would lose the value. Drawing this benefit from the loans makes it a non-Sharī'ah-compliant contract.

The Islamic Fiqh Council of the OIC in its eighth session (21–27th June, 1993) resolved the following in respect of the impact of inflation on debts:

"The creditor and debtor may agree on the day of settlement – but not before – to the settlement of the debt in a currency other than the one specified for the debt, provided the rate of exchange applied is that applicable on the settlement date. Similarly, for debts due in instalments in a specific currency, the parties may agree on the day of settlement of any instalment, to have it effected, in full, in a different currency at the prevailing rate of exchange on the date of settlement.... The two parties to the contract may, at the time of contracting, agree to the settlement of the deferred cost or salary in a specific currency to be settled in single payment or in instalments in a variety of currencies or against a given amount of gold, the settlement may also be made as indicated in the above para. A debt contracted in a specific currency should not be recorded against the debtor in its counter value in gold or other currencies because such a practice would make it compulsory to the debtor to settle the debt in gold or the other currency as agreed upon for the settlement".[111]

## 7.18  SUMMARY

While conventional banks deal in money by taking and giving loans on interest, Islamic banks and financial institutions may create debt through a variety of sale and lease contracts.

---

[108] Shariat Appellate Bench, 2000, pp. 251–253.
[109] Al Jaziri, 1973, p. 680.
[110] Ibn Qudama, 1367 AH, **4**, p. 325.
[111] Council of the Islamic Fiqh Academy, 2000, p. 163.

On the deposits side, they mobilize some deposits in current accounts that also take the form of loans. Hence, study of the rules pertaining to loans and debt in Islamic finance is of crucial importance.

Various terms like loan (Qard), debt (Dayn) and commodity loans ('Āriyah) have been explained in the chapter, with the conclusion that only the principal amount of a loan or a debt created by Islamic banks has to be paid and any addition would be Riba.

While in trading of goods it is permitted that the credit price of a commodity be different from its cash price, no value can be assigned to the time given for payment of a receivable once its amount is mutually stipulated.

Repaying a loan in excess of the principal and without a precondition is commendable and compatible with the Sunnah of the holy Prophet (pbuh). However, gracious repayment of debt is a matter of individual discretion and cannot be adopted as a system, because that would mean that a loan would necessarily yield a profit, which does not fit in the philosophy of Islamic finance.

The instructions of the Sharī'ah to debtors and creditors have also been discussed in detail. The foremost duty of the debtor is to repay his loan in fulfilment of the promise or contract made with the creditor. While creditors have been advised to be lenient in the recovery of loans, debtors have been warned that debt has to be repaid and nonpayment carries serious consequences in the Hereafter. A lender or a seller on credit can demand any security to ensure recovery of the debt if the debtor is not able to pay his liability.

Sharī'ah scholars have approved the provision of penalty clauses embedded in the con-tractual agreements to the effect that, in the case of a default in payment of the debt, the client will pay a certain amount as a penalty, which will be given to charity. Banks can claim liquidated damages or compensation for a loss arising from default through the courts or any arbitration committees that should keep in mind the actual loss suffered by the bank and not the "opportunity cost" in the conventional sense.

A rebate on prepayment of a debt *per se* is not allowed. However, the AAOIFI's Sharī'ah Standards allow banks to give rebates at their discretion if they are not stipulated in the contract.

Debts can be assigned under the rule of Hawalah, but no obligation of debt should remain unpaid, and if the assignee becomes bankrupt, dies or is unable to pay for any other reason, the original debtor (assignor) is obliged to pay. In the sale of the debt, the purchaser of the debt instrument has no recourse to the seller of the debt and, therefore, due to the involvement of Gharar and Riba, the sale of debt is prohibited, except in the case where it is subject to the rules of Hawalah.

An Islamic bank as a pledgee may derive benefit from a security in return for its services for its maintenance. However, any extra income, i.e. over and above the expenses incurred by the bank, should go to the pledger.

Finally, it has been explained that debts have to be repaid without any provision for indexation with any commodity, currency or basket of currencies. However, one can lend in terms of gold or any other currency, which, in one's perception, is not vulnerable to inflation. In this case also, the debt liability would not increase due to inflation.

# Part III
# Islamic Finance – Products and Procedures

# 8

# Overview of Financial Institutions and Products: Conventional and Islamic

## 8.1 INTRODUCTION

To understand the concepts and operations of Islamic finance, it is worthwhile giving an overview of the financial institutions, markets and instruments in the conventional set-up, as well as in the Islamic framework. This will help in understanding how financial institutions and products affect individuals, firms, societies, economies and States and how they perform to fulfil the needs of various segments in an economy.

In this chapter, we shall briefly indicate the alternatives in Islamic finance to their counterparts in conventional finance. Details of these alternatives are given in subsequent chapters and readers may like to refer to the relevant chapters for conceptual and practical explanations.

## 8.2 WHAT IS BANKING OR A BANK?

Banking is a key subsector in the economic field. The word "bank" is said to have been derived from the Italian word "banco", meaning shelf or bench, on which the ancient money changers used to display their coins. The bench of a medieval banker or money changer was broken by the people if he failed in business and this probably is the origin of the word "bankrupt".[1]

A bank is an institution authorized to take deposits for the purpose of extending long- and short-term finance facilities. Study of the history of finance reveals that the practice of banking has existed in one form or another dating back to 575 BC. People used to deposit their money in temple treasuries. These temples used to act as banks and extend finance to individuals and the State. Over time, such operations moved from religious institutions to private banks. The Igibi bank of Babylon, which existed in 575 BC, not only acted as an agent for clients, extending finance on the basis of signatures, but also accepted deposits and gave loans for agriculture.

The practice of goldsmiths in medieval England initially involved accepting deposits of gold coins and issuing receipts to depositors. For their convenience, depositors started using these receipts for the settlement of their liabilities. As these receipts established their legitimacy, depositors started making less frequent visits to the money lenders. This provided money lenders with an opportunity to extend the money lying with them to the needy on the basis of interest, while keeping a certain reserve ratio to meet the demand for withdrawals.

---

[1] Muslehuddin, 1993, p. 5, cf. *Encyclopedia of Banking and Finance*, Boston, 1962; also see the relevant text in *Encyclopedia Britannica*.

In its modern form, a bank is an establishment for the custody of money received from, or on behalf of, its customers, whose drafts it has to honour and pay. The pooled money is used by it for the purpose of making advances to others to get a return in the form of interest, dividends or others.

Traditionally, modern banking is divided into two main categories: commercial and investment banking. Commercial banking involves intermediation between depositors and fund users, and making payments on behalf of their clients. On the other hand, investment banking primarily comprises capital market activities for facilitating fundraising by the corporate sector, directly or indirectly from the investors. In the USA, the 1933 Glass–Steagall Act enforced tight regulations on the banking industry, separating the practices of commercial and investment banking. This separation was achieved in Japan by law after World War II. In the UK, this separation prevailed because of institutional history rather than any regulation.

While the financial world in past decades was clearly divided between commercial and investment banking, banks have, over time, adopted the German-style banking model, performing different functions simultaneously. Further, investment banking has become an important function of the commercial banks as well. The amendment of the London Stock Exchange regulations in 1986 eroded the distinction between commercial and investment banking in the UK. In the US, the Glass–Steagall Act was repealed in 1999, as a result of which a large number of banks started operations in the capital market and securities trading, many of them providing investment services to Muslim investors. A different and new development is emerging in the shape of Islamic banking within the banking industry in a large number of countries.

## 8.3    THE STRATEGIC POSITION OF BANKS AND FINANCIAL INSTITUTIONS

Finance is the most strategic part of modern economics that functions like blood arteries in the human body. In every society there are surplus as well as deficit households and institutions. While a large number of people have relatively smaller savings, a number of others, particularly businesses, are short of funds for their business expenses or production needs. Financial institutions provide a link between the deficit and the surplus units. In a conventional set-up, individuals and households provide funds to business and industries through financial institutions, which charge a fixed or floating but risk-free rate of return from the fund users and give a part of the return to the fund owners (savers/investors), keeping the remainder for themselves as spread.

Like all other goods and services, the availability of the funds is governed by the forces of demand and supply and the risk profiles of various stakeholders. While the supply of funds comes from individuals or households and corporate bodies, demand is generated in trade, business, industry, agriculture, corporations and government sectors. The institutions involved in this process of resources transfer are commercial banks, investment banks, savings and loan institutions, specialized institutions like micro credit, SME credit, industry, agriculture, trade, export/import, housing, leasing, venture capital, discount houses, insurance companies, fund management companies, asset management companies, etc. These institutions can be divided from one angle into two broad categories of banks and non-bank financial companies or institutions (NBFIs). Further, there are some development finance institutions (DFIs) operating both as banking and non-banking institutions and providing finance to industry, agriculture and other sectors or subsectors for developmental activities.

Commercial banks undertake the intermediation function between the saving surplus and the fund user units and entities and provide checking facilities to the savers/investors. NBFIs normally do not provide checking facilities to the savers and facilitate the raising of funds for business and industry directly from the saving surplus units/households. Investment banks are included in the NBFIs. Investment banks derive their income primarily from fee-based activities or profits from trading in securities rather than from a margin between the borrowing and lending costs. The services provided by these banks take many forms, including securities underwriting, stock and bond trading, facilitating mergers and acquisitions, arranging and funding syndicated loans and providing financial advice to companies needing funds.

The above types of institution are regulated by central banks or monetary authorities and the securities and exchange commissions in respective countries. Regulators' objectives everywhere are said to be efficiency in mobilizing resources from the surplus units and optimum allocation of these resources along with stability of prices, payment systems and the economy as a whole. In addition, there are some international financial institutions that coordinate the services of banks and financial institutions at a global level. The most important of these institutions is the Bank for International Settlements (BIS), which performs the function of coordination and standardization of the services of the financial institutions in various parts of the world.

## 8.4 CATEGORIES OF CONVENTIONAL FINANCIAL BUSINESS

### 8.4.1 Commercial Banking

The main functions of a modern commercial bank include receiving deposits of various natures, granting short- and medium-term loans by way of overdrafts, discounting of bills and commercial papers, advances against securities for business and households, long-term mortgage financing and investments in capital markets. In some markets, commercial banks are also undertaking merchant banking. All this fund-based business is conducted on the basis of interest that is charged from the fund users and paid to the depositors/investors. Commercial banks also deal in foreign currencies, money changing and perform a number of services like issuing letters of credit (L/C) and letters of guarantee (L/G), payments made/received on behalf of their clients, safe custody of valuables and a number of advisory services against service charges or commission.

However, all commercial banks might not be undertaking all of the above functions, and the majority of them undertake the business of deposit-taking with an open checking facility and lending for short periods for providing running finance to business and industry. Medium- and long-term financing is mostly arranged by investment banks by way of direct intermediation between the investors and industry/business.

*The Deposits/Liability Side of Commercial Banks*

All deposits in conventional commercial banks are the liability of the banks, because the amount of deposits has to be paid back with or without a return. Current accounts that are normally maintained by the business and corporate sectors carry no return and are used for managing their cash flow. Savings, term, notice deposits and certificates of investment/certificates of deposit (COIs/CODs) are remunerative deposits for the short, medium and long term. A brief explanation of the deposits side of banks follows.

## Current Accounts

These are a basic type of account maintained mainly by corporate clients and by individuals for availing credit facilities from the banks/financial institutions. As indicated above, normally such accounts are nonremunerative; however, many regulators allow payment of interest on such accounts and some banks give a little return as a part of their marketing strategy. Hence, a current account in the conventional system may or may not be remunerative.

## Savings Accounts

These are the normal checking accounts that commercial banks offer for fund mobilization against the payment of interest; savings accounts may have a minimum balance requirement. Different types of savings accounts offer different interest rates depending on the deposit amount. The concept of daily product is used for the entitlement of return to various depositors. Saving deposits, and to some extent term deposits, are collectively known as "demand" deposits, because one can, at any time, draw the amount without any notice.

## Fixed-term Accounts/Certificates of Investment/Certificates of Deposit

In term deposit accounts (as captioned above), the deposit holder agrees to lock in the money for a fixed period of time while the bank commits to pay an indicated interest rate depending on the term of the deposit – the longer the term, the higher the interest rate. Some banks charge a penalty in the event of premature encashment – some banks charge a prespecified penalty over the remaining period of deposit, while others use the period for which money has been with the bank. In financial markets with open competition, the return already given is adjusted in the case of early withdrawal, keeping in mind the investment and the remaining periods.

Term deposit receipts (TDRs) are issued at par or discounted value. A typical TDR issued at discount is issued at a value below its par; it grows up to the par value in the agreed timeframe. TDRs may have a life ranging from an overnight deposit to five/six/seven years, though by custom, it varies from seven days to five years. This type of deposit is also called a certificate of investment (COI) by investment banks and NBFIs. A typical COI is issued at its par value with return payment made at agreed intervals ranging from one month to the time of maturity.

## Annuities/Perpetuities

Annuities are normally built on savings accounts for commercial banks. NBFIs use COIs to offer annuities. The depositor is entitled to withdraw the amount after the deposit period. However, frequently the annuity converts itself into a perpetuity at maturity, i.e. the deposit holder is allowed to withdraw an agreed amount indefinitely at an agreed timeframe. These products are also offered by life insurance companies. Products of such a nature exist in the mutual fund industry and share markets as well, and are called "dividend reinvestment plans."

**Advance Profit-paying Products**

In these types of product, the anticipated amount of profit is discounted and paid up front. In essence, this is similar to a term deposit receipt issued at discount.

**Cash Management/Fund Management Accounts**

Historically, the NBFIs, and particularly the investment banks, used to maintain cash management accounts. But over the last decade, commercial banks have also been increasingly offering discretionary or nondiscretionary cash management and fund management accounts. A typical CMA entails the deposit of money with the bank for an agreed period that carries either a fixed rate of return or any rate linked with any other activity in capital markets. In the case of nondiscretionary accounts, the client instructs the bank about the type of investment as well. In most such cases in conventional banking, a fixed amount of return is paid. In rare cases, funds are invested on the basis of a fee, remitting all profit to the depositors.

*The Assets Side of Commercial Banks*

Commercial banks deploy depositors' funds for short-term (a year or less than one year), medium-term (one to three years) and long-term (over five years) loans and advances on the basis of interest. A prudent banker is supposed to take into consideration the character and business integrity of the borrower, his cash flow and capacity to repay, the purpose of borrowing and the security offered as collateral. The following are the possible forms of loans:

1. Productive loans: for trade, industry and other businesses and in most cases also for housing.
2. Consumption and consumer durable loans: for household goods, automobiles, etc.
3. Clean advances: on the personal surety of the borrower or of any third party, no collateral.
4. Discounting of commercial papers like notes, bills of exchange, etc.
5. Cash credit like overdrafts: customers are allowed to draw from a limit given by the bank.

The financing operations of commercial banks for various purposes in respect of industry and commerce are briefly given below:

- Working capital finance: the working capital requirement of various sectors is met by banks through grants of cash credit, overdraft facilities, demand loans, opening of L/Cs and through discounting of bills of exchange.
- Trade financing normally involves the issuance of L/Cs by commercial banks. Sight L/Cs are simply fee-based instruments issued to facilitate trade while usance L/Cs also involve financing by banks against payment of interest.
- L/Gs are issued by banks to ensure, on behalf of their clients, that the payment will be made when due or action taken as and when required in the contracts in the background. Thus, the bank acts as guarantor of the client's liability towards the counterparty. Banks get commission for issuing L/Gs, but if they are required to perform the guarantee, they have to pay the related amount for which they charge interest.
- Agricultural finance: commercial banks provide production and developmental loans to farmers. Short-term finance is required by farmers mainly for the purchase of seed, fertilizer and pesticides, while medium- and long-term finance is needed for land-levelling,

tubewells, tractors, setting up of poultry/dairy/fish farms and construction of storage facilities.

- Fixed investment finance: this is provided by way of term loans or purchase of debentures or participation in underwriting and "bridge financing" arrangements.
- Treasury products – liquidity and fund management: this involves money and capital market operations, foreign exchange operations, inter-bank borrowing and lending money on interest linked to tenor, credit considerations and liquidity amongst other factors. Treasury products are used to manage mismatches in liquidity position and to get returns. The entire activity is based on interest receipts or payments. Repo and reverse repo operations involve selling/purchasing and entering into a back to back transaction for purchasing/selling. The objective is to manage liquidity and enhance interest income.
- Nostro accounts, maintained by banks overseas to undertake trade finance activity and correspondent banking. Interest is paid and received on the balances maintained and the amounts overdrawn.

### 8.4.2 Investment Banking

Investment banks facilitate the direct flow of funds from the surplus to the deficit units in an economy. They help business firms – private and public companies – and governments in need of funds in selling their debt or equity securities in the primary financial markets and also play in the secondary markets as brokers and dealers. They derive their income primarily from fee-based activities or profits from trading securities rather than from a margin between borrowing and lending costs. The services provided by investment banks take many forms, including securities underwriting, stock and bond trading, facilitating mergers and acquisitions, arranging and funding syndicated loans, providing financial advice to companies on aspects like pricing of securities, etc.

For small and start-up companies in particular, investment banks facilitate mobilization of funds from venture capitalists. General investors are not interested in small and start-up companies and their capital needs at this stage are met through venture capital financing. Investment banks facilitate them by managing funds from the venture capitalists through private placements (issuers sell the securities directly to the ultimate investors). However, their most important job is facilitating initial public offerings (IPOs), that is the first sale of stocks by a company to the public. Companies go for IPOs to enhance their ability to raise funds. After IPO, investment banks serve as brokers, arbitrageurs and provide various corporate advisory services.[2]

Conventional investment banks normally raise medium- and long-term funds through closed- and open-ended funds, by issuance of COIs/CODs and offering guaranteed dividend accounts without checking facilities. COI holders get pre-agreed interest income. A dividend at a certain rate is guaranteed by the account-maintaining institutions during the period of deposit. In some cases the account holder is given a minimum guaranteed return, generally below the market rate, whereas the upside is kept open.

---

[2] For details about the functions of modern investment banks, see http://islamiccenter.kau.edu.sa/english/publications/Obaidullah/ifs/ifs.html; Obaidullah, n.d., pp. 146–150.

### 8.4.3   Other NBFIs

Non-bank financial institutions (NBFIs) other than investment banks are discount houses, leasing companies, venture capital companies, asset management and fund management companies, insurance companies and other specialized institutions for financing various sectors in an economy. Their activities also pertain to facilitating business and industry through direct intermediation between savers and investors and money and capital market transactions. The investors get interest or a guaranteed dividend while the fund users have to pay interest. Some NBFIs deal in real estate and manage property and other funds to get fixed and variable returns in the form of interest or dividends.

### 8.4.4   Conventional Financial Markets

Financial markets facilitate the management of liquidity for investors. When the holder of the security needs cash, he can sell the security to a third party via the financial markets. The purchaser then steps into the shoes of the previous holder and becomes entitled to receive the amount.

Financial markets in the conventional framework comprise money and capital markets. While the money market is based on receipts and payments of interest on short-term lending and borrowing and trading in short-term debt instruments, the capital market involves medium- and long-term debt and equity-based transactions. Foreign exchange markets are considered part of the financial markets.

Financial markets are further distributed in the primary and secondary markets. Instruments generated in the primary market are traded in the secondary market. More recently, global depository receipts (GDRs) – negotiable certificates held in the bank of one country representing a specific number of securities/shares of a stock traded on an exchange of another country – are being traded in the developed financial markets.

A conventional bond stands for a loan repayable to the holder in any case, and mostly with interest. It has nothing to do with the actual business undertaken with the borrowed money. A typical debt market undertakes trading of securities like bonds, debentures, commercial papers, treasury bills and derivatives in spot and future markets.

While debt instruments are entirely based on interest, many joint stock companies involve interest one way or the other. Either their core business is related to interest or Gharar or they lend or borrow on the basis of interest and undertake Gharar-based activities. The basic concept of an equity market, commonly known as a stock market, is permissible under Sharī´ah provided the stocks being traded do not involve Riba and Gharar, for which the experts have developed a number of criteria that we shall discuss in subsequent sections.

## 8.5   THE NEED FOR ISLAMIC BANKS AND NBFIS

Interest is the cornerstone of the modern financial system. Keeping in mind the strict prohibition of interest in the Islamic framework, one may consider that an Islamic finance and economic system may be developed without intermediaries like banks and financial institutions, but this is a misconception. Banks and financial institutions will remain a part and parcel of economics and finance in the Islamic framework as well. Modern businesses need huge amounts of funds, while people at large have mostly small savings. This necessitates the presence of such intermediary institutions through which business needs can be directly and indirectly fulfilled with savers' pooled money in such a way that savers/investors can also get a just return on their investments and business and industry can get the funds required for ensuring a sufficient supply of goods and services for the welfare of mankind.

Keeping in mind the role and functions of banks, based on intermediation between the savers and the fund users, the need for banks has been endorsed by Islamic economists, bankers and scholars. Al-Jarhi and Munawar Iqbal express this need in the following words:

> "Financial intermediation enhances the efficiency of the saving/investment process by eliminating the mismatches inherent in the requirements and availability of financial resources of savers and entrepreneurs in an economy. Entrepreneurs may require funds for periods relatively longer than would suit individual savers. Intermediaries resolve this mismatch of maturity and liquidity preferences by pooling small funds. Moreover, the risk preferences of savers and entrepreneurs are also different. It is often considered that small savers are risk averse and prefer safer placements whereas entrepreneurs deploy funds in risky projects. The role of the intermediary again becomes crucial. They can substantially reduce their own risks through the different techniques of proper risk management. Furthermore, small savers cannot efficiently gather information about opportunities to place their funds. Financial intermediaries are in a much better position to collect such information, which is crucial for making a successful placement of funds. Hence, we do need banks. Unfortunately, the banks' role is marred by dealing on the basis of interest and limiting their activities to mostly commercial operations, as pointed out above. Islamic banks add value on both counts".[3]

### 8.5.1   The Structure of Islamic Banking

Islamic financial institutions (IFIs) also serve as intermediaries between the saving surplus and the deficit units/households. However, the instrument of "interest" is replaced by a number of instruments. While conventional banks mainly pay and charge interest in their operations, Islamic financial institutions have to avoid interest and use more than one key instrument as the basis of their intermediary activities. The striking difference is that risks in Islamic banking remain with the ownership, as a result of which, IFIs share profit or loss arising on investments and earn return on their trading and leasing activities by dint of the risk and liability taken and adding value in real business activities. They mobilize deposits on the basis of profit/loss sharing and to some extent on the basis of Wakalah against pre-agreed service charges or agency fees.

On the assets side, they take the liability of loss, if any, in case of Musharakah/Mudarabah-based financing and bear risk in trading activities so long as the assets remain in their ownership. In leasing activities, they purchase the assets, give them on rental and bear ownership-related risks and expenses. This implies that IFIs will remain as intermediaries, as they collect savings from a large number of savers/investors for financing the needs of business, agriculture and industry, but their modus operandi will change. Their subject matter will be goods and real business activities.

The general outline of Islamic banking as we find in mainstream relevant literature and as briefly depicted by M.N. Siddiqi is as follows:[4]

> "Commercial banks will be organized with share capital and will accept demand deposits and investment accounts from the public. They will offer all the conventional banking services like safe

---

[3] Jarhi and Munawar, 2001.
[4] Siddiqi, 1983, pp. 94–96.

keeping, transfers, etc. for a fee. Demand deposits may or may not involve any service charges and they will not bring any return to the depositors. In return for the privilege of using demand deposits in their normal operations, as is the case in the fractional reserve system, the banks will be obliged to earmark part of these deposits for making short-term interest-free loans. Repayment of these loans and safety of the demand deposits will have to be ensured by the Central Bank through special arrangements.

Deposits in investment accounts may be for specific projects, or left to the discretion of the bank for suitable investment. Investment of bank funds may take the form of partnership, the banks actually participating in the management of the enterprise, or of profit-sharing advances leaving management to the entrepreneur. Banks may also buy stocks or investment certificates to diversify their portfolios. They may also resort to leasing arrangements covering such items as buildings, ships, planes, industrial equipment, etc. Actual practice may bring in other innovations in the field of profit-sharing investments. The depositors will share banks' profits on a pro rata basis according to agreed percentages.

There will be some provision for short-term interest-free loans to businesses, government and consumers. But the dominant form of transaction in the system will be investment and not lending. Additions to the supply of money will be largely contingent upon investments directed at creating additional wealth. Though the system has a built-in tendency to prevent concentration of wealth and power, the Central Bank as well as the State will guard against such a possibility and take suitable steps to maintain a balance."

Al-Jarhi and Munawar Iqbal have candidly described the operational set-up of an Islamic bank in the following words:

"An Islamic bank is a deposit-taking banking institution whose scope of activities includes all currently known banking activities, excluding borrowing and lending on the basis of interest. On the liabilities side, it mobilizes funds on the basis of a Mudarabah or Wakalah (agency) contract. It can also accept demand deposits, which are treated as interest-free loans from the clients to the bank and which are guaranteed. On the assets side, it advances funds on a profit-and-loss sharing or a debt-creating basis, in accordance with the principles of the Sharī´ah. It plays the role of an investment manager for the owners of time deposits, usually called investment deposits. In addition, equity holding as well as commodity and asset trading constitute an integral part of Islamic banking operations. An Islamic bank shares its net earnings with its depositors in a way that depends on the size and maturity of each deposit. Depositors must be informed beforehand of the formula used for sharing the net earnings with the bank."

They have identified the following approach to replace the institution of interest:

"As a rule, all financial arrangements that the parties agree to use are lawful, as long as they do not violate Islamic principles. Islam does not stop at prohibiting interest. It provides several interest-free modes of finance that can be used for different purposes. These modes can be placed into two categories. The first category includes modes of advancing funds on a profit-and-loss sharing basis. Examples of the first category are Mudarabah and Diminishing Musharakah with clients and participation in the equity capital of companies. The second category includes modes that finance the purchase/hire of goods (including assets) and services on a fixed-return basis. Examples of this type are Murabaha, Istisna‘a, Salam and leasing".[5]

There are broadly three models of organizational structure that the banks can adopt, according to their span of activities: the "Universal Banking Model", the "Bonafide Subsidiary Model" (all subsidiaries having their own capital and separate operations) and the

---

[5] Jarhi and Munawar, 2001.

"Bank Holding Company Model" (a bank holds separate organizations owned by itself for different activities, e.g. investment banking, Murabaha/trading transactions, commercial banking, etc.). The first two models may not best suit Islamic banks because of the wide difference in the nature of activities that they will have to adopt for their operations.[6] The fully owned (by the parent bank) subsidiaries model is best suited to banks if they establish a number of subsidiaries for various types of operations, namely investment banking, commodity trade-based banking, leasing-based banking, Istisna'a-based banking and the normal commercial banking. Alternatively, IFIs can have special branches for industry, agriculture, commerce, real estate and Takaful businesses.

Both on the liabilities and assets sides, the risk profile will be determining the return/charge and the nature of relationship between the savers, banks and fund users. Funds of risk-averse depositors will be used for low-risk financing and vice versa. In certain cases, the banks may also work as fund managers managing funds of investors/clients and charging commission for their services. As trustees, they will manage the clients' portfolios and the investors will have flexibility in choosing the best way and place to invest, according to their priorities and the risk profile.

The modes available to banks/their subsidiaries in order of priority will be Musharakah/equity participation, Mudarabah or profit-sharing and loss-absorbing, Ijarah and trading in real goods or sale contracts with deferred payment (Bai' Mu'ajjal) or with deferred delivery of goods (Bai' Salam and Istisna'a).

As the banks take deposits mostly from the middle class, they need to be very careful while investing their funds to safeguard the interests of the depositors as well as the shareholders. Therefore, depending upon the share of risk-averse deposits in their liabilities, they will have to use Murabaha and other debt-creating modes to reduce the risk and Shirkah-based modes for those who can take the risk of loss. Instruments for liquidity can be developed on the basis of all above modes, subject to the condition that return thereon depends upon the level of risk borne, entrepreneurship or real economic activity and involvement of real assets.

### 8.5.2 The Deposits Side of Islamic Banking

In the fast-developing world of finance, Islamic banks are obliged to innovate a set of techniques to mobilize deposits, keeping in mind the priorities and risk preferences of various categories of depositors. They will also have to cater for safeguarding the depositors from loss on PLS deposits.

Recent developments on the deposits side reveal that Islamic banks, in addition to the general categories of savings and investment deposits, have started offering commodity funds, leasing funds, Murabaha funds and COIs. The funds thus mobilized are used in lease or Murabaha operations, giving fees or fixed margins of profit to the banks. Thus, savers are in a position to get a quasi-fixed return. However, this fixity of return may create ambiguity with respect to their Sharī'ah position unless strict Sharī'ah controls are applied to the operations and distribution of returns thus achieved. The majority of authors allow third party guarantee to depositors to the extent of a nominal amount of deposits. However, for enhancing confidence of the depositors and to avoid any scares or chaos, any Takaful scheme for deposits would be desirable. This is because the provision of third party guarantee

---

[6] Khan, 1999.

has some objections, both from practical as well as Sharī´ah aspects. On the deposits side, Islamic banks will provide the products discussed below.

## Current Deposits

Generally, no return is given on current accounts on the grounds that such deposits take the form of loans given to Islamic banks and the loans cannot carry any return. They are kept as Amānah; but if the proceeds of such accounts are used by banks in their business, they are treated as loans that have to be paid back without any increase or decrease. Banks shall guarantee the principal amount of deposits. Subject to agreement, banks may have the option to use such accounts at their discretion in permissible business activities. The relationship of debtor and creditor between the bank and the depositor will continue. The bank and the depositor shall agree at the time of account opening whether the bank is allowed to use the money in its business or not. There will be no need to develop and implement a weightage system for this type of account.

However, some writers favour giving a gratis return even to current account holders. They add that it can be only at the discretion of the banks and the depositors should not have any entitlement. A further condition for such an incentive is that they should not be offered regularly. This is because, with the passage of time, the practice will become customary and, in turn, take on the ruling of benefits stipulated in a contract of deposit.[7]

## Savings Deposits/Investment Deposits/Term Deposits

All remunerative deposits in Islamic banks, including saving deposits against which banks provide a free checking facility, shall be accepted on a profit and loss sharing (PLS) basis. The ratio of profit distribution between the bank and the depositor shall be agreed at the time of account opening subject to the condition of the Sharī´ah that a partner may agree on a ratio of profit which is different from the ratio of capital but losses have to be shared strictly in the ratio of capital.

Investments/financing made by banks from their own capital and from the monies raised from PLS accounts shall form the "earning asset base", the returns from which shall be allocated between the banks and their account holders in the agreed ratio. Deposits of longer duration shall be compensated through assignment of higher weightages. Regulators may notify a range within which these allocations could be made. Alternatively, such assignment of weights may be left at the discretion of the banks. The following are the other considerations in this regard:

- Deposits of the risk-averse clients will be accepted either in current accounts as interest-free loans that will be guaranteed with no share in return from financing operations of the banks or by creating special pools or establishing Murabaha and leasing funds, wherein they will be treated as Rabbul-māl and get the quasi-fixed return out of profits or rentals earned by the respective funds.
- Risk-prone deposits will become part of the bank's equity, involving a weightage system (the longer the maturity, the higher the weight) on a daily product basis (DPB).

---

[7] Institute of Islamic Banking and Insurance (IIBI), 2000, pp. 137–138.

- Specific investment accounts can be managed as per savers' instructions on a Mudarabah or Wakalah basis. Banks can float equity funds on the principle of Mudarabah against a share in the actual profits. However, there may also be an agency relationship, wherein the bank would be managing depositors' funds against pre-agreed fees and passing on the profit/loss to the depositors.
- Banks may establish closed/open-ended mutual funds.
- Inter-bank financing will also become part of the equity of the bank, using appropriate weightage and DPB to calculate profit.

---

**Box 8.1:**   Deposit Management in Islamic Banks on Mudarabah Basis

Most of the Islamic banks are following a profit-sharing mechanism called the Mudarabah + Musharakah model or simply the Mudarabah model. Step by step, the process flow of the Mudarabah model is as follows:

The bank will create an investment pool having categories based on different tenors of deposits. We assume that the bank launches the following deposit tenors: three months, six months and one year. Each depositor of the bank will deposit its funds in a specific category of the investment pool that will be assigned a specific weightage. Weightage can only be amended at the beginning of the accounting period. Assume that the following investment is made by the depositors in pool A.

| Category | Amount in $ | Weightage |
|---|---|---|
| Three months | 3000 | 0.60 |
| Six months | 4000 | 0.70 |
| One year | 3000 | 1.00 |

All members of the pool will have a Musharakah relationship with each other, i.e. they are partners in the pool with the above mentioned weightages. The bank may also invest in the pool as a depositor.

Now the pool, in its collective capacity, enters into a Mudarabah contract. Under the agreement, pool A would act as Rabbul-māl and the bank would be Mudarib. The bank would undertake business with funds from the pool and the profit earned would be shared between the parties in an agreed ratio. Assume that the profit sharing ratio is 50:50.

The bank deploys $10 000 of the pool for a period of one month and earns a profit of $1000 at the end of the month. This profit would be shared as follows: bank (500) and the pool (500). The Mudarabah contract would be completed at this stage.

**Profit-sharing Among the Pool Members**
$500 earned by the pool would be distributed as per the weightage assigned at the beginning of the month. The relationship within the pool would be governed by the rules of Musharakah.

| Deposit ($) (A) | Weightage (B) | Weighted average (C = A*B) | Profit (D[1]) | Rate (E[2]) |
|---|---|---|---|---|
| 3000 | 0.6 | 1800 | 119 | 3.96 % |
| 4000 | 0.7 | 2800 | 184 | 4.60 % |
| 3000 | 1 | 3000 | 197 | 6.56 % |
| 10 000 | | 7600 | 500 | |

[1] C*500/7600

[2] D*100/A

### Sharing of Loss Among the Depositors

As per the rules of Musharakah, loss to the pool, if any, would be distributed among the pool members (Rabbul-māl) according to their investment ratio. For example, if a loss to pool A of $500 occurs, it will be distributed in the following manner:

| | | |
|---|---|---|
| Three months | 3000 | 150 |
| Six months | 4000 | 200 |
| One year | 3000 | 150 |
| Total loss | | 500 |

### 8.5.3  Instruments on the Assets Side

Islamic banking financing practice as of now reveals that the doors are open for utilizing all legitimate modes including those based on Shirkah, trade or lease, whether to finance trade, industry or a budget deficit through domestic or foreign sources. In order to properly manage the risk, the banks should manage diversified portfolios and select the proper modes/instruments. The volume of investment deposits determines banks' investment strategies – if depositors are risk-averse, banks should also be risk-averse – investing in less risky modes.

Musharakah/Mudarabah can be used for short-, medium- and long-term project financing, import financing, preshipment export financing, working capital financing and financing all single transactions. Banks use Diminishing Musharakah for purchase of fixed assets like houses, transport, machinery, etc.

Murabaha can be used for the purchase and sale of automobiles, consumer durables and trade financing, acquisition and holding of stock and inventory, spares and replacements, raw material and semi-finished goods. Buy-back and rollover in Murabaha are not allowed.

Musawamah can be used for the financing of huge single transactions.

Salam has a vast potential in financing the productive activities in crucial sectors, particularly agriculture, agro-based industries and the rural economy as a whole for financing agriculturists/farmers, commodity operations of public and private sectors and other purchases of homogeneous goods.

Banks' subsidiaries as trading and leasing companies can also provide finance on the basis of Murabaha and leasing. They can deal with priority areas not only on the basis of Murabaha, Salam and operating lease, but also on the basis of partnership. Ijarah, or leasing, is best suited for financing of automobiles and machinery. There could also be a combination of more than one mode like Istisna'a plus Murabaha, Salam plus Murabaha or Salam plus Istisna'a for financing of trade and industry. Finance for the purchase and construction of houses can be based on Diminishing Musharakah or Murabaha. Working capital finance can be provided on the basis of Salam, Istisna'a and Murabaha. Financing of big projects can be made through syndicate Mudarabahs using the modes of Istisna'a or Murabaha.

Appropriate modes of financing, as recommended by experts on Islamic finance, for particular areas and transactions are as given below.[8]

### Modes for Financing Trade, Agriculture and Industry

Murabaha, instalment sale, leasing and Salam are particularly suitable for trade, while Istisna'a is especially suitable for industry. More specifically, in trade and industry, financing is needed for the purchase of raw materials, inventory (goods in trade) and fixed assets as well as some working capital, for the payment of salaries and other recurrent expenses. Murabaha can be used for financing of all purchases of raw materials and inventory. For procurement of fixed assets, including plant and machinery, buildings, etc., either instalments sale or leasing can be used. Funds for recurrent expenses can be obtained by the advance sale of final products of the company using Salam or Istisna'a.

### Household, Personal Finance, Consumer Banking

Personal finance for consumer durables can be provided through Murabaha, leasing and in special cases by way of return-free loans out of the current accounts or the banks' own funds (depositors' money in PLS accounts is a trust in the hands of banks and should not be used for charitable and social purposes without their explicit approval).

Wakalah and Murabaha can be used for cash financing through charge and credit cards.

The alternatives for auto finance are Ijarah Muntahia-bi-Tamleek and Murabaha.

Housing finance is possible through Murabaha, Diminishing Musharakah and rent-sharing.

### Treasury Operations – Liquidity and Fund Management

Liquidity management means ensuring that the bank has sufficient liquid funds available for a smooth running of its operations and to meet short-term financial obligations as and when due. It has to invest surplus funds, match maturity of assets and liabilities, accommodate decreases in deposits/liabilities and increases in assets in an efficient and economic manner.

Fund management refers to securing and managing funds for the development of business.

Islamic banks may sell and purchase Sharī'ah-compliant money and capital market instruments like stocks and Sukuk. Direct placement or acquisition of funds (in the inter-bank funds market) on the basis of Mudarabah and Musharakah is also possible. The deficit bank agrees to give a share of its profits according to a Mudarabah ratio that can either be negotiated according to the market conditions or recommended by the central bank, for the duration of the contract. In the case of Mudarabah, the following process can be adopted:

1. A Mudarabah relationship will be created.
2. Funds received will be allocated to pools.
3. Weightages will be assigned periodically, based on different tiers/categories.
4. Profit earned will be allocated according to weightages assigned at the beginning of the period.

---

[8] Detailed processes for these modes of financing different areas/sectors are given in Chapter 14.

5. The bank will charge a pre-agreed Mudarib fee as a percentage of the realized profit; the bank can pay additional profit from its own share.
6. The investor will bear a loss unless it arises from misconduct or negligence of the Mudarib.

Islamic banks may also agree to an arrangement with the central bank serving as a lender of last resort. One option is financing on a Mudarabah basis; the central bank may agree to provide liquidity for, say, a three day grace period with ceilings, followed by a Mudarabah with profit-sharing ratio heavily favouring the central bank to discourage the Islamic bank from resorting to the central bank's funds for longer periods. Another option is the sale and purchase of Sharī´ah-compliant certificates/Sukuk.

Sukuk are important for liquidity management. In Sukuk, an investor gets returns on the basis of ownership rather than interest. Ijarah Sukuk are more common instruments in this regard and are issued against assets for rental. To generate liquidity, Sukuk can be sold/purchased in the secondary market. If the regulatory structure allows, Islamic banks can sell the Sukuk to the central bank to generate liquidity. Sukuk can be structured on an amortizing or bullet maturity basis.

### Foreign Exchange Operations

Exchange of currencies and monetary units has to be subjected to the rules of Bai´ al Sarf, i.e. it must be simultaneous. Accordingly, spot purchase and sale of one currency against another currency is allowed; forward purchase and sale is not allowed. However, IFIs can enter into a promise to purchase and sell agreement. On this principle, foreign currency forward cover is allowed with certain conditions, as discussed in Chapter 14. In order to ensure that the transaction actually goes through, parties may stipulate any earnest money. Negotiation of export documents is partially allowed.

### Government/Public Sector Financing

Government and public sector enterprises can obtain finance by way of Mudarabah or Musharakah certificates, which can be issued to purchase equipment or utility-generating assets in order to lease them to public sector corporations. Ijarah and Istisna'a are best suited for infrastructure projects in the public sector. Recently, Ijarah Sukuk have emerged as the most crucial instruments for financing of the public sector. Through syndication arrangements, Islamic banks can supply goods/assets of enormous value to government entities or corporations on a Murabaha basis by setting up joint Murabaha funds. In such cases, ownership of Murabaha funds can also be securitized to offer equity-based investment opportunities to the investors and the banks themselves. Returns on these funds would be distributed among Sukuk/certificate holders on a pro rata basis.

### Alternatives to Foreign Loans

For the inflow of foreign resources, the instruments of portfolio investment through stock markets, flotation of various categories of Sukuk and direct investment by foreigners can be used.

Public as well as private enterprises can issue Musharakah and Ijarah Sukuk to finance projects, especially development projects. Sukuk can be denominated in foreign as well as domestic currencies and carry a predetermined proportion of the profit earned by their respective projects. The Sukuk issued can be restricted to a particular project or earmarked to a group of projects.

Various funds can be established to finance the economic activities of public and private enterprises on equity, partnership, leasing, Salam and mixed asset pool bases. Funds can be established to finance a specific sector, for example, agriculture, industry or infrastructure; a particular industry, for example textiles, household durables, etc.; or general types of projects.

---

**Box 8.2:**    Islamic Banking Products and Services

| Nature of Product/Service | Modes and Basis |
|---|---|
| **I. Deposits – fund mobilization** | |
| Current deposits | Amānah – Qard to bank; no return payable |
| Savings deposits | Mudarabah |
| General investment term deposits | Mudarabah |
| Special investment deposits | Mudarabah, closed-and open-ended mutual funds, Wakalatul Istismār |
| Individual portfolios | Mudarabah, Wakalatul Istismār |
| Liquidity generation | Tawarruq – reverse Murabaha, sale to any 3rd party |
| **II. Trade finance, corporate finance** | |
| Project finance | Musharakah, Mudarabah-based TFCs, syndication through Mudarabah, Murabaha, Istisna'a, Ijarah/Ujrah |
| Working capital finance | Murabaha, Salam, Musharakah in single transactions |
| Export finance – preshipment | Salam/Istisna'a plus Murabaha and Wakalah, Murabaha, Musharakah |
| Import finance | Murabaha, Musharakah |
| Cash finance | Salam, Istisna'a, Tawarruq (sale to 3rd party) |
| Export finance – post shipment (bill discounting) | Qardal Hasan in local currency (spot rate) and promise to sell foreign exchange in future market – exchange rate differential bank's income; Murabaha if funds needed for next consignment |
| Letter of credit | Commission, Ujrah along with Murabaha, etc. |
| Letter of guarantee | Kafalah, service charge |
| **III. Agriculture, forestry and fisheries** | |
| Production finance for input and pesticides | Murabaha, Salam |

| | |
|---|---|
| Tubewells, tractors, trailers, farm machinery and transport (including fishing boats) | Ijarah Munahia-bi-Tamleek, Salam, Murabaha |
| Plough cattle, milk cattle and other livestock; dairy and poultry | Murabaha, Salam |
| Storage and other farm construction (sheds for animals, fencing, etc.) | Diminishing Musharakah or rent-sharing |
| Land development | Operating Ijarah, Salam |
| Orchards, nurseries, forestry | Salam, Musaqat |

**IV. Treasury**

| | |
|---|---|
| Money market – inter-bank | Mudarabah with or without allocation of assets |
| Liquidity management | Sale/purchase of permissible securities, Parallel Salam, Tawarruq |
| Fund management | Mudarabah, Wakalatul Istismār, trading in permissible stocks and Sukuk |
| Trading in Sukuk, stocks | Depending upon the nature of instruments |
| Forex operations | Unilateral promise to buy/sell foreign exchange simultaneously at pre-agreed rate |

**V. Personal advances (including consumer durables and housing)**

| | |
|---|---|
| Consumer durables | Murabaha/instalments sale |
| Automobiles | Ijarah Munahia-bi-Tamleek, Murabaha |
| Housing finance | Diminishing Musharakah, Murabaha |
| Providing cash for personal needs | Salam if possible, Tawarruq |

## 8.6   THE ISSUE OF MODE PREFERENCE

According to the majority of scholars, the main instrument by which the interest-based system has to be replaced is profit/loss sharing, encompassing Musharakah, Mudarabah and their variants. The idea of replacing interest by profit sharing in the depositor–bank and bank–business relationships, first mooted during the 1940s to 1960s, gained considerable acceptance in the 1980s and 1990s. However, there are slight differences in approach and priorities. While S.M. Hasanuz Zaman is not in favour of using Mudarabah[9] (on the assets side) for non-trade operations[10], a vast majority of scholars have recommended its extensive use. Nejatullah Siddiqi has discussed thoroughly the extended scope of Mudarabah.[11] To him, it does not involve traits like Riba, Qimār, fraud, coercion, exploitation of needs, hazard and uncertainty that could make it unlawful. He hints that although in practice the role of profit-sharing and partnership is very small at present, they continue to dominate the

---

[9] Alternatively, he recommends the use of Musharakah. As the combination of Mudarabah and Musharakah is also accepted by Sharī'ah scholars, the bank could use profit/loss sharing as a technique encompassing both modes, subject to the fulfilment of relevant conditions.

[10] Hasanuz Zaman, 1990 (1410 AH), pp. 69–88.

[11] Siddiqi, 1991, pp. 21–34.

theory of Islamic banking. They are regarded as the norm towards which practice should, and will, eventually gravitate. Like him, a large group of Islamic economists insist that Islamic banking and finance will have to rely on profit-sharing contracts if the objectives of socio-economic justice, efficiency and stability of the economic system are to be achieved.

Similarly, according to Umer Chapra, the most important and unanimously agreed upon form of financing provided by Islamic banks would be on the basis of Mudarabah, Shirkah or acquisition of shares of joint stock companies. Chapra has given its rationale in the following words:

> "The general principle, which is beyond dispute as being the criterion for determining the permissibility or otherwise of any method of financing, is that the financier cannot avert the taking of at least some risk if he wishes to derive an income. To put this in the form of an adage, one could state with respect to all financing operations: no risk, no gain".[12]

On the other hand, as pointed out by Abdul Halim Ismail, the approach of Islamic banks' practitioners is different from the general approach adopted by Islamic economists. He considers that the contracts of exchange, both for instant and deferred prices, are more relevant to Islamic financial institutions and equally legitimate as per Qur'ānic injunctions. Giving more importance to PLS modes according to the popular theory of Islamic finance has been formulated incorrectly. He has divided the writers on Islamic finance into the categories of "Islamic economists" and "Islamic bankers". While the economists group is in favour of replacing interest with a PLS system as a main policy tool, bankers have tended to give equal importance to debt-based modes involving both trade and leasing. Islamic bankers are remarkably uniform in their application of exchange contracts, including both trade and leasing. He blames Islamic economists for not deriving their theory of PLS preference from the Holy Qur'ān and considers the contracts of exchange on a par with the contracts of profit-sharing. He argues that the current practice of Islamic finance, in contrast to the general perception of Islamic finance theory, is largely based on trade/exchange-based transactions.

However, the point is that Islamic economists have not prohibited debt-creating modes; the issue is of preference only and that, too, on account of the possible impact of risk-based versus risk-free capital in an economy. As exchange-based modes also involve risk-sharing, Islamic economists have allowed them subject to the fulfilment of relevant conditions. Their stress on profit-sharing modes is for their better socio-economic impact and to avoid any back doors to interest.

Analysing the issue from another angle, the replacement of the interest-based system by an alternative profit-sharing system raises a number of fundamental theoretical, practical and policy questions. The questions being discussed in the emerging literature include, among others, the following:

- What is the theoretical framework underlying Islamic banking and finance?
- Will the Islamic system be more or less stable than the traditional interest-based system?
- What will be the effect of the adoption of an interest-free Islamic system on important macroeconomic variables like saving and investment?
- Will monetary policy have a role to play in such a system?

---

[12] Chapra, 1985.

As regards the first two questions above, Mohsin S. Khan takes the view that the replacement of interest by some type of profit-sharing arrangement makes the Islamic system an equity-based system, as opposed to a traditional debt-based system. Using the concept of equity participation, he has developed a theoretical model to examine the working of the Islamic banking system. He has shown that the Islamic system may well turn out to be better suited than the interest-based banking system to adjust to shocks that can lead to banking crises. In an equity-based system, shocks to the assets position of banks are immediately absorbed by changes in the nominal values of shares (deposits) held by the public in banks. Therefore, the real value of assets and liabilities would be equal at all points in time. In the conventional banking system, since the nominal value of deposits is guaranteed, such shocks can cause a divergence between real assets and real liabilities, and it is not clear how this disequilibrium can be corrected and how long the process of adjustment would take.[13]

On the basis of this analysis, Mohsin Khan has had an important insight that from an economic standpoint, the principal difference between the Islamic and traditional banking systems is not that one allows interest payments and the other does not. The more relevant distinction is that the Islamic system treats deposits as shares and accordingly does not guarantee their nominal value, whereas in the traditional system, such deposits are guaranteed either by the banks or by the government.

As regards the impact of adoption of the Islamic system (the third question above), Waqar Masood concludes that in a full Islamic system, the costs of monitoring would be insignificant and the equity participation arrangement would be superior to the interest-based system. Honesty and faithfulness to the terms of one's contract are an indispensable ingredient of Islamic behaviour. The driving force of a truly Islamic society is the existence of a strong ideological consensus that the success of the society and its members depends on how closely the rules of the Sharī´ah are followed.[14]

Nadeem ul Haque and Mirakhor are of the view that the adoption of a profit-sharing arrangement between the lender and investor may raise monitoring costs that could have an adverse effect on the supply of credit, and thus on investment. They are of the view that individual contracts can be designed to take into account the moral hazard problem. Avoiding an adverse effect on investment would require implementation of a legal and institutional framework that facilitates contracting. The Islamic law of contracts provides for such a framework, but it has not yet been fully adopted in countries where an Islamic banking system is being established. In the absence of this framework, monitoring costs could be prohibitive and investment could consequently be discouraged. On the other hand, if legal measures are present to safeguard the terms of contracts, the level of investment may increase.[15]

Shahrukh Rafi Khan, while discussing the implications of introducing a PLS system, has concluded that:[16]

1. Expectation-based profit-sharing ratios can serve as a pricing mechanism to bring the loanable funds market into equilibrium.
2. The elimination of risk-free assets with positive returns will leave lenders worse off.

[13] Khan and Mirakhor, 1987, pp. 15–36.
[14] Khan and Mirakhor, 1987, pp. 75–105.
[15] Khan and Mirakhor, 1987, pp. 125–161.
[16] Khan and Mirakhor, 1987, pp. 107–124.

3. Profit-sharing ratios are relatively inefficient instruments of monetary policy.
4. The introduction of interest-free banking does not necessarily lead to a situation where all profitable projects will be financed irrespective of their rate of return.

However, Mohsin Khan and Mirakhor do not feel convinced by these conclusions because they are conditional on the model and the specific assumptions under which the results are obtained. The traditional welfare comparisons made by Rafi Khan are incorrect because the welfare function itself will change with Islamization of the economy.

Regarding the impact on savings, Nadeem ul Haque and Abbas Mirakhor have concluded that the rate of return also increases as risk increases, and then savings may, in fact, rise. The structural changes accompanying the implementation of an Islamic financial system may produce favourable effects on the rate of return on financial assets. As such, there is no *a priori* reason for believing that savings in an Islamic system will necessarily be lower than in an interest-based system.

The above discussion implies that all Islamic modes have potential for development. The institution of Mudarabah serves as a basis of business to be conducted by combining funds and the expertise of different groups of people. Shirkah-based (PLS) modes that provide the much-needed risk-based funds can be used for short-, medium- and long-term project financing, import financing, preshipment export financing, working capital financing and financing of all single transactions. Mudarabah Sukuk can be issued to mobilize funds and strengthen trading and industrial activities. SPVs can manage such assets as trusts/funds for conducting business for their benefit as well as the Sukuk holders. This could generate higher rates of return for the investors relative to the return realizable on any interest-based investment.

As visualized by Homoud, if the profit rate in Mudarabah-based businesses is as low as 10 % and the annual turnover is 3, the realized profits may reach 30 % per annum. "These profits may be distributed at an equal sharing ratio or at the rate 1/3 to 2/3 between Mudarabah certificate holders and the management of the institution. . . . The idea has the potential to alleviate the hardships of low income people in many countries."[17] In the case of big projects, the IFIs may form a consortium to issue certificates to the public for subscription. Similarly, they can carry out work on infrastructure and socio-economic projects in coordination and partnership with the engineering firms.

The non-PLS techniques not only complement the PLS modes but also provide flexibility of choice to meet the needs of different sectors and economic agents in society. Murabaha with less risk has several advantages vis-à-vis other techniques and can be helpful in employment generation and alleviation of poverty. Leasing can be very much conducive to the formation of fixed assets and medium- and long-term investments.

Salam has a vast potential in financing the productive activities in crucial sectors, particularly agriculture, agro-based industries and the rural economy as a whole. It provides an incentive to enhance production and leads to the creation of a stable commodities market with stability in prices. To realize this potential, IFIs could organize a forward commodity trade market on the basis of Salam. This would provide not only a nonspeculative forward market for resource mobilization and investment but would also be a powerful vehicle for rural finance.

---

[17] Homoud, 1998.

## 8.7   ISLAMIC INVESTMENT BANKING

Islamic investment banking can be easily understood in the light of conventional investment banking. An Islamic investment bank provides exactly the same products and services as a conventional bank does. The distinguishing factor, however, is that their products and services are tailored in a Sharī´ah-compliant manner while meeting the clients' requirements. Islamic investment banks manage portfolios for institutions, corporate clients and high net worth individuals, as well as pooled investment vehicles such as unit trusts and mutual funds. Asset management companies managing conventional funds are now gearing up for Islamic funds.

The following are the opportunities for Islamic asset management:

- open and closed-end mutual funds;
- equity benchmarks;
- leasing companies involved in asset-backed financing.

Islamic investment banks provide venture capital financing to small, medium and big companies in a number of sectors. They avoid involvement in prohibited and unlawful activities and offer services to all projects except those manufacturing or dealing with forbidden products and services, such as alcohol, pork, entertainment, interest-based financial services and the like. Their services relate to venture capital and corporate finance, including syndication finance, project finance and transactions in the capital markets.

Asset management or management of funds includes equity funds, real estate funds as well as alternative investments in Ijarah and other Sukuk. They engage in treasury operations for managing the asset–liability mismatch created by different tenors of investment opportunities and different return profiles.

Islamic corporate finance activities of investment institutions are similar to conventional corporate finance except that the products and services offered are Sharī´ah-compliant. These services include:

- equity issues such as IPOs, offers for sale, rights issues;
- private placements;
- strategic reviews;
- financial restructurings;
- acquisitions, divestments, mergers;
- joint ventures, alliance searches and studies.

Islamic investment banks also undertake syndicate financing, which is usually a large financing facility granted to a key industrial or trading organization and lead-managed by a bank of strong base. Since the amount involved is large, a number of financial institutions participate in the financing. An Islamic syndication facility can be provided through Murabaha, Mudarabah, Musharakah, Ijarah or leasing (detailed processes are given in relevant chapters of the book).

## 8.8   ISLAMIC FINANCIAL MARKETS AND INSTRUMENTS

Islamic financial markets, like their conventional counterparts, comprise money and capital markets, but the instruments and the procedures of functioning are different. An Islamic financial market would be free of interest and would work on a different set of principles.[18] The Islamic Fiqh Council of the OIC has observed:

> "Although the original concept of financial markets is sound and its application is very much needed in the present-day context, yet their existing structure does not present an example to carry out the objective of investment and growth of capital within the Islamic framework. This situation requires serious academic efforts to be undertaken in collaboration between the jurists and the economists, so that it may be possible to review the existing system with its procedure and instruments and to amend what needs amendment in the light of the recognized principles of Sharī'ah".

The major instruments of Islamic financial markets are equity related. Besides equity instruments in the form of shares in any company, the Islamic financial system has other redeemable short-, medium- and long-term participating instruments representing ownership in the assets, and hence entitled to participate in the profit/loss resulting from the operations on the assets. Various types of participatory instruments can be based on (i) profit/loss sharing (Mudarabah/Musharakah), like instruments issued by Mudarabah and asset management companies and participation term certificates (PTCs), and (ii) rent-sharing in the form of Diminishing Musharakah or otherwise.

A pure debt or bonds market is not an active part of the Islamic financial markets because debt liabilities have to be paid at the nominal value subject to observance of the rules of Hawalah (recourse to the original debtor if the assignor is not able to pay the liability). The instruments on the basis of which the Islamic market has to function need to be backed by or represent real asset transactions. A debt security would result from a transaction based on any trading or Ijarah mode that can implicitly include time value of money at the stage of pricing of the underlying commodities or usufruct of the assets.

These instruments may be of either a variable or quasi-fixed/fixed return nature. Equity instruments having a claim to share in the net income and the assets of a business give a variable return, while debt-related instruments can be issued in respect of trade or leasing-based transactions subject to the observation of the principles of the underlying Islamic modes. Backing by real assets according to the rules of the relevant modes is a must and mere replacement of one paper transaction with another kind of similar paper transaction will not serve the real purpose.

Islamic financial market instruments can be of two types in terms of their nature and flow of return:

1. Fixed/quasi-fixed (stable) income securities. A bank can securitize or sell a pool of assets or offer certificates of deposit (CODs) against a fund composed of pooled Ijarah and some Murabaha and Istisna'a contracts. It will offer the investors/depositors a defined stream of cash flow constituting the return on the pooled assets. Such securities would accommodate risk-averse investors like widows, retired people, etc. and generate new resources for additional intermediation and income flow to the banks.
2. Variable income (Shirkah-based) securities. For such securities, banks can securitize a pool of Musharakah and Mudarabah contracts that are part of their asset portfolio. Such securities will offer the investors a stream of variable income with potential for growth, based on the strength of the underlying projects – profit and risk both would be higher than

---

[18] For details see Ahmad, Ausaf, 1997.

in the case of stable income securities. These would accommodate risk-taking investors with the commensurate possibility of a higher income.

### 8.8.1   Islamic Funds

Fund management can be conducted both by commercial and investment banks, but presently, mostly investment banks are involved. Due to the asset-based nature of Islamic finance, this type of business is more suitable for IFIs than short-term commercial banking.

Fund management refers to investors pooling their resources to purchase a larger number of shares through any manager collectively, which otherwise they could not purchase individually. About 150 mutual funds of various categories are providing low risk/moderate return, balanced risk/return and high risk/high return Sharī´ah-compliant investment facilities to investors in various parts of the world. While presently Islamic mutual funds are operating mainly in Saudi Arabia, UAE, Bahrain, Kuwait, Qatar, Pakistan, Malaysia, Brunei, Singapore, Germany, Ireland, the UK, the USA, Canada, Switzerland and South Africa, efforts are underway to provide investment facilities through mutual funds in all parts of the world to capture the emerging demand. Most of these funds are equity funds while a number of hybrid funds are managing leasing, real estate, Takaful and other funds.

Management of the funds can be carried out on Mudarabah or agency basis. In the case of Mudarabah, the fund manager would get any pre-agreed percentage of the realized profit, while in the case of an agency arrangement, the manager would get a fee on agreed terms that may be any specified amount or percentage of the net asset value of the fund.

Shaikh Taqi Usmani has indicated the following categories of Islamic investment fund:

1. Equity funds, the proceeds of which are invested in shares of joint stock companies, and returns in the form of capital gains and dividends are distributed on a pro rata basis among the investors.
2. Ijarah funds. The amounts of such funds are used to purchase the assets for the purpose of leasing. Rentals received from the user are distributed among subscribers of the fund. Ijarah Sukuk can be traded in the secondary market on the basis of market forces. Anyone who purchases these Sukuk replaces the sellers in the pro rata ownership of the relevant assets and all the rights and obligations of the original subscriber are passed on to him.
3. Commodity funds, in which the subscription amounts are used to purchase different commodities for the purpose of resale. The profits generated by the sales are distributed among the subscribers.
4. Murabaha funds. Any fund created for Murabaha sale should be a closed-end fund; its units cannot be negotiable in a secondary market as an Islamic bank's portfolio of Murabaha does not own any tangible assets.
5. Mixed funds, the subscription amounts of which are employed in different types of investments like equities, leasing, commodities, etc. For trading of mixed funds, the tangible assets should be more than 51 %, while the liquid assets and debts less than 50 %.[19]

*Asset Management Through Equity Funds*

As compared to a conventional equity fund, in which a fixed return is tied up with its face value, an Islamic equity fund must carry a pro rata profit actually earned by the fund.

---

[19] Usmani, 2000a, pp. 203–218.

Therefore, neither the principal nor a rate of profit (tied up with the principal) can be guaranteed. On the basis of the risk profiles of the investors and the investment strategy of the asset management companies, equity funds can be divided into four categories:

1. Regular income funds: the objective of these funds is to earn profit through dividends of investee companies. Such funds provide a regular income stream by way of dividends to their investors who are mostly risk-averse, like old and retired people.
2. Capital gain funds: the objective of these funds is to earn profit through capital gain from frequent sale and purchase of Sharī'ah-compliant stocks. These funds can provide a better return to moderate risk-taker investors by proper management and risk diversification.
3. Aggressive funds: these funds invest in high-risk securities to generate abnormal profits for their investors. They do not allow every investor to invest and limit the portfolio to high-risk investors as chances of loss are greater.
4. Balanced funds: such funds invest in high quality securities with less risk and give to the investors a regular income stream based on dividends and capital gain. These funds adopt a "capital proactive" approach.

*Screening and Purification Criteria*

Equity stocks included in the funds need to be compliant with Sharī'ah guidelines. Sharī'ah boards of IFIs develop a tolerance level in respect of investments in stocks. The selection of stocks goes through a strict screening process decided by the respective Sharī'ah boards. Keeping in mind the scenario in the markets, this tolerance level might be different in different financial institutions and markets. Generally, the screening criteria tend to ensure that:

1. The investee company's capital structure is predominantly equity based (debt less than 33 %).
2. Prohibited activities such as gambling, interest-based financial institutions, alcohol production, etc. are excluded.
3. Only a negligible portion of the income of an investee company is derived from interest on securities. (In the case of Al Meezan Islamic funds, for example, the income of an investee company from nonpermissible income should not exceed 5 % of total income.)
4. The value of share should not be less than the value of the net liquid assets of the company.

The most widely known are the Dow Jones Islamic Market Index Criteria, encompassing the following:

1. The basic business of the investee company should be Halal.
2. Debt to market capitalization: total debt divided by 12-month average market capitalization should be less than 33 %.
3. Cash and interest-bearing securities: the sum of the company's cash and interest-bearing securities divided by the trailing 12-month average market capitalization should be less than 33 %.
4. Accounts receivable: accounts receivable divided by the trailing 12-month average market capitalization should be less than 33 %.

Further, Islamic asset management companies have to purify their income by deducting from the returns on the investments the earnings emanating from any unacceptable source from the Sharī'ah point of view. It is obligatory to dole away the prohibited income that is mixed up with the earnings of the company, and this obligation is on the one who is the owner of the shares or Sukuk – the investor. Purification is not obligatory for the intermediary, agent or manager because wages or commission are their right in lieu of the work they have undertaken. In the case of fund management, it is the responsibility of the management company to exclude prohibited income.

Al-Meezan Investment Management (Pakistan), which operates a number of Islamic funds, calculates the percentage of noncompliant income to the gross revenue (net sales + other income) for each investee company and this percentage is called the charity rate. The charity rate for each investee company is multiplied by the dividend income from the respective companies to get the charitable amount. This charitable amount is then transferred to a separate account.

Islamic equity funds experienced excellent growth during the late 1990s. In 1996, for example, there were 29 Islamic equity funds on the market with $800 million in assets. By early 2000, the number of funds had grown to 98, with approximately $5 billion in assets. Today there are over 100 Islamic equity funds on the market, offering investment solutions to meet any Islamic investor's taste.

### 8.8.2   Principles Relating to Stocks

Since investment in stocks of joint stock companies is the core business of Islamic investment banks and other NBFIs, we may briefly discuss its main features and aspects. The Islamic Fiqh Council of the OIC in its seventh session (9–14th May, 1992) resolved the following in respect of shares of joint stock companies:[20]

1. Trading in stocks of companies

   — Since the essential thing about transactions is the nature of their business, the establishment of a joint stock company with unprohibited purposes and activities is permissible.
   — Trading in stocks of companies whose main purpose is a prohibited activity, such as transactions with Riba, production of, or dealing in, prohibited products is prohibited.
   — Trading in stocks of companies that deal at times in prohibited things, such as Riba, etc., but their main activities are not based on any prohibited business is permissible.

2. Underwriting: underwriting is an agreement made upon establishment of a company with someone who undertakes to guarantee the sale of all or part of the shares being issued, i.e. to undertake to subscribe for shares that remain unsubscribed by others. There is no Sharī'ah objection to this provided that the obligee subscribes to the shares at nominal value without any compensation for the commitment *per se*, though the obligee may receive compensation for work other than the underwriting – such as making feasibility studies or marketing of shares.

3. Object of the contract in the sale of shares: the object of the contract in the sale of shares is the unidentified portion of the company's assets (known as Musha'a in Islamic jurisprudence) and the share certificate is a document attesting entitlement to the said portion.

4. Preference shares: it is not permissible to issue preference shares with financial characteristics that involve guaranteed payment of the capital or of a certain amount of profit or ensure precedence over other shares at the time of liquidation or distribution of dividends.

---

[20] This is a brief summary of the resolution; for details, see Council of the Islamic Fiqh Academy, 2000.

It is, however, permissible to give certain shares such characteristics as are related to the procedural or administrative matters.

5. Borrowing on interest for investment in shares: it is not permissible to purchase a share with an interest-bearing loan offered to the purchaser by a broker or any other party against pawning of the share, as this involves Riba. Nor is it permissible to sell a share that the seller does not possess but has received as pledge from a broker, since such a deal falls within the framework of sale of something that the seller does not own. The prohibition shall be more categorical if the deal is conditional upon payment of the share price to the broker, who would then benefit by depositing this price at interest in order to obtain compensation for the loan.

### 8.8.3  Investment Sukuk as Islamic Market Instruments

Sukuk (the plural of the word Sak) were used by the Muslim societies of the Middle Ages as "papers" representing financial obligations originating from trade and other commercial activities. However, the Sukuk structures presently found in Islamic finance are different from the Sukuk originally used and are akin to the conventional concept of securitization, a process in which ownership of the underlying assets is transferred to a large number of investors through papers commonly known as certificates, Sukuk or other instruments representing proportionate value of the relevant assets.

Investment Sukuk are different in nature from common shares of joint stock companies. These are certificates of equal value representing undivided shares in ownership of tangible assets of particular projects or specific investment activity, usufruct and services.[21]

Sukuk can be of a number of types, based on the Sharī'ah mode used as the underlying contract or subcontract, the most important of which are Shirkah, Ijarah, Salam and Istisna'a. As per the basic rules of Sharī'ah, investment Sukuk have to be structured, on one side, on the Mudarabah principle. On the other side, business can be conducted through participatory or fixed-return modes/instruments. Thus, the rates of return on Sukuk will be either variable (if the modes on the second leg are participatory) or quasi-fixed (in the case of modes with a fixed return). Sukuk can be made fixed-return Sukuk through the provision of any third party guarantee.[22]

The primary markets operate on the basis of equity principles like shares, redeemable equity capital, Mudarabah/Musharakah certificates (MCs) or Sukuk representing ownership in leased assets or debt instruments resulting from trading modes issued directly to investors or fund providers. While the price of Sukuk in the primary market is derived through calculating the weighted average of the bids received for the premium to be offered over the benchmark, the price in secondary market trading depends upon the nature of the security being traded.

According to mainstream Islamic finance theory, pure debt securities do not have a secondary market in principle. However, there is the possibility of securitization of debts resulting from real trading transactions when they are pooled with other assets or instruments representing ownership in real assets. All equity or participatory instruments have a secondary market because they represent ownership in assets of the companies.

---

[21] AAOIFI, 2004–5a, pp. 298–300.
[22] Council of the Islamic Fiqh Academy, 2000, p. 65.

Sukuk can be issued by governments, corporations, banking and nonbanking financial institutions and by business/industrial concerns. As forward sale/purchase of goods through Salam rules is permissible, there is also the possibility of a commodity forward market, which, of course, will be different from the conventional commodity futures market. As such, the following types of market governed by principles of relevant contracts or modes are available in the Islamic financial structure:

• equity or stock markets;
• securities markets like nongovernment securities (banks, non-banks, corporate and housing securities);
• government and municipal securities market;
• commodity futures market;
• inter-bank money market for placement of funds on a Mudarabah basis;
• foreign exchange market (limited).

### 8.8.4  Trading in Financial Instruments

Islamic investment vehicles that are traded in Islamic financial markets include Sharī´ah-compliant stocks wherein income is derived from dividends and capital gains keeping in mind the screening criteria recommended by Sharī´ah scholars. Other instruments are Mudarabah/Musharakah certificates, units of open- or closed-ended mutual funds and investment Sukuk, wherein income is derived from buying, selling and also getting returns from the underlying businesses and assets.

Stocks/securities/certificates/Sukuk can be traded in the market depending on market signals, provided there is compliance with the following Sharī´ah rules:

• Instruments representing real physical assets and usufructs are negotiable at market prices. Certificates or Sukuk issued by Musharakah, Mudarabah and Ijarah are covered under this category.
• Instruments representing debts and money are subject for their negotiability to the rules of Hawalah[23] (assignment of debt) and Bai‘ al Sarf (exchange of monetary units).
• Instruments representing a pool of different categories are subject to the rules relating to the dominant category. If cash and debts/receivables are relatively larger, the rule of Bai‘ al Sarf applies, and if real/physical assets and usufructs are overwhelming, trading would be based on the market price.[24]

### 8.8.5  Inter-bank Funds Market

The Islamic inter-bank funds market can function on the Mudarabah principle or sale and purchase of instruments under the relevant rules of the Sharī´ah. Presently, a Mudarabah-based regular market is functioning in Malaysia. In other countries, banks place their surplus funds with deficit banks for short periods ranging from a day to a week. Mostly, these short-term deposits are treated just like other deposits mobilized from the public and profits are paid on the basis of weightages assigned and the daily product of the deposits, while

---

[23] Discussed in detail in the previous chapter.
[24] AAOIFI, 2004–5a, pp. 305–307.

sometimes a special procedure is adopted, according to which the deficit bank agrees to give a share of its general profits according to a Mudarabah ratio that is negotiated according to the market conditions. Central banks can also advise profit-sharing ratios for the duration of the fund placements.

In Malaysia, the Islamic Inter-bank Money Market (IIMM) was introduced in January, 1994 as a short-term intermediary to provide a ready source of short-term investment outlets based on Sharī´ah principles. BNM issued the guidelines on the IIMM in December 1993 to facilitate proper implementation of the IIMM. The IIMM covers the following aspects: (i) inter-bank trading of Islamic financial instruments and (ii) Mudarabah inter-bank investments (MII). Islamic banks, commercial banks, merchant banks, eligible finance companies and discount houses are allowed to participate in the IIMM.

MII refers to a mechanism whereby a deficit Islamic banking institution ("investee bank") can obtain investment from a surplus Islamic banking institution ("investor bank") based on the Mudarabah principle. The period of investment is from overnight to 12 months, while the rate of return is based on the rate of gross profit before distribution for investments of 1 year of the investee bank. The profit-sharing ratio is negotiable between both parties. The investor bank, at the time of negotiation, does not know what the return will be, as the actual return will be crystallized towards the end of the investment period. The principal invested is repaid at the end of the period, together with a share of the profit arising from use of the fund by the investee bank.

Beginning 2nd February, 1996, BNM introduced the minimum benchmark rate for the MII, i.e. the prevailing rate of the government investment issues plus a spread of 0.5 %. The purpose of the benchmark rate is to ensure that only banks with reasonable rates of return participate in the MII.

CODs and COIs, as discussed in a preceding section, can also be negotiated in the Islamic money market. In recent years, Ijarah-based negotiable Islamic money instruments have also been developed. Islamic banks can engage in trading of these instruments for liquidity management subject to observance of the Sharī´ah rules involved in the relevant modes.

### 8.8.6 Islamic Forward Markets

Based on the three types of contracts relating to future delivery, three different types of forward market can be considered in the framework of Islamic finance:

1. A Salam-based forward market (for products and commodities for which a regular market exists).
2. An Istisna‘a-based forward market, basically for infrastructural and developmental projects.
3. A Ju‘alah-based forward market for service-based activities.

Three points require serious attention in the concept of Salam trade from the point of view of future trading. First, delivery of the goods is compulsory. Second, unlike the contemporary futures market, reselling of a Salam commodity before it is received is not permitted by the Sharī´ah experts. However, Parallel Salam of the same goods, for the same date of delivery, is allowed. Third, a Salam contract strictly requires advance payment of the price of the goods. The contemporary futures market, on the contrary, does not require any advance payment to the seller.

Earning income from mere speculation on prices without having an explicit part in the real activity comes under the category of gambling. All such activities in the futures market that are meant to make a possible income simply by making good guesses with no intention to receive or deliver goods are not allowed. Unlike the conventional futures market, the actual delivery as well as its receipt will be mandatory and cannot be offset by writing a reversing futures contract in the Salam-based futures market.

In Istisna'a and Ju'alah markets too, the contract will be completed only by making or receiving actual delivery of the goods or service concerned. An Istisna'a contract can be made only for those commodities that are required to be specially produced according to the defined specifications and are not otherwise available in the market. For a Ju'alah contract, no physical goods qualify; only services qualify for such a contract.

Prices will be determined by competitive bids and offers made by traders interested in real selling and buying. For an Islamic future exchange, a bidding to purchase means a commitment to make the payment in advance. It also requires determining a certain time interval for quoting the new prices, unlike the conventional futures exchange where new prices can be offered at any time.

An Istisna'a-based futures market will be different from a Salam-based market because of longer term transactions and hence will require a different legal institutional framework. Though there is nothing in Sharī'ah to bar Istisna'a contracts for a short run, for the development of a meaningful futures market, particularly with the aim of resource mobilization for development, it will be the long-term Istisna'a-based futures contract that will serve the purpose. Prices of Istisna'a-based futures contracts in the market may not widely fluctuate over the short term, as they are expected to in the Salam-based futures market. This would make this market useful for small savers who are interested in protecting the real value of their savings. These contracts would provide them with a means to index their savings with inflation.[25]

---

**Box 8.3:**    Islamic Capital Market Instruments and Operations

Islamic financial market instruments can represent the following assets:

- ownership in a company or a business, e.g. stocks and Musharakah or Mudarabah Sukuk;
- ownership of durable assets or the usufruct of such assets, e.g. Ijarah Sukuk;
- ownership of debt arising from Murabaha, Istisna'a or Salam financing;
- a combination of the above categories.

**Tradability**

- Islamic money market instruments can either be tradable or nontradable in the secondary market;
- instruments representing ownership in business, real physical assets and usufructs are negotiable at market prices;
- instruments representing ownership of debt are not tradable in the secondary market, as sale of debt is not permissible in Islamic law;

---

[25] Khan, 1995.

**Box 8.3:** (Continued)

- instruments representing a combination of different categories are subject to rules relating to the dominant category.

**Treasury Functions**

- Debt portfolio management

  — manage the debt portfolio which emerges from the accumulation of individual financing transactions so as to achieve an acceptable cost and risk profile for the portfolio over time.

- Risk management

  — advise on and implement effective hedging of treasury type risks, especially foreign exchange, return rate, liquidity, settlement, credit and counterparty risks.

**Sukuk Structures**

- Musharakah Sukuk

  — co-ownership of assets or business with control and management rights;
  — payments supported by income generated by assets of business;
  — tradable.

- Mudarabah Sukuk

  — ownership of assets or business without control and management rights;
  — payments supported by income generated by assets of business;
  — tradable.

- Ijarah Sukuk

  — sale and lease-back structure;
  — could either be based on fixed or floating rate structures;
  — payments supported by lease rentals;
  — tradable.

- Salam Sukuk

  — ownership of debt resulting from a Salam transaction (i.e. advance payment of funds, future delivery of assets);
  — short-term maturity;
  — nontradable.

- Istisna'a Sukuk

  — ownership of debt arising from an Istisna'a transaction (i.e. advance payment of funds, in full or in instalments for construction of an asset);
  — nontradable.

### 8.8.7    Foreign Exchange Market in the Islamic Framework

A foreign exchange market can function in the Islamic financial structure keeping in mind the limitations set by the Sharī'ah. IFIs can engage in direct placement or investment in Sharī'ah-compliant F.E. denominated securities like Solidity Trust Certificates issued by IDB in 2003 and many other Sukuk.

A foreign currency forward cover facility is also available in the present Islamic financial structure. Contemporary Sharī'ah scholars have observed that forward cover is permissible subject to the following conditions:

- The amount of foreign currency is needed for genuine trade or payment transactions. This need will have to be supported by appropriate documents so as to prevent forward cover for speculative purposes. It implies that money changers or forex dealers relying on book-out transactions cannot take such cover.
- The forward cover shall be through a formal promise to sell or purchase and it shall not be a sale and purchase agreement. This means that sale/purchase shall take place simultaneously at the agreed time in future at the rate agreed upon initially at the time of agreement to sell or purchase.
- While it will be permissible to fix the price of foreign currency in terms of local currency according to the agreement, no forward cover fee shall be recovered. However, an amount may be demanded by the bank from its client in advance by way of earnest money (Hamish Jiddiyah) against foreign currency agreed to be purchased/sold at a future date. If, at the agreed time, the promisor does not perform, the bank can recover the differential and adjust the earnest money there against.

### 8.8.8    Derivatives and Islamic Finance

Conventional options, swaps and futures stem from debts and involve sale and purchase of debts/liabilities. As a group, such instruments are called derivatives, i.e. they are derived from the expected future performance of the respective underlying assets. These are very complex and risky contracts with a present market value of trillions of dollars around the world. It has been observed, however, that the global financial market is becoming increasingly fragile as more and more derivatives and "hedging" instruments emerge.

Conventional options confer merely rights and not liabilities. An option has a nominal size, this being the amount of underlying asset that the option holder may buy or sell at the strike price – the price at which the holder may like to buy or sell the underlying asset upon exercise of the option. If the price moves favourably, the option is exercised and the commodity is bought/sold at the agreed price. If the price moves unfavourably, the buyer of the option simply abandons it. This is against the principle of the Sharī'ah, according to which delivery has to be given and taken pursuant to the sale contracts without regard to movement in prices. The buyer of the option pays a price (the premium) to the seller (the writer) of the option. Hence, the feature that an option contract confers the right but not the obligation to enter into an underlying contract of exchange at or before a specified future date (the expiry date) makes the contract non-Sharī'ah compliant.

Some writers have discussed the possibility of put and call options[26] in legitimate goods and stocks on the basis of 'Arbūn and reverse 'Arbūn (for example, putting a condition in the

---

[26] A call option is the right to buy while the right to sell is referred to as a put option.

sale agreement that if the seller backs out after taking 'Arbūn, he will have to pay double the amount to the buyer), as prevalent in the legal system in some Arab countries, particularly in the Jordanian Civil Code. For example, Al Sanhuri, as a member of the committee which drafted that law, has contended that reverse 'Arbūn, which could validate put options, is in accordance with Islamic principles. Shaikh Al Dharir has, however, rejected the concept of reverse 'Arbūn and the viewpoint of Sanhuri on the grounds that such a clause in the legal system in some countries is discussed under secular legislation only and not under Islamic legal works.

As regards options relating to currencies, interest rates and stock indices, all agree that these have no place in Islamic finance.[27]

Further, among the major schools of Islamic jurisprudence, only the Hanbali uphold 'Arbūn with the condition imposed by some of them that time should be stipulated for the option. The OIC Fiqh Council has also endorsed 'Arbūn but only if a time limit is specified. Even if 'Arbūn is accepted as a valid transaction, most of the derivatives currently in the market would still be unacceptable from the Sharī´ah angle due to the involvement of Gharar and Riba. A call option can be considered near to Bai' al 'Arbūn in the sense that the seller does not return the premium or advance payment to the buyer if the latter does not exercise the purchase option and the buyer loses the option premium even if the option is exercised and the contract is confirmed. In the case of Bai' al 'Arbūn, however, the option premium is adjusted in the sale price when the contract is confirmed.

Samuel L. Hayes, after detailed discussion on derivatives, concludes:

"There are no effective derivates of Islamic debt contracts which replicate conventional risk-hedging and leveraging contracts such as swaps, futures and options. Similarly, in the equity security sector, there are no risk-hedging or leveraging contracts in Islamic finance truly comparable to available conventional derivatives . . . With respect to commodities and other goods, the Salam contract is an imperfect Islamic substitute for a conventional forward contract. The related Istisna'a contract for goods being manufactured for a buyer provides another partial Islamic proxy for a forward contract. It is also possible to construct an Islamic contract which partially replicates a conventional futures contract, via back-to-back Salam contracts."

The institutions dealing in derivatives and hedge funds claim that the diversity of hedging products protects their clients against market volatility and provides a larger spectrum of risk management to the benefit of society. But actually, volatility is caused by their activities when they trade in derivatives and the clients are sold nothing for something – protection against a danger that never needed to exist in the first place. They may produce huge profits for financial institutions at the cost of others, but these profits are not necessarily indicative of productive efforts. Mr Warren Buffet, Chairman of Berkshire Hathaway once said:

"Derivatives are financial weapons of mass destruction, mainly due to opaque pricing and accounting policies in swaps, options and other complex products whose prices are not listed on exchanges; credit derivatives and total return swaps that are agreements to guarantee counterparty against default or bankruptcy merit special concern."[28]

The macroeconomic arguments for their existence are not convincing either – they are for minimizing risks which do not need to exist. The global foreign exchange market at present is more or less an unproductive pursuit in that it exists because of an unnecessary monetary

---

[27] For details see Vogel and Hayes, 1998, pp. 156–164, 220–232, 281, 282.
[28] Buffet, 2003.

expansion. It would be better to structure the financial system such that it did not suffer from continuing volatility. What we are seeing in the Western world is the emergence of financial products that are a symptom of a system that has gone wrong. For a more efficient economy, we must promote systems in which people work in productive pursuits rather than unproductive ones. As El-Gamal states:

> "Change the system to relate it with real sector activities and all those clever dealers who earn huge profits out of thin air could become doctors, industrialists, business people and teachers instead! As such, Islamic financiers who look at the products of this system as a paradigm seem to be at mistake."[29]

Study of the behaviour of the derivatives market reveals that it has the potential to cause a serious breakdown in the financial system. The degrees of leverage that are afforded by option contracts can be so high that large unpredictable market moves in underlying prices may one day lead to the insolvency of major financial institutions. Liabilities cannot be perfectly hedged, even if that is the intention, and some traders deliberately do not hedge their option portfolios because such action would limit the potential for high returns. The case of Long Term Capital Management in the United States, rescued by a Federal Reserve bail out in 1998, demonstrates the degree of risk that can be incurred. The question is whether the central bank or other authorities would be able to move quickly enough, or in large enough measure, to prevent possible failings.

For example, collateralized debt obligations (CDOs) are a sophisticated type of derivative and a clever way of exploiting anomalies in credit ratings. A number of loans or debt securities payable by various companies are put into a pool, and new securities are issued which pay out according to the pool's collective performance. The new securities are divided into three (or more) levels of risk. The lowest, equity tranche, takes the first loss if any companies in the pool default. If enough losses eat that up, the next, mezzanine level, suffers. The most protected level, the senior tranche, would still be safe, unless the collective pool has severe losses. It takes only a couple of defaults in a pool of 100 companies to destroy the equity tranche. Downgrades of investment-grade corporate bonds in America were a record 22 % in 2002 according to Moody's, and it recorded bond defaults of $160 billion worldwide. The equity and mezzanine tranches of many CDOs suffered severe losses; some were wiped out. Even senior tranches, usually rated AAA, have been downgraded because losses may yet reach them.[30] Thus, the whole concept of CDOs as in vogue refers to absolute risk and exploitation, which is unacceptable in Islamic finance.

## 8.9  SUMMARY AND CONCLUSION

Banking and non-banking financial institutions can operate as indirect and direct intermediaries, respectively, in the Islamic framework. The instrument of "interest" will be replaced by a set of instruments comprising risk-based profit/loss sharing ratios and profit margins in trading and leasing activities. IFIs, in order to get legitimate profit/earnings, will have to take up liability, undertake risk and add value through trading and leasing transactions and services.

---

[29] El-Gamal, comment made on his personal web site: http://www.ruf.rice.edu/~ elgamal.
[30] *The Economist*, London, 15th March, 2003.

The markets that can function in the Islamic financial framework include both money and capital markets, equity markets, limited forex markets, forward markets and investment Sukuk markets, representing a variety of instruments for fund and investment management by Islamic financial institutions.

Providing Sharī´ah-compliant and feasible instruments for the functioning of Islamic capital markets in the competitive global financial environment is the real challenge facing scholars and practitioners of Islamic banking and finance. Of all the features of Islamic financial instruments, one stands out distinctly, i.e. the instruments must be real asset-based. While it is relatively easy for individual banks/financial institutions to securitize their asset-based operations, development of instruments for financing government budget deficits is a difficult task, mainly because the sovereigns needing finance do not have sufficient real assets for conversion of debt stock into Sharī´ah-compliant securities. A beginning has been made and Islamic banks and financial institutions in Bahrain, Malaysia, Saudi Arabia, UAE, Pakistan, Sudan and elsewhere in the world, including a number of non-Muslim countries like the Philippines, Germany and Japan, are using a variety of instruments based on profit/loss sharing, Ijarah and Salam. Ijarah has relatively greater potential, which needs to be realized. Sudan has developed Shirkah-based instruments and other countries need to follow.

A variety of target-specific Sukuk can be issued on the basis of various modes, keeping in mind the relevant Sharī´ah rules. This would require appropriate enabling laws to protect the interests of investors and issuers, appropriate accounting standards, study of the targeted market, monitoring of standardized contracts, appropriate flow of financial data to investors and provision of a standard quality service to customers at large. In all of this, regulators have to play a crucial role.

Governments, particularly in Islamic countries, may like to establish national mutual funds or Mudarabah/leasing companies with the dual objective of developing Islamic financial markets and mobilizing financial resources for meeting financing requirements of public sector and private sector corporations. These mutual funds may gradually replace the conventional national savings schemes, treasury bills and other government bonds.

The Bahrain-based Liquidity Management Centre (LMC) and the International Islamic Financial Market (IIFM) need to play a proactive role to coordinate the operations of Islamic banks in the world. There could be an Islamic Liquidity Management Centre established in all countries with the presence of Islamic financial institutions, which would serve as a fund manager to manage and invest the excess liquidity of IFIs working in the respective jurisdictions. The process having started, likely problems can be resolved by means of trial and error, and necessary reforms can be introduced accordingly.

# 9

# Murabaha and Musawamah

## 9.1  INTRODUCTION

Trading is one of the most common activities of Islamic banks. While conventional banks simply finance trading businesses by providing funds, Islamic banks have to be involved in the sale and purchase process for goods according to the trading rules prescribed by the Sharī´ah. They are entitled to profit by undertaking business risk like real sector businesses.

However, Islamic banks' trading pattern is different from the general trading business. Banks' clients normally need a credit facility and the banks are selling goods on credit and thus creating receivables. Credit sale (Bai' Mu´ajjal) may take a number of forms, important among which are:

1. Musawamah, or normal sale, in which parties bargain on price, a sale is executed and goods delivered while payment is deferred.
2. Murabaha, a "cost-plus sale", in which parties bargain on the margin of profit over the known cost price. The seller has to reveal the cost-incurred by him for acquisition of the goods and provide all cost-related information to the buyer.

Experts in Islamic economics and finance generally advise the use of profit/loss sharing modes and discourage extensive use of Murabaha or other trading modes. But, as its permissibility is beyond doubt and all Islamic banks operating in the world are using this technique excessively as an alternative to the conventional modes of credit, studying Murabaha from the point of view of Islamic banking is crucial, and hence is the subject of the present chapter.

The technique of Murabaha that is currently being used in Islamic banking is something different from the classical Murabaha used in normal trade. This transaction is concluded with a prior promise to buy or a request made by a person interested in acquiring goods on credit from any financial institution. As such, it is called "Murabaha to Purchase Orderer" (MPO). The AAOIFI's Sharī´ah Standard on Murabaha is also based on this arrangement. We shall discuss the general rules of Murabaha and various structures that financial institutions can adopt for sale to help their clients.

Various aspects to be discussed in this regard include the nature of Murabaha as we find in classical literature on Islamic jurisprudence, the sorts of goods eligible for selling through Murabaha on credit, disclosure to the buyer by the seller, combining other contracts or subcontracts for Murabaha arrangements by Islamic banks, the concept of Khiyar (option to rescind the sale) and possible defects in the object of sale, prepayment or late payment by the client, the possibility of liquidated damages/solatium to banks and the modern application of Murabaha along with issues involved. Fixity of price, taking ownership, risk related to ownership and possession[1] of the object of contract by the bank before sale to the client, timings of Murabaha execution and the principles regarding Murabaha receivables need more focus for their impact on Sharī´ah compliance.

## 9.2  CONDITIONS OF VALID BAI'

The conditions and rules for a lawful sale transaction have been described in detail in Chapter 6. Keeping in mind the importance given by Islamic banks to Murabaha, we give below a recap on the salient features and conditions for a valid sale:

1. The people uttering offer and acceptance in respect of a valid sale should be qualified to enter into the contracts.
2. The sale should take place with free and mutual consent of the seller and the purchaser.
3. Offer and acceptance must include certainty of price, certainty of date and place of delivery and certainty about the time of payment of the price.
4. The seller should be either the owner of the object of sale (Mabi') or an agent of the owner.
5. The Mabi' should be alienable. Transfer of title requires acquisition of title by the purchaser, which implies assuming the risks related to ownership, including the risk of damage, destruction, pilferage or theft, the risk of obsolescence and the price or market risk.
6. The subject of sale must exist at the time of sale; as such, one cannot sell the unborn calf of one's cow, or a bank cannot execute Murabaha on goods that have already been consumed or used.
7. The Mabi' should be well-defined and in the ownership of the seller. Hence, what is not owned by the seller cannot be sold; for example, A sells to B a car which he intends to purchase from C (still owned by C) Since the car is not owned by A at the time of sale, the sale is void.
8. The subject of sale must be in the physical or constructive possession of the seller at the time of sale.[2] Constructive possession means that the buyer has not taken physical delivery of the goods, but the ownership risk of the goods has been transferred to him: the goods are under his control and all rights and liabilities of the goods have passed on to him. For example, A has purchased a car from B, B has not physically handed over the car to A but has placed it in a garage which is in the control of A, who has free access to it – the risk of the car has practically passed on to him, the car is in the "constructive possession" of A and he can sell the car to any third party.
9. Sale must be instant and absolute – a sale attributed to a future date or a sale contingent on a future event is void. For example, A says to B on 1st of January: "I sell my car to you on the 1st of February". The sale is void, because it is contingent on a future event. He can give an understanding or a promise, but the sale will have to be executed on 1st February, and it is only then that rights and liabilities will emerge.

---

[1] Ownership as distinct from possession; while possession can also be constructive, the sale of unowned goods, even if existent, is unanimously prohibited, except in the case of Salam.

[2] This is based on a number of traditions of the holy Prophet, as discussed in Chapter 6. However, constructive possession is sufficient, as widely accepted by the Sharī´ah scholars. The journal *Al-Iqtisad al-Islami* of Dubai Islamic Bank reported as for back as in 1984 that possession by the banks is completed when the vendor sets it aside for it, particularly when the bank concerned is liable to bear the loss of damage to the commodity before its delivery to the buyer (*Al-Iqtisad-al-Islami*, March, 1984).

10. The subject of sale should be lawful and an object of value. A thing having no value according to the usage of trade cannot be sold; similarly, the subject of sale should not be a thing used for any prohibited purpose, e.g. pork, wine, etc.

11. The subject of sale should be specifically known and identified to the buyer, i.e. it must be identified by pointing out or by detailed specifications so as to distinguish it from other units of goods not sold. For example, A says to B: "I sell 100 cotton bales out of the bales lying in that building", if A does not identify the bales, the sale is void, because in the case of loss to the cotton, it would be difficult to ascertain who suffered how much loss.

12. The delivery of the sold commodity to the buyer should be certain and should not depend on a contingency or chance. For example, if A sells his car, which has been snatched, to a person in the hope that he will manage to get it back, the sale is void.

13. A certain price is stipulated once and for all. For example, A says to B: "If you pay in one month, the price is $50 and if in two months, the price will be $55"; as the price is uncertain, the sale is void. A can give the two options to B, but B must select one option to have one definite price to validate the sale.

14. The sale must be unconditional. A conditional sale is invalid, unless the condition is a part of any usual practice of trade not expressly prohibited by the Sharī´ah.

There are also certain other conditions which are applicable to each form of sale separately. The conditions related to Bai‘ Murabaha are discussed below.

## 9.3  MURABAHA – A BAI‘ AL AMĀNAH

For the purpose of this chapter, forms of Bai‘ can be described from the point of view of the cost of any item to the seller – we may call it the original cost. Since the original cost or purchase price is the starting point in Bai‘ Murabaha, it is appropriate to refer briefly to all such lawful forms of Bai‘ which become effective with express mention of the original cost. Such a classification of Bai‘ includes Tawliyah, Wadhi‘ah or Mohatah and Murabaha. These forms require an honest declaration of the cost by the seller and as such are referred to in the Fiqh literature as Buyoo‘ al Amānāt (fiduciary sales).[3] Among fiduciary sales, Tawliyah means resale at the stated original price with no profit or loss to the seller. Wadhi‘ah or Mohatah means resale at a discount from the original cost. The last one, Murabaha, is sale with a fixed profit margin over the cost. Another, and the most common, form is Bai‘ Musawamah, which is an ordinary sale and signifies sale for a price which is mutually agreed upon between the seller and the purchaser without any reference to the purchase price/cost to the seller. In other words, it refers to bargaining on price of the commodity being traded. All these forms could be either on a spot or deferred payment basis. While in Musawamah the parties freely agree on the price, in Murabaha the seller informs the buyer of his original cost and the parties agree on a stipulated profit to be added to that cost.

## 9.4  BAI‘ MURABAHA IN CLASSICAL LITERATURE

Murabaha is derived from Ribh, which means gain, profit or addition. In Murabaha, a seller has to reveal his cost and the contract takes place at an agreed margin of profit. This contract

---

[3] Al Jaziri, 1973, p. 300.

was practised in pre-Islamic times. Imam Malik has mentioned this sale in *Al-Mu'watta* – the first formally coded book on traditions of the holy Prophet (pbuh). A renowned Hanafi jurist Al-Marghinani has defined Murabaha as "the sale of anything for the price at which it was purchased by the seller and an addition of a fixed sum by way of profit".[4] Ibn Qudama, a Hanbali jurist, has defined it as "the sale at capital cost plus a known profit; the knowledge of capital cost is a precondition in it. Thus the seller should say: 'My capital involved in this deal is so much or this thing has cost me (Dm) 100 and I sell it to you for this cost plus a profit of (Dm) 10'. This is lawful without any controversy among the jurists".[5]

According to Imam Malik, Murabaha is conducted and completed by exchanging goods and price including a mutually agreed profit margin, then and there.[6] It is important to observe that to him, no credit is involved in Murabaha. Malikis as a whole do not like this sale as it requires so many conditions, the fulfilment of which is very difficult. However, they do not prohibit it.[7]

Imam Shaf'ie in *Kitabul Umm* expanded this concept to include credit transactions. It has been defined in similar words in other books of Fiqh.[8]

By definition, therefore, it is basic for a valid Murabaha that the buyer must know the original price, additional expenses if any and the amount of profit. Accordingly, Murabaha is a contract of trustworthiness.[9]

## 9.5  THE NEED FOR MURABAHA

Actually, Murabaha is meant for some restricted situations. Al-Marghinani has suggested that the purpose of Murabaha (and Tawliyah) is the protection of innocent consumers lacking expertise in trade from the tricks and stratagems of cunning traders.[10] A person who lacks skill in making purchases in the market on the basis of Musawamah is obliged to have recourse to a Murabaha dealer who is known for his honesty in this particular type of trade, and thus purchases the article from that person by paying him an agreed addition over the original purchase price. This leaves the actual buyer satisfied and secure from the fraud to which he was exposed for want of skill. Hence, it is evident that the main purpose of this form of Bai' is to protect innocent purchasers from exploitation by cunning traders.

Imam Ahmad prefers ordinary sale over Murabaha in the following words:

> "To me, ordinary sale (Musawamah) is easier than Murabaha, because Murabaha implies a trust (reposed in the seller) and seeking of ease on behalf of the buyer, and it also requires detailed description to the buyer; there is every likelihood that selfishness may overcome the seller, persuading him to give a false statement or that mistake may occur which makes it exploitation and fraud. Avoidance of such a situation is, therefore, much better and preferable".[11]

The same ideas have been expressed by a Jafari jurist on the authority of Imam Hussain ibn Ali.[12] After basing the sale price on the original cost of the goods to the seller, the

---

[4]  Al-Marghinani, 1957, p. 282.
[5]  Ibn Qudama, 1958, **4**, p. 179; Al Jaziri, 1973, pp. 559–564.
[6]  Malik, 1985, pp. 424, 425.
[7]  Al Jaziri, 1973, p. 559.
[8]  Al-Hilli, 1389 AH, p. 40.
[9]  Al-Kasani, 1993, **5**, p. 223, cf. Hassan, 1993, p. 95.
[10]  Al-Marghinani, 1957, p. 282.
[11]  Ibn Qudama, 1367 AH, p. 187.
[12]  Al-Kulayni, 1278 AH, p. 197.

purchaser is provided with a modicum of protection against unjust exploitation by unscrupulous merchants.[13]

It is important to observe, however, that modern Murabaha is conducted mainly by banks and financial institutions on a deferred payment basis. Upon execution of Murabaha, a receivable is created that becomes the liability of the customer. The aspect of disclosing details of the banks' cost price, though a necessary condition of Murabaha, does not remain a serious issue between the parties, particularly in view of the fact that the customer himself is involved one way or the other in locating and purchasing the goods.

## 9.6   SPECIFIC CONDITIONS OF MURABAHA

It is quite obvious that a transaction under Murabaha should meet all the general conditions applicable to an ordinary sale. The specific conditions regarding lawful transactions of Murabaha pertain to the goods subject to Murabaha, the original price paid by the seller, any additional costs to compute the total costs serving as the basis of Murabaha and the margin of profit charged on the cost so determined. An account of these conditions follows:

1. Goods to be traded should be real, but not necessarily tangible. Rights and royalties are examples of nontangibles that can be traded through Murabaha, as they have value, are owned and can be sold on credit.
2. Any currency and monetary units that are subject to the rules of Bai' al Sarf cannot be sold through Murabaha, because currencies have to be exchanged simultaneously.[14]
3. Similarly, credit documents that represent debt owed by someone cannot be the subject of Murabaha, first because debt cannot be sold except when it is subject to the rules of Hawalah and second because any profit taken on the debt would be Riba.
4. The seller must state the original price and the additional expenses incurred on the sale item and he must be just and true to his words. The additional expenses such as transport, processing and packing charges, etc. that enhance the value of the commodity in any way, and that are added as a custom by the merchant community in the original price, can be added into the purchase price to form the basis of Murabaha. It is, however, requisite that the seller, in making or including such an addition, should say: "This article has cost me so much", and not: "I have purchased this at such a rate," because the latter assertion would be false.[15] The traditional jurists had some differences in this regard. The Hanafi school permits the seller to include in the base price of Murabaha all expenses he has incurred in relation to it, which have somehow modified the object (tailoring, dyeing for cloth) and those which have not modified it but were nevertheless incurred for the object's sake (transportation, storage costs, commission).[16] The Malikis divide the expenses into three groups: expenses that directly affect the object of the sale and that can be added to the base price of the object; expenses that are incurred after the profit has been calculated and do not directly alter the sale object, like services which the seller might not have provided himself (transportation and storage expenses), which can also be added and expenses which represent the services that the seller could have

---

[13] Udovitch, 1970, p. 220.
[14] Al-Jaziri, 1973, p. 564; AAOIFI, 2004–5a, p. 128.
[15] Al-Marghinani, 1957, p. 282; Shaybani, 1953, pp. 155, 156.
[16] Al-Jaziri, 1973, pp. 564, 565; Saleh, 1986, p. 96.

provided himself but did not provide, such as packing charges, sales commission, etc. – these cannot be added.[17] According to Shafi'es also, the expenses of the last category cannot be added to the cost. The Hanbalis' view is more pragmatic, according to which all expenses can be added with mutual consent, provided the buyer is informed about the break-down of these expenses.[18]

5. The prospective seller in Murabaha is required to disclose all aspects relating to the commodity, any defects or additional benefits and the mode of payment to the original seller/supplier. All schools of thought are unanimous on the point that the buyer in Murabaha ought to be informed if the original price was on credit, since credit prices are often higher than cash prices. All also agree that the original purchase price deliberately inflated violates the concept of Murabaha. If an Islamic bank receives a rebate for goods purchased, even after the Murabaha sale of such a contract, the client/buyer is entitled to benefit from the rebate as well.[19]

6. The margin of profit on the price so reached has to be mutually agreed upon between buyer and seller. The price, once fixed as per agreement and deferred, cannot be further increased except for rebate received from the supplier as mentioned above.

7. Any Majhul (unspecified) price cannot become a basis for Murabaha, as it involves the semblance of uncertainty which renders Murabaha sale unlawful.[20] It is, therefore, a prerequisite that the price or cost paid by the seller must be expressed in identical units, such as dirhams and dinars, or specific articles of weight or measurement; because if the original price is an article of which all the units are not similar, the exact price at which the original buyer has become owner of the article will remain unknown.

8. If the seller gives an incorrect statement about the original price/cost of goods, the buyer, according to Imam Malik, may rescind the sale unless the seller returns to him the difference between his real and the stated cost, in which case the sale is binding. The Hanafis give the buyer the unqualified option to rescind, while the Hanbalis consider the sale binding after the return of the difference between the correct and the stated costs. The Shafi'es have two versions, one of which agrees with the Hanbalis and the other with the Hanafis.[21]

9. The purchaser in Murabaha has the right of option, even in the absence of this condition or its stipulation in the contract. If he discovers that the seller has defrauded him by false statement regarding particulars of the article, its price, additional expenses or if the seller himself has bought the commodity on a deferred payment basis and sold it on prompt payment without informing him, or if any practice on the part of the seller involves the semblance of illegal sale, the purchaser will be at liberty either to accept or reject the bargain as he pleases.[22] If, however, the purchaser detects cheating after he has used that commodity or it has been destroyed in his hands, he is not entitled to make any deduction from the price according to Imam Abu Hanifa and his disciple Muhammad, because the commodity against which he has to practise his right of option does not exist.

---

[17] Ibn Rushd, 1950, **2**, p. 217.
[18] See Saleh, 1986, p. 96.
[19] AAOIFI, 2004–5a, clause 4/5, p. 120; See also Saleh, 1986, p. 96.
[20] Al-Marghinani, 1957, p. 285.
[21] Ibn Rushd, 1950, **2**, p. 218; cf. Ray, 1995, p. 44.
[22] Ibn Qudama, 1369 AH, **13**, p. 78.

According to Abu Yusuf and Ibn-abi-Laila, also Hanafi, deduction will be made even after the destruction of the commodity.[23]

The message we get from the above is that Murabaha is a lawful kind of sale but has its own limitations. The Medieval Murabaha was not a mode of financing, it was a kind of trade. Contemporary jurists have accepted it as a mode of business and an alternative to financing with certain limitations. These relate to the level of transparency and justice which Islam ordains for commercial activities. It is in view of this requirement that Maliki fuqaha consider this form of sale Naqis (defective). This means that the permissibility of Murabaha is not as absolute as is the case of ordinary sale.[24]

There is no doubt that jurists have justified Murabaha on the grounds that it provides protection to the innocent, unskilled and inexperienced purchasers, but as we do not find any reference regarding its prohibition for experienced people or traders, it can therefore be adopted subject to the fulfilment of the juristic conditions, as an alternative to interest-bearing transactions for those activities which the Sharī´ah boards of various banks may allow.[25]

### 9.6.1  Bai' Murabaha and Credit Sale (Murabaha–Mu'ajjal)

Murabaha as an alternative to interest-based financial transactions assumes importance only when it is transacted on a deferred payment basis. This, therefore, calls for a study of the concept of postponement of payment in Murabaha. The terms of payment in the classical Murabaha did not necessarily involve credit; they could be either cash or credit. It may, however, be pointed out that the legality of postponement of payment is one of the general features of lawful sales – termed Bai' Mu'ajjal, which refers to sale of goods or property against deferred payment (either in a lump sum or instalments).[26] Bunched with the Murabaha, Bai' Mu'ajjal would mean sale with an agreed profit margin over the cost price along with deferred payment.

In Hidaya, permission for credit sale has been described thus:

> "A sale is valid either for ready money or for a future payment provided the period be fixed, because of the words of the Holy Qur'ān 'Trading is lawful' and also because there is a tradition of the holy Prophet (peace be upon him) who purchased a garment from a Jew, and promised to pay the price at a fixed future date by pledging his iron breast-coat. It is indispensably a requisite of business but the period of payment should be fixed. Uncertainty in the period of repayment may occasion a dispute and jeopardize the execution of the transaction since the seller would naturally like to demand the payment of the price as soon as possible, and the buyer would desire to defer it."[27]

The substitution of prompt payment by deferred payment has been justified on the grounds that upon execution of the transaction, the receipt of the agreed price becomes the sole

---

[23] Al-Sarakhsi, n.d., **13**, p. 86.

[24] Al Jaziri, 1973, p. 559.

[25] For details see Council of Islamic Ideology, 1980, pp. 15, 16, 34, 35, 38, 42–46; the CII has described the detailed application of this mode in the chapter on "Commercial Banking". According to the CII, it can be used both for "fixed investment financing" and "working capital requirements" of parties (pp. 34, 38). Farmers' short-term fund requirements, particularly for the purchase of inputs like seed, fertilizer and pesticides and for plough cattle, tractors and tubewells can be met through Murabaha (pp. 34–45). The commerce sector can also be financed through this mode (pp. 45 and 46). As regards mining, quarrying, electricity, gas, water and services, this technique may be used for financing the purchase of capital goods and machinery (pp. 46–47). In the field of personal consumption, consumer durables can be financed on a Murabaha–Mu'ajjal basis.

[26] Majallah al Ahkam refers to Bai' al Mujjal as Bai' bil Nasiah or bi al T'ajil wa al Taqsit (Al-Atasi, 1403 AH, Articles 245–251).

[27] Al-Marghinani, 1957, p. 242.

right of the seller. It is, therefore, within his discretion to postpone it for the convenience and ease of the purchaser. The fact is that he is empowered even to forego it altogether.[28] Delay in payment under Murabaha is also allowed in other schools of Fiqh, including Shiaites.[29]

As described in detail in Chapter 6, jurists slightly differ on the aspect of different cash and credit prices. The Hanafis, Shafi'es and Hanbalis permit the difference between cash and credit prices provided one price is settled at the finalization of the contract. Although Imam Malik himself forbade it, some of the Malikis hold a different view and allow it. Contemporary jurists are almost unanimous on the legality of this difference. The rationale behind this viewpoint is that exchange in respect of a loan wherein any excess is prohibited occurs between a commodity and its like, while in credit sale, one of the counter values is the money and the other any goods of trade. As, for example, in loan transactions, $100 can only be exchanged for $100 or a ton of wheat for a ton of wheat. Any increase in the mutual exchange, therefore, is Riba. In the case of credit sale, exchange has to take place between two different commodities. First, money is exchanged for goods and then goods are sold against money. Therefore, the difference between the purchase price and sale price does not amount to Riba.[30]

Further, interest charged on a loan is payable to the lender in any case. In a sale contract, this is not so because the prices are liable to change. If the price rises, the purchaser gains because he purchased a good on a deferred payment basis at a cheaper price, but if the price drops, the seller gains because he succeeded in selling the item purchased on a deferred payment basis at a higher price. Bai' bi Thaman al-'Ajil or Bai' Mu'ajjal is, therefore, in conformity with the Fiqhi principle "Al-Ghunm bil Ghurm", i.e. profit goes with loss.[31] However, the sale contract has to be finalized at one price so that the exact liability is known to the parties. This would practically imply that the whole price is in return of the sale item.[32]

However, it is not allowed to conduct Murabaha on a deferred payment basis in the case of gold, silver or currencies, because all monetary units are subject to the rules of Bai' al Sarf. Similarly, receivables or debt instruments cannot become the subject matter of Murabaha, as any profit over the principal of a debt is Riba.[33] However, Murabaha of shares of joint stock companies eligible on the basis of screening criteria is allowed.

## 9.7   POSSIBLE STRUCTURES OF MURABAHA

Trading and other real sector business activities require specific expertise, which bankers may or may not have. Further, it is not possible for banks to train all staff in trading, marketing and other real sector activities required for Islamic banking practices. One possible solution is that banks may establish specific purpose companies to undertake trading (and leasing) activities and the staff with relevant specialized expertise may be entrusted the job of trading in goods so as to fulfil the Sharī'ah essentials of Murabaha–Mu'ajjal. Those companies

---

[28] Al-Marghinani, 1957, p. 288.
[29] Al-Hilli, 1389 AH, p. 41.
[30] Nooruddin, 1977, p. 125.
[31] Nooruddin, 1977, p. 126.
[32] Nooruddin, 1977, p. 134; Al-Sanani, 1972, pp. 136–137.
[33] AAOIFI, 2004–5a, Murabaha Standard, clause 2/2/6; pp. 114, 128.

would buy commodities and assets and sell them to their customers on the basis of deferred payment. Thus, the banks' specialized entities could use their entrepreneurial expertise, like all other profit-seeking businesses, to earn profit. Otherwise, the trading activities may be conducted either through the client as agent or through a third party agency. The options for conducting Murabaha are briefly discussed below.

### 9.7.1  Direct Trading by Bank Management

Direct trading by bank officials is the most ideal option with respect to fulfilment of the Murabaha essentials, but involving the bankers in retail trading business could lead to a lot of managerial problems and open the floodgates to corruption. This issue can be resolved through the introduction of effective internal controls. In the absence of such controls, this structure could be used only in cases of selected specific assets, wherein banks could purchase any high value asset or specific goods with trademarks in bulk for building inventory and sell to its clients on a cost-plus basis. For example, a bank's subsidiary dealing with agricultural finance may purchase fertilizer/pesticides and provide them to farmers on the basis of Murabaha through dealers. In such wholesale business, an additional benefit would be that the bank's sale price could be closer to the cash market price.

### 9.7.2  Bank Purchases Through a Third Party/Agent

One option in many cases may be to purchase goods through a third party agent to maintain inventory or to purchase according to clients' requests for Murabaha operations. This structure of Murabaha is most likely to accomplish the Sharī´ah requirement of taking possession and commercial risk by the bank for the period between the purchase of the assets from the supplier and their sale to the client on Murabaha.[34] After purchase from the supplier, banks stand liable if anything goes wrong until handing the asset over to the Murabaha clients. The customer cannot guarantee the risk of transportation of the goods because the safety of the goods is the responsibility of the owner, that is, the bank.[35] Banks can mitigate this risk by stipulating to get delivery at their godowns.

Banks may appoint qualified suppliers as agents for purchase according to their inventory-creating plans or as and when required by their clients. For the latter arrangement, the package would comprise (i) an MoU or agreement to sell – the client's request and promise that he will purchase the specified commodity from the bank; it may also include a stipulation about the profit margin to be taken by the bank and, if possible, the sale price, that will include the cost price, the contract price and the payment date(s); for the profit margin, the bank may indicate at this stage any reference rate provided a definite price is stipulated at the time of execution of Murabaha;[36] (ii) the sale deed executed at the time when the commodity is in the ownership and risk of the bank; and (iii) the "promissory note" signed by the client to the effect that he will pay the price of the goods purchased on a specified date. In addition to this, the agreement may include clauses about the security/collateral, description and quality of goods and the way out in case of

---

[34] According to the AAOIFI standard, the option of a third party agent is better; it recommends that the customer should not be appointed to act as agent for purchase of items for Murabaha except in situations of dire need (clause 3/1/3, p. 117).

[35] AAOIFI, 2004–5a, p. 129.

[36] AAOIFI, 2004–5a, p. 120.

defect in the goods and nonpayment by the client at the due date(s). According to the AAOIFI Standard, a promissory note or other guarantee can be obtained from the customer at the promise stage also.[37] Of course, it is better that promissory notes be obtained after execution of the sale, because these generally contain the wording "against value received".

### 9.7.3  Murabaha Through the Client as Agent

The structure of trading through a client as the bank's agent is the safest way for banks to avoid commodity-based risks and related problems. But this arrangement is more likely to make Murabaha transactions a back door to interest and, therefore, requires extra care to keep it Sharī´ah-compliant. The foremost requirement is that goods come under the ownership and risk of the bank. Further, the customer should explain to the supplier about his agency status.[38] If the bank does not purchase and own the items and only makes payment for any goods directly purchased and received by the client from the supplier/vendor under "Murabaha", that will be a remittance of the amount of money on behalf of the client, which shall be nothing but a loan to him and any profit on this amount shall be nothing but interest. As Islamic banks are normally using this structure, we discuss it in detail.

## 9.8  MURABAHA TO PURCHASE ORDERER (MPO)

Modern Murabaha transactions by banks normally take the form of Murabaha to Purchase Orderer (MPO) (Murabaha lil 'amri bil Shira or 'Murabaha li Wa'da bi Shira), which is an arrangement wherein the bank, upon request by the customer, purchases an asset from a third party and sells the same to the customer on a deferred payment basis. This variant is being widely used by almost all Islamic banks operating in various parts of the world and by the Islamic Development Bank for its foreign trade-financing operations. The need for MPO arises from the following factors:

1. Commercial banks, and likewise Islamic banks, do not normally undertake business where they might be maintaining inventories of various goods; they do not want to become grocers or traders because inventory storage, space and holding costs might be expensive.
2. It may not be possible for Islamic banks to purchase all items in advance for Murabaha to their clients because the list of goods could be very long and there could be continuous additions to the list.
3. The clients might be in need of specific quality goods and the banks might not be even aware of the source of their availability. If banks keep similar items in inventory, these might not be acceptable to the clients.
4. Regulators/central banks normally do not allow the banks to undertake trading as their core business, with the dual purpose of keeping them liquid/saving them from the asset and market risks related to goods and to avoid cartels and monopolies in the commodity market. As such, most of the Islamic banks purchase only those goods for which they receive requisition from their clients.

---

[37] AAOIFI, 2004–5a, p. 121.
[38] AAOIFI, 2004–5a, clause 3/1/1, pp. 117, 130.

On account of the above, Islamic banks have been allowed not necessarily to maintain inventory of goods to be sold through Murabaha. According to the AAOIFI Sharī´ah Standard on Murabaha, it is permissible for IFIs to purchase items only in response to their customers' wish and application. But this wish may not be considered a promise or commitment by the client to purchase the items, except when the promise has been made in the due form.[39] For practical purposes, the promise can be incorporated into the requisition form to be submitted by the client.

The customer can also indicate the supplier from whom the items/goods are to be purchased by the bank. But the bank will have to ensure that the supplier is any third party and that the client has not already purchased the item from that supplier or made a firm commitment with him to purchase; otherwise it would be Bai' al 'Inah and the transaction would be non-Sharī´ah-compliant. The bank can obtain a performance bond from the client to ensure that the supplier identified by him will function in good faith and that the item provided by him will be acceptable to the client.[40] Similarly, the bank is not allowed to enter into a Musharakah arrangement with the client with the promise that one of the parties will buy the other's share through Murabaha on either a spot or deferred payment basis. However, the promise can be made by a partner to buy the other's share at the market price or at a mutually agreed price at the time of sale by means of a separate contract.[41]

The above permission for MPO does not imply that IFIs cannot be involved in the sale/purchase of goods or cannot create their inventories. Purchasing an item, taking its possession and ownership along with risk and reward is a major requirement of Sharī´ah, without which the transaction would not be valid. Murabaha cannot be used as a substitute for a running finance facility, which provides cash for fulfilling various needs of the client. If a bank does not keep inventory, it can purchase a commodity on a client's request and sell it to him on a cost-plus basis, but it will have to fulfil all the necessary conditions of valid Bai' as well as additional conditions applicable to Murabaha.

Merchant banking has become one of the functions of even conventional banks. Therefore, Islamic banks, in addition to conducting MPO, may like to establish specialized asset management and trading companies as non-bank financial subsidiaries to undertake active trading business by maintaining inventory of major items demanded by their clients. This way, their profit margin may be higher and the customers may also be offered such items at cheaper rates.

Banks can purchase the goods through any third person/agent and possess the goods before resale. If the bank appoints the customer its agent to buy the commodity on its behalf, the customer will first purchase the commodity on behalf of the bank and take its possession as such. But payment should be made by the bank directly to the supplier. Double agency, i.e. for making payment and for purchasing and taking delivery, should be avoided because it may become a cause of misuse, making Murabaha a back door to interest. At this stage, the commodity must remain at the risk of the financier, who is the seller in this transaction. Thereafter, the client purchases the commodity from the financier for a deferred price.[42]

---

[39] AAOIFI, 2004–5a, p. 113.

[40] AAOIFI, 2004–5a, Standard on Murabaha, clause 2/5/1, p. 116.

[41] AAOIFI, 2004–5a, Standard on Murabaha, pp. 113, 114, 116, 128; clauses 2/2/1 to 2/2/5 and 2/5.

[42] Usmani, 2000a, p. 106; for principal's ownership during agency, see Zuhayli, 2003, p. 674.

### 9.8.1   MPO – A Bunch of Contracts

Modern Murabaha also involves an agency relationship between the bank and any third party or even the client. The Murabaha to Purchase Orderer in this form would comprise three distinct contracts:

1. A master contract which defines the overall facility to be availed, followed by an agreement to purchase or promise by the client to purchase the article when offered by the bank. Instead of being a bilateral contract of forward sale, the "agreement to buy" is a unilateral promise from the client which binds him and not the bank.
2. An agency contract whereby the agent, who could be a client or any third party, has to purchase the item from the market or the supplier identified by the client and take its possession on behalf of the bank; this should be separate from the Murabaha agreement.[43]
3. The actual Murabaha contract. The actual Murabaha contract should be concluded when the bank owns the concerned commodity.

Murabaha transactions that involve other contracts like promise, agency (Wakalah) and credit along with an agreed rate of return for IFIs over the cost price lead to a number of issues: should the promise be unilateral or bilateral, binding or nonbinding? What is the remedy if the client backs out? What should be the sequencing of the various actions of the bank and the client? When the actual Murabaha is to be executed, what happens if the client makes early payment or delays in making payment of the settled price? To what extent can the bank's loss be covered and mitigated? And last, but not least, what structure and modus operandi of Murabaha can be adopted to fulfil the needs of various stakeholders along with ensuring Sharī'ah compliance? We discuss these matters in the following sections.

### 9.8.2   Promise to Purchase in Murabaha

According to classical Fiqh rules, mere promises are not binding and cannot be compelled by the process of law. Although fulfilling a promise is advisable and violation reproachable, it is neither mandatory nor enforceable through the courts.[44] However, to many other jurists, promise can be enforced through courts of law. The third view (of some Maliki jurists) is that promise is not binding in normal conditions, but if the promisor has caused the promisee to incur some expenses or undertake some labour or liability on the basis of a promise, it is mandatory on him to fulfil his promise for which he may be compelled by the courts.

Shaikh Muhammad Taqi Usmani, after detailed discussion on the subject, contends:

> "Therefore, it is evident from these injunctions that fulfilling promise is obligatory. However, the question whether or not a promise is enforceable in courts depends on the nature of the promise.... But in commercial dealings, where a party has given an absolute promise to sell or purchase something and the other party has incurred liabilities on that basis, there is no reason why such a promise should not be enforced. Therefore, on the basis of the clear injunctions of Islam, if the parties have agreed that this particular promise will be binding on the promisor, it will be enforceable. If the promisor backs out of his promise, a court or any arbitration may force him either to purchase the commodity or pay actual damages to the promisee seller. The actual damages will include the actual monetary loss suffered by him, but will not include the opportunity cost".[45]

---

[43] AAOIFI, 2004–5a, Standard on Murabaha, p. 130.

[44] This is the view of Imam Abu Hanifa, Imam Shafi'e, Imam Ahmad and of some Maliki jurists, cf. Usmani, 2000a, pp. 121, 122.

[45] Usmani, 2000a, pp. 125, 126; Resolution Nos. 2 and 3, 5th session of the Islamic Fiqh Academy.

This aspect has been discussed in detail in Chapter 5, with the conclusion that if the parties agree that the promise should be binding, it will be legally enforceable; and if the promisee has incurred expenses as a result of the promise, the promisor will have to make up the loss incurred by the promisee. A client asks a bank to purchase certain goods on the basis of Murabaha according to his specifications from a supplier and promises that, after the bank acquires the goods, he will purchase them from the bank on a cost-plus basis. In a case of the breach of promise by the client, the bank may suffer loss while trying to return or to dispose of the purchased goods. To overcome this problem, scholars have issued a verdict that the promise of the customer to enter into the sale binds him, at least to the extent that he should pay any actual loss, excluding the loss on account of conventional "opportunity cost", incurred by the bank as a consequence of its reliance on the promise. This is in line with the AAOIFI's Standard on Murabaha to Purchase Orderer.[46]

Even a mutual promise (involving two parties) is permissible in the case of a Murabaha sale provided the option (Khiyar) is given to one or both of the parties. Without such an option, it is not permissible, since in a Murabaha sale, a mutual and binding promise is like an ordinary sale contract, in which the prerequisite is that the seller should be in full possession of the goods to be sold in order to be in conformity with the tenets of the Sharī'ah forbidding the sale of anything that is not in one's possession.[47] A bank can also obtain Hamish Jiddiyah (earnest money) from the client to ensure that the latter will buy the item when purchased.

In response to a purchase request by a client, a bank can enter into a purchase agreement with the supplier, keeping for itself an option of return (Khiyaral-Shart) within a specified period. This option will expire with actual sale to the customer.[48] Hence, an option (Khiyar) can be used as a risk mitigation tool (asset risk) by an Islamic bank.

It must be kept in mind, however, that an actual sale must take place at the proper time when the bank gets possession and ownership of the item by the exchange of offer and acceptance.[49] Mere promise itself should not be taken as a concluded sale.

### 9.8.3   MPO – The Customer as the Bank's Agent to Buy and Related Matters

The general structure of this variant of Murabaha is the following:

1. The customer approaches the bank with a request for the purchase of any commodity that can be legally sold on credit.
2. The bank appoints the client its agent to purchase the item(s).
3. The bank purchases the commodity through the client as agent.
4. The bank makes payment to the vendor/supplier.
5. The customer takes delivery of the item on behalf of the bank as agent.
6. The customer makes an offer to purchase and the bank accepts the offer – the bank transfers the title over to the customer upon execution of Murabaha.
7. The customer makes payment on a deferred basis without any rollover, discount or rebate.

---

[46] The Fiqh Academy of the OIC and the AAOIFI accept this view; AAOIFI, 2004–5a, Standard on Murabaha, clause 4/2, pp. 119, 131; see also Vogel and Hayes, 1998, p. 126.

[47] AAOIFI, 2004–5a, pp. 114, 115, 127, 128.

[48] AAOIFI, 2004–5a, pp. 116, 129; clause 2/3/5 of Standard on Murabaha.

[49] AAOIFI, 2004–5a, Standard on Murabaha, clause 4/1.

The above structure involves the following stages/steps: pre-promise understanding; promise stage; agency stage; acquiring possession; execution of Murabaha; post-execution of Murabaha. Each of these steps is crucial in its own right and neglecting essentials of any stage would render the whole arrangement unacceptable from the Sharī´ah angle:

1. The client and the bank sign an MoU or "agreement to sell",[50] whereby the bank undertakes to sell and the client promises to buy a commodity for a purchase price plus a profit margin of X % that may or may not be tied with any benchmark, or a stipulated amount over the known cost.
2. The bank appoints the client as its agent for purchasing the commodity on its behalf, and both the parties sign an independent specific or general purpose agreement of agency.
3. The client purchases the commodity on behalf of the bank and takes its possession, for which the bank makes payment to the vendor/supplier. This is obligatory according to the AAOIFI Standard;[51] however, some Islamic banks do not follow this instruction due to some procedural problems. The purchase order, material receiving report and delivery challan, under whatever title, should be in the name of the bank.[52]
4. The client informs the bank that he has purchased the commodity on its behalf, has taken possession thereof, and makes an offer to purchase it from the bank at a profit margin over the cost, as agreed to in the "agreement to sell". This must be before the goods are consumed, otherwise the Murabaha will be invalid.
5. The bank accepts the offer and the sale is concluded, whereby the ownership as well as the risk of the commodity is transferred to the client.

The nature of the relationship in the above arrangement would be:

1. Bank and client: principal and agent.
2. Bank and client: promisor and promisee.
3. Bank and supplier: buyer and seller.
4. Bank and client: seller and buyer.
5. Bank and client: creditor and debtor.

Prerequisites of the various stages of MPO with the client working as agent are discussed below.

### Pre-Promise Stage – Facility Approval

The following points have to be kept in mind while approving the facility: it is essential that the transaction between the bank and the client must be genuine, involving the trade of goods. Murabaha cannot be used for providing liquidity or for cash financing. At the time of facility approval, banks should ensure that the client needs some goods. Further, this should exclude any prior contractual relationship between the client and the supplier whom the client is indicating for supply of the goods. It is not permissible to transfer a contract that has already been executed between the client and the supplier because this is tantamount to Bai‘ al 'Inah, which is prohibited. However, if any such prior understanding has not been

---

[50] This is different from the "sale agreement" in which ownership rights are transferred to the buyer upon signing of the agreement. In an "agreement to sell", a promise is made to sell any commodity in the future and it does not involve conveyance of the ownership rights.
[51] AAOIFI, 2004–5a, Standard on Murabaha, clause 3/1/4, pp. 117, 118.
[52] Usmani, 2000a, pp. 107, 108.

finalized, the bank can enter into an Murabaha arrangement. The bank must also ensure that the supplier or the party from whom the item is being purchased is a third party and not the customer, his agent or any entity with more than 50 % ownership by the customer.

The nature of the required commodity should be in the scope of valid Murabaha. Commodities that are subject to the rules of Bai' al Sarf, like gold, silver and currencies, are not valid for Murabaha, because in such commodities and monetary units, exchange has to be hand to hand.[53] The bank should also analyse the nature of goods from a risk management point of view, their marketing, any uniqueness that could affect their profitability and the cash flow and risk profile of the client.

*Promise Stage – Master Murabaha Facility Agreement*

After the initial analysis of the customer's request, the bank will enter into a master Murabaha facility agreement, or MoU, in which the limit of the facility, the nature of the commodity, the profit margin to be taken by the bank, the schedule of payment, the security to be submitted by the customer and other terms and conditions will be mutually stipulated. On the basis of one MoU there could be a number of consignments for purchase of the asset from time to time under sub-Murabahas. The MoU should also include specimens of purchase requisition, a delivery report, a promissory note and the nature of collateral required. If both parties agree, the agency agreement can also be signed at this stage.

*Purchase Requisition*

As per the MoU, the client will submit a requisition to the bank to purchase the commodity as per his specifications. The requisition will contain details of the goods required to be purchased from the bank and if possible the name of the supplier, cost price and the expected date of delivery. Also at this stage, the bank should ensure that the goods are not already owned by the client, otherwise the Sharī'ah advisor might ask the bank to credit the income from this transaction to the Charity Account. The customer will also give an undertaking to the bank that he will buy the goods which the bank will acquire on his request. Normally, a purchase requisition contains this promise. If the supplier is nominated by the client himself, the bank may demand a performance bond or guarantee for good performance to the effect that the goods provided by the supplier indicated by the client will be acceptable to him.

Earnest money (Hamish Jiddiyah) can be demanded from the customer to assess his sincerity to purchase the goods and as a security deposit. If the bank purchases the goods and the client backs out and does not purchase, the bank may sell the goods in the market and recover the actual loss, if any, from the Hamish Jiddiyah. However, the bank cannot recover the conventional "cost of funds" or liquidated damages in the form of "opportunity cost".[54]

For purchasing the commodity it is advisable that the bank makes payment directly to the supplier to ensure that the funds are used for the actual purpose. Experience has shown that if funds are given to the client, there is a chance of misutilization that could also involve non-Sharī'ah-compliance. Advance payment can also be made to the supplier, and in this case, the bank would charge a higher profit margin than the case of post-supply payment.

---

[53] AAOIFI, 2004–5a, Standard on Murabaha, clause 2/2/6, pp. 114, 128.
[54] AAOIFI, 2004–5a, Standard on Murabaha, clause 4/2, p. 119.

*Agency Stage*

An agency agreement can be signed side by side with the signing of an MoU. But it should invariably be before the purchase of goods by the client. If the client purchases the goods before the agency agreement, it would mean the goods are already owned by him and the transaction would become Bai' al 'Inah, which is prohibited. An agency agreement could be "specific agency", when the purchase of the commodity is not of a consistent nature, or "general", when the purchase of the commodity is of a consistent nature.

*Purchasing Stage*

The client should purchase the goods as the agent of the bank and as per the specifications already decided. A number of situations could evolve at this stage. If the cost price is already given and the supplier gives some rebate, it should be passed on to the client at the time of execution of the Murabaha sale by reducing the cost of sale. If there is a rise in prices and the amount escalates from the amount agreed in the Murabaha limit, the bank or the principal must be informed in order to make a decision on whether to accept it or not. The bank has the right to reject the purchase if made at other than the agreed price. If the goods to be purchased are different from those given in the agency agreement, the change of commodity can be made with mutual consent. Normally, banks indicate a time within which purchase has to be made and if there is a delay, the bank may ask the client to refund the cost of goods without any opportunity cost.

*Acquisition of Title and Possession of the Asset*

For Sharī'ah compliance, it is necessary that the bank takes ownership and actual or constructive possession of the goods before the execution of Murabaha. The forms of taking possession of items differ according to their nature and customs. The requirement from the Sharī'ah angle is that the goods must come under the responsibility and risk of the bank. The Islamic Fiqh Academy of the OIC resolved, in its sixth session, in respect of the forms of "possession":

> "Just as the possession of commodities may be physical, by taking the commodity in one's hand or measuring or weighing the eatables, or by transferring or delivering the commodity to the premises of the buyer, the possession may also be an implied or constructive possession, which takes place by leaving the commodity at one's disposal and enabling him to deal with it as he wishes. This will be deemed a valid possession, even though the physical possession has not taken place. As for the mode of possession, it may vary from commodity to commodity, according to its nature and pursuant to the different customs prevalent in this behalf".[55]

The time when the risk of the item is passed on from the supplier to the bank, and subsequently from the bank to the customer, must be clearly identified. This is why Sharī'ah scholars normally do not approve Murabaha of natural gas in pipes; the gas company cannot say that from "this" point possession of the gas and its risk has been transferred to the bank, and then from the bank to the client. Further, the goods must exist at the time of execution of Murabaha. Sometimes, it happens that the client takes delivery of the goods as agent and uses them in his process of production even before informing the bank and "offer

---

[55] Council of the Islamic Fiqh Academy, 2000, p. 107.

and acceptance". This creates a Sharī'ah objection. Before execution of Murabaha, the bank must ensure that the item exists in its form and for this purpose it is advisable that the bank appoints any person for physical inspection. Further, all ownership-related expenses like Takaful until this point need to be paid by the bank. Any loss before that date also belongs to the bank, being the principal owner of the goods.

### Execution of Murabaha Stage – Offer and Acceptance

After the customer acquires possession of the goods, as an agent, he should give a possession report and make an offer to purchase the goods acquired by him on the bank's behalf. The bank will accept the offer and the transaction will be completed. All the terms of the Murabaha transaction, such as contract price (cost plus profit), due date or schedule of payments, etc. must be mentioned in the bank's letter of acceptance. Upon execution of Murabaha, the relationship of buyer and seller between the customer and the bank changes into the relationship of debtor and creditor. After this, the bank will not be liable for any harm to the goods.

Having taken delivery of the goods as per the purchase requisition, the customer should confirm that the goods have been examined and are satisfactory in respect of quality and suitability for his use. He should also relieve the bank from any loss or third party liability in respect of the goods sold to him. The AAOIFI Standard recommends that the bank should assign to the customer the right of recourse to the supplier to obtain compensation for any established defects which would otherwise be recoverable by the bank from the supplier.[56]

### Security/Collateral against Murabaha Price

The bank can ask the customer to furnish security to its satisfaction for timely payment of the deferred price. It is also permissible that the sold commodity itself is given to the bank as a security, provided possession is once given to the customer. In such a case, the customer would own the risk and reward of the goods. The bank can obtain any of the following types of security, depending upon the amount of facility, nature of business and credibility of the customer: a hypothecation charge on assets, a pledge of goods and/or marketable securities, a lien on deposits, a mortgage charge on movable and immovable properties, bank guarantees, personal guarantees or any other security mutually agreed between bank and client. Some Sharī'ah boards allow taking interest-bearing securities as collateral (Murabaha facility against TDRs and FDRs); in such a case the bank will have recourse to the extent of principal only. However, it is preferable not to take interest-bearing instruments as securities and the customer should be asked to encash the instruments and offer any Sharī'ah-compliant securities.

## 9.9   ISSUES IN MURABAHA

The above complex type of contractual arrangement could create a number of issues relating to the sale contract, credit price and legal implications of combining promise and agency with the actual Murabaha contract. One objection sometimes raised in this regard is that

---

[56] AAOIFI, 2004–5a, clause 4/9, p. 120.

Murabaha operations by Islamic banks constitute two sales in one; the contract of promise and the sale deed. The objection is that as the promise is made binding, it takes on the character of a sale, leading to two contracts in one sale contract.[57] A very simple fact, however, is that as it does not involve violation of any major Sharī´ah principle, almost all contemporary jurists have allowed the combination, as the promise does not take the form of a formal contract. The implications of a sale contract and a promise to purchase are different. A unilateral promise remains a promise and cannot take the form of a contract.

With regard to the credit price being more than the cash market price of the goods being sold under Murabaha, we have already discussed this issue in Chapters 4 and 6. Some other issues are discussed below.

### 9.9.1   Avoiding Buy-back

Bai' al 'Inah, commonly known as "buy-back", is a double sale by which the borrower and the lender sell and then resell an object between them, once for cash and again for a higher price on credit, with the net result of a loan with interest. As such, it is a legal device to circumvent the prohibition of Riba and therefore prohibited. Although banking authorities in Malaysia consider it acceptable, the mainstream Sharī´ah experts from the Middle East and the rest of the world consider it nonpermissible. Therefore, Islamic banks, while conducting Murabaha to Purchase Orderer, have to be vigilant that the goods being required by the client are not already owned by him. The AAOIFI also holds this view.[58]

### 9.9.2   Khiyar (Option to Rescind the Sale) in Murabaha

Most scholars do not consider Khiyar (option) to be necessary in modern Murabaha. Some banks stipulate in the contract that any defect is the liability of the buyer if he examines the goods himself, or if they are described to him (in such a way) as to eliminate ignorance (about the goods), which could lead to dispute. However, any lack in the quantity of the goods or specification remains the liability of the seller. This latter case results in the sale price being reduced by an amount proportionally corresponding to the missing goods, with the buyer having the right to rescind the contract.[59]

Hence, from a juristic point of view, if the goods are defective or not according to the stipulated specifications, Khiyar al 'Aib and Khiyar al Wasf are available to the client, and if he rejects the goods on the grounds of inferior quality before the execution of the Murabaha deal, the goods can be returned to the supplier and genuine quality goods can be acquired through the same or a new Murabaha. The bank can also stipulate that, after inspection of the goods by the client and execution of Murabaha, it will not be liable for any discrepancies.[60] As discussed above, in the case of warranties, the bank can also assign such rights to the client.

If option is available to the customer, the bank will be carrying a much larger risk and may have to carry out, before agreeing to the financing, a more intensive market survey, that may not be possible for most of the Islamic banks in their present structure and state

---

[57] Ray, 1995, p. 54
[58] AAOIFI, 2004–5a, pp. 114, 128.
[59] Kuwait Finance House, n.d., **2**, Fatāwa No. 61, translation in Ray, 1995, p. 181.
[60] AAOIFI, 2004–5a, Standard on Murabaha, clause 4/9.

of infancy. To avoid the risks, what the banks are doing in practice is to make the customer their agent for the purchase of the goods as well as for taking delivery from the supplier. The client will be purchasing the goods with full care as per his requirement. Mostly, the client also identifies the supplier from which the bank should buy the goods. In this case, the bank can take from him a performance guarantee that he will be responsible in respect of the quality of the item.

### 9.9.3  Time of Executing Murabaha

Another issue is the point of time when the bank can legally sell the article to its client. The requirement in this regard is that a Murabaha contract should be conducted only after the bank gets ownership and possession and becomes responsible for any loss or any defects therein.[61] Sharī'ah scholars generally recommend that a modern Murabaha operation is allowed provided the bank takes full possession of the object before selling it, including bearing the risk of its loss and the responsibility for returning it if it is defective. Murabaha has to be executed only after the bank has taken possession and the goods exist. However, there are references in some edicts to sale occurring before the bank has taken possession of the object.[62] Such edicts might create a credibility problem for Islamic banking. Agency contracts for buying the goods by the client on behalf of the bank and immediately selling them to the client are made part and parcel of Murabaha contracts. Islamic banks must avoid this practice and treat agency contracts as being totally separate and independent from the Murabaha contracts. After the goods are taken into possession by the client as agent, there should be a separate offer and acceptance between the client and the bank.

### 9.9.4  Defaults by the Clients

In the conventional banking system, a delinquent customer has to reschedule his debt, usually at a higher rate. The additional interest cost to the customer may motivate him to pay on time. The question, therefore, is how to take care of the problem of deliberate delays in payments in the Islamic financial system. One option is that a bank stipulates in the Murabaha agreement that in the case of a customer's delay in payment without any genuine reason, all remaining instalments will become due; thus, the customer will try to be more disciplined.[63] The issue of default has also been discussed in Chapters 2 and 7. Below, we briefly mention the related matters.

By means of an undertaking by the client, Islamic banks stipulate in the contracts that the client should pay to charity in case of default. Contemporary Sharī'ah scholars have evolved a consensus that banks are authorized to impose late fees on delinquent clients (this means that the clients that are really unable to pay will not be charged any such penalty). But the proceeds of such penalties are to be used for charitable purposes. Only a court or any independent body can allocate any part of the penalty as solatium for the banks. The Shariat Appellate Bench of Pakistan's Supreme Court says, in this regard:

"The legislature can also confer a power on the court to impose penalty on a party who makes a default in meeting out his liability or who is found guilty of putting up vexatious pleas and adopting

---

[61] International Association of Islamic Banks, 1990, pp. 36, 37.

[62] Kuwait Finance House, n.d., **2**, Fatwah No. 63; See also Ray, 1995, p. 48.

[63] AAOIFI, 2004–5a, Standard on Murabaha, clause 5/1.

dilatory tactics with a view to cause delay in decision of the case and in discharging liabilities and from the amount of such penalty a smaller or bigger part, depending upon the circumstances, can be awarded as solatium to the party who is put to loss and inconvenience by such tactics. The amount of penalty can be received by the State and used for charitable purposes and in the projects of public interest, including the projects intended to ameliorate economic conditions of the sections of society possessing little or nothing, i.e. needy people/peoples without means".[64]

Therefore, courts or any resolution committees appointed by the State or the regulators can determine compensation for the actual damage but not for the loss of income calculated on the basis of the conventional concept of opportunity cost. If any part of the penalty is not allowed for the bank by a court, the proceeds must be utilized for charitable objectives only and cannot be made available as compensation to the bank.

Going further ahead on the path of Ijtihad, a Fatwah of the Sharī´ah board of Al Baraka, Sudan, authorizes Islamic banks to impose late fees to be taken as the bank's income on the basis of a profit rate actually gained by it during the period of default, as if the delayed money had also earned that profit if received by the bank.[65] However, the idea of charging a realized rate of return is more akin to the conventional concept of opportunity cost and it would be very difficult to differentiate Murabaha contracts with such stretched Ijtihad from Western trade financing involving interest. For the credibility of the Islamic financial system, such differentiation is necessary.

### 9.9.5   Rebates on Early Payment

Depending upon the cash flow, some clients may wish to pay earlier than the due date and demand a prepayment rebate as in the case of conventional banking. However, the majority of contemporary Sharī´ah scholars do not allow remission for earlier payment in Murabaha operations by banks. This issue has been discussed in detail in Chapter 7. The OIC Fiqh Academy, the Shariat Appellate Bench of the Supreme Court of Pakistan, Sharī´ah committees of Islamic banks in the Middle East and Sharī´ah scholars in general consider that it would be similar to interest-based instalments sales techniques. The AAOIFI's Sharī´ah Standard on Murabaha, however, allows a rebate if it is not already stipulated in the Murabaha contract.[66] Therefore, if the customer makes early payment and there is no commitment from the bank in respect of any discount in the price of Murabaha, the bank has discretion in allowing the rebate or not. But, it should not be made a practice and any such case should be decided on merit in consultation with the Sharī´ah advisor.

### 9.9.6   Rollover in Murabaha

"Rollover" in Murabaha means booking another Murabaha against receivables of any previous Murabaha, payment in respect of which has not been made by the client. Further mark-up is added to the receivable in default by a client. This is explicit Riba, as the bank is not entitled to any amount over and above the debt created in a Murabaha transaction, as a result of which ownership of the sold goods had already been transferred to the client. Now the bank has no right of re-pricing. Rescheduling is allowed, but re-pricing and, therefore, rollover is not allowed.

---

[64] Shariat Appellate Bench, 2000, pp. 477, para. 24 in the court order; Council of the Islamic Fiqh Academy, 2000, pp. 251, 252; AAOIFI, 2004–5a, pp. 122, 132.

[65] Fatwah translated into English, cf. Ray, 1995, pp. 182, 183.

[66] AAOIFI, 2004–5a, p. 132.

The bank, at its discretion, can reschedule the payment without any increase in the original receivable. Any amount taken from the client on account of late payment, as per his undertaking in the Murabaha agreement, would go to the charity account. However, there is the possibility of a fresh Murabaha facility through the sale of new goods.

### 9.9.7   Murabaha Through Shares

In recent years, some Islamic banks have conducted shares Murabaha, i.e. they purchase shares through a client as agent and sell them on a Murabaha basis to the clients. As shares represent tangible assets of joint stock companies, their trading is permissible provided the screening criteria recommended by the Sharī´ah scholars are taken into consideration. Their sale through Murabaha is also permissible, but Islamic banks need to take extra care with regard to Sharī´ah compliance matters. Banks should make payment directly to the brokers and the client should not be appointed agent for purchasing the shares. After the payment is made by the bank and the shares are transferred to it actually or through any central depository, the bank can sell them onward on a Murabaha basis. If settlement takes time, the bank shall wait for actual transfer. Generally, transfer takes three days; so the risk of price for three days has to be taken by the bank. Further, the shares in respect of which Murabaha is to be conducted should not be of any sister concern of the client; otherwise it will be "buy-back" and therefore prohibited.

### 9.9.8   Commodity Murabaha

Some banks in the Middle East and the West have been using commodity Murabaha on international commodity exchanges as a treasury operation. This is a very tricky issue and needs a special role of the Sharī´ah advisors of the concerned banks. It refers to a short-term placement mechanism involving purchase and sale of commodities in the international markets, e.g. London Metal Exchange (LME). Internationally, Islamic banks have relied mainly on this product for liquidity management.

The banks use Tawarruq and appoint a broker to purchase any metal and then sell the same on deferred payment to any third broker on the same date. Normally, Islamic banks make an agent of a conventional bank to buy on their behalf any metal from broker A against cash payment and then sell that to broker B on deferred payment. Nobody cares whether any actual transaction has taken place or not, and at which point in time risk was transferred to the bank. There are doubts about the quantity of metal being sufficient to cover the transaction volumes. As the brokerage cost makes the product less competitive, there is a chance that no actual transactions might be taking place. Islamic bankers need to understand that the Tawarruq arrangement, even in its genuine form, should be used in extreme cases where no option is available to avoid interest. It has not been approved by all scholars. Widespread use of such products is harmful to the Islamic banking industry in the long run.

## 9.10   PRECAUTIONS IN MURABAHA OPERATIONS

In Murabaha, Islamic banks have to face additional asset risk, greater fiduciary risks, greater legal risk and the Sharī´ah compliance risk. To mitigate the legal risk, special care has to be given to completing documentation for various contracts under the guidance of the bank's legal department. Adherence to the AAOIFI's Sharī'ah Standards would enable the bank to get Sharī'ah compliance. In this regard, the role of Sharī'ah supervisory boards/advisors is of crucial importance in applying proper internal controls for Sharī'ah compliance. Mistiming in documentation may lead to loss of income. Therefore, an Islamic bank must strengthen its internal Sharī'ah control and risk management departments. Risk mitigation measures in Murabaha are given in Box 9.1.

## 9.11  MUSAWAMAH (BARGAINING ON PRICE)

Musawamah is a general and regular kind of sale in which the price of the commodity to be traded is bargained between the seller and the buyer without any reference to the price paid or cost incurred by the former. Thus, it is different from Murabaha in respect of the pricing formula. Unlike Murabaha, the seller in Musawamah is not obliged to reveal his cost. Both the parties negotiate on the price. All other conditions relevant to Murabaha are valid for Musawamah as well. Musawamah can be used where the seller is not in a position to ascertain precisely the costs of commodities that he is offering to sell.

From a juristic point of view, Musawamah can be either cash or credit sale, but when used by banks it will generally be a deferred payment sale in which they will bargain with clients on the price of goods/assets. They will add their profit margin to their cost but will not be required to tell their clients the details of cost price and their profit in any transaction. A few Islamic financial institutions have a practice of obtaining a discount from the supplier in the case of retail goods. In such a case, since actual profit is not brought to the notice of the customer, it is necessary that such a sale should be conducted through Musawamah and not Murabaha.

---

**Box 9.1:**  Risk Management in Murabaha

| **Nature of Risk** | **Mitigating Tool(s)** |
|---|---|
| Customer refuses to purchase goods after taking possession as agent. | Promise to purchase the ordered goods is obtained from customers. Also, Hamish Jiddiyah may be taken, from which the bank can cover its actual loss. |
| Customer did not purchase fresh assets/goods; has already purchased and now wants funds for the payment to the supplier; involves Bai' al 'Inah, so non-Sharī'ah-compliant. | • Make direct payment to supplier through DD/PO.<br>• Obtain invoice of goods purchased. Date of invoice should not be earlier than the date of agency agreement and not later than the declaration or offer to purchase.<br>• In addition to invoice, obtain any other evidence, e.g. gate pass, inward register, entry in stock register, truck receipt.<br>• Physical inspection of goods. |

| | |
|---|---|
| Goods/asset have been used by customer before offer and acceptance; do not exist when Murabaha is executed, so non-Sharī'ah-compliant. | Reducing the time interval when offer is to be made periodically; physical inspection of goods on a random basis. |
| In transit, risk of destruction of goods before offer and acceptance without agent's negligence. | During transit, goods are owned by the bank and all risks belong to the bank. This risk can be mitigated through obtaining Takaful cover. |
| Overdue. | Undertaking from the customer is obtained to give a certain amount to charity in the case of late payment. |
| Default risk. | Securities/collateral can be realized to recover loss. |
| Supplier may not perform his obligation. | The agent, in his personal capacity, can guarantee the performance of the supplier. |
| Purchase from or resale to associates/subsidiaries. | Obtain related party information from the financial statements of the company or by any other source. |

---

### Box 9.2: Possible Steps for Murabaha in Import Financing

**Step 1:** The Islamic bank and the customer will sign a master murabaha agreement (MoU) and an agency agreement; as per the agency agreement, the customer will purchase goods from foreign suppliers on the bank's behalf by opening L/Cs with the bank.

(The difference between a general Murabaha agreement and a sight L/C Murabaha agreement is that it is possible in sight L/C Murabaha that an item may be sold at cost price in the case of a spot Murabaha. In order to accommodate such a transaction, the agreement needs to mention that it can be covered both under Murabaha and Musawamah.)

**Step 2:** The customer will negotiate a deal with some foreign supplier (exporter) for the purchase of assets as agent of the bank. It should be ensured that such a deal should be finalized only after execution of the agency agreement.

(Otherwise, it could be a problem for the bank in the case of sight L/C; if the customer delays in making payment, the bank will have to suffer the loss, as it would not be able to earn any profit on the amount paid to the exporter through the negotiating bank.)

**Step 3:** The importer will request the bank to open an L/C by submitting all relevant documents. Takaful should be arranged by the importer on behalf of the bank (cost to be borne by the bank) and the relevant policy should be forwarded along with the L/C application form. The bank will issue an L/C in the favour of the beneficiary (exporter).

**Box 9.2:** (Continued)

**Step 4:** On receipt of the L/C, the exporter will ship the goods and deliver the related shipping documents to the negotiating bank for the payment of the bill amount. If the documents are found to be in order, the negotiating bank will send the documents to the Islamic bank.

**Step 5:** On receipt of the documents, the Islamic bank will contact the customer and inform him of the availability of the documents. The customer will negotiate the FX rate for the required foreign currency amount. The Islamic bank will discuss the payment terms with the customer and settle the bill.

### Settlement: Sight L/C

If the customer is not in need of credit and wishes to settle the transaction, the bank will issue a Musawamah declaration to the customer. Through spot Murabaha or Musawamah, the bank will sell the assets at the following spot price to the customer: L/C cost + all charges + Takaful charges. After receiving payment, the bank will release the shipping documents to the customer. However, the bank's risk on the goods will end only after delivery of the assets to the customer.

### Settlement: Customer Requires Financing

The Islamic bank will discuss the payment date with the customer and execute the Murabaha, which means the signing of a declaration by the customer and the acceptance of its offer to purchase by the Islamic bank. Profit will be charged from the day the bank's Nostro was debited to the Murabaha settlement date according to the agreed profit rate. The bank will release the shipping documents to the customer and record a Murabaha receivable.

(MPO is being using widely for local and foreign trade financing by Islamic banks. Such Murabahas include: (i) local currency: simple Murabaha, advance payment Murabaha, suppliers' credit murabaha; (ii) foreign currency: sight L/C spot Murabaha, sight L/C deferred Murabaha, usance L/C Murabaha.)

**Box 9.3:**   Accounting Treatment by Islamic Banks in Murabaha

**Measurement of asset value at acquisition:** asset is measured and recorded at historical cost.

**After acquisition:** (1) asset available for sale on Murabaha to the purchase orderer who is obliged to fulfil his promise shall be measured at historical cost and any decline in value shall be reflected in the valuation of the asset at the end of the financial period. (2) If there is an indication of nonrecovery of costs of goods, the asset shall be measured at cash equivalent value (net realizable value). This value is obtained by creating a provision for decline in the asset value to reflect the difference between acquisition cost and the cash equivalent value.

**Potential discount after acquisition:** (1) the discount shall not be considered as revenue, however it should reduce the cost of goods. (2) The discount may be treated as revenue if this is decided by the Islamic bank's Sharī'ah supervisory board.

**Murabaha receivables:** These shall be recorded at the time of occurrence at their cash equivalent value.

**Profit recognition:** profit shall be recognized at the time of contracting if the sale is for cash or on credit but the term does not exceed the current financial period. Profits of credit sale whose payment is due after the current financial period shall be recognized using any of the following methods:

- Proportionate allocation of profits method; may be adopted whether or not cash is received, which is the preferred method.
- Profit may also be recognized as and when received. Disclose the accrued amount of profit if the accrual method has not been followed.
- Deferred profits shall be offset against Murabaha receivables in the statement of financial position.

**Early settlement with deduction of part of profit (deduction of profit at the time of settlement):** the bank may deduct the part of the profit agreed upon from the payment of one or more instalments.

**Deduction of part of profit after settlement:** the above criteria should be applied for payments of one or more instalments before the time specified, the Islamic bank may ask the client to pay the full amount and thereafter reimburse with part of the profit.

**Failure to fulfil promise having paid Hamish Jiddiyah:** Hamish Jiddiyah shall be treated as a liability on an Islamic bank.

**Treatment for nonbinding promise:** Hamish Jiddiyah shall be returned in full even if the asset is sold at a lower amount to another client.

**Treatment for binding promise:** the amount of actual loss shall be deducted from Hamish Jiddiyah. In the absence of any guarantee or Hamish Jiddiyah, any loss incurred shall be recorded as a receivable due from the defaulter client.

**Procrastination:** the amount received as a penalty shall be treated as revenue or an allocation to the charity fund, as any arbitration or Sharī´ah board deems appropriate.

**Insolvency:** the Islamic bank cannot ask the client to pay any additional amount by way of penalty.

---

**Box 9.4:**   Murabaha Financing for Exports: Process and Steps

1. Exporter and bank sign an agreement to enter into Murabaha.
2. Exporter is appointed as agent to purchase goods on the bank's behalf.
3. Bank gives money to supplier/vendor for purchase of the goods.
4. Exporter purchases goods on the bank's behalf and takes their possession.
5. Exporter makes an offer to purchase the goods from the bank.
6. Bank accepts the offer and sale is concluded.
7. Exporter pays the agreed price to the bank according to an agreed schedule.

### 9.11.1   Musawamah as a Mode of Financing

Businesses normally use Musawamah, in that they are interested only in profit, which they earn through pricing, while Islamic banks mostly use Murabaha. This is because direct use of any benchmark is relatively easier in Murabaha than in the case of Musawamah. It is easier for the bank management and the regulators to manage the return rate structure in Murabaha. Further, chances of corruption are minimal in Murabaha, because whatever the level of price of the asset, the bank will be charging a profit margin tied up with the cost price of the asset.

Musawamah is more suitable for single huge transactions, wherein decisions are made normally at the top level and the price is bargained between the parties. For example, an airline in the Middle East may require credit purchase of an aeroplane costing about $500 million. An Islamic bank may purchase the aeroplane for $450 million, for example, and sell it to the airline after adding its profit of $50 million, keeping in mind the credit period and the payment schedule. Details of the cost price to the bank will not be needed and the airline will be interested in the final price only. Similarly, Musawamah could be used in financing of all such purchases where it is not possible for banks to tell a number of minute details, as required in Murabaha.

The agency structure can also be used in Musawamah, but it is better and preferable that the bank directly purchases the assets, particularly expensive assets. However, the bank may involve the clients in selection of the supplier and the assets to ensure that the assets being purchased by the bank have all the specifications requested by the client. In the case of assets with a huge price, the structure used by banks will be Musawamah to Purchase Orderer, while in the case of less expensive goods, generally demanded by businesses and the public, banks or their specially created subsidiaries can maintain inventory for sale to the clients on a Musawamah basis as and when demanded by the clients.

The conditions of taking ownership, possession and business risk of the asset are equally applicable in Musawamah as in the case of Murabaha. Goods required for onward sale must come under the risk of the bank before execution of the sale contract with the customer. Similarly, all conditions regarding subject matter, payment of the stipulated price and the treatment in case of default, etc. will be the same as in the case of Murabaha. The only difference is that the bank is not required to disclose details about its cost price or profit margin, and bargaining will be on the final price of the goods.

## 9.12   SUMMARY

Musharakah or Mudarabah (PLS modes) may not necessarily be suitable for all the financial needs of modern businesses. In many cases, such modes may neither be feasible nor desired by the banks or their clients. The majority of the traditional as well as the contemporary jurists have, therefore, allowed a number of other modes which facilitate the sale (or purchase) of goods and usufruct of such goods, the corpus of which is not consumed with their use. One such trade-based mode is Murabaha, which takes the form of Murabaha–Mu'ajjal (cost-plus sale with deferred payment of price) when used by banks.

Murabaha refers to a mutually stipulated margin of profit in a sale transaction, where the cost of the commodity is known or made known to the buyer. The parties negotiate the profit margin on cost and not the cost *per se*. If payment of the sale price is deferred, it also becomes Mu'ajjal. The due date of payment of the price must be fixed in an unambiguous manner. Other terms used for similar transactions are instalments sale, cost-plus/mark-up based sale, etc.

According to contemporary Sharī´ah scholars, Murabaha–Mu'ajjal is legitimate provided the risk of the transaction is borne by the financier until the possession has been passed on to the Murabaha customer. For such a transaction to be legal, the bank must purchase a commodity through a contract and sell it to the customer under a separate contract.

Notwithstanding the fact that dangers are associated with the use of Murabaha by banks as an Islamic mode of financing, the reality is that Islamic banks all over the world are resorting heavily to this mode for one reason or another. An important consideration in this regard is that banks hold depositors' money as trustees. Investment of money should be undertaken keeping in mind the depositors' aspirations/advice and their risk profiles. If any classes of society, like the old and widows or others depending on their savings for their sustenance, do not want to take the risk of loss possible in PLS modes, their money has to be invested in less risky avenues on the basis of trade- or leasing based modes. Faced with this dilemma, the available way out is that it has to be used with utmost caution, with such a structure that fulfilment of the Sharī´ah essentials is ensured.

Credit sale is allowed by the clear texts of the Sharī´ah. Instalments sale with a price higher than the cash market price is also permitted as a normal reflection of market based commercial activities. A deferred Murabaha price, higher than the cash-n-carry price, is objected to by some of the theoreticians working on Islamic banking and finance. But this aspect needs to be seen on the two separate fronts of permissibility and preference of one mode over the other. There is no doubt about the permissibility of Murabaha with a credit price higher than the cash market price of the related commodity. PLS modes are preferable, but in order to safeguard the interests of the depositors, these modes need to be used keeping in mind the risk profiles of various businesses and the parties involved.

Murabaha, as currently being used in Islamic banking, is something different from the Murabaha discussed in Fiqh literature. This transaction is concluded with a prior promise to buy or a request made by a person interested in acquiring goods on credit from any financial institution. Further, the customer is normally appointed an agent of the bank for the purchase of the item on behalf of the bank. As such, it is called "Murabaha to Purchase Orderer" (MPO), which normally comprises three separate deals including a promise to buy or to sell, an agency contract and the actual Murabaha contract. Islamic banks also enter into an MoU or Murabaha facility agreement which contains the overall structure of the transaction, the profit rate to be charged in various sub-Murabahas, the nature of collateral/security, treatment in the case of default or other developments.

Banks must make sure that the client intends to purchase a commodity capable of being the subject of Murabaha. Payment of the price may be made directly to the supplier and, if it becomes necessary due to the nature of the item that funds be given to the client, purchase of the commodity should be evidenced by invoices or similar other documents which the client should present to the bank.

Buy-back arrangements and rollover in Murabaha are not allowed. Therefore, the banks must ensure that the goods requested by the client are not already in his ownership.

In order to ensure that the buyer pays the instalments promptly, he may be asked to promise that in the case of a default he will pay a certain amount of penalty for any charitable purpose. Such a penalty shall not constitute bank income and shall be utilized for charitable purposes only.

# 10
# Forward Sales: Salam and Istisna‘a

## 10.1  INTRODUCTION

As discussed in Chapters 5 and 6, there are three basic conditions for the validity of a sale. These are: the commodity to be sold must exist; the seller should have acquired the ownership of that commodity and as such its possible risks; and the commodity must be in the physical or constructive possession of the seller. These conditions are imposed to avoid the possibility of Gharar and dispute regarding the subject matter. However, there are two exceptions: Salam and Istisna‘a. Exception is accorded on the ground that some conditions have been advised, fulfilment of which renders them free from Gharar. As in both of these sales delivery of the subject matter is deferred to the future, these can be termed forward sales. In the Islamic framework, commodity markets can exist for the future delivery of goods subject to the rules relating to Salam and Istisna‘a. The modern futures markets that deal in futures like options, derivatives, swaps, etc. do not qualify under these rules.

## 10.2  BAI‘ SALAM/SALAF

Bai‘ Salam is an ancient form of forward contract wherein the price was paid in advance at the time of making the contract for prescribed goods to be delivered later. The two terms "Salam" and "Salaf" have been used interchangeably in Hadith literature to describe the contract for future delivery of specified goods with up-front payment of the price. The parties stipulate a certain time for supply of goods of specified quantity and quality. This is contrary to Bai‘ Mu'ajjal, in which goods are delivered to the purchaser in advance and the agreed price is paid at a stipulated date in the future. The word Salaf or Taslif, which literally means payment in advance, referring to a sale by advance payment, was used by jurists of Hijaz, while the jurists based in Baghdad, Iraq mainly used the term Salam for forward sale transactions. As the commodity to be delivered in future against prompt payment becomes a debt on the part of the seller, the transaction is termed Salaf and implies a loan without any benefit.[1] As, in the emerging Islamic finance movement, Salam is normally used to denote a forward transaction of a defined nature, we have used the word "Salam" throughout the book.

Salam has been permitted by the holy Prophet (pbuh) himself, without any difference of opinion among the early or the contemporary jurists, notwithstanding the general principle of the Sharī‘ah that the sale of a commodity which is not in the possession of the seller is not permitted. Upon migration from Makkah, the Prophet came to Madinah, where the people used to pay in advance the price of fruit (or dates) to be delivered within one, two

---

[1] AAOIFI, 2004–5a, pp. 163, 172; Standard on Salam, clause 2/2. Also see Ibn Hajar, 1998, pp. 85, 86.

and three years. But such a sale was carried out without specifying the quality, measure or weight of the commodity or the time of delivery. The holy Prophet ordained: "Whoever pays money in advance (for fruit) (to be delivered later) should pay it for a known quality, specified measure and weight (of dates or fruit) of course along with the price and time of delivery".[2]

The rationale for this permission, as described by S.M. Hasanuz Zaman, is the concept of "necessity". He adds:

> "It is stated that the practice, as qualified by the Prophet (pbuh), continued during his life and subsequently. The later jurists unanimously treated it as a permissible mode of business. The list of items covered by Bai' Salam suggests that it benefited the owners of farms and orchards. For example, the Madinan list of cultivation covered wheat, barley, dates and grapes. The conquest of Syria added to it such items as olives and dried large grapes.... Barring a few exceptions, the jurists have expanded the list of items, in regard to which Salam is permissible, to cover all the commodities that could be precisely determined in terms of quality and quantity."[3]

## 10.3 BENEFITS OF SALAM AND THE ECONOMIC ROLE OF BAI' SALAM

Forward sale in the form of Salam has been allowed by the Sharī'ah with such a structure that it becomes free from Riba, Gharar and, therefore, from exploitation of one party by the other. It is rather based on genuine need of the business and, therefore, beneficial to both buyer and seller. The seller gets in advance the money he needs in exchange of obligation to deliver the commodity later. Thus, he benefits from the Salam sale by covering his cash/liquidity needs in respect of personal expenses or for productive or trading activity. The purchaser gets the commodity he has planned to trade at the time he decides. He will also benefit from cheap prices, because usually the Salam price is cheaper than the cash market price. This way he will also be secured against fluctuations of price.

S.M. Hasanuz Zaman has given a detailed account of this aspect of Bai' Salam.[4] The Hadith legalizing the practice suggests that it was meant to meet the financial requirement of farmers who needed funds for a period ranging from one to three years. The economic role which Bai' Salam is supposed to perform can be summarized as follows:

- The period of delivery ranging from one year to three years suggests that the amount of advance was not small; otherwise this should have been adjusted earlier than the harvesting of crop or fraction of the garden.
- In view of the period involved in the deal, it can be claimed with confidence that the buyers were not consumers of the product; they were traders or prospective traders.
- The popularity of this practice leads us to believe that the price received in advance might have met both the productive and consumption requirements of the cultivators.
- Fixation of three years as the time of delivery suggests that money was also required for fixed investment like improvement of land and growing gardens. In the context of Syria,

---

[2] The Hadith reported by Imam Bukhari, Muslim and others. See AAOIFI, 2004–5a, p. 171. For the legal status and permission of Salam as a special case, see Zuhayli, 2003, **1**, p. 256.

[3] Hasanuz Zaman, 1991, pp. 443, 444.

[4] Hasanuz Zaman, 1991, pp. 448–450.

digging of wells and providing irrigation facilities could also be a possible purpose of the request for advance payment.

From the point of view of the farmers, Bai' Salam might be a preferable way of taking financing as compared to a loan with interest, because first, it did not make an increase in cost as interest did and, second, it saved them from the hardships and the risk involved in marketing their produce. It is not certain whether the institutions of Bai' Salam brought about any change in the role of intermediaries in the rural economy. It is, however, certain that it paved the way for a direct relationship between the grower and the trader in the city, who generally was the supplier of funds.

As the buyer in a free market would always choose to purchase at a price which gives him good income on resale on the stipulated date and during the supply season, Bai' Salam could prove an effective means of stabilizing the price at a moderate level during periods of seasonal fall in demand. And because the Sharī'ah does not allow resale of Salam goods before they are actually transferred to the buyer, this would protect the prices from exposure to speculative rise and stabilize them at a lower level. Contrary to this, financing production/inventory building through loans with interest automatically increases the cost of production/stocks. This increase is further shot up by speculative transactions for anticipated brisk trade seasons.

Salam provides a price hedge for the buyer and protects both the buyer and the seller from the respective risks of revenue and price-indexed debts. There is less incentive on the part of the seller to transfer any additional risks to the buyer by manipulating his reported revenues, as could happen in the conventional commodity forward market. Part of the variation in revenue has been already transferred to (and accepted by) the buyer in the form of a predetermined price, and the other (quantity) part is contractually fixed.

As a forward contract, it gives the buyer the required hedge against possible future price increases. It gives the seller the required price protection and does not involve any predetermined cash debt on either party. One can get financing directly from buyers without involving any intermediary. However, banks can participate as a buyer on a Salam basis in a competitive environment. Hence, a Salam contract can bring about the benefits of a swap[5] without the involvement of interest and at a lower cost. The transaction costs associated with a Salam contract are likely to be much lower than those of a swap.

## 10.4    FEATURES OF A VALID SALAM CONTRACT

A valid Salam contract requires the following conditions[6] (it goes without saying that it should also fulfil the conditions of a normal valid sale).

---

[5] A swap is an agreement whereby one party replaces one cash flow (or commitment) by another that is indexed to some price or interest rate. A country that obtains a loan, for instance, exchanges its debt obligation with another firm that undertakes to assume the obligation in exchange for payments based on the price of some commodity. In spite of the expected benefits of swap agreements, they may not be among the best instruments, for the overall transaction costs associated with them may be very high. For detail, see Uthman, 2003.

[6] In the Fiqh literature there are lengthy details regarding subject matter, price, delivery of the commodity, substitution of the subject matter and other aspects of Salam sale. We are skipping those details for the purpose of brevity. Those interested, may like to see *Financial Transactions in Islamic Jurisprudence* by Wahbah Zuhayli (Zuhayli, 2003, **1**, 237–265).

### 10.4.1  Subject Matter of Salam

On which items Salam can be conducted is the first important aspect. There is a consensus that everything that can be precisely determined in terms of quality and quantity can be made the subject of Salam sale. There is also unanimity on the point that the commodity should be well-defined but not particularized to a specific unit of farm, tree or garden. Only those fungible (Mithli) things various units of which do not differ from each other in a significant manner can be contracted under Salam. Salam cannot take place where both items of exchange are identical, e.g. wheat for wheat and potato for potato. Similarly, the commodity to be sold through Salam should, in itself, not be of the nature of money, like gold, silver or any currency.

Differences existed among the traditional jurists regarding the list of commodities that can be sold under Bai' Salam. The advocates of Bai' Salam in animals and their flesh argue that the quality of these items can be defined in terms of their species, kind and quality. Similarly, controversy existed in respect of items like cane, grass, fodder, bread, honey, milk, vegetables, oils, cheese, birds, fish, trained dogs, leopards, precious stones, heaps of charcoal wood, musk, aloe, perfumes, hide and skin, wool, hair, animal fats, paper, cloth, carpets, rugs, mine dust construction bricks, bowls, bottles, shoes and drugs. The cause of controversy is understandable, because standardization of most of these items was a very difficult job in the days when the jurists compiled their Fiqh (fourth–sixth century Hijrah). They were generally inclined to approve only the sale of those items where various units did not differ, so as to remove any possibility of Gharar and dispute at the time of delivery.

The contemporary scholars have come to the conclusion that all goods that can be standardized into identical units can become the subject of Salam. For example, wheat, rice, barley, oil, iron and copper or other grains of this type, products of companies which are regularly and commonly available at any time, like carpets, tin packs of various consumption items, etc., can be sold through Salam.[7] The commodity should be generally available in the market. Jurists of all schools of thought agree that the contracted commodity in Salam should be such that it is normally available in the market at least at the agreed time of delivery.[8] Thus, it should not be nonexistent or a rare commodity out of supply, or out of season, making it inaccessible to the seller at the time when it has to be delivered.

The buyer must unambiguously define the quality and quantity of the goods and the definition must be applicable to the generally available items of the subject matter. The specifications of goods should particularly cover all such characteristics that could cause variation in price. The jurists have devoted a large portion of discussion on the subject of the specifications and qualities of the subject of Salam which cause variation in value of the same item. The aim is to plug any possible causes of dispute as to the basic spirit of the Islamic law of sale. It is because of the spirit of ensuring mutual consent that the jurists have tried to remove all the possible causes of dissent throughout the deal.

Salam is not allowed for anything identified like "this car" or things for which the seller may not be held responsible, like land, buildings, trees or products of "this field", because that particular field may not ultimately give any produce. Similarly, Salam is not possible for items whose value depends upon subjective assessment, like landscapes, precious gems and

---

[7]  AAOIFI, 2004–5a, Standard on Salam, clause 3/2/2, p. 164.
[8]  AAOIFI, 2004–5a, Standard on Salam, clause 3/2/8, pp. 165, 173.

antiques.[9] Hence, the Salam commodity of defined specifications is made the responsibility of the seller, so that he can supply them by taking them from the market. As reported by Imam Bukhari in his Sahih, Abdur Rahman bin Abza and Abdullah bin Abi Aufa, Companions of the holy Prophet (pbuh), upon asking about Salam goods said, ". . . when the peasants of Syria came to us, we used to pay them in advance for wheat, barley and oil to be delivered within a fixed period". They were again asked, "Did the peasants own standing crops or not?" They replied, "We never asked them about it". Therefore, it is not necessary that the Salam seller himself produces the goods to be delivered in the future; rather, such specification has to be avoided to enable the seller to make available the item from where he can arrange.

### Salam in Currencies

The majority of jurists do not allow Salam in gold, silver, currencies or monetary units, although a few jurists have allowed it and, as such, a few Islamic banks have been using Salam in currencies as an alternative to bill discounting. As this issue is of far-reaching implications, it needs to be discussed in detail.

As discussed in various foregoing chapters of the book, money is treated differently from other commodities. Gold, silver and other metallic money like Fulus[10] of copper or other metals can be used for some purposes other than for making payments; hence, they can be traded keeping in mind the Sharī'ah principles. However, paper money can be used only in payment of a price, it cannot serve as a commodity to be sold. The currency notes in vogue are monetary values. They have no value in the absence of government commitment and are wanted only for the purpose of exchange and payments and not for themselves. Accordingly, the present fiduciary money in the form of currency notes is cash money or monetary value and unlimited legal tender for making payment, as creditors are obliged to accept it for the recovery of debts.

The counter values to be exchanged in Salam include prompt price payment on the one hand and deferred delivery of the commodity on the other. However, if the price in Salam is US Dollars, for example, and the commodity to be purchased/sold is Pak Rupees, it will be a currency transaction which cannot be made through Salam, because such exchange of currencies requires the simultaneous payment on both sides, while in Salam, delivery of the commodity is deferred.

In exchange/trade transactions, the commodity to be sold (Mabi') and the price (Thaman) should be differentiated. A commodity is the principal object of sale from which the benefit is ultimately to be derived, in lieu of a price as settled between the contracting parties. The Thaman, on the other hand, is only a medium of exchange. Currency notes represent Thaman and money. A lawful sale, therefore, is the sale of commodities for money or for any other consideration measurable in terms of money possessing utility, but money sold for money is generally not a lawful contract and is qualified with a number of conditions.[11] Money, being a medium of exchange and a measure of value, cannot be taken as a "production good" which yields profit on a daily basis, as is presumed by the theories of interest.

---

[9] AAOIFI, 2004–5a, Standard on Salam, clause 3/2/3, p. 164.

[10] Fulus were copper or other inferior metal coins. Every district/area had its own Fulus of different genus, quality and quantity. For example, one district had 100 coins of one kilogram of copper, while another had 50 coins of the same amount of copper. They were commodities having intrinsic value. (Lewis et al., 1965, **2**, p. 49.)

[11] See Shariat Appellate Bench, 2000, Taqi Usmani's part, para. 152.

Justice Khalil-ur-Rehman, in his part of the Judgement of the Supreme Court of Pakistan on Riba says about Fulus:

"... their position was not that of an independent currency. They were a form of sub-money used only to make payments of the fractions of a silver coin because it was not easy to break one silver dirham into two equal parts for making payment of half, nor was it easy for the government or the money changers to issue smaller silver coins to facilitate such fractional payments. Therefore, the principles developed by the jurists to regulate the exchange of copper Fulus will not be applicable to the paper currency and fiat money of today. Today's paper money has practically become almost like natural money, equal in terms of its facility of exchange and credibility to the old silver and golden coins. It will, therefore, be subject to all those injunctions laid down in the Qur'ān and the Sunnah, which regulated the exchange or transactions of gold and silver".[12]

A study conducted by the IRTI of the IDB (Umar, 1995) on Salam has thoroughly discussed the issue of whether money can be used as a commodity in Salam. It says:

"The second form: when the principal is money (Saudi Riyals) and the commodity sold is another type of money (US Dollars); this is a currency exchange transaction that cannot be made through Salam, which requires deferred delivery of the commodity sold while such exchange requires simultaneous payment of the two exchanged amounts. Allama Shirbini gives the following opinion in the case where the principal (price) is money and the commodity sold is also money: 'It is not permissible to pay one of them as Salam principal for the other because Salam requires payment of only one of the two exchanged objects of the contract at the time of signing the contract, while the currency exchange requires simultaneous payment of both the exchanged amounts'."[13]

According to all schools of thought of Islamic jurisprudence, and particularly to the Hanafi and Maliki Fuqaha, the principal paid in Salam should be in the form of money and the two transacted items should not be of the kind whose exchange would lead to Riba.[14] According to the jurists, it is a condition of Salam that the price and the commodity sold should be of the kind that can permissibly be dealt in on a deferment basis. Allama Ibn-e-Rushd explained this issue in a comparative manner when he said about this condition: "If they are not of that kind, Salam cannot be practised in them."[15]

In view of the above, it is concluded that forward sale or purchase of currencies to take the form of Salam is not a valid contract. Fulus that were a form of metallic money could be used for trading on the basis of their metal content. But currency notes are Thaman, wanted only for exchange and payments and not for themselves. Allowing the exchange of heterogeneous currencies through Salam would open a floodgate of explicit Riba. The objects of Salam sale are commodities of trade and not currencies, because these are regarded as monetary values, exchange of which is covered under the rules of Bai' al Sarf.

### 10.4.2 Payment of Price: Salam Capital

Price is normally stipulated and paid in the form of any legal tender. However, it can be in terms of goods as well, on the condition that it should not violate the prohibition of Riba in barter transactions as laid down by the Sharī'ah. Usufruct of assets can also be considered as Salam capital, which is regarded, particularly by Maliki jurists, as immediate receipt of

---

[12] Shariat Appellate Bench, February, 2000, pp. 269–273.

[13] Umar, 1995, p. 39, with reference from Shirbini, 1958, p. 114.

[14] Umar, 1995, pp. 42, 43.

[15] Umar, 1995, p. 43.

the capital on the basis of the legal maxim that says: "Taking possession of a part of a thing is like taking possession of the whole thing". Hence, making usufruct capital of Salam does not mean debt against debt, which is prohibited.[16]

Outstanding loans/debts due on the part of the seller cannot be fully or partially fixed as price, nor can a loan outstanding on a third party be transferred to the seller in future adjustment towards the price, as this amounts to an exchange of obligation for obligation (debt for debt), which is forbidden. This is also to avoid Gharar. This emphasis by the jurists is justified since the equity in Salam contracts depends on the very existence of the Salam capital, otherwise such transactions are invalid. The very term Salaf (Salam) means advance payment; if payment is delayed, it cannot be called Salam.[17]

The buyer in Salam should advance the whole price of the commodity at the time of making the contract. However, while the jurists are agreed on immediate payment of the price, they differ on defining the term "immediate". According to the majority of the jurists, the buyer must pay the amount at the time of signing the contract, in that very meeting. Imam Shafi'e emphasizes that the time must be fixed and payment of the price must take place on the spot and before separation of the parties. But some jurists allow delayed payment provided this delay is not prolonged to make it like a debt. Imam Malik allows a delay of up to three days.[18] Contemporary jurists also allow a delay of two to three days, if it has been stipulated between the parties, provided it is before the delivery period of the commodity involved (in the case of Salam for a short period of a few days).[19]

As regards barter transactions in Bai' Salam, any number or quantity of goods, as the case may be, cannot be advanced for deferred delivery of the same species of goods. As an example, a bank cannot advance ten tons of an improved variety of wheat seed for sowing against twenty-five tons of wheat at harvest. It may advance, for example, a tractor as the price for an agreed amount and quality of cotton or rice. Practically, however, the bank would avoid this and all purchases would be made against money.

*Mode of Payment*

Cash payment is not necessary in Salam; the price can be credited to the seller's account. Crediting the agreed amount in the seller's account can be termed, in letter, a debt for a debt, but in spirit, it does not fall under the prohibited form of a debt for a debt. Hence, it will not be necessary for banks to pay hard cash for Bai' Salam; they may credit the seller's account or issue a pay order in favour of the seller, which may be cashable on demand. In all such cases, money may remain in the bank but is placed at the disposal of the seller.

### 10.4.3   Period and Place of Delivery

In Salam it is necessary to precisely fix the period/time of delivery of goods. Place of delivery also has to be agreed. As regards the time or the period of delivery in Salam, the early compilations of the Hadith mention the practice of fixing a period of one to three years for delivery of farm products. The later jurists, who expanded the application of Salam,

---

[16] AAOIFI, 2004–5a, p. 172.
[17] See AAOIFI, 2004–5a, p. 164, clause 3/1/4; also p. 172 for the rationale of prepayment; references have been given from a number of books of Hadith/Fiqh.
[18] Zuhayli, 2003, p. 261.
[19] AAOIFI, 2004–5a, p. 164.

reduced the period to fifteen days, some even to one day, which, as they argued, was the minimum period necessary for the transport of a commodity from one market to another. Some jurists believed in precise fixation of the date on which delivery was to be made, while some others approved of a rough date but a definite period or occasion of delivery; for example, on harvest.[20]

Contemporary scholars recommend that the due date and place of delivery must be known. The period could be anything from a few days to a number of years, depending upon the nature of the commodity involved. Delivery can also be made in different consignments or instalments if mutually agreed.[21] Before delivery, goods will remain at the risk of the seller. Delivery of goods can be physical or constructive. After delivery, risk will be transferred to the purchaser. Transferring of risk and authority of use and utilization/consumption are the basic ingredients of constructive possession.

If a place of delivery is not stipulated at the time of the Salam agreement, the place at which the contract was executed will be regarded as the place where the goods will be delivered. The parties can also mutually decide about the place, keeping in mind the customary practice.[22]

### 10.4.4   Khiyar (Option) in Salam

The jurists disallow the operation of the Islamic law of option (Khiyar alShart) in the case of Bai' Salam because this disturbs or delays the seller's right of ownership over the price of the goods. The purchaser also does not have the "option of seeing" (Khiyar al Ro'yat), which is available in the case of normal sales. However, after taking delivery, the purchaser has the "option of defect" (Khiyar al'Aib) and the option of specified quality. This means that if the commodity is defective or it does not have the quality or specification as agreed at the time of contract, the purchaser can rescind the sale. But in that case, only the paid amount of price can be recovered without any increase.

### 10.4.5   Amending or Revoking the Salam Contract

In Salam, a seller is bound to deliver the goods as stipulated in the agreement. Similarly, the buyer has no right to unilaterally change the conditions of the contract in respect of the quality or quantity or the period of delivery of the contracted goods after payment is made to the seller. Both parties, however, have the right to rescind the contract with mutual consent in full or in part. The buyer will thus have a right to get back the amount advanced by him; but not more or less than it.[23]

The seller may often be willing to rescind the contract if the market price of the contracted goods is higher at the time of delivery than what the bank has paid to him. Similarly, the bank may be inclined to withdraw from the purchase if the price of the contracted item goes down at the time of delivery. It is, therefore, advisable, to make Bai' Salam between a bank and a supplier an irrevocable contract. The only exception may be the complete absence of the goods in the market or their becoming inaccessible to the seller just at the time of

---

[20] Hasanuz Zaman, 1991, p. 447.
[21] AAOIFI, 2004–5a, clause 3/2/9, p. 165.
[22] AAOIFI, 2004–5a, clause 3/2/10, p. 165.
[23] See, Hasanuz Zaman, 1991, p. 453 and AAOIFI, 2004–5a, clauses 4/2, 4/3, 5/5, pp. 165, 166, 173.

delivery. Only in this situation may the seller be allowed to rescind the contract, provided the bank refuses to extend the period of delivery until the next supply season. In the case of revocation of the contract, the bank will charge exactly the same amount that it had paid.

If the seller supplies the goods before the stipulated time, generally the jurists do not bind the buyer to take possession of it. Those who relax the rule subject it to the interest of the buyer. The buyer can refuse to accept the goods only if they are not according to the stipulated specifications. Any change in prices would allow neither the seller nor the buyer to rescind the contract or to refuse to give or take delivery. Hence, according to the majority of jurists, Salam is considered a nonrevocable sale except with free mutual consent.

Jurists allow the purchaser to take any goods in place of the agreed goods, after the due date falls, provided both parties agree and the new item is of a different genus from the original commodity and the market value of the substitute is not more than the value of the original commodity at the delivery date. Further, it should not be stipulated in the Salam contract.[24]

### 10.4.6  Penalty for Nonperformance

The seller can undertake in the Salam agreement that in the case of late delivery of Salam goods, he shall pay into the Charity Account maintained by the bank an amount which will be given to charity on behalf of the client. This undertaking is, in fact, a sort of self-imposed penalty to keep oneself away from default. Clause 5/7 of the AAOIFI's Salam Standard says: "It is not permitted to stipulate a penalty clause in respect of delay in the delivery of the Muslam Fihi (Salam commodity)." This implies that any such penalty cannot become part of the bank's (seller's) income. A penalty can be agreed in the contract in order to avoid wilful default, as discussed in Chapters 4 and 7. If the seller fails to fulfil his obligation due to insolvency, he should be granted an extension of time for delivery.[25]

## 10.5  SECURITY, PLEDGE AND LIABILITY OF THE SURETIES

It is permissible to ask for security or a pledge in a Salam transaction as proved from the Sunnah of the holy Prophet (pbuh). Imam Bukhari has captioned two chapters "Kafeel fis Salam" and "Al-Rihn fis Salam" and reported the Hadith of the holy Prophet borrowing grain from a Jew against the pledge of an iron breastplate. This Hadith has no mention of Kafeel. Ibn Hajar in *Fathul Bari* has explained this by saying that Imam Bukhari intended to describe the permissibility of Kafeel in Salam by copermitting Rihn and Kafeel.[26]

The seller can be required to furnish any security, personal surety or a pledge. In the case of a pledge, the bank, in the event of the seller's default, has the right to sell out the pledge and purchase the stipulated goods from the market in collaboration with the customer or take away his advance payment out of the sale proceeds and return the balance to the owner. If the bank gets its money back, it cannot be more than the price paid in advance, as the advance price is like a debt outstanding on the seller. Purchase of the stipulated commodity by the bank from the sale proceeds of the pledge should not result in any exploitation of the customer. He, therefore, may be involved in the process.

[24]  AAOIFI, 2004–5a, clauses 4/2 and 5/4, pp. 165, 166, 173.
[25]  AAOIFI, 2004–5a, Standard on Salam, clause 5/6, p. 166.
[26]  Ibn Hajar, 1981, **4**, pp. 433–434; see also AAOIFI, 2004–5a, Standard on Salam, clause 3/3, p. 165.

If a seller has furnished a personal surety, the latter will be liable to deliver the goods if the former fails to do so. If revocation of the contract is required, only the seller is authorized to revoke and not the surety; only the price paid will be taken in that case. The seller can, with the permission of the purchaser, shift the liability to the transferee on the basis of Hawalah, subject to acceptance by the latter. The liability of the surety or the transferee will automatically cease if the contract of Bai' Salam is rescinded. As a result, the pledge will also be released.

## 10.6   DISPOSING OF THE GOODS PURCHASED ON SALAM

First, the Salam buyer cannot sell the commodity onward before taking its delivery. There is a difference of opinion among Muslim jurists regarding the legality of selling the purchased goods in a Salam contract prior to taking delivery. The majority maintain that the Salam purchaser is not allowed to enjoy ownership rights nor he has the right of disposal of such goods until he has received them.[27] Therefore, the seller cannot resell an item, even at cost, cannot contract its transference and cannot make it partnership capital. These jurists rely on the tradition reported by Abu Daud and Ibn Majah: "Whoever makes Salam should not transfer it to others".[28] It is argued that in this Hadith, it is clear that the buyer should not exchange the subject matter of Salam with any person. However, this is a weak tradition, as pointed out by Hafiz Ibn Hajar.[29] Therefore, it cannot be the basis for any ruling. As indicated earlier, Salam is an exception and the basis on which a person purchases a commodity on Salam can be invoked for selling that commodity onward; from here we derive the permission for Parallel Salam for disposal of the commodity.

Therefore, many jurists have given some relaxation. Ibn Taymiyah and Ibn al-Qayyim maintained that there is no legal problem in exchanging the subject matter of Salam before taking possession. If it is sold to a third party, it may be at the same price, a higher price or a lower price. However, if it is sold to the seller himself, it should be at the same price or a lower price but not at a higher price. Companion Ibn Abbas (Gbpwh) and Imam Ahmad have the same view on the issue. This is also the Maliki view. However, they also disapprove of reselling the subject matter of Salam before taking possession if it is a foodstuff.[30]

The contemporary position of Muslim scholars is also divergent. Shaikh Nazih Hammad, for instance, maintains that it is permissible to resell Salam goods before taking possession, as maintained by Ibn Taymiyah and Ibn al-Qayyim, because there is no text from the Qur'ān or Sunnah, Ijma'a or Qiyās to prohibit this. On the contrary, the texts as well as the Qiyās convey its legality.[31] This view has also been backed by some other scholars. On the other hand, many scholars have maintained that it is illegal to resell anything before taking possession of it.[32]

It seems logical to take into consideration the opinion of those who uphold the legality of reselling Salam before taking possession, since there is no genuine text to prohibit that and as

---

[27] Ibn Abideen, n.d., **4**, p. 209; al-Buhuti, Kashshaf al-Qina, **3**, p. 293; Al-Kasani, 1400 AH, **5**, p. 214; Ibn Qudama, 1367 AH, **4**, p. 334.
[28] Abu Daud, 1952, **2**, p. 247.
[29] Among its narrators is one person named Atiah, rejected by Muhaddiseen; see, Ibn Hajar, 1998, **3**, No. 1203, p. 69.
[30] Ibn Rushd, 1950, **2**, p. 231.
[31] Majalla Majma' al-Fiqh al-Islami, No. 9, **3**, pp. 628–629.
[32] Majalla Majma' al-Fiqh al-Islami, No. 9, **3**, pp. 643–654.

a result the ideas of parallel Salam and Sukuk, or certificates based on Salam, that are crucial for the functioning of Islamic banks can be materialized. Transfer of ownership to the purchaser means transfer of risk to him and at least the price risk of the commodity is transferred as soon as the Salam agreement is executed. Otherwise, the legality of parallel Salam as has been allowed in the current framework of Islamic finance would become doubtful.

The possibility of having negotiable Salam certificates is yet to be decided. So far, the majority of the contemporary scholars have not accepted this. To be on the safer side, we may not allow actual or constructive delivery of the Salam goods before taking possession, but if banks maintain inventory of various types of goods, any units of which are sold out of inventory without identification of the particular units, it could be acceptable.

### 10.6.1 Alternatives for Marketing Salam Goods

There are a few options for disposing of or marketing the goods purchased through Salam. The options available to Islamic banks are: (i) enter into a Parallel Salam contract; (ii) an agency contract with any third party or with the customer (seller); and/or (iii) sale in the open market by the bank itself by entering into a promise with any third party or direct selling upon taking delivery. One thing must be clear, however, that such goods cannot be sold back to the Salam seller. Hence, Parallel Salam cannot be entered into with the original seller – this is prohibited due to being buy-back. Even if the purchaser in the second contract is a separate legal entity but owned by the seller in the first contract, this would not amount to a valid Parallel Salam agreement.

One deviation from the above principle would be that after settlement of the Salam transaction, i.e. transfer of ownership/risk to the bank (buyer), there might be a totally separate Murabaha or Musawamah deal with the same client. The State Bank of Pakistan, while giving the Sharī'ah essentials of Islamic modes of financing, has allowed this option.[33] Accordingly, one Islamic bank in Pakistan had been selling carpets purchased through Salam, the day after the culmination of Salam, to the Salam seller, who used to export the carpets as per the concerned L/C. However, as the majority of Sharī'ah scholars were not inclined to accept this arrangement, the bank shifted to the alternative of appointing the client as agent to export the goods on behalf of the bank. We give hereunder the procedure of the above options.

A bank may take a promise from any third party that he will purchase the goods of stipulated specification at any stipulated price. This promise would be binding on the promisor, and in case of breach of promise, he would be liable to make up the actual loss to the promisee. The bank also has the option of waiting to receive the commodity and then selling it in the open market for cash or deferred payment. In this case, it may have to create an inventory that could be useful for the bank from a business point of view, subject to proper risk mitigation and the concerned regulatory framework.

*Agency Contract*

If the bank considers that it is not suitable for it to keep inventory of the goods and/or it has no expertise to sell the commodities received under a Salam contract, it can appoint any third party or the customer as its agent to sell the commodity in the market. It is

---

[33] SBP website: http://www.sbp.gov.pk/departments/ibd.htm

necessary, however, that the Salam agreement and agency agreement should be separate and independent from each other. A price can be determined in the agency agreement at which the agent will sell the commodity, but if the agent is able to get a higher price, the benefit can be given to the agent.[34]

### *Parallel Salam*

In Salam, both the seller and the buyer can enter into a parallel contract. The bank, as seller, can sell the goods on Parallel Salam on similar conditions and specifications as it previously purchased on the first Salam, without making one contract dependent on the other. The date of delivery in the parallel contract can be the same as that of the original Salam. This does not come under prohibition in any way. Similarly, the seller can enter into a parallel contract to enable him to deliver the agreed commodity at the agreed time.

If the seller in the first Salam contract breaches his obligation, the buyer (the injured party) has no right to relate this breach/default to the party with whom he concluded a Parallel Salam. The two contracts cannot be tied up and performance of one must not be made contingent on the other. The delivery date in the parallel contract can be the same as in the original Salam contract, but not earlier than that, as this would mean sale of goods which one does not possess. There must be two separate and independent contracts, one where the bank acts as buyer and another in which it is a seller.[35]

### *Getting Promise for Purchase*

A Salam purchaser may like to get a promise from any third party whereby the latter will buy the commodities of specified quality and quantity at a mutually agreed price. The delivery date of the Salam goods can be the delivery date in the promise. The bank (as promisee) may take earnest money (Hamish Jiddiyah) from the promisor and if the latter backs out, the bank will have the right to cover the actual loss from the earnest money. In the case of promise, prepayment of price by the promisor would not be necessary, and this is the edge of the promise option over the option of Parallel Salam for disposing of goods purchased on the basis of Salam.

## 10.7  SALAM – POST EXECUTION SCENARIOS

After execution of the Salam contract, a number of situations could arise.

### 10.7.1  Supply of Goods as Per Contract

The seller delivers the commodity with the stipulated features at the due time and place of delivery. The bank (buyer) takes delivery and the transaction culminates smoothly; the bank will dispose of the commodity as per its plan.

---

[34] The AAOIFI has described the permission for appointing the client bank's agent for sale of the subject matter of Istisna'a (see p. 185, clause 6/6 of Istisna'a Standard; this implies that such agency is also possible in the case of Salam. See also Hasanuz Zaman, 1991, p. 457).

[35] AAOIFI, 2004–5a, Standard on Salam, clause 6, pp. 167, 173.

### 10.7.2  Failure in Supply of Goods

The seller defaults and does not deliver the goods, saying, for example, that he was unable to produce goods of the agreed quality or the required quantity. The Salam buyer shall have the following options:[36]

- to wait until the commodity is available;
- to cancel the contract and recover the paid price;
- to agree to a replacement with mutual consent and subject to the relevant rules.

The bank will ask the client to acquire the goods, or part thereof, from the market for supply to it as per the contract, and if the customer is unable to do so, the bank will sell the pledge/collateral given by the client in the market, purchase the commodity (the subject of Salam) from the market with the proceeds and give the remainder amount, if any, to the customer. If the proceeds are not sufficient to procure the goods as per the contract, the bank has the right to ask the customer to make good the deficit.

It is pertinent to observe here that the bank has the right to take the goods that it is purchasing from the proceeds of the security, but if it decides to get cash from the customer, it has the right to get only the price given in advance at the time of the contract. The price paid in advance by the bank amounts to a debt in the hands of the seller for the entire period until the goods are delivered. If the contract stands rescinded, the amount of debt will have to be refunded without any increase or decrease. The same amount of money will be returned without any consideration to the increase or decrease in its relative value.

### 10.7.3  Supply of Inferior Goods

Another situation may be that the seller supplies goods inferior to what had been agreed upon and thus forces the bank to either accept those inferior goods or to rescind the contract. This will put the bank in an embarrassing situation. Disputes regarding quality of the goods can be adjudicated by any institution having expertise in the area. A clause to this effect can be inserted in the Salam agreement at the time of the contract. The bank would not be obliged to accept the goods if their quality is judged to be inferior. It may, however, agree to acceptance, may be even at a discounted price. It may also make adjustment for superior quality or additional quantity.[37] There may be a number of solutions to this problem, and some of these are as follows:

1. The bank may refuse to accept the goods and insist on the supply of the agreed goods according to the procedure given in Section 10.7.2, or get the price paid at the time of contract back.
2. If the seller is not able to supply the agreed item, and the item is absolutely out of stock in the accessible market, the bank may ask the seller to supply any other goods.
3. If the seller can only partly supply the agreed goods, the bank may accept the same and revise the purchase order to the extent of the remaining quantity, or it may claim a refund of the balance.

Solution 1 above will be permissible provided it does not involve the return of a price that is different from what the bank had paid. As to solution 2, the substitution is allowed

---

[36] AAOIFI, 2004–5a, clause 5/8.
[37] AAOIFI, 2004–5a, clause 5/3.

with some conditions. The rules applicable for substitution are that the new commodity must also be fungible and not nonfungible – every unit of which is different in quality and price than the other units – and its value should not be more than the value of the Salam commodity. The new commodity should not be of the same genus as that of the original Salam commodity; for example, if the subject of the Salam was wheat, it can be substituted by cotton but not by corn or other animals owned by the customer. Both parties will mutually decide the present market price of the original Salam goods and enter into a sale agreement for the new commodity.

This will be done only when the agreed item is absolutely out of stock in the accessible market. If the item is available, the seller is obliged to buy it for delivering the same to the bank, whatever the market price may be. It is possible that the seller may require additional finance for purchasing the item to deliver it to the bank. He may approach the same bank for a facility to discharge the liability, but the new facility or advance so made by the bank will have to be treated as a separate transaction. Under no circumstances may the two contracts be tied up.

As regards solution 3 involving part delivery of the item, the bank may resort to any of the solutions given above for the remainder amount of the goods. It has to accept the available quantity of the contracted item; for the remaining amount, it can get back the part of the price it has paid. If the seller becomes insolvent and absolutely incapable of honouring the commitment at any time in the near future, he will be treated like an insolvent debtor.

## 10.8   SALAM-BASED SECURITIZATION – SALAM CERTIFICATES/SUKUK

Salam certificates representing a sort of forward contract can be issued against the future delivery of a commodity, product or service. In countries with large public sectors or where the governments have substantial deposits of natural resources, such as petroleum, copper, iron, etc., they can issue certificates for the future delivery of such products, which are fully paid for on the spot by investors, who receive certificates of purchase in return. For example, a country that produces oil may want to expand its refining facilities. It may sell oil products through Salam instead of borrowing on the basis of interest and use the price received in advance.

The Salam purchaser can choose to hold onto the Salam contract and receive the shipment on the designated date, or he may elect to sell the goods involved in the contract through Parallel Salam before the date of delivery, at whatever possible market price, to another investor. He could also issue Salam Sukuk or certificates (SC) against the price paid for future delivery of the oil products. An SC may change hands between the beginning of the contract and its date of maturity. Actual delivery and receipt, and not just paper settlement, are binding on the SC issuer or the final holder of the certificate. The essential feature of Salam certificates is the fact that the issuer's obligation towards the investor is not different from what the market in the real sector pays on the due date of payment.

Salam certificates are geared to a specific commodity or project. People who purchase SCs share income from those commodity/projects, and as such their income is not guaranteed, although it can be quasi-fixed. Since the Salam certificates tie finance, production and sale of the items involved into one contract, the risk of changing prices of the subject of Salam belongs to those who invest in them, i.e. the Salam purchasers.

The investors in Sukuk have to bear counterparty as well as market risks. The counterparty risk would arise with regard to the possibility of the seller being unable to deliver the goods.

The market risk would result from the buyer being unable to market the goods at the time of delivery, or selling them at a sale price lower than the cost to him. These risks can be mitigated by the structure of the deal.

In Bahrain, for example, aluminium has been designated the underlying asset for issuing Salam Sukuk. The Bahrain government sells aluminium to the buyer in the future market. The Bahrain Islamic Bank (BIB) purchases the aluminium and it has been nominated to represent the other banks wishing to participate in the Salam transaction. As consideration for this advance payment, the government of Bahrain issues Salam certificates and undertakes to supply a specified amount of aluminium at a specified date.

## 10.9   SUMMARY OF SALAM RULES

- In Salam, the seller undertakes to supply specific goods to the buyer at a future date in exchange for an advanced price fully paid on the spot.
- As the object of sale in Salam is a debt, payment of the price cannot be delayed, otherwise it will be a sale of debt for debt, which is prohibited.
- The capital (price) of Salam is money, but it can also be a service or a usufruct.
- A debt of the buyer in Salam against the seller or against any third party cannot be used as capital in Salam.
- The object of exchange must be fungible, clearly describable in terms of weight, size, volume, colour, quality, grade, and the like in a way that avoids disputes in the future. Negligible variation can be tolerated. Salam has to be in things that usually exist in markets but are not in the possession of the seller at the time of contracting. The objects of Salam can be agricultural, industrial or natural goods or any well-defined service.
- Salam cannot take place in money or currencies. Salam is not permitted for anything specific like "this car", land, buildings or trees or for articles whose value changes according to subjective assessment.
- It must also be ensured that the commodity is able to be delivered when it is due.
- The place and time of delivery of the object have to be specified. Instalments in delivery of the Salam goods are permissible.
- Salam goods can be delivered before the stipulated date if it does not cause the buyer inconvenience/loss.
- Salam involves no cash settlement. Actual physical delivery is a must. However, if the contract is rescinded for any reason, the actual price paid has to be recovered.
- The seller in Salam need not necessarily be an owner or a producer of the goods.
- The Salam contract is conclusive and binding. It can be altered or revoked only with the consent of both parties.
- Banks should not offset their receivables for payment of the Salam price, as a Salam sale cannot be contracted against a loan, or partly cash and partly loan, in which case the contract will be effective only to the extent of the cash payment.
- If a bank advances money for more than one item, it will be advisable to lay down a breakdown of the value of each item. This will facilitate readjustment of the contract in case of its partial fulfilment. The contract should also expressly provide for the periods of delivery of different items. The same will apply if the contract stipulates different places of delivery.
- If the seller is willing to hand over the contracted goods on the due date, the bank is duty-bound to take possession of the goods, failing which the former will be absolved of his liability. The bank can refuse to accept the goods only if the goods do not fulfil the

stipulated specifications or the same have been offered to it before the fixed date. The bank's refusal will be optional in the latter case.

- The bank, after entering into a Salam contract, can enter into a parallel contract or a promise with any third party to sell the same commodity with the same specifications and date of delivery. The two contracts would be enforceable separately and independently.

**Box 10.1:** Flow of Salam Transactions by Banks

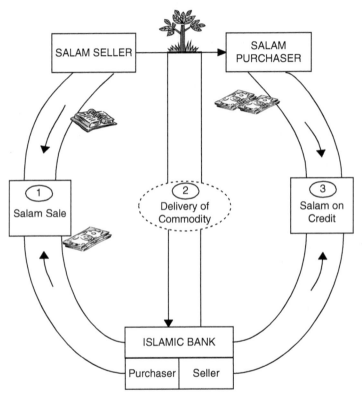

1. The bank will purchase the item from client A with full prepayment of the price and delivery on an agreed specified date.
2. The customer (seller) will deliver the commodity at the agreed time and place.
3. The bank will sell the commodity to any third party C by way of any of the following alternatives:

   — Parallel Salam with C for receipt of full payment;
   — get a promise to purchase from C at any agreed price;
   — appoint A its agent to sell it to any third party;
   — wait until the goods are received and then sell in the market.

4. After taking delivery from A on the agreed date, the bank may make delivery to C or any other purchaser.

## 10.10   SALAM AS A FINANCING TECHNIQUE BY BANKS

Islamic banks have been in operation in various parts of the world for about a quarter of a century, but they have not generally used Bai' Salam as a financing mode. The reason may be that Salam has no practical advantage over (mark-up based) Murabaha–Mu'ajjal. Its main conditions emphasize that the price fixed in the contract must be paid in full in cash, immediately at the time of contract, and banks have to take delivery of goods in the future, not money. Marketing the goods so received and any type of default, e.g. delivery of inferior goods or failure in timely delivery, etc. may also cause problems for the banks.

The practical problems in using this mode to finance agriculture, industry and other commodity sectors can be easily imagined: taking delivery of the produce, assessing its quality, then storing and disposing of it. But the banks perceive such problems when they compare this with the conventional banking practice of not dealing in goods or the easier way of entering into a Murabaha to Purchase Orderer with the client serving as the bank's agent. Once they realize the requirement of actual involvement in business, avenues of risk mitigation in Salam and the fact that Salam is the only mode allowed expressly by the holy Prophet (pbuh) himself, they will surely be inclined towards its greater use.

Salam has its own benefits as well, particularly for farmers and SMEs. Further, it can be more profitable for Islamic banks provided they are equipped with expertise in dealing in commodities. It has great potential, which Islamic banks and financial institutions need to realize. Of late, a number of IFIs have used Salam as a separate mode and also in combination with Murabaha in respect of export financing. Below we shall discuss some aspects of Salam as a financing mode.

---

**Box 10.2:**   The Difference between Salam and Murabaha

**Salam**

- In Salam, delivery of the purchased goods is deferred; the price is paid on the spot.
- In Salam, the price has to be paid in full in advance.
- Salam is not executed in the particular commodity but the commodity is specified by specifications.
- Salam cannot be executed in respect of things which must be delivered on the spot, e.g. Salam between wheat and barley.

**Murabaha**

- In Murabaha, the purchased goods are delivered on the spot; the price may be either on the spot or deferred.
- In Murabaha, the price may be on the spot or deferred.
- Murabaha is executed in particular commodities.
- Murabaha can be executed in those things.

### 10.10.1    Risks in Salam and their Management

In Salam, Islamic banks may face the following risks:

- counterparty risk;
- commodity price risk;
- delivery risk/settlement risk;
- quality risk/low investment return or loss;
- asset holding risk/possibility of extra expenses on storage and Takaful;
- asset replacement risk (in case the bank has to buy from the market);
- fiduciary risk in case of Parallel Salam (the original Salam seller might not properly perform with regard to delivery).

---

### Box 10.3:   Possible Risk Mitigation in Salam

| Risks | Management |
|---|---|
| **1. Counterparty and delivery risk** | |
| • Since the price of Salam goods is given in advance, the customer may default after accepting the payment. | • The bank can liquidate the security and can purchase the same goods from the market. |
| • In the case of different goods and consignments, there could be disputes regarding price, quantity and quality. | • In the Salam MoU, time, quality, quantity and the time of each commodity must be given. |
| • Defective goods could be supplied. | • Collateral/security and performance bonds can be taken to mitigate the loss. |
| • Goods may be delivered late. | • A penalty clause can be embedded in the contract as a deterrent against late delivery. The penalty amount would go to charity. |
| **2. Commodity – price risk** | |
| • Since the nature of a Salam contract is the forward purchase of goods, the price of the commodity may be lower than the market price or the price that was originally expected/considered to be in the market at the time of deliver. | • The bank can undertake Parallel Salam and can also take a "promise to purchase" from a third party. |
| **3. Commodity – marketing risk** | |
| • The bank might not be able to market the goods timely, resulting in possible asset loss and locking of funds in goods. | • The bank should purchase only those goods which have good marketing potential and take binding promises from prospective buyers along with a sufficient amount of Hamish Jiddiyah. |

### 4. Asset-holding risk

- The Islamic bank has to accept the goods and bear the holding cost up to the point of onward delivery.

### 5. Early termination chances

- The client may refund the price taken in advance and refuse to supply the goods.

### 6. Parallel Salam

- The original seller might not supply the goods at the settled time; the buyer in Parallel Salam may sue the bank for timely supply.

Making the Salam seller the bank's agent to dispose of the goods is also a good risk-mitigating tool.

- This cost may be recovered in parallel transactions with proper market survey, feasibility and study of the traders' practice in the relevant area.

- Salam is a binding contract; the seller cannot unilaterally terminate the contract. A penalty can be embedded in the contract to discourage this practice; the penalty amount would go to charity.

- The bank may purchase a similar asset from the spot market for supply to the buyer and recover the loss, if any, from the seller in the original Salam.

---

**Box 10.4:   Case Study**[38]

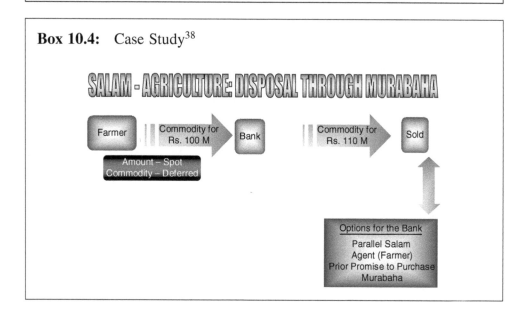

SALAM - AGRICULTURE: DISPOSAL THROUGH MURABAHA

Farmer → Commodity for Rs. 100 M → Bank

Amount – Spot
Commodity – Deferred

Bank → Commodity for Rs. 110 M → Sold

Options for the Bank
Parallel Salam
Agent (Farmer)
Prior Promise to Purchase
Murabaha

---

[38] The author is grateful to Mr Omer Mustafa Ansari of Fords Rhodes Sidat Hyder & Co., Karachi for his help in the preparation of the case studies on Salam and the flowcharts.

---

**Box 10.4:** (Continued)

1. Farmer A or a grain dealer executes a Salam contract on 1st January to sell 5000 tons of wheat in advance for Rs. 100 million to bank B.
2. Bank B pays Rs. 100 million on the spot on 1st January to A and also stipulates from where to take delivery on 1st May.
3. B enters into a promise with C – C undertakes that he will purchase wheat from B for Rs. 115 million on 1st May against Hamish Jiddiyah of Rs. 15 million.
4. A supplies 5000 tons of wheat to B on 1st May; B informs C to execute sale and take delivery.
5. C executes the sale and takes delivery from B and signs a promissory note for Rs. 100 million.

---

**Box 10.5:** Salam – Preshipment Export Financing

1. Customer A gets a purchase order from abroad for the export of rice costing Rs. 1.1 million.
2. A approaches Islamic bank B to get finance on the basis of Salam.
3. The foreign importer opens an L/C in favour of B to the amount of Rs. 1.1 million and sends it through a negotiating bank to B. (an L/C can also be opened in the name of A under an agency agreement.)
4. The bank enters into a Salam agreement with A; pays Rs. 1 million in advance for purchase of 1000 tons of defined quality rice to be delivered on 1st January, 2007. B also signs an agency agreement with A to export rice as the bank's agent.
5. A supplies 1000 tons of rice to the bank on 1st January, 2007. Henceforth, B is the owner of the risk and reward of the rice.
6. A arranges shipment of the rice, as agent of B under the L/C.
7. The bank gets the proceeds of the L/C as per its terms and conditions.
8. As B is the owner of the rice, it will be responsible if the order is cancelled for any reason, or the consignment is damaged. The Takaful expense, if any, will be borne by B.

---

**Box 10.6:** Salam and Refinance by the Central Banks (CBs)

The process flow will be as below:

1. The CB and an Islamic bank B will create a Musharakah investment pool; the bank's part of the capital will consist of mutually decided assets of B, like its investment in stocks fulfilling the Sharī´ah compliance criteria, Ijarah assets/contracts and Murabaha receivables (less than 33%), etc.
2. B will provide export finance to exporters under Salam and inform the CB, along with its proof.
3. The CB will invest in the pool the amount equivalent to the export finance given by B.

4. It would be agreed while opening the Musharakah pool that all the time, the share of the CB will be (_____) % of the total pool size.
5. Income received from the pool assets will be distributed between the CB and B as per the ratio agreed in the beginning of each accounting period, may be a month or a quarter.
6. The CB and B can agree that profit over and above a certain level will be used for creating "Reserves" that could be used for any shortfall in profits in future.

---

**Box 10.7:**   Salam for Working Capital Finance[39]

1. Sugar mill A needs working capital and approaches bank B on 1st October, 2007.
2. B offers A a Salam agreement for the purchase of sugar from it (at this point the bank can appoint A its agent for sale of the sugar when received, or get a promise to buy from any third party, or arrange for Parallel Salam; let us assume that it enters into an agency agreement that is independent of the Salam agreement).

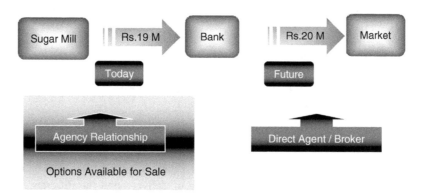

3. B indicates a target price, i.e. Rs. 20 per kg for the sale of sugar in the market by A as its agent.
4. A sells sugar of a defined quality at Rs. 19 per kg to be delivered on 31st December, 2007 and receives the proceeds in advance.
5. A delivers the sugar on 31st December, 2007; upon taking physical or constructive possession, it comes under the liability/risk of B.
6. If A sells sugar in the market as an agent of B at Rs. 21 per kg, for example, one rupee per kg could be his service fee, if the bank agrees.
7. If prices fall and sugar is sold at Rs. 18 per kg (for example), despite effort by A, B will have to suffer the loss.

---

[39] Prepared by Mr Omer Mustafa Ansari of Fords Rhodes Sidat Hyder & Co., Karachi.

**Box 10.8:**  Accounting Treatment by Islamic Banks in Salam and Parallel Salam

**Initial recognition**

- Salam financing is recognized when paid to the seller or made available to him.
- Parallel Salam is recognized when the bank receives the price.
- Initial measurement of capital/price will be made at the amount of cash paid or at fair value of the asset if capital is provided in kind.

**Measurement at the end of the financial period**

- Capital is measured in the same way as in the initial measurement; however, if delivery of the commodity is not probable in full or in part or its value declines, the Islamic bank will make provision for the estimated deficit.
- Salam financing transactions are presented as "Salam Financing" in financial statements.
- Parallel Salam transactions are presented as "Liability" in financial statements.

**Receipt of the commodity**

1. A commodity received is recorded as an asset at historical cost.
2. For receipt of commodities of different quality:

   - if the market value is equal to the contracted value, the commodity shall be recorded at book value;
   - if the market value is lower than the book value, the commodity shall be measured and recorded at market value at the time of delivery and the difference shall be recognized as loss.

3. Failure to receive the commodity on the due date:

   - if delivery is extended, the book value shall remain as it is;
   - if the Salam contract is cancelled and the client does not repay the capital, the amount shall be recognized as a receivable due from the client.

4. Failure to receive the commodity due to the client's misconduct:

   - if the Salam contract is cancelled and the client does not repay the capital, the amount shall be recognized as a receivable due from the client;
   - in the case where securities pledged for the commodity are less than its book value, the difference is recognized as a receivable due from the client, or, alternatively, a credit to the client if the proceeds are more than the book value.

**Measurement of the value of the commodity at the end of a financial period**

- A commodity acquired through Salam shall be measured at the lower of the historical cost or the cash equivalent value, and if the cash equivalent value is lower, the difference shall be recognized as loss.

**Recognition of result – delivery of the commodity**

- Upon delivery of the commodity in a Parallel Salam transaction, the difference between the amount paid by the client and the cost of the commodity shall be recognized as profit or loss.

# 10.11   ISTISNA'A (ORDER TO MANUFACTURE)

### 10.11.1   Definition and Concept

Istisna'a, like Salam, is a special kind of Bai' where the sale of a commodity is transacted before the commodity comes into existence. The legality of Istisna'a is accepted by the Sharī'ah scholars because it does not contain any prohibition, it has always been a common practice in the world and also because of ease for human beings. Renowned contemporary jurist Zuhayli writes:

> "Istisna'a evolved into Islamic jurisprudence historically due to specific needs in the areas of manual work, leather products, shoes, carpentry, etc. However, it has grown in the modern era as one of the contracts that make it possible to meet major infrastructure and industrial projects such as the building of ships, airplanes and other large machinery. Accordingly, the prominence of the commission to manufacture contract has increased with the scope of the financed projects."[40]

Istisna'a is a valid contract and a normal business practice. As a financing mode it has been legalized on the basis of the principle of Istihsan (public interest).[41] Istisna'a is an agreement culminating in a sale at an agreed price whereby the purchaser places an order to manufacture, assemble or construct (or cause so to do) anything to be delivered at a future date. It becomes an obligation of the manufacturer or the builder to deliver the asset with agreed specifications at the agreed period of time.

As the sale is executed at the time of entering into the Istisna'a contract, the contracting parties need not renew an exchange of offer and acceptance after the subject matter is prepared.[42] This is different from the promise in a contract of Murabaha to Purchase Orderer, which requires formal offer and acceptance by the parties when possession of the items to be sold is taken by the bank. Istisna'a can be used for providing the facility of financing the manufacture/construction of houses, plant, projects, building of bridges, roads and highways, etc. The price must be fixed with the consent of the parties involved.

---

[40] Zuhayli, 2003, p. 267.

[41] Islamic Fiqh Council of the OIC, Resolutions, No. 65 (3/7), pp. 137, 138; AAOIFI, 2004–5a, p. 191. For details about Istisna'a, see Zuhayli, 2003, pp. 267–279.

[42] This is because Istisna'a is a sale contract and not a mere promise; see Zuhayli, 2003, pp. 269, 270; See also AAOIFI, 2004–5a, Standard on Istisna'a, clause 2/2/2, p. 179.

In Istisna'a, the manufacturer arranges both the raw material and the labour. If material is supplied by the purchaser and the manufacturer is required to use his labour and skill only, this is the contract of Ujrah (doing any job against an agreed wage/remuneration) and not of Istisna'a. In the following sections we discuss elements of Istisna'a in detail.

An Istisna'a contract is binding on the contracting parties; the manufacturer is obliged to supply the subject matter with the agreed specifications and the orderer or buyer is obliged to accept the asset of stipulated type, quality and quantity and make the agreed payment. The parties may agree to a period during which the manufacturer will be responsible for any defects or the maintenance of the subject matter.[43]

### 10.11.2   Subject Matter of Istisna'a

Istisna'a is a sale contract applicable to items to be manufactured that are identified by specification not by designation. This contract is valid only for those objects that have to be manufactured or constructed. But it is not necessary that the seller himself manufactures the item, unless stated in the contract. The subject of Istisna'a (the thing to be manufactured or constructed) must be known and specified to the extent of removing any ignorance or lack of knowledge of its kind, type, quality and quantity.

The sellers agree to provide the subject matter transformed from raw materials through manufacturing or goods manufactured by human hands. It is invalid for natural things or products like animals, corn, fruit, etc. Both unique and homogeneous types of assets are covered under Istisna'a provided their specifications are agreed at the time of the contract. For example, items of unique description that have no regular market, have no substitute in the market and where the value of each unit of that type of goods may be different, are covered by Istisna'a.

Istisna'a is not confined to what the manufacturer himself makes after the contract. The specifications demanded by the buyer and agreed between the parties are important. The seller/manufacturer will be fulfilling his obligation if he brings in an asset conforming to all agreed specifications, unless otherwise agreed in the contract that the seller will himself manufacture the asset. In other words, the contract is binding according to specifications.

It is not permissible that the subject matter of an Istisna'a contract be an existing and identified asset.[44] For example, it is invalid for an Islamic bank to conclude a contract to sell a particular designated car from a factory on the basis of Istisna'a. But an asset that has already been produced by the seller or by another can become the subject matter of Istisna'a provided that it is not identified in the contract and the contract identifies speciation only.[45]

An Istisna'a contract may be drawn for real estate developments on designated land owned either by the purchaser or the contractor, or on land in which either of them owns the usufruct. It is allowed because the contract involves the construction of specified buildings that will be built and sold according to specification and, in this case, the contract of Istisna'a does not specify a particular identified place.

---

[43] AAOIFI, 2004–5a, clause 3/1/7, p. 181.
[44] AAOIFI, 2004–5a, clauses 3/1/2, 3/1/3, pp. 180, 191.
[45] AAOIFI, 2004–5a, p. 192.

An Istisna'a contract must definitely state, in clear terms, the type, dimensions, period and place of delivery of the asset. The asset can be manufactured or produced by any or a specific manufacturer, or manufactured from specific materials or any materials available in the market, as may be agreed between the two parties.

The manufacturer (seller) may enter into a contract with a manufacturer to provide the subject matter of Istisna'a. On this basis, the banks may undertake financing based on Istisna'a by getting the subject of Istisna'a manufactured through another such contract. Thus, Islamic banks can serve both as manufacturers (sellers) and purchasers in Istisna'a.

### 10.11.3   Price in Istisna'a

The price in Istisna'a can be in the form of cash, any tangible goods or usufruct of identified assets. Usufruct as consideration for an Istisna'a contract is relevant to situations where government institutions offer usufruct of the asset being built for an agreed time period, commonly known as "build, operate and transfer" (BOT).

The price should be known in advance to the extent of removing ignorance or lack of knowledge and dispute. It is permissible that the price of Istisna'a transactions varies in accordance with variations in delivery date. There is also no objection to a number of offers being subject to negotiation, provided that eventually only one offer is chosen for concluding the Istisna'a contract. This is to avoid uncertainty and lack of knowledge that may lead to dispute.

The price, once settled, cannot be unilaterally increased or decreased. However, as manufacturing of huge assets may involve more time, sometimes necessitating many changes, the price can be readjusted by the mutual consent of the contracting parties because of making material modifications to the item to be manufactured or due to unforeseen contingencies or changes in prices of the inputs.

It is not necessary in Istisna'a that the price is paid in advance (unlike Salam, in which spot payment of price is necessary).[46] The price can be paid in instalments within the agreed time period and can also be linked with the completion stages.[47] Against the general rule set out for Salam, contemporary scholars have legalized it on the basis of analogy and Istihsan as it involves personal labour, effort and commitment of the seller, which makes the contract similar to a leasing contract, in which it is permissible to defer the payment of the rental without that being considered a sale of debt for debt.[48] Further, the construction of huge plants may require a long gestation period and also payment through instalments, according to the pace of implementation of such projects.

A contract of Istisna'a cannot be drawn up on the basis of a Murabaha sale, for example, by determining the price of Istisna'a on a cost-plus basis. This is because the subject matter of Murabaha should be something already in existence, its cost should be known and it should be owned by the seller before conclusion of Murabaha, so that a profit margin may be added to that. None of these is a requirement of Istisna'a.[49]

The bank may be acting either in the capacity of the manufacturer or of the purchaser, and may give or demand a security deposit ('Arbūn), which may be considered as part of the

---

[46] This is the view of most of the Hanafi jurists; many jurists, including Imams Malik, Shafi'e, Ahmad, Zufar (Hanafi) and others, allow Istisna'a on the conditions of Salam, the most important of which is full prepayment; The majority of Hanafi jurists allow some relaxations on the basis of juristic approbation (Istihsan) and analogy and also because of common usage of this contract without any explicit prohibition. See Zuhayli, 2003, pp. 271, 272.

[47] AAOIFI, 2004–5a, clauses 3/2/2 to 3/2/4, p. 182.

[48] AAOIFI, 2004–5a, p. 192.

[49] AAOIFI, 2004–5a, p. 193.

price if the contract is completed, and can be forfeited if the contract is rescinded. However, the amount forfeited may be restricted to the amount of actual damage suffered and the remaining amount may preferably be returned to the customer.[50]

### 10.11.4 Penalty Clause: Delay in Fulfilling the Obligations

An Istisna'a contract may also contain a penalty clause stipulating an agreed amount of money for compensating the purchaser adequately if the manufacturer is late in delivering the asset. Such compensation is permissible only if the delay is not caused by intervening contingencies (*force majeure*). Further, it is not permitted to stipulate a penalty clause against the purchaser for default in any payment because this would be Riba.[51] A voluntary rebate for prepayment is permissible, provided it is not agreed in the contract.

It can be agreed, in other words, between the parties that in the case of delay in delivery, the price shall be reduced by a specified amount. The scholars have contended this on the basis of analogy. The classical jurists allowed such a condition in Ijarah, e.g. if a person hires the services of a tailor, he may tell him that the wage will be 10 dirhams if he prepares the clothes within a week and 12 if within two days. By analogy, experts allow a penalty clause in the Istisna'a agreement in the case of a delay in delivery, supply or construction of the subject of Istisna'a.

In Fiqh, this principle is termed Shart-e-Jazāi (penalty condition), or the condition of decreasing the price on account of a delay in delivery of the subject matter of Istisna'a.[52] This reduction will enhance the income of the orderer (purchaser) and it will not go to charity, as in the case of all other modes. This special permission is on account of the fact that, in Istisna'a, timely completion of the work depends on labour and commitment of the manufacturer (seller). If he does not devote full time to completion of the job of a particular contract and engages in other contracts in his quest for more and more orders and maximum earnings, he can be fined. This benefit would go to the purchaser, who might suffer in the case of nondelivery at the stipulated time. Any such undertaking by the manufacturer would be binding on him.

Contrary to this, in Salam, any penalty taken for late delivery by the Salam seller will go to charity, because in Salam, the price paid in advance creates a debt liability on the seller which has to be paid without any increase. Even this penalty is permissible only if the delay is not caused by intervening contingencies (*force majeure*). However, it is not permitted to stipulate a penalty clause against the purchaser (from the bank, for example) for default on payment.

### 10.11.5 The Binding Nature of an Istisna'a Contract

Istisna'a is nonbinding as long as the manufacturer does not start work on the subject matter of the contract. Therefore, before the manufacturer starts the work, any one of the parties may cancel the contract by giving notice to the other. However, after the manufacturer has started the work, the contract cannot be cancelled by the buyer unilaterally. The majority

---

[50] AAOIFI, 2004–5a, clause 3/3/1, p.182.

[51] AAOIFI, 2004–5a, clause 6/7, pp. 186, 193, also see p. 32.

[52] Zuhayli, 2003, p. 279.

of contemporary Sharī'ah scholars, Civil Law in some Muslim countries like Jordan and Sudan, the "Unified Arab Law" proposed by the League of Arab Countries and the Fiqh Council of the OIC treat Istisna'a as a "binding contract" provided that certain conditions are fulfilled. If the asset conforms to the specifications agreed at the time of the Istisna'a contract, the purchaser is bound to accept the asset and he cannot exercise the option of inspection (Khiyar al Ro'yat). He, however, has the "option of defect" (Khiyar al 'Aib) and the option of specified quality, meaning that if the asset has any proven defect or lacks the agreed specifications, the purchaser has the right to be indemnified.

### 10.11.6    Guarantees

The bank, acting either in the capacity of the manufacturer or of the ultimate purchaser, can give or demand security, collateral or a performance bond to ensure that the work is performed within the agreed time and as per specifications. It can also get 'Arbūn, which will either be part of the price if the contract is fulfilled, or forfeited if the contract is rescinded. However, it is preferable that the amount forfeited be limited to an amount equivalent to the actual damage suffered.[53]

### 10.11.7    Parallel Contract – Subcontracting

Istisna'a is not confined to what the manufacturer himself makes, and if the contract is silent or it expressly allows such, the seller/supplier can get it manufactured as per the specifications given in the contract from anyone else. Financial institutions, as sellers, would contract with someone else to manufacture the same. This could be a case of a Parallel Istisna'a contract.

An Istisna'a contract shall be entered into, on the one hand, between the bank and a customer, while on the other hand, the bank may enter into a Parallel Istisna'a with a third party (contractor) for preparation of the subject matter of the first Istisna'a. The delivery date of the parallel contract must not precede the date of the original Istisna'a contract. In one contract, the bank will be the buyer and in the second, the seller. Ownership-related risks of the two contracts will remain separate and will have to be borne by the respective parties so long as the asset is not transferred to the other.[54] Each of the two contracts shall be independent of the other. They cannot be tied up in a manner whereby the rights and obligations of one contract are dependent on the rights and obligations of the other contract. Further, Parallel Istisna'a is allowed with a third party only.

It is permissible for the bank to buy items on the basis of a clear and unambiguous specification and to pay, with the aim of providing liquidity to the manufacturer, the price in cash when the contract is concluded. Subsequently, the bank may enter into a contract with another party in order to sell, in the capacity of manufacturer or supplier, items whose specifications conform to the wishes of that other party, on the basis of Parallel Istisna'a, and fulfil its contractual obligation accordingly.

---

[53] AAOIFI, 2004–5a, clause 3/3, p. 182.
[54] AAOIFI, 2004–5a, clauses 7/1, 7/3, pp. 182, 186.

### 10.11.8   Istisna'a and Agency Contract

The bank, acting either as a seller or as a buyer in Istisna'a, can appoint any agent, with the consent of the other party, to supervise the manufacturing process or to sell the asset when received. It can ask the client/manufacturer to act as an agent to sell the subject matter. The agency agreement should be separate and independent from the Istisna'a agreement. Banks that are using Istisna'a normally appoint an agent for sale of the asset in the local or foreign markets.

An agency contract can also be used if there is a delay on the part of the purchaser in taking delivery of the subject matter within a particular period of time. The seller can sell that asset in the market and pay the amount over and above his dues, if any, to the purchaser.

The bank can also engage any consultant firms to supervise the construction work and to determine whether the subject matter conforms to the stipulated specifications or for other advisory services.[55] The parties may mutually decide who will bear the related supervision expenses.

### 10.11.9   Post Execution Scenario

*Work in Progress*

Before the manufacturer starts work on the subject matter of Istisna'a, both of the parties have the right to rescind the contract. Once the seller/manufacturer initiates the work, the contract becomes binding and any change is possible only with mutual consent.

The parties to the contract are inevitably bound by all obligations and consequences flowing from their agreement. The purchaser will make the payment as per the agreed schedule and the manufacturer/seller will supply the asset as per the specifications agreed. If the subject matter does not conform to the specifications agreed upon, the customer has the option to accept or to refuse the subject matter. The purchaser shall not be regarded as the owner of the materials in the possession of the manufacturer for the purpose of producing the asset.

If the actual cost incurred by the bank (as seller) on an asset sold on Istisna'a is less than the forecast cost, or the bank gets a discount from the subcontractor on a Parallel Istisna'a basis, the bank is not obliged to give a discount to the purchaser and any additional profit, or loss if any, pertains to the bank. The same rule adversely applies when the actual costs of production are greater than the forecast costs.[56]

If so desired by a customer, the Islamic bank (as purchaser) may replace an existing contractor to complete a project which has already been commenced by the previous contractor. For this purpose, the existing status of the project needs to be assessed, whereby the cost of such assessment and all liabilities as of that date shall remain the responsibility of the customer.

The bank, working as a manufacturer (seller), must assume liability for ownership risk, maintenance and Takaful expenses prior to delivering the subject matter to the purchaser as well as the risk of theft or any abnormal damage. The manufacturer cannot stipulate in the contract of Istisna'a that he is not liable for defects. Therefore, if the bank is the manufacturer for the purpose of an Istisna'a contract, it cannot absolve itself from loss on

---

[55] AAOIFI, 2004–5a, clauses 5, 6/6, p. 184.
[56] AAOIFI, 2004–5a, Standard on Istisna'a, clause 3/2/6.

this account. The orderer (purchaser) has the right to obtain collateral from the manufacturer for the amount he has paid and as regards delivery of the commodity with specifications and time of delivery.

A voluntary rebate for prepayment is permissible, provided it is not agreed in the contract.

### Delivery and Disposal of the Subject Matter

1. Before delivery of the asset to the purchaser, it will remain at the risk of the seller; any loss to the raw material or to the item in the process of manufacturing will be borne by him.
2. After delivery, risk will be transferred to the purchaser.
3. Possession of goods can be physical or constructive, depending upon the nature of the asset and transfer of ownership/risk. Transferring risk and delegating authority of use and utilization/consumption are the basic ingredients of constructive possession. For this, there should be a demarcation line between handing over and taking over of possession.[57]
4. If a manufactured asset is delivered before the agreed date, the purchaser should accept it if the asset meets the stipulated specifications. He can refuse to accept the goods if these are not as per the agreed specifications or there is some other genuine justification for not accepting before the agreed date (Istisna'a Standard, clauses 6/1 to 6/3).
5. If the condition of the subject matter does not conform to the contractual specifications at the date of delivery, the ultimate purchaser has the right to reject the subject matter or to accept it in its present condition, in which case the acceptance constitutes satisfactory performance of the contract.

### 10.11.10   The Potential of Istisna'a

Islamic banks can use Istisna'a for manufacturing of high technology goods like aircrafts, ships, buildings, dams, highways, etc. It can also be used for housing and export financing, meeting working capital requirements in industries where sale orders are received in advance.[58] Potential areas are given below:

- financing the construction industry – apartment buildings, hospitals, schools and universities;
- development of residential/commercial areas and housing finance schemes;
- financing high technology industries such as the aircraft industry, locomotive and ship-building industries.

### 10.11.11   Risk Management in Istisna'a

Banks could face the following risks in Istisna'a-based financing:

- settlement risk;
- price risk;
- delivery risk;
- possession risk;
- market risk.

---

[57] AAOIFI, 2004–5a, Standard on Istisna'a, clause 6/4, p. 185.
[58] For the potential of Istisna'a, see Zuhayli, 2003, pp. 278, 279.

As a whole, risks in Istisna'a would be mitigated by taking proper collateral, performance bonds, technical expertise in the relevant areas for timely and effective marketing and for ensuring cost effectiveness, by resorting to suitable Takaful policies, by choosing good clients and by adopting suitable capital budgeting and liquidity management policies. Mitigation for some of the risks is shown in Box 10.9. As little is available so far on the practical application of Istisna'a, we shall also give a number of hypothetical case studies.

---

**Box 10.9:**   Risk Mitigation in Istisna'a

**Ownership of material**

| | |
|---|---|
| The Islamic bank is not the owner of the materials in the possession of the manufacturer for the purpose of producing the asset. It can have no claim on it in the case of any nonperformance. | Security is available with the bank. |

**Delivery risk**

| | |
|---|---|
| The bank may be unable to complete the manufacturing of goods as scheduled due to late delivery of completed goods by the subcontractor in Parallel Istisna'a. | On the basis of the rule of "Shart-e-Jazāi", the bank can put in the Istisna'a agreement a clause to reduce the Istisna'a price in the case of delay. |

**Sale not permissible before delivery**

| | |
|---|---|
| Sale of Istisna'a goods is not allowed before taking physical possession. This may lead to asset, price and marketing risk. | The bank can take a "promise to purchase" from a third party and can make arrangements for sale through agency. |

**Quality risk**

| | |
|---|---|
| The Islamic bank gets delivery of inferior quality manufactured goods, which also may affect the original contract. | The bank can obtain a guarantee of quality from the original supplier. |

---

**Box 10.10:**   Differences between Istisna'a and Salam and Ijarah (Ujrah)

| **Istisna'a** | **Salam** |
|---|---|
| 1. The subject of Istisna'a is always a thing which needs manufacturing. | 1. The Salam subject can be either natural products or manufactured goods. |
| 2. The price in Istisna'a does not necessarily need to be paid in full in advance. | 2. The price has to be paid in full in advance. |

3. Istisna'a can mainly be conducted for Qimi goods, all units of which are different from one another in terms of price/specification. But it can also be used for items having trademarks wherein all units might be similar in price and specification.
4. Penalty in the form of a reduction in price on account of a delay in delivery will reflect the income of the purchaser (the principle of Shart-e-Jazāi approved by the jurists.)
5. As long as work has not started, Istisna'a is nonbinding; any of the parties can revoke the contract.

3. The subject of Salam is a liability on the seller and thus must consist of fungible (Mithli) goods, all units of which are similar, so that if the seller is not able to produce the goods by himself, he can get the same from the market.
4. Penalty for late delivery shall go to charity and the P&L Account of the purchaser (bank) will be unaffected.
5. Salam is a binding contract; once executed, it cannot be rescinded without the consent of the other.

**Istisna'a**

1. The manufacturer uses his own materials and the sale price is fixed.

2. Istisna'a can be of anything that needs manufacturing.

3. In Istisna'a, asset risk is transferred to the purchaser soon after delivery of the item to him and he has to pay the price irrespective of what happens to the asset.

**Ijarah (Ujrah)**

1. The manufacturer on an Ujrah basis uses the material provided by the buyer and he is paid the agreed wages.
2. Ijarah can be only on those assets the corpus of which is not consumed with use.
3. In Ijarah, asset risk remains with the owner (lessor) and the lessee has to give rental only if the asset is capable of being used as per normal market practice.

---

**Box 10.11:** Accounting Treatment by Islamic Banks (as Seller) in Istisna'a[59]

**Istisna'a costs**

- Istisna'a costs, including direct and indirect costs relating to the contract, shall be recognized in an Istisna'a work in progress account or Istisna'a cost account in the case of a parallel contract.
- The amount billed to al-Mustasni (buyer) shall be debited to an Istisna'a receivable account and credited to an Istisna'a billing account.

---

[59] See AAOIFI, 2004–5b, Accounting Standard on Istisna'a, pp. 300–321.

**Box 10.11:** (Continued)

- The balance of the Istisna'a billing account shall be offset against the Istisna'a work in progress account.
- Any precontract cost shall be recognized as deferred costs and transferred to the Istisna'a work in progress account upon signing of the contract.

### Contract costs in Parallel Istisna'a
- Istisna'a costs shall include the price fixed in a Parallel Istisna'a contract.
- Progress billings to al-Mustasni (buyer) shall be debited to the Istisna'a receivable account and credited to the Istisna'a billing account.
- The balance of the Istisna'a billing account shall be offset against the Istisna'a work in progress account.

### Istisna'a revenue and profit
Istisna'a revenue is the price agreed, including the Islamic bank's profit margin on the contract, and recognized in the financial statements using either of the following methods:
- percentage of completion method;
- completed contract method.

### Deferred profits
These shall be recognized using either of the following methods:
- proportionate allocation (preferred method);
- as and when each instalment is received.

### Early settlement
- On advance payment made by the buyer, the Islamic bank may waive part of its profit that shall be deducted from both the Istisna'a receivable account and the deferred profits account.
- The above shall apply if the facts are the same except that the bank did not grant a partial reduction of the profit when the payment was made, but reimbursed this amount to the buyer after receiving the payments.

### Parallel Istisna'a revenue and profit
- Revenue and profit in Parallel Istisna'a shall be measured and recognized according to the percentage of completion method.
- The recognized portion of Istisna'a profit shall be added to the Istisna'a cost account.
- If the contract price or part is to be paid following the completion of the contract, accounting treatments of deferred profits shall be applicable.

### Change orders, additional claims and maintenance costs
Change orders and additional claims

- The value and cost of change orders shall be added to Istisna'a revenue and costs, respectively.
- If the required conditions for additional claims are met, an amount of revenue shall be recognized equal to the additional cost caused by the claim.

- If the required conditions are not met in full or in part for recognizing additional claims, the estimated value of these claims shall be disclosed in notes to the financial statements.
- If Parallel Istisna'a exists, accounting treatments as mentioned above shall apply; however, the cost of such shall be determined by the contractor with the approval of the Islamic bank.

Maintenance and warranty costs

- These shall be recognized on an accrual basis and matched with recognized revenue. Actual costs shall be charged against the maintenance and warranty allowance account.
- If Parallel Istisna'a exists, these shall be accounted for on a cash basis.

**Measurement at the end of the financial period**

- Istisna'a work in progress shall be measured and reported at cash equivalent value if applying the percentage of completion method for recognition of profit and revenue.
- Any expected loss at the end of the financial period shall be recognized and reported in the income statement.
- In the case of Parallel Istisna'a, the Istisna'a cost shall be treated as mentioned above.
- Additional costs due to failure of a subcontractor shall be recognized as loss in the income statement.

---

**Box 10.12:** Accounting Treatment by Islamic Banks (as Buyer) in Istisna'a

**Istisna'a billings of completed jobs**

- Progress billings shall be debited to the Istisna'a cost account and presented as assets in financial statements and corresponding credit shall be made to the Istisna'a accounts payable account.
- The above accounting treatments shall also be applicable to a Parallel Istisna'a contract.

**Receipt of commodity**

- The commodity received, if meeting the specifications required, shall be recorded at historical cost.
- If Parallel Istisna'a exists, on delivery of the commodity to the client, the balance of the Istisna'a costs account shall be transferred to an asset account.

**Box 10.12:** (Continued)

**Late delivery of commodity**

The Islamic bank shall take compensation from the performance bond in the case of negligence or fault on the part of the seller. An allowance for doubtful debts shall be made if the performance bond is not sufficient to cover the amount of compensation.

**Commodity not conforming to the specification**

- If the commodity is declined by the bank due to nonconformity to specifications, any unrecovered progress payments made to the seller shall be recorded as accounts receivable and an allowance for doubtful debts shall be made, if necessary.
- If the bank does not decline a discrepant commodity, it shall be measured at the lower of the cash equivalent value or the historical cost. Any loss shall be recognized in the income statement in which the loss is realized.

**Buyer refuses to receive the commodity (parallel contract)**

On refusal to receive a commodity due to its being discrepant, it shall be measured at the lower of the cash equivalent value or the historical cost. Any loss shall be recognized in the income statement in which the loss is realized.

---

**Box 10.13:** Housing Finance through Istisna'a[60]

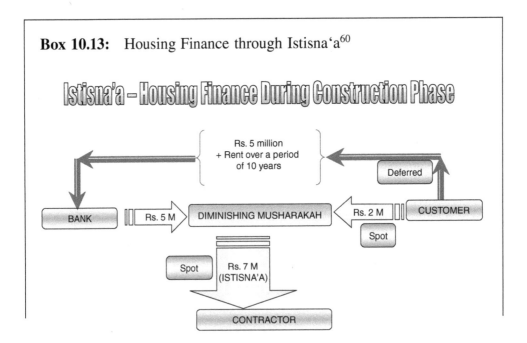

---

[60] The author is grateful to Mr Omer Mustafa Ansari of Fords Rhodes Sidat Hyder & Co., Karachi for his guidance on accounting treatment and help in preparation of case studies on Istisna'a and the flowcharts.

The following could be the flow process:

1. Suppose a builder/contractor C has announced a scheme for the construction and sale of apartments costing Rs. 7 million each. (He demands cash and has no financial relationship with the bank.)
2. Client A decides to have an apartment; he has Rs. 2 million and needs financing from bank B of Rs. 5 million for ten years.
3. A and B create a Musharakah pool of Rs. 7 million under the principle of Shirkatul-milk and jointly enter into Istisna'a agreements with C for the construction and sale of an apartment of defined specifications and pay Rs. 7 million in four instalments.
4. C starts building the apartment as per the requirements of the Istisna'a contract.
5. The bank appoints A its agent to supervise the construction work.
6. C hands over the apartment to A; B leases out its part of ownership to A in rent.
7. A purchases one unit of the bank's part every month; the rental starts decreasing after each payment and after ten years, the bank's investment is redeemed and ownership is transferred to the client. (See the rules of Diminishing Musharakah for the purpose of housing finance in Chapter 12.)

---

**Box 10.14:**   Istisna'a for Preshipment Export Finance

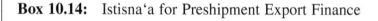

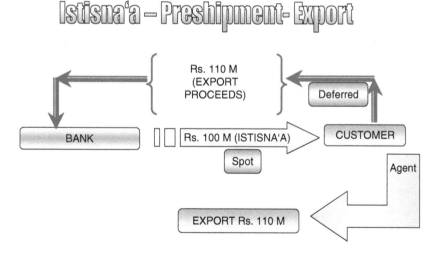

**Hypothetical case study:**

1. Client A gets an export order for the export of ready-made garments of value Rs. 110 million.
2. A approaches bank B for financing and indicates that he has the expertise to prepare the consignment.

**Box 10.14:** (Continued)

3. B enters into an Istisna'a agreement with A for the supply of garments of a specified nature for Rs. 100 million within a period of three months. This contract will be a sale; A will make delivery at the agreed time.
4. B also appoints A its agent for export of the garments when they come under its ownership.
5. A foreign importer opens an L/C of value Rs. 110 million in the name of B (the L/C can also be in the name of A but that would be under an agency agreement). If an L/C has already been opened, Istisna'a is not possible (avoiding Bai' al 'Inah).
6. A prepares the garments and informs B to take delivery; the bank takes actual/constructive delivery of the garments and henceforth the garments come under its risk/liability.
7. A exports the consignment as agent of B, sending documents on behalf of B. B gets Rs. 110 million, as per the terms of the L/C.

**Box 10.15:** Parallel Istisna'a for Building Project Finance

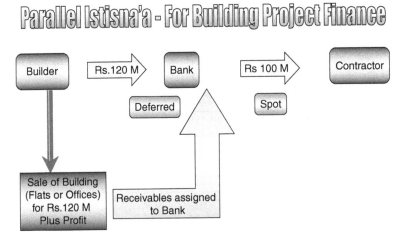

Hypothetical Case Study on a Building Project Financed through Istisna'a:

1. Builder A enters into an Istisna'a agreement with bank B for the construction of 100 economy flats within a period of 12 months, say up to 31/12/2007. The total cost is agreed at Rs. 120 million.
2. A starts booking the flats and all the flats are booked with any amount of downpayment.

3. B enters into a Parallel Istisna'a with contractor C for the construction of flats of the same specifications against the total cost of Rs. 100 million up to the end of 2007 and makes payment in four instalments, as per the agreement.
4. B appoints A its agent to supervise the construction of flats, as per the agreed specifications.
5. C gives possession of the flats at the end of December, 2007 to B, which hands them over to builder A.
6. A sells the flats to the allottees on an instalment basis and assigns the receivables to bank B.
7. The allottees will make periodical payments for rental and purchase of units from the bank; ultimately, the ownership will transfer to the allottees.

**Box 10.16:**   Parallel Istisna'a – Government Projects

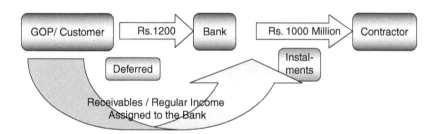

1. Government G wants a road to be built and enters into an Istisna'a contract under which bank B has agreed to build the road by the end of December, 2007 for Rs. 1200 million, payable in instalments over ten years.
2. B enters into a Parallel Istisna'a with contractor C for building the road up to 31st December, 2007 for Rs. 1000 million and pays the amount in four equal instalments.
3. C hands over the road to B on 31st December, 2007. Use of the road starts against the payment of tolls.
4. G assigns the toll receipts to the bank, and in the case of a shortfall, pays rental according to the agreement.

# 11

## Ijarah – Leasing

### 11.1  INTRODUCTION

According to contemporary jurists and experts on Islamic finance, Ijarah has great potential as an alternative to interest in respect of evolving a Sharī'ah-compliant financial system. Ijarah is permissible according to Ijma'a of jurists and the Sharī'ah scholars. As viewed by Imam Shafi'i and many other jurists, two verses of the Holy Qur'ān, because of their general nature, refer to the legality of Ijarah. Literally, Ijarah is derived from al-'Ajr and means compensation, substitute, consideration, return or counter value (al'Iwad). As a contract, it refers to hiring or renting any asset/commodity to benefit from its usufruct. It also encompasses the hiring of labour and any contract of work for anyone against a return (wage). Therefore, broadly the rules and principles of labour, renting, Ju'alah and all other contracts for usufruct of goods and services are covered by the term Ijarah. Other terms, used less frequently, for such contracts are Kirā 'a and Istijār.

In Islamic law, Ijarah is a contract of a known and proposed usufruct of specified assets for a specified time period against a specified and lawful return or consideration for the service or return for the benefit proposed to be taken, or for the effort or work proposed to be expended.[1] In other words, it is the transfer of usufruct for a consideration, which is rent in the case of hiring assets or things and wages in the case of hiring people. According to the jurists, Ijarah is the sale of usufruct (and not of 'Ain or corporeal goods) of any commodity in exchange of Ujrah, wages or rent, and covers houses, shops, riding/work animals, jewellery, clothes, etc.[2]

The permissibility of Ijarah is given in the Holy Qur'ān, Sunnah of the holy Prophet (pbuh) and consensus (Ijma'a) of the Islamic jurists.[3] Letting goods for use is a general kind of business activity legalized by the Sharī'ah as it is a convenient means for people to acquire the right to use any asset that they do not own, as all people might not be able to own the tangible assets for use.[4] This permissibility is subject to a number of conditions described in books of Hadith and Islamic jurisprudence.

In this chapter we shall discuss in detail the rules relating to Ijarah of usufruct of goods or leasing as a form of investment and a mode of financing that normally takes the form of Ijarah Muntahia-bi-Tamleek. Ijarah of work or services will be discussed briefly where deemed necessary.

---

[1] Lane, 1956; Also see Al-Atasi, 1403 AH, Majallah, Articles 405, 420, 421; Zuhayli, 2003, **1**, pp. 386, 387; Qastalani, 1304 H, **IV**, p. 124.

[2] Al-Kasani, 1993, **4**, pp. 452–457.

[3] Al-Kasani, 1993, **4**, pp. 552–556; Zuhayli, 2003, **1**, pp. 385–388.

[4] AAOIFI, 2004–5a, Standard on Ijarah, p. 151.

## 11.2    ESSENTIALS OF IJARAH CONTRACTS

As can be seen from the above given definition, the essentials of Ijarah are:

1. It is a contract.
2. Known usufruct is transferred.
3. Of a particular asset.
4. For a specified time period.
5. Against agreed-upon rental.

Like other contracts, parties to Ijarah have to be capable of entering into contracts. The lessor provides the asset for benefit against rental. The lessee is considered "Ameen", entitled to use the asset against payment of the agreed-upon rental only for the purpose specified in the agreement.[5] He is liable for loss to the asset due to his negligence, but cannot be made liable for loss caused by factors beyond his control.

For the purpose of Ijarah, the subject matter giving usufruct can be divided into two types: property or assets, like houses, vehicles, residences, etc., and labour, like the work of an engineer, doctor, tailor, carpenter, etc. While the latter involves employing the services of a person for a wage, the former relates to usufruct of any asset or property that is transferred to another person in exchange for rent. Majallah divides the subject matter of leasing into three types, where the third one is letting animals.[6] In this sense, the term Ijarah is analogous to the term leasing as used in modern business terminology.

In terms of the factors of production, the asset being leased should belong to the category of land – real assets that do not alter in original/physical form due to usage – meaning that it should not be among the things that cannot be used without consuming their corpus, or a financial or monetary asset. It also implies that the lessor, as owner of the asset, must bear the expenses and risks that are related to ownership.

The consideration of lease is Ujrah (rent or hire of things) or Ajr (wages in hiring of people). If consideration is fixed in the contract, it is called Ajr al-Musammah (agreed rent or wage) and if it has to be determined by a judge or arbitrator, it is called Ajr al-Mithl.

### 11.2.1    Ijarah and Bai' Compared

Ijarah, in a way, is similar to the contract of sale, because in both cases something is transferred to another person for a valuable consideration. Accordingly, the benefit and the consideration in Ijarah must be known comprehensively to avoid conflict. However, the difference between Ijarah and sale is that in the latter case, ownership of the corpus of the property is transferred to the purchaser, while in the former, the corpus of the property remains in the ownership of the transferor (lessor), and only its usufruct, i.e. the right to use it, is transferred to the lessee against an agreed consideration and the ownership is not transferred. Ownership-related risks and expenses have to be borne by the lessor. If the lessee becomes owner of the corporeal property let in any way, such as by gift or inheritance, the Ijarah ceases to be in force.[7]

Another big difference between sale and lease contracts is that the latter is always time-bound, meaning that the lease has to terminate at any point in time, while sale implies

---

[5] AAOIFI, 2004–5a, Standard on Ijarah, clause 7/1/4, p. 144.
[6] Al-Atasi, 1403 H, Majallah, Article 421.
[7] Al-Atasi, 1403 H, Majallah, Article 442.

definite transfer of ownership of the sold asset just after the sale is executed, along with its risk and reward.

## 11.3   GENERAL JURISTIC RULES OF IJARAH

Jurists are almost unanimous that Ijarah is valid for things which possess Manafa'ah and which can be hired or utilized but their corpus or substance ('Ayn) is not consumed.[8] Goods like candles, cotton, food or fuel are suitable for sale, not for leasing or hiring.[9] The great Hanafi jurist Kasani explains that dirhams, dinars, bullion, etc. that are 'Ain, not usufruct, and all those goods taking benefit from which is not possible without consuming them cannot be given on lease. Further, the genus of the subject matter (asset leased) and the rent should not be the same, e.g. house for house, ride for ride, etc.[10]

Therefore, lease cannot be undertaken in respect of money, edibles, fuel, ammunition, etc. because their use is not possible unless they are consumed. If anything of this nature is leased out, it will be deemed to be a loan and all the rules concerning the transaction of loan shall accordingly apply. Any rent charged on this invalid lease would amount to interest charged on a loan. Further, the assets/goods taking usufruct from which is almost impossible, cannot become the subject of Ijarah, e.g. land hit by salinity to the extent that it is not capable of any production cannot be leased out.[11]

Ijarah is valid for permissible usufruct only with the consent of both parties to the lease contract. The asset should belong to the lessor as owner or as lessee of the actual owner with permission for sub-leasing. An asset jointly acquired or belonging to a number of people can be leased to more than one lessee.[12] The contract should be free from any Gharar element with respect to the nature of usufruct and its counter value and both parties should have knowledge of the nature of the contracted usufruct.[13]

The rent or rate of hiring or renting a property can be assessed/fixed only when the property is known, whether by inspection, viewing or description. It is permissible to stipulate conditions for expediting the payment of rent or for salary and its delay or deferment, as agreed by the parties. The amount of rent or salary should be in accordance with the convention or the tradition of the locality and must be just and acceptable to both parties. The Holy Qur'ān has ordained in respect of suckling infants/offspring that the recompense of the suckling women should be just and reasonable.[14]

Al-Kasani has mentioned a number of conditions for the validity of an Ijarah contract with respect to the contracting parties and the asset or service hired. Important among these conditions are the following:

- The contracted usufruct has to be ascertained to avoid any dispute.[15]
- The lease period must be specified. However, in the case of a wage/service, any of the two, i.e. the amount of work or the time period for a job should be known.[16]

[8]  Zuhayli, 2003, pp. 387, 388; see also Jassas, 1999, **2**, p. 395; AAOIFI, Standard on Ijarah, clause 5/1/1, pp. 142, 153.
[9]  Ibn-Hazm, 1988, **8**, pp. 182–183.
[10]  Zuhayli, 2003, p. 402.
[11]  Al-Kasani, 1993, **4**, p. 458.
[12]  AAOIFI, 2004–5a, Standard on Ijarah, clauses 3/3, 3/6, pp. 140, 152.
[13]  Zuhayli, 2003, p. 391; Al-Kasani, 1993, p. 465.
[14]  Holy Qur'ān, 65: 6.
[15]  Al-Kasani, 1993, p. 471.
[16]  Al-Kasani, 1993, pp. 475–483.

- Benefiting from the hired goods should be possible. As such, lease of a nonexistent asset for usufruct of which a description cannot be determined precisely is not allowed, because such Gharar about the description and the time may lead to disputes. In other words, the purpose of the contract must be capable of being fulfilled and performed.[17]
- The handing over/delivery of the contracted goods for taking their benefit is essential. No rent becomes due merely because of execution of the contract, unless the subject of the lease is delivered and made available to the lessee. However, advance rent can be taken when availability is ensured for the period of the lease.
- In the case of workmen or service, the contracting person should be capable of undertaking the job. Therefore, hiring a runaway animal for riding, or usurped assets is invalid.[18]
- The usufruct of contracted goods must be lawful, meaning that the purpose of Ijarah should not be unlawful or Haram.[19]
- The usufruct should be conventional or according to the tradition of the people.[20]

As indicated above, according to Hanafi jurists, rent does not become due merely with the lease contract; the emergence of usufruct is necessary for this. Shawafi'i however, are of the view that rent becomes due and payable when the lease contract is finalized, because they presume that the existence of the usufruct will be materialized by use of Mu'jar (asset being leased) by the lessee. This implies that even according to Shawafi'i, rent becomes due when the asset is in the possession of the lessee and he is in a position to use it according to his requirement.[21]

If the asset to be leased is yet to be purchased as per the request of the prospective lessee, the lessor can demand payment of earnest money to ensure the latter's commitment to take the asset on lease when purchased by him. If the customer breaches his promise and the Ijarah contract is not executed for any reason attributable to the lessee, the lessor may retain the amount of loss incurred by him in making and processing the lease contract, purchasing the asset, leasing it to any other or disposing of it in the market, and give back what is in excess of the actual cost and damage he has suffered.

According to the AAOIFI Standard, rental can be paid whenever it becomes due, in instalments or at any time that is mutually agreed between the parties. The lessor can demand advance rent that will be adjusted for rent becoming due when the lease takes effect. In other words, earnest money can also be taken in respect of lease at the execution of the contract of lease and this may be treated as an advance payment of rental.[22]

### 11.3.1 Execution of an Ijarah Contract

Depending upon the nature of the asset, an Ijarah contract can be executed before or after the possession of the asset by the lessor for its instant or future enforcement/commencement. If the asset to be leased is existing, like an existing liveable house, a lease contract can be

[17] Al-Kasani, 1993, p. 491.
[18] Al-Kasani, 1993, pp. 469, 470.
[19] Al-Kasani, 1993, p. 500; see also Zuhayli, 2003, p. 397.
[20] Al-Kasani, 1993, p. 505.
[21] Al-Kasani, 1993, p. 469; accordingly, contemporary jurists are unanimous that rental becomes due only after the asset comes into the possession of the lessee in useable form and there is nothing to inhibit him from its normal use (AAOIFI, 2004–5a, Standard on Ijarah, clause 5/2/2, p. 143).
[22] AAOIFI, 2004–5a, clauses 2/1, 2/2, 2/3, 5/2/2, pp. 139, 153.

executed either for instant or future enforcement, because the usufruct of the house is clear to the parties who can stipulate the rental, keeping in mind the benefit. Future enforcement in Ijarah, as against Bai', is allowed also for the reason that ownership remains with the lessor, who is responsible for the risk of damage to the asset. Similarly, in Ijarah Mosufah bil Zimmah, wherein the nature or quality of the asset is specified and destruction of or damage to a particular unit of the asset does not terminate the contract, a contract can be executed either for instant or future enforcement.

However, if a particular asset is specified for Ijarah, a lease contract cannot be executed before existence or getting ownership of the asset or its usufruct (in the case of sub-lease). If the asset is destroyed in such leases, the contract will terminate. If the lessor does not own the asset, he can enter into a promise to lease from the prospective lessee. Advance rent can also be taken from the prospective lessee, but this will not be considered accrued rent and will be adjusted against the rental becoming due from time to time. Islamic banks' leases normally belong to this category. As per the requirement of the promise, the lessor can purchase the asset from the market or, in special cases, from the promisee, in which case it will be a case of "sale and lease-back" and the sale/purchase contract should precede the lease contract. The Ijarah contract should not be stipulated as a condition of the lease contract.[23]

### 11.3.2  Determination of Rent

The determination of rental on the basis of aggregate cost incurred in the purchase, construction or installation of the asset by the lessor is not against the rules of Sharī'ah, if both parties agree to it, provided that all other conditions of valid lease prescribed by the Sharī'ah are fully adhered to. Therefore, subject to mutual agreement of the parties to the lease contract, rental can be determined on the basis of aggregate cost incurred by the lessor for purchase/acquisition of the assets being leased. After the agreement is finalized, the lessor cannot increase the rent unilaterally and any agreement to affect the contrary would be void. If rental is once determined, there can be different rates for different phases based on any agreed benchmark during the lease period. Further, parties to the Ijarah contract can mutually agree during the lease period to review the lease period or rental or both.

Accordingly, in leases of long duration, it can be agreed upon that the rent shall be increased after a specified period, like a year or so. Contemporary scholars have also allowed in long-term leases tying up the rent with a variable and well-defined reference rate or benchmark or enhancing the rent periodically according to a mutually stipulated proportion (e.g. 5 % every year) if the other requirements of Sharī'ah for a valid lease are properly fulfilled. Using any well-defined benchmark or price index for long-term lease is recommended to determine rentals for subsequent periods, as it helps in avoiding any dispute or injustice with any of the parties due to possible fluctuations in the market rate structure and binding nature of the lease contract.[24] It can also be provided in the lease agreement that in the case of an increase in property tax or other government taxes, the rental will increase to the extent of the amount of the tax. Rent can also be tied up with the rate of inflation, i.e. if the inflation rate is 5 %, the rental will increase by 5 %.

---

[23] AAOIFI, 2004–5a, Standard on Ijarah, clauses 3/1, 3/2, pp. 140, 141, 152.
[24] AAOIFI, 2004–5a, Standard on Ijarah, clause 5/2/3, pp. 143, 154.

The question arises whether any interest rate benchmark like LIBOR (London Inter-bank Offer rate) can be agreed as the benchmark for rental. According to a minority of the scholars, with such benchmarks the transaction becomes similar to an interest-based transaction and, therefore, is not permissible. This is not the correct viewpoint, because as long as the basic requirements of Sharī'ah are being complied with, any benchmark can be used to price sale or lease transactions. Benchmarking the transaction's pricing to an interest-based rate does not render it Haram.

The rate of inflation, any price index, growth rate or any well-defined return rate in real sectors of an economy can be used for benchmarking. However, the Sharī'ah scholars do not like any interest-related benchmark for determining periodical increases in the rental due to the resemblance to interest. In principle, however, they allow it because the basic difference between valid lease and interest-based financing is that in leasing, the lessor assumes full risk in respect of the corpus of the leased assets. If the leased asset loses its usufruct without any misuse or negligence on the part of the lessee, the lessor cannot claim the rent and he will have to bear the loss of destruction. In the case of interest-based lease financing, however, the lessee is made to bear all ownership-related expenses and responsibility. So far as this basic difference (of assuming the risk) between lease and interest-based financing is maintained, any transaction will not be categorized as an interest-bearing transaction. It seems, therefore, that the use of any rate merely as a benchmark (floating rental) does not render the contract invalid, provided the amount of the rental of the first period of the Ijarah contract is specified. It is, however, desirable to use benchmarks other than interest benchmarks, so that an Islamic transaction is totally distinguished from an un-Islamic one, having no resemblance to interest whatsoever.[25]

In order to avoid Gharar and/or Jahala for both parties, the scholars suggest that the relation between the rent and the reference rate should be subjected to a ceiling or limit.[26] For example, it can be provided that rent in no case will increase or decrease by more than 5%.

### 11.3.3  Sub-lease by the Lessee

In principle, sub-lease is permissible subject to the consent of the lessor. This can be provided in the lease agreement. All the recognized schools of Islamic jurisprudence are unanimous on the permissibility of sub-lease if the rent agreed to be taken from the sub-lease is equal to or less than the rent payable to the owner/original lessor. However, the opinions are different if the rent charged from the sub-lessee is higher than the rent payable to the owner. Shafi'is allow it and hold that the sub-lessor may enjoy the surplus received from the sub-lessee. This is the preferred view in the Hanbali school as well. On the other hand, Imam Abu Hanifa is of the view that the sub-lessor cannot keep the surplus received from the sub-lessee and he will have to give that surplus to charity. However, if the sub-lessor has developed the leased property by adding something to it or has rented it in a currency different from the currency in which he himself pays rent to the owner/the original lessor, he can demand a higher rent from his sub-lessee and can enjoy the surplus.

According to the contemporary Sharī'ah scholars, the viewpoint of the Shafi'i and Hanbali schools is preferable, meaning that leased assets can be sub-leased regardless of the amount

---

[25] Usmani, 2000a, pp. 168–171; AAOIFI, 2004–5a, p. 154.
[26] AAOIFI, 2004–5a, Standard on Ijarah, clauses 5/2/3, 5/2/5, pp. 143, 154.

of rental.[27] However, if a lessee sub-leases the property to a number of sub-lessees or invites others to participate in his business by making them share the rentals received from his sub-lessees without transferring the part of ownership, or for making them participate in rentals he charges a specified amount from them, this is not acceptable in Sharī´ah, because he does not transfer the part of ownership and enters into contracts to simply share the rentals received by his sub-lessees. In this way, he simply assigns his right to receive rent against some payment. This right cannot be traded in because it amounts to selling a receivable at a discount, which amounts to Riba.

### 11.3.4    Security/Guarantee in Ijarah

As Ijarah creates a debt in the form of payable rental, the lessor can demand security and/or a guarantee from the lessee. Taking security is also permissible for the reason that the leased asset is handed over to the lessee as a trustee and he is required to protect the asset in his fiduciary capacity. He can be held liable for any damage to the asset if it is proved that damage has occurred due to any negligence on his part. In cases of such loss or defaults in payment of rental by the lessee, the lessor can recover the actual loss, excluding the cost of funds or opportunity cost in modern terminology, from the security. Any amount taken as income over and above the due rent would be Riba.[28]

### 11.3.5    Liabilities of the Parties

There is no liability on a lessee or employee except when it is established that he has transgressed or wilfully wasted or damaged the property.[29] In such cases he is liable to compensate the lessor for harm to the leased asset caused by misuse or negligence, or to replace the property.

All liabilities emerging from the ownership shall be borne by the lessor, but the liabilities relating to the use of the property shall be borne by the lessee. For example, in the case of lease of a house, the taxes relating to the property shall be the responsibility of the owner of the house, while the water tax, electricity bills and all expenses referable to use of the house shall be borne by the lessee.[30] Contemporary Sharī´ah experts and Islamic banks' Sharī´ah boards link the responsibility of the owner (lessor) to bear expenses on the asset on which the continued performance and usufruct of the asset is customarily understood with the free agreement of the parties, i.e. in the case of agreement to the contrary, expenses could be borne by the lessee.[31]

The leased property shall remain in the risk of the lessor throughout the lease period in the sense that any harm or loss caused by factors beyond the control of the lessee shall be borne by the lessor. However, as discussed earlier, the lessee is liable to compensate the lessor for harm to the leased asset caused by any misuse or negligence on his part. A property jointly owned by two or more people can be leased out, in which case they shall be responsible for its risk and the rental shall be distributed between them according to the proportion of their respective shares in the property.

---

[27] AAOIFI, 2004–5a, Standard on Ijarah, clause 3/3, p. 140.
[28] AAOIFI, 2004–5a, Standard on Ijarah, clauses 5/2/5, 6/1–6/3, 7/1/4, pp. 142–144, 153.
[29] Ibn-Hazm, 1988, **8**, p. 201; Zuhayli, 2003, pp. 421–424.
[30] AAOIFI, 2004–5a, Standard on Ijarah, clause 5/1/7.
[31] Institute of Islamic Banking and Insurance (IIBI), 2000, p. 23.

## 11.3.6    Termination/Amendment of the Contract and Implications

Ijarah is basically a binding contract, meaning that once executed, it cannot be revoked unilaterally. Unilateral and unconditional option to terminate a lease by any of the parties is contrary to the principles of justice and equity and, therefore, un-Islamic.[32] However, both parties can amend or terminate the contract with mutual consent.[33]

If the leased asset is damaged to the extent that it is no more able to give usufruct, the contract of Ijarah is terminated.[34] Similarly, in the case of an impediment to achieving the normally expected objective of the contract, the lessee can terminate the contract. In this situation, the parties may adjust the rental to avoid injustice to the lessee, keeping in mind the partial damage to the asset and possibility of beneficial use. If an unidentified unit of asset is leased (Ijarah Mosufah bil Zimmah), the contract will not terminate and the lessor will be required to replace it with another asset of the agreed specifications.[35]

If the lessee stops using the asset without the lessor's consent, accrual of the rental will continue.[36]

If the asset is sold to the lessee, the Ijarah contract is terminated due to the transfer of ownership to him. If the asset is sold to any third party, the contract does not terminate and the rights and obligations transfer to the purchaser of the asset. The lessee's consent is not necessary if the lessor wants to sell the leased asset to any third party. If the purchaser is not informed about the lease contract, he can terminate the sale contract. If he knows of it and consents to it, he takes the place of the previous owner.[37]

The traditional jurists differed regarding the termination of lease due to death of any of the parties, i.e. the lessor or the lessee. But contemporary jurists have come to the conclusion that an Ijarah contract is not terminated with the death of either party. However, the heirs of the lessee can terminate if they feel that the contract has become too onerous for their resources to pay the rental.[38]

The lessor is allowed to provide in the lease contract that he will have a right to terminate the lease if the lessee contravenes any term of the lease agreement. In that case, the lessee would be obliged to pay the due rent and not the rent of the remaining period.[39] In conventional leases, it is generally provided in the agreement that in the case of termination of the lease, even at the option of the lessor, the lessee would pay full or a part of the rent of the remaining period. The basic reason for inserting such conditions is that the main concept behind the agreement is to give an interest-bearing loan under the cover of lease. This condition is obviously against the Sharī´ah and the principles of equity and justice.

The logical consequence of the termination of lease is that the lessor should take the asset back. In this case, the lessee should be asked to pay the rent as due up to the date of termination. If the termination has been effected due to misuse or negligence on the part of the lessee, he can also be asked to compensate the lessor for the loss caused by such misuse or negligence. But he cannot be asked to pay the rent of the remaining period. It can

---

[32] Zuhayli, 2003, pp. 405, 411, 433, 434.

[33] AAOIFI, 2004–5a, Standard on Ijarah, clause 4/1/1, 7/2/1, pp. 141, 152.

[34] AAOIFI, 2004–5a, Standard on Ijarah, clauses 7/1/3, 7/2/4; Ibn-Hazm, 1988, 8, pp. 184–185.

[35] AAOIFI, 2004–5a, Standard on Ijarah, clause 7/1/5.

[36] Al-Atasi, 1403 AH, Majallah, Article 443; AAOIFI, 2004–5a, clauses 7/1/5, 7/1/6, 8/8.

[37] AAOIFI, 2004–5a, Standard on Ijarah, clause 7/1/2.

[38] AAOIFI, 2004–5a, Standard on Ijarah, clause 7/2/3, pp. 145, 156.

[39] AAOIFI, 2004–5a, Standard on Ijarah, clause 7/2/2.

also be provided in the contract that in the case of a default in payment of rental by the lessee, the lessor could terminate the lease.

If a lessee has paid rental for any stipulated period in advance and he is obliged to return the asset because of any compelling circumstances (*force majeure*), the remainder of the advance rental must be returned to the lessee, because the lease will be considered to have been dissolved for a valid reason. The remainder, if any, will also have to be returned in the case of mutual dissolution. If, however, the asset is not returned by the lessee, enabling the bank to re-lease it, the remainder will not be returned.[40]

### 11.3.7  Failure in Payment of Due Rent

Rental in respect of any lease contract when it becomes due takes the form of a debt payable by the lessee. It will be subject to all rules prescribed for a debt. Therefore, a charge from the lessee on the agreed rental would be Riba, prohibited by the Sharī´ah.[41] Unscrupulous lessees could exploit this aspect and cause loss to the lessor by wilful default. To provide a deterrent, Sharī´ah scholars allow that a donation or any amount of penalty payable to charity can be provided *abinito* in the lease agreement; the amount of donation can vary according to the period of default and can be calculated on a percentage per annum basis. Any amount charged over and above the agreed rental must not become a part of the income of the lessor and has to be given to charity.[42] As this late payment penalty cannot become part of the income of lessor banks, it is advisable that a suitable clause be incorporated in the lease agreement to the effect that in cases of wilful default, the bank will take possession of the leased asset or enforce the collateral to recover its dues.

## 11.4  MODERN USE OF IJARAH

Leasing in one form or another comprises a sizeable part of financial services in the world today. In its origin, leasing is one of the normal real sector business activities like sale and not a mode of financing. However, for certain reasons, and in particular due to some tax concessions it carries, leasing is being used in many countries for the purpose of financing, and the financial institutions lease many types of assets and equipment to their customers. In Islamic finance also, leasing is an important instrument with a lot of potential in the business of Islamic financial institutions, not only because of these benefits but also because of the "Asset-based nature" of investments in Islamic finance. From the Islamic perspective, leasing operations by banks and financial institutions are governed by the rules prescribed in Fiqh for Ijarah transactions.

To study Ijarah as a mode of financing, we shall discuss the process of entering into modern Ijarah, purchase of the asset to be leased, treatment of Takaful and other expenses, miscellaneous rules relating to determination of rental, commencement and payment of rental, some common mistakes, commonly raised objections and their answers, termination of the contract and the possibility and modus operandi of transfer of ownership to the lessee.

Non-bank financial institutions or companies (NBFIs/NBFCs) in almost all countries of the world, and banking institutions in countries like Germany, Japan, etc. are using leasing as

---

[40] Institute of Islamic Banking and Insurance (IIBI), 2000, p. 19; AAOIFI, 2004–5a, Standard on Ijarah, clauses 7/2/1, 8/8.
[41] AAOIFI, 2004–5a, Standard on Ijarah, clauses 5/2/5, 6/3, pp. 143, 144, 154.
[42] AAOIFI, 2004–5a, Standard on Ijarah, clause 6/4, pp. 144, 155.

a business mode. The forms of leasing these institutions are using are "financial lease", also termed hire–purchase; "financing lease", also referred to as "security lease"; and "operating lease". We briefly describe modern forms of leasing below.

### 11.4.1   Financial Lease or Hire–Purchase

In modern financial leases, the lease period is long enough (usually the entire useful life of the leased asset) to enable the lessor to amortize the cost of the asset with a market return on its capital. The banks pay the price of the asset to the supplier, either directly or through the lessee. While fixing the rent, the banks calculate the total cost they have incurred for purchase of those assets and add the stipulated interest they could have claimed on such an amount during the lease period. The aggregate amount so calculated is divided by the total months of the lease period, and the monthly rent is fixed on that basis. The lease commences on the day on which the price is paid by the lessor, irrespective of whether the lessee has made payment to the supplier and taken delivery of the asset or not. This means that the lessee's liability for the rent starts even before he takes delivery of the asset. The risk of ownership is borne by the lessee, i.e. the client.

The lessor recovers the cost and interest thereon and has no further interest in the asset. The lessee purchases the asset at a price specified in advance or at its market value at that time. The lease is not cancellable before the expiry of the lease period without the consent of both parties. However, the lessee is normally allowed to prepurchase the asset before the lease termination. In such situations, the lessor normally charges an extra amount (say 5 % of the remaining amount of the bank's funds) as a fine/liquidated damages for discontinuation of their income stream. The leased asset serves as security and, in the case of default on the part of the lessee, the lessor can take possession of the equipment without a court order. It also helps reduce the lessor's tax liability due to the high depreciation allowances generally allowed by tax laws in most countries. The lessor can also sell the equipment during the lease period to the effect that the rental payments accrue to the new buyer. This enables the lessor to get cash when he needs liquidity.

Normally in such contracts, compound interest is involved in the case of default or delay in payment of the instalments. As such, the end result of financial lease may turn out to be worse and more exploitative than the outright purchase of the asset by the lessee on credit instalments. For example, in a conventional lease contract of five years, the lessee is required to continue to make payments even if he no longer needs the asset, say after two years. In the case of a credit purchase on the basis of interest, he could sell the asset in the market to repay his liability. He cannot do this in financial lease and could even lose his stake in the asset, even though he has paid a part of the price of the asset in addition to the rental charges in normal operating lease.

### 11.4.2   Security or Financing Lease

A security lease in the conventional set-up is just a financing transaction and nothing more than a disguised security agreement for the amount financed to the lessee. It involves the effective transfer of all risks and rewards associated with the ownership to the lessee.

### 11.4.3 Operating Lease

In operating lease, the owner of the asset gives possession of the asset to the lessee, retaining its ownership, to have its use in return for rental. The lessor takes back the equipment/asset when the lease ends. This method is considered fully compatible with Sharī´ah provided some other conditions are fulfilled. Operating lease is particularly suitable for high cost assets that require large amounts of money in order to possess and have long production times, for example, aircraft, ships, etc.

Operating lease is rarely used by banks. Non-bank financial institutions sometimes use this mode of leasing in respect of specialized machinery. They maintain a number of assets to respond to the needs of different customers. The assets remain the property of the institution to re-lease them every time the lease period terminates. As such, NBFIs have to bear the risk of obsolescence, recession or diminishing demand.

### 11.4.4 Appraisal of Conventional Leases from the Sharī´ah Angle

Important features of most modern leases are:

1. At expiry of the hiring contract, ownership of the leased article is transferred to the lessee, either free of any additional charge or at a nominal/token price. Particularly in hire–purchase, it is mutually agreed at the very beginning that the contract of Ijarah also includes sale of the asset and the amounts received periodically from the lessee will include both rental and the cost of the asset. In finance lease, the amount periodically paid by the lessee is the rental; however, the parties may or may not agree in the lease agreement that at the termination of the lease the lessee will get ownership of the asset. We shall discuss this aspect in detail in the next section.
2. The lessor starts charging rental as soon as he gives funds to the supplier of the asset. As such, he leases an asset before buying it and taking its possession and gets reward without bearing its ownership risks. As per Sharī´ah principles, rent has to be charged from the date when the lessee is in a position to take benefit from the leased assets, i.e. after he has taken delivery of the asset, and not from the day funds are released to the lessee or the price has been paid to the supplier.
3. The lessor shifts all the risks to the lessee, particularly when the residual value of the asset is also fixed in advance in the lease contract. According to the Sharī´ah principles, all expenses incurred to rectify defects which prevent the use of the equipment by the lessee are the lessor's responsibility, while the lessee is responsible for the day-to-day maintenance and running expenses. This is the major difference between conventional and Islamic leases.
4. In conventional operating leases also, all risks and expenses are the responsibility of the lessee. But in Islamic operating leases, the lessor must bear the upkeep responsibilities and bear all the risks and costs of ownership. Further, the operating lease is not for the entire useful life of the leased asset, but rather for a specified time period and ends at the end of the agreed period unless renewed by the mutual consent of both the lessor and the lessee.

### 11.4.5 Combining Two Contracts

Ijarah and sale are two different types of contract with different governing rules, particularly in view of the principle that while in sale contracts, ownership is transferred to the buyer instantly even if it is a credit sale, in Ijarah, ownership remains with the lessor. Transfer of the ownership in the leased property cannot be made by executing a sale contract that will become effective on a future date. In most commercial leases, the lessee pays, in addition to the rental, a sum which goes toward buying the leased property. If the lessee is given credit for his payments by becoming, in ever-increasing degree, the owner of the property, the proportion of his payments that goes to rent should also continually reduce and justice would require that upon making full payment along with rental, the ownership title should transfer to him. But the question is how can the lease agreement be structured to make it Sharī'ah-compliant and also justifiable for the lessee, who has paid the full cost of the asset and the rental?

Contemporary Sharī'ah scholars recommend that a lease agreement should not contain a precondition of sale or gift after the lease period. However, the lessor may enter into a separate unilateral promise to sell the leased asset at termination of the lease. The principle, according to them, is that a unilateral promise to enter into a contract at a future date is allowed, whereby the promisor, say the bank, is bound to fulfil the promise, but the promisee is not bound to enter into an actual purchase contract. This means that the lessee would have an option to purchase, which he may or may not exercise. However, if he wants to exercise his option to purchase, the promisor cannot refuse it because he is bound by his promise. This is to avoid a bilateral promise by the two parties, which is prohibited in Sharī'ah because it becomes a contract. Similarly, scholars suggest that instead of sale, the lessor signs a separate promise to gift the asset to the lessee at the end of the lease period. This is because normally the bank, as lessor, recovers the whole cost incurred on the asset and also a return thereon as its profit margin from the lessee. As such, it seems to be the lessee's right that he gets ownership of the asset, and the best way to transfer ownership is to give him the asset as a gift.[43]

There may be an objection that Ijarah Muntahia-bi-Tamleek also comprises two contracts in one bargain and as such it is not Sharī'ah-compliant on the basis of the prohibition of two bargains in one. This perception is set aside on the following grounds:

1. Mainly the transaction is one whereby the lessor leases the asset and fixes the rental in such a way that during the lease period his cost and the rent are received. Both parties agree on this nature of the transaction.
2. It consists of an Ijarah contract, which immediately goes into effect, and a unilateral promise that may or may not become effective in a later stage or at the end of the lease period. The second part is only a unilateral promise and is not binding on the promisee; as such it is not a transaction until actually entered into by the parties.
3. This arrangement does not involve any injustice to any of the parties, Riba or any element leading to dispute among the parties. It is rather justifiable in that the lessee, who has paid the cost along with the rental, is able to get ownership title of the asset at the end of the lease period.

From this perspective, a sale executed at the end of the lease period is not in contravention of any basic principle of the Sharī'ah.

---

[43] The OIC Fiqh Academy allowed this in its third session. Also see Institute of Islamic Banking and Insurance (IIBI), 2000, p. 23.

### 11.4.6 Takaful/Insurance Expenses

It is a regulatory requirement in many countries of the world that the leasing entities should insure the leased assets. Islamic banks should use Takaful that has been approved by the Sharī´ah scholars as an alternative to insurance and should avoid conventional insurance due to the involvement of Riba and Gharar. However, a large number of Islamic banks are using insurance due to the nonavailability of Takaful-based policies. Sharī´ah scholars have allowed this only for the transitional period.

There is criticism by many scholars of a practice whereby the Islamic banks make the lessee the actual payer of the Takaful contribution or premium by passing on the premium costs as part of the lease instalments to be paid by the lessee. This criticism is based on the understanding that the lessor has an insurable interest in the subject matter and he/it should pay the insurance premium and not the lessee. It is correct that, as owner of the asset, the bank should be the insurer and the beneficiary of the Takaful policy. Islamic banks normally include the Takaful expenses in the acquisition cost of the asset for determining the rental. Sharī´ah scholars allow this on the grounds that rental in leases is subject to mutual consent of the two parties and if the lessee agrees to the amount of rental, the contract is acceptable from the Sharī´ah angle. As regards the insurable interest, it rightly belongs to the bank as lessor. But if the transfer of ownership becomes impossible without any cause attributable to the lessee, the lessee must be protected from the loss by paying to him the difference between the rent received from him as per the lease agreement and the market rental of such assets.[44] Some Islamic banks are not abiding by this rule; it is against the spirit of Islamic finance and the Sharī´ah advisors should look into the matter.

The issue of primary focus in this regard is determining the effects of loss or damage to the asset. It is usually stipulated in the agreement that the lessee will be provided with a copy of the policy and he will observe the conditions of the policy. Therefore, if the asset is destroyed and there is lack of observance of the conditions of the Takaful policy that has barred the lessor from recovery, the lessee is held liable. In the absence of any fault or negligence on the part of the lessee, the lessor bears all responsibility for damage to or loss of the leased asset. If, however, the claim paid by the Takaful company is less than the loss incurred by the Islamic bank, the remainder of the loss cannot be charged to the lessee and the bank itself should bear the loss.

## 11.5   ISLAMIC BANKS' IJARAH MUNTAHIA-BI-TAMLEEK

The above section implies that the Sharī´ah objections to modern leases relate mainly to (i) the procedure of ownership transfer to the lessee; (ii) accrual of the rentals and (iii) the responsibilities of the lessor in respect of ownership-related risks and expenses. If these aspects are taken care of by Islamic banks, they can use leasing as a mode of finance. For this purpose, they have adopted the modus operandi of Ijarah Muntahia-bi-Tamleek, according to which the transaction basically remains one of Ijarah and the ownership transfer is kept separate from the main Ijarah contract. This is closer to the conventional finance lease with the following differences:

---

[44] AAOIFI, 2004–5a, Standard on Ijarah, clause 8/8, pp. 147, 157.

1. In a finance lease, the rental starts accruing as soon as the payment for purchase of the asset being leased is made by the lessor; in Ijarah Muntahia-bi-Tamleek, rental starts at the time when the asset is supplied to the lessee in useable form.
2. In a finance lease, the payment of the cost price of the asset is made either to the supplier or to the lessee so that he may pay the supplier and get the asset on lease. In Islamic lease also, the price of the asset can be paid either to the supplier or to the lessee, but if it is paid to the lessee, there must be an agency agreement in addition to the lease agreement. The agency agreement will precede the lease agreement and all elements of Wakalah should be applicable to it. If the asset is destroyed before its delivery to the lessee in useable form, the loss will be that of the principal and not of the agent.
3. In Islamic lease, the risk of the asset will be that of the bank as long as the client serves as its agent for purchase of the asset, while in a finance lease, all risks are borne by the lessee.

As a hire–purchase contract includes both lease and sale at the very beginning, it is not suitable for Islamic banks. For Ijarah Muntahia-bi-Tamleek, Islamic banks normally purchase the asset in response to specific requests from customers to get the asset on a lease that ends with transfer of ownership after the lease term through a separate and a formal sale or gift contract. According to the AAOIFI Standard on Ijarah, transfer of ownership in the leased property cannot be made by a sale contract (along with the Ijarah) to be made effective on a future date. Ownership can be transferred using one of the following means:

1. By means of a promise to sell for a token or other consideration or by accelerating the payment of the remaining amount or by paying the market value of the leased property.
2. By promise to give it as a gift (for no consideration) at the end of the lease period.
3. By promise to gift contingent on a particular event, for example, upon the payment of the remaining instalments.

The transfer of ownership in all the above forms should be independent of the Ijarah contract and not an integral part of the transaction as a whole. The promise should be unilateral and binding on the promisor and the other party must have the option not to proceed. In cases 1 and 2 above, a new contract should be drawn up because ownership will not transfer merely by virtue of the earlier promise. In respect of 3, where an Ijarah transaction has separate documentation giving the asset as gift contingent upon the condition that the remaining instalments are paid, the ownership will be transferred to the lessee if the condition is fulfilled without any other document being signed.[45]

The ownership can also be transferred prior to the end of the lease period at a price stipulated in advance or at the market price or through the contract of Diminishing Musharakah, in which case the financier's part of ownership is gradually transferred to the lessee upon payment of rental according to an agreed schedule and the rental will decrease accordingly.

Some Islamic banks take an undertaking or a unilateral promise from the lessee that at the end of the lease or in the case of premature termination at his discretion and mutual consent, he will pay the market or a prestipulated price. A price schedule is agreed in advance that implicitly includes the bank's possible loss in the case of termination of lease before the agreed period.

---

[45] AAOIFI, 2004–5a, Standard on Ijarah, clauses 8/1–8/4, 8/6, 8/7, pp. 146, 156.

If the case is one of "sale and lease-back" – the bank purchases an asset from the client and then leases the same to him – on the basis of Ijarah Muntahia-bi-Tamleek, there should be a reasonable period between the purchase and lease contract and the transfer of ownership back to the customer, long enough that the leased property or its value might have changed. The period of one year is normally suggested for this purpose. It is necessary to avoid a contract of Bai' al 'Inah.[46]

### 11.5.1  Procedure for Ijarah Muntahia-bi-Tamleek

Islamic banks' Ijarah Muntahia-bi-Tamleek, broadly speaking, comprises an arrangement in which leasing is the real and major contract, which is subject to all the rules of an ordinary Ijarah contract where the standard Sharī´ah principles of defining the asset to be leased, its terms and essential prerequisites of contracts have to be observed. Islamic banks normally adopt the following procedure to conduct Ijarah, remaining within the limits of the Sharī´ah:

1. The client conveys his requirement to the bank and enters into an MoU for stipulating the overall structure of the deal. The bank takes an undertaking from the lessee along with some earnest money (Hamish Jiddiyah) to ensure that the client is serious in his dealing and will take the asset on lease when purchased by the bank. The amount of earnest money is kept as trust, but if the bank gets permission from the client for its use, it takes the form of a debt and becomes the liability of the bank. The AAOIFI Standard recommends that it should be kept as an investment trust to be invested by the bank on the basis of Mudarabah. As such, it should be kept as a PLS deposit in the name of the client. With the consent of the client, this amount can also be treated as advance payment of rental.[47]

2. The bank can directly purchase the asset or appoint any agent for the purpose. If the asset is to be imported, the bank can appoint the customer its agent who may open an L/C and place an order with the foreign supplier on behalf of the bank. He will pay the relevant duties, taxes, transportation and other charges to the port authorities for releasing the asset. All such payments made by the importer will be reimbursed by the bank and will constitute part of the total cost of the asset. According to the AAOIFI Standard, any third party agent is preferable, but the client can also be appointed as agent. If the vendor of the asset is also indicated by the client, the bank can get a performance bond from him to the effect that the asset supplied will be acceptable to him. The bank, however, will remain liable for ownership-related risks and expenses.[48]

   Unlike sale (through Murabaha), it is not necessary in lease that the bank should first take possession of the asset and then deliver the same to the lessee. If the bank has agreed to lease the asset to a client with effect from the date of delivery and the client is appointed as agent to purchase that asset, the lease can be made operative on the date when the lessee takes delivery as agent, without any additional procedure. While in Murabaha to Purchase Orderer, simultaneous transfer by the bank and the agent is not allowed, in leasing, the lease period may begin right from the time when the client takes delivery as agent. This is because ownership of the asset remains with the lessor along with risk and reward during the leasing period.

---

[46] AAOIFI, 2004–5a, Standard on Ijarah, clauses 3/4, 8/6, pp. 140, 146.

[47] AAOIFI, 2004–5a, Standard on Ijarah, clause 2/3.

[48] AAOIFI, 2004–5a, Standard on Ijarah, clause 3/7, pp. 140, 154.

3. Sometimes the bank and the client jointly purchase the asset and create a partnership by ownership (Shirkatulmilk) and the bank leases out its share to the client on the principle of Diminishing Musharakah. The rental to be received by the bank should be in proportion to its share in the ownership. Hence, if clients periodically purchase any parts of the bank's share, the rental should go on decreasing.[49]

4. When the asset is purchased by the bank and taken into its possession or that of the client serving as agent, the formal lease agreement is executed. Rental starts accruing from this point of time onward if all installation work is complete and the asset is in useable form. If the lessee delays in using the asset due to any problem attributable to him, he will have to pay the rental.

5. If the client defaults in paying the rental, the bank can ask for acceleration of payment, provided it is agreed in the lease agreement. This would be the case of early termination of the lease; the bank would take the asset back or the lessee would purchase the asset as per the terms of the agreement. In the case of foreclosure of security, only the due rent can be deducted and not the rent for the remaining period.[50]

The other subsequent contract is a contract for gift or sale, independent of the earlier lease contract. For transferring ownership title, Islamic banks use any of the three methods described above, i.e. promise/undertaking to sell (by the bank) or purchase (by the client) and executing a formal sale agreement at the time of the sale; promise to gift; or promise to a contingent gift.

The lessee pays rental that also includes the cost of the asset incurred by the lessor on acquiring the asset. Therefore, a part of the rental effectively goes towards buying the leased property, although, legally, the whole rent represents rental for use of the asset. As the parties can agree on any amount of rental with mutual consent, and the arrangement is equally beneficial for both the parties, Sharī'ah scholars have accepted this as Sharī'ah-compliant.

As the rental implicitly includes the cost of the asset, the AAOIFI Standard directs that if transfer of property to the lessee is not possible for any reason, like destruction or theft of the asset, or if continuity of the lease becomes impossible as per the lease contract without any cause being attributable to the lessee, the rental should be adjusted based on the prevailing market value – the difference between the prevailing rate of rental and the rental specified in the contract must be refunded to the lessee if the latter rental is higher than the former. This is to save the lessee from loss having agreed to pay a higher rental compared to the market rental of a similar asset in consideration of the lessor's promise to pass the ownership title to him upon expiry of the lease term.[51] It also implies that if the bank has taken Takaful cover of the asset, which normally is the case, the amount received from the Takaful company, over and above the bank's cost and expenses, should be given to the client.

There might be some problems in the leasing procedure of IFIs that are working without intensive surveillance by Sharī'ah supervisory boards or Sharī'ah scholars, and this practice will have to be discontinued if Sharī'ah compliance is the objective. The conventional hire–purchase structure cannot be dubbed Sharī'ah-compliant merely by renaming it Ijarah Muntahia-bi-Tamleek or Ijarah-wal-Iqtina'. But a large number of institutions are using the mode of Ijarah Muntahia-bi-Tamleek and are observing the Sharī'ah principles under the

---

[49] AAOIFI, 2004–5a, Standard on Ijarah, clause 3/6, p.140.
[50] AAOIFI, 2004–5a, Standard on Ijarah, clauses 6/5, 7/2/1, 7/2/2, pp. 144, 154.
[51] AAOIFI, 2004–5a, Standard on Ijarah, clause 8/8, pp. 147, 157.

guidance of the Sharī´ah scholars. As long as the Sharī´ah-compliant procedure recommended by the Sharī´ah scholars is adopted in letter and spirit, IFIs should not be unnecessarily criticized.[52]

*Sale and Lease-back Arrangement*

In a sale and lease-back arrangement, a customer requires finance on the basis of an asset already in his ownership. He sells the asset and then takes on rent for his use. This arrangement is legally permissible but ideally should be avoided, and Islamic banks should not adopt this as a major mode of business. However, if a client wants to get rid of Riba and does not have any other alternative, he can be accommodated by Islamic banks. It, therefore, should be used in exceptional cases and care should be taken to ensure that all parts of the arrangement conform to the related Sharī´ah rules. In case of need, it can be used both for financing of a new asset (machinery, equipment, etc.) and for conversion from conventional to Islamic financing. The sale agreement must be executed before entering into the lease agreement and in order to avoid Bai' al 'Inah, such a leased asset can be sold back to the client only after a reasonable period, long enough that the leased property or its value might have changed.

*Destruction/Theft of the Asset*

If the leased asset is totally destroyed, the Ijarah contract concluded on an identified asset is terminated. The leased asset is held by the lessee in a fiduciary capacity on behalf of the lessor; he will be held liable for any damage or destruction of the leased asset due to his misconduct or negligence. In the case of partial destruction in a manner that impairs the benefits expected from the asset, the lessee can terminate the Ijarah contract. The lessee and the lessor may also agree to amend the rental in the case of partial destruction of the leased property. The lessor is not entitled to rent for the period during which the lessee is not able to benefit from the asset, particularly if the fault occurred without any negligence on his part.

## 11.5.2   Issues Concerning Modern Use of Ijarah

With respect to the modus operandi of modern leasing business, Islamic banks face five sets of issues and problems.

1. One problem in Ijarah relates to burdens of the asset on the lessee or the lessor. For example, the Sharī´ah provides that the duty of repairing the goods, other than normal maintenance, falls solely on the lessor, since the repairs benefit him as the owner. A clause in the contract purporting to shift ownership-related costs, other than the normal operating expenses, to the lessee is invalid, because it unjustly enriches the lessor.
2. Another problem arises due to Islamic banks' lack of knowledge of the Ijarah principles. If a specified unit of asset is to be leased, the Ijarah agreement should be executed only after the asset is in the possession of the lessor (or that of the lessee in capacity of agent of the lessor). If the agreement is signed at the time of disbursement of the money to the

---

[52] See, in this regard Vogel and Hayes, 1998, p. 145.

supplier and there is any delay in delivery of the asset to the lessee – the bank fails to deliver the asset to the lessee on the date specified in the Ijarah agreement – no rental is due for the period between the agreement date and the date of actual delivery. Therefore, Islamic banks should enter into a "promise to lease" at the beginning and the actual Ijarah contract should be executed at the time when the asset is made available by the supplier. While determining the rental, they can keep in mind the whole period for which their funds remain invested, i.e. the supply period and the lease period.

3. If any damage occurs to the asset during the supply stage, the lessee (client) serving as agent is not responsible for it until any fault on his part is proved. The rental, if received in advance, should be adjusted accordingly, unless it is agreed that the lease be extended by an equivalent period after its original expiry date.

4. Another problem relates to the fact that the usufruct is extended to the future and may therefore be risky and unstable, particularly if the usufruct is reduced materially in the future. In this respect, Islamic law has the provision of cancellation of lease if any factors or events cause the usufruct to be less than normally expected. For example, nearly all schools of Islamic jurisprudence allow the reduction or abolition of rental of land if the produce of leased farmland is damaged due to any natural calamity like drought, floods, etc. According to Imam Muhammad, if the crop of leased land is destroyed due to any natural calamity, Ijarah will become invalid and the lessee will be entitled to a conventional wage.[53]

5. A big problem emerges in the case of a default in payment of rental by the lessee, as the penalty taken for late payment has to be given to charity.

Another important aspect is that the general perception that Ijarah gives a fixed return to the bank is not correct. As Islamic banks have to purchase assets for leasing, they have to pay all expenses incurred in the process of their purchase, import, etc. The bank can, of course, include all these expenses in its costs and can take them into consideration when fixing the rental, but as a matter of principle, it is liable to bear all these expenses as owner of the asset. This also implies that discounts allowed by suppliers for the purchase of leased assets would be the right of the Islamic bank, as it is the owner of the leased asset during the lease period. Banks also have to pay the major expenses related to ownership, like that of Takaful and other expenses necessary for the upkeep of the asset. A claim received from a Takaful company might not be sufficient to cover the loss or expense of repair. Hence, banks might not be able to get the targeted net return with certainty.

The solution to the above problems does not lie in stratagems leading to objectionable practices and integrity problems for the movement of Islamic finance. IFIs must take care on two points. First, risk cannot be separated from ownership; as the leased asset remains in their ownership, it must remain under their responsibility (Dhamān) and they must take that responsibility. Second, lease and sale are contracts of two different natures; they must be kept separate and independent of each other. If the above two aspects are taken care of, they can adopt any procedure for leasing the assets, mitigating the risks and transferring ownership to the lessee through any of the methods discussed in the preceding paragraphs.

---

[53] Al-Kasani, 1993, **4**, p. 514.

### 11.5.3  Assignment of the Leased Assets and Securitization of Leases

Sharī´ah experts allow the lessor to sell the asset, in whole or any part of it, to any third party along with its rights and obligations, in which case the sale will be valid and Ijarah may continue. The sale of leased assets may particularly be required in respect of high cost assets like aircraft, ships, industrial equipment, machinery, roads, bridges, etc. However, if ownership is not transferred and the lease is simply assigned to the extent of rental only, the assignment of lease for a monetary transaction is not allowed, because in that case, money (rental) would be sold for money, which must be equal for equal, i.e. one cannot charge rent more than one is paying.

The new party to whom the leased asset is sold will enjoy every right as lessor due to the former party, while he will be responsible for every liability under the lease transaction. This gives the Ijarah technique good potential for securitization and creation of a secondary market for investors on the basis of Ijarah.

If the asset is sold to a larger number of investors, the purchase of a proportion of the asset by each individual may be evidenced by certificates, which may be called "Ijarah Sukuk" or leasing certificates. The certificates will represent the holder's proportionate ownership of physical assets tied to the Ijarah contract, and the holder will assume the rights and obligations of the owner/lessor to that extent. Certificate holders are also required to maintain the asset in such a manner that the lessee is able to derive as much usufruct from it as possible.[54] Therefore, Ijarah Sukuk are subject to risks related to real market risks arising from potential changes in asset pricing and in maintenance and insurance/Takaful costs and to the ability and desirability of the lessee to pay the rental instalments. In the case of total destruction of the asset, Sukuk holders will suffer the loss to the extent of their pro rata ownership. Hence, Ijarah Sukuk may generate a quasi-fixed return since there might be default or some unexpected expenses that could not be envisaged in advance. As such, the amount of rent given in the contractual relationship represented by Ijarah Sukuk represents a maximum return subject to deduction on account of unexpected expenses.

### 11.5.4  Potential of Ijarah

Ijarah is the most important mode for financing operations of Islamic banks for meeting the needs of the retail, corporate and public sectors, and it has huge, as yet unrealized, potential. It is used directly for plant and machinery, automobiles, housing, consumer durables, etc. and indirectly for Sukuk issues by the corporate and government sectors. Ijarah is conducive to the formation of fixed assets and medium- and long-term investments in the economy. The potential is by dint of a number of features of Ijarah as given below:

- Payment of Ijarah rental can be unrelated to the period of taking usufruct by the lessee, i.e. it can be made before the beginning of the lease period, during the period or after the period, as the parties may mutually decide. Accrual of rent, however, is based on the possibility of usage of the asset by the lessee.
- Ijarah can be contracted on an existing asset or a building and even an asset that is yet to be constructed, as long as it is fully described in the contract and is not for identified

---

[54] Kahf, 1994, p. 207.

items, provided that the asset and the rent both are clearly known to the parties at the time of the contract.

- The Ijarah rate can be fixed or floating, provided a clear formula is mutually agreed with a floor and a cap. Rental has to be stipulated in clear terms for the first term of lease, and for future renewable terms it could be constant, increasing or decreasing by benchmarking.
- Holders of Ijarah Sukuk jointly acquire ownership in the asset, bear the price risks and the ownership-related costs and share its rent by leasing it to any user(s).

The flexibility described above can be used to develop different contracts and Sukuk that may suit different purposes of issuers and holders. Governments can use this concept as an alternative tool to interest-based borrowing, provided they have durable useable assets. Use of assets is necessary, while it does not matter whether these assets are commercially viable or not. Funds mobilized by issuance of Ijarah Sukuk may be used to purchase assets for leasing and the rentals received from the users distributed among the Sukuk holders. Ijarah Sukuk can be traded in the secondary market on market price; the purchasers replace the sellers in the pro rata ownership of the relevant assets and all rights and obligations of the original subscribers pass on to them. Hence, they may help in solving the problems of liquidity management faced by the Islamic banks and financial institutions.

Hence, Ijarah has great potential for financing public sector projects without the involvement of interest. Ijarah Sukuk/certificates can be issued to raise funds from the primary financial market for projects to be started afresh, or they can be issued against already existing projects. They can also be sold in the secondary market at a price to be determined by the market.

Suppose a government intends to build an airport but is short of funds. It may sign a contract with a contractor to build the airport, but at the same time, it may undertake to lease the airport and sell it to the public by issuance of Ijarah Sukuk. The value of the lease (equal to or greater than the cost of construction) will be divided over a large number of Ijarah Sukuk/certificates of different denominations and maturities. In other words, different investors may participate in the lease contract for different periods. The government will pay the contractor from the proceeds of the Sukuk. The government is not obliged to pay investors anything different from the actual income from the facility.

## 11.6   SUMMARY OF GUIDELINES FOR ISLAMIC BANKERS ON IJARAH

1. According to Islamic principles of finance, there is no difference between operating and finance leases; if all of the four essential elements relating to contracting parties, subject matter, consideration and the period in Ijarah are taken care of, Ijarah can be used as the mode of modern business by the financial institutions in the form of Ijarah Muntahia-bi-Tamleek. The deciding factor in this regard is the risk relating to ownership that must remain with the lessor and sale should be separate from the lease.
2. The lease of an identified asset cannot commence before the bank takes the possession of the asset to be leased. If the time of possession of the asset to be leased is unknown, the whole arrangement will be provisional.
3. Any arrangement of two contracts into one contract is not permissible in Sharī´ah. Therefore, IFIs cannot have the agreement of hire and purchase built into a single agreement.

4. When the period of lease comes to an end, the bank can transfer the ownership to the client or dispose of it in the open market. If the bank transfers the ownership to the lessee, the proper sale agreement or gift deed should be executed. The promise to transfer the ownership is binding on the promisor only; the other party must have the option not to proceed. The AAOIFI Standard provides for promise by the lessor, while many Islamic banks, as in the case of Pakistan and other jurisdictions, take undertaking from the lessee and deem it binding on him. Abiding by the AAOIFI's Standard in this regard seems to be justifiable and nearer to the spirit of the Sharī´ah.

5. The lessor bears expenses relating to the corpus of the asset, i.e. Takaful, accidental repairs, etc., while operating expenses related to running the asset have to be borne by the lessee. Takaful and other costs incurred by the bank can be recovered in the lease rental, subject to transparency and mutual understanding. If the customer pays the Takaful cost as agent of the bank, it will be reimbursed to the client by the bank.

6. A bank can jointly acquire an asset with a customer who wishes to get the asset on lease; the bank can then lease its share of the asset as per the undertaking of the customer. The rental to be received by the bank should be in proportion to its share in the ownership of the asset.

---

**Box 11.1:**   Risk Mitigation in the Case of Ijarah

| **Nature of risk** | **Mitigating tool** |
|---|---|
| 1. The bank has purchased the asset as per the undertaking by the customer, but the latter refuses to take the asset on lease. | A binding promise to lease should be obtained from the customer at the time of booking/purchase of the asset by the bank. Hamish Jiddiyah should also be taken from the client. The bank can sell the asset in the open market and the actual loss can be recovered from the Hamish Jiddiyah. |
| 2. The customer may default in payment of the due rental. The bank might not be able to recover even its investment; the asset is taken back, but it does not cover the loss. | An undertaking should be obtained from the customer to pay a certain amount to charity in the case of late payment of rental. This amount will go to the Charity Account. Any actual loss can be recovered from Hamish Jiddiyah. Securities/collateral can also be realized. |
| 3. Asset risk of major maintenance/destruction. | This risk can be managed through a Takaful facility. |
| 4. Early termination of lease agreement. | Keeping in mind the market value, the bank can also take the asset back and sell in the market to redeem its investment. In more risky cases, an undertaking to purchase the asset at a pre-agreed price schedule can be obtained from the customer. |

**Box 11.1:**   (Continued)

| Nature of risk | Mitigating tool |
|---|---|
| 5. The lessee may use the asset carelessly, requiring the bank to bear major maintenance expenditure. | A trust receipt should be obtained from the customer to bind him to use the asset as a trustee. It may be mentioned in the trust receipt that loss due to negligence of the customer shall be borne by the customer himself. |
| 6. Rate of return risk due to inflation. | This risk can be covered through a benchmarked floating rental rate, which is permissible subject to a floor and a cap. |
| 7. Sale of asset at maturity – the customer may not buy. | Only those assets should be leased that have sufficient resale value that the bank could sell them in the market. Alternatively, a separate promise to purchase at the end of the lease term can be obtained from the customer. |

**Box 11.2:**   Auto Ijarah Compared with Conventional Leasing Products

| Conventional auto lease products | Islamic Ijarah Muntahia-bi-Tamleek |
|---|---|
| Conventional financing leases contain hire–purchase arrangements, which are not permissible by Sharī´ah. | The Ijarah contract does not contain any condition that makes the contract void under Sharī´ah. The lease remains subject to all Ijarah rules; sale is not a part of it. |
| In conventional leasing schemes, the customer is responsible for all kinds of loss or damage to the vehicle, irrespective of circumstances being out of his control. | All risks pertaining to ownership are borne by the Islamic bank. The customer only bears usage-related expenses. |
| Insurance is independent of the lease contract. The insurance expense of the asset is borne directly by the lessee. | Takaful should be at the expense of the lessor. The lessor, however, may increase, with the consent of the lessee, the lease rent to recover the Takaful cost. |
| If the insurance company does not compensate the entire outstanding amount in the case of loss/damage, the customer is liable to pay the balance. | The Islamic bank bears the risk of Takaful claim settlements. |

If the leased vehicle is stolen or completely destroyed, the conventional leasing company would continue charging the lease rent until the settlement of the insurance claim.

Under the Islamic system, rent is consideration for usage of the leased asset, and if the asset has been stolen or destroyed, the concept of rental becomes void. As such, an Islamic bank cannot charge the rental.

In some conventional leases, the lessor is given an unrestricted power to terminate the lease unilaterally at his sole discretion.

Ijarah is a binding contract and if there is no contravention on the part of the lessee, the lease cannot be terminated by any one party. It can be provided in the agreement that if the lessee contravenes any terms of the agreement, the lessor has a right to terminate the lease contract unilaterally.

In most contemporary financial leases, an extra amount is charged if rent is not paid on time. This extra amount is taken by the leasing institutions into their income. This is prohibited due to being Riba.

Under Ijarah, the lessee may be asked to undertake that if he fails to pay rent on its due date, he will pay a certain amount to a charity but the bank cannot charge any further return.

Under conventional leasing contracts, the vehicle is automatically transferred to the name of the customer upon completion of the lease period.

In Ijarah, the customer is not obliged to purchase the vehicle. He may purchase the asset through a formal sale deed if he considers it beneficial for him.

Upfront payment has to be made in the form of downpayment, the first year's insurance premium and other insurance expenses, first month's rental, etc.

Islamic banks normally take only a security deposit, which is refundable if the lease is not finalized. The bank has the authority to recover only actual expenses not including the cost of funds.

---

## Box 11.3: A Hypothetical Case Study on Ijarah

ABC Textile Mills (Pvt.) Ltd, one of the customers of Merit Islamic Bank, has requested an Ijarah facility for the following assets. The client will deposit 10 % of the value of the Ijarah asset as a security deposit/earnest money.

1. Company cars  20  Rs. 10 000 000 (L/C has been established with XYZ bank)
2. Trucks  20  Rs. 360 000 000
3. Dyeing plant  Rs. 140 000 000 (already owned by the client)
4. Looms  50  Rs. 15 000 000 (operating for about 1 year)

The Islamic bank's employee is required to decide:

**Issue # 1**

Which asset will the bank finance through a direct lease and which through sale and lease-back? What factors will it consider before allowing sale and lease-back transactions?

## Box 11.3: (Continued)

### Issue # 2

One year after leasing the looms for his factory, ABC reports to the bank that five of the looms have broken down and have to be repaired. The bank asks the evaluator from the Takaful company to calculate the cost of repair and damage. The evaluator reports, after inspection, that the looms broke down due to poor maintenance on the part of the client and will take a month to be repaired at a cost of Rs. 20 000 per loom. How should the bank calculate future rentals and the rental for the time when the looms are being repaired?

### Issue # 3

ABC has already leased 20 cars from the bank for a tenure of five years and has used them to varying degrees. Two years down the line, ABC requests the bank to sell him ten vehicles at a price of Rs. 400 000 each. Should the bank accept his offer and what consideration should determine the decision? Prepaid expenses, including Takaful outstanding, are Rs. 20 000 per vehicle. The outstanding Ijarah investment is Rs. 350 000 per vehicle.

### Issue # 4

In the same year, one of the cars is destroyed in an accident without any negligence on the part of the client. The remaining outstanding Ijarah investment is the same as given in Issue # 3 above. The Takaful amount recovered by the bank is Rs. 450 000 and the client deposited a security deposit of Rs. 50 000. What amount is the bank legally bound under the Ijarah agreement to give to the client? In view of the satisfactory payment behaviour, in what ways can the bank accommodate the client without burdening itself?

### Answers to the above Issues:

### Answer 1

| Direct lease/Ijarah | Sale and Lease-back |
|---|---|
| The assets that can be financed under direct lease are trucks, because the bank has to purchase the same from the market. | The assets that can be financed under a sale and lease-back arrangement are the dyeing plant, looms and company cars (already owned by the client). |
| Documentation required | Documentation required |
| <ul><li>Agency agreement and letter of agency</li><li>Undertaking to Ijarah</li><li>Ijarah agreement<ul><li>— description of the Ijarah asset</li><li>— schedule of Ijarah rentals</li><li>— receipt of asset</li><li>— demand promissory note</li></ul></li><li>Ijarah rental schedule</li><li>Unilateral promise to sell/purchase Ijarah asset</li><li>Sale deed at the end.</li></ul> | <ul><li>Sale deed of cars and plant</li><li>Undertaking to Ijarah</li><li>Ijarah agreement</li><li>Description of Ijarah assets</li><li>Ijarah rental schedule</li><li>Demand promissory note</li><li>Promise to sell/purchase Ijarah assets.</li></ul> For sale and lease-back, an IFI must consider the need and willingness of the client to avoid interest and work with an Islamic bank. Further, it will add the condition that ABC Textile will not ask for early retirement before one year. |

**Answer 2**

As per the inspection report, the asset was not handled with care and proper maintenance was not made by the client. Therefore, the bank should ask the client to repair
the asset at his cost; the bank will not bear the loss. Apparently, the rental will continue
to become due and rescheduling of the Ijarah payment plan should not be needed.
However, the Sharī´ah advisor should be involved and may decide, on merit, whether
the client may be given any relaxation or not.

**Answer 3**

In the given scenario, the bank can accept the offer of the client for the purchase of
ten cars with the consideration that the price offered by the client covers the current
outstanding liabilities, i.e. 3.7 million, and through this offer the bank can earn a profit
of Rs. 300 000, i.e. Rs. 30 000 per car, even after returning the security deposit, with
the assumption that the security deposit is included in the offer price.

**Answer 4**

As per the Ijarah agreement, any loss that occurs to the asset without negligence of
the client will be borne by the bank. The client has the right to take back the security
deposit as the agreement has come to an end due to the destruction of the asset.
Therefore, he will be paid Rs. 50 000 of his security deposit. The bank has been paying
the Takaful premium as owner of the asset. As such, legally the bank is entitled to
receive the Takaful claim. However, the client has been paying rental more than the
mere rental of similar assets as prevalent in the market, due to the inclusion of the cost
by the bank in the normal rental, and he has paid all the instalments as per agreement.
As per clause 8/8 of the AAOIFI Standard on Ijarah, the bank should allow/give the
customer Rs. 130 000 that includes Rs. 50 000 of security deposit and the claim
recovered from the Takaful company after deducting the liabilities outstanding as per
# 3 above, making the amount Rs. 80 000.

---

**Box 11.4:**  Accounting Treatment of Ijarah

**1. Operating Ijarah**

**Assets acquired by the bank as lessor**

- are recognized at historical cost;
- depreciate as per normal depreciation policy;
- are presented as investments in the Ijarah assets A/c.

**Ijarah revenue/expense**

- is allocated proportionately in financial periods over the lease term;
- is presented as Ijarah revenue.

**Initial direct costs**

- are allocated over the lease term or otherwise charged directly as an expense.

## Box 11.4: (Continued)

**Repairs of leased assets**

- a provision for repairs is established if repairs are material and differ in amount from year to year;
- repairs undertaken by the lessee with the consent of the lessor are to be recognized as expense.

### 2. Ijarah Muntahia-bi-Tamleek through gift
**Assets acquired**

- are recognized at historical cost;
- are presented as Ijarah Muntahia-bi-Tamleek, with assets measured at book value;
- depreciate as per normal depreciation policy;
- however, no residual value shall be subtracted since it is to be transferred to the lessee through gift.

**Ijarah revenue/expense**

- is allocated proportionately in financial periods over the lease term;
- is presented as Ijarah revenue.

**Initial direct costs**
- material costs are allocated over the lease term or otherwise charged directly as an expense.

**Repairs of leased assets**

- a provision for repairs is established if repairs are material and differ in amount from year to year;
- repairs undertaken by the lessee with the consent of the lessor are to be recognized as expense.

**At the end of the financial period/lease term**

- legal title passes, subject to settlement of Ijarah instalments.

**Permanent impairment/sale of lease asset**

- If the Ijarah instalments exceed the fair rental amount and impairment is not due to action or omission of the lessee, the difference between the two amounts shall be recognized as liability due and charged to the income statement.

### 3. Ijarah Muntahia-bi-Tamleek for token consideration or specified amount
**Assets acquired**

- are recognized at historical cost;
- are presented as Ijarah Muntahia-bi-Tamleek assets and measured at book value;
- residual value is subtracted in determining the depreciable cost. Depreciation is charged as per normal depreciation policy.

**Ijarah revenue/expense**

- is allocated proportionately in financial periods over the lease term;

- is presented as Ijarah revenue.

### Initial direct costs

- material costs are allocated over the lease term or otherwise charged directly as an expense.

### Repairs of leased assets

- a provision for repairs is established if repairs are material and differ in amount from year to year;
- repairs undertaken by the lessee with the consent of the lessor are to be recognized as an expense.

### At the end of the financial period/lease term

- legal title passes, subject to settlement of Ijarah instalments and on purchase of the asset by the lessee;
- if the lessee is not obliged to purchase and decides not to do so, the asset shall be presented as assets acquired for Ijarah and valued at the lower of the cash equivalent value or the net book value. If the cash equivalent is less than the net book value, the difference between the two shall be recognized as loss;
- if the lessee is obliged to purchase the asset due to his promise but decides not to do so, and the cash equivalent value is lower than the net book value, the difference between the two amounts shall be recognized as a receivable from the lessee.

### Permanent impairment/sale of lease asset

- if the Ijarah instalments exceed the fair rental amount and impairment is not due to action or omission of the lessee, the difference between the two amounts shall be recognized as liability due and charged to the income statement.

### 4. Ijarah Muntahia-bi-Tamleek through sale prior to the end of the lease term for a price equivalent to the remaining Ijarah instalments

### Assets acquired

- are recognized at historical cost;
- are presented as Ijarah Muntahia-bi-Tamleek assets and measured at book value;
- depreciate as per normal depreciation policy.

### Ijarah revenue/expense

- is allocated proportionately in financial periods over the lease term;
- is presented as Ijarah revenue.

### Repairs of leased assets

- a provision for repairs is established if repairs are material and differ in amount from year to year;
- repairs undertaken by the lessee with the consent of the lessor are to be recognized as expense.

### Permanent impairment/sale of lease asset

- as in the above case.

# 12
# Participatory Modes: Shirkah and its Variants

## 12.1 INTRODUCTION

Islamic modes are asset-based and entail real economic activity and undertaking responsibility or liability. The modes that form the basis of Islamic finance belong to participatory or profit/loss sharing (PLS) or risk-sharing techniques and as such are considered the most desirable modes by the majority of jurists on Islamic finance. This does not imply that non-participatory modes, as discussed in the previous few chapters, do not involve business risk; taking risk and responsibility is rather a precondition for the legality of profit in any business. Shirkah-based participatory modes of business, however, involve direct participation in profits and losses by the parties.

Two contracts, namely Mudarabah and Musharakah, that lend themselves to the system of profit/loss sharing are based on the concept of Shirkah. A partnership may be in the right of ownership (Shirkatulmilk), wherein a profit motive may not necessarily exist, or it may be contractual (Shirkatul'aqd), in which the partners enter into a contract to conduct a joint business with the objective of earning profit and agree to share the profit on a pre-agreed ratio and bear the loss, if any, to the extent of the investment of each partner. Another variant may be wherein one partner may provide the capital and the other may manage the business (Mudarabah) for earning profit. These modes are the means of providing risk-based capital and are jointly termed participatory modes of finance. In this chapter we shall discuss variants of Shirkah, namely Musharakah, Mudarabah, modern corporations and Diminishing Musharakah, as modes of business by Islamic financial institutions (IFIs).

Partnership-based business was widely practised in the pre-Islamic period. The holy Prophet (pbuh) himself did business on the basis of partnership before his prophethood and many of his Companions did it during his life and later. Islam approved the concept of business partnership.[1] The practice was so commonly prevalent among the Arabs and other Muslims that, perhaps under their influence, the Christians of the areas in Europe where Muslims went also conducted it and introduced it far inside Europe.[2]

In the early/conventional books of Fiqh, joint businesses are discussed mainly under the caption of Shirkah, which is a set of broad principles that can accommodate many forms of joint business. According to the majority of the classical jurists, Mudarabah is also a type of Shirkah when used as a broad term. In Fiqh books, discussion on Mudarabah is available both in the chapters on Shirkah and under the separate caption of Mudarabah.

---

[1] Hassan, 1993, p.104.
[2] See Postan and Rich, 1952, **2**, pp. 173, 267.

Musharakah is a term used by the contemporary jurists both for broad and limited connotations. In the limited sense, it is used for contractual partnership in which all partners provide funds, not necessarily equally, and have the right to work for the joint venture. In the specific sense, it is an amalgam of Musharakah and Mudarabah wherein a Mudarib, in addition to the capital provided by the Rabbul-māl, employees his own capital as well. This arrangement is also permissible according to the jurists.[3]

While in Musharakah all parties contribute to the joint business and work for it, in Mudarabah, one party contributes funds and the other acts as entrepreneur and the profit is shared in a predetermined, mutually agreed ratio. In Mudarabah, the financier bears the loss while the entrepreneur loses his already expended labour.

In this chapter we shall discuss the traditional concept of Shirkah as discussed in books of Fiqh followed by a discussion on the application of the system of profit and loss sharing in the contemporary world.

The modern Shirkah takes the form of partnerships, joint stock companies and cooperative societies and, in a sense, that of pools, cartels, trusts and syndicates, etc. In modern law, all these forms are treated differently in accordance with the differences in their objectives and the nature of combination. An important difference between the Islamic and the modern partnership laws exists in the former's religious character. To describe the rules of partnership, we shall discuss the subject in the three main sets of Musharakah, Mudarabah and Diminishing Musharakah, the last being the latest development of Islamic jurisprudence based on the broad principles of Shirkah.

## 12.2  LEGALITY, FORMS AND DEFINITION OF PARTNERSHIP

The legality of Shirkah is proved by the texts of the Holy Qur'ān and Sunnah and the consensus of the Islamic jurists.[4] In particular, the two forms of Shirkah al Inan (general partnership) and Mudarabah, which we will be discussing in the following pages, enjoy acceptance by all jurists without any difference of opinion. Jurists normally divide Shirkah into two broad categories of Shirkatulmilk (partnership by ownership or in right of ownership) and Shirkatul'aqd (partnership by contract). With these two forms, traditional Shirkah is the main source of rules governing the operations of Musharakah, Mudarabah and Diminishing Musharakah by Islamic financial institutions in the present age.

Keeping in mind the discussion by classical jurists and the modern business environment, Shirkah can be defined as a business where two or more people combine their capital or labour or creditworthiness together, having similar rights and liabilities, to share the profits or a yield or appreciation in value and to share the loss, if any, according to their proportionate ownership. This implies that capital is not necessary in certain structures of Shirkah. "Profit" in the context of this definition and according to Islamic law can be made through purchase, sale, hire or wages and excludes income arising from the contracts of marriage, divorce, subsistence payable to wives and children or in the case of penalties and fines. We define various forms of Shirkah in the following section.[5]

---

[3] Usmani, 2000a, pp. 27–33, 53, 54.

[4] Holy Qur'ān, verses: 4: 12 and 38: 24; the holy Prophet is reported to have conveyed the message of Allah (SWT), who says: "So long as the two partners remain honest to each other, I am the 3rd". (Abu Daud and Sahih al Hakim).

[5] For various forms of Shirkah, see Ibn Qudama, 1367 AH, **5**, p. 1 and Usmani, 2000b, pp. 139–144.

### 12.2.1   Partnership in Ownership (Shirkatulmilk)

The basic element of Shirkatulmilk is the mixing of ownership, either mandatorily or by choice. Two or more people are joint owners of one thing. It is further subdivided into two categories: optional and compulsory. Optional partnership by ownership is explained in the words: "where two persons make a joint purchase of one specific article or where it is presented to them as a gift, and they accept of it; or where it is left to them, jointly, by bequest and they accept of it". Basically, it is not for sharing of profit. The co-owners may use the property jointly or individually. Compulsory partnership is where the capital or goods of two people become united without their act and it is difficult or impossible to distinguish between them, or where two people inherit one property.

In other forms of partnership, a partner is treated as an agent to the other partner's share, but in partnership by ownership, partners (co-owners) are not agents of each other; here, a partner is a stranger and in the absence of the other partner, he has no right to use the absent partner's property, nor can he be responsible for any liability arising out of the latter's share. He cannot use even his own share if it is detrimental to the interest of the other partner's share. It is, however, lawful for one partner to sell his own share to the other partner, and he may also sell his share to others, without his partner's consent, except only in cases of association or a mixture of property, for in both these instances, one partner cannot lawfully sell the share of the other to a third person without his partner's permission. If joint property is used by one partner, the owner may demand rental for his part of the property from the benefiting partner. The distribution of the revenue of Shirkatulmilk is always subject to the proportion of ownership.

### 12.2.2   Partnership by Contract (Shirkatul'aqd)

This is the main form of Shirkah, which is created by offer and acceptance and is applicable in most of the cases of modern business where two or more persons are involved. The AAOIFI Standard has defined it as an agreement between two or more persons to combine their assets, labour or liabilities for the purpose of making profit.[6] It is created through a contract – offer and acceptance is its basic element – partners are agents of each other and one partner cannot sell his share without the other partners consent and cannot guarantee capital or any profit of the other partners.

This form can be further divided into: Shirkatulamwal, where all the partners invest some capital into a commercial enterprise that comes under the collective ownership of the partners as per the ratio of their capital; Shirkatula'mal, where the partners jointly undertake to render some services to their customers and share the fee charged by them according to the agreed ratio and each partner brings his own resources, if needed, for the business; and Shirkatulwujooh, meaning partnership in creditworthiness where all partners avail credit from the market using their credibility and sell the commodity to share the profit so earned at an agreed ratio.

In Shirkah, the rights and liabilities of all the partners should be similar, although not necessarily equal. The basic principle of Shirkah is that a man who shares in profits must also bear the risks. This principle is based on the Prophet's saying that earnings are concomitant to risks.

---

[6] AAOIFI, 2004–5a, Standard on Shirkah (Musharakah), clause 2/1, p. 200.

Contractual partnership (Shirkatul'aqd) is subdivided into several kinds depending upon the subject matter of partnership: capital (or goods), labour or personal creditworthiness, as discussed briefly in below.

### Shirkah-al-Mufawadah, or Universal Partnership

According to the Hanafi jurists, Shirkah-al-Mufawadah is where two persons, being the equal of each other in respect of property, privileges and religious persuasion, enter into a contract of partnership. This form is very cumbersome to operate because it refers to sharing everything on an equal basis. Therefore, it is factually nonexistent. It is, in fact, advocated by Hanafi jurists only. Imam Shafi'e, Imam Ahmed ibn Hanbal, Imam Malik and the Jafari jurists do not support this form.[7]

### Shirkah al 'Inan, or General Partnership

Shirkah al 'Inan, involving collective capital of the partners, is where any two persons become partners in any particular business or where they become partners in all matters of commerce indifferently. It is contracted by each party, respectively, becoming the agent of the other and not his surety. This form enjoys consensus among all Islamic jurists. It is the most important form and seems to be nearer to the modern concept of a business partnership. We shall be discussing in detail mainly the rules of this general form of contractual partnership.

### Shirkatula'mal

Shirkatula'mal, or Sanāi' (partnership in labour or crafts), signifies a situation where two persons become partners by agreeing to work jointly, and to share their earnings, in partnership. It is also known as Shirkah Taqabbul, or Shirka al Abdān. Some classical examples of such a partnership are the partnerships between medical practitioners, teachers, miners, transport owners and farmers.[8]

### Shirkatul Wujooh, or Partnership in Creditworthiness

Shirkatul Wujooh is where two persons become partners by agreeing to purchase goods jointly, upon their personal credit (without immediately paying the price) and to sell these goods on their joint account. Partners undertake to fulfil their obligations according to the percentages determined by the parties. They also agree on the ratio of liability for which each partner is responsible while paying such debt.[9] According to Imam Shafi'e, it is unlawful. The Maliki jurists observe that such a form of partnership has an element of random chance and is, therefore, invalid. They have, however, permitted it on the condition that the element

---

[7] Jurists of the Shafi'e school of thought have legalized only Shirkatul 'Inan. (Usmani, 2000b, p.186, with reference from Mughni al-Muhtaj of Ramly and Takmelah Sharah Muhazzab).

[8] Al Mudawwanah al Kubra, Cairo, 1323 AH (Matba al Sadah), 12, p. 51.

[9] AAOIFI, 2004–5a, Standard on Musharakah, clause 3/2.

of obligation is made clear before the contract is effected, for example, joint credit purchase of a specific commodity and sale at a profit.[10]

Hanafi and Hanbali jurists, however, agree upon the validity of such a form of partnership. Loss in this form of Shirkah will have to be borne as per the liability taken at the beginning. If such a contract is enforced without first stipulating the extent of liability of each partner, they will be responsible for credit taken by each of them individually and the working partner will be entitled to wages for his work and not to a share in profits.

## Mudarabah

Mudarabah, or partnership in the profits of capital and labour, signifies a contract of partnership in which one party is entitled to profit on account of its Māl, while the other party is entitled to profit on account of its labour.

Of the above-mentioned kinds, Shirkah al 'Inan and Mudarabah are the most popular kinds of partnership and enjoy Ijma'a of the jurists. Shafi'e, Jafari and Zahirites like Ibn Hazm treat only these two forms of Shirkah as lawful modes of joint venture. For the Shafi'e and Jafari schools, Shirkah is a contract between two or more (persons) made with a view to making all profits common between the two (or among all the partners); the object of contract preferably being trade. Hanafi and Maliki jurists believe in a broader circle of joint business practices.

Shirkahal 'Inan is suitable for joint businesses, adaptable to any situation and practicable in the present day's advanced commercial practices. It refers to a joint enterprise formed for conducting any business with the condition that all partners shall share the profit according to a specified ratio, while the loss will be shared according to the ratio of contribution to the capital of the joint business. Two or more partners that are considered agents (Wakil) of other partners share the business on the basis of the following conditions:

1. Capital can be invested by the partners in any proportion.
2. Power of appropriation in the property and participation in the affairs of the Shirkah may be different and disproportionate to the capital invested by the partners.
3. Profit may be divisible unequally and disproportionate to the capital invested, and may be according to the agreement of the partners.
4. Loss is to be shared in proportion to the capital invested.
5. Each partner is an agent to the other partners.
6. No partner is responsible for indemnification of the acts of commission and omissions on the part of other partners.

There are a number of views regarding the last-mentioned condition above. Regarding rights and liabilities of partners, jurists contend that partners are allowed to sell partnership capital/assets, perform trading business with it, give it as deposit or collateral with others and hand it over to any person for business on a Mudarabah basis.[11] Further, jurists consider that the partners can perform all other acts that are according to the custom or common practice, subject to compliance with the main Sharī'ah principles. If any partner takes a loan for the joint business, all partners will be (jointly) liable to pay.[12]

---

[10] Al Mudawwanah, 1323 AH, **12**, p. 5.
[11] Al-Kasani, 1993, **6**, pp. 68, 69.
[12] Al-Kasani, 1993, **6**, p. 72.

A Musharakah (and also Mudarabah) contract may be for any specific project up to its completion or in the form of a redeemable investment by a partner,[13] particularly the financial institutions – also known as Diminishing Musharakah. If the Musharakah lasts as long as a business operates without any midway termination, it is considered a continuous Musharakah.

The above discussion implies that Shirkah in Islamic law refers to all forms of partnership, also including Mudarabah. Some of the jurists observe that Mudarabah is a form of Shirkah, while some others treat this as different from Shirkah. It seems that the difference is due to variation in analysis of business conditions more than the differences in Shirkah principles. The former view is held by some of the jurists of the Maliki and Hanbali schools, while the latter by the Hanafi school. The Hanafi jurists argue that Mudarabah should not be treated as a form of Shirkah, because in Shirkah, the contracting parties become partners and, therefore, liable to losses soon after the business is started or the capital of the partners is combined, while in Mudarabah, the working party does not become a partner and is not liable to any losses unless and until profits arise. Before the creation of profits, the position of the working party is that of an agent, although the contract of Mudarabah becomes effective.

## 12.3  BASIC RULES OF MUSHARAKAH

In this section we shall be discussing the rules relating mainly to a general partnership conducted with joint capital of the partners (Shirkatulamwal-cum-Shirkah al 'Inan). All conditions necessary for any valid contract, e.g. free consent of the parties that must be without deception, misrepresentation and duress, etc., should be fulfilled in the Shirkah contract. Certain other conditions must also be fulfilled, and these are outlined in the following paragraphs.

### 12.3.1  Conditions with Respect to Partners

The word "persons" as used in the definitions refers to both individuals and legal persons or corporate bodies. As regards individuals, it is unanimously agreed that they should be free and of sound mind. The study of relevant rules in Fiqh suggests that insolvency and prison are disqualifications for making the contract of sale; as the contract of partnership comprehends mutual agency, anybody who is handicapped in exercise of this right cannot act as a partner in the true sense and a contract so made should be deemed to be ineffective. On this ground, minors and the insane are incompetent to become partners. A minor can enter into a partnership if allowed by his guardian.[14] Imam Shafi'e extends the state of incompetence to all those who, for any reason, lose their power of decision, like a man who is intoxicated. This is, however, a temporary incompetence. A man who is put under inhibition by a court either because of insolvency or due to any other reason is also not competent to enter into a contract of partnership, because his partner could be prevented from making use of the inhibited partner's property. The Jafari scholars give five reasons which inhibit one from making a contract of sale. These are minority, stupidity, insanity,

---

[13] Ibn-Qudama, 1367 AH, **5**, p. 63.
[14] Al-Atasi, 1403 AH, Majallah, Article 1335.

fatal disease and insolvency.[15] This is also applicable to Shirkah. The other jurists do not disagree with this.

However, there is some difference of opinion about indebtedness as a cause of incompetence or inhibition. Some jurists are inclined to accept that inhibition will not be imposed if there is any possibility of the recovery of debt.[16] According to Imam Abu Hanifa, an indebted person cannot be inhibited because, in this way, he is restrained from improving his economic condition. He can, however, be imprisoned if he fails to repay his debts.[17] But the later Hanafi law, based on the views of Imam Abu Yusuf and Muhammad, provides for inhibition of the debtor if the creditors so demand.[18] Indebtedness here indicates a state in which the total liabilities of a debtor exceed his total assets and he is unable to pay off the debts. In the case of a businessman, it is a state of near insolvency. Inhibition does not apply in the case of businessmen in the present age who run their entire business on credit and command sufficient resources to dispose of their liabilities.

Musharakah can be concluded with non-Muslims and also interest-based banks to carry out operations acceptable in the Sharī'ah. In this respect, arrangement has to be made to obtain all necessary assurances and guarantees that the rules and principles of Sharī'ah will be observed during the operation of the partnership.[19] It excludes all those businesses which are not lawful in Islam, i.e. trade in swine flesh or liquor, etc. and unlawful activities like pornography and gambling. For example, if a syndicate of banks comprising Islamic as well as conventional banks is financing any huge project or corporate firm, the Islamic bank's portfolio must comprise valid contracts like Ijarah to ensure its Sharī'ah compliance. In this respect, a distinction has to be made between the goods and activities which are absolutely prohibited for all and the goods and activities which are prohibited for Muslims alone. Interest, for example, is prohibited for all in an Islamic state, while alcoholic drinks and flesh of the swine, etc. are prohibited for Muslims alone. A non-Muslim citizen of an Islamic state can be permitted to trade in the objects of the latter category but partnerships in any such trade will be declared void if any of the parties is a Muslim.

### 12.3.2   Rules Relating to Musharakah Capital

According to the majority of jurists, capital invested by a partner should be in the form of liquid assets, i.e. money or prevalent currency units, and its value should be known without any ambiguity, particularly according to Maliki, Hanbali and Shafi'e jurists. Hanafites, however, consider that knowing the amount of capital at the time of contract is not necessary; it can be agreed before the commencement of business.[20] It should not be a debt or a nonexistent commodity.[21] Al-Sarakhsi, a great Hanafi jurist, points out that the forms of capital change from place to place according to 'Urf of the place. Al-Kasani says that if the practice of the people is to invest the capital in the form of currency, the matter shall be decided according to this and if the practice of the people is to invest the capital in the form of goods, the matter shall be decided accordingly. However, contemporary jurists are

---

[15]  Hussain, 1964.
[16]  Ibn Qudama, 1367 AH, **2**, p. 168.
[17]  Al-Marghinani, **3**, p. 342.
[18]  Al-Atasi, 1403 AH, Majallah, Article 959.
[19]  AAOIFI, 2004–5a, clauses 3/1/1/2, 3/1/1/3, p. 201.
[20]  Al-Kasani, 1993, **6**, p. 63.
[21]  Ibn-Qudama, 1367 AH, **5**, p. 16; Al-Sarakhsi, n.d., **11**, pp. 156, 159.

unanimous that the value of goods should be assessed in terms of monetary units. Debt cannot become part of partnership capital until it is received.

In the case of limited companies, capital is given the form of equal units called shares, and the intended partners can buy as many of these shares as possible disproportionately.

The objects which, according to Islamic law, cannot be sold or utilized cannot form the basis of a partnership contract. Broadly, Shirkah rules require that the capital of the partners should be merged and commingled. The implication of commingling is that individual ownership is replaced by the collective ownership of the joint venture and any appreciation in value of the Musharakah assets will reflect the right of all the partners with the ratio of their capital; any partner cannot say that his part, a shop for example, that he contributed to the business at the beginning, has appreciated more in the case of a rise in its price, and hence only he is entitled to the enhancement. Commingling does not necessarily imply an indistinguishable character that the amount of capital should be in the form of cash, or identical goods or transfer of money or goods towards the partnership capital just at the time of contract. The merger can be actual or constructive, the latter being made on the basis of valuation on any agreed standard like market value. In the case of goods, the share of the partners will be calculated in terms of their money value at the time of contract.

After analysing the views of jurists of all schools of thought regarding the nature of capital, Shaikh Muhammad Taqi Usmani has concluded:

> "We may, therefore, conclude that the share capital in a Musharakah can be contributed either in cash or in the form of commodities. In the latter case, the market value of the commodities shall determine the share of the partner in the capital".[22]

Other aspects relating to the nature of partnership capital in the modern age include the following: a person can become a partner of a running business having fixed assets by investing capital in cash/kind, merger of various partnership firms is also possible.[23]

This implies that the capital of all the partners has to be quantified and specified. In the case of running business, valuation should be made in such a way that cash/receivables are taken at face value and the conversion rate in the case of different currencies should be that of the day of execution of the Musharakah contract. In the case of fixed assets, an agreed-upon value will be taken, while the average utilized amount should be considered as Musharakah capital if financing is made on the basis of running Musharakah, as in the case of deposit management by Islamic banks on the basis of Shirkah.

### 12.3.3   Mutual Relationship Among Partners and Musharakah Management Rules

Shirkah business is managed by the will and equal right of all the partners. As indicated earlier, parties to a contractual Musharakah are agents of one another. When a contract of Musharakah is executed, the conditions of agency are automatically presumed to be in existence in the contract. The actual possession of one partner over property of the Musharakah business is in the constructive possession of the other partners. However, if a partner purchases something for himself only, it is exclusively for him and not for the joint business.

---

[22] Usmani, 2000a, pp. 38–41.
[23] This is according to Ahnaf, Malikis and Hanbali (Al-Kasani, 1993, 6:60; Ibn-Qudama, 1367 AH, 5:129; Usmani, 2000b, pp. 257–261).

All partners in a Shirkah have a right to take part in management of the joint business in the following transactions: cash or credit sales, rejecting defective goods, renting the partnership's commercial assets, cancellation of contracts, requesting credit facilities for the partnership, taking the partnership's receivables, making payments or giving deposits and providing or receiving pledge for the partnership and doing all that is customary in the interests of the joint business. They can give short-term/minor loans that may not, according to customary practice, affect the operation of the partnership. However, the partners are not permitted to give out grants or loans unless all the partners have given their consent to such an action.[24]

Working for the joint business by each partner is not necessary and it can be agreed in the partnership agreement that the management will be restricted to a single or some identified partners, in which case the other partners should not act on behalf of the partnership. The partners can also agree to appoint a manager other than from the partners and pay him a fixed remuneration that will be treated as an expense of the Shirkah. An outside manager can also get a part of the investment profit as a good management bonus plus a fixed salary. However, if the management is carried out from the outset for a share in the profit earned by the venture, meaning that the manager is working as a Mudarib, he will be entitled only to the share in the realized profit and will not be given any additional remuneration for his management services. If a partner contributes to managing the venture or provides some kind of other service which other partners are not providing, such as accounting, he can be given, with mutual consent of the other partners, a share of the profit of the venture greater than that he would receive solely as a partner. A partner can be appointed for any of the services required by the Shirkah on the basis of an independent employment contract; he can also be dismissed from the service without the need to amend or terminate the Shirkah contract.[25]

The matter of indemnification is not the same in the different forms of Shirkah. In Shirkah al 'Inan, which is more relevant to us, a partner is Wakil, but not Kafil (agent, but not indemnifier) of the other partners. Thus, a partner is not liable to indemnify an outsider on behalf of another partner for a loss during such agency. Al-Kasani opines that the matter of indemnification is based on and regulated by usage ('Urf) of the people. This means that if, in a society, some type of partnership has a presumptive and potential condition of indemnification as a common usage, the condition will be considered valid.

Partners also have the following rights in the absence of any condition to the contrary:[26]

1. To invest the Shirkah capital in Mudarabah.
2. To make any person an agent for any work in the Musharakah.
3. To keep the property of Musharakah with any person as Amānah or deposit or give it as a loan.
4. To mortgage the property of Shirkah.
5. To travel for the concerned business at the expense of Shirkah.
6. To become a partner in any other Musharakah on behalf of his own Shirkah business.
7. To mix the property of Musharakah with that of his own.
8. To accept the mortgage of property of any outsider on behalf of his Musharakah.
9. Depending upon consent of the other partners and the 'Urf, spending any sum out of the Musharakah property.
10. To purchase and sell goods necessary for the conduct of business.

---

[24] AAOIFI, 2004–5a, clause 3/1/3/1, p. 202.
[25] AAOIFI, 2004–5a, clauses 3/1/3/4, 3/1/3/5, p. 203.
[26] Al-Sarakhsi, n.d., **11**, p. 158.

In all modern forms of Shirkah as well, the partners have equal rights, as mentioned above. In a partnership concern, the partners, by a mutual agreement, distribute among them their responsibilities, duties and jobs. In limited companies and cooperative societies, the shareholders delegate their powers to some of them to be called directors, or some such name. The partners may appoint a managing partner by mutual consent. Some of the partners may decide not to work for the Musharakah and work as sleeping partners.

### 12.3.4    Treatment of Profit and Loss

Profit and loss sharing is a crucial aspect in partnership. As the amount of the share towards the capital subscribed by each partner can be unequal (except in the case of Mufawadah, briefly discussed in Section 12.2.2), the share in profits and losses can also be unequal. It is, however, necessary that the share of all the partners should be decided without any ambiguity. The generally accepted view, which is based on the views of Imam Ahmad and Imam Abu Hanifa, is that the ratio of distribution of profit must be agreed upon at the time of execution of the agreement, otherwise the contract will not be valid in Sharī´ah.

There is a slight difference of opinion among jurists about a ratio of profit distribution different from the ratio of investment of two (or more) partners when both of them are obliged to work on the basis of a Musharakah contract. As a general rule, the shares of profit and of loss should be commensurate with the share in capital subscribed by each partner. According to Imam Malik, Imam Shafi'e and Imam Zufar, each partner shall get the profit exactly in the proportion of his investment. On the other hand, according to Imam Ahmad and the majority of Hanafi jurists, the ratio of profit may differ from the ratio of investment, provided it is agreed with free consent of the parties.[27] The viewpoint of Imam Abu Hanifa is a combination of both of these views. He says that, normally, the profit distribution ratio may differ from the investment ratio. But if a partner has made an express condition that he will not work for the Musharakah and will only be a sleeping partner, then his share of profit cannot be more than the ratio of his investment.[28] But it can be less than the ratio of a partner's capital according to all jurists. Therefore, it is permissible that a partner with a 40 % investment may get 50 % of the profit, provided he has not declared that he will be a sleeping partner.[29] Hanbali jurists allow even a sleeping partner more than the ratio of his share in a Musharakah investment.[30]

The difference of opinion is not generally taken care of and the general ruling is given as per the views of Imam Abu Hanifa and Imam Ahmad, according to whom the profit ratio can differ from the investment ratio on the basis of the amount of work to be done by the partners, because along with capital, labour and work are also factors for accrual of profit. Thus, any partner can make a condition that he will get more than the ratio of his investment as compensation for the work he will be doing for the Shirkah. According to all

---

[27] Ibn-Qudama, 1367 AH, **5**, p. 31; Al-Kasani, 1993, **6**, p.63.

[28] Al-Kasani, 1993, **6**, pp. 62, 63.

[29] For details see Usmani, 2000b, pp. 213–215. The principle that "profit is based on agreement of the parties, but loss is always subject to the ratio of investment" has been derived from the Fiqh of Imam Abu Hanifa and Imam Ahmad. (Ibn-Qudama, 1367 AH, **5**, p.140; Al-Kasani, 1993, **6**, pp. 162, 163). As regards loss, there is complete consensus of the jurists on this part of the principle (Ibn-Qudama, 1367 AH, **5**, p. 147).

[30] Ibn-Qudama, 1367 AH, **5**, pp. 140; Usmani, 2000b, pp. 210–218.

contemporary jurists, a loss must be shared exactly in accordance with the ratio of capital invested by the partners. This principle is given in a famous maxim based on the following saying of the fourth Pious Caliph of Islam, Ali (Gbpwh): "Profit is based on agreement of the parties, but loss is always subject to the ratio of investment".[31] The rationale of this principle is that earning profit is legitimized by engaging in an economic activity and thereby contributing to the socio-economic welfare of society. It encompasses equitable risk-sharing between the provider of capital and the entrepreneur.

The profit ratio must relate to the actual profit accrued to the business and not to the capital invested by any partner. For example, a profit earned may be distributed between two parties 50:50, 60:40, 30:70, etc. The contract should not lead to any stipulation that profit will be ( ) % on capital or so many dollars/rupees for all or any of the partners. It can also be agreed that partners A, B and C, for example, will get 30 %, 40 % and 30 % of the net profit earned by the joint business.[32] It is not allowed to fix any lump sum amount of the profit for any partner, or any rate of profit tied up with the capital invested by a partner.[33]

If a partner subscribes less capital but works more for the partnership than the other partners, he may be entitled to an equal share in profits or even more.[34] In the same way, if both partners have an equal share of subscription, their share of profits may be unequal provided that in all such cases, the working partner is entitled to a bigger share. In the case of loss, there is complete unanimity among all jurists that each partner in Shirkah shall suffer the loss according to the ratio of his investment.[35]

Any partner can withdraw any lump sum amount of profit subject to adjustment at the time of final settlement and distribution, meaning that any amount drawn by any partner will be deducted from his share of the profit. But if there is no profit or the actual profit is less than the anticipated profit, the amount drawn by any partner shall have to be subtracted from his capital.

Partners can amend, at any point in time, the terms of the partnership contract. They can amend the ratio of profit-sharing, taking into account that losses are shared according to the share of each partner in the partnership capital.[36] Once the profit is realized, it has to be shared as per the agreed ratio. Rules relating to profit in general kinds of Shirkah are given in Box 12.1.

In a partnership in creditworthiness, the partners should determine at the very beginning the percentage of profit-sharing and also liability-sharing for all the partners. The ratio of loss-sharing may differ, downward or upward, with mutual consent, from the percentage of profit-sharing: "The profit shall be distributed according to the agreement. However, the loss will be borne by each partner according to the ratio that each partner had undertaken to bear in proportion to overall assets that are purchased on credit. It is not permitted that the contract of partnership incorporates a provision that specifies a lump sum from the profit for any partner".[37]

---

[31] AAOIFI, 2004–5a, Standard on Musharakah, p. 221.
[32] Al-Kasani, 1993, **6**, p. 62.
[33] Ibn-Qudama, 1367 AH, **5**, pp. 32, 34.
[34] Al-Sarakhsi, n.d., **11**, p. 157.
[35] Ibn-Qudama, 1367 AH, pp. 33, 62.
[36] AAOIFI, 2004–5a, Standard on Musharakah, clauses 3/1/1/4, 3/1/5.
[37] AAOIFI, 2004–5a, Standard on Musharakah, clause 3/2, p. 207.

### 12.3.5  Guarantees in Shirkah Contracts

All partners in Shirkah maintain the assets of the partnership as a trust. Therefore, no one is liable except in cases of breach of the contract, misconduct or proven negligence. Negligence will be considered to have occurred in any of the following three cases: (i) a partner does not abide by the terms and conditions of the contract; (ii) a partner works against the norms of the concerned business; and (iii) the established ill-intention of a partner. Hence, the profit or even capital of any partners cannot be guaranteed by the co-partners. However, one partner can demand from another partner to provide any surety, security or pledge to cover the cases of misconduct and negligence.[38]

Therefore, in the case of a Musharakah agreement between a bank and the business community, the bank, as a part of risk management and for the judicious use of funds of the depositors, can obtain adequate security from a partner against his misconduct, breach of contract and negligence (if any).

*Third Party Guarantee in Musharakah*

Any third party can also provide a guarantee to make up the loss of capital of all or some of the partners. This is subject to the conditions:

1. The third party should not be legally and financially related to the Musharakah by owning more than 50 % of the capital of the guaranteed joint venture.
2. The guaranteed joint venture should not own more than half of the capital of the guarantee-providing entity.
3. The Shirkah contract should not be conditional on such a guarantee.
4. The guarantee should not be provided for any consideration. In other words, fulfilment of promise by a third party is not a condition for validity of the contract.

It is important to observe that the third party's undertaking is actually a "promise to guarantee" and does not create the right for the beneficiary to relate the Shirkah contract with fulfilment of the guarantee. The partners in whose favour third party guarantee is given can neither claim that Shirkah should become null and void nor can they refuse to meet their obligations under the contract on the grounds that they had entered into Shirkah taking into account the third party's undertaking to guarantee the profit or the capital.[39]

### 12.3.6  Maturity/Termination of Musharakah

Musharakah is basically a nonbinding contract, meaning that any partner can withdraw his share from the partnership at his will. But the partners can agree on any timeframe of Shirkah business. A traditional Shirkah agreement is terminated in any of the following situations:

1. When the purpose of forming Shirkah is achieved in the case of a specific purpose Musharakah. While the profit will be distributed according to the agreed profit distribution ratio, any loss will be borne by each partner according to the ratio of his investment.
2. When, after sufficient information or notice, any partner withdraws from a partnership after giving his partners due notice to this effect. His withdrawal will not necessitate

---

[38] AAOIFI, 2004–5a, Standard on Musharakah, clauses 3/1/4/1, 3/1/4/2.
[39] AAOIFI, 2004–5a, Standard on Musharakah, clause 3/1/4/3, pp. 203, 220, 221.

termination of the partnership between the remaining partners. Assets will be distributed pro rata among the partners with mutual consent and then the profit, if any, will be distributed on the basis of the agreed ratio. It is preferable that assets are assessed in terms of monetary value with mutual consent.

3. When any partner dies. However, his heirs can replace him with the consent of the other parties.
4. When the whole of the Musharakah capital is exhausted or lost.
5. When any partner is prevented or prohibited from exercising his legal powers over his property.

In the past, the need for early termination of Shirkah contracts normally did not arise, due to the short life and liquidating nature of joint enterprises that were of the nature of caravan trade. The classical jurists, therefore, did not feel any need to impose any restrictions on withdrawal of the partners. Latter jurists have contended that in the case of a partnership among more than two persons, the contract remains intact even after withdrawal by any partner.[40]

According to modern practice ('Urf), a shareholder of a limited company cannot withdraw from it his capital. He can, however, sell his share to any person desirous of becoming a shareholder of that company. In the present complicated commercial scenario, public control and legal structures require a considerable period for all related activities and no partner or shareholder can be absolved of his liabilities as easily as in the old days. In businesses that require long gestation periods and huge amounts of capital investment, termination of the project in between is considered out of the question. The jurists have, however, allowed changes of ownership through the sale and purchase of shares.[41]

Partners can enter into a binding promise for continuity of the partnership for a stipulated period of time. However, they can terminate the partnership with mutual consent before such a fixed period. One partner can give a binding promise to buy, within the operation period or at the time of liquidation, the assets of the partnership at their market value or as per agreement at the date of buying. A promise to buy at a pre-agreed price or at the face value of the shares of a company is not allowed in contractual partnerships, as this implies guarantee of capital of other partner(s), which is not allowed in Shirkatul'aqd.[42]

---

**Box 12.1:**   Rules Relating to Sharing of Profit/Loss in Shirkah

**Rules relating to profit**

1. The ratio or the basis for sharing profit should be decided at the beginning of a partnership.
2. Profit should be allocated in percentages of net earnings (after deducting the operating costs and expenses) and not in a sum of money or a percentage of the capital or investment by the partners.

---

[40] Al-Atasi, 1403 AH, Section 352, 4: 277.
[41] For details see Usmani, 2000b, pp. 220–231.
[42] AAOIFI, 2004–5a, clause 3/1/6/2, pp. 207, 222.

**Box 12.1:** (Continued)

3. It is not necessary that agreement for sharing profit should be proportionate to capital contribution.
4. A sleeping partner cannot share the profit more than the percentage of his capital. If a partner did not stipulate that he would be a sleeping partner, he is entitled to get an additional profit share over his percentage of contribution to the capital even if he did not work.[43]
5. The partners may, at a later stage, agree to change the profit-sharing ratio, and on the date of distribution, a partner may surrender a part of his profit to another partner.
6. One partner can cap his share of profit to a certain amount of money, giving the profit over and above that cap to the other partner(s).
7. The final allocation of profit is not allowed to be based on expected profit. However, it is permissible to distribute a provisional profit, subject to final settlement after actual or constructive liquidation.
8. If the subject matter of Shirkah is a leased asset, the rental amount distributed to the partners should be on account, subject to settlement and reimbursement according to the final position.[44]
9. It is permissible for partners to decide not to distribute a portion of profit for the purpose of creation of various reserves.[45]
10. Different profit-sharing formulas can be agreed for different periods or the magnitude of the realized profits, provided such a formula does not lead to the likelihood of a partner being precluded from participation in profit.[46]
11. Profit distribution/allocation should be made on the basis of actual or constructive liquidation (valuation of assets) of the venture. Receivables must be valued at the cash value, i.e. after deduction for an allowance for doubtful debts. For receivables, it is not permitted to take into account the concept of time value of money or the notion of discount of the debt amount as consideration for earlier payment.[47]

**Rules relating to loss**

1. All partners will have to share the loss in proportion to their investment.
2. However, it is valid according to the AAOIFI Standard that one partner can take responsibility for bearing the loss, at the time of loss, without any prior condition.[48]

## 12.4  THE CONCEPT AND RULES OF MUDARABAH

Mudarabah is a special kind of Shirkah in which an investor or a group of investors provides capital to an agent or manager who has to trade with it; the profit is shared according

---

[43] AAOIFI, 2004–5a, Standard on Musharakah, clause 3/1/5/3; also see, for the basis of Sharī'ah rulings in respect of profit/loss sharing, pp. 221, 222.
[44] AAOIFI, 2004–5a, Standard on Musharakah, clause 3/1/5/13.
[45] AAOIFI, 2004–5a, Standard on Musharakah, clause 3/1/5/15.
[46] AAOIFI, 2004–5a, Standard on Musharakah, clause 3/1/5/5.
[47] AAOIFI, 2004–5a, Standard on Musharakah, clause 3/1/5/10.
[48] AAOIFI, 2004–5a, Standard on Musharakah, clause 3/1/5/4.

to the pre-agreed proportion, while the loss has to be borne exclusively by the investor.[49] The loss means a shortfall in the capital or investment of the financier. The loss of the agent (Mudarib) is by way of expended time and effort, for which he will not be given any remuneration. There is no restriction on the number of persons giving funds for business or any restriction on the number of working partners.[50] As discussed in the case of Musharakah, profit cannot be in the form of a fixed amount or any percentage of the capital employed.[51] Any ambiguity or ignorance regarding capital or ratio of profit makes the contract invalid.[52] If a Mudarabah contract becomes invalid for any reason, the Mudarib will be working for the necessary period as a wage-earner and will get Ujratul-mithl (fair pay) for his job. He will not be given any share of the profit.

As evident from various books of Fiqh, the term Mudarabah is interchangeably used with Qirād and Muqaradah. It is presumed that while the latter two originated in Hijaz, Mudarabah was of Iraqi origin. Subsequently, the difference appears to have been perpetuated by the legal schools, the Malikis and Shafi'es adopting the terms "Qirād" and "Muqaradah" and the Hanafis using the term "Mudarabah".[53]

Al-Sarakhsi, in his book *Al-Mabsut*, explains the nature of Mudarabah in the following words:

"The term Mudarabah is derived from the expression 'making a journey' and it is called this because the agent (Mudarib) is entitled to the profit by virtue of his effort and work. And he is the investor's partner in the profit and in the capital used on the journey and in its dispositions.

The people of Madina call this contract Muqaradah, and that is based on a tradition concerning 'Uthman, (Gbpwh), who entrusted funds to a man in the form of a Maqarada. This is derived from al-Qard, which signifies cutting; for, in this contract, the investor cuts off the disposition of a sum of money from himself and transfers its disposition to the agent. It is therefore designated accordingly. We, however, have preferred the first term (Mudarabah) because it corresponds to that which is found in the book of Almighty Allah. He said: 'while others travel in the land (yadribuna fil-ard) in search of Allah's bounty,' that is to say, travel for the purposes of trade."[54]

With regard to the legality of Mudarabah, Al-Marghinani says in Al-Hidaya:

"There is no difference of opinion among the Muslims about the legality of Qirād. It was an institution in the pre-Islamic period and Islam confirmed it. They all agree that the nature of the Mudarabah business is that a person gives to another person some capital that he uses in the business. The user gets, according to conditions, some specified proportion, e.g. one-third, one-fourth or even one-half."

A number of sayings of the holy Prophet (pbuh) and reports by his Companions on the subject indicate that Islamic jurists are unanimous on the legitimacy of Mudarabah.[55] The terms of the Mudarabah contract offered by the Prophet's uncle Abbas were approved by the Prophet (pbuh). Abu Musa, the governor of Kufa, wanted to remit public money to the Bayt al Māl. He gave the amount to Abdullah bin Umar and his brother, who traded with it. The Caliph's assembly treated it as an ex post facto Mudarabah and took half of the profits

---

[49] Ibn-Qudama, 1367 AH, p.33.
[50] Ibn-Qudama, 1367 AH, **5**, p. 32.
[51] Al-Marghinani, 1957, **3**, p. 256.
[52] Ibn-Qudama, 1367 AH, p.30.
[53] Udovitch, 1970, pp. 174–175; AAOIFI, 2004–5a, Standard on Mudarabah, clause 4, p. 231.
[54] Al-Sarakhsi, n.d., **12**, p. 18.
[55] Al-Sarakhsi, n.d., **12**, p. 18.

earned by the two brothers, because the public money in their hands was not the loan. Caliph Umar also used to invest orphans' property on the basis of Mudarabah.

This practice was rather needed, since weaker members of society could not undertake long journeys for trading the way that most important professions of Arabs could at that time. Al-Sarakhsi, in this regard, says:

> "Because people have a need for this contract. For the owner of capital may not find his way to profitable trading activity and the person who can find his way to such activity may not have the capital. And profit cannot be attained except by means of both of these, that is, capital and trading activity. By permitting this contract, the goal of both parties is attained".

By allowing Mudarabah, Islam has intended to fulfil an important economic function by way of encouraging the hiring of capital and that of trade skills on judicious terms of risk-sharing, leading to the benefit of society and the concerned parties. The Mudarib has to work in various capacities like trustee, agent, partner, indemnifier/liable and even wage-earner if the contract becomes void. Being an agent to the Rabbul-māl, he undertakes the business and shares the profit.[56]

There could also be multilateral and sub-Mudarabahs. A multilateral Mudarabah may take various forms. A number of financiers may make a contract of Mudarabah with a single person, or a financier may contract Mudarabah with more than one worker, severally or jointly. Similarly, a number of workers may associate in order to work for one or more than one subscriber. As regards a sub-Mudarabah, there seems to be a unanimity of opinion that a Mudarib may give the Mudarabah capital to a third party on Mudarabah terms only if the financier has allowed it either in clear terms or has left the business of the Mudarabah to the discretion of the Mudarib. The absence of the owner's permission will make the former contract voidable.[57]

Mudarabah, like other contracts, calls for lawful items of trade, failing which the contract will become void or voidable, as the case may be. Thus, a worker is not allowed to trade in wine or swine with the Mudarabah capital. The classical jurists generally restricted the use of Mudarabah to the act of trade (buying/selling)[58], but an overwhelming majority of contemporary jurists and scholars allow the use of Mudarabah with a wider scope for use by Islamic banks as an alternative to interest-based financing.

Mudarabah is a contract of fidelity and the Mudarib is considered trustworthy with respect to the capital entrusted to him. He is not liable for the loss incurred in the normal course of business activities. As a corollary, he is liable for the property in his care as a result of the breach of trust, misconduct and negligence.[59] A guarantee to return funds can be taken from him but can be enforced only in two situations: if he is negligent in the use of funds or if he breaches the stipulated conditions of Mudarabah.[60] Hence, his actions should be in consonance with the overall purpose of the contract and within the recognized and customary commercial practice. In some situations, he becomes an employee when he performs some duty after the Mudarabah contract becomes invalid.

---

[56] For legality and rationale see AAOIFI, 2004–5a, pp. 240–241.

[57] Al Jaziri, 1973, **2**, pp. 858–862.

[58] This is particularly the view of Shafi'e jurists (Al Jaziri, 1973, **2**, 847–848; see also the relevant chapter in *Badai lil Kasāni*). Among the contemporary jurists, Hasanuz Zaman is in favour of a limited role for Mudarabah (Hasanuz Zaman, 1990).

[59] AAOIFI, 2004–5a, Standard on Mudarabah, clause 4/4, p. 232.

[60] AAOIFI, 2004–5a, Standard on Mudarabah, clauses 4/4, 6.

### 12.4.1    The Nature of Mudarabah Capital

As described in the discussion on Shirkah, Mudarabah capital should preferably be in the form of legal tender money, because capital in the form of commodities may lead to uncertainties and disputes. The value of illiquid assets must be clearly determined in terms of legal tender at the time of entering into the Mudarabah contract and there should be no ambiguity or uncertainty about its value. It is not permitted to use a debt owed by the Mudarib or another party to the capital provider as capital in a Mudarabah contract.[61] This is because the capital to be given for Mudarabah business should be free from all liabilities. The conversion of debt into a Mudarabah is prohibited to safeguard against the abuse of usurious loan being camouflaged as a Mudarabah, where, in essence, the financier would possibly ensure for himself not only the recovery of his debt but also an illegal return on his loan under the cover of his share in Mudarabah profits.[62] A financier cannot give the Mudarib two different amounts of capital with the stipulation that profit earned from one should go to him and from the other to the Mudarib. Similarly, he cannot specify different periods to state that profit earned in a specific period will be his and that of another period, the Mudarib's. It is also not allowed to stipulate that profit from a particular transaction should go to the financier and the profit from another transaction will belong to the Mudarib.[63]

*Mixing of Capital by the Mudarib*

A Mudarib is normally responsible for the management only and all the investment comes from the financier. But there may be situations where the Mudarib also wants to invest some of his money into the business of Mudarabah. In such cases, Musharakah and Mudarabah are combined. Jurists allow the Mudarib to add his own capital to the capital of Mudarabah with the permission of the Rabbul-māl. If a Mudarib subscribes his portion of profit or a portion of capital in the Mudarabah business, he will become a partner to the extent of his subscription, in addition to his remaining a worker. His rights and liabilities will be governed by Musharakah rules so long as his capital remains part of the business to the extent of his share of subscription. For example, A gives $100 000 to a Mudarib B, who also invests his own funds amounting to $50 000. This is the situation where Mudarabah and Musharakah have been combined. In this combined business, B (the Mudarib) can stipulate for himself a certain percentage of profit against his own investment and another percentage for his work as a Mudarib. In the above example, he has invested one-third of the capital. Therefore, according to normal business practice, he will get one-third of the actual profit on account of his investment, while the remaining two-thirds will be distributed between them equally. However, they may agree on another ratio for distribution.

Islamic banks normally mobilize deposits on Mudarabah principles and invest them in the business. If a bank also provides funds, it is entitled to get a profit on its own capital in proportion to the total capital of the Mudarabah. In addition to such a share in the profit, the bank shall also be entitled to share the remaining profit as Mudarib in an agreed proportion. For example, depositors provide $2000 for Mudarabah and the bank contributes $1000 to the business, and it was agreed to share the profit in the ratio 50:50. Let us assume that the profit earned by the bank as Mudarib is $300. The bank will get $100 as profit on its own

---

[61]  AAOIFI, 2004–5a, Standard on Mudarabah, clause 7/3; also see p. 242.
[62]  AAOIFI, 2004–5a, Standard on Mudarabah, p. 242.
[63]  AAOIFI, 2004–5a, clause 8/6.

investment of $1000. The remaining profit of $200 will be distributed between the bank and the depositors on the agreed ratio of 50:50. In other words, out of the profit of $200, the bank will get $100 and the depositors $100.

### 12.4.2  Types of Mudarabah and Conditions Regarding Business

Mudarabah business can be of two types: restricted and unrestricted Mudarabah. If the finance provider specifies any particular business, the Mudarib shall undertake business in that particular business only for items and conditions and the time set by the Rabbul-māl. This is restricted Mudarabah. But if the Rabbul-māl has left it open for the Mudarib to undertake any business he wishes, the Mudarib shall be authorized to invest the funds in any business he deems fit. This is called un-restricted Mudarabah. In both cases, the actions of the Mudarib should be in accordance with the business customs relating to the Mudarabah operations: the subject matter of the contract.[64]

Accordingly, a Mudarabah contract can be conditional or unconditional. The conditions may pertain to the nature of the work, the place of work and/or the period of the work. Conditions binding the worker to trade with a particular person or in a particular commodity, etc. are, according to Hanafi and Hanbali jurists, permissible, but these make the contract a special Mudarabah.

It is not legally necessary that the financier directly makes a contract with the Mudarib.[65] Thus, a banker may act as an agent to an investor and become a middle man doing business on the basis of investment agency (Wakalatul Istismār).

The financier has a right to impose conditions on a Mudarib, provided they are not prejudicial to the interests of the business and are not counterproductive to the purpose of the Mudarabah. For example:

1. He may fix a time limit for the operation of the contract.
2. He may specify the articles to be traded in or whose trade is to be avoided.
3. He may stop the worker from dealing with a particular person or a company.
4. He may stop the worker from travelling to a particular place or may also specify the place where trade is to be carried out.
5. He may ask the worker to make sure to fulfil his fiduciary responsibilities (but not profitability).[66]
6. According to some jurists, he may also compel his worker to sell the goods if the bargain is profitable (while the worker wants to hold then).
7. He also has a right to stop the worker from contracting a Mudarabah with any other party.

The Mudarib, on his part, is bound to follow the financier's conditions. If he violates a restriction or contravenes a beneficial condition, he becomes a usurper and will be responsible in respect of capital to the capital owner. He is not entitled to sell the Mudarabah goods at less than the general market price or buy goods for Mudarabah at a price higher than the common market price. He is also not allowed to donate Mudarabah funds or waive receivables of the business without explicit permission from the financier.[67]

---

[64] AAOIFI, 2004–5a, Standard on Mudarabah, clause 5/1.
[65] Al Jaziri, 1973, **2**, p. 815.
[66] Al Jaziri, 1973, **2**, p. 851.
[67] AAOIFI, 2004–5a, Standard on Mudarabah, clauses 9/5–9/7, pp. 236, 244.

### 12.4.3    Work for the Mudarabah Business

According to the majority of the traditional jurists, a financier in Mudarabah is not allowed to work for the joint business. He is not permitted to stipulate that he has a right to work with a Mudarib and to be involved in selling and buying activities, or supplying and ordering. However, he has the right to oversee and ensure that the Mudarib is doing his fiduciary duties honestly and efficiently.

It is only according to Hanbali jurists and, to some extent, Hanafi jurists that the owner is allowed to work for the business with the Mudarib. The reason for disapproval by the majority is that it jeopardizes the freedom of the worker to act according to his discretion.[68] This classical position is understandable if the basic idea that a person enters into a Mudarabah contract because he lacks business skill is presumed to exist. But if the financier also has skill and has contracted Mudarabah simply because he cannot do the entire work single-handedly, the rationale behind prohibiting him to work is not understandable. Moreover, it now seems more reasonable to allow the owner to ensure honesty and efficiency of the worker by taking a personal interest in the affairs of the business. Even some Hanafi jurists have allowed the financier's sale of Mudarabah goods if it is profitable.[69]

In present circumstances, it can be left to the parties, who may agree on any role by the investor keeping in mind its impact on profitability of the joint business. After transfer of the capital by the financier, the Mudarib needs to be given independence for the normal conduct of business. However, the financier can impose restrictions on the Mudarib in terms of place, object and method of trade. He may also want to have quick and direct access to his capital and may, for instance, stipulate that the Mudarib may trade within a certain marketing zone.

### 12.4.4    Treatment of Profit/Loss

Both parties in Mudarabah are at liberty to agree on the proportion or ratio of profit-sharing between them with mutual consent. This ratio has to be decided at the time the contract is concluded. They can agree on equal sharing or allocate different proportions. A lump sum amount as a profit/return on investment for any of the parties cannot be allowed or agreed upon. In other words, they can agree on, for example, 50, 40 or 60% of the profit going to the Rabbul-māl and the remaining 50, 60 or 40%, respectively, going to the Mudarib. Different proportions can be agreed upon for different situations. For example, the financier can say to the Mudarib: "If you deal in wheat, you will get 50%, but if you deal in cloth, you will be given 40% of the profit. Or if you do business in your town, you will get 40% and if in another town, your share in the profit will be 50%." Loss, if any, has to be borne by the financier. Loss means erosion of capital; no profit can be recognized or claimed unless the capital of Mudarabah is maintained intact.[70]

The distribution of profit depends on the final result of the operations at the time of physical or constructive liquidation of the Mudarabah. Reserves can be created with mutual consent and if a Mudarabah incurs a loss, the loss can be compensated by the profit of the future operation of the joint business or the reserves created in the past. At the time of profit

---

[68] The same is the view taken by the AAOIFI, as per its Standard on Mudarabah (clause 9/3; also see p. 244).

[69] See Hasanuz Zaman, 1990, pp. 69–88.

[70] See, for its basis, AAOIFI, 2004–5a, p. 243.

allocation, one partner can donate a part of his profit to the other partner(s). A financier can also award a good management bonus to a Mudarib. If losses are greater than profits at the time of liquidation, the balance (net loss) has to be deducted from the capital.

Profits are shared when they accrue, but this accrual does not mean a transaction-wise calculation of the profits; it means the overall adjustment of profits and losses over a particular period of time, which will be treated as the closing of the accounts but not necessarily the winding up of the business. However, the partners can provisionally draw the profit that will be subject to adjustment at the time of finalization of the accounts.

The Mudarib is entitled to a share of profit as soon as it is clear that the operations of the Mudarabah have led to the realization of a profit. However, this entitlement is not absolute, as it is subject to the retention of interim profits for the protection of the capital. It will be an absolute right only after distribution takes place. For valuation, receivables should be measured at the cash equivalent, or net realizable, value, i.e. after the deduction of a provision for doubtful debts. In measuring receivables, neither time value nor discount on current value for an extension of the period of payment shall be taken into consideration.[71]

Parties can change the ratio for profit distribution at any time, but that ratio will remain effective for the period for which it has been mutually fixed. If the parties did not stipulate the ratio, they should refer to the customary practice, if any, to determine the shares of profit. If there is no customary practice, the contract will be regarded void *ab intio* and the Mudarib will get the common market wage for the kind and amount of service he has rendered.[72]

Although one party in Mudarabah cannot stipulate for himself a lump sum amount of money, the parties can agree with mutual consent that if the profit is over a particular ceiling, one of the parties can take the greater share of the profit and if the profit is below or equal to the stipulated ceiling, the distribution will be according to the agreed ratio. The profits realized from Mudarabah cannot be finally distributed until all expenses have been paid, in accordance with custom and the original agreement. Final accounting will be undertaken against the net profits of the Mudarabah operations. The part of profit of the Mudarib becomes secure after the liquidation of the Mudarabah and the capital owner recovers its capital and part of profit.

The Mudarib cannot claim any periodical salary or a fee or remuneration for the work done by him for the Mudarabah business over and above his share as agreed in the contract. However, Imam Ahmad has allowed the Mudarib to draw his daily expenses of food only from the Mudarabah account. Hanafi jurists have also restricted the right of the Mudarib to claim expenses incurred during business journies. The financier and the manager can enter into a separate agreement, independent of the Mudarabah agreement, for assigning any job that is not by custom a part of the Mudarabah business against a fee. This means that the Mudarabah contract will not be affected if the Mudarib is terminated from the service.[73]

As a principle, in Mudarabah it is only the financier who bears the loss. However, if a Mudarib has also contributed capital, which he can do with mutual consent, he will bear the pro rata loss. If profit has been distributed upon constructive or actual liquidation of business, it cannot be withdrawn in order to make up for a later loss or for any other purpose.[74] If loss has occurred in some transactions and profit has been realized in some others, the profit can

[71] AAOIFI, 2004–5a, Standard on Mudarabah, clause 8/8.

[72] AAOIFI, 2004–5a Standard on Mudarabah, clause 8/4.

[73] AAOIFI, 2004–5a, Standard on Mudarabah, clause 8/2.

[74] Al Jaziri, 1973, **2**, pp. 862–865.

be used to offset the loss at the first instance, then the remainder, if any, shall be distributed between the parties according to the agreed ratio.

### 12.4.5   Termination of a Mudarabah Contract

The general principle is that Mudarabah is not a binding contract and each of the parties can terminate it unilaterally except in two cases: (i) when the Mudarib has already commenced the business, in which case the contract becomes binding up to the date of actual or constructive liquidation; and (ii) when the parties agree on a certain duration of the contract, in which case it cannot be terminated before expiry of that period except with mutual agreement. For termination, the Mudarib will be given time to sell the illiquid assets so that an actual amount of profit may be determined.[75]

The unlimited power to terminate the Mudarabah may create difficulties in the context of the present circumstances, because most commercial enterprises today need time to bear fruit. Modern businesses also demand continuous and complex efforts. Therefore, if the parties agree, while entering into the Mudarabah, that no party shall terminate it during a specified period, except in specified circumstances, it does not seem to violate any principle of Sharī´ah, particularly in the light of the famous Hadith which says: "All the conditions agreed upon by the Muslims are upheld, except a condition which allows what is prohibited or prohibits what is lawful in Sharī´ah."

If all assets of the Mudarabah are in cash form at the time of termination, and some profit has been earned on the principal amount, it shall be distributed between the parties according to the agreed ratio. However, if the assets of the Mudarabah are not in cash form, the Mudarib shall be given an opportunity to sell and liquidate them, so that the actual profit may be determined.

A restricted Mudarabah will automatically wind up after the object is achieved. If the Mudarabah is general, it will be in the interests of both parties to wind up at will whenever both of them mutually agree to do so. The difficulty may arise if one of the parties wants to continue business. Reconciliation on this point should be sought through a court or any arbitration.

## 12.5   MUDARABAH DISTINGUISHED FROM MUSHARAKAH

Mudarabah is distinguished from Musharakah briefly on the following grounds:

1. The investment in Musharakah comes from all the partners, while in Mudarabah, investment comes from a person or a group of persons, but not from the Mudarib.[76]
2. In Musharakah, all partners have a right to participate in the management of the business and can work for it, while in Mudarabah, the Rabbul-māl has no right to participate in management. With mutual consent, however, he can work for the venture. Further, the financier has the right to ensure that the Mudarib is doing his fiduciary duties in the true sense.
3. In Musharakah, all the partners share the loss according to the ratio of their investment, while in Mudarabah, the loss, if any, is suffered by the Rabbul-māl only. However, if

---

[75] AAOIFI, 2004–5a, Standard on Mudarabah, clause 10.
[76] Usmani, 2000a, pp. 47–49.

the Mudarib has conducted business with negligence or has been dishonest, he shall be liable for the loss caused by his negligence or misconduct.

4. The liability of the partners in Musharakah is normally unlimited. However, if all the partners have agreed that no partner shall incur any debt during the course of business, then the liabilities exceeding assets shall be borne by that partner alone who has incurred a debt on the business in violation of the aforesaid condition. Contrary to this, in Mudarabah, the liability of the Rabbul-māl is limited to his investment unless he has permitted the Mudarib to incur debts on his behalf.[77]

5. In Musharakah, profit can be distributed on an annual, quarterly or monthly basis by valuation of the assets.[78] In the case of Mudarabah, final distribution can take place only after liquidation of the Mudarabah business. However, on account payment of profit is possible subject to ultimate adjustment.[79] To avoid problems in perpetual Mudarabah, the contemporary jurists have accepted the concept of constructive liquidation of assets by determining the market value of nonliquid assets.[80]

6. In Musharakah, all assets of the Musharakah become jointly owned by all of the partners according to the proportion of their respective investment. Therefore, each one of them can benefit from the appreciation in the value of the assets, even if profit has not accrued through sales. In Mudarabah, however, all the goods/assets purchased by the Mudarib are solely owned by the Rabbul-māl, and the Mudarib can earn his share in the profit only if he sells the assets profitably. However, there are some exceptions to this rule according to a minority view.

7. If the Mudarabah business is dissolved, its assets and profit, if any, can be distributed only after assessing its value in terms of money. In the case of Shirkah, this is not necessary.[81]

## 12.6   MODERN CORPORATIONS: JOINT STOCK COMPANIES

Modern corporate bodies can be considered to be based on the concept of Shirkah al 'Inan or a combination of Musharakah and Mudarabah, which is allowed by the generality of the contemporary jurists.[82] There are a number of forms of modern corporations, including joint stock companies with limited liability, joint liability companies (a form of personal partnership), companies limited by shares (also a kind of personal partnership), partnerships in commendum (a form of financing partnership), etc.[83] The general principles governing these forms are the same and we will be discussing mainly the modern stock companies with limited liability of the shareholders.

The main ingredient of modern corporate business is the issuance of shares or certificates to the investors in a joint business. A large number of people provide funds and are issued any specific type of receipts that are called shares or a variety of certificates that represent the proportionate ownership of the shareholders. The AAOIFI Standard on Musharakah has defined a stock company as an entity, the capital of which is distributed into equal units of

---

[77] Ibn-Qudama, 1367 AH, pp. 18, 35.
[78] Ibn-Qudama, 1367 AH, pp. 5, 64.
[79] AlJaziri, 1973, **3**, p. 61.
[80] Usmani, 2000b, pp. 276–283.
[81] Al-Kasani, 1993, **6**, p. 77.
[82] Usmani, 2000b, pp. 313–329.
[83] See, for details, AAOIFI, 2004–5a, Standard on Musharakah, pp. 208–213.

tradable shares with limited liability of the shareholders to their pro rata capital. The rules relating to Shirkah al 'Inan are applicable to it except on the issue of the limited liability of the shareholders. In other words, shareholders are owners of the assets of the company to the extent of shares held by them. They can sell/transfer the shares to any other persons but have no discretion over the assets of the company.[84]

A company incorporated by law is considered a juristic personality, and as such, cannot avoid its obligations to people dealing with it. This separates the liability of the company from the liability of the shareholders. The company's liability can be limited to its paid-up capital if it is made public in order to make the customers aware of its financial position. It involves a binding contract for continuity in terms of its Articles of Association. Therefore, no one is entitled to terminate the company in terms of his shares. However, a shareholder can sell his shares or relinquish title to them in favour of other people.

The capital contribution for subscription to shares can be made in a lump sum or in instalments. Unpaid instalments would constitute an undertaking to increase the share in the company subsequently. It is permissible to issue new shares in order to increase the capital, provided the new shares are issued at the fair value of the old shares – this can be at a premium, discount or at the nominal value of the shares.[85] Preference shares having special financial characteristics that give their holders a priority for profit allocation at the time of the company's liquidation do not conform to the Sharī´ah principles.[86]

IFIs can purchase or sell shares of any company subject to the condition that the company is undertaking a Halal business. The price of the shares can be less or more than their nominal value, provided more than 50 % of its shares comprise fixed assets, i.e. liquid assets (cash plus receivables) are less than 50 %. If the major business of any company is not against Sharī´ah and some of its transactions involve un-Islamic elements, like dealing with interest-based institutions, its shares can also be purchased, provided the part of income representing interest, if identified, is given to charity.

One cannot sell shares that one does not own and a promise by a broker to lend a share to a short-seller at the date of delivery does not refer to ownership or possession of the shares. Shares can also be pledged, because anything that can be sold can also be given as pledge.[87]

Shares that are gradually redeemed before the termination of the company only through the distribution of profits by the company do not conform to the Sharī´ah principles. This is because the funds the certificate holders receive constitute profit in respect of their shares. The claim that the participations be redeemed in consideration for the distributed profit is invalid. Therefore, the certificate holders remain owners of the shares and are entitled to proceeds when the company is liquidated.[88]

Preference shares, on the basis of which some of the partners in a concern are earmarked a fixed percentage of dividends, do not fulfil the principles of Sharī´ah. The basic principle of distribution of profit is that no gain can be had without undertaking to bear the risk of loss. In this respect, all the subscribing partners of a company should be treated alike, based on the number of shares held by them. Similarly, if any of the partners has been privileged to share in profits only without sharing in losses, the partnership contract is deemed to have

---

[84] AAOIFI, 2004–5a, Standard on Musharakah, clause 4/1/1; Usmani, 2000b, p.330.

[85] AAOIFI, 2004–5a, Standard on Musharakah, clause 4/1/2/3.

[86] AAOIFI, 2004–5a, Standard on Musharakah, clause 4/1/2/14.

[87] AAOIFI, 2004–5a, Standard on Musharakah, clause 4/1/2/7; also at p. 223.

[88] See Resolution No. 63(1/7) of the International Islamic Fiqh Academy; AAOIFI, 2004–5a, Standard on Musharakah, clause 4/1/2/15, pp. 210, 224.

become void due to the element of interest. The case of qualification shares is, however, different, as it determines the minimum extent of attention and devotion of the directors without any preferential treatment in pecuniary entitlement.

Underwriting is a crucial part of the business related to modern corporations. A shareholder or any third party can underwrite an issue of shares without any consideration. The underwriter will undertake, by an agreement at the time of incorporation of the company or shares issue, to buy all or a part of the shares issue. It undertakes to buy the remaining shares at nominal value that are not subscribed through public or private placements. The underwriter can charge for services provided, other than the underwriting, such as conducting feasibility studies or marketing the shares.[89]

The actual rules of modern corporate business require more detailed analysis. Shares/certificates are floated for raising liquid assets. Trading in assets that represent the underlying assets is permissible as long as real assets and services constitute the majority of the total assets. As such, the instruments or shares represent only the money, they cannot be traded so long as the capital is in liquid form, i.e. in the form of cash raised or receivables or advances due from others. This is because the shares represent pro rata ownership of shareholders in the joint business/project. If the capital is still in liquid form, the shares may be sold only at face value, otherwise it would mean that money is being exchanged for more money, which is Riba. However, when the raised money is employed in purchasing nonliquid assets, like land, buildings, machinery, raw material, furniture, etc., the shares/Musharakah certificates will represent the holders' proportionate ownership in these assets. In this case, it will be allowed by the Sharī´ah to sell these certificates in the secondary market for any price agreed upon between the parties, which may be more or less than the face value of the shares/certificates, because the subject matter of the sale is a share in the tangible assets and not in money only; therefore, the certificate may be taken as any other commodity which can be sold with profit or at a loss.

Another major feature of the present corporate structure is that running projects are normally a mixture of liquid and tangible assets, e.g. in the form of raw material, fixed assets, inventory of finished goods, sales proceeds, receivables (that being debt is treated as liquid, like money), etc. The opinion of contemporary jurists regarding the Sharī´ah position of trading in shares of entities having mixed liquid and nonliquid assets is different. According to the classical jurists of the Shafi'e school, combined assets of a business cannot be sold unless the tangible assets are separated and sold independently. Hanafi jurists, however, are of the view that a combination of liquid and tangible assets can be sold/purchased for an amount that is greater than the amount of liquid assets in the combined assets. They prescribe no specific proportion of tangible assets to qualify for permission of such a sale/purchase. However, most of the contemporary scholars, including those of the Shafi'e school, have allowed trading in the shares and certificates only if the nonliquid assets of the business are more than 50%, while some reduce this floor to 33%.

Other principles relating to stocks have been discussed in Chapter 8.

## 12.7 MODERN APPLICATION OF THE CONCEPT OF SHIRKAH

Keeping in mind the broad principles and the concept of Shirkah, Musharakah and Mudarabah can be used for evolving a new system, both on the liabilities and assets sides of the financial

---

[89] AAOIFI, 2004–5a, Standard on Musharakah, clause 4/1/2/4; also at p. 223.

system, that conforms to the requirements of Sharī´ah and also fulfils the needs of trade and business. It may take the form of corporate firms, mutual funds, Mudarabah companies, individual or multi-investment portfolios by fund managers, business participation certificates, Musharakah agreements, project financing, running Musharakah and partnership businesses, certificates of investment or Diminishing Musharakah for facilitating financing fixed assets, trade and services. A combination of Shirkatulamwal and Shirkatula´mal can be used for service firms of the modern age in medicine, law, IT, architecture and other fields.[90]

### 12.7.1  Use of Shirkah on the Deposits Side of the Banking System

According to the Sharī´ah principles, whatever is permissible for an individual is also permissible for a group of people. Based on this principle, Shirkah, which conventionally was an individual contract carried out by an owner of funds with a Mudarib, has now become a group activity. The main relationship between depositors and Islamic banks is that of financiers and Mudaribs. All deposits are pooled, the bank invests the pooled amount in business, all direct expenses are charged to the pool while expenses related to the general management or Head Office expenses are borne by the bank (Mudarib) itself, and the net proceeds are distributed among depositors according to the stipulated ratios. Different weightages can be assigned to different depositors depending upon their tenure and size, subject to the condition of sufficient disclosure to all depositors. For the purpose of profit distribution among partners, there is constructive liquidation after a tenure or accounting period and then the joint relationship starts afresh for the next accounting period.

Banks normally also put a part of their equity into the pool. In terms of the rules, the relationship will be of Musharakah if they put their part in the pool at the beginning of pool creation and that of Mudarabah if subsequently. In the latter case, the bank will be an investor just like the other depositors. All pool members will be partners among themselves and the bank will serve as Mudarib. The overall relationship will remain one of Mudarib and Rabbul-māl, because in the case of Musharakah, all partners would have the right to participate in the appreciation of the business as a whole, which is not the case for the banks' depositors. Further, depositors are like sleeping partners and normally have no right in management and business decisions. This Mudarabah relationship is clearer in the case of special investors or portfolio accounts maintained by depositors, investment of which is made by banks in the light of depositors' directives.

The longer the tenor of deposits, the greater the weightage assigned to them. Banks can assign preferential weightages to various categories of deposits, like those of the old/pensioners, welfare associations, etc. But assigning different weightages to bigger sizes of deposit as a matter of course would not be a good practice, keeping in mind the principle of justice.

According to the rules of Mudarabah, all financial losses, if any, should be borne by the pool as Rabbul-māl. However, in such a case, the bank should also not earn any amount against its services. A loss attributable to the pool should be distributed among the pool members according to their investment as per the rules of Musharakah, i.e. according to their investment ratio.

The bank should cover all expenses from its own share of profit within the Mudarabah arrangement. Weightages can only be amended at the beginning of the accounting period, which can be a month or a quarter. The bank can have a right to reduce/withdraw the

---

[90] Ibn-Qudama, 1367 AH, **5**, p. 9; Usmani, 2000b, pp. 292–308.

profit-sharing ratio in the Mudarabah arrangement in favour of the pool. The bank may also invest in the pool as a depositor.

All accounts should be linked to respective pools containing more than 50 % Ijarah or other fixed assets to allow premature withdrawal. However, if the Hanafi view is adopted, early withdrawal will be allowed even if the nonliquid assets are more than 10 % of its total worth.

Savers/investors offer funds to Islamic mutual funds or banks on a Mudarabah basis, who mix those funds with their own funds and offer them to users who seek Sharī´ah-compatible financing. Hence, Islamic financial institutions play the role of intermediary along with that of partner, as reflected in taking the funds, considering customer requests, following up repayments, distributing realized profits and many other functions.

The system of profit allocation between the banks' equity and investment account holders is important, because it deals with fundamental and ethical aspects relating to the concept of fairness in the Islamic alternative that Islamic banks offer as opposed to interest-based banks. It requires disclosure of information regarding the business and the profit-sharing formulas. The principles of fairness and trust emphasize the importance of the individuals' confidence in the Islamic banks' ability to achieve their investment goals. Disclosure should be made about significant accounting policies, weightages assigned on the basis of the tenor and the size of accounts, expenses to be charged and the basis applied by the Islamic bank in the allocation of profits between owners' equity and unrestricted investment account holders.

### 12.7.2   Use of Shirkah on the Assets Side

The best alternative to interest for financing by banks is considered to be a Shirkah arrangement that could be in the form of Mudarabah, Musharakah or investments through Shirkah-based certificates or Sukuk. Mudarabah can be best used for financing of import trade on a single transaction or consignment basis in the case of a firm order and L/C without margin, where the whole investment has to be made by the bank. Its use is also possible for running businesses, project financing and for the purpose of securitization.

Musharakah can be applied in trade finance without complexities, since the chances of fraud, negligence and other problems are relatively lower in international trade than in other Musharakah-based projects. A bank may enter into a Musharakah arrangement with a client who intends to import; the bank may also appoint him as agent for acquisition and disposal of the goods after the same are imported; an L/C could be opened in the bank's or the client's name. The net profit out of this limited purpose Musharakah will be shared between the bank and the client in an agreed ratio. The above procedure can also be adopted in respect of bills drawn under inland L/Cs. Detailed procedures for import financing under Musharakah are given in Chapter 14.

In the case of export finance under L/C, the goods will be acquired and made ready for shipment on a Musharakah basis. The client will prepare the export documents strictly in accordance with the terms of the L/C and undertake to indemnify the bank for any loss in case of his failure to honour his commitment. Export proceeds will be distributed according to the agreed ratio. If there is no L/C involved, the merchandise will be made ready for export under joint ownership of the bank and the client. However, details of all such transactions will have to be worked out in consultation with the commercial bankers who are actually involved in the business.

The following could be the procedure for export financing on the basis of Shirkah: the exporter receives an order from abroad to export a specific commodity/goods at a known price. He estimates its expected profit. If he needs financing for manufacturing/procurement of the goods, the bank can provide financing on the basis of Shirkah. Profit would be shared on a pre-agreed percentage. The bank can secure itself from any negligence on the part of the exporter. However, being a partner of the business, the bank will be liable to bear any loss which may be caused due to any reason other than the negligence of the exporter. However, in order to undertake such an operation, banks need to understand the nature of the exporter's business and other requirements.

Banks can also provide Musharakah-based financing through Musharakah agreements with their clients. It is observed that a Sharī´ah expert would not have any objection if the banks make a provision in the Musharakah agreements giving them the right, on an agreed formula, to convert their investment outstanding at any time during the currency of the agreement into ordinary shares of the company. The details can be worked out by the experts. The client may be required to seek clearance from the bank before declaration of any dividend. There should also be a provision for adjudication to resolve any differences between the parties. There may be a review or a resolution committee with members named in the Musharakah agreement to deal with the issues of breach of contract by either of the parties. It seems imperative that banks shall employ some mechanics for monitoring the affairs of the concerned companies. They will have to gear up their machinery for a more thorough appraisal of the project feasibility and other aspects in the preliminary stages as well as for subsequent monitoring of projects' implementation.

In the case of project financing, the traditional method of Shirkah can be easily adopted. If the financier wants to finance the whole project, the form of Mudarabah can be used. If investment comes from both sides, the form of Musharakah would be more suitable. In this case, if the management is the sole responsibility of one party, a combination of Musharakah and Mudarabah can also be used according to the rules.

The following may be the flow of transactions in the case of Musharakah for running business:

1. A running Musharakah Account for the client will be opened in the books of the financing bank.
2. The client's proceeds from the sale of finished of goods will be credited in the Running Musharakah Account.
3. The client's cash flows generated from investment activities (for example, sales proceeds from the disposal of fixed assets) and cash flows from long-term financing activities (for example, long-term finance availed for the project) cannot be credited in the Running Musharakah Account.
4. For determination of the period of running Musharakah limit, all the clients of the bank will be divided into the following three categories: seasonal, cyclical and continued operation.
5. At the end of each quarter or month, as the case may be, the profit earned by the client in the Musharakah will be paid to the bank.
6. The profit-sharing will be based on the computed operating profit for the same period for which the running Musharakah limit was awarded.[91]

Shirkah can also be used for financing through the purchase of Musharakah/Mudarabah certificates like Shirkah-based Sukuk, term finance certificates (TFCs) or participation term

---

[91] For details, see Usmani, 2000a, pp. 55–81.

certificates (PTCs). Certificates issued on the principle of Shirkah are negotiable instruments issued by a company in consideration of any fund, money or accommodation received or to be received by it whether in cash or in kind, or against any promise, guarantee, undertaking or indemnity issued for its benefit. The problem of moral hazard would be much less in the case of TFCs/PTCs than in the case of direct Musharakah investments.

However, banks indicate a number of risks and problems in the case of Shirkah-based financing. For example, the managing partner may manipulate the financial reporting in order to deceive the Islamic bank. They may be unwilling to disclose actual profits to the bank, exposing it to the risk of return on its investment. Guarantee/collateral can be taken only to safeguard against negligence and misconduct. The partners may allocate indirect and personal expenses in Musharakah operations. Legal capacity and financial stability of the guarantors have to be independent from the Musharakah contract. The Islamic bank, as the buying partner in a Diminishing Musharakah, may be exposed to fluctuations in unit price if it is not fixed at the beginning of the contract.

The main obstacles in the way of widespread use of Musharakah stem from the lack of documentation, defective taxation systems and the lack of effort on the part of the bankers themselves. In the view of this author, Islamic banks have not made serious efforts to apply this system simply because of the easy and less risky alternatives based on Murabaha and leasing. Musharakah could have been safely applied at least for trading and project financing if they had undertaken some research and taken initiatives to realize the potential of this most preferable mode of Islamic finance. In the following pages we shall give some case studies in this regard.

### 12.7.3   Securitization on a Shirkah Basis

A security, in financial terms, can be defined as an asset in the form of a paper whose cash flow is backed by a pool of liquid and tangible assets. Through securitization, tangible or nonliquid assts of joint business are made negotiable through the sale of shares/certificates in the financial market.

Musharakah can easily be adopted as a basis for securitization, especially in the case of big projects where huge amounts are required. Every subscriber can be given a certificate representing his proportionate ownership in the assets of the joint business, and after the project is started by acquiring substantial nonliquid assets, these Musharakah certificates can be treated as negotiable instruments and can be bought and sold in the secondary market.

Musharakah and Mudarabah Sukuk can be issued as redeemable certificates by or to the corporate sector or to individuals for their rehabilitation/employment, for purchase of automobiles for their commercial use or for the establishment of high-standard clinics, hospitals, factories, trading centres, endowments, etc. This we shall discuss in detail in Chapter 15.

---

**Box 12.2:**   Case Study on the Use of Musharakah for Trade Financing

Islamic banks normally use Murabaha in trade financing and Musharakah and Mudarabah are avoided because of the perception of more risk. Shirkah-based modes can be applied in export and import finance without complexities, particularly in respect of single transactions and export/import consignments. However, in order to undertake such operations, Islamic banks need to understand the nature of the exporter's business and other requirements. A possible procedure for trade financing under Musharakah and Mudarabah is given below:

1.  The exporter receives an order from abroad to export a specific commodity/good at a known price. He prepares estimates of cost and his expected profit.
2.  He needs financing for manufacturing/procurement of the goods and asks the bank to provide finance on the basis of Shirkah. The bank enters into an agreement, according to which profit will be shared on a pre-agreed percentage.
3.  The bank can get a guarantee/security to protect itself from misconduct, breach of contract or negligence on the part of the client. However, being a partner of the exporter, the bank will be liable to bear any loss which may be caused due to any reason other than the negligence of the exporter.

A practical application of a similar transaction of import finance is discussed in the following case study.

A huge utility organization awards a contract to a local supplier (ABC & Co) for the supply of equipment that has to be imported. ABC & Co is interested in financing the transaction through a Musharakah arrangement with an Islamic bank. The structure of the product is developed on a partnership by creditworthiness basis (Shirkatul Wujooh), in which the partners have no investment at all. They purchase goods on credit and sell them at spot. The profit so earned is distributed between them at an agreed ratio. The process of the transaction consists of the following steps:

1.  ABC & Co opens a Usance L/C of Rs. 10 million, which is issued by an Islamic bank (bank financing on a participation basis) in favour of M/s XYZ Machines, Italy.
2.  XYZ Machines agrees to give a credit period of 180 days.
3.  Equipment is shipped to the importing country through air cargo due to the sensitivity of the equipment.
4.  ABC & Co inspects the goods and confirms its satisfaction to the bank, upon which the Islamic bank conveys its acceptance of the documents to the negotiating bank.
5.  Customs take 30 days for the clearing of the equipment.
6.  ABC & Co take around 50 days to install the equipment.
7.  After the installation, the utility organization inspects and tests the equipment for its performance.
8.  As soon as the satisfaction certificate is issued, a bill is lodged for payment.
9.  Payment is received within 150 days of shipment.
10. Profit is distributed among the partners as per the agreed ratio.
11. The Islamic bank settles the L/C on the due date.

---

**Box 12.3:**   Musharakah-based TFCs Issued by Sitara Industries, Pakistan

An excellent example of Musharakah-based financing through the issuance of participatory instruments is that of the 5-year term finance certificates (TFCs) worth Pak Rupees 360 million issued by Sitara Chemical Industries, a public limited company in Pakistan, in June 2002. The amount raised through the TFC issue was utilized to meet

**Box 12.3:** (Continued)

a part of the cost of an expansion project of the company. The TFCs are based on the mechanism of Shirkah and are tradable in the securities market. The payment of profit or sharing of loss is linked to the operating profit or loss of the company. The investors assume the risk of sustaining losses proportionate to their principal amount in the case of any operating losses incurred by Sitara. Changes in any government regulations may also affect the profitability of the TFCs. By investing in the TFCs, an investor also assumes the risk of not being able to sell the TFC without adversely affecting the price.

Profit is paid on a six-monthly basis. For the purposes of sharing profit with the TFC holders, the level of yearly operating profit is divided into two tiers, as described below under the headings of Level I Profit and Level II Profit.

**Level I Profit**

On the first Rs. 100 million operating profit at 12 % p.a. of the outstanding principal. The rate of 12 % has been taken as a projected rate by reverse accounting on the basis of a sharing ratio. The rate of percentage profit entitlement shall be proportionately reduced if operating profit is less than Rs. 100 million, as follows: (Actual operating profit / Rs.100 million) × 12 % = Actual profit entitlement rate for Level I profit.

**Level II Profit**

2 % p.a. of the outstanding principal on each subsequent Rs. 100 million operating profit (over and above Rs.100 million). One quarter of this profit will be transferred into the Takaful reserve and the balance will be distributed to the TFC holders. The rate of profit entitlement shall be proportionately reduced if the actual figure of subsequent operating profit falls in between two successive slabs of Rs. 100 million of operating profit, as follows: (Actual operating profit / Rs.100 million) × 2 % = Actual profit entitlement rate for Level II profit.

If the final profit payment of a year is in excess of the on-account profit payments already paid to the TFC holders, the excess amount will be paid along with the next six-monthly on-account profit payment. However, if the on-account payments that have already been made for the year are in excess of the final profit share of the TFC holders, then the excess will be adjusted as per a predecided procedure. If the operating profit is more than Level I profit, the profit-sharing arrangement applicable on Level II profit is followed.

If, upon finalization of the annual audited accounts, a loss is incurred, the on-account profit payment has to be adjusted. The loss attributable to the TFC holders will be offset against the Takaful reserve created for the purpose. If the amount available in the Takaful reserve is insufficient to absorb the entire loss attributable to the TFC holders, the unabsorbed losses will be adjusted against the principal amount at the time of redemption of the principal amount.

The face value of each TFC issued to the general public is Rs. 5000. The principal amount has to be redeemed at the end of the third, fourth and fifth years from July 1, 2002. The amount of principal redemption at the end of the third year may be Rs. 1650/-, at the end of the fourth year Rs. 1650/- and at the end of the fifth year

Rs. 1700/-. The principal redemption in each above-mentioned year will be subject to profit/loss adjustments.

NB: Sitara TFCs remained highly profitable; they gave a profit between 15 and 24% per annum. The TFCs are not available in the secondary market as the holders locked in, keeping in mind the high profitability.

## 12.8   DIMINISHING MUSHARAKAH

The participatory contracts that may be more suitable for financing of fixed assets and present-day ongoing projects, particularly for financial intermediaries, can be based on the concept of "Diminishing Musharakah" (DM). In the Diminishing Musharakah contract, a party, after participation in ownership of any business/project, can liquidate his investment from the asset or the ongoing business. The jurists are unanimous on the permissibility of this arrangement.[92] DM contracts contain a sale provision, according to which, one partner makes a promise to sell his part of ownership to the other party periodically. As discussed earlier, jurists have opined that promises are enforceable, and a court of law can compel a promisor to fulfil his promise, especially in the context of commercial activities.[93]

Diminishing Musharakah as a financing technique, however, is a new type of contract, suggested by contemporary jurists keeping in mind the problems perceived while discussing the traditional Musharakah/Mudarabah principles in the broader economic perspective. This involves the concept of Musha'a, which means undivided ownership of the asset by the partners. All co-owners are owners of each and every part of the joint property on a pro rata basis and one partner cannot claim a specific part of the property leaving other part(s) for other partners. Further, it is allowed to lease Musha'a to another joint owner.

A DM arrangement may consist of two or three subcontracts, i.e. in the case of assets that could render any service, and hence they could be leased, there would be three subcontracts: partnership by ownership between two or more persons, leasing by one partner its share in the asset to the other partner(s), selling by one partner its share to the other partner(s); and in the case of partnership in trade of assets that do not involve leasing, it would involve two subcontracts: partnership and sale. This factually becomes a general partnership and all rules of Shirkahal 'Inan are applicable to it. One major point to be taken into consideration in this type of DM arrangement is that one partner cannot sell his part to the other partner at a pre-agreed price.[94]

All, two or three subcontracts are considered permissible by the jurists, particularly when the sale/lease contracts are stipulated among the partners, i.e. assets are sold/leased to the partners.[95] Thus, the combination of Shirkah and lease contracts does not create any Sharī'ah-related problem. Sale of a part by a partner to the other partner should be separate and independent from the Shirkah or leasing arrangement.

There is some difference of opinion regarding leasing out an undivided share to a third party. While Imams Malik, Shafi'e and Abu Yusuf allow it, Imams Abu Hanifa and Zufur disallow the letting out of the undivided share to any third party. As per the present practice

---

[92] Al-Kasani, 1993, **4**, p. 493.

[93] For details, see Usmani, 2000b, pp. 363–368.

[94] Usmani, 2000a, pp. 91, 92.

[95] Ibn-Qudama, 1367 AH, **6**, p. 137; for details see Usmani, 2000b, pp. 357–360; AAOIFI, 2004–5a, p. 215.

of Islamic financial institutions, DM is being used in such a manner that lease/sale is made to the co-partners, in respect of which there is no difference of opinion among the jurists.

We can infer from the contemporary juristic opinion that any arrangement in which three separate agreements of partnership, leasing and sale are made in such a way that they are not conditional upon one another and are separately enforceable, will be according to the principles of Sharī´ah and therefore Sharī´ah-compliant. However, if the three contracts are stipulated collectively, this is not approved by the jurists, as discussed in Chapter 5. Even the Hanbali jurists, who allow imposing some conditions in a sale contract, do not approve of a contract, the enforcement of which depends upon any other contract. The relationship among the parties in this arrangement is that of partners and lessor/lessee in the first instance and seller and buyer at the later stage. The sale has to be kept independent from the first part, comprising partnership and leasing.

Diminishing Musharakah can be conducted both in respect of partnership in ownership (Shirkatulmilk) and contractual partnership (Shirkatul'aqd). But some crucial differences between the two have to be taken into consideration to ensure Sharī´ah compliance:

1. In Diminishing Musharakah through contractual partnership, the ratio of profit distribution for each partner should be clearly determined, this may be disproportionate to the ratio of equity of both parties. This ratio can be changed with mutual agreement due to a change in the ratio of equity share of the parties. A loss would necessarily be allocated in accordance with the ratio of equity at the time when the loss is incurred. No partner can be given a lump sum amount out of the profits.[96]

   As regards partnership by ownership, the major objective of its forming is not profit-earning through business; therefore, the ratio of profit distribution need not be stipulated in this arrangement. Each partner will own both risk and reward proportionate to his share. As one partner can lease his part to the co-partner, he can get rental on the leased part. The lessee, who is owner of a part of the asset, will get the reward of his part by using the asset without paying any rent. As the lessee partner goes on purchasing the share of the financier partner, the rental goes on decreasing. Both parties will bear ownership-related expenses/liabilities and losses, if any in the case of sale, on a pro rata basis.

2. In Diminishing Musharakah through partnership by contract, the lessee partner can promise to buy periodically the share of the financier partner according to the market value or at a price to be agreed at the time of sale of units of the asset. It is not permitted to stipulate that the ownership units will be bought at a pre-agreed price or at their original or fair value, as this would constitute a guarantee of share capital of one partner by the other partner, which is prohibited by the Sharī´ah.

   In Diminishing Musharakah through partnership by ownership, one partner can purchase ownership units of the co-partner at a pre-agreed price. This is a crucial difference between the two, particularly in respect of Sharī´ah compliance of the procedure and the payment of price for transfer of ownership from the Islamic financial institutions to their clients. The IFIs that provide housing finance on the basis of DM in Shirkatulmilk generally take promise from the clients that they will purchase the banks' units of shares at pre-agreed prices, and this is permissible as per Sharī´ah rules.

Diminishing Musharakah in trade is conducted for the purpose of profit-earning; therefore, the price of units of the financial institution cannot be fixed in the promise to purchase by

---

[96] AAOIFI, 2004–5a, Standard on Musharakah, clauses 5/4, 5/5, 5/6.

the other partner (client) because it would practically mean that the client has guaranteed the principal invested by the financier with or without profit. Therefore, the financial institution either has to agree to sell the units of his ownership on the basis of valuation at the time of the sale of each unit, or allow the client to sell these units to anybody else at whatever price he can, but at the same time it would offer a specific price to the client, meaning thereby that if he finds a purchaser of that unit at a higher price, he may sell it to him, but if he wants to sell it to the financier, the latter will be agreeable to purchase it at the price fixed by him beforehand. However, this does not seem to be feasible as it does not serve the purpose of decreasing the equity in any business, as required under a Diminishing Musharakah arrangement. Therefore, Diminishing Musharakah is feasible only in respect of fixed or other assets that can be leased or given for use to the other partner.[97]

## 12.9   DIMINISHING MUSHARAKAH AS AN ISLAMIC MODE OF FINANCE

Diminishing Musharakah can be easily used for the purpose of financing fixed assets by Islamic banks. It includes house financing, auto financing, plant and machinery financing, factory/building financing and all other fixed asset financing. In the case of housing finance, for example, a joint ownership is created for the purpose of Diminishing Musharakah. The financier partner gives his undivided share on lease to the partner using the house. The client gives rent on the part of the financier and periodically purchases the units of the partner's ownership.

The modus operandi approved by Sharī´ah scholars is that three contracts are entered into separately, ensuring that each contract is independent of the other two contracts. The sequencing of contracts should be:

1. A contract between partners to create a joint ownership. The client partner makes a promise, before or after the lease agreement is finalized, to purchase the share of the financier partner.
2. The financing partner gives units of his share to the client on lease.
3. The client partner goes on purchasing the units of ownership of the financing partner as per his promise. Accordingly, the rent goes on decreasing.

Financing by a bank on the basis of Diminishing Musharakah can take different forms depending upon the assets involved. Some assets can be leased out, e.g. in the case of house financing and financing the purchase of plant and machinery. Assets of a commercial nature would not involve leasing.

### 12.9.1   Diminishing Musharakah in Trade

If leasing is not involved and there is a simple partnership in which two partners start a business, for example on a 40:60 basis, they can agree that the share units of one partner will be periodically sold to the other partner, who will keep on purchasing them on a gradual basis until the second party is out of the business. As this contract has been entered into for profit-earning by the partners and also does not involve leasing, like the case of a house or a vehicle, the price of share units cannot be fixed in the promise to sell. One partner may agree to sell the units on the basis of valuation of the business at the time of the purchase of each unit. Such valuation may be carried out in accordance with the recognized principles by experts, whose identity may be agreed upon between the parties when the promise is signed. At the time of purchase, the sale should be executed through offer and acceptance.

Although the entrepreneur partner in DM for trade has an inherent motivation to acquire full ownership by purchasing shares from the financier, the Sharī´ah experts are not inclined to make the purchase binding on him. According to Resolution No. 2 of the Jeddah-based OIC Fiqh Academy, and also research undertaken by the IRTI, the sale provision of the contract can be made binding only on the financier partner and the sale will be effected at the prices prevailing in the market at the time of actual sale. After creating joint ownership, the bank may sign a one-sided promise to sell different units of the share of its ownership periodically and may undertake that when the client purchases a unit of its share, the rent of the remaining units will be reduced accordingly. Thus, an Islamic bank will be making a binding promise to offer a specific part of its ownership of the project for sale on a specified future date for a price that will be determined at the time of actual sale. The entrepreneur partner may voluntarily buy the share of the financier at the prices prevailing at the time of sale in the stock market or at a price determined with the free consent of the parties.

### 12.9.2   Procedure and Documentation in Diminishing Musharakah

The following is the sequence of documentation in a typical Diminishing Musharakah arrangement, as being used by Islamic financial institutions for housing finance business on the basis of partnership by ownership:

1. Creation of joint ownership through a Musharakah agreement; the customer and the IFI become co-owners in a joint property. If legal title to the property is already with the customer, there can be an agreement to the effect that the IFI will acquire a certain share in the Musha'a property and this would involve a sale and lease-back arrangement.
2. Rent agreement. Both parties agree that the IFI will lease its undivided share to the client partner against a stipulated rental to be governed under the rules of Ijarah. This agreement is signed after the Musharakah agreement. It contains details about rent, the formula of its calculation and a schedule for the period of lease.
3. Undertaking to purchase units of the bank's share in the joint property. This is a unilateral promise binding on the promisor only. Either the client or the bank can make this promise. If the arrangement is based on Shirkatulmilk, it may contain a price schedule at which the client has to purchase the units from time to time. It also gives details about the situation if the client wants at any time, to purchase more shares than provided in the mutually agreed schedule. The arrangement also contains details about the nature of security/guarantee to be provided by the client. Normally it is the equitable mortgage of the financed property. The bank may require additional security to secure its interest, particularly in view of the financial position of the client.

Thus, the customer pays rent for the use of the bank's share in the property and goes on purchasing a part of the bank's share periodically until the ownership of the asset is transferred to him. The facility can be provided for buying a house, building a house, renovation of a house and for replacing interest-based housing loans with a Sharī´ah-compliant arrangement (balance transfer facility). Other fixed assets can also be financed through Diminishing Musharakah.

**Box 12.4:** Construction of a House on a Customer's Land or Renovation of a House

Construction of a house on land owned by the customer would involve purchase/sale and lease-back. Suppose the plot of land is worth one million dirhams and the customer needs 800 000 Drs from the Islamic bank. The bank would purchase a part of the land from the customer (say 8 units of 100 000 Drs each out of a total of ten units) to form a joint ownership on the basis of Shirkatulmilk. The customer would undertake that he would pay rent on the bank's part of ownership and would periodically purchase the share of the bank according to a pre-agreed schedule of price.

With the proceeds of the land (800 000 Drs that could be provided in four equal instalments), the client would construct the house; when the house was complete and habitable, the bank would lease its part of ownership to the client at the agreed rental. Up to one year, the client would pay only the rent on the bank's part of the house. Accordingly, the rent would not decrease during that period.

One year after the disbursement of the last instalment, the bank would start selling its units of ownership to the client as per the undertaking of the customer; rent would decrease with every rental paid, and ultimately the title of the house would transfer to the client. The period of one year has been suggested by the Sharī'ah scholars for sale of units by the bank to avoid buy-back (Bai' al 'Inah), which is prohibited.

Renovation of a house owned by the customer would also involve purchase/sale and lease-back. The client would sell, say, four units of his ownership to the bank to create a joint ownership. With the proceeds of the sale, the client would renovate the house or make alterations to it. The bank would start taking rent from the first month after disbursement of the first tranche because the customer is already living in the house. The process of the units' sale back to the client would start one year after the disbursement of the last tranche.

---

**Box 12.5:** Hypothetical Case Study on Housing Finance Through Diminishing Musharakah (Partnership by Ownership)

**Calculation of the monthly payment plan for home purchase:**

Cost of house: Drs or Ryls 1. 0 Mm

Bank financing: 80 %

Tenure: 10 years

Rental (return rate equivalent to) : 7 % p.a. (of investment)

Purpose: home purchase from the market

**Box 12.5:** (Continued)

**Key structure**

Monthly payment consists of unit purchase and rent components. Unit purchase will remain constant over the entire tenure. Rent is calculated based on the number of units outstanding. The rent component will decrease every month with the purchase of units.

*(Construction of a house on a plot of land already owned by the client, renovation/additions to a house owned by him or a balance transfer facility (BTF) for the payment of an interest-based mortgage loan on a client's house are subject to a different procedure, as discussed in the previous Box.)*

**Working**

Bank's share: Ryls. 800 000; full payment is made in one tranche

Client's share: Ryls. 200 000

No. of bank's units (equal to number of months): 120

Price per unit: 6666.67

(Principal/number of units)

Rent per unit (annual): 466.67

[(((outstanding investment * rate) / 12) for monthly rent]

| Month | Unit | Rent per month | Total | Units | Investment |
|---|---|---|---|---|---|
| 0 | — | — | — | 120 | 800 000.0 |
| 1 | 6666.67 | 4666.67 | 11 333.33 | 119 | 793 333.3 |
| 2 | 6666.67 | 4627.78 | 11 294.44 | 118 | 786 666.7 |
| 3 | 6666.67 | 4588.89 | 11 255.56 | 117 | 780 000.0 |
| 4 | 6666.67 | 4550.00 | 11 216.67 | 116 | 773 333.3 |
| 5 | 6666.67 | 4511.11 | 11 177.78 | 115 | 766 666.7 |
| 6 to 115 | xxxx | xxxx | xxxx | xxxx | xxxx |
| 116 | 6666.67 | 194.44 | 6861.11 | 4 | 26 666.7 |
| 117 | 6666.67 | 155.56 | 6822.22 | 3 | 20 000.0 |
| 118 | 6666.67 | 116.67 | 6783.33 | 2 | 13 333.3 |
| 119 | 6666.67 | 77.78 | 6744.44 | 1 | 6666.7 |
| 120 | 6666.67 | 38.89 | 6705.56 | — | 0.0 |

In all three above cases, i.e. the construction of a house, renovation of a house or purchase of a built house, if the client regularly pays the rental and periodically purchases the bank's share, the ownership is transferred to him. If he delays, the rental will not decrease and the bank's loss in terms of income will be far less than in the case of Murabaha or even simple leasing, as the customer will go on paying rental on the units owned by the bank.

The client can also purchase more than one unit if his cash flow allows him to do so. In this case, Islamic banks normally conduct a valuation of the house and share in the capital gain, if any, generally up to a prestipulated rate. For example, if the client intends to purchase five units at one time, the bank will conduct a valuation and will share the appreciation up to 3 or 4% on its part of the investment, giving the remainder to the client. Thus, Diminishing Musharakah on the basis of Shirkatul milk has a built-in element of risk mitigation. The rental rates to be taken by the banks can be fixed or floating; if floating, they should be subject to a proper "floor and cap" to avoid Gharar, which could render the transaction non-Sharī´ah-compliant.

## 12.10  SUMMARY AND CONCLUSION

We may summarize the basic principles of Shirkah in the following way:

1. Of the various kinds of Shirkah used in the books of Islamic jurisprudence, Shirkah al 'Inan is of more relevance to partnership business by banks and financial institutions. There is a consensus of the jurists that Shirkah is not only a legitimate contract in Islam but is also preferable over the modes based on trade and leasing. The term "Musharakah" introduced by contemporary Sharī´ah scholars also means joint commercial enterprise doing any economic activity by joint funds.[98]
2. Capital to be invested by the partners can be unequal and should preferably be in the nature of any prevalent currency. If it is in the shape of commodities, the market value should be determined with mutual consent to determine the share of each partner for sharing the profit or bearing the loss, if any. It may also be in the form of equal units representing currency, called shares in the case of perpetual Musharakah and certificates or Sukuk in the case of a redeemable partnership. The shares/Sukuk are negotiable and a shareholder can sell his shares to anyone in the market. Obtaining formal consent about the entry or exit of members into limited companies is not compulsory from an Islamic point of view.
3. Power of appropriation in the property and participation in the affairs of the Musharakah may be disproportionate to the capital invested by the partners.
4. In Musharakah (and also in Mudarabah), the ratio of profit distribution may differ from the ratio of investment, but the loss must be divided exactly in accordance with the ratio of capital invested by each of the partners.
5. It is not allowed to fix a lump sum amount of profit for any of the partners, or any rate of profit tied up with his investment.
6. Scholars have approved the concept of "projected profit", but this is subject to final settlement at the end of the term, meaning that any amount so drawn by any partner shall be treated as an "on-account payment" and will be adjusted to the actual profit he may deserve at the end of the term.
7. If all the partners agree to work for the joint venture, each one of them shall be treated as an agent of the other in all the matters of the business and any work done by one of them in the normal course of business shall be deemed to be authorized by all the partners. The partners may agree upon a condition that the management shall be carried out by one of them, and no other partner shall work for the Musharakah. In this case, the ratio of profit allocated to a sleeping partner shall not exceed the ratio of his investment.
8. In the case of running Shirkah business, the concept of "daily product" can be used for determining the share of each partner in the profit accrued.

---

[98] Usmani, 2000a, pp. 32, 33.

lusharakah or Mudarabah should never mean the advancing of money to get an ex ante return. It means participation in the business and sharing the actual results in the form of both profit and loss, subject to certain conditions.

10. A financier on the basis of Shirkah must share the loss incurred by the business to the extent of his financing.
11. The loss suffered by each partner must be exactly in the proportion of his investment.
12. The basis of profit-sharing has to be defined beforehand without any pre-emptive right to any of the parties.

Mudarabah is an essential mode for the establishment and operation of Islamic financial institutions. It serves as a basis of business to be conducted by combining funds and the expertise of different groups of people. For the assets side, however, Mudarabah is considered to be a very high-risk financing activity, mainly due to the moral hazard, adverse selection and lack of banks' expertise in project evaluation and related technical matters. Islamic banks may use Mudarabah, albeit with proper care and risk management, to finance the business of those who are capable to work, whether they are professionals like physicians or engineers or traders and craftsmen. It can also be used without much risk of loss in foreign trade financing.

Musharakah can be used for foreign and inland trade financing, project financing directly or through securitization.

Mudarabah Sukuk can be issued to mobilize funds and strengthen trading and industrial activities. Asset management companies can manage such funds for conducting business for their benefit, and also that of the Sukuk holders. This could generate higher rates of return for the investors relative to the return realizable on any interest-based investment. In the case of big projects, the IFIs may form a consortium to issue certificates to the public for subscription. Similarly, they can carry out work on infrastructure and socio-economic projects in coordination and partnership with engineering firms.

---

### Box 12.6: Accounting Treatment of Mudarabah (Financing Side)

**Recognition of Mudarabah capital at the time of contracting**

- recognize when paid to Mudarib or placed under his disposition;
- if capital is paid in instalments, each instalment is recognized when paid;
- presented as "Mudarabah financing". If capital is provided in the form of nonmonetary assets, it is reported as "nonmonetary assets".

**Measurement of Mudarabah capital at the time of contract**

- capital provided in cash is measured by the amount paid or amount placed under the disposition of the Mudarib;
- capital provided in kind is measured at fair value of the assets and any difference between the fair value and the book value is recognized as profit or loss;
- expenses incurred are not considered part of the Mudarabah capital, unless otherwise agreed by both parties.

**Measurement at the end of the financial period**

- apply the same measurement criteria as used at the time of contracting, however, any repayment made to the bank is to be deducted from the Mudarabah capital;
- any loss at the inception of work shall be borne by the Islamic bank and if the loss occurs after the inception of work, it shall not affect the measurement of Mudarabah capital;
- if the whole of the capital is lost without any misconduct or negligence of the Mudarib, the Mudarabah shall be terminated and the Islamic bank shall recognize it as loss;
- if the Mudarabah is terminated or liquidated and capital is not paid, it shall be recognized as a receivable due from the Mudarib.

**Recognition of the bank's share in profits or losses**

- profits or loss on Mudarabah transactions which commence and end during the same financial period are recognized at the time of liquidation (constructive or actual);
- the Islamic bank's share of profits on Mudarabah financing that continues for more than one financial period is recognized to the extent of profit distribution and the loss is deducted from the Mudarabah capital;
- share of profits is recognized as a receivable due from the Mudarib if he does not pay after liquidation or settlement of account is made;
- losses are recognized at the time of liquidation by reducing the Mudarabah capital.

---

## Box 12.7:   Accounting Treatment of Musharakah[99]

**Recognition of the bank's share in Musharakah capital at the time of the contract**

- recognized when it is paid to the partner or made available to him on account of Musharakah;
- presented as "Musharakah financing" in the financial statements.

**Measurement of the bank's share in Musharakah capital at the time of contracting**

- capital provided in cash is measured by the amount paid or made available to the partner on account of Musharakah;
- capital provided in kind is measured at fair value of the assets and any difference between the fair value and the book value is recognized as profit or loss;
- expenses incurred are not to be considered part of Musharakah capital, unless otherwise agreed by both parties.

---

[99] The author is grateful to Mr Omer Mustafa Ansari of Fords Rhodes Sidat Hyder & Co., Karachi for his help in respect of the accounting treatment in various modes of financing.

**Box 12.7:**   (Continued)

**Measurement at the end of the financial period**

- share in constant Musharakah capital is measured at historical cost;
- share in Diminishing Musharakah is measured at historical cost after deducting the share transferred to the partner. Such transfer is made by sale at fair value (in DM on Shirkah al 'Aqd). The difference between the historical cost and the fair value is recognized as profit or loss;
- if Diminishing Musharakah is liquidated before complete transfer is made to the partner, the difference between the book value and the recovered amount is recognized in the income statement of the bank;
- if Musharakah is terminated or liquidated, any amount that remains unpaid is recognized as a receivable due from the partner.

**Recognition of the Islamic bank's share in profits or losses**

- profits or loss on Musharakah transactions which commence and culminate during the same financial period are recognized at the time of (constructive) liquidation;
- the Islamic bank's share of profits on Musharakah financing that continues for more than one financial period is recognized to the extent of profit distribution and share of loss is deducted from the Musharakah capital;
- the treatment mentioned in the above point shall apply to a Diminishing Musharakah after taking into consideration the decline in the Islamic bank's share in Musharakah capital and its profits or loss;
- share of profits is recognized as a receivable due from the partner if he does not pay the Islamic bank's due share of profits after liquidation or settlement of account is made;
- loss incurred due to negligence or misconduct of the partner is recognized as a receivable due from the partner.

# 13
## Some Accessory Contracts

## 13.1  INTRODUCTION

Major contracts being used by Islamic financial institutions like Shirkah, Bai', Ijarah and similar contracts have been discussed separately in various chapters. However, there are some ancillary contracts that are used as part of the major contracts or could be used under various modes. Out of these, two contracts, namely Wakalah (agency) and Ju'alah (rendering a service against reward), are discussed in this chapter. Tawarruq (monetization or generating cash through purchase/sale activity) basically carries the concept of Murabaha in one way or the other, but it has taken the form of a separate mode that Islamic banks use along with some other major modes. Hence, it is also discussed in this chapter. Istijrar, a kind of repeat sale that could take place under some major modes, has been discussed briefly. Other subcontracts like Hawalah (assignment of debt), Kafalah (guarantee) and Bai' al Dayn (sale of debt) have been discussed in the relevant chapters.

## 13.2  WAKALAH (AGENCY)

The literal meaning of "Wakalah" is looking after, taking custody or application of skill or remedying on behalf of others. From this, the word "Tawkeel" is derived, which means to appoint someone to take charge of something, and also to delegate any job to any other person. Wakalah is also a responsibility. It is therefore necessary for a Wakil to discharge his responsibility in the way a trustee discharges his responsibility in the case of Amānah.

### 13.2.1  Types of Wakalah

- Wakil-bil-Kusoomah (to take up various disputes/cases on behalf of the principal);
- Wakil-bil-Taqazi al Dayn (receiving debt);
- Wakil-bil-Qabaza al Dayn (possession of debt);
- Wakil-bil-Bai' (agency for trading);
- Wakil-bil-Shira (agency for purchase).

Agency or delegated authority is proved by the texts of the Sharī'ah. The holy Prophet (pbuh) himself delegated the job of purchasing a goat for him to a Companion named 'Urwah al Barqi.[1] Similarly, the fourth Pious Caliph, Hadhrat Ali, and a number of other Companions (Gbpwth) delegated their business to others.

---

[1] Abu Daud, 1952, cf. Mansoori, 2005, p. 62.

The subject matter of agency or the act to be performed by the agent should be known/defined. If the agency is for the purchase of a thing, the genus, kind, quality and other necessary attributes of the commodity to be bought should be mentioned. Agency is not permissible in acts prohibited in the Sharī'ah or acts of disobedience such as theft, usurpation of property or conducting Riba-based business.

An act to be carried out by an agent should be one that admits representation. Hence, appointment of an agent for an act such as prayer, fasting, giving evidence or for taking an oath is not permissible, because these acts should be performed by the principal himself. An eyewitness to an incident, for instance, is required to give testimony himself. He is not allowed to delegate this task to another person. Some of the acts for which the agency contract can be invoked include sale and purchase, letting and hiring, borrowing and lending, assignment of debt, guarantee, pledge, gifts, bailment, taking and making payments, marriage and divorce, litigation and relinquishment, admission and acknowledgement of rights.

An agency contract may be specific or general. A bank, for example, may appoint an agent to purchase some kinds of goods as and when asked by it. This will be a general agency contract. If a bank asks an agent to sell his particular asset at a given price or as per its instruction, it will be a specific agency contract. Even in a general contract, the nature of job to be undertaken has to be clearly defined to avoid any disputes.

Delivery of the subject matter, claiming the price, exercise of the right of option of defect or inspection and returning goods in the case of reclaiming and similar rights and liabilities are attributed to the agent, who is responsible for making payment and receiving goods on behalf of the principal. He would demand the price from the purchaser in case of sale. The agent can be sued for not performing as per the agency agreement in the case of purchase or sale. However, there are certain contracts which are attributed explicitly to the principal, such as marriage, divorce and settlement of murder.

The agent must perform according to the instructions of the principal and exercise due care and skill. He cannot entrust the job to another person without the consent of the principal. He must also avoid conflicts of interest. Hence, for example, he cannot sell his own property to the principal without fully disclosing that it belongs to him. Agency could generate third party liabilities. Banks, while appointing an agent for the conduct of any business, should take care of this aspect to ensure that the agent performs the function in good faith and with due diligence, and the contract may contain a clause to make him liable in the case of negligence on his part.

An action performed by an agent on behalf of the principal will be deemed an action by the principal. According to the preferred juristic view, particularly of Shafi'is and Hanbalis, ownership of a commodity purchased by an agent for the principal will stand transferred from the seller to the principal, without first entering into the ownership of the agent.

Sometimes jobs are undertaken without the proper authority of the principal. Such an unauthorized person is termed Fuduli in Islamic jurisprudence. There are two opinions regarding the legal status of contracts concluded on behalf of another without proper authority. The preferred view is that these are valid subject to ratification by the principal.

A Wakalah contract comes to an end by mutual agreement, unilateral termination, discharging of obligation, destruction of the subject matter or death or loss of legal capacity.

A Wakalah contract is used by Islamic financial institutions in respect of almost all modes like Murabaha, Salam, Istisna'a, Ijarah, Diminishing Musharakah and activities like

L/C, payment and collection of bills, fund management and securitization. Wakalah may be both commutative and noncommutative. Islamic banks mostly do not pay a fee to their clients who purchase/sell goods on their behalf or perform other functions. However, banks normally charge fees for agency services rendered by them on behalf of their clients. Fund management on the basis of Wakalatul Istismār is one such example, wherein banks charge a fixed fee remitting all profits/losses to the investors. We discuss this briefly below.

### 13.2.2   Wakalatul Istismār

Islamic financial institutions can manage funds of investors on the basis of Wakalatul Istismār, meaning agency services for the management of the funds. For their services, banks can get a pre-agreed fee irrespective of the profit or loss on the relevant portfolio. This fee may be fixed in a lump sum or as a monthly or annual remuneration in percentage of the amount of investment or the net asset value of the fund. For example, it may be agreed that the management will get 2 % or 3 % of the net asset value of the fund at the end of every financial year.

However, it is necessary to determine any one of the aforesaid methods before the launch of the fund. The practical means of doing this would be to disclose in the prospectus of the fund the basis on which the fees of the management will be paid. It is generally presumed that whoever subscribes to the fund agrees with the terms mentioned in the prospectus. Therefore, the manner of paying the management fee will be taken as agreed upon by all the subscribers.

## 13.3   TAWARRUQ

Tawarruq means to buy on credit and sell at spot value with the objective of getting cash, meaning that the transaction is not the need of the buyer; he simply wants liquidity, which he gets by purchasing a commodity on credit and selling the same forthwith for cash. If he sells to any third party, it is acceptable from the Sharī'ah point of view, but if he sells to the person from whom he purchased on credit, it is not Sharī'ah compatible according to the majority view. Despite being a grey area, Tawarruq is being used by many Islamic banks for liquidity management and as a mode of financing, especially for personal financing and credit cards.

In the traditional books of Islamic jurisprudence, Tawarruq has been discussed mainly by the Hanbali and Shafi'e jurists; but they also differentiate it from Bai' al 'Inah. The difference between 'Inah and Tawarruq is that "Mutawarriq" (the person who acquires liquidity in this way) sells the commodity to a third party, while in 'Inah, the buyer resells it to the same seller from whom he had bought the commodity with a difference in the sale and purchase price.

The Hanbali and Shafi'e jurists generally allow Tawarruq. There are two versions reported from Imam Ahmad Ibn Hanbal about the permissibility of Tawarruq. The majority of the Hanbali jurists have preferred the version according to which Tawarruq is permissible. However, Ibn Taymiyah and Ibn Qayyim have held it as impermissible. Maliki jurists, who are very strict about 'Inah, do not see a major problem in Tawarruq. They consider it a way to avoid Riba.

Some Hanafi jurists of later days have held that Tawarruq is 'Inah, and hence abominable. But the majority of the Hanafi jurists have preferred the view of Ibnul-Hummam that 'Inah is restricted to a situation where the commodity is sold back to the person from whom it was purchased; if it is sold in the market, the transaction is valid and permissible. However, Qardal Hasan (lending money without interest) is more preferable. Thus, the preferred view in all the four schools of Islamic Fiqh is that Tawarruq is permissible. The AAOIFI has also taken up the view that if a commodity is sold back, either directly or indirectly (through any agent), to the original seller from whom it was purchased on a deferred payment basis, this will be invalid, while if the commodity is sold to a third party, it is acceptable in the Sharī´ah.

This is the position with regard to the original concept of Tawarruq, but the ruling changes if the transaction is infiltrated by some other elements. If a bank purchases a commodity having brisk market and sells the same to the Mutawarriq, who sells it in the market, there is no Sharī´ah problem. But, if the bank appoints the Mutawarriq its agent to purchase the commodity on its behalf and then to sell the same to himself, the transaction will not be valid, as the two transactions of purchase and sale are interdependent and the bank has not taken the possession and the business risk. However, if the bank appoints him as an agent only for the purchase of a commodity on behalf of the bank, then, once it is purchased, the bank itself sells it to him through a separate contract with proper offer and acceptance, the transaction is valid, but not advisable.

If a Mutawarriq appoints the bank his agent to sell a commodity that he would purchase from the bank for Tawarruq in the market and this agency is stipulated in the contract of sale as a condition, the transaction is not valid. However, if the agency was not a condition in the sale contract and has been effected after unconditional sale, the transaction is valid, but even then not advisable.

If Tawarruq is carried out through the national or international commodity exchange, wherein only brokers are doing some agency services and the goods always remain where they were without transfer of ownership from the seller to the buyer, it is vulnerable to violation of Sharī´ah rules one way or another, because a number of conditions of a valid sale may be lacking. Some Islamic banks are conducting Tawarruq by way of shares of joint stock companies, Ijarah Sukuk (of tangible assets and also of services) and even "bundles of assets", comprising real assets as well as cash and receivables (the real assets being in the majority in the bundle). Despite permissibility on legal grounds, use of such financing on an extensive level needs to be avoided. The Sharī´ah scholars and experts in Islamic finance advise that Tawarruq practice must be of limited use only for meeting unavoidable liquidity needs of the corporate sector. "For individual consumers it must be completely out of the Islamic banking practices," says Monzer Kahf, a renowned scholar of Islamic economics and finance.[2] Nejatullah Siddiqi has observed in this regard: "The client approaches the Islamic bank with a wish to have cash and a collateral and comes back with the desired cash after signing a number of papers".[3] This trend of wide and careless use of Tawarruq would create systemic risk for the nascent finance industry. However, if all the conditions of a valid sale are properly observed, the transaction may be valid, but even then its extensive use could be problematic.[4]

---

[2] Kahf, 2004.
[3] Siddiqi, 2006, pp. 15, 16.
[4] For further details, see Obaidullah, n.d., pp. 109–111; http://islamiccenter.kau.edu.sa/english/publications/Obaidullah/ifs/ifs.html.

### 13.3.1  Use of Tawarruq for Liquidity Management

Some Islamic banks use Tawarruq to place and obtain funds. It can give a fixed return to the banks and, hence, it is widely used as Commodity Murabaha or Shares Murabaha in the Middle East. Acceptable Tawarruq arrangements can be executed in the following manner: one bank (in need of funds) and another bank (intends to place funds) select any commodity/stocks which are liquid in nature (such as blue chip stocks); the surplus bank purchases the commodity on cash payment from the market; the deficit bank purchases it from the surplus bank on credit (Murabaha) and after taking delivery, sells it in the market at spot price.

The Tawarruq process seems to be very simple. However, extreme care should be taken while undertaking such transactions and it should be ensured that the transaction does not become a mere exchange of papers between two brokers and one or two banks. Islamic banks need to understand that Tawarruq arrangements should be used in extreme cases where no option is available to avoid interest. Widespread use of such products is harmful to the Islamic banking industry in the long run. Sharī'ah boards need to strictly monitor all Tawarruq-based transactions.

# 13.4  JU'ALAH

Ju'alah is a contract in which one party (the Jā'il) undertakes to give a specific reward (the Jua'l) to anyone who may be able to realize a specific or uncertain required result, for example, finding a stolen car. Ju'alah is permissible on the authority of the Holy Qur'ān and the Sunnah. There is reference in Surah Yousuf to the announcement about the lost beaker of the King that the person who would find the beaker of the King would be given reward of a camel load grain.[5] As regards the Sunnah, the holy Prophet (pbuh) approved a deal by some Companions who stipulated that if the Chief of the tribe was cured, they would be given compensation for that. Although some jurists restrict Ju'alah to a reward for the return of a runaway slave, the majority of them consider it permissible for a number of activities.

The determination of the required end result of the transaction is considered to be sufficient to make it permissible. Ju'alah is a relevant and useful transaction in events that cannot be accomplished through Ijarah, such as bringing back a lost property from an uncertain location, because the Ijarah contract requires that the work must be specified. Accordingly, Ju'alah may be used by Islamic banks for recovery of overdue debts and certain other services whereby the subject of the required work cannot be minutely specified.

### 13.4.1  Parties to Ju'alah

The two parties of Ju'alah are the offeror and the worker; the former offers specified compensation to anyone (the worker) who has to realize a determined result in a known or unknown period. The worker may be any specified person(s) or the general public. In this respect also, it is different from Ijarah. Realization of the end result is necessary in Ju'alah for payment of the compensation to the worker(s). In other words, if the worker, despite his effort, is unable to realize the objective, he will not be entitled to any compensation for

---

[5] Holy Qur'ān, 10: 70–72.

his effort or time spent. Therefore, Ju'alah is not affected by the uncertainty with respect to the subject matter or the work to be done. This is why it is suitable for activities for which Ijarah is not.

It is not a condition of Ju'alah that the worker be specified and it is sufficient that an offer is issued to the general public, in response to which any person can undertake the work himself or with the help of others. However, if any worker is specified, then he himself will have to undertake the work or he can involve others with the express consent of the offeror. Ju'alah is similar to agency, in which seeking help from others is valid.

Ju'alah *per se* is not a binding contract. Parties in a Ju'alah contract are entitled to terminate the contract unilaterally. However, when the worker commences the work, it becomes binding and if the offeror revokes in between, he will have to give a reasonable wage to the worker. The basis for the entitlement of the worker to receive reasonable wages when the contract is revoked after commencement of work is that the work done by the worker is legally valid and loss is not to be caused to him. When the parties undertake not to terminate the contract within a specified period, they must observe such an undertaking. If the worker himself revokes the contract after commencing the work, he has no claim against the offeror, unless they had agreed to the contrary.

The worker is considered a trustee as to the property of the offeror in his possession. As such, he is not liable for any loss except in the case of negligence, misconduct or violation of the stipulated conditions.

### 13.4.2  Subject Matter of Ju'alah and Reward

The subject matter of Ju'alah is the work required to be done and the compensation agreed for the work. As Ju'alah is a contract of exchange, it is necessary to indicate a task and the reward. The task should not be a legal or an employment obligation upon the worker and must involve some effort. The reward should be known and valuable, i.e. is permissible consideration, and deliverable when required, so as to avoid any uncertainty when the result is realized. The reward can also be a certain portion of the realized result.

If the work to be realized is determined, a Ju'alah contract is valid, despite uncertainty about the amount of work to be put in by the worker and the possibility of realization of the result. Ju'alah can be used for undertaking various activities like extraction of minerals, finding any lost asset or property, collection of debts, getting any information for the benefit of the offeror, such as presenting a report on any subject or the project or undertaking any scientific invention, etc.

For example, governments may ask some firms for extraction of minerals with the condition that a specified amount of money will be given only to those who find any agreed-upon mineral with specified features. Ju'alah can also be used for collection of due but defaulted debts, where the entitlement to compensation is contingent upon collection of agreed upon-debts/receivables. Compensation in this case can also be related to the amount of realized debts on a proportionate basis.

For innovations, scientific discoveries and designs such as trademarks, the entitlement to compensation is contingent upon realization of the discovery or the accomplishment of the stipulated job.

If Ju'alah is used for brokerage activities, the entitlement to compensation will be contingent upon completion or execution of the contract for which the brokerage service has been sought.

An offeror can specify a time for accomplishment of a job, after which the worker will not be entitled to any reward except any stipulation or adjustment otherwise. For example, parties can agree that if work on the job is at an advanced stage but remains incomplete due to any genuine problem, the completion time may be increased with mutual consent.

### 13.4.3   Execution of a Ju'alah Contract

Ju'alah can be concluded by an open or informal offer to the public. In this case, any person who hears or receives the offer and is interested to do the job may do so, either himself or through the assistance of another person. However, if a Ju'alah contract is concluded with a specified worker, such a worker is obliged to perform the work himself.

Conclusion of a Ju'alah contract does not require a counter acceptance by another party (as is required in Ijarah), because the requirement of counter acceptance in Ju'alah is practically unattainable, except when it is concluded with a specific worker who is obliged to perform the work himself.

As against Ijarah/Ujrah, the claim to the reward is not enforceable until the completion of the required work. (In Ujrah, the worker who had agreed to work for a stipulated time is entitled to a wage if he has worked for the settled time, irrespective of the work being completed or not.) However, the worker is entitled to the reward prior to the completion of the work in the following situations:

1. When it is found that the worker has worked to realize a result in respect of a property that does not belong to the offeror and a legal decision to that effect has been issued.
2. When an accident that was not due to the negligence or misconduct of the worker causes impairment of the value of the subject matter of the contract; here, the worker is entitled to the full reward.

The worker is not entitled to a reward if Ju'alah is terminated unilaterally by either party before the commencement of work. However, when the contract is terminated by the offeror after the work is commenced, the former is obliged to pay to the worker the common market remuneration.

### 13.4.4   Parallel Ju'alah Contracts

A bank, after taking work, can get it done by others on the basis of a Parallel Ju'alah. The two contracts will be independent of each other. The bank may play the role of the worker by signing a Ju'alah contract. It may carry out the work itself or through another parallel contract with a third party, provided the first Ju'alah contract does not require it to do the work itself.

It is also possible for the bank to play the role of the offeror for performance, irrespective of whether it needs the work for its own benefit or for the fulfilment of its obligation in a Parallel Ju'alah contract, taking into account that the two contracts remain independent.

### 13.4.5   Practical Process in Ju'alah by Islamic Banks

Ju'alah can be used by Islamic banks for a number of services, directly or through a Parallel Ju'alah contract with the following process (see Figure 13.1):

1. The customer negotiates with the bank for performance of uncertain work in a specified time for an agreed reward.

2. The bank agrees to perform the work after conducting a cost versus benefit analysis, and a Ju'alah contract is entered into between the bank and the customer.
3. The bank finds a worker with the expertise to perform such uncertain work on his behalf and a Parallel Ju'alah contract is made with him.
4. The work is completed by the worker and an agreed wage or reward is paid to him by the bank.
5. The bank collects its reward from the customer with whom the initial Ju'alah contract had been entered into.

Similarly, banks can take services from others on the basis of Ju'alah. Recovery of nonperforming debts is one such example.

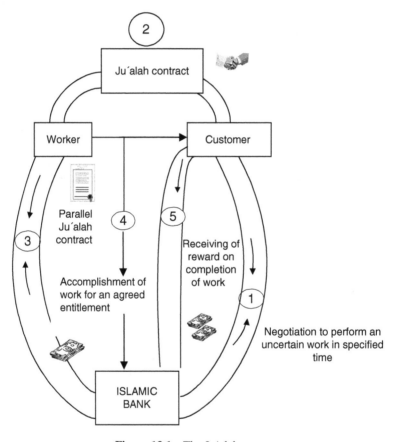

**Figure 13.1**   The Ju'alah process

### 13.4.6   Some Islamic Financial Products Based on Ju'alah

*Collection of Debts*

Ju'alah contracts can be used for collecting due debts where the entitlement to the reward is related to realization of all or part of the debt. For example, a Ju'alah contract for recovery of debt is entered into between "A Bank" and "B Ltd". The contract provides for the reward as a percentage of the amount collected on the basis of Ju'alah. The reward can also be paid in advance in full or in part, before completion of the work. However, in such a case, the worker shall not be absolutely entitled to reward until the required result is realized and the payment shall be made "on account" to him.

### Securing Permissible Financing Facility

Ju'alah contracts can be used to secure permissible financing, in which a worker is required to do some form of service, like preparing of feasibility, that will make the bank agree to provide the facility to the offeror.

### Brokerage

Ju'alah contracts may also be used in brokerage activities, where entitlement to reward is attached to the signing of a contract which is intermediated by the broker.

## 13.5   BAI' AL ISTIJRAR (SUPPLY CONTRACT)

Istijrar is not a specific mode; it is rather a repeat sale/purchase arrangement of normal sale in which a seller agrees to sell various amounts/units of a commodity from time to time. The seller may also deliver the commodity agreed upon once in a number of consignments and the price may be determined in advance, with every consignment or after the delivery of all consignments.

The terms and conditions of repeat sale may be of any normal cash or credit sale. An agreement may take place between the buyer and the supplier, whereby the supplier agrees to supply a particular product on an ongoing basis, for example monthly, at an agreed price and on the basis of an agreed mode of payment.

This is a modus operandi by which a master agreement is signed for financing on an ongoing basis under any suitable normal modes. As it is a normal day-to-day business, Sharī'ah scholars give some relaxation on the matter of fixation and payment of price if the arrangement does not involve Gharar.[6] Such types of arrangement take place between wholesalers and retailers. Normally, the seller goes on delivering specified goods at the price known to the buyer and the buyer makes payment on a monthly basis or as agreed between them. A supplier of bread may go on supplying bread to a retailer for a month and may take payment once after the month.

However, if any formal or informal contracts take place on the basis of any specific mode, like Murabaha or Salam, their conditions and Sharī'ah essentials have to be fulfilled. In the case of Murabaha, for example, separate offer and acceptance would be needed for every consignment, based upon requisition of the client.

---

[6] Obaidullah, n.d., pp. 101, 177.

# 14

## Application of the System: Financing Principles and Practices

### 14.1  INTRODUCTION

By now we have discussed the philosophy and features of Islamic finance, given an overview of the products and financial services possible in the Islamic framework and also the major modes that form the basis of Islamic financial products. Direct or indirect financial intermediation by banking or non-banking institutions involves mobilization of resources from the surplus units in an economy and their supply to the deficit units. The deposits side of banks has been discussed in the necessary detail in Chapters 8 and 12. Some areas of financing by Islamic banks have also been discussed in chapters on the basic modes; but the investments or financing side needs detailed discussion in terms of the principles underlying prudent Sharī´ah-compliant investment practices and some specific areas of financing, enabling readers to fully understand the functioning of Islamic banking and finance. In the present chapter we shall discuss the principles governing Islamic financing and how these can be implemented for proper functioning of the system.

Prudent financing requires vigorous product development and implementation along with prudence, proper risk management and Sharī´ah compliance. It is pertinent to observe that "money earning money" does not fit into the Islamic structure; money has to be invested in goods that may yield profit on the basis of risk/liability-taking and value addition. Islamic banks have to conduct business in a win–win scenario, just like any other business, while avoiding non-Sharī´ah compliant elements like interest, Gharar, gambling and other unethical practices. For this purpose, they have to design instruments and diversified investment portfolios that may generate profit with sufficient liquidity to fulfil the expectations and demands of the depositors. To maximize profits, they need to look for investments that yield the highest return, minimize risks and provide adequate liquidity, albeit keeping in mind the business ethics prescribed by the Sharī´ah.

The Islamic banking and finance industry is facing a number of challenges. The biggest challenge is to develop products of investment and financing which not only are in accordance with the Sharī´ah principles but also meet the ever-growing and changing needs of trade, business and industry, both in the private and public sectors. Only this way can they meet the challenge of confidence-building and enhancing the integrity of Islamic financial institutions.

Innovation is the most critical success factor in the current financial era. A Sharī´ah inspired and compliant product innovation process is different from the conventional product development process, as it has to follow the additional parameters of conformity with Sharī´ah tenets. It requires common efforts of the Sharī´ah scholars and the bankers.

## 14.2   PRODUCT DEVELOPMENT

Product development means creating business, suggesting means to it, keeping in mind the realities and business prospects for the future. Product development with reference to Islamic finance refers to the process of developing assets, through innovation and research, in the form of products and services to cater to the customers' demands in the most suitable way within the parameters of Sharī´ah and the governing regulatory and legal boundaries. It also includes re-engineering of existing products in accordance with Islamic economic principles and the changing requirements of businesses. It helps banks to create more business opportunities and provides a competitive advantage over other market players. Effective product development creates synergy between the customers and the bank and thus assists the bank in better understanding the needs of its customers. A satisfied customer is often a repeat customer and tends to enhance the credibility of the bank.

### 14.2.1   Procedure for Product Development

Product development requires assessment of need, generation of ideas, discussion with the Sharī´ah advisor/board for deciding detailed procedures for the operation and implementation of the product, development of the procedures (preparation of an operational manual for guidance of staff members) and the final approval by the Sharī´ah department of the bank. All possible risks have to be carefully analysed and risk mitigants devised to manage the risks. The Risk Management Division should also be involved to take into account the operational, asset-related and credit risks, accounting, taxation, regulatory and legal issues at the stage of product development. Deciding factors in this regard are: market survey; Sharī´ah compliance (in terms of mode, nature of assets involved, process and documentation); risk profile of depositors; cash flow of clients on the assets side; risk mitigation measures; legal matters and managing mismatch – liquidity versus profitability.

The product manual has to be discussed with the operations staff to ensure the smooth operation of the product in accordance with recognized procedures.

IT support is an integral part of today's business and needs to be properly worked out.

Training of marketing and operational personnel is necessary before launching and implementing the product. They must know the salient features of the product and, more specifically, its advantages over other available products in the market.

Launching the product is the start of another process, i.e. revision and modification of the product's features. In the light of the feedback, the product features may be modified to cater to the customers' requirements in a more effective manner.

A product may involve more than one mode to cater to the needs of the business in a Sharī´ah-compliant and efficient manner. For example, a housing finance product based on Diminishing Musharakah may comprise the concepts of Shirkah, Ijarah, Istisna‘a and Wakalah. Product developers have to observe the rules of all the related modes.

## 14.3   THE NATURE OF FINANCIAL SERVICES/BUSINESS

The major players in the finance industry include Islamic commercial banks, Islamic investment banks and other non-banking Islamic financial institutions, Islamic funds and unit trusts, equity and debt market players, pilgrimage funds and other cooperative institutions and Takaful companies. The regulatory framework for these institutions is different in different countries. While banks and non-banking institutions like investment banks are managed mostly by the central banks, equity and debt market businesses, funds, unit trusts, venture capital, etc. are governed by the Securities and Exchange Commissions in respective jurisdictions. But there may be some slight differences in regulatory set-up in various jurisdictions.

Islamic financial institutions (IFIs) obtain funds from a number of sources, which include: shareholders' equity, customers' general or investment deposits, inter-bank borrowings and, in some cases, the central banks. The bases for mobilization of funds are Mudarabah and Wakalatul Istismār (agency). Unrestricted or restricted investment deposits are based on the principle of Shirkah, while current accounts are normally kept as loans and are not entitled to any return.

### 14.3.1 Management of Deposit Pools and Investments

For the purpose of investment of funds, IFIs maintain common and separate pools or general and individual portfolios. The volume of investment deposits determines the banks' investment strategies. If depositors are risk-averse, banks should also be risk-averse, investing in less risky modes and avenues. Keeping in mind the depositors' risk profiles, profitability and liquidity, they should invest through PLS modes in high-risk ventures and through debt-creating modes in low-risk investments. They should also deploy funds in financial markets and make fee-based earnings through investment management and services.

The financing assets of Islamic banks are grouped into different investment pools with respect to the source of funds. The funds and financing assets can be allocated to the following investment pools:

- general deposit pools (domestic or foreign currencies);
- central bank's refinance scheme pools (like the Islamic export refinance scheme of the State Bank of Pakistan);
- treasury/financial institutions pool;
- equity pool;
- specific customers' pools.

The above pools are managed at the Head Offices or the Area Offices of the banks. The internal auditor and/or Sharī´ah advisor have to take the following steps to ensure the Sharī´ah compliance of deposit management with respect to investments by an Islamic bank:

- Distinguish between various kinds of deposits offered by the bank under various schemes and to see that proper ratios for sharing profits/losses have been given and weightages assigned based on the tenors of deposits and disclosed to the depositors; assigning different weightages on the basis of size of accounts of the same tenor, although permissible with proper disclosure to all depositors, has to be generally discouraged, as it may lead to favouritism and injustice. It should also be ensured that the profit is allocated using the concept of daily product and the weightages system.
- Ensure that the bank has not assured any fixed return to any individuals or group of depositors; if any projected rates have been quoted, the same must be subject to

adjustments on the basis of actual performance of the relevant general or restricted pools of deposits. For example, an Islamic bank can tell any corporate client that it will invest its deposit in Ijarah and Murabaha activities, upon which it will be earning fixed return/rentals. But as there could be some defaults, and hence a loss of cost of funds to the bank, and the bank may also have to incur some ownership-related expenses in leases, it might not be possible to give any pre-fixed return; Sharī´ah auditors should ensure that all such issues have been properly taken care of in respect of all pools maintained by the bank. In the case of large numbers of pools, they may take up a sampling method. They may like to obtain the bank's correspondence with high-valued accounts to ensure that no fixed return is committed with them.

- Auditors may also select a sample of transactions booked under various pools and obtain their respective agreements to check that the documentation and agreements approved for various activities have been used or there are some deviations.
- It must also be ensured that the bank is performing its fiduciary responsibility as a Mudarib and Rabbul-māl in cases where the deposits are kept on a Shirkah basis and agency-related responsibilities in cases where deposits are based on a Wakalatul Istismār basis. Any remunerative deposits should not be taken as loans by the bank.
- If the bank's own funds are also invested with those of the depositors in various pools, it should be ensured that the profits earned during the period have been distributed between the bank and depositors and among the depositors as per the agreed terms. After the distribution of the profit is made between the bank and the pools, the bank can donate a part of its own profit to any pool, provided it is not pre-agreed with the depositors/pool members.

### 14.3.2  Selection of the Mode for Financing

The deployment of funds is still a major issue for IFIs as they do not have vanilla products available for meeting the needs of their customers. Islamic banks need to focus on the modes which best suit the requirements of the customers. Once a customer approaches the bank, they need to evaluate his requirements and offer the best possible product. Using Murabaha or Ijarah for every kind of need is neither feasible nor advisable.

For example, Murabaha is not the right mode to provide financing for the purchase of sugar cane. Similarly, it may not be feasible for housing or other longer term investments in economies with high rates of inflation. Ijarah may not be feasible for projects entailing asset, market and counterparty risks, particularly for longer term project financing. In addition, Murabaha and Ijarah may not give better profit margins for the banks. Therefore, Islamic banks need to evaluate the flexibilities available in other modes of finance. Diversification is the best strategy for any bank – Islamic or conventional. It helps them in providing better customer service and earning better profit margins. A quick overview of the basic business features of Islamic modes of finance is given below:

- Murabaha: Islamic banks purchase the goods and sell them on a profit margin; banks have to take ownership-related risks until the goods are sold to the customer; the asset risk is transferred to the client upon execution of Murabaha; there is less risk and a fixed return; normally for short-term financing.

- Ijarah: Islamic banks purchase nonconsumable assets and give them on lease, getting risk and reward of the ownership of the assets; conducive to the formation of fixed assets and medium- and long-term investments; the bank is an "accumulator" (if it keeps the assets in its ownership) or "distributor" (if it transfers the ownership and risks through securitization); return can be fixed or floating but asset-related risks remain with the bank until the termination of Ijarah. Ijarah is most suitable for financing the public sector and big corporations, provided they have unencumbered useable assets, and this is possible through the issuance of Ijarah certificates and Sukuk.
- Salam: a forward sale with prepayment in full; fulfils the seller's needs by providing him funds that he may use anywhere and offers the buyer a profitable business asset. It has vast potential, particularly in agriculture, agro-based industries and financing of overhead expenses of trade and industry; can be used for short- and, in selected cases, for medium-term financing.
- Istisna'a: also a forward sale with an order to manufacture or construct an asset with given specifications. It has the flexibility of payment of price, which can be immediate, deferred or in instalments. As manufacturing or construction also depends on the personal effort and commitment of the seller/manufacturer, Istisna'a has an additional flexibility for controlling any delay in delivery of the asset by the seller.
- Musharakah/Mudarabah: particularly suitable for consignment-based trade transactions, for short-, medium- and long-term project financing, import financing, preshipment export financing and working capital financing. Project financing can be conducted under Musharakah through the issuance of TFCs or Sukuk.
- Diminishing Musharakah: for financing of fixed assets like houses, motor vehicles, machinery, etc. In particular, it is suitable for financing the purchase, construction and renovation of houses and commercial buildings. It may also involve "sale and lease-back" arrangements in cases where the property is already in the ownership of the customer.

**Box 14.1:**   Salient Features of Major Modes of Financing

| Features | Diminishing Musharakah | Ijarah | Murabaha |
|---|---|---|---|
| Period | Long-term | Long-term | Short/long-term |
| Rate | Fixed/variable | Fixed/variable | Fixed |
| Prepayment allowed | Yes | Yes | Not allowed as a system |
| Risk of the asset | Joint | Financier | Financier/customer |
| Uses | Nonconsumable assets | Nonconsumable assets | Any Halal assets |
| Late payments | Controllable | Controllable | Loss to the bank |

**Box 14.1:**   (Continued)

| Features | Salam | Istisna'a | Musharakah/ Mudarabah |
|---|---|---|---|
| Period | Short-term | Short/long-term | Short/long-term |
| Rate | Fixed | Fixed | Variable |
| Prepayment allowed | No | May be structured | Yes |
| Risk of the asset | Financier/customer | Customer/financier | Joint |
| Uses | Salam compatible | Assets to be manufactured | Any Halal business |
| Late payments | Loss to the bank | Controllable | No issue |

**Box 14.2:**   Example of Using Salam and Murabaha Combined

An Islamic bank can purchase cotton on the basis of Salam from growers while operating in the agricultural finance sector. In order to sell the cotton, it can take promise from a textile mill that it will purchase the cotton against an agreed price. Once the cotton is ready for delivery, the bank may appoint the textile mill its agent to take delivery of the cotton from the grower. When the mill informs the bank that it has taken delivery, the bank may sell the same to the mill (the promisor) for the already agreed price under a Murabaha transaction.

The product is beneficial to the farmer as he gets cash for the future produce and manages the risk of a fall in price or his inability to market the cotton at the harvest time.

The product is beneficial to the bank for the following reasons: funds are deployed for an extended tenure, with exposure on two different customers in different sectors; thus, risk is minimized. In a Salam transaction, a bank may end up with inventory, which creates problems for the bank. However, under the proposed structure, all problems related to inventory will be resolved. If structured properly, the bank can earn a better margin on the transaction.

The product is also beneficial to the textile mill as the mill can shield itself from price fluctuation in the cotton season. It is a hedging mechanism for the mill.

### 14.3.3   Tenor of Financing

Analysis of the cash flow of the customer is extremely important in Islamic banking for deciding the tenor of financing for any client. In conventional banking, bankers and customers focus on interest rates and obtain financing even in scenarios where the cash flows of the project mismatch with the repayment capacity. The customers believe that they will manage it through rollovers and other related facilities. Although this approach is not considered prudent, even according to the rules of conventional finance, it can work in individual cases.

It is, on the other hand, suicidal in Islamic finance, mainly because an Islamic bank cannot claim any liquidated damages against the loss of the cost of funds in cases of default. If the situation is not managed properly, the bank will face problems in payments by its customers. Therefore, the tenor of any financing facility must be determined carefully in consultation with the customer.

### 14.3.4  Sharī'ah Compliance and Internal Sharī'ah Controls

Ensuring Sharī'ah compliance is the most important job in Islamic banking. Any failure in this regard may cause systemic risk for Islamic banking and income loss for any bank. Audit should be conducted with regular intervals to ensure Sharī'ah compliance. Internal auditors have to identify gaps in the process of financing and the operations department has to refine and amend the products and the procedures. Sharī'ah compliance guidelines should be issued in specific formats with each product programme so that the Sharī'ah audit may be carried out systematically. The product developers and implementers should adopt the policy of learning and improving from mistakes. Another purpose of the audit should be the education of staff members.

Sharī'ah boards of the banks have to play a crucial role in this regard. They should be in a position to offer recommendations as to how to amend the proposed structure of any product in order to make it feasible and Sharī'ah-compatible. They should finalize the model documents and agreements for the modes of financing and try to ensure that banks follow them in all their transactions, in letter and spirit. Whenever a situation arises where there are difficulties in applying any of the formats, the management should bring the problem to the notice of its Sharī'ah board to resolve the related issues.

The personnel of Islamic banks have often been trained in conventional banking and are not familiar with Islamic banking. As Islamic banking is still in a process of evolution, even the senior management may not be experienced or up to date in the latest applications of the Sharī'ah principles. Quite unintentionally, they may fail to carry out their Sharī'ah board's resolutions. For this reason, the board may like to inspect the bank's transactions in detail and give advice as to where they could be improved for compatibility with the Islamic principles. This would not only ensure that the bank is operating in accordance with Islamic law, but would also give the Sharī'ah board itself an opportunity of gaining a deeper insight into the practical problems that arise. In addition, both the staff and the management would be given an opportunity to enhance their understanding and competence.

Similarly, a large part of Islamic banks' assets may comprise investments in equities/capital markets. Sharī'ah boards must ensure the compliance of criteria for Islamic banks' investments in shares, equities, Sukuk and other avenues of business. This aspect of Sharī'ah control should include prohibition of investment in companies with unacceptable business lines, which produce prohibited products and provide prohibited services like:

- alcoholic beverages and tobacco products;
- grocery stores dealing in Haram goods;
- restaurants, casinos and hotels with bars for prohibited activities;
- amusement and recreational services likely to involve indecent activities;
- financial institutions which deal with interest;
- companies of which:

— the interest income ratio is more than (5) %;
— the debt ratio (leverage) is more than (10–33) %;
— total illiquid assets are less than 10–33 % of its total assets.

If investment is made in the equity of such companies, Haram or interest-related income will have to be given to charity and the Sharī´ah boards must ensure its credit to the Charity Account.

The major functions of a Sharī´ah supervisory board in the light of the AAOIFI's Sharī´ah Standard are given in the appendix to this chapter.

*Sharī´ah Controls in Respect of Various Modes*

In order to ensure Sharī´ah compliance, Sharī´ah boards should specify certain controls for modes which respective banks are using, particularly in respect of commonly used products like Murabaha and Ijarah, which are susceptible to being used as back doors to interest. Murabaha in various goods may involve different aspects needing close monitoring, for example, Murabaha in perishable goods, shares of joint stock companies, particularly when the transactions involve dual side agency agreements (the client is appointed agent to purchase the asset on behalf of the bank and also given funds for payment to the supplier), Tawarruq and other by-products of major Islamic modes. We outline internal controls in respect of some commonly used modes below.

**Murabaha – Internal Sharī´ah Controls**

1. The Internal Control Department/Sharī´ah Board should ensure that accounting in Murabaha is made similar to that of a trade transaction instead of a financial transaction. In this respect, the AAOIFI's Accounting Standard on Murabaha may be consulted or there could be adaptation keeping in mind the international accounting standards and the local business practices. Some banks record only the disbursement of the total amount including mark-up. This is against the substance of Sharī´ah-compliant Murabaha.
2. To ensure that banks are not involved in rollover of Murabaha transactions, strict internal controls should be applied. The price of the goods cannot be changed if the customer does not pay on time. Accordingly, there is no prospect for a rollover of Murabaha transactions. Nevertheless, it should also be kept in mind that a master Murabaha facility that a bank approves for a client as MoU, entails multiple Murabaha transactions, and if it is necessary to extend credit, a new Murabaha should be initiated against new goods with a fresh offer and acceptance and complete process of trade. However, some banks resort to arrangements in which they disburse the amount payable by their client against a new but fictitious Murabaha (only book entries), credit the amount to the client's account and then debit his account against the old Murabaha. In some cases, banks might not be making even the book entry for the new Murabaha and there might be simple rollover of the previous Murabaha, including the previous receivables plus mark-up for the new term. Sharī´ah boards will have to restrict the banks from such operations. Return on such rollovers must go to the Charity Account.
3. The client who is being paid an amount for purchase of the commodity on behalf of the bank may not purchase the commodity for a long time and use the funds for arbitrage or any other asset that might not be permissible, e.g. for purchase of interest-based securities or shares in interest-based companies. Therefore, it has to be ensured that the client

purchases the commodity within a given maximum time and gives declaration to the bank. It may also be indicated in the agency agreement that the given funds are an Amānah and their use for any unauthorized purpose is not allowed by Sharī'ah. The Sharī'ah board may also advise the bank to make payment directly to the supplier.

4. It also has to be ensured that the goods purchased by the client in Murabaha to Purchase Orderer exist at the time of offer and acceptance – i.e. have not been consumed by the client in his production cycle. For this purpose, the bank should identify the time within which declaration has to be made by the client in respect of various goods.

5. Although legal title is not necessary from a Sharī'ah point of view and simple transfer of ownership transfers the risk and reward to the buyer, for genuine Murabaha, it is recommended that the title of ownership is transferred to the bank in the form of any documentary evidence. But banks, in order to avoid payment of transfer charges, purchase the goods in the name of the client; thus, they do not become owner of the goods in any way. A Sharī'ah board must ensure that not only is the title of goods in the name of the bank at the time of sale to the client, but also the bank retains all risks and rewards related to ownership until the goods are sold to the client. This reduces the chances of making the Murabaha a back door to interest.

6. It must also be ensured that all documentation requirements, particularly if the client is also an agent of the bank, are being fulfilled properly. The board should not allow any change in the format of the master Murabaha agreement without its prior approval.

7. Mark-up should be charged from the time when the bank sells the commodity on credit to the client and not from the date of disbursement of funds to the supplier or to the client (as agent). Any part of the mark-up should not be referable to the intervening period, i.e. between disbursement and declaration/acceptance by the bank. Hence, Islamic banks should calculate their Murabaha profit from the date they sell the commodity to the client. However, they may apply any rate in consultation with the customers.

8. A Sharī'ah board should put in place effective controls to ensure that banks do not resort to buy-back techniques in the case of Murabaha transactions. The companies from which goods are being purchased for sale on a Murabaha basis should not be the sister concerns of the customer's company, i.e. the customer's share in ownership of such companies should not be more than 50 %.

9. Banks, upon financing, normally take demand promissory notes (DP notes) from the client. As Islamic banks' financing is based on the underlying trading/leasing contracts, they should get DP notes only after executing the Murabaha sale and creation of liability, e.g. after the sale of goods. If such a note is necessary at the time of disbursement for the sake of security, it can be of the principal amount only, i.e. excluding the mark-up or profit margin.

Auditors have also to look into the overall or master agreement, a kind of MoU, between the bank and the purchaser/customer, whereby the bank promises to sell or the purchaser promises to buy the commodity from time to time on an agreed rate of profit added to the cost.

Some Sharī'ah boards have also allowed in the Murabaha structure the use of Tawarruq, i.e. the client selling the goods in the market purchased from the bank to get cash for any consumption or business activity. In this case, the Sharī'ah board must ensure that the process of genuine Murabaha is completed, fulfilling the Sharī'ah essentials, and that the cash realized by the client is intended for any Halal business/purpose.

With regard to documentation in Murabaha, the auditor should ensure that the bank has received proper invoices for the goods and has taken delivery of the assets either by itself or through an agent authorized for this purpose. The date on invoices must not be later than the date of declaration by the client serving as agent. Sale is concluded when the bank accepts the offer, whereby the ownership, as well as the risk relating to the asset, is transferred to the customer.

### Ijarah – Internal Sharī´ah Controls

The other major mode Islamic banks are using is Ijarah, along with its variants like the leasing part of Diminishing Musharakah in financing of fixed durable assets. The following may be some of its controls:

1. The Sharī´ah board should ensure that ownership title of the leased asset is transferred to the bank, i.e. the lessor. If it involves import, the bank should import in its name directly or through an agent/client. It has been observed that to avoid some taxes/charges, assets are imported in the name of the client/lessee. This is not advisable and the minimum that should be ensured is that a "counter deed" should be signed between the bank (lessor) and the client (lessee) for transfer of the ownership to the lessor.
2. If an identified asset is to be leased, e.g. a 2007 model Toyota car manufactured by company 'ABC', it must be ensured that the bank acquires the ownership before entering into an actual Ijarah agreement. Prior to that it would only be a "promise to lease".
3. The Ijarah asset, the lease period and the rental must be defined properly. It also needs to be seen that the intended use of the asset is permissible.
4. In situations where a floating rental is stipulated, the first rental should be specified and then a certain benchmark applied for determination of future rental along with a proper floor and cap. In addition, rental for the subsequent period should be agreed in absolute value before the start of the period.
5. It has to be ensured that conventional insurance is not taken, particularly when Takaful is available.
6. Ijarah and Bai' are entirely different types of transactions in terms of their implications for the parties involved. Therefore, the two transactions should not be mixed in such a way that their respective Sharī´ah essentials are not fulfilled. Transfer of ownership to the lessee should not be an integral condition of the lease agreement. It could be a unilateral undertaking or promise, not binding on the other party. A separate contract has to be entered into for transfer of ownership of the asset to the client at the end of the lease term.
7. A Sharī´ah board should ensure that expenses relating to purchase and ownership of the asset are borne by the bank. As such, expenses that are necessary to maintain the overall corpus of the asset are the lessor's responsibility.
8. As per the AAOIFI's Accounting Standard for Ijarah, accounting for Ijarah-based financing should be similar to that of operating lease and not that of finance lease.
9. It should be ensured that if rental is received in advance, the same cannot be treated as bank's income, even if an accounting period is lapsed. An auditor should check the delivery orders to ensure that the asset had been delivered at the time of commencement of the lease period and accrual of the rent.
10. Any penalty received by the bank in cases of default or late payment of lease rentals should be given to charity, as approved by the Sharī´ah board.

## Other Modes – Internal Sharī'ah Controls

Similarly, for all other modes which an Islamic bank is using, a Sharī'ah board should identify the minimum controls which must be ensured so as to maintain the sanctity of Islamic business products. For example, in Diminishing Musharakah, different documents relating to the creation of partnership, leasing and sale of units to the other party must be independently enforceable. All expenses relating to ownership must be borne by the parties in the proportion of their ownership. If a jointly purchased asset is not capable of being leased (like an open plot of land), it cannot be leased to charge rental, because it is only a commercial asset and can give profit only upon its sale. If commercial assets are involved, the nature of the partnership will be that of Shirkatul'aqd and the units may be sold only at market or agreed-upon value at the time of sale. Similarly, they can be revalued only keeping in mind their actual value, and if it is prestipulated that units will be revalued by ( )% per month/annum, without regard to the actual value, the transaction will become usurious.

In the case of Musharakah agreements for financing, profit rates are projected in the agreements with the customers on the assets side. The Sharī'ah department will need to ensure that payments to banks under projected rates are subject to an approved final adjustment procedure. Treatment of loss, if any, by the bank management is also crucial and it must be ensured that loss is borne by the partners in proportion of their share in the joint investment. Further, investments in shares of joint stock companies should be subject to the screening criteria approved by the Sharī'ah board and in the case of any non-compliance, the dividend income or the capital gain from non-Sharī'ah-compliant investments must go to the Charity Account.

An Islamic bank's placements with other institutions should be only on any of the Sharī'ah-compliant bases and any income from non-Sharī'ah-compliant placements must go to charity. It should also be ensured that the bank fulfils the necessary disclosure requirements and profits are distributed among shareholders and various categories of depositors according to the already disclosed criteria/ratios/weightages.

Finally, the use of charity fund proceeds has to be overseen by the Sharī'ah board. Generally, it is left to Islamic banks themselves as to whom and how they disburse such funds. However, if regulators in respective countries do not advise any procedure/avenues for disbursement of charity funds, Sharī'ah boards must ensure that these are used for the uplift of the poor or for social welfare projects in the respective economies/societies and are not used for any other purpose not conforming to the Sharī'ah tenets.

### 14.3.5  Operational Controls

Islamic banks' assets are normally risk-based. They may finance projects on the basis of equity participation and profit-sharing in addition to debt-based modes of trade and leasing. Therefore, the soundness of their operations needs a type of control that goes beyond merely ensuring the solvency of debtors. To ascertain operational soundness, the regulators need to undertake the following procedures:

1. The application of consolidated and acceptable accounting standards suitable for Islamic modes of financing.
2. A review of project financing operations to ensure soundness of the bank's performance in preparing feasibility studies and evaluations and follow-ups on project implementation.

3. An evaluation of the performance of the bank in monitoring and controlling the enterprises it finances by way of equity participation. This would also include looking into the ability of the bank to deal with the problems facing enterprises, and providing them with necessary technical assistance.

### Structural Issues

1. It is better that each and every aspect of the transaction structure is clarified by the Sharī´ah board.
2. It may also happen in Islamic banking that a slight change in process flow may lead to transfer to charity of the whole income due to non-Sharī´ah-compliance. Therefore, all issues related to the structure of the transaction/product should be clarified beforehand with the Sharī´ah advisor/Sharī´ah board.
3. As IFIs have to deal in goods and tangible assets, they may suitably change their business structure, enabling them to fulfil the requirements of the Sharī´ah.

### Asymmetric Risk and Moral Hazard Issues

1. Asymmetric risk arises from information asymmetry, which occurs when one party to a transaction has more or better information than the other party – also called asymmetrical information.
2. Moral hazard is the name given to the increased risk of problematical (immoral) behaviour, and thus a negative outcome because the person who caused the problem doesn't suffer the full (or any) consequences, or may actually benefit. Such a concern typically arises in the context of contracts like Takaful of the financed assets.
3. As discussed earlier, Islamic modes of finance give certain rights/liabilities to both parties. Bankers need to understand these rights and liabilities in detail. For example, in Ijarah, the client may stop using the asset on his own, ask the bank to take the asset back and refuse to purchase the asset at the price given by the bank, despite his promise. Ijarah principles in fact allow him to do so, but the bank will have to see at the very beginning how to mitigate such risks or overcome possible problems. Taking the past history of the client in respect of financial matters could be useful.

### Documentation

Documentation in Islamic banking is a very important area which needs to be focused on. Proper preparation and development of documents for various contracts and adequate execution could save the bank from many unforeseen losses during the course of business. For example, a client wants to import something under sight L/C, needs the bank's help only for opening the L/C and does not want to get finance from the bank. In such a case, if the bank has not taken full cover in advance, it might be in trouble if the client does not pay in time, while the bank's Nostro account has been debited. Now the bank can do nothing and will have to suffer loss for the period of nonpayment by the client. An agency agreement with the client, if entered into at the time of opening the L/C, could save the bank from the loss, as it could undertake Murabaha with the client, covering the cost of funds for the credit facility availed by the client.

The sequence and timing of various documents is extremely important and should be properly taken care of. The master facility agreement in respect of various modes is the basic document that must cover all aspects of the related facility. To do this effectively, all relevant staff of the bank should be trained to execute the documentation in the appropriate manner.

*Legal Framework*

Another issue with Islamic banking is conformity with the legal framework in vogue. Unlike conventional banking, Islamic banking products might need complete re-engineering with a slight change in the legal framework, for which Islamic banks may get regulators' guidance. It is possible that an Islamic bank may have to develop the same product on an entirely different structure to accommodate the legal framework. As Islamic banks cannot recover the liquidated damages through any contractual arrangement in cases of default in timely payment, they must keep in mind the legal options available in such situations. The issues of third party obligations and guarantees are also very important and have to be kept in mind while undertaking asset-based business of trade and leasing.

## 14.4   PROSPECTS AND ISSUES IN SPECIFIC AREAS OF FINANCING

We shall briefly discuss financing in the following areas:

- working capital financing;
- trade financing;
- project financing;
- syndicate arrangements;
- inter-bank financing;
- liquidity management;
- Tawarruq arrangements;
- debit, charge and credit cards;
- securitization;
- central bank's Islamic refinance.

### 14.4.1   Working Capital Finance

The banks, in order to facilitate trade or meet working capital requirements, may provide facilities in connection with purchase/import and sale/export of goods and machinery, and acquisition and holding of stock and inventory, spares and replacements, raw material and semi-finished goods. Financing genuine trading activities could promote a number of performance criteria in the economy. The most popular mode of finance for working capital is Murabaha. Islamic banks have to purchase the raw material for sale to the clients on a Murabaha basis. However, Murabaha alone cannot fulfil all the requirements of business and industry. Customers, especially exporters, sometimes need financing for the processing of raw material and to meet labour and overhead expenses.

Murabaha combined with Istisna'a and Wakalah can fulfil banks' requirements more properly. The following may be the procedure for this purpose:

1. Murabaha is provided for the purchase of raw material.
2. Istisna'a is provided to manufacture the required goods and pay overhead expenses.

3. The customer will manufacture and deliver the goods to the bank as per the L/C. Once the goods are manufactured, the same will become the property of the bank.
4. The exporter can be appointed as agent to export the goods on behalf of the bank. The export proceeds will be remitted to the bank, which will deduct from the proceeds the cost of goods (Istisna'a price) and profit; the client will pay the Murabaha price to the bank as per the agreed schedule.

The Musharakah mode can also be adopted for working capital requirements by using the concept of daily product, subject to fulfilment of the relevant Sharī´ah essentials. The bank and the client can also agree that they will share the gross profits, so that indirect expenses like depreciation of fixed assets, salaries of administrative staff, etc. shall not be deducted from the distributable profits, meaning that the client will voluntarily bear all indirect expenses. This aspect may be kept in mind while fixing the sharing ratio between the bank and the client, by allocating a larger share to the latter. Expenses like those related to raw materials, labour directly involved in production, electricity, etc. should be borne jointly by the Musharakah.

Salam can also be used to finance the working capital needs of customers. It can be very effectively used to finance the sugar, fertilizer and cement industries. The process in the case of a sugar mill, for example, will consist of the following steps:

1. An Islamic bank enters into a Salam agreement with the sugar mill, under which the bank will purchase sugar from the mill by paying the full price in advance. The mill is liable to deliver the sugar on the agreed date. The bank may take a charge on the mill's asset against the payment made under the Salam agreement.
2. The bank enters into an agency agreement with the mill, under which the mill will sell the sugar in the market at a mutually agreed solidus/advised price. It can also be provided in the agency agreement that if the mill sells the sugar at a price higher than the agreed price, it may keep the extra amount as a bonus.
3. On the delivery date, the mill informs the bank to take delivery from its godowns; the bank takes delivery and authorizes the mill to sell the sugar on its behalf.
4. The sugar mill sells the sugar and pays the price to the bank; if the price is higher than the agreed price, the bank may pay the extra amount to the mill, if so promised in the agency agreement. However, if the market price falls below the agreed price, the bank will suffer the loss.

### 14.4.2    Trade Financing by Islamic Banks

Trade finance operations of banks play an important role in the overall economic development of any country, through facilitating imports and exports. Since it usually involves assets, the conversion of the trade finance operation to Islamic modes is relatively easier. Islamic banks can use Musharakah/Mudarabah in trade finance to build a profitable and secure portfolio. So far, Musharakah use in this sector is minimal, but Islamic banks need to realize the potential in trade financing through Shirkah arrangements, which can safely be used on a consignment basis or for single transactions in financing of foreign trade, as already explained in Chapter 12.

Banks should take service charges for opening L/Cs. Funds may be provided for imports on the basis of profit/loss sharing or Murabaha. Similarly, banks can charge fees as negotiating banks in exports. They can provide preshipment export financing on the basis of PLS or

Murabaha. Discounting of bills, as in the case of post shipment financing, will have to be replaced by a fee for agency services of the banks, which they will render for collection of the bills' amount on behalf of the exporters and the amount of the bills will be given to the clients as interest-free loans.

Some other areas of trade financing are discussed below.

*Alternative to Post Shipment Discounting*

Exporters mostly need post shipment financing in the form of bill discounting. The practice of bill discounting, being Riba-based, will have to be changed. The banks may provide interest-free loans against the bills and take over the bills for collection from the drawee. As collecting agent of the bills, the banks can receive agreed service charges. Negotiation of the bills will be at the face value and the service charge will be amount-related and not time-related. This will apply to inland as well as export bills. There should be no objection if they use any of the Sharī´ah-compliant modes like Musharakah, Mudarabah, Istisna'a, etc.

Islamic banks cannot provide the facility of bill discounting. However, Musawamah can be used to partially help exporters in this regard. For example, on 1st January, 2007 an exporter approaches an Islamic bank with a bill of US$100 000/- to be realized after 55 days (25th February, 2007) for discounting. Suppose the spot rate of the Dollar is Rs. 57.75; the Islamic bank may agree to quote the rate of Rs. 57.60/US$ and the transaction will be executed in the following manner:

1. The client identifies his needs for raw materials worth Rs. 5 760 000.
2. The bank disburses funds of Rs. 5 760 000/- to the client under the agency agreement for the purchase of the agreed commodities.
3. The client purchases the material, gives declaration about possession of the stock and makes an offer to the bank to purchase the stock held by it as agent, at US$ 100 000/- to be paid on 25th February, 2007. The Islamic bank accepts the offer and a sale is concluded.
4. On the due date, a foreign bank remits US$100 000/- in the client's account maintained with the Islamic bank. As per the authority given by the client, the Islamic bank debits US$100 000/- from the client's account and the transaction is completed.

There could be a number of other alternatives for interest-free post shipment finance. Exporters normally require discounting of bills for preparation of the next consignments; Islamic banks may facilitate this through Murabaha, Salam, Istisna'a and a combination of various modes and submodes. One case study involving a trade transaction is discussed below.

Let's assume a valued client, Abdul, of Islamic bank B has prepared an export consignment of 100 million dollars from his own resources or through borrowing from the informal sector; the consignment is almost ready for shipment as per a negotiable L/C already opened and accepted in Abdul's favour, involving the period of 90 days. Now, for payment of some urgent liabilities, problems in the plant or other unexpected expenses, Abdul needs a huge amount of liquidity within one week and approaches bank B for a solution without the involvement of interest-based discounting. One solution that B can offer is that it purchases the goods from Abdul on a cash payment basis; the L/C would be assigned in its favour, it would appoint Abdul its agent and he would arrange to ship the goods on behalf of the bank. The bank would get its profit margin while purchasing the goods from Abdul and receive the proceeds of the bill after 90 days. In this way, the client would be helped without the involvement of interest.

### Commodity Operations

Islamic banks can undertake commodity operations of various government institutions on the basis of Murabaha. For example, presently the governments in a number of countries announce 'support price' of wheat to be procured by federal units or provincial governments in the harvest season. The central banks advise the major commercial banks about the purchase limits for the wheat procurement centres that are established by the provincial governments. The farmers/suppliers supply the wheat at centres, the officials of which issue purchase bills to them for the quantity received. Conventional banks provide interest-based finance to the provincial governments and make payments to the farmers/suppliers. Upon completion of the purchase process, the central banks adjust the account by debiting the amount to the concerned provincial accounts.

To undertake Sharī´ah-compliant commodity operations, Islamic banks may form a syndicate or establish a company to purchase goods from the farmers/suppliers and sell the same to the provincial governments with their profit margin. The company will undertake trading functions through agencies like food departments and other well-established trade entities that may serve as agents to the company. The company will be having tangible assets along with some inventory of the goods purchased.

### Murabaha–Istisna'a Financing for Exports

Exporters need financing for the processing of raw material to prepare exportable goods. For example, textile composite units purchase cotton to manufacture finished cloth; these units cannot rely on Murabaha-based finance, since they also need huge amounts of liquidity for meeting labour and other overhead expenses. They can be helped out through combining Murabaha with Istisna'a and Wakalah, as explained earlier. Istisna'a is an exception where forward sale is allowed without making full pre-payment. It relates to goods that require manufacturing and the manufacturer (seller) undertakes to manufacture goods. It is, however, necessary for an Istisna'a transaction that the price is fixed and necessary specifications of the product are clearly defined.

### Import Financing through Murabaha

An Islamic bank and a customer will sign a master Murabaha agreement and an agency agreement to finance L/Cs of the customer. As per the agency arrangement, the customer will purchase goods from foreign suppliers on the bank's behalf. The difference between a general Murabaha agreement and an L/C Murabaha agreement lies in the fact that it is possible in L/C Murabaha that a commodity may also be sold at cost price in the case of a spot Murabaha. In order to accommodate such a transaction, agreements need to mention that such transactions are regarded as Musawamah. Such a deal should be finalized only after execution of the agency agreement.

An importer will request the bank to open an L/C by submitting all relevant documents. On receipt of the L/C, the exporter will ship the goods and deliver the shipping documents to the negotiating bank for payment of the bill amount. If the documents are found to be in order, the negotiating bank will send documents to the Islamic bank. On receipt of the documents, the Islamic bank will contact the customer and inform him of the availability of the documents. The customer will negotiate the FX rate for the required foreign currency amount. The bill may be settled in the following ways:

- Normal payment: the Islamic bank will discuss the payment date with the customer and if the customer wishes to settle the transaction, it will issue a Musawamah declaration to the customer and sell the goods to the customer at the following price: L/C cost + all other charges/expenses. After receiving the payment, the bank will release the shipping documents to the customer. However, the bank's risk on the goods will end only after the asset is delivered to the customer.

  If the customer requires financing, it will enter into a sub-Murabaha, which means giving declaration and offer by the customer and its acceptance by the bank. Profit will be charged from the day the bank's Nostro is debited to the Murabaha settlement date, according to the agreed profit rate. The bank will release the shipping documents to the customer and record a Murabaha receivable.
- Settlement – payment against documents (PAD): sub-Murabaha will be booked on the day the customer can arrange funds and shipping documents will be released on the same day. The price will include profit from the day the bank's Nostro account is debited until the sub-Murabaha settlement date.
- Settlement – trust receipt (TR) Murabaha: TR Murabaha is the same as the case of normal payment. The only difference is that the financing by the bank is done for a relatively longer period, such as 120 days or more.
- Shipping guarantees or delivery orders (DO): if the goods have arrived prior to the shipping documents, which is possible in the case of air cargo, the customer may request the Islamic bank to issue a shipping guarantee or delivery order. The bank may take, for example, 110 % margin from the customer and execute a sub-Murabaha based on the FX rate prevailing on that date. The selling price will be fixed at that stage. If, however, upon arrival of the documents, the final cost of the goods turns out to be higher or lower than the cost price of the sub-Murabaha, the bank will settle the difference with the customer by paying or receiving the differential amount. This adjustment in price after the execution of Murabaha is permissible because Murabaha is a cost-plus-profit transaction and it can be mutually stipulated that if the seller discovers after execution of the Murabaha that the cost was higher or lower, he can settle the difference with the buyer. However, only the cost portion may be adjusted, the profit portion should not be adjusted.

### 14.4.3   Project Financing

Project financing can be provided through various modes of financing. Currently, Ijarah is a popular mode of finance for undertaking project finance. However, if the project needs to be installed or constructed, Ijarah cannot be used effectively. Some alternate products are discussed below.

*Construction/Erection of a Cement Plant (for example)*

A bank can provide finance on Musharakah basis and enter into an Istisna'a contract with any industrial concern by appointing the customer its agent for supervision of the erection of the plant. The bank will enter into a Musharakah contract with the client to operate the plant and get a periodic profit payment in the form of rental on its part of ownership. Principal can be recovered through selling of units to the client at the market price with proper offer and acceptance. The client may go on purchasing the bank's units until the bank's investment is redeemed. Ownership transfer can also be once, at the end of the investment period. Partnership can also be for sharing of profits of the plant when it goes into production.

### Syndication Arrangements for Construction of an Oil Terminal

Islamic banks can form syndicates for huge financing requirements of corporate customers. A financing consortium and the terminal operator may enter into an agreement to Ijarah – a kind of unilateral but binding promise. An Istisna'a agreement may be executed between a construction contractor and the financing consortium. The consortium may appoint the terminal operator (the ultimate customer) its agent to supervise the construction. When the terminal is ready for operations, the consortium and the terminal operator should enter into an Ijarah agreement. However, Sharī´ah essentials and requirements of the Islamic modes should be taken care of in syndication arrangements also.

### Syndication Arrangements for Sukuk Issue and Securitization

Banks may also form syndicates to finance the projects of the public sector and the big entities of the corporate sector through securitization and Sukuk issue. The securities created through securitization of assets represent the proportionate ownership of the holders in the assets underlying the Sukuk issue. The pool of assets of different natures being securitized should comprise Ijarah or fixed assets valuing more than 50 % of the total worth of the pool, according to the majority of the Islamic schools of jurisprudence. In this case, Sukuk can be traded at any value in the secondary market. However, if the Hanafi view is adopted, trading will be allowed even if the illiquid assets are more than 10 % of its total worth. Investors in the pool will have a Musharakah relationship and each one will be a proportionate owner of the pool.

The Sukuk holders assume the rights and obligations of the pool up to the extent of their ownership. However, if the pool contains any debt instruments, i.e. Murabaha receivables, the price of the Sukuk cannot be less than the value of such debt instruments. Other details about Sukuk and securitization will be discussed in the next chapter.

### 14.4.4  Liquidity Management

Liquidity can be managed by dealing in the Islamic inter-bank fund market. There could be direct placement of funds in the open market by surplus banks for use by deficit banks. The Mudarabah contract is the most useful instrument for transactions in the inter-bank market. A deficit bank would agree to give a share of its general profits according to a Mudarabah ratio that could be negotiated according to the market conditions. The central bank may also issue some guiding principles in this regard.

Liquidity management in Islamic banks can also be done through securitization of the pool of income-generating assets. An Islamic bank (IB) would purchase Sukuk from the government at par at the time of primary issue, and earn rental or profit. If the bank requires liquidity, it may sell the Sukuk in the secondary market to another bank to generate cash, and if the IB is in surplus, it can purchase Sukuk from the market. This would be similar to the repo–reverse repo operations of conventional banks. However, the IB would sell and buy on an outright basis as two separate transactions. If the market is not liquid, the IB can sell the Sukuk to the central bank to obtain liquidity.

If the IB requires financing without selling/purchasing Sukuk, it can do so by creating an asset pool of its Murabaha and Ijarah assets and invite other banks and NBFCs to invest in its pool. The share of Murabaha receivables should be less than 50 % of the total assets of the pool. At the time of maturity, the investing bank would redeem its investment and the IB would pay its share of profit.

Liquidity needs can also be met by way of Parallel Salam contracts, in which case the purchaser would pay the whole sale price in advance.

The Tawarruq arrangement is also used by Islamic banks to place and obtain liquidity. For this purpose, an Islamic bank in need of funds and a surplus bank select any commodity/stocks of liquid nature (such as metals sold in the Commodity Exchange or blue chip stocks). The IB purchases the commodity from another bank or any institution on credit (Murabaha) and after taking delivery, sells it in the market at spot price. The process can be reversed if the Islamic bank has to place liquidity with any other bank. On the face of it, the process seems to be very simple; however, extreme care should be taken while undertaking such transactions and it should be ensured that the transaction does not become a mere exchange of papers.

The Tawarruq arrangement when used on the assets side gives a fixed guaranteed return to the banks and can also be executed with conventional banks. Credit cards used by Islamic banks in Malaysia are based on this concept combined with a buy-back arrangement. The majority of the Sharī'ah scholars consider such cards non-Sharī'ah-compliant.

The product "Commodity Murabaha" based on Tawarruq is used by a number of IFIs working in the Middle East. However, it is considered a grey area and Islamic bankers need to realize that it should be used only in extreme cases to avoid interest where no other option is available and even then under the guidance of the Sharī'ah board. Widespread use of such products is harmful to the Islamic banking industry in the long run.

### 14.4.5  Forward Contracts and Foreign Exchange Dealings

In a forward market, the currency or commodity is sold for a future date and delivery of the article as well as the currency is given on any future date. However, the specifications of the article, time and place of delivery, as well as the currency and amount, are all settled in advance. So the seller is hedged against any fall in price of the commodity and the buyer is assured of the supply on time, as well as being covered against a possible increase in price by the time he needs the commodity. But this feature of conventional Forex markets results in the creation of fictitious assets and exploitation of any of the parties. As deliberated upon in Chapters 3, 4 and 6, trading rules in respect of currencies are different from trading in commodities other than monetary units. The Sharī'ah rules for trading in currencies are briefly given in the following paragraphs.

Both parties to the exchange of currencies must take possession of the counter values before dispersing, such possession being either actual or constructive. If the currency on both sides is the same, the counter values must be equal in amount, even if one of them is in paper money and the other is in coin of the same country, like a note of five pounds for five pound coins. The exchange would be simultaneous without any deferment clause regarding the delivery of one or both counter values. Return-free loans based on Tabarru', which are noncommutative contracts, are exempt from this general rule. Some of the implications of this rule of Islamic finance in respect of modern transactions are discussed below.

When a contract is concluded for the sale of an amount of currency, possession must be taken for the whole amount at the time of concluding the transaction. Possession may take place either physically or constructively. The form of taking possession of assets differs according to their nature and customary business practices. Physical possession takes place by means of simultaneous delivery by hand. Constructive possession of an amount of currency or an asset is deemed to have taken place by the seller enabling the other party to take its delivery and dispose of it, even if there is no physical taking of possession. Some of the forms of constructive possession that are approved by both the Sharī´ah and business norms are the following:

1. Crediting a sum of money to the account of the customer directly or through bank transfer.
2. A customer entering into a spot contract of currency exchange with the Islamic bank against another currency already deposited in his account.
3. The bank debiting – by the order of the customer – a sum of money to the latter's account and crediting it to another account in a different currency, either in the same bank or another Islamic bank, for the benefit of the customer or any other payee.
4. Receipt of a cheque constitutes constructive possession, provided the balance payable is available in the account of the issuer in the currency of the cheque and the bank has blocked such a balance for payment.
5. The receipt of a voucher by a merchant, signed by the credit card holder (buyer), is constructive possession of the amount of currency entered as payable on the coupon, provided that the card-issuing Islamic bank pays the amount without deferment to the merchant accepting the card.

Islamic banks are allowed to deal in foreign exchange remittances and the buying and selling of foreign exchange on a spot basis. However, differences in time zones between different foreign exchange markets require allowing two days' delay for the clearing of such operations, but the operation will be finalized on the rates of the date on which the transaction was executed.

Islamic banks can undertake remittance transactions domestically and externally. Externally, they will need to have a correspondent relationship with many banks. Given the predominance of interest-based banks, this will pose a great challenge to Islamic banks. Some banks have managed to enter into agreements with correspondent banks without the giving or taking of interest on the basis of reciprocal treatment. They keep foreign exchange balances for agreed amounts and periods, i.e. they normally maintain credit balances and are, in return, allowed debit balances to a limited level.

An exchange of two amounts that are debts, denominated in different currencies and established as obligations, is permissible if it is in the fulfilment of the obligations in respect of these debts and does not becomes a bilateral exchange of currencies. This covers the following cases: for discharging two debts where one party owes an amount from another party denominated in (say) dinars and the other party owes an amount from the first party denominated in (say) dirhams, both may agree on the rate of exchange between dinars and dirhams in order to settle the debts wholly or partially. This type of transaction is known as set-off (discharge of a receivable debt against a payable debt). A creditor can take payment of a debt due to him in a currency other than the currency in which the debt was incurred, provided the settlement is made as a spot transaction at the spot exchange rate on the day of settlement.[1]

As per the rules of exchange of monetary units, it is not permitted for one of the partners in contractual Musharakah or Mudarabah to be a guarantor for the other partner, to protect the latter from the risks of dealing in currencies. However, it is permissible for a third party to volunteer to be a guarantor for that purpose, provided this guarantee is not stated in the contract.

*Forward Currency Cover*

Islamic forward currency contracts are permissible when executed with the firm intention of delivering and receiving the currency on the specified future date. If delivery and receipt of the counter currencies bought and sold is not made, this will not be a valid transaction. Due to the Sharī'ah restrictions, it can only be a unilateral promise to sell in the future at a pre-agreed rate rather than an actual sale contract. The unilateral promise or moral obligation is considered binding and is effective and well-recognized in the market; a defaulting party is debarred from doing any further business. A bilateral promise to purchase and sell currencies is forbidden if the promise is binding.

Accordingly, contemporary Sharī'ah scholars have observed that forward foreign currency cover is permissible subject to the following conditions:

1. The amount of foreign currency is needed for genuine trade or payment transactions. The need will have to be supported by appropriate documents so as to prevent forward cover for speculative purposes. This means that a currency dealer would not be permitted to get a cover.
2. The forward cover shall be through a unilateral promise to sell or purchase and it shall not be a sale/purchase agreement. This means that sale/purchase shall take place simultaneously at the agreed time in future at the rate agreed upon initially at the time of agreement to sell or purchase.
3. While it will be permissible to fix the price of foreign currency in terms of domestic currency according to the promise, no forward cover fee can be recovered. However, an amount may be demanded by the bank from its client in advance by way of earnest money against foreign currency agreed to be purchased/sold at a future date. If, at the agreed time, the party does not perform, the bank can recover the actual loss, if any, and adjust the earnest money there against.

### 14.4.6  Refinancing by the Central Banks

In order to promote investment in certain priority areas like agriculture, exports or structural overhead projects, some central banks provide to the commercial banks or NBFCs a refinance facility against their disbursement to the priority areas. This refinance is normally based on interest, but it is possible to provide such refinance in a Sharī'ah-compliant manner. For example, the central bank in Pakistan (SBP) provides an Islamic export refinance scheme (IERS) on the basis of Musharakah. Its main features are given below.

---

[1] For details relating to the above, see AAOIFI, 2004–5a, Standards on Set-off, 2004–5, pp. 46–48; Standard on Trading in Currencies, clause 2/10, p. 8.

The framework of the IERS is based on the concept of Shirkah. The State Bank shares in the actual profit of the Musharakah pool maintained by the Islamic bank that provides export finance under various Islamic modes. However, if the actual profit of the pool is more than ongoing rates under a conventional export finance scheme (EFS), the excess profit so received by SBP is credited to the Takaful fund, a reserve fund to be maintained by SBP for risk mitigation; the Takaful fund can be used to meet future losses arising on implementation of the IERS. The salient features of the scheme are:

1. The facility initially is allowed only against an underlying transaction, designed on the basis of Islamic modes of financing approved by the Sharī´ah board of the concerned bank.

2. An Islamic bank desirous of refinance has to create a Musharakah pool (having a minimum of (ten) blue chip companies – to be achieved in the first year of operations). Blue chip companies mean such companies involved in the export business or other business or both, or manufacturing concerns marketing their products in Pakistan or abroad, who have (i) a good track record on the stock exchange or (ii) a rating of minimum $B^+$ or equivalent by the rating agencies approved by the State Bank for rating banks in Pakistan, such a rating should be acceptable to the bank as per its own lending policies for advancing loans or (iii) a return on equity (ROE) during the last three years higher than the rates of finance prescribed by the State Bank during those years on its conventional EFS. In the case of a company which has been in operation for less than three years, the ROE of the available number of years shall be considered. The Islamic bank has to ensure that companies selected for the Musharakah pool under the above criteria do not have adverse "Credit Information Bureau" reports.

3. The State Bank shares the overall profit of the pool (gross income less any provision created under prudential regulations during the period plus any amount recovered against prior periods' losses and reversal of provision) earned by the Islamic bank on the Musharakah pool under the provisions of the IERS calculated on a daily product basis.

4. If, on the basis of the annual audited accounts of the Islamic bank, the profit accruing to the SBP is more than the profit paid to the SBP on a quarterly basis, as per the unaudited accounts of earnings of the pool, the difference has to be deposited by the Islamic bank, within seven days of its determination, in a special nonremunerative reserve fund, "Takaful fund," to be maintained at the office of the State Bank where the Head Office/Country Office of the concerned bank is situated.

5. If, on the basis of the annual audited accounts of the pool, the share of the State Bank in the profit works out to be less than the amount already paid to the State Bank on a provisional basis, the State Bank has to refund the excess amount involved out of balances held in the Takaful fund, if any.

6. In the event of loss suffered on the Musharakah pool on the basis of the annual audited accounts, the Islamic bank and the State Bank shall have to share the loss in the proportion of their share of investment in the pool expressed on a daily product basis. The share of loss to the State Bank will first be met out of the credit balance in the Takaful fund, if any. Any loss not met from the Takaful fund shall be borne by the State Bank.

7. In the case of loss, the Islamic bank is entitled to claim a refund on account of the share of profit paid by it to SBP on a provisional basis, along with the SBP's share in the loss of principal amount extended to the Musharakah pool.

### 14.4.7   Cards: Debit, Charge, Credit and ATM

Four types of card representing plastic money, which are issued by banks and other institutions to withdraw cash from their accounts, to obtain credit or to pay for goods purchased or services received, are debit cards, charge cards, credit cards and ATM cards. These cards provide all or some of the benefits of liquidity, safety, mobility and flexibility to manage the budgets of the card holders. The AAOIFI has issued a Sharī´ah standard on these cards (Standard # 2), which provides a useful basis for developing electronic money by Islamic banks remaining within the Sharī´ah framework.[2] Below, we briefly give the general characteristics of the various cards.

A debit card, which is issued against the available funds in a customer's account, gives its holder the right to withdraw cash from his account and to pay for goods and services to the limit of the available funds. The debit to the customer's account is immediate and the card doesn't provide any credit. The issuing institutions normally do not charge customers for using the card, except when it is used to withdraw cash or to purchase another currency through another institution different from the institution that has issued the card. The issuing institution may or may not charge a fee for issuing the card. Some institutions charge the party accepting payment by means of the card by charging a certain percentage on such transactions.

A charge card provides a credit facility up to a certain ceiling for a specified period of time, along with providing a means of payment. It is used to pay for goods and services and also to obtain cash. However, it does not provide a revolving facility and the card holder is obliged to make payments for the goods and services on the basis of the statement sent by the institution. In the case of a delay beyond the free credit period, the institution charges interest to the card holder. It does not charge the card holder any commission on use of the card. Rather, it receives a commission in percentage from the party accepting the card for payment. The card-issuing institution has a personal and direct right against the card holder to be reimbursed for any payments, irrespective of the relationship between the card holder and the party accepting the card for payment.

A credit card provides a revolving credit facility, by which the borrower may use or withdraw funds up to a pre-approved credit limit and the amount of available credit increases and decreases as funds are borrowed and then repaid. In other words, the credit may be used repeatedly. The borrower makes payments based only on the amount he has actually used or withdrawn, plus interest. The borrower may repay over time (subject to any minimum payment requirement) or in full at any time. Within the prescribed credit limit, the card holder may purchase goods and services or withdraw cash. The free credit period is determined by the issuing bank/institution. No interest is charged if the payment is made within the given free credit period. In the case of cash withdrawals, there is no free credit period. The card holder may defer the payment subject to an interest charge that is normally higher than the general interest rate prevalent in the formal sector in an economy. The issuing institution doesn't charge the card holder any percentage commission on usage. Instead, it receives a commission from the party accepting the card for payment. The institution is obliged to pay the party accepting the card for purchases made by the card holder and this obligation is independent of the relationship between the card holder and the party accepting the card for payment. The institution has a personal and direct right against card holder to be

---

[2] For details, see AAOIFI, 2004–5a, Standard on Cards, pp. 16–27.

reimbursed for any payments, irrespective of the relationship between the card holder and the party accepting the card for payment.

The most important of the above cards are credit cards, which provide revolving credit, emergency buying power, worldwide payments through a single instrument and financial security. The Jeddah-based OIC Fiqh Council has defined the credit card as follows:

> "A credit card is a document that a bank issues to a natural or legal person according to a contract between them. The card holder purchases goods or services from those who accept the card without immediate payment of the price. Payment is made from the account of the bank, who, afterwards, charges the card holder at regular time intervals depending upon the terms of the contract and the situation".

### Sharīʿah Position on Various Cards

The Islamic Fiqh Council, in its twelfth session (23–28th September, 2000) resolved that:

> "It is not permissible to issue a credit card or use it if its conditions include imposition of interest. This is so even if the card holder has the intention to pay (the price) within the moratorium period that precedes imposition of interest. However, it is permissible to issue credit cards that do not carry a condition of imposing interest on the credit. The bank can take from the card holder a specific amount of money at the time of issuing or renewal of the card as fee that the issuer deserves according to the services it provides to the card holder and any charge over and above this fixed amount is impermissible because of being usurious. It is also permissible for the bank to take a commission from the merchant on the goods or services purchased by the card holder, provided that such goods or services are sold at the same price, whether in cash or credit".

This, therefore, implies that charging an initial membership or periodic fee on credit cards does not pose any Sharīʿah problem. However, financing through credit cards on the basis of interest is prohibited. Thus, Islamic credit cards can take the form of "charge cards", where charges for the issuance of the card and recurring annual charges can be recovered from the card holders, and transaction charges and commission can be recovered from the merchants. However, if a loan or debt is created, no return can be charged thereon from the card holders.

A debit card can be issued and used as long as the card holder does not exceed the balance available in his account; no interest charge arises out of the transaction. Charge cards can also be issued subject to the following conditions:

1. The card holder is not obliged to pay interest in the case of delay in paying the due amount.
2. If the cardholder is required to deposit a sum of money as a guarantee and this amount is not available for use by the card holder, then the issuing institution should invest it for the benefit of the card holder on the basis of Mudarabah; any profit accruing on it should be shared by the card holder and the institution according to the specified ratio.
3. The institution must stipulate and ensure that the card holder will not use the card for purposes prohibited by the Sharīʿah.
4. It is permissible to purchase gold, silver or currency with a debit card or a charge card in cases where the issuing bank is able to settle the amount due to the party accepting the card without any credit period.

An Islamic bank or institution is not permitted to issue credit cards that provide an interest-bearing revolving credit facility, whereby the card holder pays interest for being allowed to pay off the debt in instalments. IFIs can charge the card holder membership fees, renewal fees and replacement fees. They can also charge a commission from the merchants accepting the card in the form of a percentage of the purchase price of the items and services availed using the card. Islamic banks and financial institutions can take membership of international card regulatory organizations, remaining within the limits of the Sharī'ah, and pay membership fees, service charges and other fees to them, as long as these do not include interest payments, even in an indirect way, such as in the case of increasing the service charge to cater for the granted credit.

A card holder can withdraw cash within the limit of his available funds, or more with the agreement of the institution issuing the card, provided no interest is charged. The issuing institution can charge a flat service fee for cash withdrawal, proportionate to the service offered, but not a fee that varies with the amount withdrawn.

IFIs cannot grant the card holder privileges prohibited by the Sharī'ah, such as conventional life insurance, entrance to prohibited places or prohibited gifts. They can grant privileges that are not prohibited, such as a priority right to services or discounts on hotel, airline or restaurant reservations and the like. Thus, possible features of a Sharī'ah-compliant credit card may be the following:

- an annual fee charged for issuing the card in order to cover expenses related to card issuance and usage;
- an interest-free revolving credit line;
- the card confers on its holder the right to pay for goods or services purchased up to a certain limit;
- a cash limit provided for emergency cases;
- a percentage commission from merchants accepting the card;
- the card holder to repay a certain amount of principal every month and the remaining amount is deferred to the next month with no interest charged;
- a penalty levied as a deterrent against defaults for charity;
- the card holder must not use the card for purposes prohibited by the Sharī'ah.

*Structures of Islamic Credit Cards Currently in Use*

**Credit Card of Emirates Islamic Bank**
This card is based on Ujrah or a service charge. A yearly service charge is levied depending on the credit card type, which is payable on a quarterly basis. The EIB credit card is not the same as a charge card. It allows a customer to pay a minimum monthly amount of 10 % of the outstanding balance (a minimum payment of UAED 100), as opposed to a charge card, where the full amount is payable on the due date. It offers the following benefits:

- free card delivery;
- free supplementary cards;
- a free EIB account with no minimum balance requirement;
- settlement by cash/cheque or direct debit to the EIB account;
- worldwide acceptance;
- a 100 % cash advance facility;
- free online access;

- a grace period up to 55 days;
- utility bill payments;
- 24-hour assistance through a dedicated call centre;
- no interest charge on the outstanding balance – the customer pays a fixed quarterly fee, which allows him to use the card up to an approved limit.

Any amount over the actual credit limit immediately falls due and is payable once the bank statement is delivered to the customer. A fixed fee of D75 is charged for any over limit, irrespective of the amount over the limit. A fixed fee of D25 is levied, irrespective of card type, for retrieval of one transaction slip. A fee of D20 is levied for each copy of the statement, provided the requested statement is for less than three months. For any request of a statement for more than three months, a fee of D100 per copy is levied, irrespective of the card type.

The annual fee charged by the Emirates Islamic Bank on its credit card may be higher than the annual fee charged by other conventional banks, but it is totally free from any element of interest and there is no hidden cost associated with the usage of the card; all fees are explicitly made known to the customer. Therefore, depending on usage, it may not necessarily be expensive, vis-à-vis conventional credit cards in the competitive market.[3]

### Bank Islam Malaysia Card (BIC)

BIC is based on three contracts, namely Bai' al 'Inah (buy-back), Wadi'ah (deposit for safe-keeping) and Qard al Hasan. The bank sells a piece of land to the customer at an agreed cash price and repurchases at a lower deferred price. The difference in the price is the bank's maximum return, which is determined in advance, unlike a conventional credit card whereby the interest charged is undetermined and it may further increase. The amount is credited to the customer's account under the concept of Wadi'ah, and the customer can use his/her BIC for retail purchases and cash withdrawals just like conventional credit cards, except that each transaction is backed by the cash held in his/her Wadi'ah BIC account. The facility of an interest-free loan is granted in emergency situations and the card holder is allowed to utilize funds above the available financing limit upon approval. The loan amount needs to be settled in full within a specified period and in this case no charge or fee is levied.

Due to the involvement of Bai' al 'Inah, the Sharī'ah position of this card is questionable; the scholars, other than some in the Far East, do not allow Bai' al 'Inah. Islamic banks' clients, as a whole, are also not inclined to accept it as a genuine Sharī'ah-compliant product.

### AmBank Bank Berhad Al-Taslif Card

This is also based on the Bai' al 'Inah concept through two contracts, namely a cash sales contract and a deferred purchase contract; at times the deferred sale precedes the cash purchase, but this is not an issue because the end result is the same, i.e. buy-back. AmBank has identified some assets for the purpose, which are used for sale and then purchase, giving the bank a profit margin and the customer an amount to be used through the card. The bank does not allow transactions for six prohibited activities: bars, discos, night clubs, purchase of beer, escort and massage services and gambling.[4]

---

[3] http://www.emiratesislamicbank.ae/eib/faqs/products/creditcardsfaqs.htm.
[4] http://search.msn.com/results.aspx?srch=105&FORM=AS5&q=AmBank+Bank+Berhad+Al+-Taslif+Card.

## Kuwait Finance House Al Tayseer Credit Card

An annual fee is charged on the cards, which may be more than that of comparable conventional credit cards, but no interest is charged. The bank also earns revenue from transactions initiated through the cards. The monthly balance repayment is one-third of the outstanding balance. The remaining two-thirds of the outstanding balance are rolled over to the next month in a revolving credit scheme, but no interest is added. To ensure that at least one-third of the outstanding balance is paid off every month, card holders should have either a salary account with KFH or any other lien in favour of KFH.[5]

The Al Tayseer card allows card holders to hold both a Visa and a Master Card with a single joint credit limit and a single PIN number for both cards. Card holders can then choose to use either card according to merchant preference and to exploit any special offers made available by Visa and Master Cards. Therefore, the "dual card, one account" system is the main advantage of choosing KFH's Islamic credit card offering. Sometime back, KFH had around 400 000 retail customers on its books, a customer base equivalent to approximately 35 % of Kuwait's retail market.

## Kuwait Finance House (Bahrain) Ijarah Card

This is an innovative product based on the concept of Ijarah, but its detailed features are not available. The Ijarah Card enables users to finance their purchases of durable goods over a tenure of up to 25 months.[6]

*Other Possible Structures of Cards*

Credit cards can also be designed on the basis of Murabaha, whereby the bank may buy the goods from the store and then sell them on deferred payment to the customer, the merchant being the agent. This could be when an Islamic bank is issuing its own credit card. The following may be the possible features of Murabaha-based credit cards:

- a pre-agreed master Murabaha contract with the card holder – the format for offer and acceptance can be built into the receipt for every transaction;
- the bank can offer different packages with different tenures and different profit rates;
- a time value of money concept may be used but only for pricing the related goods;
- the issuer may agree with the card holder to any of the following two options:

  — pay the price stipulated according to the Murabaha tenure, e.g. $100 + 5 = 105$;
  — pay within the given credit time, e.g. 100; bank gets a discount from the merchant.

A Musharakah basis could also be used, whereby the bank would enter into an agreement with some stores, according to which it would provide funds to the stores on the basis of profit-sharing and the bank would issue credit cards which customers could use to purchase goods from such stores; the stores would administer the act of selling while the banks would administer all other banking services. The bank and the stores would agree as to how they would share the profits.

---

[5] http://www.kfh.com/english/index.asp.
[6] http://www.islamic-commerce.net/index.php?name=News&file=article&sid=331.

## 14.5    ISLAMIC BANKS' RELATIONSHIP WITH CONVENTIONAL BANKS

Islamic banks represent a link in the chain of the financial system. It seems inconceivable that they could operate totally in isolation, disregarding conventional banks on the basis of the prohibition of interest. An Islamic banking system set-up has been introduced in a number of Muslim majority and Muslim minority countries. There is a lot of scope and also the need for cooperation and business relationships between conventional and Islamic banks in many areas, at national and international levels. This may be in respect of corresponding services, foreign trade financing and cofinancing of the projects. Temporary placement of funds with each other (on a basis other than interest) is unavoidable for banks, and particularly for the Islamic banks, to ensure an adequate supply of liquidity at the time of need. Exchange of information between the two and training programmes for orientation of the banks' employees in the fields of feasibility studies, accounting, auditing, supervising, the latest IT and communication-related techniques are also very important areas of cooperation between the conventional and Islamic banks.[7]

## 14.6    FEE-BASED ISLAMIC BANKING SERVICES

### 14.6.1    Underwriting

In investment banking services, underwriting is an important function of banking and non-banking institutions which yields fee-based income to the underwriters. In the Islamic framework, the underwriter shall bind himself to provide services of procuring the under-written amount of capital, for which he can charge a fee/commission. Accordingly, it shall be entitled to charge an underwriting fee only in consideration of arranging procurement of the underwritten capital. Take-up commission by the underwriter for subscribing to any unsubscribed amount of shares is not permissible. Shares to be subscribed by the underwriter shall have to be at the offer price, as applicable to all other shareholders, without any increase or decrease from the face value of such shares.

The Council of the Islamic Fiqh of the OIC, in its seventh session (9–14th May, 1992) resolved that:

> "Underwriting is an agreement made upon establishment of a company with someone who under-takes to guarantee the sale of all or part of the shares issued, i.e. to subscribe to the shares that would remain unsubscribed by others. There is no Sharī´ah objection to this provided that the underwriter subscribes to the shares at nominal value without any compensation for the commitment *per se*, though he may receive compensation for services other than underwriting that he may have offered, such as preparation of studies or marketing of shares."

### 14.6.2    Letters of Guarantee (L/G)

Jurists generally do not allow fees or remuneration based on guarantees. However, some jurists consider that the bank can take commission and fees, since a guarantee represents a bunch of services including, Wakalah, against which banks can charge fees. Banks' services

---

[7] For details, see Ayub, 2002, pp. 214–218.

involve some administrative expenses, therefore, they can recover expenses by way of fees or guarantee commission. However, if the guarantee is called, banks will be entitled to recover their principal amount only.

### 14.6.3   Letters of Credit (L/C)

Letters of credit are essential banking services, particularly in the area of international trade. Sharī´ah scholars have different views on how letters of credit should be treated. In literature on Islamic banking, L/Cs are covered under various contracts like Wakalah and Kafalah for businesses under Musharakah and Murabaha. Some say that they should be treated as a service and charged at a fixed rate that will not vary with the duration or the volume of the letter of credit. Other scholars allow for the fees to vary with the volume of L/Cs, as more or less work and effort may be needed when officials of middle, senior and even top management are involved, depending upon the volume of the L/Cs. Some Sharī´ah boards have suggested a rate structure based on brackets rather than on a percentage basis. Other Sharī´ah boards have decided that L/Cs should be treated on the basis of an agency arrangement at a fixed percentage. However,  the general view so far is that banks may be allowed to charge commission or fees for L/Cs as service charges which may not be time-related.

It is suggested that we treat L/Cs as a banking service and not as a guarantee, except in the case of standby letters of credit, which are used as a form of guarantee. However, L/Cs differ in that some allow partial shipment, some are revolving, some need confirmation and others have a red clause. In each case, the fee will differ, as the effort exerted will differ with each type of L/C. Time will not be an element in the variation of fees, except as it involves more or less administrative work.

Letters of credit may be opened for business on the basis of Murabaha or Musharakah. In the former case, the bank would open the L/C for itself (or in the name of a client under agency), and when it possesses the goods, it would sell them to the customer either on an FOB or on a CIF basis. The fee could be added to the total cost of the goods.

Musharakah is more flexible, as the L/C may be in the name of the customer or the bank; when the goods are received, the partner may sell them and the Musharakah liquidated or the partner may buy the share of the bank. In the case of Musharakah, either the bank or the customer can administer the L/C; this gives more flexibility to both parties and solves some legal, Sharī´ah-related and procedural problems which are encountered in Murabaha L/Cs. It is also possible for the bank to act as an agent to the beneficiary on behalf of the issuing bank and, in return, charge a fee against the L/C.

There is no objection to Islamic banks opening documentary credits at conventional banks. Islamic banks may ask correspondent banks to add their confirmation to an L/C opened on behalf of foreign suppliers to importers. They would keep surplus in their accounts with the correspondent bank to cover their obligations to the third party (the supplier). In this regard, there are certain considerations to be taken into account:

1. An Islamic bank should not delay the transfer of the value of the L/C to the correspondent abroad lest the correspondent bank should charge interest.
2. Import business conducted by an Islamic bank should not involve facilities for payment on the part of suppliers in return for interest. This procedure often entails drawing drafts on importers, guaranteed to be honoured for the benefit of the supplier, by the bank opening the credit. Experience has shown that, in addition to the surplus maintained by

the Islamic banks, foreign banks have been accepting dealing on the basis of mutual agreements by simple exchange of letters, to enable Islamic banks to avail confirmation facilities up to an agreed ceiling without charging interest if the accounts are overdrawn. In consideration, Islamic banks undertake to abide by the following:

— to keep a reasonable amount of cash in their current accounts with the confirming banks;
— to endeavour to cover any debit as soon as possible (it is part of the understanding that the Islamic bank does not ask for any return on any balance due to it, should the other bank utilize these funds profitably. Therefore, there is no condition set by the other party if the Islamic bank's account remains overdrawn for some time).

As partial security, the correspondent bank will, on adding its confirmation, debit the Islamic bank with a certain "cash margin", which it will transfer immediately to its own account. Thus, Islamic banks need, in fact, only to keep sufficient balances in their correspondent bank's account to cover the cash margins on the letters of credit.

Transfer of funds in a specific currency to be paid in the same currency is allowed with or without a fee. In traditional Islamic finance literature, we come across the instrument of "Suftajah" for cash transfer/payment, which involved the act of depositing a certain amount of money with someone for settlement to the benefit of the depositor or his representative at another place or in another country. If the transfer involves payment in any other currency, the exchange operation at the agreed rate is carried out before the transfer.

## 14.7  SUMMARY AND CONCLUSION

IFIs are capable of covering almost all types of financial services being provided by the conventional financial institutions, with the exception of conventional derivatives and some Forex-related dealings. This exception may be rather good for them as it makes them avoid overexposure and could save them from financial crises. Through indirect or direct intermediation by commercial banking and investment banking institutions respectively, they can effectively facilitate investment of funds profitably, remaining within the rules prescribed by the Sharī´ah. Solid conceptual bases have been provided and now the practitioners need to be innovative in the development of products, services and the financial business as a whole, with commitment and Sharī´ah inspiration. Practice with Sharī´ah inspiration is more likely to help enhance the credibility of the Islamic financial system and develop it on a sustainable basis.

For R & D, Sharī´ah scholars and finance experts need to collaborate more frequently. Support at the regulators' level is necessary, and this should be eagerly provided, as IFIs are capable of deepening the financial markets and providing healthy financial services to investors and the business community by enhancing the ambit of banks' clientele.

IFIs may mobilize funds on the basis of Mudarabah and Wakalatul Istismār by offering general or specific pools to individuals and the corporate sector. They may invest the funds to facilitate business and industry, both through Shirkah-based and debt-creating modes, keeping in mind the risk profile of the investors and the profitability and cash flow of the fund users. They can provide working capital finance, trade finance, consumer finance and project finance to public and private sector entities through individual or syndicate arrangements.

Along with Sharī'ah compliance, profitability and liquidity, Islamic banks need to keep in mind the impact of their financing policies and products on the socio-economic development of society, so as to play a role in employment generation, reducing income disparity and poverty alleviation. As a part of their marketing strategy, they should promote the institution of Qard al Hasan for SME and microfinance out of shareholders' profits, reserves or the funds credited to the Charity Account on various grounds.[8]

## Appendix: The major Functions of a Sharī'ah Supervisory Board In the Light of the AAOIFI's Sharī'ah Standard

The Accounting and Auditing Organization of Islamic Financial Institutions (AAOIFI) has prepared a standard for a Sharī'ah supervisory board, its composition and related aspects like rulings, report, etc. According to this standard, a Sharī'ah board should be an independent body of specialized jurists in Islamic commercial jurisprudence. It may also include other experts in areas of Islamic financial institutions with knowledge of Islamic jurisprudence relating to commercial transactions.

The Sharī'ah board is entrusted with the duty of directing, reviewing and supervising the activities of the Islamic financial institution in order to ensure that it is in compliance with Islamic Sharī'ah rules and principles. The Fatwahs, and rulings of the Sharī'ah supervisory board are binding on the Islamic financial institution.

According to the AAOIFI Standard, a Sharī'ah board should consist of at least three Sharī'ah scholar members. It may seek the services of consultants having expertise in business, economics, law, accounting and/or others. It should not include directors or significant shareholders of the Islamic financial institution.

The following is the illustrative wording of any Sharī'ah board's report on operations of Islamic financial institutions:

> "We have reviewed the principles and the contracts relating to the transactions and applications introduced by the Islamic Financial Institution (IFI) during the period ended... We have also conducted our review to form an opinion as to whether the institution has complied with Sharī'ah rules and principles and also with the specific Fatwahs, rulings and guidelines issued by us.[9]
>
> We conducted our review, which included examining, on a test basis of each type of transaction, the relevant documentation and procedures adopted by the Islamic Financial Institution. We planned and performed our review so as to obtain all the information and explanations which we considered necessary in order to provide us with sufficient evidence to give reasonable assurance that the institution has not violated Islamic Sharī'ah rules and principles."[10]

The Sharī'ah board should particularly focus on the Sharī'ah compliance of financial structures, including products, documentation and the process of transactions. Where appropriate, the report of the board should include a clear statement that the financial statements have been examined for the appropriateness of the Sharī'ah basis of allocation of profit between the equity holders and the depositors.

---

[8]  The author is grateful to Mr Faisal Shaikh of Bank Islami Pakistan for sharing knowledge on practical issues of Islamic finance, particularly for this chapter.

[9]  AAOIFI, 2004–5b, Governance Standard No. 1, Sharī'ah Supervisory Board, para. 13.

[10]  AAOIFI, 2004–5b, Governance Standard No. 1, Sharī'ah Supervisory Board, para. 16.

The Sharī'ah board's report should also include a clear statement that all earnings that have been realized from sources or by means prohibited by Islamic Sharī'ah rules and principles have been disposed of to charitable causes. In the case of violation of any Sharī'ah rules or rulings of the Sharī'ah board, the board should indicate the violations in its report. The central Sharī'ah boards may also approve the fit and proper criteria for appointment of Sharī'ah advisors in Islamic banking institutions.

The AAOIFI has also issued standards on Sharī'ah review by the Sharī'ah boards (Governance Standard No. 2) and internal Sharī'ah review (Governance Standard No. 3) by an independent internal audit department of the respective banks. Sharī'ah review is to be carried out in the following stages:

1. Planning review procedures.
2. Executing the review procedures and preparation of working papers.
3. Documenting the conclusion and report.

Internal Sharī'ah review should be conducted to examine and evaluate the extent of compliance of the Sharī'ah rules in the light of the guidelines provided by the Sharī'ah supervisory board.

# 15

# Sukuk and Securitization: Vital Issues in Islamic Capital Markets

## 15.1   INTRODUCTION

The growth of Islamic banking and finance has gained momentum during the last decade, particularly in the areas of Sukuk and securitization. In addition to a large number of products for retail banking and investment instruments, securitization in the framework of the Islamic finance industry has developed a lot of momentum. While Shirkah-based instruments of investment like Mudarabah certificates and participation term certificates (PTCs) have been in use since the early 1980s, local currency instruments/Sukuk based on modes other than Shirkah have been issued since 1992. The first issue of dollar-denominated Sukuk of $600 million was offered in Malaysia in 2002. This was followed by the launching of $400 million Solidarity Trust Sukuk of the Islamic Development Bank in September 2003. Since then, about forty sovereign and corporate Sukuk issues have been offered in Bahrain, Malaysia, Saudi Arabia, Qatar, UAE, the UK, Germany, Pakistan, Indonesia, The Philippines and a number of other countries. Prominent Sukuk issues include PCFC's's Sukuk of USD 3.5 billion to help fund DP World's acquisition of the UK's P&O, $3.52 billion Sukuk offered by Nakheel, the property arm of Dubai's DP World, and Pakistan's sovereign Sukuk of $600 million.[1]

Sukuk are gaining popularity as an alternative source of funding, particularly for sovereigns and corporate bodies. Their growth has been fuelled by strong demand in the global capital market for Sharī´ah-compliant instruments. Standard & Poor's, the well-known rating agency, has put the market for Islamic financial products – banking, mortgages, equity funds, Sukuk, Takaful, project finance, etc. – at $400 billion.[2] Sukuk have taken a crucial position among the instruments of Islamic capital markets by providing an alternative to conventional fixed-income securities issued for funding large developmental and capital expenditures of the big entities and facilitating IFIs and investors in managing liquidity with profitability.

Two decades back, it was considered that only an equity market is possible in an Islamic finance framework for financing long-term projects. This may be partly true, as debts cannot be sold as per Sharī´ah principles unless their trading is subject to the rules of Hawalah, i.e. at face value with recourse to the assignor. Hence, debts cannot generate any return. But the emergence of Sukuk, particularly Ijarah Sukuk and the Sukuk backed by a mixed asset pool, has tended to imply that some features and benefits of a debt market are possible even in an Islamic financial structure.

The major requirement for making an investment certificate Sharī´ah-compliant is that it should not represent interest-bearing debt as dominant part of the underlying assets. The

---

[1] See http://www.lmcbahrain.com.
[2] *The Economist*, 9th–15th December, 2006, p. 73.

Sukuk issued on the bases of Shirkah and Ijarah represent the ownership of the underlying assets by the Sukuk holders; hence, the same can be traded in the secondary market at the price determined by the market forces. A typical debt market provides a fixed return and secondary market trading facilities; Sukuk issued on the basis of Ijarah and pools of mixed assets – fixed as well as intangible like receivables – can also provide the same facility, subject to the fulfilment of certain criteria. Near alternatives of conventional bonds can, therefore, be developed through securitization of assets. The instruments created through securitization of assets represent the proportionate ownership of their holders in the assets.

Like the two categories of modes in Islamic finance, i.e. participatory and fixed-return/debt-creating, Sukuk or investment instruments can also be variable-return Sukuk (VRS) and fixed-return Sukuk (FRS). But the FRS are different from the conventional debt-related instruments like bonds and debentures because, in principle, the return on Islamic instruments will be quasi-fixed, as we shall explain in this chapter, unless an independent third party guarantee is provided, as admissible under the Sharī´ah rules.

## 15.2  THE CAPITAL MARKET IN AN ISLAMIC FRAMEWORK

Before discussing Sukuk and securitization, we may briefly see the salient features of the capital market comprising debt, equity and the Sukuk markets. An equity market, commonly known as a stock market, is the trading place for the stocks of joint stock companies. A debt market, which deals in debentures and bonds, normally involves Riba and Gharar and, therefore, is not an active part of Islamic financial markets. Debts can only be assigned to others on a par value without transferring the risk of default. This process is called Hawalah in Fiqh terminology. The difference between sale and assignment is that transfer in Hawalah is with recourse, while transfer in ordinary sale is without recourse.

Key components of an Islamic capital market are Sharī´ah-compliant stocks, Islamic funds and Sukuk/Islamic investment certificates. The basic concept of a stock market is permissible under Sharī´ah. However, there are certain conditions which need to be followed for investments in stocks conforming to the Sharī´ah principles. Sharī´ah guidelines in respect of stocks have already been given in Chapter 8 and to some extent in Chapter 12.

An Islamic capital market can be developed by developing Sukuk, introducing Islamic depository receipts (IDRs) at a mass level, replacing debt financing with Shirkah-based indirect and direct financing, securitization and fund management. While IDRs refer to an arrangement for trading of stocks in countries other than their origin (see Box 15.1), Sukuk represent common undivided shares in the ownership of underlying assets with the effect that the Sukuk holders share the return as agreed at the time of issuance and bear the loss, if any, in proportion to their share in investment. Issuance of Sharī´ah-compliant Sukuk would result in enhanced supply of risk-based capital with limited risk-taking on account of the prohibition of Riba, gambling and Gharar and a balanced return rate structure based on real-asset-backed economic activities.

---

**Box 15.1:**   Developing Islamic Depository Receipts (IDRs)

A GDR is a negotiable certificate held in the bank of one country representing a specific number of shares of a stock traded on an exchange of another country. It is an arrangement for trading of stocks in countries other than their origin. The following are a few specialized GDRs: American depositor receipts (ADRs); European depository receipts (EDRs) and Islamic depository receipts (IDRs). Parties to an IDR would be the originator of the underlying asset, an investor and the custodian bank. Sharī'ah-compliant stocks and other instruments are to be traded under IDRs.

**Advantages of IDRs**

For the originators

- expansion of investor base;
- low cost of funds in highly liquid markets;
- better image of securities by trading in more organized markets.

For the investors

- diversification of portfolio in other markets;
- IFIs to have Sharī'ah-compliant stocks;
- higher returns for IFIs than conventional placements in Murabaha;
- liquidity management facility for IFIs.

**Importance of IDRs**

- convergence of Islamic capital markets;
- an alternative to cross-listing;
- better regulatory environment due to listing of IDRs;
- generation of development funds for developing Muslim countries;
- standardization of Sharī'ah compliance standards across jurisdictions;
- growth of Islamic capital markets.

**Institutions supporting IDR development include**

- Islamic Development Bank (IDB);
- International Islamic Financial Market (IIFM);
- rating agencies;
- International Financial Services Board (IFSB);
- local regulatory bodies;
- Islamic financial institutions.

# 15.3 SECURITIZATION AND SUKUK

The traditional business model of financial institutions revolved around originating an asset and holding it until maturity. But now, financial institutions increasingly resort to securitization, which is a process of pooling/repackaging the nonmarketable and illiquid assets into tradable certificates of investment. Securitization transforms the originator's role from being an accumulator to that of a distributor. In Islamic finance it has become a stimulating factor, which refers to the process in which ownership of the underlying assets is transferred to a large number of investors in the form of instruments, presently termed Sukuk (the plural of the word Sak, or Sanadat, meaning certificate of investment or simply certificates).

The ownership of the securitized assets is transferred to a special purpose vehicle (SPV) or special purpose Mudarabah (SPM) that is set up for the dual purpose of managing the assets on behalf of the Sukuk holders and for the issuance of the investment certificates. The SPV that serves as Mudarib manages both the liabilities and assets of the issues. The contractual rights attached to Sukuk determine the mutual ownership and benefits of the securitized assets for the individual investors who subscribe to the Sukuk. The Sukuk holders earn any revenue generated by the project and/or capital appreciation of the assets involved.

The AAOIFI has defined investment Sukuk as certificates of equal value representing undivided shares in the ownership of tangible assets, usufruct and services or (in the ownership of) assets of the particular projects or any specified investment activity.[3] Investment Sukuk should be distinguished from common shares and bonds. While shares represent the ownership of a company as a whole and are for an indefinite period, Sukuk represent specified assets and are for a given period of time (so far issued for periods ranging from three months to ten years). Sukuk, unlike bonds, carry returns based on cash flow originating from the assets on the basis of which they are issued.

Islamic financing being asset-backed by nature, provides ample opportunities for issuance of Sukuk on the basis of assets already booked by IFIs or by purchasing the assets with proceeds of a variety of Sukuk created on the principle of Shirkah. The process and the procedures applied for Sukuk issue are almost same as those used for securitization in the conventional set-up, with the exception of avoiding Riba, Gharar and the activities prohibited by the Shari´ah.

Securitization involves evaluating, isolating and efficiently allocating specific risks, evaluating the taxation, accounting and legal implications, designing appropriate credit enhancement structures[4] and pricing the (residual) risk for pricing the units of the securitized assets or pools. Securitization provides a premium over equivalent related plain securities and better stability than vanilla papers. Other benefits of securitization for investors include: focused risks associated with securities, portfolio diversification, tailored cash flow structures backed by the securitized assets, a flexible range of maturities and experienced risk assessment.

Securitization is also beneficial for the originator, as it provides incentives for developing a transparent fund approval process, efficient collection procedures, and a well-built mechanism to control this process. Public availability of information about pool performance adds to confidence in securitized papers. New forms of securities in the form of Sukuk assist the development of capital markets, attract conservative buyers, draw international capital and facilitate the efficient sharing of risks.

Securitized papers are generally traded at a premium over vanilla corporate papers of similar rating and tenor. The premium depends on the liquidity/active secondary market for the securitized paper, the complexity of the transaction structure, investors' comfort with the underlying collateral and investors' demand at the time of issuance. It makes them

---

[3] AAOIFI, 2004–5a, Standard on Investment Sukuk, p. 298.

[4] Credit enhancements in respect of Sukuk could be internal and/or external collateral aspects, in addition to the underlying assets, to reduce the risk to investors and to enhance the rating of the issue. Some examples are: cash reserves, Takaful cover, overcollateralization, early warning triggers performance guarantee by originators of facilities and third party guarantee, if possible.

an effective and attractive tool for mobilizing long-term funds for financing development projects in industry, agriculture and real estate development.

### 15.3.1   Parties to Sukuk Issue/Securitization

Various parties are involved in Sukuk transactions. Key players in various issues of Sukuk are:

- The originator or the issuer of Sukuk, who sells its assets to the SPV and uses the realized funds. Originators are mostly governments or big corporations, but they could be banking or non-banking Islamic financial institutions. The issuers may delegate, for a consideration or a commission, the process of arranging the issue.
- The SPV – an entity set up specifically for the securitization process and managing the issue. It purchases assets from the originator and funds the purchase price by issuing Sukuk. Sometimes, the SPV is also referred to as the issuer.
- Investment banks – as issue agents for underwriting, lead managing and book-making services for Sukuk against any agreed-upon fee or commission. These services are provided by syndicates of Islamic banks and big multinational banks operating Islamic windows.
- Subscribers of Sukuk – mostly central banks, Islamic banks and NBFIs and individuals who subscribe to securities issued by the SPV.

Other parties to the general securitization process may include:

- the obligor: a contractual debtor to the originator who pays cash flows that are securitized;
- the lead manager: as structurer for designing and executing the transaction and as arranger for the securities – may be a company/trust/mutual fund that provides services for managing the issues;
- the servicer: collects and administers the rentals from obligors, monitors and maintains assets;
- the cash administrator or receiving and paying agent: the banker for the deal who manages inflows and outflows, invests interim funds and accesses cash collateral;
- the credit enhancement provider: provides credit enhancement by way of guarantees, Takaful/insurance, etc.;
- the credit rating agency: provides a rating for the deal based on structure, rating of parties, legal and tax aspects;
- the legal and tax counsel: provides key opinions on the structure and underlying contracts with respect to their legal and tax implications;
- the auditor: appointed for conducting due diligence, both initial and during the deal;
- the custodian/R&T agents: appointed for registration/transfer of securities and safe custody of the underlying documents. It actually holds the assets as agent and bailee for the trustee.

Classes of securitized papers include:

- asset-backed securitization (ABS);
- pool-based securitization:

  — mortgage-backed securitization;

— CDO/CLO: collateralized debt/loan obligations (not Sharī'ah-compliant unless subjected to the rules of Hawalah);
— lease rentals securitization (for Sharī'ah compliance of Ijarah Sukuk, ownership of the assets must also be transferred to the Sukuk holders);

- future flow securitization (FFS):

— securitization of receivables to be generated in future;
— road toll securitization (transfer of pro rata ownership to Sukuk holders necessary for Sharī'ah compliance);
— telecom receivable securitization;
— credit card receivable securitization (not Sharī'ah-compliant unless subjected to the rules of Hawalah).

A flow diagram of the typical securitization process is given in Figure 15.1.

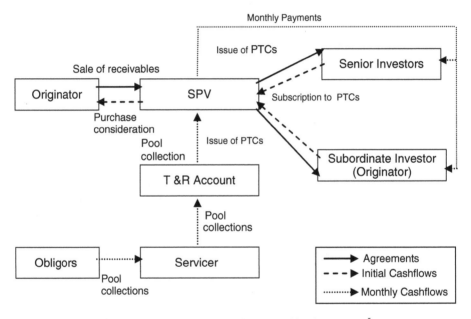

**Figure 15.1**   Flow diagram of the securitization process[5]

### 15.3.2   Special Purpose Vehicle (SPV)

SPVs are formed as separate legal entities for the specified purpose of managing the securities issues. As such, an SPV is capital and tax efficient – it does not add to the costs of the transaction. Major characteristics of a typical SPV include bankruptcy remoteness and thin capitalization.

[5] The author is grateful to M/s Ashar Nazim, Arsalan Siddiqi and Shazia Farooq of Islamic Capital Partners, Karachi and Mr Muhammad Sajid, CEO, JS Finance, Karachi for their help in preparing flow diagrams and charts and also for sharing vital information on securitization and Sukuk.

The legal structure of an SPV depends upon the regulatory and legal environment in which it has to work. It has to be ensured that the sale to the SPV is true and there is a proper segregation of the asset from the original owner. Once the ownership has been transferred to the SPV, the discretion of the original owner in respect of the asset comes to an end, and it cannot be reversed in the case of insolvency of the original owner or otherwise.

Alternative payment structures adopted by SPVs include the "pass-through structure" – the SPV remits any funds collected completely and immediately to the investors – and the "pay-through structures" – desynchronization of servicing of the securities from the underlying cash flows. SPVs may also have discretion to reinvest the funds and pay investors according to a predetermined schedule. They may also serve as "conduits" – vehicles set up for multiple issuances (typically in the case of securitization of receivables of credit cards and commercial papers).

### 15.3.3   Risk, Contract and Cash Flow Analysis

The lead bankers have to undertake minute risk analysis in respect of credit and bankruptcy risk (the ability of the entity to pay its obligations and survive as a viable entity); performance risk (the ability to fulfil contractual obligations); asset/collateral risk (variation in the value of the underlying asset); payment risk (the ability of other parties, particularly credit enhancement providers, to meet their obligations); return rate risk (variation in return rate structure); exchange rate risk; liquidity risk (the ability to liquidate the underlying assets or the collateral to service the investor); risk of loss of money collected and retained by the servicer for a short period before remitting to the SPV; prepayment risk (variation in maturity of the investments made by the investors due to prepayment by obligors); reinvestment risk in pay-through structures (variation in the returns earned on investments made by the SPV for the period until the prespecified dates, and the legal/regulatory/tax related risk (interpretation of various laws, regulations and complex documentation).

Contract analysis focuses on rights and obligations, performance requirements, termination, events of default and consequences of defaults, with the purpose of knowing the ability to fulfil the rights and obligations. It also includes study of transaction documentation.

Cash flow analysis is conducted to identify key variables and expected patterns of the underlying cash flows under various scenarios and to determine the rating.

---

**Box 15.2:**   Securitization Mitigates the Risks

Originator's perspective

- mitigates liquidity risk of an illiquid asset;
- reduced cost of funding;
- takes assets off balance sheet, without loss of use;

- reduced cost of finance if SPV is serving as multiple originators by pooling assets.

Investors' perspective

- foreign exchange risk is reduced if underlying asset is denominated in multiple currencies;
- pooling of diversified assets with heterogeneous risk mitigates earnings risk;
- undivided ownership of the asset is an added protection.

### 15.3.4  Sharī´ah Bases of Sukuk Issue

The AAOIFI, in its Sharī´ah Standard for Investment Sukuk, has discussed the following types of investment certificates or Sukuk:

1. Sukuk of ownership in leased assets: further divided into Sukuk of ownership of usufruct of existing assets, Sukuk of ownership of described future assets, Sukuk of ownership of services of a specified party and Sukuk of ownership of described future services.
2. Salam Sukuk.
3. Istisna‘a Sukuk.
4. Murabaha Sukuk.
5. Musharakah Sukuk: further divided into participation certificates, Mudarabah Sukuk and investment agency Sukuk.
6. Muzara‘ah (share-cropping) Sukuk.
7. Musāqah (projects involving irrigation of fruit-bearing trees) Sukuk.
8. Mughārasah (projects involving plantation of gardens) Sukuk.

The most important of the above Sukuk or certificates of investment with sizeable potential are those issued on the basis of Shirkah, Ijarah, Salam and Istisna‘a. As per the basic rules of Sharī´ah, investment Sukuk have to be structured, on one side, on the principle of Shirkah. However, depending upon the nature of the asset, usufruct of assets or services involved, certificates can be structured to be designated as Ijarah Sukuk, Salam Sukuk and Istisna‘a Sukuk. On the other side, business could be conducted through participatory or fixed return modes/instruments. Thus, the rates of return on Sukuk will be either variable (if the modes on the second leg are participatory) or quasi-fixed (in the case of cash flow from assets securitized through modes with fixed return). However, any third party guarantee can make the Sukuk fixed-return certificates of investment.[6]

The issuers or the Sukuk holders can adopt any permissible methods of managing and mitigating risks, such as creating a Takaful fund with contributions from certificate holders, or taking cover from Islamic Takaful companies and paying the contributions from the income of the issue or donations of the Sukuk holders. It is also permissible to set aside a certain percentage of the profit in order to mitigate fluctuations of distributable profit, subject to the condition that proper disclosure was made in the prospectus of the issue.

*Disgusting Bases of Sukuk Issues and Trading*

Most of the Sukuk issues so far are based on the concept of Ijarah, while a few Sukuk are based on Shirkah, Salam or pooled assets. A number of Sukuk issues are subject to severe criticism due to the involvement of Bai‘ al ‘Inah, Bai‘ al Dayn and other non-Sharī´ah-compliant traits that make the Sukuk as good or as bad as interest-based bonds. Bai‘ al ‘Inah is a double sale by which the borrower and the lender sell and then resell an object between them, once for cash and once for a higher price on credit, with the net result of a loan with interest. As such, it is a legal device to circumvent the prohibition of Riba. Sukuk issues of Malaysia are mostly based on the concepts of Bai‘ al ‘Inah of underlying assets and the concept of Tabarru‘ (donation to the investor irrespective of the cash flow of the project

---

[6] Council of the Islamic Fiqh Academy, 2000, p. 65; AAOIFI, 2004–5a, Standard on Guarantees (No. 5), clause 7/6 and Standard on Sukuk (No. 17), clause 5/1/8/7.

underlying the Sukuk or certificates), while their trading in the secondary market takes place through Bai' al Dayn. (Lately, they have also been issuing Ijarah Sukuk, which is a healthy development.)

Rosly and Sanusi have concluded in this regard:

> "The use of a legal device is therefore evidence that the Niyyah (intention) factor is undermined or made secondary in the securitization process of Islamic bonds in Malaysia... To retain the basic structure of traditional bonds in Islamic finance, that is providing fixed return to investors, practitioners and the relevant Sharī'ah experts may have wrongly applied Sharī'ah laws, which implies now that the legitimacy of Islamic bonds issued using Bai' al 'Inah is suspect."[7]

In the case of a variety of Malaysia-based Sukuk, secondary market trading of Sukuk is conducted on the basis of Bai' al Dayn. However, the majority of jurists do not accept this, even though the debt represented by Sukuk is supported by the underlying assets. The traditional Muslim jurists are unanimous on the point that Bai' al Dayn with discount is not allowed in Sharī' ah. The overwhelming majority of contemporary Sharī'ah scholars are also of the same view. However, some scholars from Malaysia have allowed this kind of sale. They normally refer to the ruling of the Shafi'e school, but they do not consider the fact that the Shafi'e jurists allowed it only in a case where a debt was sold at its par value.[8] Rosly and Sanusi have observed in this regard:

> "The trading of Islamic bonds at a discount using Bai' al Dayn has been found unacceptable by the Jamhur Ulama, including al-Shafi'e. As such, the position of Malaysian Islamic bonds remains unacceptable among the Middle Eastern jurists, although some Malaysian jurists found this the opposite."

The OIC Islamic Fiqh Council, which has the representation of all Islamic countries, including Malaysia, has also approved the prohibition of Bai' al Dayn unanimously, without a single dissent.

In contrast to the Bai' al 'Inah concept, which is prohibited, the experts in Sharī'ah principles allow the use of a sale and lease-back technique. This is because of the flexibility in the Ijarah contract, as discussed earlier. An asset can be purchased from a party and then leased to that party. In this case, the Ijarah contract should not be executed unless and until the IFI has acquired the asset.[9] As such, the sale and lease-back technique does not create any Sharī'ah-related problem, particularly in respect of Sukuk issue on the basis of Ijarah, provided the sale of the asset is complete in all respects and then the Ijarah rules are made applicable. (Use of sale and lease-back in the case of consumer durables is not considered desirable by many Sharī'ah scholars and even practitioners, and they allow it only where the client wants to avoid interest-based financing and there is no other way out.) Assets leased under this technique can again be sold to the original owner, as in the case of most of the sovereign Ijarah Sukuk issued so far. Sharī'ah scholars suggest, however, that sufficient time should pass before the lessee repurchases the asset, in which time there is the possibility of a change in the value and structure of the asset being sold and leased back. They recommend that in such cases, the client should purchase back the asset at least after one year of sale. This is to ensure that the technique is not used as a back door to interest.

---

[7] Rosly and Sanusi, 1999, **1**(2) (http://islamic-finance.net/journal.html).
[8] Usmani, 2000a, pp. 216–217.
[9] AAOIFI, 2004–5a, pp. 140, 152.

Ijarah has great flexibility and a large potential for Sukuk issue, but some of the features of Ijarah Sukuk issues or the agreements involved in the process are pointers to different Sharī´ah-related problems. As per Sharī´ah rules, Sukuk holders have to jointly bear the risks of an asset's price and the ownership-related costs and share its rent by leasing it to any user. As discussed in Chapter 11, due to the possibility of nonpredictable expenses relating to the ownership of relevant leased assets and possible defaults, the returns could be quasi-fixed and not absolutely fixed or unmodified when pegged to any benchmark. However, the returns on most of the Sukuk are absolutely fixed or unmodified. This aspect carries systemic risk of non-Sharī´ah-compliance, which nullifies the very basis of the Islamic financial system and contravenes the investors' aspiration based on their belief.

Sukuk originating from Sudan, Bahrain and other Middle Eastern countries are based on Shirkah, Ijarah, Salam, Istisna'a, Istisna'a-cum-Ijarah or a pool of mixed assets. Such Sukuk are acceptable to almost all of the Islamic scholars and banking experts, subject to the fulfilment of minimal Sharī´ah essentials associated with underlying contracts.

### 15.3.5   Categories of Sukuk

Below we discuss various categories of Sukuk.

*Muqaradah or Mudarabah Sukuk*

Mudarabah or Muqaradah[10] Sukuk or deeds can be instrumental in enhancing public participation in investment activities in any economy. These are certificates that represent projects or activities managed on the Mudarabah principle by appointing any of the partners or any other person as Mudarib for management of the business. As regards the relationship between the parties to the issue, the issuer of Mudarabah certificates is the Mudarib, subscribers are the owners of the capital and the realized funds are the Mudarabah capital. The certificate holders own the assets of the Mudarabah and the agreed upon share of the profits belongs to the owners of capital and they bear the loss, if any.

In terms of the Resolution of the Islamic Fiqh Council of the OIC (fourth session, 1988), the following are the salient features of Mudarabah Sukuk/certificates:

1. Mudarabah Sukuk (MS) represent common ownership and entitle their holders to a share in the specific projects against which the MS have been issued.
2. The MS contract is based on the official notice of the issue or the prospectus, which must provide all information required by Sharī´ah for a Qirād contract, such as the nature of capital, the ratio for profit distribution and other conditions related to the issue, which must be compatible with Sharī´ah.
3. The MS holder is given the right to transfer the ownership by selling the Sukuk in the securities market at his discretion. The market value of Muqaradah Sukuk varies with the business status and anticipated or expected profits of the concerned project. The sale of MS must follow the rules listed below:

---

[10] Muqaradah or Qirād have the same meaning as that of Mudarabah, as explained in Chapter 12 (in the part relating to Mudarabah).

— if the Mudarabah capital is still in the form of money before the operation of the specific project, the trading of MS will be like the exchange of money for money and it must satisfy the rules of Bai' al Sarf;[11]

— if the Mudarabah capital is in the form of debt, it must be based on the principles of debt trading in Islamic jurisprudence;

— if the capital is in the form of a combination of cash, receivables, goods, real assets and benefits, trade must be based on the market price evolved by mutual consent.

4. The manager/SPV who receives the funds collected from the subscribers to MS can also invest his own funds. He will get a profit for his capital contribution in addition to his share in the profit as Mudarib.

5. Neither prospectus nor MS should contain a guarantee, from the issuer or the manager of the fund, for the capital or a fixed profit, or a profit based on any percentage of the capital. Accordingly, (i) the prospectus, or the MS issued pursuant to it, may not stipulate payment of a specific amount to the MS holder, (ii) profit is to be divided, as determined by applying the rules of Sharī'ah; that is, an amount in excess of the capital, and not the revenue or the yield, and (iii) the Profit and Loss Account of the project must be published and disseminated to MS holders.

6. It is permissible to create reserves for contingencies, such as loss of capital, by deducting from the profit a certain percentage in each accounting period.

7. The prospectus can also contain a promise made by a third party, totally unrelated to the parties to the contract, in terms of legal entity or financial status, to donate a specific sum, without any counter benefit, to meet losses in a given project, provided such commitment is independent of the Mudarabah contract. However, it is not permissible for the issuer to guarantee the capital of the Mudarabah.[12]

IFIs can offer Mudarabah Sukuk or certificates to the investors who would subscribe and participate in the investment transactions. The funds mobilized would be the variable capital (class B share) of any bank to be marketed regionally through the selling of the issued Mudarabah Sukuk.

*Musharakah Sukuk*

Musharakah is a mode which can serve as a basis for securitization easily, especially in the case of big projects where huge amounts are required. Every subscriber is given a Musharakah certificate, which represents his proportionate ownership in the assets of the project. These are certificates of equal value issued for mobilizing funds to be used on the basis of partnership, so that their holders become owners of the relevant project or the asset as per their respective shares that are part of their asset portfolios. Musharakah Sukuk can be issued as redeemable certificates by or to the corporate sector or to individuals for their rehabilitation/employment, for the purchase of automobiles for their commercial use or for the establishment of high-standard clinics, hospitals, factories, trading centres, endowments, etc.

---

[11] Bai' al Sarf refers to the exchange of gold, silver, monetary values/receivables or currencies; this has to be equal for equal and simultaneous if the items of exchange are homogeneous, like gold for gold or US Dollar for US Dollar; and simultaneous if the items being exchanged are heterogeneous, e.g. gold for silver or Pound for Dollar.

[12] Council of the Islamic Fiqh Academy, 2000, pp. 61–66.

Musharakah redeemable Sukuk are almost similar to Mudarabah Sukuk. Therefore, basic Sharī'ah rules relating to Mudarabah also apply to Musharakah certificates. The only major difference is that the intermediary party will be a partner of the group of subscribers represented by a body of Musharakah certificate holders, in a manner similar to a joint stock company.[13]

After the project is started, these Musharakah certificates can be treated as negotiable instruments. Certificates based on Musharakah/Mudarabah can be bought and sold in the secondary market, subject to the condition that the portfolio of Musharakah comprises nonliquid assets valuing more than 50 %. Profit earned by the Musharakah is shared according to an agreed ratio. Loss is shared on a pro rata basis. Whenever there is a combination of liquid and nonliquid assets, it can be sold and purchased for an amount greater than the amount of liquid assets in the combination or in the pool.

Investment Sukuk can be issued on a Musharakah basis to mobilize short-term deposits for the development of long-term projects or for investment in general financial activities or specific projects. The proceeds of the Sukuk can be used to buy and lease certain equipment or for the construction of projects and factories, the expansion of projects or for working capital finance. The Musharakah structure is considered more equitable and also safer for the investors than the Mudarabah structure, as it involves both profit- and loss-sharing between the fund manager and the Sukuk holders, not only profit-sharing. In addition, Musharakah Sukuk holders will have added comfort and security from the cushion provided by the manager's participation in the Musharakah capital.

In Sudan, a number of assets of the Ministry of Finance and the Bank of Sudan, Bank of Khartoum, Nilain Bank and other public entities have been identified for the purpose of securitization on a Musharakah basis. Instruments known as central bank Musharakah certificates (CMCs) and government Musharakah certificates (GMCs) have been issued since 1998 for investors and are used in place of treasury bills and other interest-bearing securities for open market operations and monetary management by the central bank. The CMCs are sold (or bought) by the central bank through auctions and can be traded in the secondary inter-bank market.[14]

### Ijarah Sukuk

The concept of Ijarah can be used for mobilizing funds for the development of long-term infrastructure projects. This is possible through securitization of tangible assets such as airports, roads, buildings, schools and hospitals and offering Sukuk to a large number of institutional and individual investors. It is also possible to create a secondary market instrument for financiers on the basis of Ijarah.

If a lessor, after executing an Ijarah contract, wishes to recover his cost of purchase of the asset to get liquidity or for the purpose of profit, he can sell the leased asset wholly or partly, either to one party or to a number of individuals. The purchase of proportion of the asset can be evidenced by issuing certificates, which may be called Ijarah certificates or Sukuk. The certificates must represent ownership of the pro rata undivided parts of the asset with all related rights and obligations. Hence, Ijarah Sukuk are the securities representing

---

[13] Homoud, 1998.
[14] Ayub, 2002, pp. 128–131; Eltejani, 2005, pp. 411–413.

ownership of well-defined and known assets tied up to a lease contract, rental of which is the return payable to the Sukuk holders.

By virtue of flexibility in the rules of Ijarah, securitizing the Ijarah contracts is a key factor for solving liquidity management problems and financing the public sector needs in developing countries. Payment of Ijarah rentals can be unrelated to the period of taking usufruct by the lessee, i.e. it can be made before the beginning of the lease period, during the period or after the period, as the parties may mutually decide. This flexibility can be used to evolve different forms of contracts and Sukuk that may suit different purposes of issuers and investors.

If funds are raised through issuance of Sukuk for purchasing assets like buildings, motor vehicles or other equipment for the purpose of leasing them out to their ultimate users, these may be termed Ijarah funds. The ownership of the assets remains with the fund manager or SPV and the rentals received from the users are distributed by the fund managers pro rata among the subscribers. As discussed in detail in Chapter 12, most of the jurists are of the view that such a fund cannot be created on the basis of Mudarabah, because Mudarabah, according to them, is restricted to the sale of goods and does not extend to the business of services and leases. However, in the Hanbali school, Mudarabah can be used in services and also leases. This view is preferred by the majority of contemporary scholars.

Rental in Ijarah must be stipulated in clear terms for the first term of lease, and for future renewable terms it could be constant, increasing or decreasing by benchmarking or relating it to any well-known variable like the inflation rate, any periodically announced price index, or otherwise by any settled percentage. The mainstream Sharī´ah experts have permitted benchmarking with any interest rate reference, although it is not an ideal practice to them.[15]

Governments can use Ijarah Sukuk as an alternative tool to interest-based borrowing, provided they have durable assets useable in the process of performing government functions. Use of assets by governments is necessary, while it does not matter whether these assets are income-generating or not.

The following types of Sukuk can be issued on the concept of Ijarah:

1. Sukuk of ownership in leased assets. These are certificates of equal value that are issued either by the owner of a leased asset or an asset to be leased (by promise), or by his financial agent, with the aim of recovering the value of the asset through subscription. The subscribers are buyers of the asset. The certificate holders become owners of the asset jointly, with its benefits and risks.
2. Sukuk of ownership of usufruct of assets. Such certificates have various types, including the following:

   — Sukuk of ownership of usufructs of existing assets. These are documents of equal value issued either by the owner of usufruct of an existing asset or a financial intermediary acting on the owner's behalf. The mobilized funds from subscription are the purchase price of the usufructs, and the certificate holders become owners of the usufruct along with the risks and rewards. It is permissible to trade in certificates of ownership of usufructs of tangible assets prior to a contract of sub-leasing the assets. When the assets are sub-leased, the certificate then represents the rent receivables, which makes it a debt certificate. Therefore, in that case, the certificate is subject to the rules and

---

[15] Usmani, 2000a, pp. 168–171.

requirements of debts. It is permissible for the issuer to redeem, either at the market price or as agreed upon at the time of purchase, the Sukuk of ownership of usufruct of tangible assets from the Sukuk holder after allocation of Sukuk and payment of subscription amounts.

— Certificates of ownership of usufructs to be made available in the future as per description. These are documents of equal value issued for the sake of leasing assets that the lessor is liable to provide in the future, whereby the rental is recovered from the subscription income, in which case the holders of the certificates become owners of the usufruct of the future assets. The subscribers are buyers of usufructs and will have both the risks and rewards. Such Sukuk can be traded after the asset is identified. It is not valid to sub-lease or trade in usufructs of an asset to be made available prior to identification of the asset, in which case trading must be carried out in line with the rules of currency exchange. The trading rules in the case of sub-leasing of such usufructs would be the same as those discussed above.

— Certificates of ownership of services of a specified supplier. These are documents of equal value issued for the sake of providing or selling services through a specified supplier (such as educational programmes in a particular university) and obtaining the value in the form of subscription income, in which case the holders of the Sukuk become owners of the services.

— Certificates of ownership of services to be made available in the future as per description. These are documents of equal value issued for the sake of providing or selling services through a nonexisting supplier with the description of the subject matter (such as educational programmes of a specific quality, schedule, duration, etc. without mentioning the educational institution) and obtaining the value in the form of subscription income, in which case the holders of the certificates become owners of the services.[16]

The following features may be kept in mind for securitization under Ijarah. It is necessary for an Ijarah contract that the asset being leased and the amount of rent both are clearly known to the parties at the time of the contract, and if both of these are known, Ijarah can be contracted on an asset or a building that is yet to be constructed, as long as it is fully described in the contract, provided that the lessor should normally be able to acquire, construct or buy the asset being leased by the time set for its delivery to the lessee. The lessor can sell the leased asset provided it does not hinder the lessee in taking benefit from the asset. The new owner(s) will be entitled to receive the rentals for the remaining period. Similarly, they can dispose of their share in the asset to the new owners individually or collectively.

As an Ijarah certificate represents the holder's proportionate ownership in the leased asset, the holder will assume the rights and obligations of the owner/lessor to the extent of his ownership. The holder will have the right to enjoy part of the rent according to his proportion of ownership in the asset. In the case of total destruction of the assets, he will suffer the loss to the extent of his ownership. So, it is essential that the Ijarah certificates are designed to represent real ownership of the leased assets, and not only a right to receive the rent.

As per Sharī´ah rules, expenses related to the corpus or basic characteristics of the asset are the responsibility of the owner, while maintenance expenses related to its operation

---

[16] AAOIFI, 2004–5a, pp. 298–302.

are to be borne by the lessee. Therefore, the expected return flow from such Sukuk may not be completely fixed and predetermined. From this perspective, Ijarah Sukuk should be taken as quasi-fixed return instruments in Islamic finance. There is one possibility that the owner/lessor of the asset may assure the purchaser (SPV/Sukuk holder) about – performance of the lessees, as in the case of IDB Trust. But if the asset is destroyed without any fault or negligence of the lessee, the loss has to be borne by the lessor – the Sukuk holders.

It can be agreed between the parties that the rental should consist of two parts – one for payment to the lessor and the other as an "on account" payment, to be held by the lessee for any costs relating to ownership of the asset.

As regards the procedure for issuance of Ijarah Sukuk, an SPV is created to purchase the asset(s), and this serves as a manager and issues Sukuk to the investors, enabling it to make payment for purchasing the asset. The asset is then leased to the government or any corporate body for its use. The lessee makes periodic rental payments to the SPV, which, in turn, distributes the same among the Sukuk holders. As the lessor can stipulate the rental in advance, the rental on Sukuk issue can be indicated in advance with the possibility of very small variation that might be possible due to payment of ownership-related unpredictable expenses by the lessor or the possibility of any default by the lessee.

Ijarah certificates can be negotiated and traded freely in the market and can serve as an instrument easily convertible into cash. But, this should be after transfer of ownership to the Sukuk holders, necessarily implying that the Sukuk represent real assets and not the monetary capital, and that the holders have become owners of the assets (after which they can sell). It is also permissible for the issuer to redeem, before maturity, certificates of ownership of leased assets at the market price or at the price agreed upon between the certificate holder and the issuer. Similarly, Ijarah Sukuk representing ownership of the usufruct of ascertained assets can be traded prior to the contract of sub-leasing (because in that case they would represent the monetary rent receivable).

## Salam Securities/Sukuk

Salam is a contract in which advance payment of a price is made for goods to be delivered later on. As per the AAOIFI Standard, a Salam purchase can onward sell the Salam commodity by another contract which is parallel to the first. In this case, the first and the second contracts should be independent of each other. Specifications of the goods and delivery dates of the two contracts may conform to each other, but both the contracts should be independently enforceable.

Salam Sukuk are certificates of equal value issued for the sake of mobilizing capital that is paid in advance in the shape of the price of the commodity to be delivered later. The seller of the Salam commodity issues the certificates, while the subscribers are the buyers of that commodity, i.e. they are the owners of the commodity when delivered. In the case of Parallel Salam, the holders of Salam Sukuk are entitled to the Salam commodity or the selling price at the time when the commodity is delivered.

Salam sale is attractive to the seller, whose cash flow is enhanced in advance, and to the buyer, as the Salam price is normally lower than the prevailing spot price. The BMA, in June 2001, developed Salam-based securities with LIBOR-related three-month tenures used by Islamic banks for maintaining SLR. The Bahrain government sells aluminium to Bahrain Islamic Bank (BIB), which has been nominated to represent the other banks wishing to participate in the Salam contract. The government undertakes to supply a specified amount of aluminium on the basis of Salam at a future date. At the same time, BIB appoints the government its agent to market the aluminium at the time of delivery through its channels of distribution at a price which provides a return to the security holders. Such short-term Sukuk can be developed on the basis of commodities being heavily traded, like crude oil and cotton, and the produce of big industrial projects having firm demand.

So far, secondary market trading of Salam Sukuk is considered impermissible on the grounds that the certificates represent a share in the Salam debt, in which case they are subject to the rules of debt trading. The issue needs further analysis in respect of reselling the goods purchased under Salam before taking possession by the original buyer, especially in the situation when he maintains inventory of that kind of goods, in which case banks would be selling those goods out of the stock maintained by them without specifying any units of the goods.

The Salam seller is bound to deliver the goods at the agreed date/time. The possibility of a change in price of tangible goods during the Salam contract/the delivery period gives rise to a business risk needed for getting a return through sale. Secondly, Salam deals have been allowed as an exception from the general rule of not selling goods without having their ownership and possession by dint of some conditions that are put in place to avoid excessive Gharar in transactions. If it is allowed, the Salam Sukuk may be negotiable. The purchaser of Sukuk would be the owner of the commodity to be delivered at the specified date and the price of Sukuk would be determined by the market, depending upon the demand and supply of the underlying commodity.

## Istisna'a Sukuk

Istisna'a is a contractual agreement for manufacturing goods, allowing cash payment in advance and future delivery or a future payment and future delivery of the goods manufactured, as per the contract. It can be used for providing the facility of financing the manufacture or construction of houses, plant, projects, bridges, roads and highways. By way of a Parallel Istisna'a contract with subcontractors, Islamic banks can undertake the construction of any project/asset and its sale for a deferred price, and subcontract the actual construction to any specialized firms.

In Istisna'a, full ownership of the constructed item is immediately transferred upon delivery of the item to the purchaser, against the deferred sale price that normally covers not only the construction costs but also profits, which could legitimately include the cost of tying funds for the duration of the repayment period. The payable deferred price can be documented in the form of Sukuk (certificates of indebtedness), known as Istisna'a Sukuk, which are documents that carry equal value and are issued with the aim of mobilizing the funds required for producing a certain item. The issuer of the certificates is the manufacturer (seller), while the subscribers or certificate holders are the buyers of the item to be produced.

It is permissible to trade in or redeem Istisna'a certificates if the funds have been converted through business or trade into assets owned by certificate holders during the operation of Istisna'a, as the Sukuk represent properties that can be disposed of. If the realized funds are immediately paid as a price in a Parallel Istisna'a contract or the manufactured item is submitted to the ultimate purchaser, then trading in Istisna'a certificates is subject to the rules of disposing of debts. This is because the Sukuk represent a price that is a monetary debt owed by the ultimate purchaser to the manufacturer.[17]

The prohibition of Riba precludes the sale of these debt certificates to a third party at any price other than their face value. Therefore, such certificates, which may be cashed only on maturity, cannot have a secondary market. However, they can be transferred at face value to a third party. Builders, big industrial concerns and wholesale suppliers can sell to the IFIs certain assets on an Istisna'a basis on deferred payment and issue Istisna'a Sukuk redeemable periodically according to their payment dates. The holders of Istisna'a Sukuk may acquire against them property or merchandise for a deferred price. Once acquired, such property or merchandise can be disposed of in any manner. As indicated earlier in the book, the deferred price of goods acquired against such certificates would be higher than the spot price of the same goods. The certificate holder acquiring the goods now at higher than the spot price is, in fact, relinquishing to the seller of the goods some (all, or even more) of the price differential which the former obtained from the client above the construction cost of the project he financed. This means that the market forces can play a role in encouraging or curtailing the exchange of these certificates for goods.[18]

### Securitization on the Basis of Murabaha and Murabaha Sukuk

Any paper representing a monetary right or obligation arising out of a credit sale transaction by banks cannot create a negotiable instrument. Therefore, Murabaha receivables cannot be securitized for creating negotiable Sukuk to be traded in the secondary market. The purchaser on credit in a Murabaha transaction signs a note or paper to evidence his indebtedness towards the seller. That paper represents a debt receivable by the seller. Transfer of this paper to a third party must be at par value and subject to the rules of Hawalah, meaning that its assignment also has to be at face value. However, if a commodity has been purchased but not yet sold, trading in certificates issued against it is allowed, as the certificates represent the asset that can be traded.

A mixed portfolio consisting of a number of transactions, including Murabaha, may issue negotiable certificates subject to certain conditions. For this purpose, the pool of the assets should consist of Ijarah or other fixed assets valuing more than 50 % of its total worth. However, if the Hanafi view is adopted, trading will be allowed even if the nonliquid assets are more than 10 % of its total worth.

Murabaha Sukuk are more likely to be used in respect of purchases of goods by the public sector. If the government needs items of huge price, it may purchase them through credit sales by paying in instalments. The seller will amortize his cost and return (profit margin) over the period of instalments. The government will issue certificates according to the number of instalments. Each certificate having a maturity date will represent a property right of the seller, which can change hands provided the amount of the claim does not change. The seller or the original certificate holder can transfer his collection rights to another party, subject to recourse to him against payment that would be equal to the face value of the certificate minus the collection cost at the transferee's end. Any "Murabaha funds" can also issue Murabaha Sukuk, the proceeds of which could be used for sale of prespecified and

---

[17]   AAOIFI, 2004–5a, p. 311.
[18]   Al-Bashir and Al-Amine, 2001.

general assets on the basis of Murabaha to give a quasi-fixed return to the Murabaha Sukuk holders.

Arcapita Bank B.S.C (Bahrain) issued five-year multicurrency Murabaha-backed Sukuk in 2005 with a five-year bullet maturity. The proceeds of the Sukuk are used for sale and purchase of assets via a series of commodity Murabaha transactions. As Murabaha may yield a fixed return, the Sukuk holders have been offered a return equivalent to three-month LIBOR + 175 bps. The SPV will have full recourse to Arcapita and, therefore, the Sukuk are a freely transferable instrument on the basis of a mechanism approved by Arcapita's Sharī'ah supervisory board. It is presumed that the SPV will be maintaining a sufficient amount of inventory or fixed assets, making its Sukuk negotiable.

*Mixed Portfolio Securities/Sukuk*

Banks may securitize a pool of Musharakah, Ijarah and some Murabaha, Salam, Istisna'a, and Ju'alah (a contract for performing a given task against a prescribed fee in a given period) contracts. The return/risk on such securities depends on the chosen mix of the contracts. A prominent example of such mixed portfolio Sukuk are IDB's Solidarity Trust Sukuk for US$ 400 million issued in 2003. Salient features of IDB Solidarity Trust Sukuk are given below.

Solidarity Trust Services (STS) served as trustee to issue the fixed-rate trust certificates that were issued to purchase a portfolio of Sukuk assets comprising Ijarah, Murabaha and Istisna'a contracts originated by the IDB. Each certificate represented an undivided beneficial ownership in trust assets and ranked *pari passu* with other trust certificates. Most of the assets (over 50 %) would, at all times during the period, comprise Ijarah assets. If, at any time, the proportion of assets evidenced by Ijarah contracts fell below 25 %, a dissolution event would occur, and IDB, by virtue of its separate undertaking, would be obliged to purchase all of the assets owned by the trustee pursuant to the terms of the "purchase undertaking deed". Profit on Sukuk assets, net of expenses of the trust, would be used to give a periodic return to the certificate holders. Certificates would be redeemed at 100 % of their principal value. In the case of any early dissolution event, the redemption would be according to adjustment, keeping in mind the return accumulation period. Principal amounts of Sukuk would be reinvested in Ijarah and Musharakah contracts to form a part of Sukuk assets.

On the basis of a separate undertaking, IDB has guaranteed payments in respect of assets owed by the trustee by reference to the schedule of payments given by IDB at the time of sale of assets to the trustee. Certificate holders will not have any recourse for payment of any amount in respect of certificates in case the trust assets are exhausted.

As such, IDB's guarantee (for the rate on the certificates) does not comprise a guarantee of payments in respect of the trust certificates, but represents a guarantee, *inter alia*, of the amount scheduled as being payable by the obligors of the underlying transactions in respect of the assets. In the case of any shortfall in return on the Sukuk assets, the IDB has agreed to meet the shortfall. IDB has also agreed to provide an interest-free facility to the STS to ensure timely payment of any periodic distribution amounts on the trust certificates. Thus, the ability of the trust to pay the due on certificates ultimately depends on IDB.

On the basis of the "purchase undertaking deed" between IDB and the trust, the IDB will purchase the Sukuk assets on the earlier of the maturity date or the dissolution date. The proceeds will be distributed by the trust among the certificate holders, who will periodically receive a fixed rate of return net of any withholding or any other taxes.

Under Islamic banking principles, IDB has to retain the risk of default on the Sukuk assets sold to the trust. As such, it is an unconditional and irrevocable guarantor to provide liquidity to the trust to cover costs and expenses, periodic distribution payments and the principal amount of investment to Sukuk holders. A flow-chart of IDB Trust Sukuk is given in Figure 15.2.

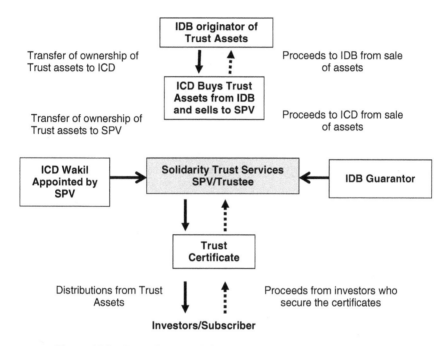

**Figure 15.2**   Flow diagram of IDB mixed portfolio Sukuk issue, 2003

The modus operandi of issuing mixed portfolio Sukuk is an effective tool for converting nonmarketable and illiquid assets to negotiable instruments having a secondary market, particularly suitable for investment banks and DFIs.

### 15.3.6   Tradability of Sukuk

Sukuk representing tangible assets or usufruct of such assets can be traded in the secondary market, depending upon the quality, risk and profitability of the securitized assets. Tradability is a highly important feature that has to be kept in mind while issuing Sukuk as well as for making investment. A deciding factor in this regard is whether the Sukuk create any debt obligations or they represent an ownership stake in the underlying assets or project; in the former case, the certificate will not be tradable, while in the latter case, it will be negotiable/tradable. As discussed above in the case of various categories of Sukuk in the light of the AAOIFI Standard, the Sharī´ah position of their trading in the secondary market is given in Box 15.3.

**Box 15.3:**   Tradability of Sukuk in the Secondary Market[19]

| | |
|---|---|
| Mudarabah/Musharakah certificates or Sukuk | Tradable at market price after the commencement of the activity for which the funds were raised. |
| Ijarah Sukuk based on freehold existing assets | Tradable at market price. |
| Ijarah Sukuk of existing assets subject to head lease | Tradable at market price or at a rate agreed upon at the date of redemption. |
| Ijarah Sukuk based on future tangible assets | Tradable at market price only after the asset is ascertained and leased. |
| Sukuk based on existing specified services | Tradable prior to sub-leasing of such services. |
| Sukuk based on described future services | Tradable at market price only after the source of the service is ascertained. |
| Salam Sukuk | Not tradable except at the face value. |
| Istisna'a Sukuk | Tradable if funds converted into assets and before sale to the orderer. |
| Sukuk issued on Mudarabah basis for Murabaha sales – Murabaha Sukuk | Tradable before sale of the goods to the end-buyer or if receivables (if inventory is maintained) are less than 50 %; after sale of the goods and without inventory of more than 50 %, tradable only at face value with recourse. |

**Box 15.4:**   Prominent Sukuk Issues in Various Countries[20]

| Name of Sukuk | Type | Amount | Period | Pricing |
|---|---|---|---|---|
| Malaysian Global First | Corporate | US$ 150M | 5 years | Floating rate on underlying Ijarah |
| IFC Wawasan Ringgit Sukuk (Bai' bil Thamanal Ajil) | Corporate | US$ 132M | 3 years | Fixed, 2.82 % |
| Malaysian Global Ijarah Sukuk | Sovereign | US$ 500M | 7 years | Floating, LIBOR-related |
| Qatar Global Ijarah Sukuk | Sovereign | US$ 700M | 7 years | 0.4 % above LIBOR |
| Tabreed Global Ijarah Sukuk | Corporate | US$ 100M | 5 years | Fixed, 6 % |
| Sukuk Al Intifaa Makkah | Corporate | US$ 390M | 24 years | Sale of usufruct rights as weekly time shares |
| Ijarah Sukuk Saxony-Anhalt Germany | Sovereign | Euro 100M | 5 years | 1 basis point over 6-month EURIBOR |
| Dubai – Civil Aviation (DCA) Ijarah Sukuk | Corporate | US$ 750M | 5 years | Floating reference rate on underlying Ijarah |

---

[19] AAOIFI, 2004–5a, Standard on Investment Certificates (No. 17), clause 5/2.
[20] Web sites of LMC (http://www.lmcbahrain.com) and respective entities.

| | | | | |
|---|---|---|---|---|
| Sitara Musharakah Term Finance | Corporate | Pak Rs. 360M | 5 years | Shirkah-based profit/loss |
| Solidarity Trust Certificates IDB | Corporate | US$ 400M | 5 years | Based on performance of mixed portfolio, IDB guarantee |
| Bahrain Monetary Agency (BMA) | Sovereign | US$ 100M | 5 years | Fixed, 4.25 % |
| GoB – BMA | Sovereign | US$ 70M | 3 years | Fixed, 4 % |
| BMA | Sovereign | US$ 80M | 5 years | Fixed, 4 % |
| BMA | Sovereign | US$ 50M | 3 years | Fixed, 3 % |
| BMA | Sovereign | US$ 80M | 3 years | Fixed, 3 % |
| BMA | Sovereign | US$ 100M | 5 years | Fixed, 3.75 % |
| BMA | Sovereign | US$ 250M | 5 years | 0.6 % above LIBOR |
| BMA | Sovereign | US$ 200M | 5 years | Floating rate reference |
| BMA | Sovereign | US$ 106M | 10 years | Fixed, 5.125 % |
| 1st Islamic Investment Bank, Bahrain | Corporate | US$ 75M | 3 years | LIBOR-related |
| Malaysia Global Ijarah | Sovereign | US$ 600M | 5 years | 0.95 % above LIBOR |
| Dubai Civil Aviation Sukuk | Sovereign | US$ 1000M | 5 years | Fixed |
| Durrat Real Estate Sukuk | Sovereign | US$ 120M | 5 years | 1.25 % above LIBOR |
| Sarawak Ijarah Sukuk | Sovereign | US$ 350M | 5 years | 1.25 % above LIBOR |
| Nakheel Sukuk | Corporate | US$ 3.52B | 3 years | 1.20 % above LIBOR |
| Ijarah Sukuk, Pakistan | Sovereign | US$ 600M | 5 years | 2.20 % above LIBOR |

### 15.3.7   Issues in Terms and Structures of Sukuk

Notwithstanding the exceptional growth of Sukuk in the last five years, there are some concerns that have to be taken care of for more vigorous and sustained support for the emerging financial system. The first and foremost crucial issue is that of conclusively pre-fixed rates of return in almost all Sukuk, in some cases even without any provision for third party guarantee. Profit rates in deferred-payment Murabaha and rentals in Ijarah are no doubt fixed, but while there could be default in receipt of Murabaha receivables, in leases there is the possibility both of ownership-related expenses and default in receipt of the due rental. The loss of the cost of funds that cannot be recovered under Islamic finance and expenses that could be incurred by the lessor as owner of the leased asset may not make it possible to give a return to Sukuk holders that is fixed and guaranteed in all respects. This concern is particularly genuine in respect of sovereign Sukuk, as a guarantee by the sovereign itself may give rise to doubts about Sharī´ah compliance. Payment of rental is guaranteed in the main contract itself in the form of a contractual obligation on sovereigns to pay the rent.

In this regard, the general public interested in Islamic finance and practitioners need to be educated about the flexibilities and the limits of each mode/product so that the integrity of the system is not damaged. The Sharī´ah scholars are unanimous that any pre-fixed return or guarantee of the investment by any of the partners in contractual Shirkah-based modes is not acceptable. According to the AAOIFI's Standard on Sukuk, a prospectus to issue any certificates (not only those which are Shirkah-based) must not contain any clause that the issuer is liable to compensate certificate holders up to the nominal value in situations other than torts and negligence, or that he guarantees a fixed percentage of profit. (An independent third party can, however, provide such a guarantee free of charge and subject to relevant conditions).[21] But the way in which various Sukuk are structured and marketed tends to assure the subscribers/holders that the issue carries a fixed return rate, like any fixed income security in the conventional interest-based structure.

One view is that the financier partner can give a part of its own profit or even out of its own wallet to the client partners, as in the case of deposits kept on the basis of Mudarabah. But even there the banks are not free; they can accommodate the clients up to the limit of a pre-agreed ratio only and any arrangement of payment of an agreed amount of profit out of the banks' own income may dilute the sanctity of the institution of Shirkah, particularly when adopted as a system. In the case of Sukuk, even this is not possible and the SPVs have to distribute among the Sukuk holders the net proceeds of the business in which the raised funds have been used.

Ijarah has flexibility in the sense that the rental rate can be fixed or floating and the lessor may know in advance his future expected receipts. But the lessor is exposed to losing rental collection when the lessee fails in timely payment. He may also lose his property because of both systematic and unsystematic risks. So, how can Sukuk holders be given a guarantee of investment and assured of a fixed income? One possibility is that the owner/lessor of the asset may assure the purchaser of the asset (while selling it to the SPV) about the performance of the lessees, as in the case of IDB Trust Sukuk issued on the basis of a mixed portfolio of assets booked by the IDB. In the case of Murabaha or other receivables, the SPV may have recourse to the institution that has undertaken the underlying transactions. It seems pertinent that the Sharī´ah scholars may explain the limits within which such guarantee or assurance can be given, particularly in respect of future assets to be leased by the SPV. If the asset is destroyed without any fault or negligence of the lessee, the risk has to be borne by the lessor – Sukuk holders. They may also like to clarify how the requirement of taking up the ownership-related risks would be fulfilled if Ijarah Sukuk holders were guaranteed a fixed return on their investment, as in the case of conventional securities.

Another important issue is that a number of contracts are combined in one arrangement of Sukuk issue in such a way that they are interdependent on one another. The Ijarah Sukuk issue with a sale and lease-back arrangement involves about six agreements. If these are made integral parts of the main contract, Sharī´ah compliance is at stake. Sequencing of these agreements, which has a bearing on Sharī´ah compliance, also needs to be taken care of.

Further, it has been observed that most of the issues lack transparency in respect of documentation and rights and liabilities of various parties to the issue. Proper care of all the aspects and transparency would lend enhanced credibility to the concept of Sukuk and widen the Islamic finance market. According to the AAOIFI's Standard, a prospectus of any issue must include all contractual conditions, rights and obligations of various parties and the party covering the loss, if any. The Sharī´ah boards should not only approve the procedure of the issue but also monitor the implementation of the project throughout its duration. This necessarily includes matters relating to the distribution of profit, trade and redemption of the certificates.[22]

A related point of concern is that of reliance on Ijarah Sukuk only; the potential of Shirkah-based or even mixed portfolio Sukuk is not being properly realized. Most of the Sukuk issued for public sector financing are not based on the best possible structures of

---

[21] AAOIFI, 2004–5a, Standard on Investment Certificates, clause 5/1/8/7; see also clause 6/7 of Standard No. 5 on Guarantees.

[22] AAOIFI, 2004–5a, Standard on Investment Certificates, clause 5/1/8.

Islamic finance. Salam Sukuk in Bahrain and some Shirkah-related certificates in Sudan are the only exceptions. Experience of Shirkah-based certificates of investment issued by corporate bodies has proved their suitability and profitability. Further, the procedures of Ijarah Sukuk issues need some refinement in consultation with a team of Sharī´ah scholars.

### 15.3.8   Potential of Sukuk in Fund Management and Developing the Islamic Capital Market

Sukuk, a by-product of the fast-growing Islamic finance industry, have confirmed their viability in mobilization of resources and their effective use for the benefit of both investors and the fund users. Their growth is attributable to a number of factors, including, among others, their potential for liquidity and fund management. They could also be used as a tool for monetary policy and open market operations. As is the case in Sudan, central banks can issue Sukuk for the purpose of controlling liquidity.[23]

Previously, IFIs had to rely on Tawarruq and Murabaha-based dealings in the international metals market and equity markets for the purpose of short-term and medium- to long-term fund and cash management respectively. The modus operandi of the transactions in the metals market was not fully acceptable to the Sharī´ah scholars, as the Murabaha conditions were not accomplished in letter and spirit. The emergence of Sukuk in general since 2001, and IjarahSukuk in particular, and that of the market makers and servicers facilitates IFIs in short-term fund placements in a Sharī´ah-compliant manner. Due to a shortage in supply of such instruments vis-à-vis their demand, Sukuk were tightly held until the recent past, resulting in the absence of a secondary market. Lately, the position has eased and active trading has started. The average volume of trading in PCFC Sukuk has been $10 million a day since their launch.[24] An active secondary market dealing in Nakheel Sukuk just after their issue in December 2006 also points to a healthy signal in this regard.

According to Sameer Abdi of Ernst & Young, about one-third of investors in countries with a Muslim majority are seeking Sharī´ah-compliant products; another 50–60 % would use products conforming to Sharī´ah tenets if they were commercially competitive. At the company level, a large number of businesses and institutions in the world, where Sharī´ah-compliant products are available, particularly in the Middle East, are shifting to public vehicles offering Sharī´ah-compliant solutions to financial problems. This confirms the huge potential of Sharī´ah-compliant certificates of investment.

In a Sukuk issue of $800 million from Abu Dhabi Investment Bank that closed on December 4, 2006, nearly 40 % of the investors came from Europe. In the Nakheel Sukuk issue of $3.52 billion also, 40 % of investors are from Europe. A number of European and Japanese corporations are planning to explore the Sukuk market for raising long-term funds.

A huge amount of funds is needed for infrastructure projects in the Muslim world, and if managed properly and carefully without compromising on the Sharī´ah principles, this can not only be arranged through the vehicle of Sukuk, but also it could be a stepping stone for broad-based development of these economies. This requires developing Islamic countries to increasingly use the vehicle of Sukuk for financing their infrastructure and other development projects.

---

[23] See Eltejani, 2005, pp. 411–413.
[24] *The Economist*, December 9th–15th, 2006, p. 73.

The development of Sukuk depends on factors like a proper regulatory framework, Sharī'ah compliance and convergence, the development of market professionals, investors' education and knowledge-sharing.

## 15.4  SUMMARY AND CONCLUSION

Sukuk provide a tremendous potential for growth in the global Islamic capital market that is critical for the sustained development of the Islamic finance industry. Their emergence has attracted a large number of investors across the world. Sukuk create a framework for participation of a large number of people in financing projects in the public and private sectors, including those of infrastructure, such as roads, bridges, ports, airports, etc. A variety of target-specific Sukuk can be issued on the basis of various modes, keeping in mind the relevant Sharī'ah rules. The return on the Sukuk depends on the income realized by the underlying assets/projects. Sukuk issue requires appropriate enabling laws to protect the interests of investors and issuers, appropriate accounting standards, study of the targeted market, monitoring of standardized contracts, appropriate flow of financial data to investors and provision of a standard quality service to customers at large.

Islamic banks' credibility is a very fragile issue, especially in countries such as the GCC states and Pakistan. The role of Sharī'ah scholars is crucial in this regard; anything to do with the Sharī'ah should be the exclusive domain of the Sharī'ah scholars, who are careful and responsible enough to find solutions to financial problems without compromising on the tenets of the Sharī'ah.

The international institutions set up during the last decade to lend the Islamic finance industry a global acceptance, namely the Bahrain-based LMC, IIFM and IIRA, have to do a lot to make Islamic capital markets increasingly active and efficient. They have to lead the industry players to exploit the potential of Shirkah-based Sukuk, as reliance on Ijarah Sukuk alone, as has been witnessed over the last few years, may not be sufficient to realize the securitization potential of the industry as a whole. It may not be able to generate the sustainable support critically needed for realization of the market potential.[25] The creation of Islamic universal Sukuk, structured by IIFM as SPV, fulfilling the Sharī'ah essentials of Ijarah could serve as a basis to promote cooperation among Muslim countries and their financial markets.

---

**Box 15.5:**  DP World's Nakheel Sukuk

Initial offering – US$ 2.5 billion
Final offering – US$ 3.52 billion (amount raised by US$ 1.02 billion)
Financial institutions involved – Barclays Capital and Dubai Islamic Bank as joint lead managers and joint bookrunners for the offering
Listed on – Dubai International Financial Exchange
Sukuk tenor – 3 years
Structure – Sale and lease-back (convertible)
Pricing – LIBOR + 120 basis points

---

[25] Adam, 2005, pp. 371–400.

**Investors' Profile**

Around 100 accounts were allocated notes, of which 38 % were from the Middle East, 40 % from Europe and 22 % from the rest of the world. By type, 55 % of the deal went to banks, 35 % to both fixed-income and convertible funds and the remainder to asset managers and wealthy individuals.

The bonds will continue until maturity in 2009. There is an extensive security package featuring a mortgage on land, a pledge on shares in the operating company and a guarantee from Nakheel's parent company, Dubai World.

**Box 15.6:**  Ijarah Sukuk Offering by the Government of Pakistan

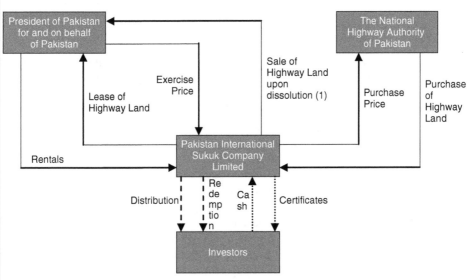

Pakistan's first ever Islamic Sukuk, worth USD 600 million, were launched in January 2005. Pakistan International Sukuk Company Limited (PIS) bought highway land (M-2 motorway) from the National Highway Authority and issued the trust certificates. The Sukuk issue was assigned a B+ rating by Standard & Poor's Rating Services.

**Issue structure**

An SPV was created – Pakistan International Sukuk Company Limited – wholly owned by the government of Pakistan. The property in collateral is the M-2 motorway.

**The offer**

- the offer attracted orders from 82 accounts worth USD 1200 million, of which USD 600 million were accepted;
- sold at par to yield 220 basis points above six-month LIBOR.

---

**Box 15.6:** Continued

**Transaction structure**

- Pakistan International Sukuk Company Limited bought highway land (M-2 motorway) from the National Highway Authority and issued the trust certificates;
- the land was then leased to the government of Pakistan for a period corresponding to the tenor of the trust certificates;
- the government of Pakistan is making periodic payments under lease agreements to PIS to pay off periodic liabilities arising on the trust certificates;
- on completion of the term, the government of Pakistan will repurchase the land from PIS at an agreed price, enabling it to redeem the Sukuk.

---

**Box 15.7:** Ijarah Sukuk Issue by WAPDA, Pakistan

The Water and Power Development Authority (WAPDA), is an autonomous body working for the development of water and hydel power in the country. It needed finance to enhance its power-generating capacity, which it did through the issuance of local currency Ijarah Sukuk. An SPV, "WAPDA First Sukuk Co" (WFS) was formed, which purchased from WAPDA ten power generation turbines installed at Mangla Hydel Power Station for lease back to WAPDA for seven years. Rentals are benchmarked against the Karachi Interbank Offer Rate (KIBOR).

WAPDA pays semiannual rental to WFS to pay periodic rental to the Sukuk holders. At the end of the lease term, WAPDA will purchase the underlying assets by fulfilling its unilateral undertaking to purchase the turbines. This will enable WFS to pay back the investment amounts to the Sukuk holders.

The payment obligation of WAPDA under the WAPDA Sukuk issue is guaranteed by the government of Pakistan, this characteristic has made them eligible for maintaining a statutory liquidity requirement (SLR) by Islamic banks. The transaction structure, in brief, is:

> Rental rate: 6 months KIBOR + 35 bps
> Principal amount: PKR 8000 million
> Underlying asset: WAPDA's ten Mangla Hydel power generation units
> Issuance format: privately placed LCY floating-rate notes
> Specific feature: Sukuk eligible for maintaining SLR.

---

**Box 15.8:** Case Study of Hanco Fleet Securitization (Saudi Arabia)

**Issue structure**

> Principal amount: USD 27 200 000
> Periodic distribution: 6%
> Tenor: 3 years

Issuance format: privately placed LCY fixed-rate notes
Issuer: two-tier SPV/SPC
Underlying assets: motor fleet.

A two-tier special purpose vehicle/special purpose company (SPV/ SPC) structure was established to issue Sukuk certificates, where the SPC was incorporated in a foreign country because of stringent Saudi laws.

**Transaction structure**

- the SPC issues Sukuk certificates and proceeds are used by the SPV to fund the purchase of assets from the originator;
- the SPV owns the assets and allows an agent to manage the assets. The SPV forwards all cash flows into an off-shore bank account, managed by the SPC;
- in the case of lack of cash flow to fulfil the payment flow obligations, this bank account is used to meet the obligations;
- the SPC pays the certificate holders and, at maturity, sells the assets to fund the redemption of certificate holders.

# 16
# Takaful: An Alternative
# to Conventional Insurance

## 16.1 INTRODUCTION

Insurance has become a need of businesses and individuals for mitigating risks and losses and lessening the impact of catastrophes on their lives and wealth. Financial institutions also have to take out insurance cover to safeguard against losses. When Islamic banking started functioning in the 1970s, it also required a Sharī´ah-compliant alternative to conventional insurance, considered against the Sharī´ah tenets due to the involvement of Riba, Gharar and gambling. To fill the gap in the cycle of Islamic finance, the system of Takaful has been developed and a large number of Takaful companies are providing services in various regions of the world.

In this chapter we shall briefly discuss the reasons why conventional insurance is frowned upon, the need for and evolution of Takaful, the Sharī´ah basis and features of Takaful, various models of Takaful, the status, opportunities and the challenges facing the Takaful industry. Giving details about the technicalities and working of the Takaful industry is not the objective. As the nature of business of banking and Takaful is different, and bankers are mostly not involved in Takaful business, the purpose of this chapter is only to introduce the reader to the main features of the Takaful system that is compliant with the Sharī´ah tenets.

## 16.2 THE NEED FOR TAKAFUL COVER

All human beings are exposed to risks in respect of their lives and belongings. Man is required by instinct, and as such has always strived, to safeguard himself from the risks and hazards to his life and property. As human society developed and business grew, this instinct took the form of the business of life and general insurance. Today, the insurance industry has become a necessary part of business and part and parcel of the financial system.[1]

However, Muslim societies in general have been avoiding commercial insurance, mainly for two reasons. First, it has been considered unnecessary, as members of a Muslim society are required to help each other, particularly the victims of any misfortune. Hence, some arrangements to help traders and other communities have been in existence in Muslim societies for centuries. Many people believe that true belief in Allah and destiny means there is no need for any such cover against death or losses to a man himself or his wealth. Things happen with the will and order of God and to get insurance against them is considered to

---

[1] Insurance products are mainly of two categories: life insurance and general insurance. The latter has three main branches: marine, fire and accident (as in the case of motor vehicles, aeroplanes, etc.); life insurance is broadly classified into whole life policies and endowment policies. While whole life policies promise the face value of the policy whenever the insured dies, endowment policies are confined to limited periods.

be questioning His actions. Second, the severe prohibition of Riba, Gharar and gambling are believed to indicate the nonpermissibility of conventional insurance. Further, insurance companies are involved in other forbidden businesses, including alcohol, pork, indecent entertainment and hotels with clubs and prohibited activities.

While the second reason is genuine and must be observed in order to avoid prohibitions, the first is only a myth. All human beings are invariably exposed to the likelihood of meeting catastrophes and disasters, giving rise to misfortune and suffering such as death, loss of limbs, accident, destruction of business or wealth, etc. Notwithstanding the belief in Allah and destiny, Islam provides that one must find ways and means to avoid such catastrophe and disaster wherever possible, and to lighten one's or one's family's burden should such an event occur.

Sharī'ah intends to save human beings from hardship. The Holy Qur'ān says: "Allâh intends for you ease, and He does not want to make things difficult for you." (2: 185). It further says: "Allah wishes to lighten (the burden) for you, and man was created weak" (4: 28). One day the holy Prophet (pbuh) saw a person leaving a camel in the jungle, he asked him: "Why don't you tie down your camel?" He answered: "I put my trust in Allah." The Prophet said: "Tie your camel first, then put your trust in Allah."

The idea of getting cover against risks is not intrinsically bad. In the case of genuine problems and remaining within the main Sharī'ah constraints, the rule of necessity comes into play to find the proper solutions. Therefore, the scholars deemed it necessary to develop a scheme or system enabling human beings to avoid misfortune and lessen the losses in a manner not against the principles of the Sharī'ah.

The insurance business is conducted mostly by non-bank financial institutions (NBFIs) and the commercial banks are not allowed, in most countries, to be involved in the insurance business. However, all commercial and investment banks and other NBFIs have to resort to insurance services, either as a regulatory requirement or as an unavoidable business need. Similarly, business, industry and individuals have been increasingly taking on the services of insurance companies to safeguard against unfortunate incidents and losses to life and wealth. While Islamic banking emerged in the 1960s and early 1970s, Islamic insurance started no earlier than 1979. This reveals that the Takaful system developed in response to demand for risk cover by Islamic financial institutions, due mainly to the fact that banking and insurance go hand-in-hand and complement each other's operations. However, it may also have positive implications for those individuals, households and businesses who have been avoiding insurance on the basis of belief.

### 16.2.1   Why Conventional Insurance is Prohibited

As indicated above, efforts to avoid risk are not against the Sharī'ah tenets. Belief in God or destiny does not mean that man should be exposed to unnecessary risks, and Sharī'ah accepts the basic safety requirement of human beings and their belongings. This includes protection of self, protection of one's offspring and wealth, protection against disease, illiteracy and poverty and other misfortune. Why, then, is conventional insurance not acceptable in the structure of Islamic finance?

Marine insurance was the first form of commercial insurance, initiated probably at the end of the 12th century. It took the form of a formal system in the 17th century, when the marine business developed on a massive scale. Among the Islamic jurists, Ibn Abdin, a widely respected jurist of the 19th century, was the first scholar who wrote about modern commercial insurance in detail and particularly discussed the marine insurance of his time; but he did not approve it from the Sharī'ah point of view.

Different views have been expressed about the Sharī'ah status of conventional insurance.[2] The difference of opinion has arisen for two reasons: one, jurists who did not know the details and complexities involved in various forms of insurance and its structure were asked to issue edicts without sufficiently explaining the background and perspective of the issues involved, and two, there is no direct reference to practices like insurance in the Holy Qur'ān and Sunnah. As Islamic economics and finance developed, Sharī'ah scholars gained more and more knowledge and, hence, it became easy for them to analyse the system proactively. As a result, an overwhelming majority of the Sharī'ah scholars have come to the conclusion that commercial insurance is unlawful due to the involvement of Riba (interest), Qimār and Maisir (gambling), Gharar (excessive uncertainty) and the invalid transfer of risk from the insured to the insurer. As a whole, it contains the element of temptation and cheating and is incompatible with the natural and ethical methods of earning money.

Riba is involved in conventional insurance both directly and indirectly: an excess on one side in the case of exchange between the amount of premiums and the sum insured is the direct involvement of Riba, while investment in interest-based businesses by the insurer refers to the indirect involvement of the policyholder in Riba-based transactions. If a claim is not made in non-life policies, the insurance company keeps almost the whole amount. There is a loss of premiums in the case of cancellation of a life insurance policy by the policyholder, while only a proportional refund is made if the insurance company terminates the cover.

Gharar means Khatar and uncertainty about the subject matter and the price and the rights and liabilities of parties in commutative contracts and also involves Maisir and Qimār. Khatar refers to stipulating transfer of ownership of a property or profitability in a deal where commercial benefit is involved on both sides for any uncertain event. Hence, Khatar/Gharar would be found if the liability of any of the parties to a contract was uncertain or contingent; delivery of one of the exchange items was not in the control of any party, or the payment from one side was uncertain. Qimār is found in a deal if the profit of one party is dependent on the loss of the other. It also involves Maisir, which means any deal in which monetary gains come from mere chance, speculation and conjecture and not from work, taking responsibility or real sector business.

Conventional insurance involves Khatar as a policyholder enters into a business deal in which his liability and the right both remain contingent. He loses the amount given as premium if the event of insurance does not occur, as in the case of general insurance. The insurer (company) does not know how much he will owe to the insured. In many cases, an insured also does not know how much he will pay ultimately to the insurer. In life policies, a policyholder has generally to lose all premiums that he has paid if he cancels his policy within the first two or three years of the contract.

The insurer receives premiums and undertakes to fulfil the loss or damage to life or property of the insured. It is either in surplus or in deficit if the claims are less or higher than the premiums received, respectively. This becomes a monetary or commercial transaction in which the insurer owns an underwriting surplus (UWS) or underwriting loss (UWL).[3]

---

[2] For different views on insurance, see Khorshid, 2004, pp. 12–15, 60–78; Fatawah in respect of insurance/Takaful are given (without text) in the appendix to this chapter.

[3] UWS means the net amount of money which the insurer gets from the premiums paid by the policyholders after payments of the claims, if any. Conversely, UWL is the amount of money which the insurer has to pay in the form of claims in excess of the premiums received from the policyholders.

Any of the parties gains at the cost of the other. The hope of "chance profit" or gain motivates the taking of risk, the feature which makes the insurance contract a money stake or a gamble. It is pertinent to keep in view in this regard that Gharar, or uncertainty, is prohibited when it is involved in commercial/commutative contracts. As conventional insurance is a commutative contract, any involvement of uncertainty would invalidate the contract.

At the present stage of human life, individuals, businesses and societies cannot afford to avoid such cover against losses to business. The only requirement is that the elements prohibited by the Sharī'ah are excluded from any such scheme. Hence, an Islamic alternative to insurance was urgently required to fill the gap in Islamic finance. In many cases it is a legal requirement that assets underlying Islamic banking contracts have to be insured, as in the case of auto Ijarah, storage, shipment and transportation of goods, etc. Further, Islamic banks' clients criticized the involvement of conventional insurance as they wanted to avoid interest in all respects. In addition to that, there was a need for an alternative to life insurance, as in the case of housing finance by an increasing number of IFIs and for the benefit of individuals. IFIs also needed to offer savings and protection-related Takaful products to their customers. As such, the development of the Takaful industry was necessary to complete the cycle of Islamic finance.

# 16.3   THE SHARĪ'AH BASIS OF TAKAFUL

The approximate Sharī'ah equivalent word for insurance in Arabic is "Ta'mein", which means to reassure, safeguard and guarantee through indemnity to losses. It also denotes fidelity, loyalty, confidence and trust and refers more to guarantee than to cooperative sharing of losses among a group. This concept remained under discussion of the scholars for about a century. But the concept which finally gained Sharī'ah scholars' acceptance on a large scale is that of Takaful, which requires that the nature of the main insurance contract should be converted to a contributory arrangement in which the losses to members may be covered from the Takaful pool on the basis of mutual help and sacrifice.

Shaikh Abu Zahra, an eminent jurist of the 20th century, has deliberated upon the subject in detail and concluded that a cooperative and social insurance scheme is, in principle, legitimate, and that noncooperative insurance is unacceptable because it contains the traits of gambling, temptation and usury that invalidate the contract.[4] The Islamic Fiqh Council of the OIC approved the Takaful system based on mutual cooperation as an alternative to conventional insurance in 1985.

Takaful is not a new concept for Islamic commercial law. Islam accepts the right of human beings to protect their religion (belief), life, dignity and honour, property and talent. Some similar practices were in vogue in early Islamic Arab Society, like 'Āqilah (kinsmen; further explained below), Qasāmah (an oath that was taken from the kinsmen of the murdered; in one such case the holy Prophet paid blood money of one hundred camels of Sadaqah[5]) and Mawālāt (a contract in which one party agreed to bequeath his property to the other on the understanding that the benefactor would pay any blood money that may eventually be due by the former)[6].

---

[4] Khorshid, 2004, pp. 58, 59.
[5] Muslim, 1981, Book 16, Kitab al Qasamah.
[6] Khorshid, 2004, p. 24.

Contemporary jurists acknowledge that the principle of shared responsibility in the system of " 'Āqilah" (kinsmen or people in a relationship) laid the foundation for Takaful. It was practised in the ancient Arab tribes and the holy Prophet (pbuh) approved it. In the case of any natural calamity, everybody used to contribute something until the disaster was relieved. Similarly, the idea of 'Āqilah in respect of blood money was based on the concept of Takaful, wherein payments by the whole tribe distributed the burden of the family in trouble. Islam accepted this principle of reciprocal compensation and joint responsibility.[7] In addition, such an institution of mutual help was established in the early second century of the Islamic era when the Arabs expanding trade into Asia mutually agreed to contribute to a fund to help anyone in the group that incurred mishaps or robberies during the sea voyages.

On the basis of the above principles, the Takaful system as an alternative to conventional insurance embodies the elements of shared responsibility, common benefit and mutual solidarity. Every policyholder pays his subscription in order to assist those among them who need assistance. The theory of Islamic finance does not accept Gharar or excessive uncertainty in respect of rights and liabilities of the parties to a commercial contract. Hence, the concept of Tabarru' (donation) has been incorporated in the arrangement as the main ingredient of the contract. A participant of a Takaful policy agrees to relinquish, as Tabarru', the whole or a certain proportion of his Takaful contributions that he undertakes to pay, thus enabling him to fulfil his obligation of mutual help should any of his fellow participants suffer a defined loss.

Another concept and institution which provides support to the idea of mutual help is that of Waqf (endowment). Waqf in Islamic Sharī'ah refers to the retention of a property for the benefit of a charitable or humanitarian objective, or for a specified group of people such as members of the donor's family. There are three kinds of Waqf in Islamic jurisprudence: religious Waqf, philanthropic Waqf and family Waqf. Waqf becomes a separate entity which has the ability to accept or transfer ownership. The ownership of the Waqf property is transferred from the person creating the Waqf forever. Waqf property cannot be sold; only the usufruct is assigned to the beneficiaries. According to the Waqf principles, a member (donor) can also benefit from the Waqf. The beneficiaries of the Waqf in Takaful arrangements are the creator of the Waqf and the group whose members contribute for the purpose of mutual help and covering the losses to any of them.

Keeping the above in mind, the jurists have developed, over the last two or three decades, a system of cooperative risk-sharing in such a way that on the one hand, the basic prohibitions of Sharī'ah are taken care of and, on the other hand, the requirements of the socio-economic and financial framework are fulfilled. The losses of the unfortunate few are shared by the contributions of the fortunate many that are exposed to the same risk on a cooperative risk-sharing basis. The funds are used by the manager/trustee for payment of claims and for business in any Sharī'ah-compliant manner. The underwriting surplus or deficit belongs to the group members. The manager of the pool gets a return in the form of a fee and/or share from the profit made from the investments of the funds in Sharī'ah-compliant avenues (this is the "investment profit" – different from the UWS/UWL as discussed above).

---

[7] Muslehuddin, 1982, p. 62; Nyazi, 1988, p. 339.

### 16.3.1  Main Objective of the Takaful System

The above discussion reveals that the main objective of the Takaful system from the policyholders' point of view is mutual help and not earning profit or any windfall gains, as in the case of conventional insurance. In all forms of Takaful, like family Takaful (alternative to life insurance) or general Takaful, the participants agree to help one another out of their contributions at the time when any of them faces any catastrophe or incurs any defined loss. As a business venture, however, the operators can get fees and/or share the profits against their services and the policyholders/partners can share the realized profit, if any, after making up the losses incurred by the group members.

Having a family Takaful or Islamic life policy is not against virtue or piety. It does not mean that one has insured one's life; it is one of the means of providing a safeguard for offspring and is thus in line with the saying of the holy Prophet (pbuh): "It is better for you to leave your offspring wealthy than to leave them poor, asking others for help". The holy Prophet (pbuh) also encouraged the providing of security for widows, orphans and the poor, as he highlighted in one of his sayings: "The one who looks after and works for a widow and for a poor person (dependent), is like a warrior fighting for the cause of Allah (SWT), or like a person who fasts during the day and prays throughout the night".

Mutual help in the case of any catastrophe is also acclaimed in the Sharī´ah. There was a concept of mutual protection practised in the Islamic era by establishing common pools amongst Muslim traders to jointly compensate the loss to any group member due to robberies or misfortune during their trade journeys. As such, the concept of Tabarru' and virtue with other fellow beings is the main feature of Takaful business and any Takaful-based policy. However, there is no Sharī´ah issue in viewing Takaful as a business when conducted with Sharī´ah compliance, transparency and fairness to all stakeholders.

## 16.4  HOW THE TAKAFUL SYSTEM WORKS

A Takaful company serves as a trustee or a manager on the basis of Wakalah or Mudarabah to operate the business. The operator and the partners who take any policy contribute to the Takaful fund. Claims are paid from the Takaful fund and the underwriting surplus or deficit is shared by the participants. In life policies, a part of the contribution is also kept as an investment fund. The operator uses the funds in the business on the basis of Wakalah or Mudarabah. The underwriting surplus or deficit belongs to the policyholders/partners, while distribution of profit arising from the business depends upon the basis of Wakalah or Mudarabah.

The modus operandi of Takaful can be divided mainly into two types: family Takaful or life policies and general Takaful. The contribution paid by the life policyholders is divided into a "protection part" (for the Takaful fund/payment of claims) and a saving/investment part if the company is working as Mudarib; if the company is working on a Wakalah basis, contributions are divided into three parts, i.e. a part as a management fee, a protection part and the investment part. The protection part works on a donation principle, according to which individual rights are given up in favour of the Waqf. In the investment/savings part, individual rights remain intact under the Mudarabah principle and the contributions, along with the profit (net of expenses), are paid to the policyholders at the end of the policy term or before, if required by them. In the case of general Takaful, the whole contribution is considered a donation for protection and the participants relinquish their ownership right in favour of the Takaful fund, and the UWS/UWL belongs to the participants. There is a provision of Qard al Hasan by the company to the fund if claims at any time exceed the amount available in it and the reserves are insufficient to meet the shortfall.

On the same bases of Tabarru', Waqf and Mudarabah, Takaful companies can arrange re-Takaful, for which they pay an agreed-upon contribution from the Takaful fund to a re-Takaful operator, which, in return, helps the Takaful companies in case of losses.

Here, a question arises about the treatment of Tabarru' or donation: some people consider it synonymous with Sadaqah, or charity, that, once given, can neither be taken back nor can any benefit be derived from it.[8] This, however, is not the case; every donation is not necessarily Sadaqah. The operators who are working on the Mudarabah model are of the view that the Takaful fund becomes a separate legal entity and the protection part of the contribution of the policyholders is considered its part in case of any claims; it is conditional on being used to pay the claims and there is an element of surplus, which may be given back to the participants. Proportionate ownership of the contribution remains that of the participants to the extent that the funds are not used for payment of the claims.

Even if the amount is considered Tabarru' from the very beginning, donations to Waqf are used for the beneficiaries in favour of whom the Waqf has been created. Like Sadaqah, here also, the person who contributes to the Waqf relinquishes his right of individual ownership; but in contrast to Sadaqah, he can benefit from the fund as one of the beneficiaries. This is why the model involving the concept of Waqf, as introduced in the Takaful business in recent years, is considered preferable to the models that operate without Waqf. The whole contribution by the policyholders or a part of it is considered a donation to the Waqf fund. Policyholders have no claim on the donation part that is used for payment of claims. The operator invests the funds in the business and shares the profits with the Waqf fund and the policyholders get any share in the profit as beneficiaries of the fund.

In the early years when Takaful developed as a system, no distinction was made by the Takaful operators between the underwriting surplus and the "investment profit". Even now, in many cases, sharing of profit or surplus that may emerge from the overall operations of Takaful is made only after the obligation of assisting fellow participants has been fulfilled. But in the continuing process of research and discussion, the scholars felt that the whole UWS/UWL should belong to the participants/policyholders and the Takaful operator should get a Takaful fee and/or a share in the "investment profit".

### 16.4.1  Models of Takaful

Any form of insurance business acceptable to Islam must contain the virtues of cooperation, solidarity and Tabarru'. Sharī'ah scholars are also unanimous that there can be a commercial basis conforming to the basic characteristics of Islamic business principles. Towards this end, the scholars have suggested from time to time various models, like that of Wakalah, Mudarabah, Waqf (a kind of endowment) or Wakalah with Waqf. According to the latest research by over forty Sharī'ah scholars conducted under the guidance of Shaikh Muhammad Taqi Usmani, a renowned contemporary jurist and member of the Sharī'ah councils of the OIC/IDB and the AAOIFI, a Waqf model or a combination of Wakalah and Waqf is the best basis for evolving a practical Takaful system in line with the Sharī'ah principles. Even prior

---

[8] Billah, 2002.

to that, some jurists advocated the use of a Waqf mechanism to develop a Sharī'ah-compliant insurance system.[9]

In a pure Wakalah model, generally practised in the Middle East, the Takaful operator acts as a Wakil for the participants and gets a fee in the form of an agreed percentage, say 30 % of the participants' donations, and the whole UWS/UWL and the investment profit/loss belongs to the policyholders or the participants. The Wakalah fee is to cover all management expenses of business. The fee rate is fixed annually in advance in consultation with the Sharī'ah committee of the company. In order to give incentive, a part of the UWS is also given to the operator, depending upon the level of performance. However, the loss (UWL), if any, has to be borne only by the participants. The operator simply provides Qard al Hasan. For this reason, the Sharī'ah scholars have expressed some reservation on this model, due to it not being equitable.

Under a pure Mudarabah model, practised mainly in the Asia – Pacific region, the participants and the operator enter into a Mudarabah contract for cooperative sharing of losses of the members and sharing the profits, if any. The profit, which is taken to mean return on investments plus any underwriting surplus (as in the case of conventional insurance), is distributed according to the mutually agreed ratio, such as 50:50, 60:40, etc. between the participants and the company. The Sharī'ah committee of the Takaful company approves the sharing ratio for each year in advance. Most of the expenses are charged to the shareholders. An issue in this model is that the amount donated as Tabarru' cannot simultaneously become capital for the Mudarabah relationship. Moreover, the Takaful operator gets the UWS, but does not bear the UWL. Therefore, Sharī'ah scholars have raised serious objections to this model.

In some cases, a model involving the combination of Mudarabah and Wakalah has been adopted. Under the combined model, the sharing of profit between participants and operators is an entitlement embedded in the contract, i.e. UWS and the investment profit both are shared. There is, however, a structural issue in the way such profit/surplus is determined. The issue is that, under Mudarabah, the operator, as the Mudarib, cannot charge its management expenses from the Takaful fund separate from its share as Mudarib, whereas under Wakalah, the operator, being the agent of the participants, can take its management fees from the fund as per pre-agreed terms. Further, the operator does not bear the UWL. Therefore, it also smacks of trouble from the Sharī'ah angle.

In the Waqf model introduced in recent years, the shareholders create a Waqf fund (Takaful fund) through an initial donation to extend help to those who want cover against catastrophes or financial losses. More than one Takaful fund can be formed for different classes of service. Contributions of the participants, appropriate to the risk of the participants/assets, are divided into two parts: one as donation to the Takaful fund and the other for investment on the basis of Mudarabah. The donation part always remains with the Waqf. Operational costs like re-Takaful, claims, etc. are met from the fund. The underwriting surplus or loss belongs to the fund, which can be distributed to the beneficiaries of the Waqf, kept as a reserve or reinvested to the benefit of the Waqf. There is no obligation to distribute the surplus. Rules for management fees, distribution of profit, creation of reserves, the procedure, extent or limit of compensation to the policyholders are decided beforehand. In the case of need, shareholders give Qard al Hasan to the fund. For investment purposes, a Mudarabah contract takes place between the Takaful fund and the company working as Mudarib. The investment

---

[9] For details, see Khorshid, 2004, pp. 20–22.

part is invested by the company on a Mudarabah basis and is redeemed to the policyholder on a NAV basis at maturity of the policy. The investment profit is shared between the company and the fund. As per the contents of the policies, the company distributes the profit among the beneficiaries.

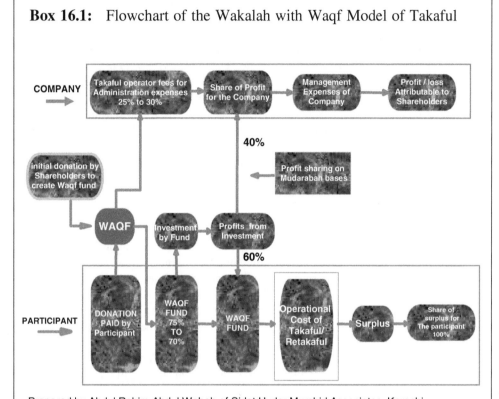

**Box 16.1:**  Flowchart of the Wakalah with Waqf Model of Takaful

Prepared by Abdul Rahim Abdul Wahab of Sidat Hyder Murshid Associates, Karachi

1. Shareholders create a Waqf for the purpose of Takaful; policyholders/participants donate to the Waqf fund.
2. The company invests 70 % to 75 % of the Waqf fund on a Wakalah basis. 25–30 % is the management fee for the company, from which it shall incur all management expenses.
3. Claims/operational costs of Takaful and re-Takaful are charged to the Takaful fund and the UWS or UWL belongs to the participants as a group.
4. A Mudarabah contract for investment purposes takes place between the fund and the company. The profit-sharing ratio between the company and the fund in this case is 40 % and 60 % (it can be any ratio as per agreement).

Besides the usual technical reserves, the Waqf fund is allowed to create a contingency reserve fund from the contributions and the profit earned on investment. This reserve is also the property of the Waqf. The company's sources of income are the Waqf management fee, paid from the Waqf fund, a share in the investment profit as Mudarib or a service charge as investment agent and the profit from shareholders' money.

### 16.4.2 Issues in the Mudarabah Model

While the concept of Mudarabah is highly suitable as a basis for Islamic banking business, particularly on the deposits side, it is not suitable for the insurance business. In a Mudarabah model of Takaful, amounts paid by the participants and the investment incomes are used to pay the claims, re-Takaful costs and other claims-related expenses from the general Takaful fund. Normally, the shareholders meet all management and marketing-related expenses from their share and any remaining amount is their net profit. However, in some cases, the companies charge management expenses from the Takaful fund, which is against the rules of Mudarabah. Some part of any underwriting surplus is also given to the operator, depending upon his performance.

Sharī´ah scholars have raised certain issues about the validity of the Mudarabah model for Takaful on account of the following:

- In this arrangement the cooperative nature of the contract is undermined. The relationship between the participants should base on Tabarru´ and not Mudarabah; profit-sharing cannot be applied here. A donation cannot be the Mudarabah capital at the same time.
- Sharing in any UWS makes the Takaful contract essentially the same as conventional insurance, in which the shareholders become the risk-takers – they get the UWS or bear the UWL; Mudarabah-based Takaful is rather worse, because the Takaful operators/shareholders take only the UWS, but do not bear the UWL, if any. The point is that a Takaful operator should not be a risk-taker, which he becomes in the case of the Mudarabah model.
- In Mudarabah, invested capital has to be returned along with the profit, if any; and if there is a loss, that has to be subtracted from the capital. In non-life Takaful, the paid premiums are not returned.
- The requirement to provide Qard al Hasan (in case of a deficit) in a Mudarabah contract is against the concept of Mudarabah by definition, which is a profit-sharing contract. Further, a Mudarib cannot be a guarantor to the financier.

### 16.4.3 Issues in Wakalah and Wakalah–Mudarabah Models

- Wakalah combined with Shirkah arrangements (as in the case of most Takaful companies in the Middle East that give a part of any UWS to shareholders) is subject to the same objections as the Mudarabah model. The problem arises when the Takaful operator is given a part of the UWS in addition to the operating fee as a performance incentive. Sharing of surplus should be among the pool members of the fund.
- The risk premium should be separately defined and related to the risk; this should be the same for similar risks, regardless of who the client is.
- For large clients, the company should reduce the operator's fees and not the risk premium rates.
- Expenses related to initial set-up should be borne by the shareholders.

## 16.5   TAKAFUL AND CONVENTIONAL INSURANCE COMPARED

Takaful and conventional insurance are different with respect to the objectives, structure, investment policies and returns. In conventional insurance, risk is transferred to one party – the company – and the prohibited factors of Riba, Gharar and gambling are involved. The policyholders have to pay the premiums against unknown risks in the case of general insurance. In life insurance, they get back the premiums along with interest in the case of survival and the insured amount in the case of death before maturity of the policy. In Takaful, the participants or the group members relinquish their ownership right of the amount of the donation and then the Waqf fund bears the losses to any of them and the members share the UWS/UWL. The Takaful companies manage the business and share the investment profit with the policyholders.

Although there still remains some uncertainty, it is within the group itself, all members have jointly contributed to help those among them who incur any loss and share the remainder, if any. This is why the model of Takaful in which UWS/UWL fully belongs to the participants is considered to be the best model as per the latest research. Uncertainty is further minimized by recourse to reserves and access to Qard al Hasan to the Takaful fund from the shareholders in case of need.

The risk premium in the conventional system is commercially driven, motivated by the desire for maximum profit for the shareholders; while in Takaful, its adequacy is the main consideration and the profit element is subject to the rules of equity, justice and ethics.

Losses in terms of underwriting or on investment, if any, are first absorbed by the reserves, then from the interest-free loans from shareholders and then by a general increase in pricing by the company. Hence, the Takaful system has a built-in mechanism to counter any overpricing policies of the insurance companies, because whatever the amount of premium, the surplus goes back to the participants in proportion to their contributions.

There are some basic differences between life policies in the two systems. A life insurance policy under the conventional system revolves around the element of Riba, whereas the Islamic model of life policy is based mainly on the principles of Waqf, Tabarru' and Mudarabah. Under the conventional policies, payments to the agents are made from the assureds' paid premiums, whereas under the family Takaful policy, the agents work for the company and thus they are paid by the company itself. With regard to the insurable interest, under the conventional system, it is usually vested to the policyholder himself should he be alive upon the expiry of the policy period. But, in the case of death of the assured within the period, the insurable interest is to be vested to the nominee, who could be the husband/wife, parents or children or any other person or entity. In contrast, under the Islamic model, the insurable interest is to be vested to the assured himself or to his heirs, according to the principles of inheritance and wills.

The idea of a conventional life policy is that if the assured dies at any time before the maturity of the policy, the nominee is entitled to recover from the insurer the whole amount agreed in the policy, while if the assured is alive upon the expiry of the policy period, he is entitled to the whole amount agreed in the policy plus interest, dividends and bonus subject to the company's policy. On the contrary, in the Takaful system, if the assured dies at any time before the maturity of policy, the company gives to the beneficiary the amount projected in the policy, which includes his investment part along with profit, any amount from the Takaful fund and the donation from the company at its discretion. In the case where the policyholder is alive upon the expiry of the maturity period, the company gives him the investment part along with profit, a pro rata share in the underwriting surplus and a dividend/bonus according to the policy of the company. In the case of premature termination, the partner is given the investment part along with profit and a pro rata share in underwriting surplus (with reduced weightages depending upon the number of years). He gets no assistance from the Takaful fund.

The distinction between conventional insurance and Takaful business is more visible with respect to investment of funds. While insurance companies invest their funds, among others, in interest-based avenues and without any regard to the concepts of Halal and Haram, Takaful companies undertake only Sharī´ah-compliant business and the profits are distributed in accordance with the pre-agreed formula/basis in the Takaful agreement.

## 16.6  STATUS AND POTENTIAL OF THE TAKAFUL INDUSTRY

The Takaful business has proved its viability in a period of only two decades. The first Takaful company was established in 1979 – the Islamic Insurance Company of Sudan. Malaysia started Takaful business in 1984. The system gathered momentum in Saudi Arabia and other Middle Eastern countries. It has been growing at a rate of 10–20 % p.a., compared to the global average growth of the insurance industry which is, 5 % p.a. A large number of Takaful companies exist in the Middle East, Far East and even in some non-Islamic countries.

There are over 60 companies offering Takaful services (including windows – 5 %) in 24 countries around the world. These countries are: Bahrain, Bangladesh, Brunei, Egypt, Ghana, Indonesia, Iran, Jordan, Kuwait, Luxembourg, Malaysia, Pakistan, Qatar, Saudi Arabia, Senegal, Singapore, Sri Lanka, Sudan, Trinidad & Tobago, Tunisia, Turkey, United Arab Emirates and Yemen. Takaful products are available to meet the needs of all sectors of the economy, both at individual and corporate levels, to cater for short- and long-term financial needs of various groups in society. Re-Takaful business has also been developed in Malaysia, Bahrain, Saudi Arabia and UAE.

At global level, however, the Takaful system has not met with such a major degree of success as has been witnessed in the case of Islamic banking. This is for two reasons:

1. The huge investment required to compete with the conventional insurance industry.
2. The changes required in regulatory requirements, as seen in the case of Malaysia, to allow Takaful to compete on equal terms with the conventional industry.

Takaful business has a huge potential as there is increasing demand for a Sharī´ah-compliant system, particularly with the development of the Islamic banking industry. There has been low insurance density (premiums per capita) and low penetration (premiums as a percentage of GDP) in Islamic countries, mainly because of the belief of the majority of Muslims that insurance is un-Islamic, and that there is no alternative available to that system. With the development of Islamic banking, there has been a significant increase in the Ijarah and home mortgages which necessitate Takaful. Also, there is a need for Takaful in cases of personal policies, like motor vehicles, health and family security.

The potential may be realized only if people are given education and awareness about the features of the Takaful system, particularly about life Takaful. So far, only a small number of companies are providing comprehensive family Takaful policies. In the Middle East, only Bank Aljazira of Saudi Arabia is offering exclusive Takaful Ta'awani (family Takaful) with a full range of products like retirement, marriage, education and protection to the general public and corporate clients. Other companies are engaged mainly in composite operations.

Takaful operators need to approach the large number of individuals and groups who have not been taking out insurance cover in the past due to religious reasons.

Islamic banks may like to realize this potential and thus complete the cycle of Islamic finance more quickly. In the markets or countries where a viable Takaful facility is not yet available, they may jointly establish well-capitalized Takaful companies, as long as there are no legal constraints. The main objective of these companies may be to provide Takaful services to the Islamic banks, keeping in mind all Sharīʿah principles. They may also be allowed to do other market business. This would create competition in the market and a large number of general Takaful companies would be entering into the market to undertake Sharīʿah-compliant business with competitive pricing.

## 16.7  TAKAFUL CHALLENGES

The basic structure of a Sharīʿah-compliant insurance system has been generally accepted by the Sharīʿah scholars to be essentially based on the principle of mutual help by group members. The way ahead is to improve/reform and develop the existing operational structures in respect of the models and procedures. A number of conceptual issues need to be addressed to ensure credibility and thus enhance the acceptability of the new industry. Takaful operators should come forward to incorporate the institution of Waqf in the Takaful arrangement, as it fully conforms to the requirements of the concept of Tabarruʿ and is free from Sharīʿah-related objections. Other problems that have to be addressed are adequate capitalization, enabling the Takaful operators to work in competition with the conventional companies, developing human resources, re-Takaful facilities and Sharīʿah-compliant avenues for investment of funds, standardization/harmonization of the practices and providing legal and regulatory frameworks for healthy operation of the industry.

The most important challenge that the Takaful industry is facing is creating awareness about the concept itself. The majority of the Muslim population, who have been avoiding insurance because of religious reasons, need to be assured that taking out cover against catastrophes in a manner conforming to the principles of Sharīʿah does not involve any prohibitions.

A Sharīʿah board or an advisor and periodical Sharīʿah audit are required for every Takaful company, not only for ensuring Sharīʿah compliance but also for enhancing the confidence of the public with regard to Sharīʿah-related issues.

Takaful companies are mostly providing general business policies. The real potential lies in family Takaful or Takaful Taʿawani, to realize which, practitioners need to mobilize the general public in Muslim societies. For this they also need a sound financial basis. Composite business has the benefit of offering annual products, which are expense and surplus driven, allowing an early and much-needed cash flow for successful Takaful business. Family Takaful programmes, on the other hand, are cash-absorbing businesses in the early years of establishment of the company. This problem can be solved only by enhancing the capital base of the companies, which, of course, would benefit them in subsequent years.

Besides this, working in a competitive environment side by side with conventional insurance companies is, in itself, a challenge. Takaful companies must offer competitive products/services in terms of price, quality of coverage and delivery time. They will have to work with a new mindset, avoiding malpractices and using the best professional expertise. Policy holders also need to support Takaful companies and be proactive to ensure that the companies are competitive and their operations are Sharīʿah-compliant in all respects. Re-Takaful availability is a problem, as only a few companies are providing re-Takaful facilities in Malaysia, UAE, Bahrain and Saudi Arabia, and that too on a Mudarabah basis, which is objectionable, as discussed in the chapter.

Providing well-aware and competent manpower for the nascent Takaful industry is another challenge. Only committed, trained and experienced personnel can enhance the acceptability of the system among the public. While there are some facilities available for training in Islamic banking, facilities in respect of Takaful are almost entirely lacking. In this respect, the IRTI (IDB), the AAOIFI, training arms of the central banks and the Securities and Exchange Commissions in countries where Islamic financial services are being developed need to work proactively in collaboration with the Takaful companies.

Lastly, in view of the process of globalization of financial services, there must be standardization of the Takaful products. This will require efforts by the AAOIFI and IFSB to prepare the Sharī'ah and performance standards respectively (as in the case of Islamic banking) for standardization of services and structures feasible in the framework of mutual help. Differences of opinion with regard to the Takaful models have to be resolved. This is because reservations/differences, once expressed, would keep agitating the minds of stakeholders and thus hinder the growth of the emerging industry. To avoid this and to harmonize the practice, the Sharī'ah scholars and the practitioners should collaborate for convergence on the basis of the Wakalah–Waqf model that is nearest to the principles of the Sharī'ah. The regulators need to provide flexibility and ensure that the operators or practitioners perform their functions, keeping in mind the generally accepted key benchmarks, like the CAMELS tests and other performance criteria.[10]

## Appendix: Fatāwa (Juristic Opinions) on Different Aspects of Insurance

| Source(s) | Issue(s) |
| --- | --- |
| Fatwah by Shaikh al-Azhar Shaikh Jad al-Haq Ali Jad al-Haq in 1995 (al-Iqtisadul Islami, July 1995) | Against life insurance |
| Fatwah issued in a judicial conference held in Makkah in Shaban 1398 AH | Against the validity of insurance |
| The unanimous decisions of the Muslim scholars in a seminar held in Morocco on 6th May, 1972 | Against life insurance |
| Verdict of the Supreme Court of Egypt on 27th December, 1926 | Against life insurance |
| Fatwah issued by the National Religious Council (Malaysia) in 1972 | Against the validity of conventional insurance |
| Two Fatāwa issued by Shaikh Mohammad Abduh (the ex-Grand Mufti of Egypt) in 1900–1901 | In favour of the validity of insurance |
| A unanimous fatwah issued by the ulama in the Muslim League Conference, held in Cairo in 1965 | Against life insurance |
| Fatāwa issued by the Higher Council of Saudi Ulama in 1397 AH | In favour of insurance under an Islamic model |
| Fatāwa issued by the Fiqh Council of Muslim World League in 1398 AH | In favour of insurance under an Islamic model |
| Fatāwa issued by Shaikh Mohd Baqit (the ex-Mufti of Egypt) in 1906 | In favour of insurance |

---

[10] The author is grateful to M/s Hassan Kaleem, Sharī'ah Advisor, Al Baraka Islamic Bank, Pakistan and Abdul Rahim Abdul Wahab of Sidat Hyder Murshid Associates, Karachi for their conceptual and technical help in writing this chapter.

| | |
|---|---|
| Fatāwa issued by the Fiqh Council of the Organization of the Islamic Conference in 1405 AH | In favour of insurance under an Islamic model |
| Unanimous decision by the ulama in the First International Conference for the Islamic Economy held in Makah in 1396 AH | In favour of insurance under an Islamic model |
| Fatwah issued by the State of Trengganu in 1974 | Against the validity of conventional insurance |
| Fatwah issued by the State of Selangor in 1970 | Against the validity of conventional insurance |
| Fatwah issued by the State of Negri Sembilan in 1972 | Against the validity of conventional insurance |
| Fatwah issued by the State of Kelantan in 1975 | Against the validity of conventional insurance |
| Fatwah issued by the State of Perak in 1974 | Against the validity of conventional insurance |

Source: http://islamic-finance.net/Islamic-insurance/fatawa.html.

# An Appraisal of Common Criticism of Islamic Banking and Finance

## 17.1 INTRODUCTION

Islamic banking and finance has seen impressive growth in the world over the last three decades. It has come a long way towards providing most of the financial services that only interest-based banking and non-bank financial institutions had been providing. But its share in the financial sector as a whole at national and global levels is very low, even in Muslim majority countries. Almost all Muslims believe that any involvement in Riba – taking, giving, witnessing and even documenting Riba-based transactions – is a great sin that is tantamount to waging war with Allah (SWT) and his Prophet (pbuh). So why, despite the lapse of over three decades since the start of the Islamic finance movement in the modern age, is the share of Islamic banking in the financial system 1.5 % in Indonesia, 2.2 % in Pakistan, 12 % in Malaysia and 24 % in Bahrain? Bahrain is the hub of Islamic banking, where a lot of work has been done in finalizing the Sharī´ah standards for Islamic modes, innovation in Sharī´ah-compliant products, providing a suitable regulatory framework for Islamic banks and the establishment of an Islamic capital market. If so much preparatory work has been accomplished, why has the whole system not been transformed on a Sharī´ah-compliant basis and why is a vast majority of the Muslim population still involved in waging war with Allah and His holy Prophet?

The major factors behind this phenomenon, among others, are a number of myths and a lot of confusion about the Islamic theory of finance among the public and the intelligentsia and unattended common criticism of the concepts and practice of Islamic banking. The misconceptions about Islamic banking and criticisms about its theory and practice have been discussed directly or indirectly in various places in the book. The need for removing the myths and analysing the criticism to impart convincing clarity and confidence to readers and to create commitment among the practitioners for development of the emerging financial discipline in its true perspective cannot be overemphasized. Hence, a full-fledged chapter is devoted to this cause. In this chapter we shall analyse the myths and the criticism generally made on Islamic banking on conceptual and practical grounds. In places, we shall refer to the relevant parts of the book where the issue has already been discussed in detail.

## 17.2 THE COMMON MYTHS AND OBJECTIONS

As indicated above, the stakeholders of Islamic finance have a number of questions and objections about the emerging system; there also exists a significant amount of confusion. Some common objections and misconceptions will be discussed here; however, answering all frequently asked questions is not the objective.[1] Criticisms related to the philosophy and concepts of Islamic banking and finance are briefly listed below.

1. The connotation of the word Riba is not expressly given in the original sources of the Sharī´ah, i.e. the Holy Qur´ān and the Sunnah. There are two extremes: while many people consider that commercial interest as in vogue is not Riba, which is prohibited, many others believe that a "bank" cannot be Islamic and that any return over savings and financial investments is prohibited as Riba. Other major objections related to the concept of Riba are:

   — Money is like other commodities used, bought or sold; if someone borrows money, he should pay for it and the interest is the payment for its use; a lessor can charge rent from the lessee for use of the asset or for benefiting from its usufruct. A lender of money or a debtor should also be allowed to charge rent from the borrower or the debtor.
   — Riba that is prohibited in the Qur´ān was a specific kind of increase over the principal. Riba at the maximum would be where any charge is added on any old unpaid debt or loan and if some charge is added to the loan at the very beginning, it would not be Riba.
   — There was no commercial interest in Arabia at the time of the revelation of the Holy Qur´ān. As such, commercial interest as is found in the present age is not prohibited. Only a high rate of interest (termed "usury") is prohibited and any normal charge on loans or debts does not come under the purview of prohibition.
   — Some people legalize interest on account of inflation and decrease in purchasing power of the lent money. They say that the borrower must indemnify the lender in case of depreciation of the loan amount due to inflation. They criticize the theory of Islamic finance as it does not accept indexation of financial liabilities with gold, baskets of goods or any stable currency.
   — It is also argued that debtors in the present age are not poor people; therefore, charging interest from them is not unjust.

2. "Interest" is based on the concepts of time value of money or opportunity cost; rejecting interest should imply rejecting time value of money. Hence, Islamic banks should neither give any return on deposits nor charge any rate from the users of funds; they should operate only on the basis of Musharakah/Mudarabah or give return-free loans. If they are involved in trading activities, the credit price they may charge should be equal to the cash-n-carry price of the relevant commodity in the market. Otherwise, Islamic banks would be involved in Riba.

3. If Islamic banking means avoiding predetermined/fixed returns as found in the form of conventional interest, it should be based on the two-tier Mudarabah/Musharakah – mobilizing and advancing funds on the basis of profit/loss sharing. Hence, debt should not be part of Islamic banking and finance. Banks should either give return-free loans for providing assistance to the needy and the poor or operate on the basis of Musharakah/Mudarabah to provide risk-based capital for the development of business, industry and economies.

---

[1] For answers to FAQs, readers may like to see Jarhi and Munawar, 2001.

4. Banks are intermediaries by nature and deal in documents only; they should not involve themselves in trading or other direct business; otherwise they will be taking unnecessary risk exposure and leaving themselves open to possible loss to the investors and the financial system.

5. There are differences of opinion in respect to a number of concepts, modes and products of Islamic finance, due to which a standardized system cannot be developed. Many products developed in the Far East and other parts of the world are almost identical to interest-based products. Those products provide the same or similar return to the investors without any possible impact on socio-economic growth, as claimed by the pioneers of Islamic finance. Examples of this are sale of debt and debt instruments, giving returns to the investors in the form of gifts and last but not least, Tawarruq, for which Islamic banks simply engage one or two brokers to sign a few documents to get or place liquidity at fixed rates of return.

With regard to the practice of Islamic banking, the generally made criticism pertains to the following:

1. There is divergence between the theory of Islamic finance and its practices. The pioneers of the theory prescribed the use of Musharakah and Mudarabah (PLS modes); but practically, the share of PLS modes is negligible and the mainstream business is based on debt-creating modes to earn fixed returns as in the case of the interest-based system.

2. Islamic financial institutions (IFIs) operate on the basis of predetermined and fixed rates and earn fixed returns. So-called Islamic Sukuk also carry fixed returns, just like conventional fixed-income securities. How, then, are they Sharī'ah-compliant?

3. Islamic banks price their products on the basis of interest-related benchmarks like LIBOR; charge predetermined rates to the clients on the assets side and give benchmarked rates to depositors, just as conventional banks give to their investors in a given jurisdiction.

4. There is no factual difference between the operations of conventional and Islamic banks. Islamic banks are performing as intermediaries working on the same grounds on which the conventional institutions are working.

5. The net result of conventional and Islamic bank financing is the same. In leasing, for example, Islamic banks add all costs, including insurance, transportation, registration of the leased assets, etc., to determine the rental related to the interest-based benchmark; and at the end, they transfer the leased asset to the client, as in the case of conventional lease finance. In mortgage financing also, they charge the profit/rent on the basis of an IRR/benchmark. Even in the case of Shirkah-based modes, their main concern is to get a market-based rate of return on their investment.

6. IFIs do not actually get involved in trading activities. They have no inventories of the goods to be sold, make the clients their agents for purchasing the goods requisitioned by them and many a time engage in buy-back and Tawarruq (monetization or cash procurement through tailored trade contracts) activities.

7. Islamic banks normally are working in the same regulatory frameworks in which the conventional banks are working. "Islamic windows" or stand-alone Islamic banking branches (IBBs), allocate interest income as the seed or base capital. By offering such "Windows" they are only befooling the public, who avoided interest on the basis of belief, for mobilizing petrodollars in the Middle East and the excess wealth in the Muslim majority and minority countries. How can a Riba-based institution ensure Sharī'ah

compliance while working in a Riba-ridden environment? It gives rise to doubts about their Islamicity/credibility.

8. Islamic banks take collateral/security like their counterparts in conventional finance. They should facilitate people who are not in a position to offer any security without any requirement of collateral, while practically they demand security, even in the case of Musharakah/Mudarabah.

9. For the legality of fixed returns, Islamic banks prepare a number of documents and enter into different agreements in respect of one overall transaction. They make the clients their agents for various activities without payment of any agency fee, enter into "promise" in almost all modes of financing and combine a number of contracts against the Sharī´ah injunction that prohibits two contracts in one contract.

10. If money has always to be linked to real assets and real sector business, as claimed in Islamic finance theory, how can the needs for cash for paying salaries to employees, utility bills, etc. be fulfilled?

11. The Holy Qur´ān advises granting more time to a debtor who is in difficulty, or even forgiving/writing-off the whole debt; but Islamic banks charge penalties from defaulting clients.

In the following paragraphs, we critically examine the above myths and criticisms. In some cases, we briefly touch on the area by referring to different chapters of the book.

## 17.3   APPRAISAL OF CONCEPTUAL CRITICISM

### 17.3.1   The Connotation of the Word Riba

The meaning and connotation of Riba has already been discussed in detail in Chapter 3 (Section 3.2.1) and Chapter 7 (Section 7.3). Here, we shall briefly analyse the related objections and try to remove the common myths. First, saying that the Qur´ān and the Sunnah have not explained the connotation of Riba is not correct. Although the Qur´ān has not given any legal definition of Riba, as in the case of other terms used by the Holy Book, it has quite sufficiently elaborated its connotation. In the related verses of Surah Al Baqarah (2: 274–281), it differentiates between business and charity on the one hand, and trading and usurious activities on the other hand, permitting the trade and its profit and prohibiting Riba. It ordains that whatever is sought over and above the principal of a loan or a debt is Riba and therefore prohibited. This explicitly or implicitly describes the liabilities and rights of human beings and ordains the avoidance of exploitation of each other's rights. Similarly, the holy Prophet (pbuh) has categorically prohibited any increase sought over and above the principal of a loan or a debt, due to its being Riba.

While Islam encouraged Qard al Hasan, or loaning free of any charge, it prohibited the business of exchanging monetary units and other goods of the same 'Illah (effective cause of prohibition), except for hand to hand (in case of heterogeneous goods) and hand to hand and equal for equal (in case of homogeneous items of exchange). This is to ensure that when one party to exchange is giving resources/purchasing power to the other along with the opportunity to use, the other party should also give in exchange the stipulated resources forthwith so that the other may also use the same at his discretion. If monetary units are not exchanged simultaneously, a person can take benefit by use of a money/currency which he has received while he has not given its counter value from which the other party could derive benefit.

Thus, it is established from the texts of the Sharī´ah that modern commercial interest comes under the purview of Riba and no form of loans/debts based on interest is exempt from this prohibition. No differentiation can be made between a low and a high rate of interest expressed on a fixed or floating percentage of the principal or with regard to the purpose of the loan, i.e. for consumption or production. "Rate" is a relative term and, based on the principle given by the Holy Qur´ān, any addition over the amount of debt *per se* is prohibited, irrespective of the rate. We have explained in detail in Chapter 3 that commercial interest was a major feature of business at the time the Holy Qur´ān was revealed, and financing on the basis of Riba was a profession of the rich at that time. The common feature of all Riba-based transactions was that an increased amount was charged on the principal amount of debts. At times the debt was created through a transaction of sale and sometimes it was created through a loan. Similarly, the increased amount was, at times, charged on a monthly/yearly basis, while the principal was to be paid at a stipulated date, and sometimes it was charged along with the principal. All these forms used to be called Riba. Hence, all loans that embody any benefit over and above the principal as a precondition are void, irrespective of the fact that the condition embodies a rate, low or high, or any gain in quantity or quality.

## 17.3.2    Rent on Money Capital

Money is to facilitate socio-economic activities of human beings by serving as a medium of exchange. Islamic Sharī´ah encourages the use of money (in whatever form it may be) to avoid exploitation of one another. In a number of well-known Aḥādith, the holy Prophet (pbuh) advised not to exchange low-quality commodities of a genus with better-quality commodities of the same genus (except in equal amounts) and ordained that one should first sell the low-quality goods and then purchase, with the money so received, the superior quality goods, and vice versa. The rationale behind this is to save both parties from possible losses or exploitation of one party by the other.

Financial transactions, in order to be permissible and for the purpose of earning profit, should be associated with real assets or instruments representing real assets. Money cannot be awarded a fixed charge for its use. It is pertinent to observe in this regard that in Islamic economics, human efforts and economic activities have been given more strategic position in the distribution of produce and profits than capital in the form of money. Linking money to productive purposes brings into action labour and other resources bestowed by Allah (SWT) to initiate a process from which goods and services are produced and the benefits pass on to society. Unlike the conventional system, where money is considered a commodity that may be sold/bought and rented against profit, or rent that one party has to pay irrespective of the use or role of lent money in the hands of the borrower, the Islamic system links capital in the form of cash to the actual business activities and their results.

Capital as a factor of production in Islamic finance constitutes those things which can be used up in the production process in such a way that they are wholly consumed or used, such as gold, silver in the past and/or paper currency in the present age. Such goods cannot be leased because their corpus is consumed with their use, as in the case of fuel or edible goods, and their provider is not in a position to bear the risk related to the ownership. Monetary units, also including paper money, serving as capital are entitled to profit, provided they also accept the risk of loss. In other words, monetary units cannot be leased, because the risk of loss is attributable to the money capital itself and its form changes altogether. Fixed assets like buildings and machinery have claims on rent because the lessor retains their ownership and bears the related risks. Therefore, one cannot derive any benefit from money unless one gives it up in exchange for commodities or services using the structure of any of the valid contracts of sale or lease.

Real sector business transactions take any of the following three forms: sale/purchase that may be either on cash or credit, loaning or leasing. When executed, these transactions have different implications in respect of transfer of ownership, risk and liability. Earning of profit depending upon the outcome of the business is permissible. Whether it is a real sector business or a financial activity, risk always remains with the ownership. A person who gives a loan has the right to get it back; he bears no risk irrespective of whether the borrower earned any profit or incurred loss or even used the borrowed money in consumption. Hence, he cannot claim any return on his loaned capital. If a person who is providing the funds wants any profit over his money, he will have to agree to bear the loss, if any. In this case, the realized profit would be distributed as per a pre-agreed ratio, while a loss would be shared in proportion to the investment made by each financier; a fund user's loss being his unrewarded labour. Hence, there is no place for "interest". That is to say, one is entitled to profit only if one bears the risk of loss.

If a person purchases a commodity, gets its possession/risk, he can sell it with a margin of profit on cash or credit. As soon as the (credit) sale is executed, his right is the receivable thus created, while the asset risk is transferred to the buyer. If he transforms his money capital into a fixed/nonconsumable asset, he has the right to lease it on rent provided he bears the ownership-related risks and expenses. Keeping in mind this principle, it can be said that one can earn profit on his investment or financing but that has to be related to certain assets exposed to direct or indirect business risk. As a lender or a creditor bears no risk and is entitled to repayment of the whole amount of the loan or the debt, he has no right to claim any return or rent.

### 17.3.3   Inflation and Interest

Interest cannot be legalized on the basis of inflation, mainly because of the fact that loaning in Islam is a noncommutative and virtuous activity. It should not be mixed with a business that is conducted with the objective of earning profit. Profit can be earned if capital is linked to any liability, risk or responsibility. Islamic finance does not have the provision of linking any debt or receivable with any currency/commodity. The clear injunctions of the Holy Qur'ān and Sunnah reveal that if financial contribution takes the form of a loan or a debt, it is to be paid back exactly in the same kind and quantity, irrespective of any change in the value of the concerned currency or price of the commodity lent or borrowed at the time of return of the loan. If one wants to avoid the risk of depreciation in value, one should transform one's money into a real asset, undertake any business, earn profit thereby and get a rental or a share in the realized profit by taking liability of the loss. In the presence of the Nass of the Holy Qur'ān (verse 2: 279), the idea of linking loans/debts to the purchasing power of money cannot be justified on the basis of Ijtihad, because Ijtihad is carried out only where a clear directive by the Qur'ān or Sunnah does not exist.

During an inflationary period, the intrinsic characteristics of money, i.e. its role as a medium of exchange and as a unit of account, remain intact. Only the relative characteristic changes, i.e. the future value of money in terms of its exchange value; but this has been changing since the introduction of money, even in respect of full-bodied coins. The value of silver dirhams depreciated in terms of gold dinars even during the early Caliphate.[2] But we do not find any reference in the whole literature on Islamic jurisprudence to the concept of indexation on account of fluctuation in the value of money. Prohibition of Riba essentially requires that all like-for-like exchanges be executed on an equal basis in terms of the relevant units of exchange. If this does not suit someone, he is free to avoid such an exchange and to pursue an alternative permissible course of action, like sale, lease or any partnership-based arrangement. For example, through credit sale, a need of the buyer may be fulfilled, while concerns of the seller may be accommodated through the margin added in the deferred price. But, here again, the price, once agreed, has to remain fixed.

Gold, silver and other monetary units like paper currencies are among the six commodities whose exchange must be like for like, equal for equal and hand to hand. If someone borrows 100 dollars payable after one year, and this amount, after indexation, becomes 105 dollars, it falls into the category of Riba. As elaborated in Chapter 7 (Section 7.17), renowned jurists like Al-Kasani and Ibn Qudama have clearly expressed the view that the borrower should pay the same coins or currency as he took, irrespective of any increase or decrease in its value.

As per the Sharī´ah principle, a loan/receivable that seeks any increase involves Riba. In the case of inflation, the value of a currency decreases across the board; it makes no difference whether a person has lent it or is keeping it with himself in liquid form. If he lends it by indexing with gold, for example, in order to avoid a decrease in its value, this implies that he has drawn benefit from the loan, as the debtor would make good the deficiency to the amount of lent money, while money kept in his own coffer would also lose its value. Drawing this benefit from the loan violates the Sharī´ah. The crux of the matter is that a loan is a nonremunerative contract; as such, it should remain noncommutative and not used as a means for earning or getting compensation.

Even in conventional finance, indexation is not normally used to make up for a loss occurring due to inflation. Conventional institutions make a provision for a floating rate in the agreements, keeping in mind the future inflationary pressures. As such, any new rate is applied on the remaining period, while it does not affect the liability already accrued. In certain modes/products, Islamic banks are also allowed to stipulate a floating or variable rate, as in the case of leasing, but this does not affect any debt liability once created. For example, in leasing, Islamic banks can charge rental at a higher rate, if already provided in the agreement, for any remaining period of the lease; but the rentals for a particular period, once accrued, cannot be indexed.

We come to the conclusion, therefore, that if the financial contribution takes the form of a loan or a debt, it is to be paid back exactly in the same kind and quantity, irrespective of any change in the value of the currency in which it is denominated or the price of the commodity lent or borrowed at the time of return of the loan.

## 17.3.4 Time Value of Money and Islamic Banking

Some people who believe in prohibition of interest criticize Islamic banking on charging time value of money through pricing, while some others are of the view that avoiding interest means negation of time value of money; therefore, they argue that either Islamic

---

[2] See Maududi, 1982–1991, **1**, pp. 382, 383 (4: 92).

banks who charge higher credit prices than the spot prices of the goods are not Islamic or the present-day bank interest is not prohibited. Both views are based on misconception. We have discussed this issue in detail in Chapter 4. It was explained that time value is approved by the Sharī´ah in trading/exchange of real goods but not in Qard or Dayn, against which one cannot derive any benefit. Pricing of goods and their usufruct is a major part of any business transaction, and for the purpose of pricing, the place and the time of transaction are crucial factors. A commodity might be cheaper in one part or market of a city than another part or market of the same city. Similarly, a commodity might be cheaper at the peak of the season than at its beginning. The Sharī'ah does recognize differences in value due to place and time elements, and does not prohibit realizing the time value of money in a genuine business transaction based on exchange (sale and leasing). What is prohibited is any claim to the time value of money as a predetermined quantity calculable at a predetermined rate not related to any real sector business.

There is almost a consensus among the Sharī´ah scholars that the credit price of a commodity can genuinely be more than its cash price, provided one price is agreed at the time of execution of the contract (discussed in detail in Chapter 6; Sections 6.5.3 and 6.8). Similarly, it is quite natural that in forward contracts like Salam, the future delivery price is less than the price at the time of delivery of goods. This is tantamount to the acceptance of time value of money in the pricing of goods. What is prohibited is any addition to the price once agreed because of any delay in its payment. This is so because the commodity, once sold (on credit), generates debt and belongs to the purchaser on a permanent basis and the seller has no right to re-price a commodity that he has sold and which no longer belongs to him. The concept of time value of money in the context of Sharī´ah is also established from the disapproval of Riba Al-Fadl, which involved gold and silver in addition to some other commodities that perhaps were used as media of exchange. Exchange of these commodities on a deferred basis is banned as a rule. Only hand-to-hand exchange is allowed, on the condition that the quantity on both sides is the same. This implies that the Sharī´ah prohibits mutual exchange of gold, silver or monetary values except when it is done simultaneously. This is so because a person can take benefit by a medium of exchange which he has received while he has not given its counter value from which the other party could take the benefit.

Valuation of a credit period for pricing the goods or their usufruct is different from the conventional concepts of "opportunity cost" or the "time value". As such, "mark-up" in trade is permissible, provided the Sharī´ah rules relating to sale of goods are adhered to, but interest is prohibited, as this is an increase over any loan or debt. Therefore, no time value can be added to the principal of a loan or a debt after it is created or the liability of the purchaser fixed.

Islamic economics has the genuine provision of converting money into assets, on the basis of which one can measure its utility. While most of the jurists uphold the concept and practice of a higher credit price than the cash market price of goods, none of them allows generating rent on the principal amount of loans and debts. Hence, there is no justification to assume a zero rate of time preference in an Islamic economy. Similarly, one cannot add value to loans and debts on account of time. Economic agents can have positive time preferences and there will be indicators available in the economy to approximate the rates of their time preferences, generally determined by the forces of demand and supply.

### 17.3.5   Charging Interest from Rich Debtors

The argument that, in the present age, the borrowers from financial institutions belong mostly to the rich business community, and charging interest from them is not unjust, is not convincing at all. This argument would be tenable only if all indebted businesses were earning a profit significantly higher than the interest rate. But if some earn less than the interest rate, some earn out of proportion while some others incur a loss, the claim loses ground. This criticism rather strengthens the case against interest, because the relatively richer class takes funds at much cheaper rates vis-à-vis their profits from the business. They give a small part of their profit in the form of interest to the banks, which is treated as an expense and ultimately charged to the consumers. If some of them incur a loss in the business, they normally resort to different unethical practices to avoid the loss, causing harm to society as a whole. Thus, the rich become richer, leaving the poor poorer. The solution to the problem lies in making available a framework in which one may earn profit/return/income only through exerting mental or physical labour, or taking responsibility and business risk. Interest leads to exploitation of any of the parties, i.e. the debtor or the creditor, and hence it is prohibited, irrespective of who is the exploiter in any particular transaction. Due to the involvement of interest and gambling on a massive scale, the conventional financial system has become a means for exploiting savers or depositors and the general public.

### 17.3.6   Different Sharī'ah Interpretations

Another criticism of Islamic finance is that its products are not standardized because a number of its concepts are subject to different Sharī'ah interpretations. Islamic scholars do not resort to Ijtihad and therefore, Islamic finance cannot become a solid basis for a financial system to replace the present conventional system. However, as the Islamic banking movement has already passed a significant milestone of having evolved a general consensus on the philosophy and products for business, with large-scale acceptance of mainstream theory and practice, slight differences in the concepts are no longer an issue of concern. As regards standardization of the products, this will take time. For the time being, evolving the products along with their process and procedures is the main challenge. Further, institutions like the IDB, the AAOIFI and the IFSB are working on this line; this may increasingly lead to standardization in the future.

Islamic Sharī'ah has provided flexibility for Ijtihad to respond to changes and diversity in day-to-day life. Remaining within the Sharī'ah boundaries, a great deal of Ijtihad is needed to infer from the original sources the appropriate rules relating to transactions of business and finance. In the recent past, the Sharī'ah scholars have very rightly used this source of deriving principles to facilitate the growth of Islamic finance on a wider scale. But Ijtihad has its own limitations. It is neither a source of anarchy nor a means of transforming the Islamic Sharī'ah from Divine to man-made law. The concepts of custom, general good, utility and necessity are also taken into consideration in the process of Ijtihad, based on proper analogy, but these factors are relevant only when the basic principles given in the Nass (clear texts of the Qur'ān and Sunnah) are taken care of and the outcome conforms to the objectives (Maqasid) of the Sharī'ah.

The development of ethical and belief-based disciplines depends on the acceptability of their conceptual underpinnings and their implementation procedures. The mainstream theory of Islamic finance has got this acceptance and the industry has to be developed on the basis of the acceptable concepts. Some concepts that serve as the basis for application in some areas have not obtained general acceptance, and many scholars, even those belonging to such areas, have pointed out convincing arguments against these concepts. For example, products that involve Bai' al Dayn (sale of debts/receivables) and Bai' al 'Inah (buy-back arrangements) are not genuine products for Islamic banking business, as they do not fit its philosophy.

Islamic finance provides a firm basis for a sound and efficient financial system by dint of supply of risk-related capital and a balanced return rate structure through prohibition of interest and Gharar and undertaking only asset-based business activities according to a well-defined set of rules for the related businesses. Keeping in mind the genuine need of IFIs and the rules of Sharī´ah, Sharī´ah scholars have given a number of relaxations. Allowing the levy of penalty on a percentage per annum basis on defaulters, albeit for charity; foreign currency forward cover through unilateral promise to exchange two currencies simultaneously at a pre-agreed rate; the practice of sale and lease-back, particularly in the case of the corporate sector and sovereigns; a number of flexibilities in respect of Sukuk and securitization, like the provision of third party guarantee for the possibility of making the Sukuk "fixed-income securities" and permission for Tawarruq where actual trade takes place and the goods are sold in the market or to any third party, are some major areas where Sharī´ah scholars have provided a helping hand to the Islamic finance movement by way of Ijtihad. One should not expect edicts in favour of every new product in the conventional market, as this would dilute the sanctity of Islamic finance. Hence, we can conclude that major issues relating to interpretation have been resolved and now the practitioners should proceed with standardization on the basis of the settled principles, which provide solid and sufficient grounds for conducting business.

### 17.3.7  Islamic Banks Using Debt-creating Modes

A number of authors on Islamic finance, both economists and financial experts, have been saying that Musharakah and Mudarabah are the only modes to serve as an alternative to interest in the Islamic framework. They contend that if IFIs have to avoid interest, they should either operate on a return-free basis or conduct business only on the basis of Mudarabah/Musharakah. This is, however, a myth and misconception. It is neither a Sharī´ah requirement nor possible in actual life. Trading has been an overwhelming part of human activities forever. The major economic activities of human beings, besides producing goods, involve trading, leasing or rendering services for others. These activities can be conducted in different structures like self-entrepreneurship, hiring others' expertise and services on payment and partnership. Any individual or institution can opt for any structure by observing the related rules of business. The only requirement that the Sharī´ah makes is that in order to get a return, one must make a value addition by way of labour, risk or responsibility. If one chooses the business of trading, one must get a commodity, take its ownership and risk and then sell it by adding profit. In leasing, one has to take ownership-related risks to be entitled to get rental. In partnership-based business activities, the financier has to bear the business loss, if any, for entitlement to profit in the joint venture. If Islamic banks fulfil the relevant requirements, they can do business through any of the above structures. This aspect requires discussion on two aspects: permissibility versus preference of some modes over others and suitability/possibility of use of various modes, keeping in mind the ground realities and the risk profile and requirements of the investors and the banks. This is discussed below.

*Preference versus Permissibility of Various Modes*

Debt has been prevalent forever, and will remain an important part of individuals' and nations' economies. The holy Prophet (pbuh) himself borrowed and incurred debt (through credit purchase and borrowing), both for personal and the State's requirements, as we have discussed in Chapter 7. The only point to be taken care of is that a debt should not carry any charge over its principal. Therefore, debt-creating modes like Murabaha, Salam and Ijarah will remain as operating tools in the hands of Islamic financial institutions, and spot, credit and/or forward trade will remain a major economic activity in the Islamic framework. The issue is not of the permissibility of such modes, but of a preference for equity-based modes over debt-creating modes.

However, some people mix the aspect of permissibility with preference or priority. Some modes/products are considered borderline techniques, due mainly to fixity of profit rates for the banks. But that fixity of profit margin *per se* is not any problem at all. All transactions of Islamic banks should be based on exchange of commodities, goods, services or labour. If there is exchange of commodities or services along with the application of the relevant Sharī'ah principles, the transaction is permissible. Murabaha and Ijarah are permissible and there should be no doubt in this regard. When applied by banks, any of the modes may involve irregularities, making the same non-Sharī'ah-compliant. In this sense, someone may label any modes borderline techniques, because a little negligence on the part of the banker or the client may cause a Sharī'ah compliance problem. But such problems are faced even in the case of Musharakah and Mudarabah; should we avoid them for the reason that some IFIs have not applied the Musharakah conditions in letter and spirit? Certainly not. So the issue is not one of "debt versus equity" but one of putting greater reliance on equity and subjecting the debt to the principle of the Sharī'ah that debt, once created, should not increase as it increases in the conventional system.

For example, it was due to the careless functioning of Islamic banks in Pakistan in the 1980s that their Murabaha operations involving "buy-back" and "rollover" were merely a change of name. (This may be possible even now in cases of "windows" operated by conventional financial institutions without any Sharī'ah supervision by regulators or Sharī'ah advisors.) As a result, the Federal Shariat Court in Pakistan altogether prohibited the use of Murabaha in its judgement given in November, 1991. The government of Pakistan preferred an appeal to the Shariat Appellate Bench (SAB) of the Supreme Court of Pakistan, which allowed the use of Murabaha with the condition that all Sharī'ah essentials of Murabaha are applied and banks actually become involved in trading and undertake trading risks.

Similarly, Ijarah is a crucial mode that can be helpful in enhancing capital formation in an economy. But if banks do not fulfil its conditions relating to risk and reward of the leased asset, the transaction will not be Sharī'ah-compliant and the Sharī'ah advisor would be justified in rejecting this.

Islamic banks can charge fixed profits/rentals if they engage in trading and leasing; so much so that if the price or the rental is not fixed in clear terms, the transactions lose validity. Therefore, the permissibility of debt-creating modes is intact and established. Financing through these modes, in order to be Sharī'ah-compliant, is necessarily linked to real sector activities and, therefore, is a source of productivity and just profitability. Any of the products or modes should not be questioned simply because some bankers do not fulfil the requisite Sharī'ah conditions. If an effective Sharī'ah compliance framework is in operation and the Sharī'ah advisors and/or regulators are vigilant about the operations of IFIs, their products should be acceptable.

*Suitability of Shirkah-based Modes for Financing*

As regards the application of the preferable modes based on Shirkah principles, banks' management or the regulators may like to issue instructions to the practitioners in the banks to apply them keeping in mind the risk profile of the fund owners and ground realities of the business in respective areas. In many areas of business, use of Shirkah-based modes might not even be possible. A person doing family business may be in need of bridge finance and not of permanent or long-term funding. His requirement can be met through trade-based modes or leasing. In some other cases, their use may not be advisable due to a low-risk profile of the investors. Banks keep depositors' money as a trust and they are bound to invest such money according to the wishes or instructions of the depositors, without compromising on the Sharī´ah principles. If the depositors are risk-averse, their money will have to be invested in leasing or trade-based modes. For example, a pensioner or a widow may require an Islamic banker to invest his/her money in less risky but Sharī´ah-compliant business because he or she is not in a position to bear the risk of loss that could arise in Shirkah-based business. The bank, as a trustee, would be bound to invest the funds of such risk-averse investors in trade and Ijarah-based activities. Similarly, on the assets side, the bank's clients may either not be willing to make the bank a partner in their business or may not be keeping proper and correct records of the joint business; this may cause loss to the bank and, in turn, to the savers/investors.

However, it should be accepted that Musharakah and Mudarabah or other PLS products are the best alternatives to interest. They not only make the capital risk-bearing, a badly needed factor in growth and development even in developed countries, but also encourage entrepreneurship. But this should not lead to negation of non-PLS modes, which can also play a role in capital formation and development of economies. Accordingly, there has been a gradual change in the approach of Islamic banking experts, and it is being increasingly felt that all Islamic modes of financing, if properly used in line with their Sharī´ah-related requirements, can have a positive role in the development process. Islamic banks, while functioning on a basis other than interest, have to perform a crucial task of resource mobilization, their efficient allocation on the basis of both PLS and non-PLS categories of modes and strengthening the payments systems to contribute to economic growth and development.

### 17.3.8   Islamic Financial Institutions – Banks or Trade Houses?

Islamic banking is also criticized on the basis that banking means intermediation between savers and borrowers; banks do not deal in real sector business. They facilitate trade and business, but in that case also they deal in documents only. Islamic banks should not get involved in trading or other direct business, otherwise they would be exposing themselves to unnecessary risk and possible loss to the investors and the financial system. But this objection has no solid base. Even conventional financial business is conducted on the basis of different structures, namely commercial banks, universal banks, investment banks and other non-banking finance institutions or companies. In countries like Japan, Germany, Switzerland and the Netherlands, banks are involved in real sector merchant and universal banking. Investment banks, mutual funds and other asset management companies are involved in almost all countries in non-commercial business activities.

Therefore, Islamic banks, which are not supposed to work on a purely financial intermediation model, are not something absolutely new and unique in global finance. As lending and borrowing is not a major activity of IFIs, the universal banking model and investment banking are more suitable for their operation and certainly more useful for the economy and the society in which they operate. In this structure, they are in a better position to deal with problems like information asymmetry that the commercial banks working for pure financial intermediation have to face. Besides, they are in a position to earn a higher profit, enabling them to pass on higher profits to the depositors. It is normally suggested, therefore, that Islamic banks should establish trading companies to finance the credit purchases of their customers. As regards the risk, Islamic finance has the provision of mitigating asset, market and return-related risks. Further, the banks' management or the regulators can establish firewalls so that Islamic financial institutions may avoid unnecessary exposure in various sectors.

### 17.3.9    Islamic Banks to Act as Social Welfare Institutions?

Another, less common, criticism of Islamic banking is that IFIs charge the clients a market-related rate; they should get no return on the facilities they provide and serve as social security or charity institutions. This does not have any firm basis from the point of view of the Sharī´ah or economic principles. Giving return-free loans may be an activity of individuals at their discretion, or of States in some special circumstances. Providing funds by business institutions without any return is not possible according to the rules of demand and supply. Where will the funds come from if banks do not give any return to the depositors/investors? Profit earning is not the issue; the issue is how to earn profit – through interest-based lending or through real sector business? Islamic banks normally do not lend money; they undertake real sector business keeping in mind the Sharī´ah principles.

IFIs have to work as business institutions so as to properly perform the functions of mobilization and efficient allocation of resources. The myth in some circles that Islamic banks need to work as social security centres providing charity to the needy and for benevolence has to be removed, because business and benevolence are two separate things. Individuals have a right to spend for benevolence out of their incomes, for which they will be rewarded in this world and in the Hereafter. But banks that hold depositors' money with a particular mandate have no right to dishonour the mandate.

Islamic banks will sell goods purchased by them on profit, lease assets against rentals and share the profit (or bear the loss) accruing from Shirkah-based investments. They will help society to develop by facilitating asset-based investment and supply of risk-based capital. The State or the regulators will be required to oversee their functions to ensure that the interest of various stakeholders is properly safeguarded. Subject to the policies of their boards and in consultation with stakeholders, they can also take part in social and welfare activities, but this will not be their normal course of business.

## 17.4    APPRAISAL OF CRITICISM ON ISLAMIC BANKING PRACTICE

We analyse various objections and criticism of Islamic banking practices below.

### 17.4.1    Divergence between Theory and Practice

A number of scholars writing on Islamic banking are of the view that Islamic banks have deviated to a great extent from their philosophical basis and that the concept of Islamic banking and finance has changed visibly from the concept envisaged in the second half of the nineteenth century. In the initial stage of evolution of Islamic banking (the 1940s to the early 1980s), it was considered that, mainly, the profit/loss sharing modes would be the alternative to interest to rectify the socio-economic injustice caused by the institution of interest. For example, neither Dr Nejatullah Siddiqi's *Banking without Interest* nor Dr Uzair's *Interest-free Banking* make any reference to Murabaha. The Report of the Council of Islamic Ideology, Pakistan (1980) that is the pioneering work on the subject, allowed the use of Murabaha only hesitantly and limited its use to unavoidable cases in the transformation process. Shaikh Muhammad Taqi Usmani writes about Murabaha and Ijarah in the concluding chapter of *An Introduction to Islamic Finance*:

> "The Sharī'ah scholars have allowed their use for financing purposes only in those spheres where Musharakah cannot work and that, too, with certain conditions. This allowance should not be taken as a permanent rule for all sorts of transactions and the entire operations of Islamic banks should not revolve around it".[3]

Practically, however, Murabaha and Ijarah are being used to a very large extent and the use of PLS modes is negligible, even in institutions in which the honourable Shaikh serves as Sharī'ah supervisor or member of the Sharī'ah board. This divergence has to be seen in the correct and larger perspective, as this will determine the level of credibility of the emerging system. As a matter of fact, this phenomenon refers more to evolution of the concept of Islamic finance than to its divergence. Islamic finance is still evolving on the basis of the basic philosophy and principles given by the Sharī'ah.

One major cause of the apparent divergence between theory and practice is the excessive use of Murabaha, which gives a fixed rate of return to the banks. This has been dubbed "Murabaha Syndrome", with an ironic feeling about operations of IFIs.[4] Conceptually speaking, it is not a true feeling. Trading is an accepted activity in the Islamic system and if the prohibitions and the recommended ethics of business, as identified in the books of Hadith and jurisprudence, are taken care of, it leads to many facilities for human beings, growth of wealth and broader distribution of bounties of the Almighty. In many cases, trade or leasing are the only options. A vast majority of depositors, particularly in developing countries, are low income people like pensioners, widows and other lower middle class groups. Their money should not be invested in risky ventures. However, in the case of single trade transactions or where satisfactory documentation is available, Islamic banks should use Musharakah, as this will give them higher returns.

### 17.4.2  IFIs using Interest Income as Seed/Base Capital

Some quarters criticize Islamic banking on the grounds that conventional interest-based banks are using their interest income for setting up "Islamic windows", stand-alone Islamic banking branches (IBBs) or full-fledged Islamic banking institutions. The objection is that income earned from prohibited sources should not be used for business based on Sharī'ah principles. But the argument is ill-founded. If a person doing any prohibited/illegal business intends, at any time, to stop the wrong-doing, he needs to be encouraged. There must be a start-up time to transform to valid, good and socially useful activities from illegal, harmful

---

[3] Usmani, 2000a, p. 241.
[4] Yousef, 2005.

and bad professions. The Qur´ānic verses give the principle that "those who listen to the order of the Almighty and desist from engaging in interest (in future), may keep their previously received gains, their case being entrusted to the Almighty (for accountability in the Hereafter)" (2: 275) and "if you repent (on taking interest), you have the right to get your principal" (2: 278). This principle gives a clear line of action: income of an interest-based institution can become the seed capital for an Islamic financial institution – a window, a branch, a full-fledged bank or NBFC. The only requirement is that its operations should be Sharī´ah-compliant and totally segregated from the interest-based business. Further, in many cases, the whole capital of the bank would not be the interest income. Initially generated capital remains a part of it.

A related objection could be that, as per the direction of the Holy Qur´ān, such institutions should altogether leave the interest-based business and transform their entire operations to Sharī´ah-compliant ones. This is the ideal requirement and the policymakers/regulators, particularly in Muslim majority countries, must have the target of transformation of the whole system within a well-defined period. But this could have exceptions: a mega multinational conventional financial institution cannot be expected to transform its whole operations overnight; but it should certainly be encouraged to launch Sharī´ah-compliant business at whatever level it can afford, as this would possibly be a driving force for promotion of the emerging system across the globe.

### 17.4.3    Difference between Islamic and Conventional Banking

The most common criticism pertaining to the practice of Islamic banking is that there is no real difference between the conventional and the Islamic banking operations. The objection is raised on the following grounds: IFIs charge time value of money on the basis of reference rates, like the conventional institutions, to earn the same level of income; they do not actually deal in goods and only facilitate the purchase of goods and services by the clients, like their counterparts in the conventional system, and thus earn fixed income; they require collateral from the clients, penalize them in cases of default, give almost the same return to the depositors and the investors and have never passed any loss to the depositors. The following sections consider these objections.

*Charging Time Value of Money as Conventional Banks Charge*

IFIs cannot and generally do not charge the time value of money in the conventional sense. They have to undertake trading or leasing, for which they can genuinely take into consideration the time factor for the purpose of pricing of goods or their usufructs, as discussed in detail in various parts of the book. But once the receivable is created upon execution of any valid contract, they cannot add anything to the receivable, not only in debt-creating modes like trade and leasing but also in respect of the profits realized in Musharakah or Mudarabah. The "cost of funds" in terms of conventional opportunity cost is not any consideration in Islamic finance. Time value of money is accepted for the purpose of pricing of goods/usufruct only and not for pricing of money or debts/debt instruments. Hence, the view that Islamic banks charge time value of money like conventional banks is a misconception.

*Use of Interest Rates as Benchmarks*

Use of any interest-related benchmark by Islamic banks is also a subject of criticism. An important point to be observed in this regard is that benchmark or reference rates are a genuine need of all types of business. Reference rates may differ from sector to sector, market to market and time to time – a formal market rate would be different from that of the informal market; a real estate rate would be different from the commodities market rate; similarly, the financial sector's rate would be different from that of industry or agriculture. But any such rate must be there, enabling the related market players to price their goods and services. Accordingly, IFIs also need reference rates or benchmarks. As the market in which they have to function is financial, they can use only the financial market's reference rate, otherwise there would be distortion or chaos.

A related question could be why don't Islamic banks develop their own benchmark rates? It has to be accepted that a benchmark reflective of fictitious assets will not be helpful in realizing the socio-economic objectives of Islamic banking and finance. But the point to be noted is that in the present scenario, wherein Islamic banks' share in the national and global financial markets is very small, they are obliged to use the benchmark of the formal conventional market in which they are operating. Governments and big public and private sector corporations are raising huge funds on the basis of interest. Also, they place their excess liquidity at the highest possible risk-free rates of return. Even most of the stocks do not fulfil the screening criteria for Sharī'ah-compliant investment in shares of joint stock companies. This is why IFIs are currently using the interest-based benchmarks in almost all parts of the world. No doubt Islamic banking, which is inherently different from the conventional system, needs its own benchmarks, but evolving separate rates in every jurisdiction requires time and sustained efforts, which should remain part of the future agenda of economists, bankers, policymakers and Sharī'ah scholars.

For the time being, conventional benchmarks can be used by IFIs because these are used only as a tool and a basis for pricing the goods or their usufruct, which Sharī'ah accepts. A seller can charge any price with the consent of the buyer and to remain competitive in a market. The use of a conventional benchmark does not mean that Islamic and conventional banking are similar. As discussed earlier, different subject matters of the two systems (money in the former and goods in the latter) make a lot of difference in terms of rights and liabilities of the parties.

*Pre-fixed Rates of Return in Islamic Finance*

A common myth, particularly among laymen, is that an Islamic financial institution should charge and give only variable returns on financial accommodation and deposits respectively; a fixed deposit or facility rate is interest. This myth needs to be removed, as the return rate depends on the nature of the contract or the agreement. In all transactions, the Sharī'ah requirement is that one should sufficiently know what one is giving and getting in exchange in a contract. This implies that certainty about the subject matter and its exchange value, transparency, disclosure and free consent of the parties for entering into the contracts are important factors in Islamic business and finance.

It all depends on the nature of the transaction. In a money transaction or a debt, no fixed or floating/variable charge can be taken. If the deposits with a bank are in the form of a loan, as in the case of current account liabilities of banks, they should carry no return. Deposits mobilized on the basis of Mudarabah should generate a variable return for both the bank and the depositors. In the case of loss on such deposits, the depositor's capital will decrease while the bank will not be able to get any return against its services as fund manager. If deposits are managed on a Wakalatul Istismār basis, the bank will charge a fixed fee, while the depositor will take the entire profit or bear the loss, if any.

The rule that one should sufficiently know what one is giving and what one is getting in exchange in a contract implies that the price or the rent has to be fixed with certainty. In the case of trade, Islamic banks are required to fix the price once and for all and, therefore, they can charge a fixed profit in Murabaha, while in Salam, the bank's return depends on the price at which it is able to market the Salam commodity. In Ijarah, the rental has to be fixed, otherwise the transaction is void. But, as the lessor has to bear the ownership-related risks and expenses, the net return to the bank as lessor or to the Ijarah Sukuk holders is quasi-fixed and not absolutely fixed. On money lending or debt-based instruments, Islamic banks cannot get any return. Shirkah-based investments can be attached to fixed earning modes like trade and Ijarah. Examples are Diminishing Musharakah on the basis of Shirkatulmilk and securitization through Ijarah and Shirkah. Islamic investment products can be structured in such a way that investors get a variable or quasi-fixed return. Hence, fixity of charge *per se* is not an issue; it all depends on the nature of any transaction or its result and implications.

A linked objection in respect of rates is that although Islamic banks get deposits on the basis of Mudarabah, they have never passed on any loss to the depositors. The factual position is that IFIs constitute a number of pools of deposits, and investments on the basis of sharing and debt-creating modes are made out of the respective pools, keeping in mind the principle of diversification. The greater the pool and broader the level of diversification, the lower the possibility of loss to the bank and, in turn, to the pool members. For example, a pool belonging to one thousand depositors of different categories (tenors) has to be invested; the bank invests in four, five or even more sectors/subsectors of the economy by facilitating 200 entrepreneurs on the basis of various modes like Murabaha, Ijarah, Diminishing Musharakah and Musharakah, by observing all risk management tools. As a result, in many cases of trade and leasing, the bank will be earning a prestipulated return; in the case of Shirkah-based financing, it may incur loss in a few cases, while in most cases, it will earn a profit, as it has applied all risk mitigation tools allowed by the Sharī´ah. Even if it has to incur loss in respect of a few cases or some of the receivables come under default, it will be earning a profit on an overall basis. The overall profit earned from the pool is distributed between the pool and the bank (Mudarib) and then the pool's share is distributed among the pool members on the basis of average daily products and the weightages assigned to each category at the beginning of the period.[5] If a projected rate of profit is indicated in advance, it has no impact on the final profit distribution; only the net realized amount has to be distributed on the basis of pre-agreed criteria and the bank has a limited "tool kit" to make up the shortfall, if any.

We can say, therefore, that any loss has to be charged to the pool, but the profit earned by the bank in most cases covers the loss. Further, IFIs can create reserves from the profits, from which any losses in the future can be met.

Another important aspect is that Islamic banks are business entities for the purpose of earning profit. They are required to be more prudent businessmen than their counterparts in the conventional set-up, as they are holding public money as a trust. All businesses avoid loss by way of proper management and risk mitigation tools. Likewise, Islamic banks holding

---

[5] The procedure of deposit management on the basis of Shirkah has been described in Chapter 8, Section 8.5.2.

depositors' money as a trust are required to apply all legal and possible measures to avoid losses.

Conclusive fixity of return on various types of Sukuk is, of course, a critical issue. We have discussed this matter in detail in Chapter 15 (Section 15.3.7). The gist of the discussion is that "fixed-income" securities or Sukuk in the sense of conventional investment instruments are not possible in Islamic finance. The prospectus to issue any Sukuk/certificates (not only those which are Shirkah-based) must not contain any clause that the issuer is liable to compensate the certificate holders up to the nominal value in situations other than torts and negligence, or that he guarantees a fixed percentage of profit. In Shirkah-based Sukuk, only an independent third party can provide guarantee without any remuneration for the capital or any profit. But the third party's commitment does not create the right for beneficiaries to relate the Shirkah contract with fulfilment of the guarantee. In the case of inability or refusal by the third party to perform as per commitment, the Sukuk holders cannot claim for redress on the grounds that they had purchased the Sukuk taking into account the third party's undertaking to guarantee the profit or the capital.[6]

In the case of Ijarah or mixed portfolio Sukuk, there could be default in receipt of Murabaha receivables; in leases, there is the possibility both of ownership-related expenses and default in receipt of the due rental. The owner/lessor of the asset may assure the purchaser (Sukuk holder), while selling it to the SPV, about the performance of the lessees, as in the case of IDB Trust. But what should be the course of action if the asset is destroyed without any fault or negligence of the lessee? This loss has to be borne by the lessor – Sukuk holders. In the case of Murabaha or other receivables, the SPV may have recourse to the institution that has undertaken the underlying transactions, but even then there could be shortfalls. Hence, the return rate can be quasi-fixed but not fixed in any way in respect of any category of Sukuk. Therefore, the matter should be taken care of for integrity and sustained support for the emerging financial system.

*Actual Involvement in Real Sector Business*

Islamic banks are also criticized on the grounds that they are not actually involved in real sector business. This is not true; Islamic banks have to be involved in real business, with all its implications, as they are not allowed to charge cost of funds or rent on money in short-, medium- or long-term loans, overdrafts, guarantees, financing against bills, receivables or other instruments or sell their debt instruments. The most strategic difference between Islamic and conventional rules is that, in the latter case, both items of exchange in a transaction can be delayed/deferred and the goods purchased, and even the "options" can be sold onward without taking ownership of the underlying assets and possession of the related risk. In Islamic finance, only one of the items of an exchange contract can be delayed while delivery/possession of the item of exchange has to be given and taken, as stipulated in the contract, along with transfer of the risk to the buyer. Islamic banks' operations involve exchange of goods for money, which may take a number of forms like simultaneous exchange on the spot, spot delivery with deferred payment and spot payment with deferred delivery.

The subject matter of Islamic banking is goods; IFIs use money only as a medium of exchange for purchasing the goods for the purpose of leasing or selling onward, thereby

---

[6] AAOIFI, 2004–5a, Standard on Musharakah, clause 3/1/4/3.

earning rental or profit. As discussed in Chapters 4 and 5, they have to virtually purchase a commodity, take it into ownership and possession, necessarily implying transfer of ownership risk to them; only then are they entitled to earn a profit by selling it onward. After execution of the sale, asset risk is transferred to the clients, who are bound to pay the price at the settled time. In Salam, the bank has to take delivery of the goods purchased in advance, irrespective of a fall or rise in their price. In Istisna'a, the manufacturer delivers the asset to the bank along with all asset-related and market risks. In Ijarah, ownership of leased assets remains with the banks and according to well-established rules of the Sharī'ah, risk also remains with them.

Islamic banks, however, do not and cannot maintain inventory of all the goods they trade in; they are not grocery stores. Neither is it a Sharī'ah requirement that a person should necessarily place the wares on counters of a store before selling it onward. The procedure that IFIs may purchase the goods for onward sale upon requisition of the clients is based on very common real sector business practice and, therefore, is acceptable from the Sharī'ah angle. Accordingly, the Sharī'ah Standard on Murabaha prepared by the AAOIFI has been named the Standard on Murabaha to Purchase Orderer.

Making the client an agent for the purchase or sale of goods by Islamic banks is also accepted in the Sharī'ah without any difference of opinion. Goods held by an agent are in the risk of the principal so long as any negligence or breach of trust on the part of the agent is not proved. It seems to be preferable that Islamic banks establish some asset management or trading companies that may maintain inventories of the commonly required goods and assets for undertaking merchant banking; but it is neither possible to keep inventory of all the goods and brands of goods required by the clients, nor is it a Sharī'ah condition for the genuine business of trade and Ijarah.

## Taking Security/Collateral and Documentation

Another objection raised is that Islamic banks, like their counterparts in the conventional system, take collateral/security in all financing, also including Musharakah/Mudarabah. A related objection is that Islamic banks ask for too much documentation. It is misunderstood that IFIs should facilitate their clients on the assets side without any requirement of collateral. In principle, this objection is baseless. Islamic banks are commercial institutions; they can take pledge/collateral to the level of their satisfaction for recovery of their receivables.[7]

As IFIs deal in goods and create receivables, they need collateral and also documentation more than the conventional institutions need. The Holy Qur'ān and Sunnah emphasize documentation, transparency and collateral in all credit transactions, as we have discussed in detail in Chapter 7. The Holy Qur'ān enjoins one to write down and take witnesses in all transactions that involve credit one way or another. Similarly, the holy Prophet (pbuh) encouraged disclosure of all features of goods being traded and the competitive environment in which people get sufficient information about the goods and their prices in the market.

Hence, in all debt-creating modes, banks may ask the client to furnish security in the form of a mortgage, a lien or a charge on any of his assets. In forward purchase, banks can ask the client to furnish security to ensure that he shall deliver the commodity on the agreed date. In PLS modes as well, the bank can ask for a guarantee against negligence or breach of the contract; but the bank will not be entitled to enforce the collateral if a loss in the

---

[7] Wilson, 2002, pp. 210, 211.

business has occurred without any misconduct or negligence on the part of the client who is a partner of the bank.

Practically, however, there may be a requirement that, in certain cases, the condition relating to collateral be relaxed to enable clients of small means to conduct some micro-level business. Experience has shown that small businesses and the middle class clients of financial institutions do not adopt dilatory practices in payment of their liabilities. Therefore, IFIs should also launch some schemes to facilitate the unemployed and poor people to start some business to earn sustenance on the basis of personal and/or group sureties.

## Risk Profile of Islamic Banks

Another misconception is that Islamic banks, like conventional banks, do not take on risk; they adopt modes and techniques such that they are able to get targeted income, as in the case of conventional banking. The point to be emphasized in this regard is that risk-taking and risk management are two different aspects. Islamic banking involves risk-taking by its very nature; risk can be minimized by way of valid risk management tools but not totally avoided or eliminated. Conventional banks give and take risk-free returns in the sense that the principal and an addition over it in the form of interest is guaranteed; depositors and the banks are entitled to get the full amount of the loan along with interest. If an amount goes into default, it is due to a management/governance problem, as the contractual right to receive the amount remains intact. This is not the case in Islamic finance; IFIs have to conduct real business, as a result of which they may earn a profit or incur a loss, and hence they take on risk.

The additional risks that Islamic financial institutions have to face as compared to conventional institutions are asset risk, market risk, Sharī´ah-non-compliance risk, greater rate of return risks, greater fiduciary risks and greater legal risks. Asset risk is involved in all modes, particularly in Murabaha (before onward sale to the client), Salam (after taking delivery from the Salam seller) and Ijarah, as all ownership-related risks belong to the bank so long as the asset is in its ownership; if the asset is damaged without any fault on the part of the lessee and it is not able to deliver the normally intended benefit, the bank's right to get rental will cease. In Shirkah-based modes, risk is borne as per the share in the ownership. Market risk is involved as the bank might not be able to market the goods purchased on the basis of Salam, Istisna'a, etc. at a profitable price. Rate of return risk is involved as the price, once fixed in Murabaha/Salam, cannot be increased. Remaining within the Sharī´ah principles, Islamic banks are allowed to take risk mitigation/management measures. But transfer of risk to anyone else without transferring related reward is not permissible. Therefore, the criticism that Islamic banks, like conventional banks, do not take business risk is not valid.

## Identical End Result of Conventional and Islamic Banking

Islamic banking is also criticized on the grounds that the end results of Islamic banking operations are the same as those of conventional banking. Apparently, this may be true, for the reason that IFIs are using the same benchmarks, working in a competitive environment and, as such, are not in a position to give or charge rates significantly different from those of the conventional banks. The financial sector's benchmarks make the administration and regulation by the banks' management and the regulators easy, effective and transparent. Hence, Islamic banks generally use the benchmarks that conventional institutions use. But mere use of a benchmark does not imply that the end result will be the same. While conventional banks use a benchmark for pricing their lending or money-based transactions, Islamic banks use them for pricing of goods, their usufruct and services; and this feature makes a lot of difference between the two systems. Islamic banks will not be able to create money out of nothing or without the backing of real assets, as is the case in the conventional system. They can only securitize their asset-based operations for the purpose of generating liquid funds, transferring thereby their ownership to the security holders along with their risk and reward. Financing government budget deficits by Islamic banks and financial institutions will not be possible until the governments have sufficient real assets for raising funds in a Sharī´ah-compliant manner or for the conversion of debt stock into Sharī´ah-compliant securities. (The issue of money creation is discussed in detail in Chapter 4, Section 4.7.3.)

The two systems are different even in respect of commercial operations. While conventional institutions provide loans for consumption or for purchasing raw materials/finished goods/assets and keep on charging interest so long as the receivable is not paid, Islamic banks sell the relevant asset/commodity after taking its ownership and risk at one stipulated price that remains the same even in the case of default. In leasing, they bear the ownership-related risks and expenses. If the leased asset is destroyed for any reason other than the negligence of the lessee, they incur the loss and if the amount received from insurance/Takaful is not sufficient to cover the whole loss, they cannot claim the difference from the lessee. Similarly, in Salam they receive the goods and if they have to get back the prepaid price for any reason, they cannot claim any "cost of funds" for use of money by the Salam seller.

Therefore, it is not true to say that the end result of the practices of Islamic and conventional banks is the same, so long as Islamic banks fulfil the Sharī´ah requirements of Islamic modes of business. Islamic finance enhances the supply of risk-based capital and helps in capital formation in the economy, which ultimately benefits the general public, while conventional finance tends to create individuals who earn money from money without participation in real business activities – making the rich richer and the poor poorer.

### IFIs' Combined and Complicated Contracts

Another point of criticism regarding Islamic banking is that IFIs combine a number of contracts in respect of one overall transaction, while, as per the theory of Islamic finance, entering into "two contracts for one contract" is prohibited. But the factual Sharī´ah position is that only two interdependent agreements are prohibited. The combination of some contracts is permissible subject to certain conditions. Shirkah and Ijarah can be combined, meaning that a partner can give his part of ownership in an asset on lease to any co-partners, as in the case of Diminishing Musharakah. In contrast, Bai´ and Ijarah are two contracts of totally different impacts; while in Bai´, ownership and risk are transferred to the buyer, in Ijarah, neither ownership nor risk is transferred from the lessor to the lessee. It is necessary, therefore, that lease and sale are kept as separate agreements. However, one of the parties can undertake a unilateral promise to sell, buy or gift the asset at the termination of the lease. This will not be binding on the other party. Similarly, sale of ownership units to the client in Diminishing Musharakah will have to be kept totally separate, requiring "offer and acceptance" for each unit and the partners will bear the pro rata risk on the basis of share in ownership at any point of time.

Musharakah and Mudarabah can also be combined. For example, banks manage depositors' funds on the basis of Mudarabah; they can deploy their own funds in the business with the condition that the ratio of profit for a sleeping partner shall not be more than the ratio that its capital has in the total capital.

Contracts of agency (Wakalah) and suretyship (Kafalah) can also be combined with sale or lease contracts, with the condition that rights and liabilities arising from various contracts are taken as per their respective rules.

Islamic banks can structure products by combining different modes, subject to the fulfilment of their respective conditions. For example, they can combine Salam or Istisna'a with Murabaha for preshipment export financing. Diminishing Musharakah is a combination of Shirkah and Ijarah added by an undertaking by one party to periodically sell/purchase the ownership to/from the other partner. In all major contracts like Musharakah, Ijarah, Salam and Istisna'a, Islamic banks enter into promise and agency contracts with the clients or any third parties. This is acceptable in Sharī'ah provided all agreements and accessory contracts are independently enforceable with their implications. However, interdependent agreements or stipulations leading to uncertainty about rights and liabilities of the contracting parties cannot be made.

*Taking Binding Promises from Clients*

Some scholars have criticized Islamic banks for treating the "promise to purchase" by the client as binding. But as it does not involve violation of any Sharī'ah principle, mainstream Islamic finance theory has declared it binding, keeping in mind the practical problems in finalization of contracts (see Chapter 5, Section 5.6). Keeping in mind the intricacies of present-day business, particularly when conducted by Islamic banks, contemporary scholars have reached the consensus that promise by one party in economic/financial transactions is enforceable by law until and unless the promisor is not in a position to fulfil it on account of any *force majeure*. If nonfulfilment is due to any wilful act of the promisor, he shall have to make good the loss to the promisee.

The rationale behind this consensus decision is that, in many cases, binding promises become a genuine requirement, fulfilment of which does not amount to violation of any basic Sharī'ah tenet. This has important implications for Islamic banks' operations in respect of Murabaha to Purchase Orderer, Ijarah Muntahia-bi-Tamleek, Diminishing Musharakah and for the disposal of goods purchased by banks under Salam/Istisna'a. As it does not contradict any Nass (text) of the Qur'ān or Sunnah, it can be accepted on the principle of Ibāhatul Asliyah (all economic activities that are not prohibited are valid/permissible).

### 17.4.4 Imposing Penalties on Defaulters

Imposing late payment penalties by Islamic banks is also subject to criticism. The argument is that while the Holy Qur'ān recommends giving more time to debtors and even waiving the debt, IFIs impose penalties on a percentage per annum basis. As a result, the cost of financing for the clients is the same as in the case of conventional banks, or perhaps higher. Islamic banks should, therefore, give extra time without any extra charge.

Default is one of the major challenges facing the financial industry across the globe. The conventional system has a built-in tool for controlling default, as the defaulters are charged interest that becomes part of the income of the conventional financial institutions. IFIs have been allowed by the Sharī'ah scholars to charge penalties to defaulters in order to discipline them, but the penalty amount has to be spent on charity and cannot become part of the income of the bank.

The situation is not so simple. Most of the banks' clients on the assets side are resourceful businessmen. They do not pay their dues to the banks, while they continue their luxurious lifestyles. In such cases, they are not covered under the idea of debtors in difficulty being entitled to relaxation or waiver. While full and timely repayment of debts cannot be overemphasized in Islamic economics and finance, we have to differentiate between wilful and actual default arising due to real economic problems faced by the debtors. As per Sharī´ah rules, wilful defaulters are like usurpers who are made to return any profit, along with the property, made by them on the usurped property.

We also have to differentiate between Qard and Dayn, as the jurists have approved imposing penalties in the latter case only. This means that, in the case of a loan (Qard), the creditor should give more time, while if the liability to pay has been created due to any business transaction – sale or Ijarah transactions – and the client is delaying the payment by resorting to negligent tactics, he can be required to pay a fine, which goes to charity, and even to compensate the bank for the actual loss (see Chapter 7, Section 7.13). In this regard, the OIC Fiqh Council has resolved that penalty provision should become null and void when a client proves that his failure to meet an obligation was due to a reason beyond his control, or when he proves that, as a result of his breach of the contract, the bank has incurred no loss.

Default in settlement of liabilities has become a socio-economic evil of the present age, due mainly to the unjust principles of the capitalistic and interest-based system and legal loopholes. In the Islamic framework, debtors are not given such latitude that while asset-wise they are billionaires, they do not pay the liabilities on account of some legal loopholes. As Islamic banks have to work in the same overall environment, Sharī´ah scholars allow them to impose penalties in case of default, as the default hits them more than it hits the conventional institutions. They cannot claim "cost of funds" or liquidated damages as the conventional banks can charge. As default is injurious to the deposit holders, IFIs need to take every possible step to minimize its possibility.

### 17.4.5  Availability of Cash for Overhead Expenses and Deficit Financing

Another criticism made of Islamic finance is that, if money has always to be linked to real assets, how will the needs of cash for overhead expenses and for deficit financing be fulfilled? Islamic finance has a number of modes/instruments on the basis of which liquidity needs can be properly fulfilled. Forward sales like Salam/Salaf and Istisna‘a are the best examples. A producer of homogeneous goods can genuinely sell his production in advance, and thus use the cash received for any consumption or business purposes. Needs of governments and the corporate sector can be met by issuance of Shirkah- or Ijarah-based Sukuk. Therefore, this criticism is no longer valid.

### 17.4.6  Socio-economic Impact of the Present Islamic Banking System

Last but not least is the criticism that Islamic banking and finance in the present structure is not capable of achieving the socio-economic goals of an Islamic economy, as claimed in theory. Some of the pioneers have expressed their deep concern over the neglect of equity-based modes and the general prevalence of debt-creating modes. The concern is justifiable to the extent that if IFIs continue to work in the competitive environment without much support by States, policymakers and the regulators, as is the case at present, they may not be able to realize the objectives of an Islamic financial system as visualized by its pioneers, even in the long term.

But some are harsher and consider the present Islamic banking "an attempt to legitimize conventional Western banking by distorting the Sharī´ah".[8] It seems that the writers who make such remarks might not have tried to gain sufficient awareness about the concepts and philosophy of Islamic economics and finance (notwithstanding their scholarship in some other areas). Further, they should take into consideration "the tricky issues that the present generation of humanity faces in following divine guidance" (as remarked by Dr M. Nejatullah Siddiqi in his response to the article by Dr Asad Zaman; Ahmad and Siddiqi 2006). Responding to the above criticism, Professor Khurshid Ahmad says: "We all are concerned that systematic and sustained movement in that direction (equity-based economy) is yet to be made. It would be a tragedy if the Islamic movement does not move in that direction. But it would be less than generous to condemn the whole effort and regard it as an exercise in legitimization of the interest-based banking model."

Further, banking is only one part of an economy; public finance also has to follow a just and equitable system for getting the real benefit. The scope and need for the use of equity-based modes will be discussed in the final chapter, "The Way Forward".

## 17.5   CONCLUSION

The emerging system is subject to a number of myths and severe criticism, not only by those who do not accept the prohibition of interest but also by those "pious" people – both laymen and the well-educated/elite – who visualize an ideal system without giving any weightage to the evolutionary challenges and teething problems and difficulties. The concept and philosophy of Islamic finance is based on sound reasoning and is being accepted by an increasing number of people across the globe. What the practitioners need to do is to create awareness so as to remove the myths among the public.

As regards Islamic banking practice, IFIs need to apply stringent internal controls to avoid systemic and operational risks. Training of the operational staff at all levels, aimed at enhancing their vision, confidence and commitment, is a prerequisite for sustainable growth of the new discipline. They must find ways and means to apply equity-based modes, keeping in mind the risk profile of the fund owners and the nature of business on the financing side. A starting point in this direction may be financing of consignment-based trade practices, micro-business operations, Shirkah-based securitization and fund management.

Taking collateral and security is entirely valid for Islamic banks. However, they must also facilitate the clients who are capable of doing any profitable business but are not in a position to offer any tangible collateral, to enable them to start some business to earn sustenance on the basis of personal and/or group sureties.

---

[8] Zaman, 2006. For a response to this by Professor Khurshid Ahmad and Dr Nejatullah Siddiqi, see Ahmad, Khurshid, 2006 and Siddiqi, 2006b.

# The Way Forward

## 18.1 INTRODUCTION

As indicated in the Introduction to the book, I believe the socio-economic problems facing mankind today have emanated from the unbridled creation of fictitious assets, particularly reserve currencies, and the unhindered forces of demand and supply with exploitative tools of "sovereignty" of individuals, "unfettered self-interest" and the "interest"-based corrupt financial system. Human beings could have avoided massive losses to life and property had the creation of fictitious monetary assets not been so easy and rampant.[1] The solution lies in disciplining the creation of money, limiting self-interest with social interest and business ethics, and transforming the corrupt financial system to make it free from exploitation and games of chance, thus enabling mankind to optimally use the resources for benefits on a larger scale. Islamic finance provides a solid basis for these reformatory measures; it is up to human beings how they realize the potential.

The book has discussed mainly the latter part, i.e. how the financial system can be made friendly to human societies rather than individuals or a few strong and powerful players. This concluding chapter comprises observations and recommendations on two aspects:

1. Taking macro-level policy measures to discipline the financial matters of States, corporate bodies and the financial institutions, with the objective of discontinuing, in phases, the creation of fictitious assets.
2. How to develop the financial system on a sustainable basis on the principles and philosophy of Islamic finance, which essentially revolves around real tangible assets and business ethics cherished by humanity as a whole.[2]

## 18.2 AGENDA FOR THE POLICYMAKERS

The Islamic theory of finance possesses a huge potential in terms of its principles and instruments, which allow the minimum possible number of loopholes. Enhanced supply of risk-related permanent and redeemable capital – the most powerful fuel for the engines of modern economies – restricted risk-taking (implied in the prohibition of gambling and Gharar), a balanced return-rate structure based on real-asset-backed economic activities and supply of money commensurate with prospects of growth in an economy provide a sound basis for sustainable development and evenly shared income for the socio-economic benefit

---

[1] For example, in recent wars, financed in the main by deficit financing or the creation of (reserve) money, hundreds of thousands of human beings have lost their lives without any fault on their part. According to independent sources, the cost of the Iraq War has been projected at about 1 trillion US Dollars (see http://www.msnbc.msn.com/id/11880954/).

[2] Readers are recommended to review the first chapter for this.

of mankind as a whole. Advancement of societies in the long run depends on sharing knowledge and exchange of philosophies to choose the best of them on merit. It is for the policymakers and the world leaders to determine how to benefit from knowledge and wisdom, from wherever it is available.

In a survey of Islamic banking, the *South* magazine, in its issue of November, 1986, reported that:

> "Islamic banking, as the system is widely known, was first ridiculed in the West as a fundamentalist phenomenon, then just tolerated. Now, after careful scrutiny, it is being adopted in Western financing institutions and other interest-based commercial banks in the Muslim world. Islamic bankers have survived the credibility crisis and are no longer basking in the glory of divine revelation. After the splendid development since then, Islamic banks and other financial institutions have become more pragmatic and scientific".[3]

This was two decades back, but now the situation has enormously improved. It has provided good opportunities for the developed countries to tap into Muslim countries of the Middle East and also the Muslim minority markets. Asset-based Islamic banking that requires rigorous self-regulation as a part of Sharī´ah compliance and specific emphasis on ethical premises is expected to strengthen the internal controls in financial institutions and promote soundness of the financial system.

If applied widely at a global level, it could be instrumental in achieving balanced growth of national and global economies due to fewer spill-over effects that lead to excessive money and credit creation, as per the practice currently in vogue. It is possible, if the opinion makers and the intelligentsia initiate a well-thought-out movement, to persuade the economists of repute, particularly those sitting in the IMF and the World Bank and the policymakers in governments, to reframe the national and global trade and finance systems on just and equitable bases.

Already, a large number of influential people are talking of green finance and ethical investments. The strategy has to be framed to enhance the demand of such asset-based finances in all parts of the world. Islamic finance is well-placed to serve this purpose because transparency, justice and fulfilment of social responsibilities are among its core values. It has the potential to become an alternative model for the global system, beneficial to all societies and for close interaction between Muslim and non-Muslim societies. At an international level, the following measures may be required:

1. Increasing the number of reserve currencies in the global payments system for the purpose of diversification, which would require not only enhancing the role of the Euro and strong currencies like those of Japan and China, but also developing other regional or group-based reserve currencies. For example, regional currencies could be developed for inter-regional payments in South-East Asia, the Far East, Central Asia, the Middle East, Africa, Latin America and others; the OIC would be the best forum to develop such a strong and widely acceptable reserve currency acceptable on the wider scale in the world. International financial institutions should facilitate the development of multireserve currencies if the objective of avoiding possible turmoil in global finance and developing the world economy on sound footings is to be achieved. For the long-term betterment, the USA should also be required to help such a move for the future of its own people and

---

[3] *South*, London, November, 1986.

human society at large.[4] There should be an international conference like the one that was held in Bretton Woods in 1945 to discuss matters relating to the creation of reserves and of national currencies on merit.

2. Money and credit creation should be commensurate with real sector development in all economies. The economists must devise strategies such that an increase in monetary assets is matched by the real assets in an economy, with a possible allowance for realizing the growth potential of respective assets, businesses and economies during the related plan period. This has to be particularly observed in the case of currencies used for international payments. In other words, the issuance of the certificates of investment/financial assets must be based on real assets and their potential growth. For this purpose, the principles of Sukuk issue in Islamic finance can be of great help in transforming the basis for creating financial assets from thin air to some underlying real assets.

3. Loan-based finance leads to the squandering of wealth due to corrupt practices ostensibly resorted to by officials of the donors and also the recipient countries/institutions. Such finance must be replaced by (i) direct investment in commodity-producing or service sectors; (ii) project-based financing under strictly observed transparent standards; (iii) portfolio investments by sovereigns and multinational corporate bodies to strengthen equity markets in the recipient countries; and (iv) granting return-free loans or "in kind" assistance in the case of large-scale natural calamities in any part of the world, ensuring transparency and proper distribution among the affected people. Interest-based financial aid to the affected countries is fatal for their economies and could adversely affect the flow of global finance in the long run.[5]

4. "Foreign aid" or other forms of financial assistance to the poorer nations of the world must take the form of financial help, with the affected country benefiting rather tangibly, by controlling any corrupt commercial behaviour of the donor agencies as well as officials in the recipient countries.

5. If projected properly, Islamic finance should have appeal to followers of all religions. By introducing it as religious and/or ethical banking in all societies of the world, Islamic finance can become an engine of economic growth by mobilizing savings from so-far untapped groups of people and channelling them to healthy and real-asset based investments. The prohibition of Riba in all revealed religions could be instrumental in enhancing this appeal.

### 18.2.1 Muslim States and Islamic Finance

While Islamic principles of finance have proved their viability worldwide, and individual Islamic financial institutions and giant multinational groups are queuing to exploit the potential benefits, Muslim countries are not yet playing any effective role in the promotion of Islamic finance as a policy objective at the state level. Only one or two countries may be considered exceptions. To reiterate, the foundations of the asset-based and risk-related financial system have been laid down and it has already passed the significant milestones of

---

[4] The observations of John Perkins in *Confessions of an Economic Hitman*, as briefly given in the first chapter, may be kept in mind. Readers may like to study pages xi–xiv and 211–225 of his book. To quote another of his observations: "Admitting to a problem is the first step towards finding a solution. Confessing a sin is the beginning of redemption. Let this book, then, be the start of our salvation. Let it inspire us to new levels of dedication and drive us to realize our dream of balanced and honorable societies". (p. xiv).

[5] For details see Chapra, 2002, pp. 219–235.

having a rational and sound theoretical basis and increasingly wider acceptance at a global level. The measures required for building an all-pervasive structure of finance and making it free from injustice and anomalies include the creation of asset-based money and promoting retail and corporate financial services on the basis of fair play and risk-sharing.

Almost all Islamic countries are still borrowing through the conventional interest-based system and only a negligible part of their needs has been financed through Sharī´ah-compliant instruments. The firm edict of the Sharī´ah people against fixed-income securities, however, does not allow the use of conventional investment instruments. In realizing the real potential of Islamic finance, experimented and proved in recent years, these countries have to set a precedent for other countries of the world. The OIC or IDB may formulate financial packages for member countries, obliging them to resort to asset-based financing on the basis of Ijarah, Istisna´a and Shirkah. If applied wholeheartedly on a larger scale, these modes of business and investment have the possibility of being used as an efficient alternative to interest-based deficit financing, along with the added benefit of disciplining fiscal behaviour. In such a case, each economy would be able to get real benchmarks for the pricing of goods, their usufruct and services, both in cash and credit markets, representing the real demand/supply scenario and the strength of the economy. Obtaining a benchmark for Sharī´ah-compliant securities in the present situation is almost impossible. This is why, IFIs are currently obliged to adopt the interest-based benchmarks in almost all parts of the world, making the integrity of their operations vulnerable.

If Islamic finance theory is adopted for retail and/or corporate banking on a smaller or larger scale, and not for the financial system as a whole, i.e. the governments continue to generate funds primarily from the conventional markets, it is not likely to have any visible impact on any economies of the world or their general populations. Accordingly, the economists and the policymakers are required to come out with confidence and dynamism against the syndrome of allowing the creation of monetary assets without any meaningful limit on the one hand and allowing a fixed rent on such assets on the other; and be encouraged to adopt the real economic activity-based regimes that allow ex post profit- or loss-sharing and fixed or quasi-fixed returns through pricing of real goods, assets or their usufruct. This would require some bold measures that, of course, are not novel, as these are being taken in many economies in various parts of the world.

The conventional financial system has developed through a prolonged and continuous process, moving away from gold to the electronic medium of exchange. Correcting it to make it really helpful for human beings, just and conflict-free would also take a long time. However, the process of change has to be started with sincerity. Putting it on the right track would require a lot of work and sacrifice by present generations for the bright and safe future of mankind.

To transform whole economies and make them Sharī´ah-compliant, sooner or later the policymakers and planners will need well-defined phases and well-thought-out plans with committed and sustained efforts. This will require (i) identification of transformation requirements in terms of laws, rules, regulations and institutional structures in different jurisdictions, and components of policies fitting into the overall implementation timetable; (ii) laying down a phased plan and the implementation mechanism; and (iii) feedback or continuous review and evaluation in order to ensure proper application and to remove any obstacles.

Application of a real-asset-based financial system by only a few countries could cause a critical problem for them, due to exogenous factors responsible for an increase in money supply if most of the major economies of the world continue the present practices of money creation. To some extent, this problem can be tackled by facilitating closer linkages between the exogenous money and policies of the State in respect of capital flow, investment in the public and private sectors, fiscal, trade and pricing policies and the effective over-seeing role of the State.

## 18.3   POTENTIAL, ISSUES AND CHALLENGES FOR ISLAMIC BANKING

In this section we shall discuss the issues, potential and challenges for Islamic banking and how best it can meet such challenges. Islamic finance has rapidly grown from a highly specialized niche market into a multi-billion dollar global industry, expected to continue double-digit growth in the coming decades. Islamic retail banks and non-bank financial institutions operating across the world already number in the hundreds, in both Muslim majority and Muslim minority countries. The IFIs' product portfolio has significantly grown on account of innovative products, both for retail and corporate operations. Financial institutions of the West and America, including Citigroup, Deutsche Bank, ABN AMRO, HSBC and UBS, are increasingly offering products based on the Sharī'ah principles.[6]

The experiences of Islamic banks in Kuwait, Bahrain, Saudi Arabia, Sudan, Britain and in other parts of the world point towards tangible success in the areas of product innovation, venture capital, equity finance, finance for trade, housing and other consumer needs and international syndication for trade and project finance deals. Owing to the growing amount of funds available with Islamic banks, refining of Islamic financing techniques and the huge requirement of infrastructure development in Muslim countries, there has been a large number of project finance agreements in the recent past, particularly in the Middle East region. Islamic banks now participate in a wide range of financing, stretching from simple Sharī'ah-compliant retail products to highly complex structured finance and large-scale project implementation. These projects include the construction of power stations, water plants, roads, bridges and other infrastructure projects.

Electronic money has also been introduced by a number of IFIs. A number of institutions, including Kuwait Finance House, Dubai Islamic Bank, etc., are offering credit cards, while debit cards have been issued by a large number of IFIs. National Commercial Bank of Saudi Arabia has introduced an "advance card", which does not have a credit line and instead has a prepaid line. Added benefits are purchase protection, travel accident insurance without the involvement of interest and extra fees. This prepaid card facility is especially attractive to women, the young, the self employed and small establishment employees who sometimes do not meet the strict requirements of a conventional credit card facility.

Some efficient and Sharī'ah-compliant vehicles have been developed lately. Besides a large number of general Islamic funds, a number of multimanager funds have been established to ensure best practice and results without compromising on the Sharī'ah compliance matters. A number of Islamic financial market indices have been developed that are observing screening and purification criteria for investment in equity markets. Some examples are the Dow Jones Islamic Index, Al-Meezan Islamic Investment Index and the Malaysian Islamic

---

[6] For the evolution of Islamic banking and analysis of the movement, see Siddiqi, 2006a, pp. 1–48.

Index. A large number of corporate bodies and sovereigns have been using Sukuk in place of interest-based securities for more than five years. The vehicle of Sharī´ah-compliant Sukuk has been successfully introduced even in Japan and China.

International infrastructure institutions like the Islamic Development Bank, Islamic Financial Services Board (IFSB), International Islamic Financial Market (IIFM), General Council for Islamic Banks and Financial Institutions (GCIBAFI) and the International Arbitration and Reconciliation Centre for Islamic Financial Institutions (ARCIFI), Sharī´ah support institutions like the AAOIFI and Sharī´ah councils of various groups, as well as other commercial support institutions such as the International Islamic Rating Agency (IIRA) and the Liquidity Management Centre (LMC) are playing a crucial role in promotion and standardization of financial operations of IFIs. Bahrain is the main centre for Islamic finance in the Middle East region, playing a vital role in fostering Islamic banking operations and regulation. The ARCIFI is working in Dubai as a support institution to resolve disputes that may occur between industry participants and their counterparties.

From this perspective, the discussion on issues, potential, challenges and the way forward for Islamic finance must take into account the factors that provide impetus and the driving force needed for the fast promotion of the emerging Islamic finance industry. These factors include:

1. An increasing demand for Riba-free investment instruments for religious reasons, which has been a catalyst for the emergence of financial institutions working on Sharī´ah-compliant bases. Riba has been prohibited in the severest terms and a conscientious Muslim cannot harbour any idea about involvement in interest-based transactions. Islamic banking has thus enabled such people to fulfil their aspirations for doing business or investing their money without pricking their consciences.
2. The resurgence of Muslim cultural values, resulting in the desire to conduct financial business in accordance with the Sharī´ah principles.
3. The active involvement of the Sharī´ah scholars and experts in Islamic jurisprudence in coordination with bankers and the practitioners, which has been instrumental in improving the availability of innovative products and increasing awareness about the concepts and philosophy of Islamic banking.
4. The development of Sharī´ah-compliant products and instruments of investment, which has facilitated gainful deployment of excess liquidity that IFIs had in the early years of their establishment and broadened the base of the Islamic capital market.
5. The standardization of modes and products on a Sharī´ah basis and accounting and auditing procedures, particularly the AAOIFI's Sharī´ah Standards, which have played a crucial role in enhancing credibility, and hence demand, for Islamic banks' products. Risk management, capital adequacy and corporate governance standards introduced/being developed by the IFSB have also played a significant role in providing recognition for Islamic finance.
6. The growth of surplus money in the Gulf region due to increasing petroleum prices and the growth of economies in Muslim countries.
7. Flexibility in the regulatory framework in a number of regions, and deregulation and privatization of financial institutions, which has also facilitated the growth of banking and non-banking financial institutions in Islamic as well as Muslim minority countries. For example, in the USA, more than two dozen Islamic investment institutions are providing needed facilities to communities who avoid Riba. This began when the Glass–Steagall Act of 1933 was repealed in 1999. Flexibility provided by the FSA in the UK

in respect of the treatment of IFIs' deposits, stamp duty on mortgages (which needs only be paid once in a retail transaction) and accommodating Islamic banking practices has given a big impetus to the Islamic finance industry in the UK and ultimately in the whole of Europe.

8. The conversion of a few financially sound institutions in the Middle East to Islamic modes of business in recent years on account of increasing demand, which has also provided a self-enforcing impetus to the movement of Islamic finance.

9. The fact that, as investors are gaining awareness, high net worth individuals are shifting their investments to Sharī´ah-compliant institutions. This is leading to the development of Islamic finance markets and the availability of a wider range of services.

10. The real-asset-based and ethical nature of Islamic financial products based on the avoidance of gambling and interest, which has increased demand for such investments and widened the IFIs' customer base.

In the light of the above, the way forward for the Islamic banking industry is to take advantage of all the above factors and explore other such factors in order to provide even more powerful impetus for its sustainable development, enabling it to contribute to the welfare of human beings on a wider scale. In the following paragraphs we shall discuss the potential of Islamic finance and issues and challenges that Islamic banking and finance face in optimally realizing their potential and developing on a sustainable basis.

### 18.3.1  Promising Potential

The amazing development of Islamic finance in the last decade and analysis of the factors that served as driving forces for the fast growth is indicative of the huge potential for the industry in the future, because the factors will hopefully continue to provide impetus. An important observation to be made in this regard is that while firm foundations of the system have been laid down, the focus should now be on realization of the basic objectives of the theory of Islamic finance. In other words, potential should be related to the expectations of the pioneers of the concept of Islamic finance and the apprehensions of a large number of contemporary scholars, who are minutely watching the procedures, direction and trends of its growth in terms of the impact of the system in benefiting societies and removing the anomalies created by the conventional system.

Having said that, the Islamic banking and finance industry has a large potential ahead in retail, corporate and investment banking and fund management. The characteristic of Islamic finance that all transactions must be based on fixed assets, services or instruments representing such assets or services, makes investment banking, fund management, and Sukuk issues, along with retail and corporate banking, lucrative for the financial institutions. To realize this potential, IFIs require structural adjustments enabling them to deal with real sector business, implementation of trading, leasing and real-estate-related contracts using both participatory and nonparticipatory Islamic modes of financing. Structural adjustments are necessary not only to consolidate the success achieved so far, but also to realize the huge potential in the areas of fund management and securitization, provide Halal and relatively better return flow to investors and thus contribute to economic growth and prosperity.

## Potential in Fund Management

IFIs may engage in fund and portfolio management through asset management companies regulated by the central banks or the SEC, as the case may be in various jurisdictions. Broadly, the following may be the categories of funds:

- funds yielding return with minimum possible variation: these funds can be based on short-term Murabaha and leasing operations of banks in both local as well as foreign currencies and hence can be made to offer minimal risk to the investors in such funds. Such low-risk funds, which would be earmarked for purchase of goods and their resale on mark-up and short- to medium-term leasing operations giving fixed earnings to the banks, would be best suited for risk-averse savers who cannot afford possible losses in PLS-based investments.
- funds yielding high returns based on Musharakah or long-term leasing operations for those who are willing to take some risk for higher returns.

Banks may offer a type of equity exposure through restricted/specific investment accounts, where they may identify possible investment opportunities from existing or new business clients and invite existing account holders to subscribe. Instead of sharing in the banks' profit, the investors would share the profits of the project in which the funds were invested. Banks can also offer open-ended multiple equity funds to be invested in stocks.

Banks may introduce domestic currency trade funds for those who want to invest their savings with minimal risk. The amount thus mobilized can be invested for financing SMEs and domestic and international trade. The experiences of Grameen Bank of Bangladesh and the Bangladesh Islamic Bank reveal that banks may invest such funds mainly for small- and medium-level business and trading activities wherein the default level/ratio is expected to be the lowest. Keeping in mind the relatively larger mobility of capital across the nations, banks may also set up international/foreign currency trade funds, which may finance imports/exports of clients, firms and industries.

## Potential Relating to Sukuk

Sukuk, a by-product of the fast-growing Islamic finance industry, have confirmed their viability in mobilization of resources and their effective use for the benefit of both investors and fund users. Their growth is attributable to a number of factors, including their potential for liquidity and fund management. They could also be used as a tool for monetary policy and open market operations and for liquidity management.

Sukuk create a framework for participation of a large number of people in financing projects in the public and private sectors, including those of infrastructure such as roads, bridges, ports, airports, etc., on the basis of various modes. A variety of target-specific Sukuk can be issued, keeping in mind the relevant Sharī'ah rules. This requires appropriate enabling laws to protect the interests of investors and issuers, appropriate accounting standards, study of the targeted market, monitoring of standardized contracts, appropriate flow of financial data to investors and the provision of a standard quality service to the customers at large.

The international institutions set up during the last decade to provide global acceptance for the Islamic finance industry, namely the Bahrain-based LMC, IIFM and IIRA, have to do a lot to make the vehicles of Sukuk, fund management and ultimately Islamic capital markets increasingly active and efficient. They have to lead the industry players to exploit the potential of Shirkah-based Sukuk, because further reliance on Ijarah Sukuk alone, as witnessed over the last five years, may not be sufficient to realize the securitization potential of Islamic finance as a whole.[7]

*Potential in Specific Sectors*

Asset-based modes of Islamic finance are more suitable for enhancing business and for capital formation in priority sectors of small business, cottage industry and agriculture. If Islamic banks and NBFIs adopt structures and procedures to suit such sectors, it could be highly profitable for them, and beneficial for business and industrial communities and the related economies. This is because the financing of small-and medium-sized enterprises and micro finance have proved to be effective approaches for broad-based economic growth and alleviating poverty in the developing and emerging economies. Islamic micro finance institutions (IMFIs) would have fewer default, moral hazard and asymmetric information problems. In this respect, Habib Ahmed, an economist at the IDB, has undertaken a useful study for exploring problems and prospects of IMFIs, which readers may like to see for details.[8]

Enhancing the role of the financial sector in micro-level businesses could mitigate the serious problems of unemployment and the low level of exports in developing countries. If suitably planned, financing of this sector could boost the development process. The value addition generated in these industries would favourably affect the income distribution. The post investment role of the financier, as required in Islamic modes of financing, could go a long way towards the development of SMEs and the economy if a full-fledged structure of financial help is provided through industry-specific and generalist models of investment. IMFIs can also benefit from various income sources like those of Zakat and Waqf institutions and use the resources for direct financing of needy small business enterprises, without the involvement of any middleman, thus benefiting themselves and the clients.

For clients of high net worth and the big investors, banks may offer individual investment portfolios and investment funds in Shirkah-based and debt-creating modes, depending upon the risk profile of the fund owners. In such funds, banks may serve as a Mudarib or as an agent. As Mudarib, banks would get a share in the profit on a predetermined ratio, while as agent, they would get a fee and the rest of the profits/losses would go to the fund owners.

### 18.3.2  Issues in Islamic Finance

Commensurate with the prospects of growth in the Islamic finance industry are some of the issues and challenges. Some major issues are discussed below.

*Sharī'ah Interpretation: An Issue?*

A large number of experts and policymakers consider that different Sharī'ah interpretation of some modes and concepts is a major issue hindering the development of Islamic finance. Is it really an issue or merely a buzz word? This, in itself, is a question. It seems that it is not as big an issue as some people consider; it is no longer a real problem. No doubt, in

---

[7] Adam, 2005, pp. 371–400.
[8] Ahmed, 2002, pp. 27–64.

the wake of emerging issues in the fast-moving world of finance, some aspects will remain to be decided in the light of the Sharīʿah principles, and the same may be resolved as and when confronted, but the major Sharīʿah-related issues that the Islamic finance movement faced in the early years of its foundation have been resolved or cleared by dint of ample work by the jurists.

The Islamic Fiqh Council of the OIC, the AAOIFI and the Sharīʿah scholars in general have discussed at length almost all major areas and provided a number of alternatives to most of the conventional products, except derivatives based on interest or short-selling and speculative transactions in the Forex markets. Now the practitioners have to proceed on the basis of the achieved consensus. Product innovation from the Sharīʿah perspective does not mean that alternatives must be provided for each and every instrument or product used by conventional institutions. This is not possible; a discipline based on ethics and just hypotheses cannot afford to follow any unethical system step by step. Islamic finance will have to observe certain restraints so that it does not become exploitative and unjust, as is the case with its counterpart, interest-based system.

There are some unresolved issues as well, but these are not purely of Sharīʿah inter-pretation; the practical difficulties and the ground realities have given rise to these issues. Therefore, such problems and issues can be resolved once and for all by a body of Sharīʿah scholars like the OIC Islamic Fiqh Council or that of the AAOIFI. And if this is not possible, the Sharīʿah boards/Sharīʿah advisors of the respective banks may decide cases on merit by resorting to Ijtihad, subject to the widely accepted principles of the Sharīʿah.

Examples of such unresolved issues are the award of liquidated damages to the banks in cases of default on their receivables. In principle, the penalty paid by the defaulting client goes to the charity fund; if the default persists for longer periods, it will be harmful to the system, besides being unjust to the bank and the depositors. An accepted solution in this regard is that banks may claim their loss through a court or any independent arbitration; but on what firm basis the courts would be deciding is another related issue. Conventional opportunity cost *per se* should not be the basis for such award. Some Sharīʿah boards allow the banks to charge defaulters a rate based on the income that they have earned from the similar portfolio in the related period. But the deciding factor should be the financial position and the behaviour of the client and the expenses and time involved in litigation, on the basis of which the court may allow some or the whole of the penalty to go to the bank.

Another practice-related issue could be that of the liability of the banks' shareholders towards investment account holders of Islamic banks. This is a complicated issue because it also involves conflict of interests; its solution lies in a firm regulatory framework with special emphasis on safeguarding the interests of the depositors. Losses to banks could be due to overexposure, lack of diversification, imprudent banking practices and/or actual business losses. The Sharīʿah boards of the banks may decide the cases on merit, keeping in mind all such factors.

As regards the big issues of Sharīʿah interpretation, it is encouraging to observe that, lately, the practitioners in the Far East have started using genuine alternatives to interest (like Ijarah) for issuance of Sukuk, and it could be anticipated that in future, they will also change the basis of products based on the sale of debt and buy-back. Going forward, the focus of policymakers and product developers should be on development of the products, instruments and the Islamic finance industry by using the flexibilities already available and not wasting time and money on such areas that could lead only to the loss of integrity of the emerging discipline of finance. They should stick to the standards issued by the AAOIFI that are based on the deep conceptual research by Sharī'ah scholars under the aegis of the Fiqh Academy of the OIC. This is the only way to avoid inconsistencies in interpretation of Sharī'ah law by different scholars.

## Integrity and Credibility

The integrity of IFIs has unfortunately become an issue; a large number of people, intentionally or inadvertently, express doubts, not only about the credibility of the system but also about the intention and integrity of the scholars and the practitioners involved in the process of evolution. This has to be tackled with joint efforts by the Islamic banks, the central banks/regulators and the Sharī'ah scholars if rapid growth of the emerging discipline of finance is the objective. Many academicians, policymakers, regulators, religious leaders and even those who are working with Islamic banks are not confident about the Sharī'ah position of Islamic banks' products. The integrity of Islamic financial institutions depends on:

1. The status of Sharī'ah compliance of their products.
2. The impact of the products on the clients and the society or economy.
3. Professional competence and care for the interests of the stakeholders.
4. Behaviour towards and observance of Sharī'ah norms by IFIs' incumbents.

As regards the first factor, Sharī'ah scholars may play a crucial role in enhancing the credibility of IFIs. People with Sharī'ah considerations normally approach the Sharī'ah scholars to get advice for investment in Sharī'ah-compliant avenues. But the problem is that many religious leaders do not fully understand the operations of IFIs. Hence, they give edicts prohibiting people to invest in any institution called a "bank". To them, a bank cannot work on Islamic principles and any amount received or paid over and above the amounts deposited or taken from the banks is Riba, irrespective of the nature of banks' operations. It is pertinent, therefore, that an association of IFIs in different countries or the central banks should launch programmes for awareness and education of such religious leaders, not only about the functions of banking and other intermediary institutions but also about the principles and philosophy underlying Islamic banking operations. At the very least, the Sharī'ah Standards developed by the AAOIFI must be introduced to them in detail. This would enhance their confidence and enable them to create a positive impression of Islamic banking among the common people.

Factor 2 above is very important in enhancing the credibility of Islamic banking. People generally question the impact of present Islamic banking practices vis-à-vis the impact of the conventional banks' operations. Normally, Islamic bankers fail to defend themselves on this point because they do not have in mind such ideas; like conventional bankers, they are simply told how to earn profit. They must be given sound and intensive training about the philosophy and functioning of IFIs and the differences between the services of Islamic banks and those of their counterparts, and about how and to what extent Islamic banking practices could be useful for society. However, a pertinent point in this regard is that policymakers, product developers and those who are at the helm of affairs must bear in mind socio-economic considerations along with the profit consideration.

Further, Islamic bankers and the public in general must be apprised of the role various modes of financing can play in socio-economic development. The stakeholders should also have knowledge of the limitations and challenges facing Islamic banking, due to which it might not be able to achieve the results proclaimed in Islamic finance theory, at least in the short or medium terms.

The stakeholders must have the knowledge that all Islamic modes have potential for development. Shirkah-based (PLS) modes that provide the much-needed risk-related funds for development of trade, business and industry can be used for short-, medium- and long-term project financing, import financing, preshipment export financing, working capital financing and financing of most single transactions. The institution of Mudarabah serves as a basis of business to be conducted by combining funds and the expertise of different groups of people. Mudarabah Sukuk can be issued to mobilize funds and strengthen trading and industrial activities. SPVs can manage such assets and conduct business for their benefit and that of the Sukuk holders. This could generate higher rates of return for the investors relative to the return realizable on any interest-based investment, as discussed in Chapter 12. In the case of big projects, IFIs may form consortia to issue certificates to the public for subscription. Similarly, they can carry out work on infrastructure and socio-economic projects in coordination and partnership with engineering firms.

The non-PLS techniques not only complement the PLS modes but also provide flexibility of choice to meet the needs of different sectors and economic agents in society. Murabaha, with less risk, has several advantages vis-à-vis other techniques and can be helpful in meeting the needs of risk-averse investors, employment generation and alleviation of poverty. Leasing is very much conducive to the formation of fixed assets and medium- and long-term investments. Salam has a large potential in financing productive activities in crucial sectors, particularly agriculture, agro-based industries and the rural economy as a whole. To realize this potential, IFIs could organize a forward commodity trade market on the basis of Salam. This would provide not only a nonspeculative forward market for resource mobilization and investment, but would also be a powerful vehicle for rural development.

On the basis of the above, it can be said that supply of and demand for investment capital would continue in an interest-free scenario with the additional benefit of a larger supply of risk-related capital, more efficient allocation of resources and an active role of banks and financial institutions, as required in the asset-based Islamic discipline of finance. This could be helpful in achieving the objective of development with distributive justice by increasing the supply of risk capital in the economy, facilitating capital formation and growth of fixed assets and real sector business activities.

But a point of concern in this regard is that Islamic banks are obliged to work with a number of limitations and constraints, most important among which is competition with the mainstream banks. They have to use the same benchmarks and apply charges comparable with the main conventional market. As such, it may take more effort and relatively a much longer time to achieve visible socio-economic results.

As regards points 3 and 4 above, the moral dimension is the main ingredient of Islamic banking and finance. IFIs may implement a code of conduct reflecting Islamic values and principles, strictly ensuring that it is demonstrated in the management procedures, operations and overall behaviour of their incumbents (see the AAOIFI's *Code of Ethics*). This is particularly relevant in Muslim majority areas, where Islamic culture has a deep bearing on the approaches and ideas of the masses. Islamic banking is one aspect of an Islamic way of life and if an Islamic banker is involved in any unethical or prohibited practices, it could undermine the integrity and credibility of the system. Therefore, ensuring good governance by IFIs on the basis of Islamic behavioural principles and moral and business ethics is a big challenge for the integrity and long-term health of IFIs.

The ultimate objective in this regard should be to provide the best services at competitive rates and to strike a balance between the interests of the shareholders and those of the depositors. It has been observed that to compete with conventional financial institutions, some IFIs have been giving fixed rates of return, either by paying from the shareholders' part or by allocating more to the shareholders in the case of higher profits. Although profit equalization reserves can be maintained with sufficient disclosure and transparency, apportioning profits just to compete in the market and without taking the partners into confidence is against the spirit of the Sharī'ah. An effective enforcement of the code of conduct would enhance the integrity of the system.

### Structure of Financial Institutions

What the structure of Islamic banks should be is another issue. Should they become traders or business entities? In most countries, they have to operate analogously to the conventional banks, within the national banking systems in general and in respect of international financial and business transactions in particular. Although the philosophy, process and the procedures of Islamic banks differ, they do serve as financial intermediaries and as a link in the chain of the banking system. Like conventional banks, they mobilize savings and undertake the financing of economic and social development activities for the benefit of the economies where they operate. While fulfilling this objective, which is indisputably accepted by all Islamic scholars, they have to undertake real sector business instead of dealing in money on the basis of interest. This implies that Islamic banks' procedures should be different from those of the conventional banks, in the sense that the latter deal in money while Islamic banks have to deal in goods. Islamic banks' modus operandi is also different from that of the business community in general, because they do not normally hold inventories of the goods for selling or leasing. They rather purchase the goods/assets on requisition of their clients for letting or onward sale, and there is no Sharī'ah objection in this regard. Accordingly, the Murabaha Standard issued by the AAOIFI has been captioned the Standard for Murabaha to Purchase Orderer.

Concern has been shown by a number of writers that IFIs concentrate on short-term commercial financing, like the conventional banks. An active developmental role is expected of them that actually provides the rationale for their existence. The concern is genuine, but to combat it would require some structural changes and amendments in legal and regulatory frameworks, which are crucial for ensuring Sharī'ah compliance and for better performance of the IFIs.

Accordingly, banking business should not be taken as a sacred cow to preclude any change in its tools, processes or operations. Survival in the world of finance, which is undergoing rapid transformation, is possible only through adjustments and transformation, needed from time to time due to changing ground realities. In the global competitive environment, IFIs must diversify their operations to offer broader portfolio services, both to savers/investors and fund users. By providing only short-term commercial loans, they cannot compete with giant conventional banks. They should increasingly provide project and infrastructure financing through Shirkah- and Ijarah-based modes. They may also provide corporate advisory services like issuance of Sharī'ah-compliant Sukuk/certificates and balance sheet and corporate restructuring, etc. through syndication arrangements. IFIs also have to undertake all sorts of business – from retail banking to fund management and corporate services – by effecting some structural changes. This would require close coordination between central banks and SECs in respective countries, enabling the IFIs to adopt suitable models and structures for business, keeping in mind the demands of the market and the Sharī'ah principles.

IFIs might engage in portfolio management through a number of asset management, leasing and trading companies. Subsidiaries can be created for specific sectors/operations, which would enter into genuine trade and leasing transactions.

### Regulatory and Tax Issues

Another pertinent issue is the regulatory framework for Islamic financial institutions. Like the conventional institutions, IFIs, too, require regulation for the following reasons:

1. Making the needed information available to the investors.
2. Protecting the interests of savers.
3. Ensuring Sharī'ah compliance and soundness of the financial system.
4. Making the legal framework conducive to the smooth functioning of the system in which "cost of funds" cannot be recovered in the case of default.
5. Making the monetary policy and management effective.

The policy, nature and the level of regulation and supervision and the legal frameworks have important bearing on the size, growth, Sharī'ah compliance and integrity of the Sharī'ah-based finance discipline. As the nature of their operations is different, IFIs have to face different problems in respect of legal, regulatory and taxation rules. In order to foster stability in Islamic banking, there is a need to develop uniform regulatory and transparency standards that are tailored to the specific characteristics of Islamic financial products and institutions. This task, whilst taking into consideration the financial environment in each country, would also need adaptation of the international standards, core principles and good practices to the specific needs of Islamic finance. Islamic banks have to purchase assets for onward sale or lease to their clients. As such, the levy of taxation and fees on their purchases leads to an uneven playing field for them compared with their conventional counterparts. To avoid such costs, Islamic banks, except for a few countries with a tax-free environment, resort to practices creating doubts with respect to Sharī'ah compliance when seen in standards set by the AAOIFI and the Islamic Fiqh Council of the OIC.

The regulators in countries where both systems operate side by side should recognize the need to set up flexible regulatory and tax frameworks that could facilitate banking operations in line with the Sharī'ah principles. Flexibilities granted by the FSA in Britain are a welcome move; it is hoped that the process of adaptation of laws will continue in order to make London an international hub for the Islamic finance industry in coming years.[9] Other regulators are also required to amend rules and regulations to facilitate Islamic banking transactions with proper risk management and Sharī'ah compliance. For a comprehensive framework, the following steps would be needed:

1. Saving the IFIs and their customers from dual taxation, particularly in respect of mortgage financing and Murabaha and leasing operations.
2. Facilitating the IFIs to fulfil all Sharī'ah-related requirements on the deposits and assets sides.
3. Providing an effective Sharī'ah compliance framework.
4. Ensuring that banks adopt justifiable procedures for distribution of profits between the shareholders and the depositors, and then among various categories of depositors. This is more relevant in the Islamic financial system than in the conventional system.

---

[9] For changes made or required to be made in the UK taxation laws, see the article by Mohammed Amin (Amin, 2006).

5. Increasing the amount of information available to the investors to reduce the adverse selection and moral hazard problems in financial markets.
6. Enforcing prudential rules and regulations, keeping in mind proper risk management and the needs and nature of the new system.
7. Ensuring that the risks relating to current accounts, which are a liability for the IFIs, are borne by the banks themselves and not transmitted to investment accounts, particularly when the bank is in distress.
8. Vigorous training of concerned central bank staff, enabling them to effectively supervise and guide the IFIs.
9. Establishment of a research and training centre for banking regulations, supervision and education.
10. Rating institutions and feasibility study institutions with specially trained incumbents are the infrastructure of the new system that should be provided.

Protecting the rights of the depositors is said to be the foremost important objective of regulators all over the world, as per their vision and mission statements. However, practically, the situation is the reverse. Working in the "capitalist" structure, the regulators/central banks in almost all economies where the financial sector has been "liberalized" do not intervene in the rate structures of financial services, while actually they need more intensive supervision in order to protect the depositors and entrepreneurs from possible exploitation by financial institutions working with the motto of "self-interest" and maximization of their net profits. The free market policy has become a source of injustice and exploitation of the clients both of conventional and Islamic banks. As banks' income increases, they should pass on a fair part of their income to the depositors. Practically, however, only the spread has been increasing. There is a need for proper vigilance by the regulators, particularly for IFIs, because their depositors have to bear additional risks.

Keeping in mind the possibilities of business failure, some customers of IFIs may not be able to pay their liabilities in time. Sharī´ah scholars have allowed the receipt of additional amounts for charity in order to discipline customers. But the IFIs must differentiate between the wilful defaulters and those who are really in trouble. For this purpose, the regulators may introduce some parameters to ensure that while solvent/wilful defaulters are charged heavily to create a deterrent for others, those who are in genuine difficulties and unable to pay their liabilities are given respite without any charge or fine. A well-thought-out system for restructuring the liabilities of such insolvent customers and for helping them in revival of their business has to be an important part of the regulatory set-up for Islamic finance.

For an effective Sharī´ah compliance mechanism, regulators may enlist Sharī´ah advisors with the appropriate entry qualifications and skill sets. If necessary, central banks may like to help train Sharī´ah scholars to improve their understanding of finance and skills for enhancing their practice-oriented knowledge.

Regulations are also needed for transparent and proper disposal of charity amounts from the Islamic banks, keeping in mind the principles of charity in the Sharī´ah. In addition to general heads to dispense charity funds, rules can be provided on the basis of nonremunerative (e.g. current accounts) deposits and the level of net earnings of the IFIs, in terms of which some funds might be used for grants or return-free loans to the poor and the needy, like students belonging to low-income groups, widows, the sick and other destitute members of society. For this purpose, IFIs can also be required to contribute from the shareholders' income. Regulators may ensure that Islamic banks do not spend lavishly on unnecessary marketing; instead, they should use the community and social development avenues for marketing their products.

## Shari'ah Compliance Framework

The need for Shari'ah compliance of IFIs' operations is accepted by all, but what the framework should be in different situations is an issue that needs to be resolved. One option is to have Shari'ah boards in all Islamic financial institutions that could guide in product development and application and also enforce internal Shari'ah controls at a micro-level. The problem with this option is that having a Shari'ah board in all individual IFIs would not be feasible due to the shortage of competent Shari'ah scholars, and also the sheer cost. A small variation in this option could be to have one Shari'ah advisor, and not a board, in every IFI. Along with this, the central bank or an association of IFIs may facilitate the formation of a forum of Shari'ah advisors for all IFIs in a country to periodically meet for discussion and resolution of Shari'ah-related issues. This could serve the dual purpose of economizing on costs and providing an opportunity for wider level discussion on Shari'ah-related issues. It may also lead to standardization of edicts on the transactions of IFIs.

The other option is that the central banks or monetary authorities may facilitate the establishment of independent Shari'ah boards/committees in the private sector, with members having Shari'ah as well as banking knowledge, that could provide advisory and consultancy services in respect of all aspects relating to development and implementation of products and periodical Shari'ah-related inspection of IFIs. For the integrity and competence of such private sector boards, central bank accreditation based upon fit and proper and good governance criteria would be necessary. In this structure, Shari'ah boards or Shari'ah scholars would not be necessary in the central bank or the individual IFIs. But the dark side of this option is that effective monitoring of the operations and guidance and advice on Shari'ah matters needed from time to time by the bankers would not be possible.

Another option is that there should be a central Shari'ah board in a country or jurisdiction to advise the regulators on Shari'ah issues and facilitate the IFIs in ensuring Shari'ah compliance in coordination with Shari'ah advisors/boards of the individual banks. This option could be instrumental in bringing harmony in the practices of IFIs working in a jurisdiction. This seems to be the best option and could be made more useful if a forum of Shari'ah advisors, as proposed above, was also added to the scheme.

A related issue is the constitution of the Shari'ah board: should all members be Shari'ah scholars or it should comprise Shari'ah scholars as well as other experts from other disciplines like banking, accountancy, law, economics and others? Most Shari'ah boards comprise only Shari'ah scholars with understanding of banking and finance. Experts from other disciplines are co-opted for technical help as and when required. Edicts are issued mostly on the basis of unanimous decisions by the members of the boards. Sometimes, consensus is attained on the basis of majority and this happens mostly in cases where Shari'ah endorsement is outsourced. It is interesting to observe that Shari'ah endorsement of most of the Sukuk issues by an international Islamic financial institution in the recent past has been on the majority principle. The majority principle could be adopted in some cases if sufficient grounds on the basis of accepted Shari'ah principles are available. But open and frequent resort to this principle in Shari'ah matters may harm the integrity of the board and/or the system in the long run. One possible solution to avoid differences is that the AAOIFI Standards should be made the basis of the Shari'ah boards' decisions/edicts and applied meticulously.

Whichever option is taken, ensuring Sharī´ah compliance requires much more input by the banks themselves and the regulators. This refers to the need for full-fledged Sharī´ah departments in all IFIs, effective internal Sharī´ah controls and Sharī´ah inspection of Islamic banks' operations. The banks operating "Islamic windows" may be required to establish stand-alone Islamic banking branches in place of "windows" to conduct business under the guidance of Sharī´ah monitoring.

Another important aspect is that Sharī´ah boards/advisors should supervise, not only advise, the activities of Islamic banks in order to ensure Sharī´ah compliance in all respects. To this end, they should finalize the model agreements and application procedures for the modes of financing and try to ensure that banks follow them in all their transactions, in letter and spirit. A passive role, whereby they are limited to approving the products or procedures and the applications are left totally to the banks, opens the door to interest in the garb of asset-based transactions. The modus operandi adopted in many cases lacks Sharī´ah inspiration and a slight change or negligence in any of the formalities may render the transactions non-Sharī´ah-compliant. Therefore, the experts deem it necessary that Sharī´ah boards should thoroughly inspect, at least once a year, the Islamic banks' activities.

For Sharī´ah-related inspection of operations of the IFIs, the following three options have been suggested, with the scale of preference in ascending order:[10]

1. Sharī´ah-related inspection by central banks themselves.
2. Inspection by specially created Sharī´ah audit firms working in the private sector.
3. Inspection by external CA and audit firms.

But this order of preference might be different in different jurisdictions. In countries where the central bank's inspection team is competent, professionally trained and well-equipped, the first option might be the best. All depends on the expertise and integrity of the auditors and the audit firms. The regulators may decide on merit, with the ultimate objective of effectively checking that the IFIs do not undertake non-Sharī´ah-compliant practices.

---

**Box 18.1:**   Sharī´ah Compliance Framework Introduced by the State Bank of Pakistan

- A Sharī´ah board comprising two Sharī´ah scholars and three experts in the areas of banking, accounting and the legal framework was established in the central bank in December, 2003. The board advises the central bank on modes, procedures, laws and regulation for Islamic banking to ensure Islamic banks' functioning in line with the Sharī´ah principles.
- A Sharī´ah board or at least a Sharī´ah advisor has to be appointed by each Islamic banking institution (IBI) as per fit and proper criteria approved by SBP's Sharī´ah board.
- Each IBI has to conduct internal Sharī´ah audit at least once in a year.

---

[10] Chapra and Khan, 2000.

---

**Box 18.1:** (Continued)

- The State Bank of Pakistan has provided for Sharī´ah compliance audit by its inspection staff for IBIs to ensure Sharī´ah compliance and enhance the credibility of the Islamic banking system. A manual for Sharī´ah audit has been prepared in consultation with a consultancy firm of repute. For capacity building, the first Sharī´ah audit of an Islamic bank was outsourced to the same firm to develop Sharī´ah audit skills and provide hands-on training to the State Bank's inspection staff. The inspection manual has been finalized, keeping in mind the experience gained and observations made by the auditors during that inspection. Periodical Sharī´ah-compliance inspection of IBIs has to be conducted by auditors of the State Bank on the basis of that manual.

---

One problem related to Sharī´ah audit is how to resolve any possible difference of opinion between the Sharī´ah department of a bank and the Sharī´ah auditors. The best solution to this problem is that in each jurisdiction a Sharī´ah manual should be prepared with joint efforts of the auditors/regulators, different Sharī´ah boards and the practitioners and the audit should then be conducted on the basis of that manual.

The next question would be how to penalize IFIs if any lapses are proved in the Sharī´ah audit. On the assets side, the solution lies in allocating the revenue from non-Sharī´ah-compliant transactions to the Charity Account. But this loss should belong to the shareholders and not the depositors, because they furnish deposits for Sharī´ah-compliant business and if the bank fails to accomplish this, it must be penalized; the depositors should not be penalized for follies of the bank's management. For irregularities on the deposits side, the regulators will have to enforce a set of penalties in consultation with the auditors and the Sharī´ah scholars.

### 18.3.3   The Challenges

An inspiring performance so far and the huge potential ahead, combined with the resolution of issues which could boost the growth momentum of the Islamic finance industry, gives rise to a number of challenges. The future relies on the policymakers and the practitioners and how they face the challenges. The major challenges are briefly discussed below.

*Education and Awareness Creation*

The pace of growth in the future certainly depends on enhancing the clientele of the emerging industry, which is possible only through education of the people, removing the myths and creating awareness about the new system. The economists, policymakers and the general public, both in Muslim majority and Muslim minority countries, have a number of queries about Islamic finance, like: How does it work? Can it survive on a sustainable basis in competition with a centuries old financial system? Are the products offered by it really Islamic? Could it make any difference in removing the hardships of mankind? And so on and so forth. Bankers have to respond to all these queries with confidence. Similarly, the savers/investors who have so far avoided the banking channel *per se* due to the involvement of Riba will approach Islamic banks only when they are assured that their funds will be invested in Sharī´ah-compliant activities.

There is a lot of criticism that the concept of Islamic banking and finance has changed visibly from the concept envisaged in the 1970s. People need to be told in this regard that the practice is evolving from the philosophy, which has not changed – the subject matter for the banks has to be goods and services, not money *per se* and all financial transactions have to be linked to real sector transactions based on well-defined business rules. It depends on the nature of the transaction. If a transaction is one of trade or Ijarah, the price or rental has to be fixed. Further, despite the apparent divergence, Sharī´ah compliance is ensured in respect of all modes and Islamic finance is passing through the initial process of evolution.

Hence, creating understanding of the Sharī´ah principles and enhancing knowledge about Islamic modes of business and investment, both among Muslims and non-Muslims, is the greatest challenge. Efforts need to be made without further delay to create demand and appeal on the basis of principles and philosophy of the new discipline of finance. Failure in creating requisite awareness could inevitably lead to serious disruptions in the market, causing systemic risk for the nascent industry. Through a comprehensive campaign, people must be made to understand that Islamic banking does not mean free loaning to business and industry, and that savers can justifiably take a return on the basis of the nature of the transactions and results of the business activity undertaken with the help of their funds. Creating awareness about these aspects is more necessary among the religious leaders at grass-roots level.

The clients also need to be apprised that Islamic banks use the funds with professional competence and a sense of responsibility only in permissible avenues and that prohibited and indecent activities are avoided.

### *Sharī´ah Compliance and the Integrity of the Islamic Finance Industry*

Sharī´ah compliance of business and transactions is of crucial importance for ensuring the integrity and credibility of the Islamic banking industry. Therefore, Islamic bankers will have to ensure that whatever they are offering is in conformity with the tenets of the Sharī´ah, and for this purpose they must keep in mind that all human beings are individually answerable to Allah (SWT). The last revealed verse of the Holy Qur'ān (2: 281), placed next to the verses of Surah al Baqarah on Riba, clearly describes this principle of accountability. But practically, many IFIs, particularly those who are operating windows without any effective internal Sharī´ah-related controls, are using products like Tawarruq, buy-back arrangements and other grey area instruments so bluntly that if not checked forthwith, they may betray the whole movement. This is why M. Nejatullah Siddiqi, one of the pioneers of Islamic finance, suggests in one of his recent papers:

> "This leads us to the need for a redefinition of the term 'Sharī´ah-compliant'. It should not be confined to analogical reasoning and matching new with old, approved contracts. Considerations of Maslaha and Maqasid al Sharī´ah should be an essential part of the comprehensive definition. Sharī´ah advisors educated in traditional Islamic sciences only can hardly do so, as it requires a grasp of economic analysis. . . . A strong involvement of trained economists and social scientists is necessary."[11]

---

[11] Siddiqi, 2006, p. 17; also see Parker, 1999.

For achieving the objective of Sharī'ah compliance, the active involvement of people having deep understanding of Sharī'ah matters, socio-economic issues and principles of finance is crucial. Credibility has to be established, both at national and international levels. For this purpose, the involvement of IFIs in real sector business is necessary, failing which they cannot escape severe criticism. Moreover, this will have no socio-economic impact, even if implemented across the whole world. Presently, the common man understands that Islamic banks do not actually carry out businesses like trading, leasing or construction activities and hence they end up doing only financial operations. This impression needs to be removed.

Sharī'ah compliance requires Sharī'ah inspiration and complete observance of the principles of Islamic finance. It also needs internal controls and Sharī'ah-related inspection for enhancing credibility and acceptability of the IFIs. It does not mean, however, that other professional requirements for successful business are of less importance. Phillip Moore, in *Islamic Finance: A Partnership for Growth* (1997), contends that a Sharī'ah board will typically ask four questions in relation to any given transaction. These will generally be:

1. Do the terms of the transaction comply with Sharī'ah law?
2. Is this the best investment for the client?
3. Does the investment produce value for the client and for the community or society in which the client is active?
4. As an asset manager, is this a transaction in which the banker as an individual would be prepared to invest his own money?

If the answer to any of these four questions is no, the proposed transaction would usually be rejected, although the committees only have the power to reject the transaction on the grounds that it does not comply with Sharī'ah law. This author agrees with Moore and reiterates that Sharī'ah compliance must be accompanied by the best solutions for the financial problems of the clients.

## Competitiveness and Parallel Functioning

The most dominant and common model of Islamic banking in practice today comprises a dual system, whereby interest-based and Islamic financial institutions are working side by side. While the growth of the Islamic financial system is a challenge to the conventional interest-based banks, the adoption of Islamic financial modes by the conventional banks is a challenge to the Islamic banks. This situation, on the one hand, points to increasing competition in future, and on the other hand, calls for the development of cooperation between the two types of institutions.

In the present scenario, wherein the share of IFIs in the national as well as global financial systems is low, functioning of the Islamic financial institutions in the competitive environment is really a challenge. They cannot give rates to the depositors significantly different from the conventional benchmark rates because of regulatory requirements and the forces of demand and supply in the competitive markets. While conventional banks can market their liability side products by offering fixed rates of return, Islamic banks cannot do so unless they compromise on the Sharī'ah principles. This makes it much more difficult for them to get deposits from the corporate sector where the main concern of the financial managers is the highest return without any risk. The same is true on the financing side, as competing with the conventional institutions while ensuring Sharī'ah compliance is very difficult for IFIs unless they change their strategy and structure. In order to meet this challenge, IFIs have to make efforts in coordination with the regulators, Sharī'ah scholars and the customers. Prospering in the competitive environment on a sustainable basis would require;

- conformity of products and transactions with the Sharī'ah principles;
- best practice strategy for screening Islamic investments along with taking care of credit, market and other operational risks;
- innovative products;
- better quality of service to the customers.

In a highly competitive environment, IFIs would require some structural adjustments enabling them to deal with real sector business, implementation of trading, leasing and real-estate related contracts using both profit/loss sharing (PLS) and "fixed-rate" Islamic modes of financing. For example, banking laws and regulations in many jurisdictions require that deposits be treated as capital guaranteed, while Sharī'ah requires that the same should be based on profit/loss sharing. This problem could be resolved if IFIs operate in the form of mutual funds. Such an approach would enable them to earn higher profits, as businesses in the real sector normally earn, and pass on a greater part of the profits so earned to the savers/investors.

### Developing Benchmarks

Islamic financial institutions require benchmarks for pricing of goods and services and for determining sharing ratios for distribution of profit among partners of joint ventures. Such benchmarks will be different in different jurisdictions and sectors/subsectors and will require deep study, keeping in mind the level of development, the supply and demand of goods and services and also the assets and liabilities of the customers. Such studies need to be undertaken at international as well as country levels. One such effort was made by Abbas Mirakhor and Nadeem ul Haque in 1998, focusing on developing some indices for calculating rates of return on national participation papers (NPP).[12]

For the time being, conventional benchmarks are being used by IFIs in almost all jurisdictions. Although permissible from a Sharī'ah point of view as a tool and basis for pricing of goods and their usufructs, a benchmark reflective of fictitious assets, as is the case in the conventional framework, will not be helpful in realizing the socio-economic objectives of Islamic banking and finance. This will require long-term and sustained efforts on the part of the economists, bankers, policymakers and the Sharī'ah scholars.

### Product Development – Financial Engineering

The need for innovative products for cash management and financing of various sectors, particularly the government or public sector, cannot be overemphasized. It requires mutual efforts by the economists, practitioners, Sharī'ah scholars and the regulators. The major challenge in product innovation and designing the investment products is ensuring Sharī'ah compliance in line with the mainstream theory developed so far. Any resort to Sharī'ah

---

[12] Mirakhor and ul Haque, 1998.

interpretation unacceptable to the majority of the scholars would damage the image of the emerging industry in the long run.

In the area of public finance, a lot of work needs to be done by the product developers in collaboration with the fiscal authorities in various jurisdictions. The potential of Sukuk and securitization can help a lot in meeting this challenge. In case of dire need, the Sharī´ah boards may like to offer well-defined and specified relaxations without compromising on the cardinal principles of the Sharī´ah. Any vague observations or edicts may lead to anarchy and loss of integrity for Islamic finance theory and themselves.

### Liquidity and Monetary Management

Monetary management in the framework of Islamic finance is the area where sufficient work has not been done so far. A related matter is the availability of instruments for liquidity management. As compared with conventional institutions, IFIs have to place a greater part of their deposits with the central banks, on which they get no return in lieu of the statutory liquidity reserves (SLR). This harms their competitiveness in terms of giving competitive returns to the depositors. While some instruments for liquidity management have been developed and introduced, the modus operandi of their use for OMOs and repo has to be evolved.

The establishment of inter-bank Islamic money markets in each jurisdiction with a significant number of IFIs is a key element for short-term liquidity management and for monetary management and ultimately for the promotion of Islamic finance. Any mismatch between clients' demand for funds and their supply is normally covered through inter-bank transactions, which can be conducted on the Mudarabah principle. Islamic banks can also invest their funds with conventional banks offering Islamic banking business, provided the latter invest them on a Sharī´ah-compliant basis ensuring segregation of Riba-free and Riba-based deposits and financing. The latter will also have to ensure that any Sharī´ah advisor/committee has certified such segregation.

The banks may also resort to securitization of their assets or fund management by issuing certificates of deposit or investment. The certificates of the funds may be traded in the secondary market. It is, however, necessary that the cash and receivables component in the pool of assets being securitized or the assets of the funds should be less than 50%. Since the certificates will belong to funds that are based on genuine asset-based transactions, they will have a genuine secondary market.

The central bank as the lender of last resort is the most strategic part of the conventional financial system. The following could be the options in this regard in the Islamic framework:

1. A Mudarabah-based facility in case of a liquidity crisis of defined extent faced by any IFI. This could be for two or three days with a profit-sharing ratio of, say, 50:50 on the basis of the daily product; it can be provided in the Mudarabah agreement that if the IFI is unable to pay back the amount on the due date, the profit-sharing ratio will be enhanced in favour of the central bank.
2. The establishment of a common pool with the central bank to which all IFIs may contribute at a specified percentage of their deposits and from which they will have the right to get interest-free accommodation up to (three) days in the case of a defined liquidity crunch.

*Supply of Well-versed Human Resources*

One of the major bottlenecks for the development of the Islamic financial industry at this stage is the scarcity of trained human resources. Although IFIs are also intermediaries, like conventional banks, the mindset of Islamic bankers has to be significantly different and requires special orientation. All incumbents of IFIs should not only be technically competent but also well aware of Islamic finance principles and committed to their cause. Only committed and competent personnel, embedded with Islamic ethical values, can be instrumental in marketing the products in Muslim and other communities and enhancing the acceptability of the new discipline. This challenge can be met by imparting quality training to all those who are related in one way or another to Islamic financial institutions about the philosophy, products and practices of Islamic finance.

The long-term growth of Islamic finance will require developing a framework for HR development, pushing up R & D activities and enhancing training and education facilities in collaboration with the leading academic and research institutions. It will require joint efforts by the Islamic financial institutions, Sharī´ah scholars, central banks/regulators, universities, business schools and the student community. The universities should sense the huge need for providing competent human resources to the Islamic finance industry. In this context, the focus has to be on the philosophy of Islamic finance as it has evolved today and the practical operations of Islamic financial institutions, without getting involved in any unnecessary controversies.

# 18.4   CONCLUSION

The prospects for Islamic banking and finance are bright but the task ahead is challenging. Its practice is not only sustainable but also profitable in taking the form of a genuine business. However, there is a need for change in the procedures and the tools of business and the mindset of the stakeholders, and also for coordinated work in order to develop innovative products while remaining within the Sharī´ah boundaries. This will require promoting collaboration at various levels, including global and local, public and private sectors, business/industry and academia, Sharī´ah scholars and practitioners. Support from governments and regulators is crucial. They may accommodate Islamic finance for reasons both of principles and practical importance.

Realization of the potential of Islamic finance will require structural adjustments enabling Islamic financial institutions to deal with real sector business, implementation of trading, leasing and real-estate related contracts using Islamic modes of financing. Fixity of rates is no problem at all; nonfixity of prices and rentals rather makes the transactions invalid as per the Sharī´ah rules. The mindset for conducting trading, leasing or other such businesses would enable IFIs to earn higher profits, as businesses in the real sector normally earn, and pass on a greater part of the profits so earned to the savers/investors. In addition to securitizing their asset portfolios, they may resort to fund management and invest in Shirkah-based variable income and trade and leasing-based quasi-fixed income operations to provide a Sharī´ah-compliant investment facility to various classes of investors according to their risk profiles and preferences.

Islamic banks' operations must have positive socio-economic implications through real sector development and just and equitable pricing policies, in addition to cost efficiency and profit adequacy. For this purpose, IFIs should look beyond the formal abolition of interest and practically involve themselves in real business activities. In the words of Zubair Hasan, an economist at the International Islamic University of Malaysia: "One must see Islamic banking as an on-going process in a social milieu characterized with mass poverty and gross inequalities in the wealth, income and opportunities".[13]

The regulators, authorities in governments and the practitioners in Islamic banking have to work together in order to take care of areas like education, training and public awareness about the Islamic financial system, effective enforcement of contracts, strengthening recovery systems and conducting internal and external Sharī´ah compliance audit of IFIs' operations.

Strengthening the regulatory set-up, facilitating IFIs to offer suitable products, designing prudential rules to reflect the specific risk characteristics of Islamic financial contracts and application of well-thought-out risk management and accounting standards will be instrumental in deepening and widening the financial sector. Regulators need to provide an enabling environment and ensure that proper procedures for good corporate governance, transparency and ensuring Sharī´ah compliance are in place.

The use of Islamic finance principles for public sector financing needs more attention, as it could be helpful in ensuring fiscal discipline and thus giving a just basis for monetary management.

---

[13] Hasan, 2005, pp. 229–248.

# Acronyms

| | |
|---|---|
| AAOIFI | Accounting and Auditing Organization for Islamic Financial Institutions |
| ABS | Asset-backed securities |
| ARCIFI | Arbitration and Reconciliation Centre for Islamic Financial Institutions |
| ARR | Anticipated rate of return |
| ATM | Automatic teller machine |
| BIC | Bank Islam Malaysia Card |
| BIS | Bank for International Settlements |
| BMA | Bahrain Monetary Agency |
| BNM | Bank Negara Malaysia |
| BOOT | Build own operate and transfer |
| BOT | Build operate and transfer |
| BTF | Balance transfer facility |
| CAMELS | Capital adequacy, Asset quality, Management capability, Earnings, Liquidity, Sensitivity to market risks (sometimes, another S is added at the end, which stands for Systems and operations controls) |
| CBs | Central banks |
| CDC | Central depository company |
| CDOs | Collateralized debt obligations |
| CIF | Cost, insurance and freight |
| CII | Council of Islamic Ideology (Pakistan) |
| CLOs | Collateralized loan obligations |
| CMA | Cash management accounts |
| CMC | Central bank Musharakah certificates (Sudan) |
| CODs | Certificates of deposit |
| COIs | Certificates of investment |
| COT | Carried over transactions |
| DFIs | Development finance institutions |
| DM | Diminishing Musharakah |
| DO | Delivery order |
| DPB | Daily product basis (deposit management) |
| EDL | External debt liability |

| | |
|---|---|
| EDR | European depository receipts |
| EFS | Export finance scheme |
| EIB | Emirates Islamic Bank (credit card) |
| FDR | Fixed deposit receipts |
| FFS | Future flow securitization |
| FOB | Free on board |
| FRS | Fixed return securities |
| FSC | Federal Shariat Court (Pakistan) |
| Gbpwh/Gbpwth | God be pleased with him and God be pleased with them – a salutation Muslims use with the names of the Companions of the holy Prophet of Islam |
| GCC | Gulf Cooperation Council |
| GCIBAFI | General Council for Islamic Banks and Financial Institutions |
| GDP | Gross domestic product |
| GDR | Global depository receipts |
| GICs | Government investment certificates (Malaysia) |
| GIIs | Government investment issues (Malaysia) |
| GMC | Government Musharakah certificates (Sudan) |
| GNI | Gross national income |
| IB | Islamic Bank |
| IBBs | Islamic banking branches (stand-alone) |
| ID | Islamic Dinar |
| IDB | Islamic Development Bank |
| IDR | Islamic depository receipts |
| IERS | Islamic export refinance scheme |
| IFIs | Islamic financial institutions |
| IFSB | Islamic Financial Services Board (Malaysia-based) |
| IIBI | Institute of Islamic Banking and Insurance (London) |
| IIFM | International Islamic Financial Market (Bahrain-based) |
| IIIE | International Institute of Islamic Economics (Islamabad) |
| IIIT | International Institute of Islamic Thought |
| IIMM | Islamic inter-bank money market (Malaysia) |
| IIRA | International Islamic Rating Agency |
| IIU | International Islamic University |
| IMF | International Monetary Fund |
| IMFIs | Islamic micro-finance institutions |
| IPO | Initial public offering (shares) |
| IRI | Islamic Research Institute (Islamabad, Pakistan) |
| IRS | Internal rating system |
| IRTI | Islamic Research and Training Institute, research and training arm of IDB (Jeddah) |
| ITC | Islamic Trade Centre |
| JIB | Jordan Islamic Bank |
| L/C | Letter of credit |
| L/G | Letter of guarantee |
| LDCs | Least developed countries |
| LLR | Lender of last resort |
| LMC | Liquidity Management Centre (Bahrain-based) |
| LUMS | Lahore University of Management Sciences |
| MGS | Malaysian government securities |
| MII | Mudarabah inter-bank investments |
| MPO | Murabaha to Purchase Orderer |
| MS | Mudarabah Sukuk |

| | |
|---|---|
| MTB | Malaysian treasury bills |
| NBFCs | Non-bank financial companies |
| NBFIs | Non-bank financial institutions |
| NDFIs | National development finance institutions |
| NIB | Non-interest based system |
| NIBAF | National Institute of Banking and Finance |
| NPL | Nonperforming loans |
| NSS | National savings schemes |
| OD | Overdraft |
| OIC | Organization of Islamic Countries |
| OMOs | Open market operations |
| PAD | Payment against documents |
| Pbuh | Peace be upon Him (used with the name of the holy Prophet of Islam) |
| PLS | Profit/loss sharing |
| PTC | Participation term certificates (Musharakah-based investment certificates) |
| R&D | Research and development |
| Repo | Repurchase offer |
| ROE | Return on equity |
| SAB | Shariat Appellate Bench (of the Supreme Court of Pakistan) that gave an historic judgement on Riba in 1999 |
| SAMA | Saudi Arabian Monetary Agency |
| SC | Salam certificate |
| SDR | Special drawing right |
| SEC | Securities and Exchange Commission |
| SLR | Statutory liquidity reserves |
| SME | Small and medium enterprises |
| SPM | Special purpose Mudarabah |
| SPV | Special purpose vehicle |
| SSC | Sharī'ah supervisory committee |
| STS | Solidarity Trust Services (SPV to issue IDB's trust certificates) |
| SWT | Subhanahu wa Ta'ala (the term that Muslims use with the name of Allah Almighty) |
| TC | Traveller's cheque |
| TDR | Term deposit receipts |
| TDT | Trickle-down theory (in economic development and growth) |
| TFC | Term finance certificates |
| TMCL | Time multiple counter loan |
| TR | Trust receipt |
| UDCs | Underdeveloped countries |
| UWL | Underwriting loss (in Takaful/insurance) |
| UWS | Underwriting surplus (in Takaful/insurance) |
| VRS | Variable return securities |
| WTO | World Trade Organization |

# Glossary

**Ahādith**: Plural of Hadith, traditions of the holy Prophet of Islam describing his utterances, actions, instructions and actions of others (Companions) tacitly approved by him.

**'Ahd**: Generally, a unilateral promise or an undertaking, although sometimes it also covers a bilateral obligation.

**'Ain**: Determinate property; property that is not Dayn; generally the commodities of material value in themselves; plural 'Aayān.

**Ajr al-Mithl**: Rent or wage to be decided by a judge or arbitrator.

**Ajr al-Musammah**: Agreed rent or wage in Ijarah or Ujrah contracts.

**Akhlāq**: Matters for disciplining one's self regarding relationships with others.

**Al-Ajr**: Commission, fees or wages charged for services rendered or work done.

**Al Ghunm bil Ghurm**: Earning profit is legitimized only by risk-sharing and engaging in an economic venture. This provides the rationale and the principle of profit-sharing in Shirkah arrangements. Al Kharaj bil Daman has similar meaning: one can claim profit only if one is ready to take liability – to bear the business risk, if any.

**Al-Hisbah**: The institution of ombudsman, a social regulatory body empowered to check imbalances in the market for the purpose of re-establishing a better semblance of market-driven exchanges in the light of the principles of justice.

**Al Kāli bil Kāli**: Exchange of two things, both delayed, or exchange of delayed counter value for another delayed counter value – also termed Bai' al-Dayn bid-Dayn.

**Al-Sarf**: Sale of monetary value for monetary value – currency exchange. In Islamic law such exchange is regarded as "sale of price for price", and each price is a consideration of the other; has to be simultaneously paid.

**Al-Wadi'ah**: A basis for safe-keeping of deposits (Amānah) on which no profit can be sought.

**Amānah**: Refers to deposit in trust. A person can hold a property in trust for another, sometimes by express contract and sometimes by implication of a contract. It entails the absence of liability for loss, except in breach of duty. Current accounts are regarded as Amābnah. If the bank gets authority to use current account funds in its business, Amānah transforms into a loan. As every loan has to be repaid, banks are liable to repay the full amounts of the current accounts, irrespective of their loss or profit.

**Ameen**: Trustworthy, trustee – safeguarding others' entrusted property as if it was his own; not liable in case of any damage to the trust property without any negligence on his part.

**Aqāid**: Matters of belief and worship – rituals pertaining to the relationship between man and God.

**'Aqd**: Lexically, conjunction or to tie; legally, synonymous with the word "contract" in modern law.

**'Aqd Batil**: A void or invalid contract – one which does not fulfil the conditions relating to offer and acceptance, subject matter or the consideration and possession or delivery of the subject matter or involves some illegal external attributes like the involvement of Riba, Gharar or Qimar.

**'Aqd Ghair Lāzim**: A contract in which any of the parties has a right to revoke it without the consent of the other.

**'Aqd Lāzim**: A contract in which none of the parties has a unilateral right to revoke (without the consent of the other).

**'Āqilah**: Kin or persons of relationship who share any responsibility.

**'Arbūn**: Downpayment; an amount taken from the buyer as part of the price after execution of the sale agreement; the seller has the option to confiscate it if the buyer backs out and does not complete the purchase process.

**'Āriyah**: Gratuitous loan of objects. It means the loan of a particular piece of property, the substance of which is not consumed by its use, without anything taken in exchange. In other words, it is the gift of usufruct of a commodity that is not consumed on use. It is different from Qard, which is the loan of fungible objects which are consumed on use and in which the similar and not the same commodity has to be returned. It is also a virtuous act like Qard. The borrowed commodity is treated as a liability of the borrower, who is bound to return it to its owner.

**Athman**: Plural of Thaman – monetary units – medium of exchange used for payment of prices and liabilities.

**Bai'al'Arbūn**: A sale of downpayment with the condition that if the buyer takes the commodity, the downpayment will become part of the selling price and if he does not purchase the commodity, the advance money will be forfeited.

**Bai' al Dayn**: Sale of debt or debt instruments.

**Bai' al-Ghāib**: Sale of absent or concealed goods (without knowing their features/specifications).

**Bai' al Hasat**: Sale where the subject matter depends on the fall of a stone or pebble; prohibited due to Gharar.

**Bai' al 'Inah**: Double sale by which the borrower and the lender sell and then resell an object between them, once for cash and then for a higher price on credit, with the net result of a loan with interest – prohibited.

**Bai' al Khiyar**: Sale with an option of one party to rescind the contract within a specified time.

**Bai' al-Majhūl**: A sale in which the object of sale or its price or the time of payment remains unknown and unspecified – lacking any material information.

**Bai' al Mu'allaq**: Suspended sale – a sale transaction, the effectiveness of which is related to any future condition or action.

**Bai' al Sarf**: Sale of gold, silver or other monetary units on both sides.

**Bai' Batil**: Invalid sale – having no effect in respect of rights and liabilities of the parties.

**Bai' bil Wafa**: Sale with a right of the seller to repurchase (redeem) the property by refunding the purchase price – basically a pledge; treats the sold asset as collateral until the amount is paid back by the other party to sale; not permissible if the resale of the property to the original seller is made a condition for the initial sale.

**Bai' Mu'ajjal**: Literally, a credit sale. Technically, a financing technique adopted by Islamic banks; it is a contract in which the seller allows the buyer to pay the price of a commodity at a future date in a lump sum or in instalments. The price fixed for the commodity in such a transaction can be the same as the spot price or higher or lower than the spot price, but generally it is higher than the spot price.

**Bai' Murabaha**: Sale at cost price plus a mutually agreed profit – bargaining on profit margin on the cost price. (See Murabaha)

**Bai' Musawamah**: Sale without any reference to the cost price to the seller – bargaining on price.

**Bai' Salam**: A contract in which advance payment is made for goods to be delivered later on. The seller undertakes to supply some specific goods to the buyer at a future date in exchange of an advance price fully paid at the time of the contract. According to normal rules of the Sharī'ah, no sale can be executed unless the goods are in existence at the time of the bargain, but Salam sale forms an exception given by the holy Prophet himself to the general rule, provided the goods and their prices are defined and the date of delivery is fixed. It is necessary that the quality of the commodity intended to be purchased is fully specified, leaving no ambiguity leading to dispute. The objects of this sale are goods and not media of exchange like gold, silver or currencies, because these are regarded as monetary values, the exchange of which is covered under the rules of Bai' al Sarf, i.e. hand to hand without delay. Barring this, Bai' Salam covers almost everything which is capable of being definitely described as to quantity, quality and workmanship, subject to the fulfilment of other conditions for valid Salam.

**Bai' Tawliyah**: Sale at cost price – to facilitate or serve others.

**Bai' Wadhi'ah**: Sale with loss – at a price less than the cost price.

**Bai' wal Salaf**: A conditional contract combining selling and lending, like one man saying to another: "I purchase your goods for such and such if you lend me such and such" – invalid.

**Barnāmaj**: Catalogue or list of contents in a sale consignment.

**Bayt al Māl**: Public treasury of an Islamic State.

**Buyoo'al Amānāt**: Fiduciary sales like Murabaha, Tawliyah and Wadhi'ah.

**Dayn**: Debt; goods of indeterminate category that can be used for payment of liabilities; a liability to pay which results from any credit transaction like purchase/sale on credit or due rentals in Ijarah (leasing). A Dayn comes into existence as a result of any other contract or credit transaction.

**Dhamān**: Taking liability, responsibility – contract of guarantee; responsibility of entrepreneur/manager of a business.

**Dhamān Khatr al-Tariq**: An arrangement of mutual assistance in which losses suffered by traders during journeys due to hazards on trade routes were indemnified from jointly pooled funds.

**Dinar**: Currency in the form of gold coins that was prevalent in the past.

**Dirham**: Currency in the form of silver coins prevalent in the past.

**Falah**: Welfare in this world and the Hereafter; Falah means to thrive, to become happy or to have luck and success. Technically, it implies success both in this world and in the Akhirah (Hereafter). The Falah presumes belief in one God, the apostlehood of Prophet Muhammad (pbuh), Akhirah and conformity to the Sharī'ah in behaviour.

**Fāsid**: A voidable or defective contract (according to division of contracts with respect to legality as per Hanafi Fiqh) due to nonfulfilment of any condition required for valid contracts.

**Fatwah**: A religious decree or edict; plural Fatāwa.

**Fiqh**: Islamic jurisprudence; the science of the Sharī'ah. It is an important source of Islamic tenets.

**Frāidh**: Obligations – acts that are obligatory for Muslims.

**Fuduli**: A person who is neither guardian nor agent, or if he is agent, he transgresses the limits prescribed by the principal in respect of a contract.

**Fulus**: Coins of inferior metals.

**Ghaban**: Misappropriation or defrauding others in respect of specifications of the goods and their prices.

**Ghaban-e-Fahish**: Excessive profiteering with deception – a person sells a commodity stating explicitly or giving the impression that he is charging the market price, but actually he is charging an exorbitant price taking benefit of the ignorance of the purchaser – in such cases the purchaser has the option to revoke the sale and get back the price paid (see Khiyar-e-Ghaban).

**Gharar**: Literally, uncertainty, hazard, risk relating to major elements of a contract; technically, sale of a thing which is not present at hand, or the sale of a thing whose consequence or outcome is not known, or a sale in which one does not know whether it will come to be or not, such as fish in water or a bird in the air. It refers to an element of absolute or excessive uncertainty in any business or a contract about the subject of contract or its price, or mere speculative risk. It leads to undue loss to a party and unjustified enrichment of another, which is prohibited. Gambling is a form of Gharar because the gambler is ignorant of the result of the gamble. Selling goods without allowing the buyer to properly examine the goods is also a kind of Gharar. Some examples of Gharar are: selling goods that the seller is unable to deliver; selling known or unknown goods against an unknown price, such as selling the contents of a sealed box without exact information about its contents; selling goods without proper description; selling goods without specifying the price, such as selling at the "going price".

**Ghārmeen**: One head of the Zakat beneficiaries – broadly, those who are obliged to pay others' debts as sureties. An Islamic State can make up their loss by paying from Zakat proceeds.

**Ghāsib**: Usurper of property of others.

**Habal-al-Hablah**: Sale of what is in the womb of an animal; a sale where its subject matter is not clearly known – prohibited due to Gharar.

**Halal**: Anything permitted by the Sharī'ah; permissible goods, valid earnings, etc.

**Hamish Jiddiyah**: The margin reflecting firm intention of the promisee – earnest money taken from a person who intends to purchase a commodity from or enters into a contract with anyone to confirm his sincerity to actually purchase the commodity when offered. In the case of breach of promise, the promisee has the right to recover his actual loss incurred due to the breach.

**Haram**: Anything prohibited by the Sharī'ah.

**Hawalah**: Literally, transfer; legally, an agreement by which a debtor is freed from a debt by another becoming responsible for it, or the transfer of a claim of a debt by shifting the responsibility from one person to another – contract of assignment of debt. It also refers to the document by which the transfer takes place, like a bill of exchange, promissory note, cheque or draft.

**Hibah**: Gift – to give something in permanent ownership to another without any consideration in exchange.

**Hilah, Hiyal** (plural): Ruses, tricks used in transactions to circumvent the basic prohibitions.

**Hukmi (Qabza)**: Constructive possession; a situation in which the buyer has not taken the physical delivery of the commodity, yet the commodity has come into his risk and control and all the rights and liabilities are passed on to him, including the risk of its destruction.

**Husnal Qadha**: Gracious payment of loan/debt: repaying a loan in excess of the principal without a precondition; individuals' discretion; not to be adopted as a system in which a creditor, lender or an investor has expectation of getting some reward on the debt.

**Ibādāt**: Plural of Ibādah, meaning worship or a ritual act.

**Ibāhatul Asliyah**: General permissibility, which means that all economic activities that are not prohibited by the original sources of Sharī´ah, i.e. the Qurān and Sunnah, are valid/permissible.

**Ijab**: Offer, in a contract (see also Qabul).

**Ijarah**: Letting on lease. Sale of defined usufruct of any asset for a defined period in exchange of definite rent; only those assets can be leased the corpus of which is not consumed with use or the form/shape of which is not entirely changed with use. For example, cotton, yarn, fuel, milk, money can be sold/bought, but not leased against rentals. This is because the lessor has to bear the risk related to the ownership of the asset, and this is possible only if the leased asset remains intact and the lessor gets reward in the form of rental against taking risk.

**Ijarah Mosufah bil Zimmah**: A lease contract where the lessor undertakes to provide a well-defined service or benefit without identifying any particular units of asset rendering the related service. If a unit of the asset is destroyed, the contract is not terminated and the lessor provides another such unit.

**Ijarah Muntahia-bi-Tamleek**: Lease culminating in the transfer of ownership to the lessee in such a way that lease and sale are kept separate and independent transactions. Use of this term for Islamic leasing is better than Ijarah-wal-Iqtina´, as the latter tends to give the impression that Ijarah and sale are working side by side, while actually they have to be two separate deals.

**Ijarah-wal-Iqtina´**: A mode of financing by way of hire–purchase, adopted by Islamic banks but different from conventional hire–purchase. It is a contract under which an Islamic bank purchases equipment, buildings, etc., giving them on lease against agreed rentals together with a unilateral undertaking that at the end of the lease period, the ownership in the asset will be transferred to the lessee. The underlying contract is Ijarah and all rules applicable to Ijarah have to be observed to make the deal Sharī´ah-compliant. The undertaking or the promise does not become an integral part of the lease contract to make it conditional. Ownership is transferred through a separate contract of sale or gift. Another term used for this is Ijarah Muntahia-bi-Tamleek.

**Ijma´a**: Consensus – decision or resolution of generality of the Sharī´ah scholars of any time pertaining to any matters relating to Sharī´ah. Ijma´a of the Companions of the holy Prophet is considered by the overwhelming majority of Muslims as part of the Sunnah and an important source for the derivation of laws in the subsequent periods.

**Ijtihad**: An endeavor of a qualified jurist to derive or formulate a rule of law to determine the true ruling of the divine law in a matter on which the revelation is not explicit or certain, on the basis of Nass or evidence found in the Holy Qur'ān and the Sunnah. Express injunctions have no room for Ijtihad. Implied injunctions can be interpreted in different ways by way of inference from the accepted principles of the Sharī´ah.

**´Illah**: The attribute of an exchange or event that entails a particular Divine ruling for cases possessing that attribute – cause of prohibition of specific exchange contracts. ´Illah is the basis for applying analogy for determining permissibility or otherwise of any transaction.

**Imam**: Leader, guide or ruler.

**Iman**: Faith, belief.

**'Inān** (a type of Shirkah): A form of partnership in which each partner contributes capital and has a right to work for the business, not necessarily equally.

**Isrāf**: Immoderateness, exaggeration in spending wealth and waste, covers spending on objects which are permissible otherwise, spending on superfluous objects, spending on objects which are not needed and are incompatible with the economic standard of the majority of the population (see also Tabzir).

**Istihsan**: A doctrine of Islamic law that allows exception to strict legal reasoning in special circumstances when considerations of human welfare so demand.

**Istijār**: Hiring, renting – another term less frequently used for Ijarah.

**Istijrar**: Repeat sale/a continuous purchase or supply contract – an agreement between a buyer and a supplier whereby the latter agrees to supply a particular product on an ongoing basis, for example monthly, at an agreed price and on the basis of an agreed mode of payment.

**Istisna'a**: Order to manufacture (for purchase). It is a contractual agreement for manufacturing goods and commodities, allowing cash payment in advance and future delivery or future payment and future delivery. Istisna'a can be used for providing the facility of financing the manufacture/construction of houses, plant, projects, bridges, roads and highways.

**'Iwad**: Recompense or equivalent counter value in an exchange.

**Jahl or Jahala**: Ignorance, lack of knowledge; indefiniteness in a contract, non-clarity about the parties or their rights and obligations, the goods/subject matter or the price/consideration – leading to Gharar.

**Ju'alah or Ji'alah**: Rendering a service against reward; literally, wages, pay, stipend or reward for a job. Legally, it refers to doing any job or providing any service for achieving an objective which is not sure to be achieved for someone against a prize, fee or commission. Achievement of the end result is necessary for entitlement to the fee or prize. The determination of the required end result of the transaction is considered to be sufficient to make it permissible. Ju'alah is a relevant and useful transaction in events that cannot be accomplished through Ijarah, such as bringing back lost property from an uncertain location, because an Ijarah contract requires that the work and the wage must be known and specified without any hazard.

**Kafalah**: Guarantee; literally, Kafalah means responsibility, amenability or suretyship, legally, in Kafalah, a third party becomes surety for the payment of debt. It is a covenant/pledge given to a creditor that the debtor will pay the debt or any other liability.

**Khalabah**: Misleading marketing – pursuing unaware and simple clients by overprojecting the quality of a commodity.

**Kharaj bi-al-Daman**: Gain accompanies liability for loss; a Hadith forming a legal maxim and a basic principle of Islamic finance (see also Al-Ghunm bil Ghurm).

**Khatar**: A kind of Gharar – Khatar will be involved if liability of any of the parties to a contract is uncertain or contingent, delivery of one of the exchange items is not in the control of any party or the payment from one side is uncertain.

**Khiyār**: Option or a power to annul or cancel a contract.

**Khiyar al 'Aib**: Option of defect – goods can be returned if found defective – option automatically available to the buyer.

**Khiyar al-Majlis**: Option for the contracting session; the power to annul a contract possessed by both contracting parties as long as they do not separate.

**Khiyar al Ro'yat**: Option to revoke a sale contract to be exercised on seeing the goods.

**Khiyar al-Shart**: A right, stipulated by one or both of the parties to a contract, to cancel the contract for any reason within a fixed period of time.

**Khiyar al Wasf**: Option of quality – where goods are sold by specified quality, if that quality is absent, the goods can be returned.

**Khiyar-e-Ghaban**: Option relating to price – where goods are sold at a price far higher than the market price, and the client is told or given the impression that he has been charged the market price.

**Khiyar-e-Naqad**: Option of payment – to agree that if payment is not made within (three) days, the contract will be annulled.

**Ma'lum**: Known – in the knowledge of the parties.

**Mabi'**: Subject of sale – the commodity that is being traded in a transaction.

**Maisir**: An ancient Arabian game of chance played with arrows without heads and feathering, for stakes of slaughtered and quartered camels. It refers to all types of hazard and gambling – acquisition of wealth by chance/easily (without paying an equivalent compensation ('Iwad) for it or without working for it, or without undertaking any liability against it).

**Māl**: Anything that can be possessed; includes money such as gold, silver and monetary units, commodities such as clothes and foodstuffs and immovable properties such as houses and factories.

**Māl-e-Mutaqawam**: Things the use of which is lawful under the Sharī´ah, or wealth that has a commercial value. Legal tenders of the modern age that carry monetary value are included in Māl-e-Mutaqawam. It is possible that certain wealth has no commercial value for Muslims (non-Mutaqawam) but is valuable for non-Muslims. Examples are wine and pork.

**Maslaha-e-Mursalah**: The aspect of general welfare/benefit of mankind/society that is kept in mind by the scholars competent to undertake Ijtihad while resolving issues confronted from time to time. Catering to the well-being of people in the worldly life and also in the Hereafter or relieving them of hardships is the basic objective of the Sharī´ah.

**Mawālāt**: A contract in ancient Arabia in which one party agreed to bequeath his property to the other on the understanding that the benefactor would pay any blood money that may eventually be due by the former.

**Mawquf**: A contract, the effectiveness of which is suspended until any happening.

**Mithāq**: A covenant; refers to an earnest and firm determination on the part of the concerned parties to fulfil the contractual obligations; has more sanctity than the ordinary contracts.

**Mithlam-bi-mithlin**: Like for like (in exchange transactions).

**Mithli**: Fungible goods; goods all units of which are the same and that can be returned in kind, i.e. gold, silver, wheat, all currencies, etc.

**Mu'āmalāt**: All kinds of economic activities related to exchange of goods and services.

**Mua'awamah**: Sale for years – e.g. fruit of a tree or an orchard sold for more than one year to come without stipulating the amount, price or time of delivery – prohibited.

**Mubāh**: Object that is lawful (i.e. something which is permissible to use or trade in).

**Mudarabah**: A form of partnership where one party provides the funds while the other provides expertise and management. The latter is referred to as the Mudarib. Any profits accrued are shared between the two parties on a pre-agreed basis, while any loss is borne by the provider of the capital.

**Mudarib**: In a Mudarabah contract, the person or party who acts as entrepreneur.

**Muflis**: Destitute; insolvent/bankrupt debtors.

**Mughārasah**: Joint venture projects involving plantation of gardens and sharing the produce.

**Mulamasah**: Sale by touching the subject matter or its carton without knowing its detail.

**Munabadhah**: If a man throws to another a garment in exchange for a garment that the other throws to him without both of them examining them.

**Murabaha**: Literally it means a sale on mutually agreed profit. Technically, it is a contract of sale in which the seller declares his cost and the profit. This has been adopted by Islamic banks as a mode of financing. As a financing technique, it can involve a request by the client to the bank to purchase a certain item for him. The bank does that for a definite profit over the cost.

**Murabaha lil 'amri bil Shira** or **Murabaha li Wa′da bi Shira**: Murabaha to Purchase Orderer.

**Musāqah**: A contract in which the owner of a garden shares its produce with another person in return for his services in irrigating the garden.

**Musawamah**: A general kind of sale in which the price of the commodity to be traded is bargained between the seller and the purchaser without any reference to the price paid or cost incurred by the former.

**Musharakah**: Partnership between two parties, who both provide capital towards the financing of a project. Both parties share profits on a pre-agreed ratio, but losses are shared on the basis of equity participation. Management of the project is carried out by both parties. However, the partners also have a right to forego the right of management/work in favour of any specific partner or person. There are two main forms of Musharakah: Permanent Musharakah and Diminishing Musharakah.

**Mustarsal**: An unknowing entrant into the market – not aware of the market.

**Muzara‘a**: Share cropping; a contract in which one person agrees to till the land of another person in return for a part of the produce of the land.

**Najash**: Bidding up the price without an intention to purchase and take delivery of the commodity.

**Nass**: Clear texts of the Sharī′ah, i.e. the Qur′ān and Sunnah.

**Nawāhi**: Prohibitions – acts prohibited by Islam.

**Niyyah**: Intent or intention while doing a job or action.

**Qabul**: Acceptance, in a contract (see also Ijab).

**Qard**: Literally "to cut". It is so called because the property is cut off – transferred to the borrower. Legally, Qard means to give anything having value in the ownership of the other by way of virtue so that the latter may avail himself of the same for his benefit with the condition that the same or similar amount of that thing will be paid back on demand or at the settled time. The repayment of loan is obligatory. Loans under Islamic law can be classified into Salaf and Qard, the former being a loan for a fixed time and the latter payable on demand. Qard is, in fact, a particular kind of Salaf (see Salaf).

**Qard al Hasan**: A virtuous loan. A loan with the stipulation to return the principal sum in the future without any increase; in Islamic law, all loans have to be virtuous, as seeking any benefit from loaning amounts to Riba.

**Qimār**: Games of chance – gambling. Technically, it is an arrangement in which possession of a property is contingent upon the happening of an uncertain event. By implication, this applies to a situation in which there is a loss for one party and a gain for the other without specifying which party will lose and which will gain.

**Qirād**: Another name for Mudarabah – partnership in which a person or a group of people provides funds while another provides entrepreneurship for conducting the business.

**Qirād mithl**: Matching rate in Qirad/Mudarabah, which has to be paid to the Mudarib if the Mudarabah/Muqaradah contract becomes voidable due to any technical reason.

**Qirsh**: A coin of inferior metals used in ancient Iraq for making payment.

**Qisās**: A provision of Islamic law to punish those who cause any harm to human life – a murderer is executed to death in exchange.

**Qiyami or Qimi**: Nonfungible goods; the value of each unit of which is different.

**Qiyās**: Analogy – literally it means to measure or compare for analogy. Technically, it means a derivation of the law on the analogy of an existing law if the basis ('Illah) of the two is the same. It is one of the sources of Islamic law.

**Ra'asul-māl**: Principal amount of a loan or a debt or money invested in a business.

**Rā'iee**: In charge – one who is responsible for his subordinates.

**Rabbul-māl**: The person who invests the capital in a Shirkah/Mudarabah contract.

**Riba**: Literally, an excess or increase. Technically, it means an increase over the principal in a loan transaction, over a debt or in exchange transactions, accrued to the lender/creditor or a party to exchange without giving an equivalent counter value or recompense ('iwad) in return to the other party.

**Riba Al-Fadl**: The quality premium in exchange of low quality with better quality goods, e.g. dates for dates, wheat for wheat, etc. – an excess in the exchange of Ribawi goods in the case of a single genus on both sides. The concept of Riba Al-Fadl refers to exchange/sale transactions.

**Riba Al-Nasiah**: Riba of delay, due to exchange not being immediate with or without excess in one of the counter values. It is an increment on the principal of a loan or debt payable. It refers to loan/credit transactions or lending money on the understanding that the borrower will return to the lender at the end of the period the amount originally lent together with an increase on it, in consideration of the lender having granted him time to pay. Interest, in all modern banking transactions, falls under the purview of Riba Al-Nasiah.

**Ribawi**: Goods subject to Fiqh rules on Riba in sales – monetary units and items sold by weight and/or by measure, including gold, silver, paper currencies, edible goods like wheat, rice, barley, dates, salt, etc.

**Ribh-al-mithl**: Matching rate of profit.

**Rihn or Rahn**: Pledge, collateral; legally, Rihn means to pledge or lodge a real or corporeal property of material value as security for a debt or pecuniary obligation, so as to make it possible for the creditor to recover the debt, in the case of nonpayment, by selling the pledged property.

**Rukbān**: Grain dealers coming from the tribal/rural areas to the town to sell goods.

**Sā'a**: A measure that was used for exchanging/trading grains.

**Sadd al-Zarāi'**: To prohibit a transaction on the grounds of blocking the means to an illicit end.

**Sahābah**: Companions of the holy Prophet of Islam – the people who saw the holy Prophet while being firm believers (Muslims).

**Salaf**: Used in two senses: (i) literally, payment in advance; a loan which draws forth no profit for the creditor; it includes loans for specified periods, i.e. short, intermediate and long-term loans; slightly different from Qard – an amount given as Salaf cannot be called back, unlike Qard, before it is due.

Also, another name of Salam – forward sale; (ii) Forebears – jurists and scholars of early periods of Islam.

**Sanadāt**: Certificates of investment – another name for Sukuk.

**Sarf**: Contract in which both exchange items are gold, silver or any monetary units.

**Saw´ām-bi-sawaa´**: Equal for equal (in exchange transactions).

**Sharī´ah**: Divine guidance as given by the Holy Qur'ān and the Sunnah of the Prophet Muhammad (pbuh); embodies all aspects of the Islamic faith, including beliefs and practice.

**Shart-e-Jazāi**: A clause that a purchaser can put into an Istisna'a agreement whereby the price of the item being manufactured would decrease in the case of a delay in delivery by the seller/manufacturer whereby the delay benefits the purchaser – unlike all other modes in which any penalty imposed due to default or delay in payment of liabilities goes to the charity account and not to the banks' P & L accounts.

**Shirkah**: Commingling by two or more people of their money or work or obligations to earn a profit or a yield or appreciation in value and to share the loss, if any, according to their proportionate ownership. In the present Islamic banking terminology, it may include both Musharakah and Mudarabah and various kinds of Musharakah like business/commercial partnership, partnership by ownership and permanent or redeemable partnership.

**Shirkatul'aqd**: Commercial/business partnership – a contract between two or more people who launch a business or an enterprise to make profits.

**Shirkatulmilk**: Partnership by ownership or in the right of ownership; not for business.

**Shuf'ah**: Pre-emptive right of a partner in a joint ownership or a neighbour in sale of landed properties.

**Suftajah**: An instrument in traditional Islamic finance used for cash transfer/payment which involved the act of depositing a certain amount of money with someone for settlement or to the benefit of the depositor or his representative at another place or in another country. A type of instrument used for the delegation of credit during the Muslim period, especially the Abbasides period. It was used to collect taxes, disburse government dues and transfer funds by merchants.

**Sukuk**: Certificates of equal value representing undivided share in ownership of tangible assets of particular projects or specific investment activity, usufruct and services.

**Sunnah**: Literally, custom, habit or way of life. Technically, it refers to actions, sayings and utterances of the holy Prophet Muhammad (pbuh), or actions of others tacitly approved by him, as reported in the books of Hadith.

**T'azir**: Punishments not expressly provided in the Holy Qur'ān and Sunnah; awarded by a judge at his own discretion, keeping in mind the severity of the crime.

**T'aliq**: Conditions which suspend a contract to any future event.

**Ta'mein**: Arabic word used for insurance.

**Tabarru'**: Benefits given by a person to another without getting anything in exchange. For example, gracious repayment of debt, absolutely at the lender's own discretion and without any prior condition or inducement for reward is covered under Tabarru'. Repaying a loan in excess of the principal and without a precondition is commendable and compatible with the Sunnah of the holy Prophet (pbuh). But it is matter of individual discretion and cannot be adopted as a system, because this would mean that a loan would necessarily yield a profit, making it usurious.

**Tabzir**: Spending wastefully on objects which have been explicitly prohibited by the Sharī´ah, irrespective of the amount of expenditure (see also Isrāf).

**Takaful**: A form of Islamic insurance based on the principle of Ta'awon or mutual assistance. It provides for mutual assistance in cases of loss to life, assets and property and offers joint risk-sharing in the event of a loss incurred by one of the pool members.

**Taqwa**: Piety, virtue and righteousness with a sense of accountability to Allah (SWT). It encompasses not only obedience to Allah, but also the love of fellow human beings, who should be treated as part of an extended human family.

**Tawarruq**: Acquiring cash through trade activities – to buy on credit and sell at spot value with the objective of getting cash, meaning that the trade transaction was not needed by the buyer; he simply wanted liquidity, which he got by purchasing a commodity on credit and selling the same to a third party on cash.

**Thaman**: Price, monetary value of a commodity in an exchange.

**Thaman-e-mithl**: Normal/market price that has to be paid in case any issue arises in deciding the actual price in any transaction.

**Ujrah**: Wages/service fees against work done for others; Ijarah of services; different from Ju'alah which means giving a reward for accomplishment of a defined task. While in Ujrah, acceptance of "offer" by a specified person is necessary, in Ju'alah, anyone who hears the offer can undertake the work and becomes entitled to reward only upon completion of the job.

**Ujratul-mithl**: A remuneration or compensation which has to be given as per normal market rate if the underlying contract(s) become voidable.

**Uqood-e-Mu'awadha**: Commutative contracts in which one can genuinely take any return, like contracts of Bai', Ijarah and Wakalah.

**Uqood Ghair Mu'awadha**: Noncommutative contracts wherein one cannot get any return or compensation, like contracts of loan (Qard), gift (Tabarru'/Hibah), Guarantee (Kafalah) and assignment of debt (Hawalah).

**W'adah**: Promise – does not create contractual rights and obligations; may be binding or unbinding.

**Wadi'ah**: Amānah or deposit; the trustee is not responsible for loss except in the case of negligence on his part. If, however, the Amānah amount is used in business, with the permission of the owner, the amount becomes the trustee's liability.

**Wakalah**: Contract of agency, can be commutative or noncommutative.

**Wakalatul Istismār**: Investment agency – fund management in which the investor gets all the profit or loss while the fund manager gets a pre-agreed service fee or commission that could be a lump sum amount or a certain percentage of the invested capital.

**Waqf**: Retention of a property for the benefit of a charitable or humanitarian objective, or for a specified group of people such as members of the donor's family. There are three kinds of Waqf in Islamic jurisprudence: religious Waqf, philanthropic Waqf and family Waqf. The Waqf property can neither be sold nor inherited or donated to anyone.

**Yadam-bi-yadin**: Hand to hand or on the spot (in exchange transactions).

**Zakah/Zakat**: Zakah is the third out of five pillars of Islam. A religious tax on Muslims having wealth over and above an exemption limit (Nisab) at a rate fixed by the Sharī'ah. As such, it is not a tax on income, but on the assets held by a Muslim at a prescribed date (a Zakat day has to be determined for calculation of Zakat money to be paid annually) over and above the amount of Nisab after fulfilment of the normal needs of the owner. The objective is to take away a part of the wealth of the well-to-do and to distribute it among the poor and the needy. It is levied on cash, cattle, agricultural produce, minerals, capital invested in industry and business, etc. The rates are different for different natures of assets. The recipients of Zakah funds have been identified in the Holy Qur'ān (9: 60) and are the poor, the needy, Zakah collectors, new converts to Islam, travellers in difficulty, captives and debtors and for the cause of the Almighty.

**Zulm**: Injustice, usurping others' rights, not giving proper recompense in an exchange by way of any illegal act or coercion.

# Bibliography
## English Sources

AAOIFI (2004–5a) *Sharī´ah Standards*.

AAOIFI (2004–5b) *Accounting, Auditing and Governance Standards for Islamic Financial Institutions* (also including Code of Ethics for accountants, auditors and employees of IFIs).

Adam, Nathif Jama (2005) *Sukuk: A Panacea for Convergence and Capital Market Development in the OIC Countries*, compiled papers presented at the 6th International Conference on Islamic Economics and Banking in the 21st Century, Jakarta, Indonesia, 21–24th November.

Ahmad, Aftab (2005) "Poverty in the World's Richest Country", *The Dawn*, Karachi, 3rd October.

Ahmad, Alyas (1961) "Ibn Taymiyah on Islamic Economics", *The Voice of Islam*, Karachi, **IX**11), August.

Ahmad, Anis (1997) "Social Welfare: A Basic Islamic Value", *Hamdard Islamicus*, Karachi, **XX**(3), July–September.

Ahmad, Ausaf (1997) *Towards an Islamic Financial Market*, research paper 45, IRTI, IDB, Jeddah.

Ahmad, Khurshid (2006) "Response to Paper by Asad Zaman", *Market Forces: Journal of Management, Informatics and Technology*, Karachi, **2**(3), October.

Ahmad, Qadeeruddin (1995) "What is Riba?" *Journal of Islamic Banking and Finance*, January–March.

Ahmad, Ziauddin (1993) "Prohibition of Interest in Islam", in *Banking and Finance: Islamic Concept*, Mukhtar Zaman (Ed.), IAIB, Karachi.

Ahmed, Habib (2002) *Financing Micro Enterprises: An Analytical Study of Islamic Microfinance Institutions*, Islamic Economic Studies, IRTI, IDB, Jeddah, **9**(2), March.

Ahmed, Mahmud Shaikh (1967) "Semantics of Theory of Interest", *Islamic Studies*, **6**(2), 171–196.

Al Baraka, Dallah Group (1981–2001) *Resolutions and Recommendations of Al Baraka Symposia on Islamic Economy*, first English edition.

Ali, Yusuf (1989) *English Translation (with commentary) of the Holy Qur´ān*, revised edition, edited by IIIT. Amana Corporation, USA.

Amin, Mohammed (2006) *UK Taxation of Islamic Finance: Where Are We Now?* New Horizon, Institute of Islamic Banking and Insurance, London.

Ayub, Muhammad (1999) "Banks' Prize Schemes: Their Sharī´ah Position", *Journal of the Institute of Bankers*, Pakistan, June, pp. 29–38.

Ayub, Muhammad (2002) *Islamic Banking and Finance: Theory and Practice*, State Bank of Pakistan, Karachi, December.

Al-Bashir, Muhammad and Al-Amine, Muhammad (2001) "The Islamic Bonds Market: Possibilities and Challenges", *International Journal of Islamic Financial Services*, **3**(1), April–June (http://www.islamic-finance.net/journal.html).

Billah, Mohammad Masum (2002) "Takaful (Islamic insurance) Premium: A Suggested Regulatory Framework", *International Journal of Islamic Financial Services*, **3**(1). A slightly different version was also published in *Journal of Islamic Banking and Finance*, **19**(1).

Boulakia, Jean David C. (1971) "Ibn Khaldun: A Fourteenth Century Economist", *Journal of Political Economy*, **79**(5), September/October.

Brown, Gordon (2006) Opening address to the Islamic Finance and Trade Conference, New Horizon, London, July–August.

Buffet, Warren (2003) "Derivatives: Weapons of Financial Mass Destruction", *The Economist*, 15th March.

Cannan, Edwin, Adarkar, B.P., Sandwell, B.K., Keynes, John Maynard and Boulding, K.E. (1932) "Saving and Usury: A Symposium", *The Economic Journal*, **42**(165), 123–141.

Chapra, M. Umer (1979) *Islamic Welfare State and its Role in the Economy*, The Islamic Foundation, Leicester.

Chapra, M. Umer (1985) *Towards a Just Monetary System*, The Islamic Foundation, Leicester.

Chapra, M. Umer (1992) *Islam and the Economic Challenge*, The Islamic Foundation and the International Institute of Islamic Thought.

Chapra, M. Umer (1993) *Islam and Economic Development*. IRI, Islamabad.

Chapra, M. Umer (1996) *What is Islamic Economics?* IDB prize-winning lecture series, No. 9.

Chapra, M. Umer (2000a) *The Future of Economics: An Islamic Perspective*, The Islamic Foundation, Leicester.

Chapra, M. Umer (2000b) "Is it Necessary to Have Islamic Economics?" *The Journal of Socio-economics*, **29**, 21–37.

Chapra, M. Umer (2002) "Alternative Vision of International Monetary Reform", in *Islamic Banking and Finance: New Perspectives on Profit-sharing and Risk*, Iqbal Munawar and David T. Llewellyn (Eds). Edward Elgar, London.

Chapra, M. Umer and Khan, Tariqullah (2000) *Regulation and Supervision of Islamic Banks*, IRTI, IDB, Jeddah.

Choudhury, Masadul Alam (1997) *Money in Islam: A Study in Islamic Political Economy*. Routledge, London, pp. 71–103; 286–291.

Clement, M. Henry and Wilson, Rodney (Eds) (2005) *The Politics of Islamic Finance*. Oxford University Press.

Council of Islamic Ideology (CII) (1980) *Report on Elimination of Interest from the Economy*.

Council of the Islamic Fiqh Academy (2000) *Resolutions and Recommendations (1985–2000)*, IRTI, IDB, Jeddah.

Dennis, Lawrence and Somerville, H. (1932) "Usury", *The Economic Journal*, **42**(166), 312–323.

Al-Dhareer, Siddiq M. Al-Amen (1997) *Al-Gharar in Contracts and its Effect on Contemporary Transactions*, IRTI, IDB, Jeddah.

Eltejani, A. Ahmed (2005) Comments on paper by Adam, Nathif Jama on Sukuk. Papers presented at the 6th International Conference in Islamic Economics and Finance, Jakarta, Indonesia, 21–24th November, pp. 411–413.

Federal Shariat Court (FSC) (1992) *Judgement on Laws Involving Interest*. PLD Publishers, Lahore, volume XLIV.

Hasan, Zubair (2005) "Evaluation of Islamic Banking Performance: On the Current Use of Econometric Models", Islamic Economics and Banking in the 21st Century, papers from the 6th Islamic Conference, Jakarta, 21–24th November, pp. 229–248.

Hasanuz Zaman, S.M. (1990) "Mudarabah in Non-Trade Operations in Islamic Economics", *Journal of King Abdul Aziz University*, Jeddah, **2**, 69–88.

Hasanuz Zaman, S.M. (1991) "Bai' Salam: Principles and Practical Applications", *Islamic Studies*, **30**(4), Winter.

Hasanuz Zaman, S.M. (1993) *Indexation of Financial Assets: An Islamic Evaluation*. IIIT, Islamabad.

Hasanuz Zaman, S.M. (2000) "Defining Islamic Economics", *Journal of Islamic Banking and Finance*, **17**(2), April–June.

Hasanuz Zaman, S.M. (2003) *Islam and Business Ethics*. IIBI, London.

Hassan, Abdullah Alwi Haji (1993) *Sales and Contracts in Early Islamic Commercial Law*. Islamic Research Institute, International Islamic University, Islamabad.

Hatch, Charles, T. (2005) *Inflationary Deception: How Banks are Evading Reserve Requirements and Inflating the Money Supply*, May 16th, http://www.mises.org/workingpapers.asp.

Homoud, Sami Hassan (1998) "Islamic Financial Instruments based on Intermediary Contracts", in *Islamic Financial Instruments for Public Sector Resource Mobilization*, Ausaf Ahmad and Tariqullah Khan (Eds), IRTI, IDB, Jeddah.

Institute of Islamic Banking and Insurance (IIBI) (2000) *A Compendium of Legal Opinions on the Operations of Islamic Banks*, volume II, edited and translated by Yusuf Talal Delorenzo.

International Association of Islamic Banks (IAIB) (1990) *Directory of Islamic Banks and Financial Institutions*, Jeddah.

Al-Jarhi (1983) "A Monetary and Financial Structure for an Interest-free Economy", in *Money and Banking in Islam*, Ziauddin Ahmad *et al.* (Eds), IPS, Islamabad, pp. 69–101.

Jarhi, Mabid Ali and Munawar, Iqbal (2001) *Islamic Banking: Answers to some Frequently Asked Questions*, IRTI, IDB, occasional paper No. 4.

Kahf, Monzer (1994) "Budget Deficits and Public Borrowing Instruments in an Islamic Economic System", *The American Journal of Islamic Social Sciences*, **11**(2), 207.

Kahf, Monzer (1997) *Instruments of Meeting Budget Deficit in an Islamic Economy*, IRTI, IDB, research paper No. 42.

Kahf, Monzer (2004) *Framework of Tawarruq and Securitization in Shari'ah and Islamic Banking*, paper written for AAOIFI seminar in Bahrain, February 2004, available at: www.kahf.net/papers.html.

Kazmi, Aqdas Ali (2004) *Daily Dawn*, Karachi, 29th May.

Kester, W. Carl (1986) "Capital and Ownership Structure: A Comparison of US and Japanese Manufacturing Corporations", *Financial Management*, **15**, Spring.

Keynes, John Maynard (1926) "The End of Laissez-faire", lecture given at Oxford in November 1924, published by The Hogarth Press, July 1926.

Khan, M. Fahim (1987) *Time Value of Money and its Discounting in the Islamic Perspective*, IIIE, International Islamic University, Islamabad.

Khan, M. Fahim (1995) *Islamic Futures and their Markets*, IRTI, IDB, research paper No. 32.

Khan, M. Fahim (1999) "Financial Modernization in the 21st Century and Challenges for Islamic Banking", *International Journal of Islamic Financial Services*, **1**(3).

Khan, Mohsin S. (1986) *Islamic Interest-free Banking: A Theoretical Analysis*, IMF staff papers, **33**(1), 1–27.

Khan, Mohsin, S. and Mirakhor, Abbas (Eds) (1987) *Theoretical Studies in Islamic Banking and Finance*, the Institute for Research and Islamic Studies, Houston, Texas.

Khan, Tariqullah and Ahmed, Habib (2001) *Risk Management: An Analysis of Issues in the Islamic Financial Industry*, IRTI, IDB, occasional paper No. 5.

Khorshid, Aly (2004) *Islamic Insurance: A Modern Approach to Islamic Banking*. Routledge Curzon, London.

Lane, Edward William (1956) *Arabic–English Lexicon*. Frederic Publication Co.

Lewis, B., Pellat, Ch. and Schacht, J. (Eds) (1965) *The Encyclopedia of Islam*, volume 2, p. 49.

Lombard, Maurice (1975) *The Golden Age of Islam*, translated from the French by Joan Spencer. North Holland Publishing Company.

Mahmasani, S. (1961) *Falsafat Al-Tashri Fi Al-Islam*, translated into English by Farhat J. Zaideh and E.J. Bril Leiden.

Malik, Ibn-e-Anas (Imam) (1985) *Mu'watta*, translated into English by M. Rahimuddin. Sh. Muhammad Ashraf Publishers, Lahore.

Mannan, M.A. (1984) *The Making of Islamic Economic Society*. International Association for Islamic Banks, Cairo, pp. 55–74.

Mansoori, M. Tahir (2005) *Islamic Law of Contracts and Business Transactions*. IIU, Islamabad.

Al-Marghinani (1957) *Al-Hidaya*, translated into English by Charles Hamilton. Premier Book House, Lahore.

Mills, P.S. and Presley, J.R. (1999) *Islamic Finance: Theory and Practice*. Macmillan Press, Basingstoke.

Mirakhor, Abbas and ul Haque, Nadeem (1998) *The Design of Instruments for Government Finance in an Islamic Economy*, IMF working paper/98/54, March.

Moore, Phillip (1997) *Islamic Finance: A Partnership for Growth*. Euromoney Publications, London.

Muslehuddin, Muhammad (1982) *Concept of Civil Liability in Islam and the Law of Torts*. Islamic Publications Ltd, Lahore.

Muslehuddin, Muhammad (1993) *Banking and Islamic Law*. Islamic Book Service, New Delhi.

Nabhani, Taqiuddin (1997) *The Economic System of Islam*. Al-Khilafah Publications, London.

Nyazi, Liaqat Ali (1988) *Islamic Law of Tort*, Research Cell, Dayal Singh Trust Library, Lahore.

Obaidullah, Mohammed (n.d.) *Islamic Financial Services*, King Abdul Aziz University, Jeddah, available at: http://www.islamiccenter.kau.edu.sa/english/publications/Obaidullah/ifs/ifs.html.

Parker, Mushtaq (1999) "A Crisis of Credibility", editorial, *Islamic Banker*, April, p. 2.

Perkins, John (2004) *Confessions of an Economic Hitman*. Berrett–Koehler Publishers, Inc., San Francisco.

Piranie, Ashraf (2006) *Ethical Socially Responsible Investments*. New Horizon, London July–August.

Postan, M. and Rich, E.E. (Eds) (1952) *The Cambridge Economic History of Europe*. Cambridge University Press, Cambridge.

Qadri, Anwar Ahmed (1963) *Islamic Jurisprudence in the Modern World*. N.M. Tripathi Private Limited, Bombay, pp. 97–113.

Rahim, Abdul (1958) *The Principles of Mahammedan Jurisprudence*. All Pakistan Legal Decisions, Lahore, pp. 261–325.

Ray, Nicholas Dylan (1995) *Arab Islamic Banking and the Renewal of Islamic Law*. Graham and Trotman, London.

Robbins, Lionel (1962) *Essay on the Nature and Significance of Economic Science*. Macmillan, London.

Robertson, James (1990) *Future Wealth: A New Economics for the 21st Century*. Cassell Publications, London.

Rosly, Saiful Azhar and Sanusi, Mahmood M. (1999) "The Application of Bai' Al-'Inah and Bai' Al-Dayn in Malaysian Islamic Bonds: An Islamic Analysis", *International Journal of Islamic Financial Services*, July–September (http://www.islamic-finance.net/journal.html).

Saleh, Nabil A. (1986) *Unlawful Gain and Legitimate Profit in Islamic Commercial Law: Riba, Gharar and Islamic Banking*. Cambridge University Press, Cambridge.

Schacht, Joseph (1964) *An Introduction to Islamic Law*. Oxford University Press, Oxford.

Schumpeter, A. Joseph (1954) *History of Economic Analysis*. Routledge, London.

Shariat Appellate Bench (SAB) (2000) *Judgement on Riba*, Shariat Law Reports, Lahore, February.

Siddiqi, M. Nejatullah (1976) *Banking without Interest*, The Islamic Foundation, Leicester.

Siddiqi, M. Nejatullah (1981) *Muslim Economic Thinking: A Survey of Contemporary Literature in Studies in Islamic Economics*, The Islamic Foundation, Leicester.

Siddiqi, M. Nejatullah (1983) *Issues in Islamic Banking: Selected Papers*, The Islamic Foundation, Leicester.

Siddiqi, M. Nejatullah (1991) "Some Economic Aspects of Mudarabah: Review of Islamic Economics", *Journal of the International Association for Islamic Economics*, **1**(2), 21–34.

Siddiqi, M. Nejatullah (2002) *Dialogue in Islamic Economics*. IPS and The Islamic Foundation, Leicester.

Siddiqi, M. Nejatullah (2006a) "Islamic Banking and Finance in Theory and Practice: A Survey of the State of the Art", *Islamic Economic Studies*, **13**(2), 1–48.

Siddiqi, M. Nejatullah (2006b) "Response on the paper by Asad Zaman", *Market Forces: Journal of Management, Informatics and Technology*, Karachi, 2(3), October.

Somerville, H. (1931) "Interest and Usury in a New Light", *The Economic Journal*, **41**(164), 646–649.

Thani, Nik Norzul, Ridza, Mohamed Abdullah and Megat, Hizaini Hassan (2003) *Law and Practice of Islamic Banking and Finance*. Thomson, Sweet & Maxwell (Asia), Malaysia.

*The Economist*, London, various issues.

Udovitch, Abraham (1970) *Partnership and Profit in Medieval Islam*. Princeton University Press.

Umar, Halim (1995) *Sharī'ah, Economic and Accounting Framework of Bai' Al-Salam*, IRTI, IDB, Jeddah, research paper No. 33.

Usmani, Muhammad Taqi (2000a) *Introduction to Islamic Finance*. Idaratul Ma'arif, Karachi, May.

Uthman, Usamah A. (2003) "Prepaid Forward and Leasing Contracts: A Critical Analysis of a Form of Financing Employed by Enron", in *Practical Financial Economics: A New Science*, Austin Murphy (Ed.), Praeger, Westport, pp. 105–132.

Uzair, Muhammad (2001) *Interest-free Banking*, 2nd edition. Royal Book Company, Karachi.

Visser, Wayne A.M. and McIntosh, Alastair (1998) *A Short Review of the Historical Critique of Usury: Accounting, Business and Financial History*. Routledge, London, pp. 175–189.

Vogel, E. Frank and Hayes, Samuel L. (1998) *Islamic Law and Finance: Religion, Risk and Return*. Arab and Islamic Law Series, Kluwer Law International, The Hague, Netherlands.

Wilson, Rodney (2002) "The Interface between Islamic and Conventional Banking", in *Islamic Banking and Finance: New Perspectives on Profit-sharing and Risk*, Iqbal Munawar and David T. Llewellyn (Eds), Edward Elgar.

World Bank (2005) *Global Development Finance: Mobilising Finance and Managing Vulnerability*, Washington DC.

Yousef, M. Tarik (2005) "The Murabaha Syndrome in Islamic Finance: Laws, Institutions and Politics", in *The Politics of Islamic Finance*, Clement M. Henry and Rodney Wilson (Eds), Oxford University Press, pp. 63–80.

Zaman, Asad (2006) "Islamic Economics; Problems and Prospects – A Note", *Market Forces: Journal of Management, Informatics and Technology*, **2**(1).

Zaman, S.H. (1966) "Islam vis-à-vis Interest", *Islamic Culture*, Hyderabad Deccan, January.

Zaman, Arshad and Zaman, Asad (2001) "Interest and Modern Economy", in *Islamic Economic Studies*, **8**(2), 61–74, April. Also in the *Lahore Journal of Economics*, **6**(1).

Zuhayli, Wahbah (2003) *Financial Transactions in Islamic Jurisprudence* (originally *Al Fiqhul Islami wa Adillatohu*), translated into English by Mahmoud Amin El-Gamal. Dar al Fikr, Damascus, Syria.

# Arabic/Urdu Sources

Abu Daud, Sulayman al-Sijistani (1952) *Sunan Abu Daud*, Matbah Mustapha al-Halabi, volume 2.

Abu Hanifah (Imam) (n.d.) *Jami' Masanid al-Imam al-A'zam* (compiled by Muhammad ibn Mahmud al-Khwarizmi), Darul Maarif, Hyderabad Deccan.

Ali, Syed Amir (n.d.) *Fatāwa Alamgiri (Fatāwa Al Hindiah)* (Urdu translation), Lahore.

Al-Atasi, Muhammad Khalid (1403 AH) *Sharah Majallah al Ahkam al Adliah*, Maktaba Islamia, Quetta.

Al-Ayny, Umdat Al Qari (n.d.) *Tafsir Sahih al Bukhari*, volume XI.

Baihaqi (1344 H) *Sunan al Kubra*, Idaratul Maāraf, Hyderabad Deccan.

Al-Baji, Abul Walid Suleman bin Khalf (1332 AH) *Kitab al-Muntaqa, Sharah al Muwatta*, Matba al Saadah, Egypt, volume 4.

Dubai Islamic Bank (1984) *Al-Iqtisad al-Islami*, March issue.

Al-Hilli (1389 AH) *Shaair-al-Islam*, Najaf, volume 2.

Al-Hindi, Ali al Muttaqi Allauddin (1950) *Kanzulummal*, Hyderabad Deccan, volume 2.

Hussain, Ali al Hussaini (1964) *Aqd al Bai' fi Fiqh al Jafari*, Maktaba Nahda, Baghdad.

Ibn Abideen, Muhammad Amin (n.d.) *'Raddul Muhtar' alā Durrel Mukhtar*, H.M. Saeed Company, volume 6.

Ibn-abi-Hātim (1997) *Tafsir al Qur'an al Azim*, Makkah mukarramah, KSA, volume 2.

Ibn Bāz, Abdullah (1995) *Fatāwa* (Urdu translation), Maktaba Darussalam, Riyadh, KSA.

Ibn Hajar, Al-Asqalani (1981) *Fathul Bari, Sharah of Sahih al Bukhari*, Makkah.

Ibn Hajar, Al-Asqalani (1998) *Talkhis al-Habeer fi Takhrij Ahadith al-Rāfi'e al-Kabir*, Darul Kutub al Ilmiyah, Beirut, volume 3.

Ibn Hazm, Abu Muhammad, Ali bin Ahmad bin Saeed (1988/1408 AH) *Al Muhallah bil Aathar*, Darul Kutub al Ilmiyah, Beirut.

Ibn Qudama, Abu Muhammad Abdullah bin Ahmad (1367 AH) *Al Mughni*, Darul Manar, Egypt.

Ibn Rushd, Muhammad bin Ahmad (1950) *Bidāyat-al-Mujtahid wa Nihāyat-al-Muuqtasid*, Egypt.

Ibnul Qayyim, Shamsuddin Muhammad bin Abi Bakr (1955) *Ilāmul Muwaqqi'in 'an Rabbil 'Alameen*, Egypt, volume 2.

Jassas al Razi, Abu Bakr Ahmad bin Ali (1999) *Ahkamul Qur'an*, Urdu translation by Abdul Qayyum, Sharī'ah Academy, IIU, Islamabad.

Jawad, Muhammad al Mughniah (1966) *Fiqh al-Imam Jafar al-Sadiq*, Beirut.

Al Jaziri, Abdur Rahman (1973) *Kitabul Fiqh Alā Mazāib-e-Arba'a*, Urdu translation, Lahore, volume 2.

Kandhalvi, Muhammad Zakria (1984/1404 AH) *Ijāzul Masalik 'ilaMuawatta lil Malik*, Maktaba al Imdadia, volume 11.

Al-Kasani, Alauddin Abu Bakr bin Masud (1400 AH) *Badāi al-Sanā I fe Tartib-al-Sharā i*, H.M. Saeed Company, Karachi. Urdu translation, Lahore, 1993.

Al-Khazin, Ali bin Muhammad bin Ibrahim (1955) *Tafsir al Khazin*, Mustafs al babi, Egypt, volume 1.

Al-Kulayni, Abu Jafar Muhammad al-Razi (1278 AH) *al-Kafi*, Tehran, volume 5.

Kuwait Finance House (KFH) (n.d.) *Fatawa li Haiat al Riqabah al Sharī'ah*, volume 2.

Al-Marghinani, Burhanuddin abu al Hasan ali b. Abdul Jalil, *Al Hidaya*, Maktaba Imdadia, Multan.

Maududi, Abul Ala (1982/1991) *Tafhimul Qur'an*, Idara Tarjumanul Qur'ān, Lahore, volumes 1 and 2.

Mubarakpuri, Safiur Rahman (1996) *Al-Raheequm Makhtoom*, Al-Maktaba a Salafiah, Lahore.

Mubarakpuri, Abdur Rahman (n.d.) Tohfatul Ahwazi, *Sharah Jām'i al Tirmidhi*, Nashar al Sunnah, Multan.

Muslim, Ibn al Hajjaj al-Nisāburi (d. 261/875) *Sahih Muslim*, with annotation by Yahya bin Sharaf al-Nawavi (d. 676/1277) Darul Fikr, Maktabe-al-Riyadh al Hadithah, 1981/1401 AH.

Nisai, Abu Abdur Rehman, Ahmad bin Shoaib (n.d.) *Sunan*, with Sharah by Jalaluddin al Sayyuti, Maktabah al Ilmiah, Beirut, volumes 7 and 8.

Nooruddin, Atar (1977/1397 AH) *Al Muamalāt al masrafia wa rabawiah wa IlāJoha fil Islam*, third edition.

Qastalani, Ahmad bin Muhamad bin Abi Bakr (1304 H) *Irshad-al-Sari li Sharah al Sahih Bukhari*, Egypt, volume 4, p. 57.

Al-Qattan, Ibrahim, *Al Munjid*, fifth edition, Maktaba al Asriyah.

*Sahifah Ahl-Hadith*, Karachi, 24th February 1993.

Al-Sanani, Abu Bakar Abdul Razzaq (1972) *Al-Musannaf*, volume 8, Lebanon.

Al-Sarakhsi, Shamsuddin Abu Bakr Muhammad bin Abe Sahl (n.d.) *Al Mabsut*, Maktaba al Saadah, Egypt.

Sayyuti, Abdur Rehman Jalaluddin (2003/1423 AH) *Lubab al Noqool*, Darul Kutab al Araby, Beirut.

Shafi'e, Abu Abdullah, Muhammad bin Idrees (1321 H) *Kitab al Umm*, Egypt, volume 3.

Shatibi, Abu Ishaq Ibrahim (n.d.) *Muwafaqāt fi Usul al-Sharī'ah*, Cairo.

Shaybani, Muhammad (1953) *Al-Asl*, Cairo.

Shirbini, Muhammad Al Khateeb (1958) *Mughni al Muhtaj*, volume 2, Mustafa al babi, Egypt.

Shukani, Muhammad bin Ali (n.d.) *Nail al Awtār, min Asrār Muntaqa al Akhbār*, volume 5. *Nashar al Sunnah*, Multan, volume 2.

Tabari, Abu Jafar Muhammad bin Jarir (n.d.) *Jami 'al Bayan*, Darul Ma'ārif, Egypt, volume 6.

Thanwi, Zafar Ahmad (n.d.) *A'alā al Sunan*, Idarah Al Qur'ān wal Uloom al Islamia, Karachi.

Tirmidhi, Abu 'Isa Muhammad (1988) *Sahih al Sunan*, with Takhreej by Nasiruddin Albani, Riyadh, KSA, volume 2.

University of the Punjab, Lahore (1973) *Dāera-e-Maārif-e-Islamia*, volume 10.

Usmani, Muhammad Imran Ashraf (2000b) *Shirkat wa Mudaradat, 'Asr-e-Hazar Mein*, Idaratul Maaraf, Karachi.

Usmani, Muhammad Taqi (1994) *Fiqhi Maqalat*, volume 1, Memon Islamic Publications, Karachi.

Usmani, Muhammad Taqi (1999) *Islam Aur Jadeed Maeeshat wa Tijarat*, Idarah Al Maraf, Karachi.

Waliullah, Shah Dehlvi (1353 H) *Al Musawa min Ahadith al Muawatta*, volume 2.

Waqdi, Muhammad bin Umar (1966) *Kitab Al Maghazi*. Oxford University Press, Oxford.

Zuhayli, Wahbah (1985) *Al Fiqhul Islami wa Adillatohu*, Darul Fikr, Damascus.

# Suggested Further Readings

Aghnides, Nicolas P. (1961) *Mohammedan Theories of Finance*. The Premier Book House, Lahore.

Ahmad, Ziauddin (1985) *The Present State of the Islamic Finance Movement*. IIIE, Islamabad.

Ahmad, Ziauddin (1985) *Some Misgivings about Islamic Interest-free Banking*. IIIE, Islamabad.

Ahmad, Ziauddin, Munawar, Iqbal and Khan, M. Fahim (Eds) (1983) *Money and Banking in Islam*. International Centre for Research in Islamic Economics, King Abdul Aziz University, Jeddah and the Institute of Policy Studies, Islamabad.

Anwar, Muhammad (2002) *Islamicity of Islamic Banking and Modes of Islamic Banking*, Research Centre, International Islamic University, Malaysia.

El Ashker, Ahmad (1987) *The Islamic Business Enterprise*. Croom Helm.

El Ashker, Ahmad (1995) *Profit Index as a Replacement to LIBOR in Islamic Banking Operations*. IRTI, IDB, Jeddah.

Ayub, Muhammad (1983) "Ownership of Land and Land Tenure System in Islam", *Islamic Order*, Karachi, 4th quarter, pp. 94–115.

Ayub, Muhammad (2001) "Meaning of Riba", *Journal of Islamic Banking and Finance*, **18**(3/4), 7–16.

Ayub, Muhammad (2005) "Islamic Banking and Finance: A Feasible Option", *LUMS Business Recorder*, Lahore, Summer, pp. 79–82.

Bahrain Monetary Agency (2002) *Islamic Banking and Finance in the Kingdom of Bahrain*.

Chapra, M. Umer and Ahmed, Habib (2002) *Corporate Governance in Islamic Financial Institutions*, IRTI, IDB, occasional paper No.6.

Choudhury, Masadul Alam (2001) "Financial Globalization and Islamic Financing Institutions: The Topic Revisited", *Islamic Economic Studies*, **9**(1), 19–38.

Choudhury, Masadul Alam and Uzair, Abdul Malik (1992) *The Foundations of Islamic Political Economy*. St Martin's Press, New York.

Cole, Harold L. and Kocherlakota, Narayana (1998) "Zero Nominal Interest Rates: Why They're Good and How to Get Them", *Federal Reserve Bank of Minneapolis Quarterly Review*, **22** (Spring), 2–10.

Dudley, Nigel (2001) "Islamic Banks Tap a Rich New Business", *Euromoney*, issue 392, 2–97.

Errico, Luca and Farahbaksh, Mitra (1998) *Islamic Banking: Issues in Prudential Regulations and Supervision*, IMF working paper 1998/30.

El-Gamal, Mahmoud Amin (2000) *A Basic Guide to Contemporary Islamic Banking and Finance*. ISNA, Indiana.

El-Gamal, Mahmoud Amin (2001) "An Economic Explication of the Prohibition of Gharar in Classical Islamic Jurisprudence", *Islamic Economic Studies*, **8**(2), 29–58.

Ghazali, Abdel Hamid (1994) *Profit versus Bank Interest in Economic Analysis and Islamic Law*, IRTI, IDB, Jeddah, p. 61.

Ghazali, Aidit (1990) *Development: An Islamic Perspective*. Pelanduk Publications, Selangor, Malaysia.

Hammad, Nazih (1990) *Studies in Principles of Debts in Islamic Fiqh*. Taif, Dar Al Farooq, KSA.

Al Harran, Saad (1993) *Islamic Finance: Partnership Financing*. Pelanduk Publishing, Selangor, Malaysia.

Hasanuz Zaman, S.M. (1989) "Limited Liability of Shareholders in an Islamic Perspective", *Islamic Studies*, **28**(4).

Hasanuz Zaman, S.M. (1991) *Economic Functions of an Islamic State (the early experience)*, The Islamic Foundation, Leicester.

Hasanuz Zaman, S.M. (1998) "Interest-free Financing of Social Overhead", *Journal of Islamic Banking and Finance*.

Hasanuz Zaman, S.M. (n.d.) *The Economic Relevance of the Sharī'ah Maxims (Al Qawaid al Fiqhiyah)*, King Abdul Aziz University, Jeddah, KSA.

Homoud, Sami Hassan (1985) *Islamic Banking*. Arabian Information, London.

Al-Jarhi, Mabid Ali (2006) "The Case for Universal Banking as a Component of Islamic Banking", *Islamic Economic Studies*, **12**(2) and **13**(1), February/August, IRTI, IDB, Jeddah.

Ibn Khaldun (1958) *The Muqaddimah: An Introduction to History*. Princeton University Press. Complete three-volume English translation by Franz Rosenthal. Abridged English version by N.J. Dawood (1967) Princeton University Press.

Ibn Taymiyah (1992) *Public Duties in Islam: The Institution of the Hisba*, The Islamic Foundation, Leicester. Translated from the Arabic by Muhtar Holland.

Institute of Islamic Banking and Insurance (1994) *Development of an Accounting System for Islamic Banking*.

Institute of Islamic Banking and Insurance (1996) *European Perception of Islamic Banking*.

Institute of Islamic Banking and Insurance (2000) *Anthology of Islamic Banking*.

International Institute of Islamic Economics (1999) *IIIE's Blueprint for an Islamic Financial System*, Islamabad.

Islahi, Abdul Azim (1988) *Economic Concepts of Ibn Taymiyah*, The Islamic Foundation, Leicester.

Janjua, M. Ashraf (2003) *History of the State Bank of Pakistan, volume 3 (1977–1988)*. SBP, Karachi.

Janjua, M. Ashraf (2004) *History of the State Bank of Pakistan, volume 4 (1988–2003)*. SBP, Karachi, chapters on Islamization of the economy.

Khan, M. Akram (1999) *An Introduction to Islamic Economics*. Kitab Bhavan, New Delhi.

Khan, M. Fahim (1991) *Comparative Economics of Some Islamic Financing Techniques*, IRTI, IDB, research paper No. 12.

Khan, M. Fahim (1995) *Essays in Islamic Economics*, The Islamic Foundation, Leicester.

Khan, Mahmood Hasan (2002) *When is Economic Growth Pro-poor? Experiences in Malaysia and Pakistan*, authorized for distribution by Mohsin S. Khan, IMF working paper, WP/02/85.

Khan, Shahrukh Rafi (1987) *Profit and Loss Sharing*. Oxford University Press, Oxford.

Khan, Tariqullah (1999/2000) "Islamic Quasi Equity (Debt) Instruments and the Challenges of Balance Sheet Hedging: An Exploratory Analysis", *Islamic Economic Studies*, **7**(1 and 2), IRTI, IDB, Jeddah.

Khan, Tariqullah and Ahmed, Habib (2001) *Risk Management: An Analysis of Issues in the Islamic Financial Industry*, IRTI, IDB, occasional paper No. 5.

Khan, Waqar Masood (1983) *Towards an Interest-free Islamic Economic System: A Theoretical Analysis of Prohibiting Debt Financing*, The Islamic Foundation, Leicester.

Kuran, Timur (1992) "The Economic System in Contemporary Islamic Thought", in *Islamic Economic Alternatives*, K.S. Jomo (Ed.), Macmillan, London, pp. 9–47. An earlier version appeared in 1986 in *International Journal of Middle Eastern Studies*, **18**(2), 135–164.

Kuran, Timur (1995) "Islamic Economics and the Islamic Subeconomy", *Journal of Economic Perspectives*, **9**(4), 155–173.

Lewis, Mervyn K. and Algavoud, Latifa M. (2001) *Islamic Banking*. MPG Book Ltd, Bodmin, Cornwall.

Munawar, Iqbal (1987) *Distributive Justice and Need Fulfilment in an Islamic Economy*. IIIE, Islamabad.

Munawar, Iqbal (2001) "Islamic and Conventional Banking in the Nineties: A Comparative Study", *Islamic Economic Studies*, **8**(2), 1–27.

Noland, Marcus (2003) *Religion, Culture and Economic Performance*, available at: http://www. csmonitor.com/cgi-bin/encrytmail.pl?

Nyazee, Imran Ahsan Khan (1998) *Islamic Law of Business Organisation Corporations*. IIIT and IRTI, Islamabad.

Omar, Al Fuad and Abdel Haq, Mohammed (1996) *Islamic Banking: Theory, Practice and Challenges*. Oxford University Press, Oxford.

Pramanik, Ataul Haq (2002) "Islam and Development Revisited with Evidence from Malaysia", *Islamic Economic Studies*, **10**(1), 39–74.

Presley, John R. (Ed.) (1988) *Directory of Islamic Financial Institutions*. International Centre for Islamic Studies/Croom Helm, London.

Qari, M. Ali (1993) "Towards an Islamic Stock Market", *Islamic Economic Studies*, **1**(1).

Qureshi, Anwar Iqbal (1967) *Islam and the Theory of Interest*. Sh. Muhammad Ashraf, Lahore.

Rosly, Saiful Azhar (2005) *Critical Issues on Islamic Banking and Financial Markets*. Dinamas, Kuala Lumpur, Malaysia.

Saadallah, Ridha (1994) "Concept of Time in Islamic Economics", *Islamic Economic Studies*, **2**(1), 81–102.

Salama, Abdin Ahmed (2001) "Financial Instruments and Liquidity Management", *New Horizon*, July.

Shirazi, Habib (1990) *Islamic Banking*. Butterworths, London.

Siddiqi, M. Nejatullah (1985) *Partnership and Profit Sharing in Islamic Law*, The Islamic Foundation, Leicester.

Siddiqi, M. Nejatullah (1996) *Role of the State in the Economy: An Islamic Perspective*, The Islamic Foundation, Leicester.

Sundararajan, V. and Errico, Luca (2002) *Islamic Financial Institutions and Products in the Global Financial System: Key Issues in Risk Management and Challenges Ahead*, IMF working paper, WP/02/192.

Tahir, Sayyid (n.d.) *Financing of Government Budgetary Deficit in the Light of Sharn'ah Principles*. IIIE, Islamabad.

Warde, Ibrahim (2000) *Islamic Finance in the Global Economy*. Edinburgh University Press, Edinburgh.

Wilson, Charles (1979) "An Infinite Horizon Model with Money', in *General Equilibrium, Growth and Trade*, Jerry R. Green and Jose Alexandre Scheinkman (Eds), Academic Press, New York.

Wilson, Rodney (1990) *Islamic Financial Markets*. Routledge, London.

Wilson, Rodney (1994) "Development of Financial Instruments in an Islamic Framework', *Islamic Economic Studies*, **2**(1), 103–115.

Zaidi, Iqbal and Mirakhor, Abbas (1991) "Stabilization and Growth in an Open Islamic Economy", *Review of Islamic Economics*, **1**(2), 1–20.

# SUGGESTED READINGS ON TAKAFUL/ISLAMIC INSURANCE

Malaysian National Re-Insurance Bhd (1994/5) *The Malaysian Insurance Directory*, Kuala Lumpur, Malaysia.

Murtuza, Ali K.M. (1991) *Insurance in Islam: Some Aspects of Islamic Insurance*. Islamic Economics Research Bureau, Dhaka.

Murtuza, Ali K.M. (1996) *Takaful (Islamic Insurance) Concepts and Operational System from the Practitioner's Perspective*. BIRT, Kuala Lumpur, Malaysia.

Muslehuddin, M. (1995) *Insurance and Islamic Law*, 2nd edition, Delhi.

Rahman, Afzal-ur (1982) *Economic Doctrines of Islam*, volume IV. Islamic Publications.

Rispler, Vardit (1985) *Insurance in the World of Islam: Origins, Problems and Current Practices.* UMI, USA.

Shafi, Mufti Muhammad (1994) *Bima-e-Zindagi* (Urdu, English translation – *Life Insurance* – by Anwar Ahmad Meenai). Darul Ishayat, Karachi.

Siddiqi, M. Nejatullah (1985) *Insurance in an Islamic Economy*, The Islamic Foundation, Leicester.

# Index

CPSIA information can be obtained
at www.ICGtesting.com
Printed in the USA
LVHW01*0407271217
560875LV00016B/70/P